MCTS Guide to Microsoft Windows Server 2008 Network Infrastructure Configuration

Michael Bender

COURSE TECHNOLOGY
CENGAGE Learning™

Australia • Brazil • Japan • Korea • Mexico • Singapore • Spain • United Kingdom • United States

COURSE TECHNOLOGY
CENGAGE Learning™

MCTS Guide to Microsoft Windows Server 2008 Network Infrastructure Configuration

Michael Bender

Vice President, Career and Professional Editorial: Dave Garza

Executive Editor: Stephen Helba

Managing Editor: Marah Bellegarde

Acquisitions Editor: Nick Lombardi

Senior Product Manager: Michelle Ruelos Cannistraci

Developmental Editor: Lisa Ruffolo

Editorial Assistant: Sarah Pickering

Vice President, Career and Professional Marketing: Jennifer McAvey

Marketing Director: Deborah S. Yarnell

Senior Marketing Manager: Erin Coffin

Marketing Coordinator: Shanna Gibbs

Production Director: Carolyn Miller

Production Manager: Andrew Crouth

Content Project Manager: Jessica McNavich

Design Assistant: Hannah Wellman

Cover designer: Robert Pehlke

Cover photo or illustration: Getty Images

Manufacturing Coordinator: Denise Powers

Copyeditor: Bruce Owens

Proofreader: Amy Ford

Compositor: Cadmus/KGL

For product information and technology assistance, contact us at **Cengage Learning Customer & Sales Support, 1-800-354-9706**
For permission to use material from this text or product, submit all requests online at **cengage.com/permissions**

Further permissions questions can be emailed to **permissionrequest@cengage.com**

Example: Microsoft® is a registered trademark of the Microsoft Corporation.

Library of Congress Control Number: 2009922095

ISBN-13: 978-1-423-90236-2

ISBN-10: 1-423-90236-X

Course Technology
20 Channel Center
Boston, MA 02210
USA

Cengage Learning is a leading provider of customized learning solutions with office locations around the globe, including Singapore, the United Kingdom, Australia, Mexico, Brazil, and Japan. Locate your local office at: **international.cengage.com/region**

Cengage Learning products are represented in Canada by Nelson Education, Ltd.

For your lifelong learning solutions, visit **course.cengage.com**
Visit our corporate website at **cengage.com**.

Some of the product names and company names used in this book have been used for identification purposes only and may be trademarks or registered trademarks of their respective manufacturers and sellers.

Microsoft and the Office logo are either registered trademarks or trademarks of Microsoft Corporation in the United States and/or other countries. Course Technology, a part of Cengage Learning, is an independent entity from the Microsoft Corporation, and not affiliated with Microsoft in any manner.

Any fictional data related to persons or companies or URLs used throughout this book is intended for instructional purposes only. At the time this book was printed, any such data was fictional and not belonging to any real persons or companies.

Course Technology and the Course Technology logo are registered trademarks used under license.

Course Technology, a part of Cengage Learning, reserves the right to revise this publication and make changes from time to time in its content without notice.

The programs in this book are for instructional purposes only. They have been tested with care, but are not guaranteed for any particular intent beyond educational purposes. The author and the publisher do not offer any warranties or representations, nor do they accept any liabilities with respect to the programs.

Printed in the United States of America
3 4 5 6 7 12 11

Brief Table of Contents

Table of Contents

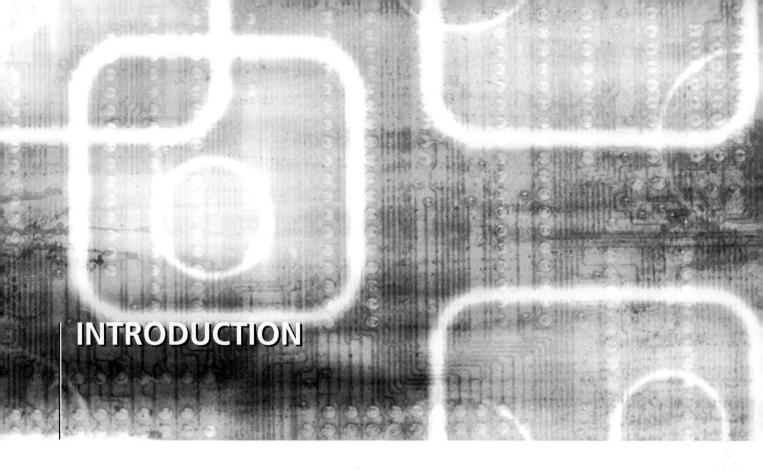

INTRODUCTION

MCTS Guide to Microsoft® Windows Server® 2008 Network Infrastructure Configuration provides in-depth coverage of the 70-642 certification exam objectives and focuses on the skills needed to manage a Windows Server 2008 network. With more than 100 hands-on activities and dozens of skill-reinforcing case projects, you'll be well prepared for the certification exam and learn valuable skills to perform on the job.

After you finish this book, you'll have an in-depth knowledge of Windows Server 2008, TCP/IP networking, Domain Name System, and related services, such as Dynamic Host Configuration Protocol, Active Directory Domain Services, File Services, Printers and Print Services, Network Policy and Access Services, security, and managing the Windows Server 2008 network infrastructure.

Several new features of Windows Server 2008 are also covered including Server Core, Windows Backup, and Server Manager.

Intended Audience

MCTS Guide to Microsoft Windows Server 2008 Network Infrastructure Configuration is intended for people who want to learn how to configure and manage a Windows Server 2008 network and are considering becoming MCTS and MCITP certified. The focus on network infrastructure configuration gives new and experienced users alike the opportunity to study in depth the core technologies in Windows Server 2008. This book serves as an excellent text for classroom teaching, but self-paced learners will also find that the clear explanations and challenging activities and case projects serve them equally well. Although this book doesn't assume previous experience with Windows servers, it does assume a familiarity with current Windows OSs, such as Windows XP or Vista. Networking knowledge equivalent to an introductory networking course is highly recommended.

This book includes:

- A Windows Server 2008 Enterprise Edition evaluation DVD is bundled with the book. It can be installed on a computer or in a virtual machine using Microsoft Hyper-V, Microsoft Virtual Server, VMware Workstation, VMware Player, or VMware Server.

- Step-by-step hands-on activities walk you through tasks ranging from a basic Windows Server 2008 installation to complex multiserver network configurations involving DHCP, DNS, and many other services. All activities have been tested by a technical editor, reviewers, and validation experts.

- Extensive review and end-of-chapter materials reinforce your learning.

- Challenging case projects build on one another and require you to apply the concepts and technologies learned throughout the book.

- Coverage of features new to Windows Server 2008, including Server Core and Server Manager, is provided as well as new roles and features, such as the Network Policy Server, Windows Backup, and improved installation options including the Windows Automated Installation Kit and ImageX.

- Abundant screen captures and diagrams visually reinforce the text and hands-on activities.

- A list of 70-642 exam objectives is cross-referenced with chapters and sections that cover each objective.

Chapter Descriptions

This book is organized to familiarize you with Windows Server 2008 features and technologies and then provide in-depth coverage of network infrastructure configuration and its related services. The book wraps up by discussing server management and monitoring. The 70-642 exam objectives are covered throughout the book, and you can find a mapping of objectives and the chapters in which they're covered on the inside front cover, with a more detailed mapping in Appendix A.

The following list describes this book's chapters:

- **Chapter 1**, "Introduction to Windows Server 2008," begins by describing the role of clients, servers, and Windows network models, and compares the Windows Server 2008 editions. Next, you're given an overview of Windows Server 2008 new technologies, such as Network Access Protection, Windows Remote Management, and Group Policy preferences. New server roles and features in Windows Server 2008 are also described. Finally, the chapter introduces the Windows Server 2008 interface.

- **Chapter 2**, "Installing Windows Server 2008," discusses the details of preparing to install the Full version of a Windows Server 2008 installation, including deployment improvements in Windows Server 2008. Next, the chapter shows how to install Windows Server 2008 with Server Core, the newest installation option. The chapter also discusses how to configure Full and Server Core versions of Windows Server 2008 for initial use.

- **Chapter 3**, "Networking with Windows Server 2008," begins by introducing networking and then discusses network addressing with TCP/IP. The chapter compares how to configure clients for IPv4 and IPv6 and how to upgrade your network to IPv6. It also explains troubleshooting considerations on a TCP/IP network.

- **Chapter 4**, "Installing and Configuring the Dynamic Host Configuration Protocol," explores the basics of DHCP, including its components and processes. The chapter explains how to install DHCP in a Windows Server 2008 environment and configure a DHCP server. DHCP administration and troubleshooting DHCP are also discussed.

- **Chapter 5**, "Introduction to DNS in Windows Server 2008," introduces the Domain Name System. The chapter explains how to configure DNS clients and install DNS in Windows Server 2008. Finally, the chapter examines the role of DNS zones on a Windows Server 2008 network.

- **Chapter 6**, "Managing and Administering DNS in Windows Server 2008," introduces Active Directory Domain Services. It examines how to manage and troubleshoot DNS in detail. It also explores the Windows Internet Name Service and new DNS features, including DNS on Server Core, support for IPv6, and link-local multicast name resolution.

- **Chapter 7**, "Configuring File Services in Windows Server 2008" provides a detailed look at File Services. After introducing the topic, the chapter explains how to install the File Server role. Access Control and its role in File Services are also explored. The chapter also discusses the Distributed File System and explains how to manage Windows Server 2008 with the File System Resource Manager.

- **Chapter 8**, "Introduction to Printers in a Windows Server 2008 Network," focuses on Windows Server 2008 printing services. The chapter begins by examining the Windows Printer model for Windows Server 2008. It then explains how to deploy printers and print services and configure printer resources. Finally, the chapter discusses managing printers and print services.

- **Chapter 9**, "Network Policy and Access Services in Windows Server 2008," provides an overview of configuring routing in Windows Server 2008. It also discusses how to configure Remote Access Services in

Windows Server 2008. The chapter also introduces you to Network Policy Server and explains wireless access configuration in Windows Server 2008.

- **Chapter 10,** "Securing Windows Server 2008," surveys security management in Windows Server 2008. The chapter explores the Encrypting File Services and using BitLocker. It also discusses using the Microsoft Baseline Security Analyzer as a basic security tool. Internet Protocol security is also discussed along with network authentication. The chapter also provides an introduction to Network Access Protection.

- **Chapter 11,** "Managing and Monitoring a Windows Server 2008 Network Infrastructure," explains how to manage Windows Server 2008. The chapter explains how to update Windows Server 2008 and use the Microsoft Baseline Security Analyzer 2.1 to measure network performance. Monitoring Windows Server 2008 is also discussed. Finally, the chapter explains how to back up and restore data in Windows Server 2008.

- **Appendix A,** "MCTS 70-642 Exam Objectives," maps each 70-642 exam objective to the chapter and section where you can find information on that objective.

- **Appendix B,** "Virtual Machine Instructions for Selected Activities," provides instructions for performing selected activities in VMware Workstation or Microsoft Virtual PC.

Features

This book includes the following learning features to help you master configuring a Windows Server 2008 network and the 70-642 exam objectives:

- *Chapter objectives*—Each chapter begins with a detailed list of the concepts to be mastered. This list is a quick reference to the chapter's contents and a useful study aid.

- *Hands-on activities*—More than 100 hands-on activities are incorporated in the book, giving you practice in setting up, managing, and troubleshooting a Windows Server 2008 server, with emphasis on network infrastructure configuration. The activities give you a strong foundation for carrying out server administration tasks in the real world.

- *Screen captures, illustrations, and tables*—Numerous screen captures and illustrations of concepts aid you in visualizing theories and concepts and seeing how to use tools and software features. In addition, tables are used often to provide details and comparisons of practical and theoretical information and can be used for a quick review.

- *Chapter summary*—Each chapter ends with a summary of the concepts introduced in the chapter. These summaries are a helpful way to recap and revisit the material covered in the chapter.

- *Key terms*—All terms in the chapter introduced with bold text are gathered together in the Key Terms list at the end of the chapter. This list gives you a method for checking your understanding of all terms introduced.

- *Review questions*—The end-of-chapter assessment begins with review questions that reinforce the concepts and techniques covered in each chapter. Answering these questions helps ensure that you have mastered important topics.

- *Case projects*—Each chapter closes with one or more case projects. Many of the case projects build on one another, as you take a small startup company to a flourishing enterprise.

- *On the DVD*—The DVD includes a free 120-day evaluation copy of Windows Server 2008, Enterprise Edition.

Text and Graphics Conventions

Additional information and exercises have been added to this book to help you better understand what's being discussed in the chapter. Icons throughout the text alert you to these additional materials:

Tips offer extra information on resources, how to solve problems, and time-saving shortcuts.

 Notes present additional helpful material related to the subject being discussed.

 The Caution icon identifies important information about potential mistakes or hazards.

 Each Hands-on activity in this book is preceded by the Activity icon.

 Case Project icons mark the end-of-chapter case projects, which are scenario-based assignments that ask you to apply what you have learned in the chapter.

Test Preparation Software CD

MCTS Guide to Microsoft Windows Server 2008 Network Infrastructure Configuration includes the exam objectives coverage map from Appendix A as well as CertBlaster test preparation questions that mirror the look and feel of the MCTS exam 70-642. The unlock code for the CertBlaster questions is c_642. For more information about dti test prep products, visit the Web site at www.dtipublishing.com

Instructor's Resources

The following supplemental materials are available when this book is used in a classroom setting. All the supplements available with this book are provided to instructors on a single CD, called the Instructor's Resource CD (ISBN 1-423-90269-6).

- *Electronic Instructor's Manual*—The Instructor's Manual that accompanies this book includes additional instructional material to assist in class preparation, including suggestions for classroom activities, discussion topics, and additional activities.

- *Solutions—The* instructor's resources include solutions to all end-of-chapter material, including review questions, hands-on activities, and case projects.

- *ExamView*—This textbook is accompanied by ExamView, a powerful testing software package that allows instructors to create and administer printed, computer (LAN-based), and Internet exams. ExamView includes hundreds of questions that correspond to the topics covered in this book, enabling students to generate detailed study guides that include page references for further review. The computer-based and Internet testing components allow students to take exams at their computers and also save the instructor time by grading each exam automatically.

- *PowerPoint presentations*—This book comes with Microsoft PowerPoint slides for each chapter. They are included as a teaching aid for classroom presentation, to make available to students on the network for chapter review, or to be printed for classroom distribution. Instructors, please feel free to add your own slides for additional topics you introduce to the class.

- *Figure files*—All the figures and tables in the book are reproduced on the Instructor's Resource CD in bitmap format. Similar to the PowerPoint presentations, they are included as a teaching aid for classroom presentation, to make available to students for review, or to be printed for classroom distribution.

System Requirements

Hardware (Without Using Virtualization)
Minimum two computers per student that meet the following requirements:

- 2 GHz or faster CPU
- 512 MB or more RAM (preferably more when using a Vista client for some activities)
- 15 GB or more disk space
- DVD-ROM drive
- Super VGA or higher resolution monitor
- Mouse or pointing device
- Keyboard
- Two Network interface cards including one connected to the classroom, lab, or school network
- Printer (to practice setting up a network printer)

Hardware (Using Virtualization)
One computer per student to act as the host machine that meets the following minimum requirements:

- Windows XP Professional or Windows Vista
- 2.4 GHz CPU
- 2 GB or more RAM (more is always better with virtualization)
- 40 GB or more disk space
- DVD-ROM drive
- Super VGA or higher resolution monitor
- Mouse or pointing device
- Keyboard
- Two Network interface cards including one connected to the classroom, lab, or school network
- Printer (to practice setting up a network printer)

Software

- Windows Server 2008 Standard or Enterprise Edition (included with DVD in the book)
- Windows Vista: Any edition except Home Edition (an evaluation virtual machine can be downloaded from the Microsoft Web site)

Virtualization
Windows Server 2008 and Windows Vista can be loaded into a virtual server environment, such VMware Workstation or Server, Microsoft Virtual PC, or Microsoft Hyper-V. The use of virtualization is highly recommended.

Acknowledgments

First, the author would like to thank Nick Lombardi and Michelle Cannistraci at Cengage for the opportunity to write this book. Thanks go out to Lisa Ruffolo for her super editing skills and keeping me on track. Thanks to the reviewers for their insight and direction during the writing process. A big thanks goes out to all of my students for whom this book is for. Last, but not least, thanks to my wife, Melanie, along with the rest of my friends and family for their understanding and patience during the writing of this book. Without their support, none of this would be possible.

Thanks also to the peer reviewers, who provided thoughtful advice, constructive criticism, and helpful encouragement: Mark Allison, Keiser University; Brian Bridson, Baker College of Flint; Robert Sherman, Sinclair College; and Daniel Ziesmer, San Juan College.

About the Author

Michael Bender is an Information Technology instructor at Madison Area Technical College in Microsoft technologies. He has taught Windows Workstation (XP/Vista), Windows Server 2003, and Exchange 2003/2007, and is the lead developer of Windows Server and Exchange curriculum for the Computer Systems Administration Associate Degree program. Mike's background includes over 10 years of experience in System Administration and Technical training covering all Microsoft platforms from Windows 95 to Server 2008. Mike is a Microsoft Certified Trainer, an MCSE on the NT 4.0/2000/2003 platforms, and an MCITP on Windows Server 2008.

chapter 1

Introduction to Windows Server 2008

After reading this chapter and completing the exercises, you will be able to:

- Discuss clients, servers, and Windows network models
- Differentiate among the editions of Windows Server 2008
- Identify Windows Server 2008 hardware requirements
- Discuss the new Windows Server 2008 technologies
- Describe the new roles and features in Windows Server 2008
- Navigate the Windows Server 2008 interface

After five years of development, Microsoft released the latest version of Windows Server: Windows Server 2008. This much-anticipated release includes many new and innovative features designed for businesses of all sizes. This book explores Windows Server 2008 networking and helps you prepare for the MCTS/MCITP Exam 70-642: Windows Server 2008 Network Infrastructure, Configuring. To prepare for this exam and the job responsibilities related to it, you need to develop extensive knowledge of Windows Server 2008. This book focuses on configuring, managing, and troubleshooting networking features and services in a Windows 2008 Server environment.

This chapter introduces you to Windows networking models to lay a foundation for the rest of the book. It continues by discussing the editions of Windows Server 2008, identifying the hardware requirements for installing Windows Server 2008, and describing how to perform a Full installation and Server Core installation. The chapter also explores the new roles and features of Windows Server 2008. Finally, the chapter tours the Windows Server 2008 user interface (UI).

Clients, Servers, and Windows Network Models

You are probably familiar with **client** computers running operating systems (OSs) such as Windows XP or Windows Vista. A client operating system is designed as a user interface, usually graphical, for users to perform tasks such as word processing, researching information on the Internet, and exchanging e-mail. Clients generally initiate requests for services from a local or network resource. For example, users in an office use client computers on their desktops to log onto the network and perform their work. The purpose of a network is to allow users to access resources using one or more computers. These resources can be printers, applications, documents, or even the Internet. Servers are the computers that provide these services and resources to network users and that have an operating system such as Windows Server 2008. Running in the background, Windows Server 2008 servers wait for requests from clients. When it receives a request, the server performs its tasks and then returns the information to the client. Rarely does a user interact directly with a server without a client intermediary. This type of interaction is known as **client-server computing** and is the basis for all types of Microsoft network models. This chapter examines the following Windows network models:

- Workgroup model
- Domain model with Active Directory

Workgroup Model

A **workgroup** is a network of computers that allow each other access to their files, printers, Internet connection, or other resources. Although Microsoft defines a workgroup as a peer-to-peer computing network, workgroups do share some of the characteristics of a client-server computing network. Even with peers, which are other computers in the workgroup, one computer often acts as a client and another as a server, such as when two colleagues share a folder of documents located on a single computer.

Within small environments, usually up to 10 computers, workgroups have a number of benefits. In a workgroup, computers can easily share resources. Also, a workgroup does not require a server or other network resources to function. Because servers can be quite expensive, the workgroup model may be a cost-effective solution for small businesses or home environments.

However, workgroups have a few drawbacks, especially for larger networks. Because of the decentralized nature of workgroups, administering and managing computers and resources can be a challenge. Each member of a workgroup is responsible for controlling access to its own resources. For example, if you are managing a company workgroup with five computers and five users, you have to create 25 user accounts in the network. If a user leaves your company, you need to remove the user's account from each computer. Because of these drawbacks, Microsoft recommends limiting your workgroup environments to a maximum of 10 computers.

By default, all Windows Server 2008 computers are placed in a workgroup named WORK-GROUP. Each computer accessing a network is defined by name, Internet Protocol (IP) address, and **membership status**, which is either a single workgroup or a domain (discussed next). Membership in a workgroup allows users to easily find shared resources, such as files and printers hosted by peers. In addition, a computer can access resources located on computers outside the workgroup. A network can have more than one workgroup.

Domain Model with Active Directory

In the client-server computing model, a **domain** is a group of users and computers that are managed by the same security database. In Windows Server 2008, **Active Directory Domain Services (AD DS)** is the technology that runs the domain security database. Servers that host this database are called **domain controllers (DCs)**. Domains provide a centralized authentication and administration for users, groups, and computers, which are generally referred to as objects in such an **Active Directory (AD)** environment.

In the domain network model, users and computers can access shared resources only if they have the appropriate permissions to do so. In addition, access permissions can be defined only for users and computers that are members of the domain and contained in the central domain security database.

First introduced with the release of Windows 2000 Server, AD continues the concept of domains started in Windows NT but improves on it. In Windows NT, DCs were one of two types: primary or backup. A **primary domain controller (PDC)** held readable and writable copies of the security database. A Windows NT network could have only one PDC. This database was replicated as a read-only copy to **backup domain controllers (BDCs)**. BDCs could process client requests for authentication; however, they could not make changes, such as deleting or adding a user. This had to be done at the PDC. Thus, Windows NT had one writable database and a single point of failure. DCs in Active Directory domains use **multimaster replication**, which means all DCs can update and replicate the directory database. This provides higher fault tolerance in a domain that has more than one DC.

Active Directory domains also use the **Domain Name System (DNS)** for name resolution. DNS is a Transmission Control Protocol (TCP)/IP-based standard for resolving computer names with IP addresses. For example, when you enter www.microsoft.com in your Web browser, your computer can connect to the Web site by requesting the IP address for www.microsoft.com from a server running DNS. (DNS is discussed in detail in Chapter 6.)

Along with the use of DNS and multimaster DCs, Active Directory introduced Group Policy. **Group Policy** is a way to set up specific configurations for users and computers within an Active Directory domain. Group Policy settings are contained in Group Policy objects (GPOs), which are linked to the following Active Directory service containers: sites, domains, and organizational units. The settings within GPOs are then evaluated by the affected targets using the hierarchical nature of Active Directory. Consequently, because it allows you to manage user and computer objects, Group Policy is one of the top reasons to deploy Active Directory.

A single network can have many domains. However, each domain must maintain an Active Directory database for managing its member objects. As with workgroups, if you are a user on a domain network, you can access resources outside your domain, but you will be asked for credentials—a user ID and password—to access outside systems. If the domain you are accessing is in the same forest, your credentials are required only once and follow you as long as you are logged on. A **forest** is a network of domains related to each other by relationships known as trusts. Some domains have a parent-child relationship where they share a contiguous namespace, such as us.microsoft.com and microsoft.com. These domains are part of the same **tree** within a forest. Other domains do not share a contiguous namespace but establish trust relationships so they can access resources from each other. An example of this is the related companies BenderTechnology.com and BenderResources.com. Each has its own namespace, but trusts allow them to share resources and information. Trusts between Active Directory domains in a forest are created automatically when you create domains in Windows Server 2008. These are called **transitive trusts**. In Windows NT domains prior to Windows 2000, administrators created all trusts manually.

Windows Server 2008 Editions

From the small business with a few employees to the Fortune 100 multinational company, an edition of Windows Server 2008 serves every business need. Each edition provides shared and unique sets of services for administrators. Microsoft offers three general editions of Windows Server 2008: Enterprise, Datacenter, and Standard. Two additional editions are designed for special-purpose server applications: Web Server and HPC Server. All these editions are available for 32-bit and 64-bit computers except HPC Server, which is available only for 64-bit machines. Standard, Enterprise, and Datacenter editions are also provided in two types of installations: Full installation (all options and features) or **Server Core** (minimal options).

Table 1-1 displays the differences among the 32-bit Windows Server 2008 editions. Many of these features are explored in this book. Each edition is described in more detail in the following sections.

Table 1-1   Features in Windows Server 2008 editions

Feature Name	Enterprise	Datacenter	Standard	Web
ADFS Web Agent	X			
Directory uIDM	X	X	X	
Desktop Experience	X	X	X	X
Windows Clustering	X	X	X	X
Windows Server Backup	X	X	X	X
Windows Network Load Balancing	X	X	X	X
Simple TCP/IP Services	X	X	X	X
SMTP	X	X	X	X
Subsystem for UNIX-Based Applications	X	X	X	X
Telnet Client	X	X	X	X
Telnet Server	X	X	X	X
Microsoft Message Queuing	X	X	X	X
RPC Over HTTP Proxy	X	X	X	X
Windows Internet Name Service	X	X	X	X
Wireless Client	X	X	X	X
Windows System Resource Manager	X	X	X	X
Simple SAN Management	X	X	X	X
LPR Port Monitor	X	X	X	X
Windows Foundation Components for WinFX	X	X	X	X
BITS Server Extensions	X	X	X	X
iSNS Server Service	X	X	X	X
BitLocker Drive Encryption	X	X	X	X
Multipath IO	X	X	X	X
Removable Storage Management	X	X	X	X
TFTP	X	X	X	X
SNMP	X	X	X	X
Server Admin Pack	X	X	X	X
RDC	X	X	X	X
Peer-to-Peer Name Resolution Protocol	X	X	X	X
Recovery Disk	X	X	X	X
Windows PowerShell	X	X	X	X

Windows Server 2008, Standard Edition

Designed for smaller environments and single-purpose installations, Windows Server 2008 Standard edition (SE) is the entry-level server edition that provides everything you most likely need to run your network. It works as a single domain server for a small business or a single file/application server in larger environments. This edition includes most of the features and support of the other editions, including the file and print services, Internet Information Services (IIS) 7, Active Directory, the distributed and encrypting file systems, and various management tools. A notable addition is Network Load Balancing, which was previously available only in Enterprise and Datacenter editions.

Windows Server 2008, Enterprise Edition

Windows Server 2008 Enterprise edition (EE) provides the following features not available with SE:

- Significant increase in maximum allowable memory
- Active Directory Federation Services (discussed later in this chapter)
- Failover clustering
- Installation of up to four virtual machines on each physical host
- Hot-add memory

The decision to use the Enterprise edition instead of the Standard edition depends on two factors: expense and functionality. Small and medium-sized businesses do not often need the additional features of the Enterprise edition, so Standard is a good choice for them. Also, large businesses not requiring these features can take advantage of a significant monetary savings. However, if an organization plans to use failover clustering, Enterprise is the best choice.

Windows Server 2008, Datacenter Edition

Datacenter edition (DE) includes all the features offered in the Enterprise edition with a few additions, including the following:

- The ability to run up to 32 processors
- The ability to hot-add and replace processors
- Installation of unlimited virtual machines on each physical host

For most instances where plans include hosting more than four virtual machine guests on a server, Datacenter is often the most economical choice. Datacenter is also licensed per processor, so each processor installed in a system needs a Datacenter license, which involves additional expense.

 Microsoft does not currently differentiate among single, dual, and quad-core processors for licensing. All are considered a single processor. This might be a factor in hardware decisions when choosing between dual and quad-core systems.

Windows Web Server 2008

Windows Web Server 2008 continues the Microsoft tradition of providing an OS edition designed specifically as a single-purpose **Web server**. Because the purpose of this server is hosting Web sites and applications, the functionality of the system is reduced to accommodate these services. Many server roles, including Dynamic Host Configuration Protocol (DHCP), DNS, and file server, are not available. Web Server 2008 includes the reengineered IIS 7.0, ASP.NET, and the .NET Framework as part of the installation. Web Server differs from other editions in that it does not require **client access licenses (CAL)** for users. You can also install the database of your choice without limitations on user access to the Web site and its related data.

The Web Server 2008 edition is available only as a 32-bit and a 64-bit OS in the Full version only. Server Core does not currently support the .NET Framework and ASP.NET.

Windows HPC Server 2008

Windows HPC Server 2008 is designed for **high-performance computing (HPC)** applications. This edition accommodates up to thousands of processing cores because it is built on the Server 2008 64-bit architecture model. For more information on Microsoft HPC Server 2008, see *www.microsoft.com/hpc*.

Windows Server 2008, Without Hyper-V

Standard, Enterprise, and Datacenter editions for 64-bit servers are offered with or without Hyper-V, which lets you consolidate multiple server roles as separate virtual machines running on a single physical machine. Hyper-V also lets you efficiently run different operating systems—such as Windows and Linux—in parallel on a single server. Currently, the retail price for Windows Server 2008 without Hyper-V is slightly less than the price of Server 2008 with Hyper-V. Note that the 32-bit versions of these SE, EE, and DE do not support Hyper-V.

Windows Server 2008 for Itanium-Based Systems

Standard, Enterprise, and Datacenter editions are available for servers using Intel Itanium processors. Itanium processors use a different architecture from other 32-bit and 64-bit processors. For more information on Intel Itanium processors, see *www.intel.com*.

Windows Server 2008 Hardware Requirements

Microsoft provides minimum and recommended hardware requirements for installing its operating systems. The minimum requirements let you install and run a system using minimal resources and services. Table 1-2 lists the Windows Server 2008 hardware requirements, including the minimum, recommended, and maximum requirements.

Note the significant differences between memory capabilities in 32-bit processor versions and 64-bit processor versions.

Table 1-2   Windows Server 2008 hardware requirements

Component	Requirement
Processor	Minimum: 1 GHz (x86 processor) or 1.4 GHz (x64 processor) Recommended: 2 GHz or faster Note: An Intel Itanium 2 processor is required for Windows Server 2008 for Itanium-based systems
Memory	Minimum: 512 MB RAM Recommended: 2 GB RAM or greater Maximum (32-bit systems): 4 GB (Standard) or 64 GB (Enterprise and Datacenter) Maximum (64-bit systems): 32 GB (Standard) or 2 TB (Enterprise, Datacenter, and Itanium-based systems)
Available disk space	Minimum: 10 GB Recommended: 40 GB or greater Note: Computers with more than 16 GB of RAM require more disk space for paging, hibernation, and dump files
Drive	DVD-ROM drive
Display and peripherals	Super VGA (800 × 600) or higher-resolution monitor, keyboard, Microsoft mouse or compatible pointing device

32-Bit and 64-Bit Processors

As noted earlier, Windows Server 2008 is available for both 32-bit and 64-bit processor architectures. Although the role and feature sets of the versions are the same, they have noticeable differences in two areas:

- Hardware limits
- Driver and application support

The 64-bit architectures have a greater theoretical limit for processing data. Basically, a 64-bit processor can handle twice the amount of data of a comparable 32-bit product.

Because the 64-bit version of Windows Server 2008 cannot run 16-bit Windows applications or use 32-bit device drivers, you cannot run some legacy applications and hardware with the 64-bit version. For legacy applications, virtual technologies are an excellent option.

Windows Server 2008 is the last server operating system from Microsoft available in a 32-bit version.

New Technologies in Windows Server 2008

Besides providing a new user interface, Windows Server 2008 also offers a new way of managing and securing your Windows network. Built on the same code base as Windows Vista, Windows Server 2008 includes many improvements to previous server operating systems along with new functionality. This section introduces the following technologies and enhancements, which are important to anyone configuring and administering a Windows Server 2008 network:

- Improved installation process
- Hyper-V
- Server Core
- TCP/IP improvements
- Network Access Protection
- Server Manager
- Windows Remote Management
- PowerShell
- Group Policy preferences

Before exploring these technologies, install Windows Server 2008 Enterprise Edition by completing Activity 1-1. Chapter 2 provides a more detailed description of installing Server 2008.

Activity 1-1: Installing Windows Server 2008, Enterprise Edition

Time Required: 30 to 60 minutes (depending on hardware configuration of lab environment)

Objective: Install a working version of Windows Server 2008.

Description: As the system administrator for your company, you have just received an evaluation copy of Windows Server 2008, Enterprise edition. You want to install the software so you can review the new features it offers. In this activity, you install Server 2008, Enterprise edition.

In all the activities, your instructor might give you additional steps to perform depending on your lab environment. All the activities in this chapter are appropriate for physical machines and virtual machine applications. Before completing this activity, verify that your environment meets the hardware requirements in Table 1-2.

Figure 1-1   Preparing to install Windows Server 2008

1. Place your Windows Server 2008 DVD in the DVD drive of your computer and then restart or power on your computer.

2. If prompted by the startup screen, press any key to boot from the DVD. You are prompted only if the computer has an existing operating system. The first part of the installation program starts.

3. When the first Install Windows window appears, confirm your time and currency format and that the keyboard layout is correct, and then click **Next**. The next Install Windows window appears, shown in Figure 1-1, to start the installation.

4. Click **Install now**. The Type your product key for activation window opens. See Figure 1-2.

5. Enter your product key if you have one and are required to enter the key. You can install Windows Server 2008 without a product key.

Depending on the type of installation media and license model you are using, you may not be prompted for a product key. Skip to Step 7.

6. Click the **Automatically activate Windows when I'm online** check box to remove the checkmark and then click **Next**. If you did not enter a product key, a message appears asking whether you want to enter a key. Click **No** to continue installing without a product key.

7. In the next window, select the version of Server 2008 you will be installing. For this activity, choose **Windows Server 2008 Enterprise (Full Installation)** and then check the **I have selected the edition of Windows that I purchased** box. See Figure 1-3. Click **Next**.

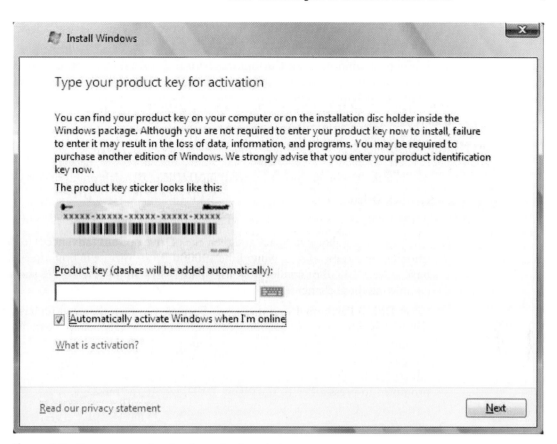

Figure 1-2   Type your product key for activation window

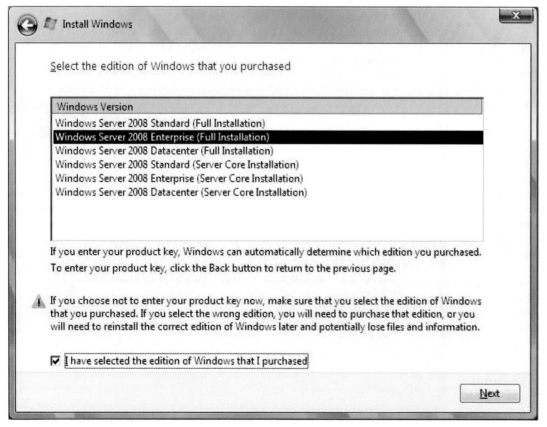

Figure 1-3   Selecting the operating system to install

8. In the next window, read the Microsoft Software License Terms, check the **I accept the license terms** box, and then click **Next**.

9. In the next window, click **Custom** to perform a custom installation, which is the appropriate option for performing a new installation. Notice that the choice to upgrade is not available. (Chapter 2 covers upgrading Windows Server 2008.)

10. If necessary, delete any existing partitions by completing the following steps in the Where do you want to install Windows? window:

    a. Click the partition you want to delete.

    b. Click the **Drive options (advanced)** link to display partitioning options.

    c. Click **Delete**.

    d. Click **OK** to confirm you want to delete the partition and lose all its data.

11. Click **Disk 0 Unallocated Space** and then click **Drive options (advanced)** to perform disk partitioning operations. Click **New**. Enter **30000** in the Size text box after ensuring that you have at least 10 GB of unallocated disk space. Click **Apply**. Figure 1-4 shows an example of completing these changes.

12. Select **Disk 0 Partition 1** and then click **Format**. Confirm that you understand that all data will be lost when you format the partition by clicking **OK**. Click **Next**. Windows performs a number of tasks that do not require your input, as shown in Figure 1-5. This portion of the installation takes approximately 30 minutes depending on the hardware setup of your lab computer. The system will reboot one or more times during the installation. If you are prompted to press a key to start from DVD, ignore the message.

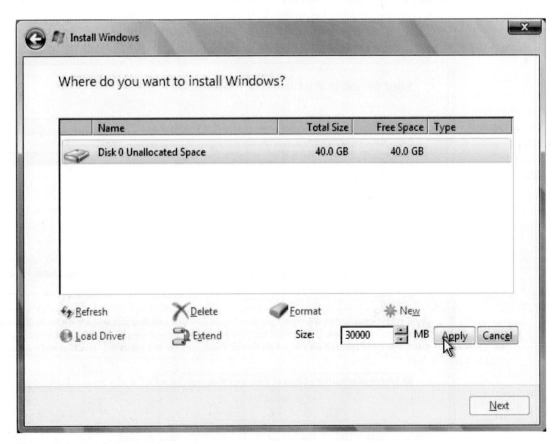

Figure 1-4   Installation location options

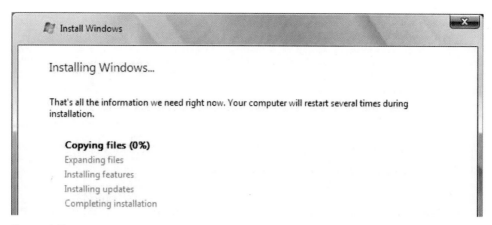

Figure 1-5 Installing Windows Server 2008

13. When advised that you need to change your password before logging on for the first time, click **OK**. Use **P@ssw0rd** as your new password. Enter the password twice to ensure it is correct and then click the arrow to submit the new password. When prompted that your password has changed, click **OK**.

    Windows Server 2008 starts for the first time, checks for and applies any updates, and then displays the Initial Configuration Tasks window shown in Figure 1-6, which remains displayed until you complete all the tasks. Then you can check the **Do not show this window at logon** box and click the **Close** button. For now, you only need to set the time zone and computer name, which you do in Activity 1-2.

14. Leave the window open for the next activity.

Improved Installation Process

Introduced in Windows Vista, the new, streamlined installation process that Windows Server 2008 uses requires minimal user input. You no longer have to wait for the installation program to ask for networking information, regional settings, and other settings. You now provide this information using the Initial Configuration Tasks window, which opens by default the first time you log onto Windows Server 2008.

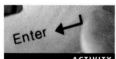

Activity 1-2: Completing Initial Configuration Tasks

Time Required: 20 minutes

Objective: Perform system configuration tasks after installation of Windows Server 2008.
Description: You just completed installing Windows Server 2008, Enterprise edition. Now you want to configure the software so you can use it regularly. In this activity, you use the Initial Configuration Tasks window to change the system time, time zone, and computer name.

1. The Initial Configuration Tasks window should still be open. If it is not, log onto your system by pressing **Ctrl+Alt+Del**, enter **P@ssw0rd** as your password, and then press **Enter**.

2. In the Initial Configuration Tasks window, click **Set time zone**. The Date and Time dialog box opens. Click **Change time zone**, select your time zone in the Time zone drop-down list, and then click **OK**. If the date and time are incorrect, click **Change date and time**, change the time to your local time, and then click **OK**. Click **OK** to accept the changes and close the Date and Time dialog box.

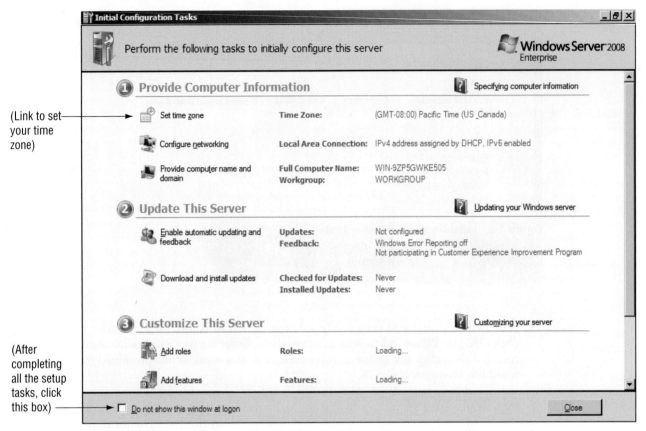

(Link to set your time zone)

(After completing all the setup tasks, click this box)

Figure 1-6   Initial Configuration Tasks window

Ask your instructor if you are not sure of the proper time zone for your location.

3. In the Initial Configuration Tasks window, click **Provide computer name and domain**. The System Properties dialog box opens.

4. On the Computer Name tab, click **Change**. The Computer Name/Domain Changes dialog box opens.

5. Replace the current computer name with **MSN-SRV-0XX**, where XX is a number supplied by your instructor. Your number should be unique so each student has a different server name.

6. Click **OK** to accept the new name. A message appears, informing you that a restart is needed. Click **OK** to close message box.

7. Click **Close** to close the System Properties dialog box. When a Microsoft Windows dialog box appears, click **Restart Now** to restart your system.

8. After your system restarts, log on by pressing **Ctrl+Alt+Del**. Enter **P@ssw0rd** as your password and then press **Enter**.

9. When the Initial Configuration Tasks window opens, click the **Do not show this window at logon** check box. If you need to open the Initial Configuration Tasks window later, click the **Start** button, type **OOBE.exe** in the Start Search box, and then press **Enter**.

You can also complete all of the initial configuration tasks using Server Manager, which you will explore later in this chapter.

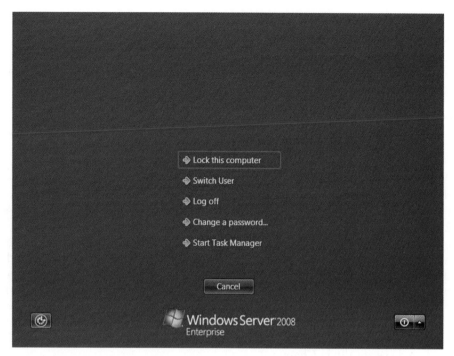

Figure 1-7   Ctrl+Alt+Del options screen

10. Click **Close** to close the Initial Configuration Tasks window.

11. Press **Ctrl+Alt+Del** and then click **Log off**, as shown in Figure 1-7, to log off.

Hyper-V

Virtualization is a popular topic in information technology because it conserves hardware resources. Using blade servers, virtual machines, and network storage are ways to consolidate data centers. In a nutshell, virtualization allows you to run one or more separate instances of an OS within a single host OS. Before virtualization, many companies had data centers full of servers that used only 5 to 10 percent of their resources. This occurs because installed applications often need to run on their own system because of performance or third-party vendor support requirements. Virtualization allows organizations to consolidate these physical systems onto high-powered servers (known as the host system). Each OS runs in its own virtual instance to take advantage of the hardware resources of the host system. Microsoft's entry into the server virtualization arena is called Hyper-V (formerly code-named Viridian). It is available with your initial investment in the 64-bit editions of Windows Server 2008 or as add-on application.

Server Core

For years, Windows administrators have battled to harden systems and roll out implementations of Windows Server without unnecessary roles and services running. Server Core, Microsoft's newest role in the Windows Server family, simplifies this task. Server Core is a stripped-down installation of Windows Server 2008 with a set of available roles and services more limited than in the Full version. To minimize the **attack surface**, or areas of the system that could expose it to security breaches, much of the UI has been removed. Server Core provides a single command-line window and tools such as the Registry Editor available for administration. Although Microsoft considers Server Core to be a role instead of a separate edition, Server Core can function as a separate entity. Server Core has a base set of installable roles and services. As a role, Server Core can be installed on Standard, Enterprise, and Datacenter editions of Windows Server 2008 but only during initial installation of the operating system. You cannot upgrade from Server Core to the Full version unless you perform a complete operating system reinstallation.

Network Access Protection

Network Access Protection (NAP) is a new platform for Windows Server 2008, Windows Vista, and Windows XP Service Pack 3 (SP3). NAP helps to protect networks, both public and private, from malware such as viruses and spyware. Threats come from many sources, including the following typical examples:

- Employees accessing the Internet from work and inadvertently install Trojan horses

- Remote access to connections from external networks that create a gateway for viruses

- Guest computers accessing an internal network that introduce malware to the network

At its core, NAP queries the health state of computers accessing a network, determines whether this state meets defined corporate health policies, and takes appropriate administrative action. For example, a **host-based stateful firewall** such as the Windows Firewall in Windows Server 2008, Windows Vista, Windows XP SP2, and Windows Server 2003 SP1 or SP2 provides a layer of defense against malicious inbound or outbound traffic. With NAP, you can define a corporate health policy that enables the Windows Firewall to your specifications. Should a user turn off the Windows Firewall on a NAP-compatible client computer, the local health policy will turn it back on to remain compliant. NAP is designed to work with third-party hardware and software. One important alliance is with Cisco Systems, a leader in networking hardware. Microsoft and Cisco have created the alliance so that NAP can interact with **Network Access Control (NAC)**, a feature of Cisco networking products. NAP and its components are discussed throughout the book and specifically in Chapter 9.

TCP/IP Improvements

Windows Server 2008 includes a number of improvements to its implementation of TCP/IP. The **Next-Generation TCP/IP stack** is a new implementation of the TCP/IP protocol stack that contains full support for Internet Protocol Version 4 (IPv4) and Internet Protocol Version 6 (IPv6). Part of the new stack is the introduction of **Teredo**, an IPv6 technology that can encapsulate IPv6 packets as IPv4 packets to allow them to traverse IPv4 networks. Included as well is **Receive Window Auto-tuning**, a feature of the new stack that optimizes the size of the data packets a server can accept. Windows Server 2008 computers can optimize network connections on the basis of whether the data being transmitted is one large packet of data or multiple small packets of data. Receive-side Scaling works with Receive Window Auto-tuning to optimize traffic flow. This is especially important for networks with 10-GB (or more) local area network speeds.

Server Manager

One of the most noticeable changes in Windows Server 2008 is the Server Manager console, shown in Figure 1-8. In previous versions of Windows Server, you had to use various windows and commands to configure your server. Server Manager centralizes these tools and allows you to easily manage your server and network.

Activity 1-3: Exploring Server Manager

Time Required: 10 minutes

Objective: Review the features of Server Manager.

Description: After installing Windows Server 2008 for your company, you want to become familiar with the tools you can use to configure and manage your server and network. You can explore Server Manager to learn about the tools it provides.

Remember that MSN-SRV-0XX is a placeholder for the name your instructor assigned you or the name added in Activity 1-2.

1. Log onto your Windows Server 2008 Enterprise computer, if necessary. If Server Manager does not start, click the **Start** button and then click **Server Manager**.

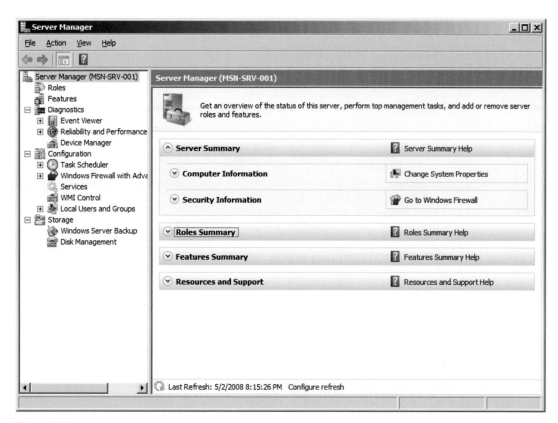

Figure 1-8   Summary view in Server Manager

2. If necessary, click **Server Manager (MSN-SRV-0XX)** in the left pane. The Server Summary options appear in the right pane, which are similar to the options provided in the Initial Configuration Tasks window along with other management resources.

3. Click **Roles** in the left pane. The Roles Summary options appear in the right pane, where you manage roles.

4. Click **Features** in the left pane. The Features Summary options appear in the right pane, where you manage features.

5. Click **Diagnostics** in the left pane. The Diagnostics Summary options appear in the right pane, including tools for analyzing your server and diagnosing problems.

6. Click **Configuration** in the left pane. The Configuration Summary options appear in the right pane, including tools for managing specific configuration settings of your server.

7. Click **Storage** in the left pane. The Storage Summary options appear in the right pane, including tools for managing disks and backups.

8. Close Server Manager by clicking **File** on the menu bar and then clicking **Exit**.

PowerShell

If you are familiar with Linux or UNIX, you have probably noted that Windows operating systems would benefit from a similar flexible and powerful **command-line interface (CLI)** with access to the operating system and its inner workings. Windows Server 2008 provides this interface with PowerShell. First introduced in Microsoft Exchange Server 2007, PowerShell is built on the Microsoft .NET Framework. PowerShell is becoming the de facto CLI and scripting language for Microsoft products. For example, in Exchange 2007, all graphical user interface (GUI) consoles are built on PowerShell commands. Although PowerShell has its own scripting language for automation, you can use PowerShell interactively instead of using the GUI-based administrative consoles. PowerShell allows you to string together commands, passing the result of one

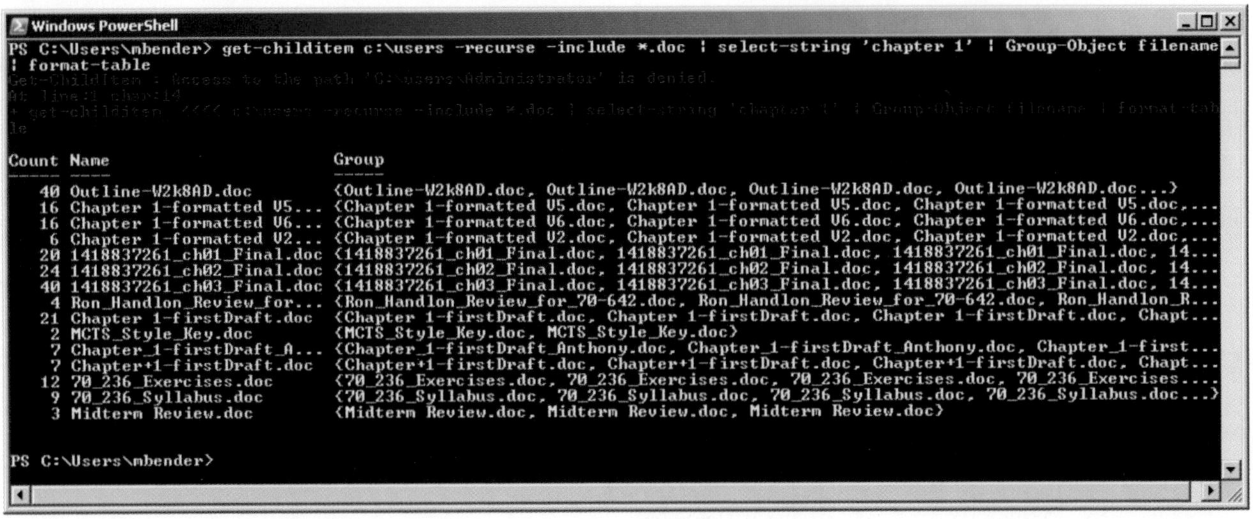

Figure 1-9   Pipelining in Windows PowerShell

command into the next, in a process known as pipelining. Instead of passing the result as text, PowerShell passes results as **.NET objects**, which are data packages containing information applications and services can use and are compatible with .NET Framework. For example, pipelining allows you to create a list of all the Microsoft Word (.doc) files in a directory that contain a specific character, word, or phrase, and then sort the output according to your preferences. See Figure 1-9.

Windows Remote Management

As a system administrator, most of your work involves managing servers. Being able to perform this work remotely decreases your administrative task load and allows you to focus on other issues. **Windows Remote Management (WinRM)** is a new feature that lets administrators manage servers remotely by running management scripts and managing data on remote machines. All connections are handled via the **WS-Management protocol**, which is a public standard for exchanging management data remotely by any device implementing the protocol, making it non–vendor specific. WinRM has features similar to those of Windows Management Instrumentation (WMI), which was installed on all computers using Windows Millennium Edition (Windows Me), Windows 2000, Windows XP, and Windows Server 2003.

WinRM allows you to access, edit, and update data from local and remote computers. You can obtain hardware data from WS-Management protocol implementations running on non-Windows operating systems such as Linux. This allows hardware and operating systems from diverse vendors to function together. For example, you can take data from all the computers in a network and store it in a folder on a single computer, thereby creating a centrally located, comprehensive network event log. Security risks are minimized by the use of encryption and authentication.

Group Policy Preferences

Group Policy preferences are a new feature of the Group Policy Management Console (GPMC). Group Policy preferences are applied but not enforced, whereas settings in a Group Policy are enforced, preventing users from making changes. Along with the GPMC and improvements in the Group Policy Editor, Group Policy preferences will help you effectively implement Group Policies within your Active Directory environments.

New Roles and Features in Windows Server 2008

Unlike previous versions of Windows Server, Windows Server 2008 makes a distinction between roles and features. In Windows Server 2008, a role is a major function or service that a server performs. For example, the File Services role allows the server to share files on a network. You can

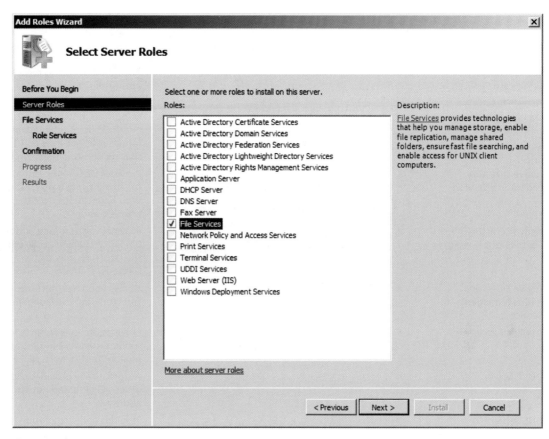

Figure 1-10   Server roles you can install on Full versions of Windows Server 2008

also add features, which enhance or support a role or provide a standalone service. For example, the Windows Server Backup feature allows you to back up and restore data.

New Roles in Server 2008

Windows Server 2008 introduces new roles and improves existing roles. Similar to a job role in a company, a server **role** defines the specific task that a server is responsible for performing. Depending on the security requirements, resource availability, and needs of the business, you can install one or many roles on a single Windows Server 2008 computer. However, some roles are not meant to be hosted together. For example, the Hyper-V role should be installed only by itself because of its security and function requirements as a virtualization platform in Windows Server 2008.

The Full versions of Windows Server 2008 editions (SE, EE, and DC) can have a total of 17 installable roles, 16 roles if you have Server 2008 without Hyper-V. See Figure 1-10. The Server Core versions have a total of eight installable roles.

Roles can be organized into three groups—Active Directory, Infrastructure, and Network roles—which are described in the following sections. Table 1-3 shows the 17 roles including the Windows Server 2008 editions for Full installations and the available roles for Server Core.

Active Directory Roles

Active Directory roles and services provide an integrated way to manage resources, both internal and external. Windows Server 2008 includes five Active Directory roles:

- Active Directory Certificate Services
- Active Directory Domain Services
- Active Directory Federation Services
- Active Directory Lightweight Directory Services
- Active Directory Rights Management Services

Table 1-3 Roles in each edition in Windows Server 2008 (including Server Core)

Server Role	Enterprise	Datacenter	Standard	Server Core	Description
Active Directory Certificate Services	X	X	X		Allows the server to create certificate authorities
Active Directory Domain Services	X	X	X	X	Stores information about users, computers, and other resources on the network; helps administrators manage this information securely and facilitates resource sharing and collaboration between users
Active Directory Federation Services	X	X			Provides Web single-sign-on capabilities to authenticate a user to multiple, related Web applications over the life of a single online session
Active Directory Lightweight Directory Services	X	X	X	X	Provides data storage and retrieval for directory-enabled applications, without the dependencies that are required for Active Directory Domain Services
Active Directory Rights Management Services	X	X	X		Allows you to protect information with Directory Rights Management
Application Server	X	X	X		Provides an environment for deploying and running custom business applications that are built with Microsoft .NET Framework 3.0
DHCP Server	X	X	X	X	Automatically provides client computers and other TCP/IP-based network devices with IP addresses
DNS Server	X	X	X	X	Provides name resolution services
Fax Server	X	X	X		Enables the users in your network to send and receive faxes
File Services	X	X	X	X	Adds file serving capabilities to your server, including replication, shared folder management, file searching, and more
Hyper-V	X	X	X	X	Provides a hypervisor-based virtualization layer
Network Policy and Access Services	X	X	X		Helps to protect your network by making sure client computers are healthy
Print Services	X	X	X	X	Allows you to share printers among client computers
Terminal Services	X	X	X		Provides users with the ability to centrally access a desktop and individual applications
UDDI Services	X	X	X		Provides Universal Description, Discovery, and Integration (UDDI) capabilities for sharing information about Web services
Web Services	X	X	X	X	Provides a Web-serving platform based on the new IIS 7
Windows Deployment Services	X	X	X		Provides a simplified and secure way to deploy Windows desktops

Active Directory Certificate Services

Active Directory Certificate Services (AD CS) provides digital certificate services for users, computers, and organizations. As a security technology, it provides customizable services for creating and managing public key certificates used in software security systems that employ public key technologies. AD CS is often used in tandem with IP, Internet Protocol Security (IPSec), and Encrypting File System (EFS) when these security technologies are deployed in a Windows network.

Active Directory Domain Services

AD DS stores information on objects such as users and groups on the network. This information is available so users can effectively access resources on the network and collaborate with other users. Network administrators can use AD CS to secure information and resources and to facilitate the sharing of these resources to users. Adding AD DS provides the base for managing your AD objects.

Active Directory Federation Services

Active Directory Federation Services (AD FS) is a secure framework for allowing simplified identity federation and single sign-on for Web services, both internal and external. Administrators can use AD FS to secure internal applications and provide single sign-on for users or to provide external business partners access to Web applications and data.

Active Directory Lightweight Directory Services

You use Active Directory Lightweight Directory Services (AD LDS) to deploy directory-enabled applications, without the dependencies that are required for AD DS.

AD LDS allows you to create and manage computer, user, and group objects that applications can use with a DC. Multiple instances of AD LDS directories can exist on a single server.

Active Directory Rights Management Services

You use Active Directory Rights Management Services (AD RMS) to deploy rights technologies to your network. Used in connection with rights management-aware applications and clients such as Microsoft Office 2007 and Windows Vista, users and administrators can protect intellectual property and data within an organization.

Network Roles

The network roles, which are covered in detail throughout this text, cover the major networking protocols and services provided by Windows Server 2008. You can install the following three Active Directory roles in Server 2008:

- DHCP
- DNS
- Network Policy and Access Services

DHCP

DHCP is a network standard protocol used to dynamically allocate and track IP addresses for clients on a network. Within a Windows network, DHCP eases the administrative burden of assigning IP addresses to clients, along with helping to populate DNS names via Dynamic DNS. DHCP and its implementation are discussed in depth in Chapter 5.

DNS

The main goal of DNS is to match a domain name to an IP address based on a client query for information. Basically, DNS acts as a phone book for the Internet by translating easy-to-remember host names such as www.MyExample.com into IP addresses such as 202.76.190.166, a numbering format required by networks to communicate. Besides providing domain names, DNS provides information necessary for services such as e-mail to route electronic messages to the proper destination. These records are called **mail exchanger (MX) records**. In an Active Directory environment, DNS provides information to clients so they can connect with necessary network services such as domain controllers and **global catalog** servers. DNS is discussed in detail in Chapter 6.

Network Policy and Access Services

Network Policy and Access Services (NPAS) provides networking technologies for deploying virtual private networking, dial-up networking, and 802.11-protected wireless access in Windows Server 2008. NPAS allows you to implement the following services on your network:

- Network Policy Server
- Routing and Remote Access Service
- Health Registration Authority
- Host Credential Authorization Protocol

All these technologies are covered in depth in later chapters.

Infrastructure Roles

Finally, the infrastructure roles provide the major services for clients. Following are the eight Active Directory roles that can be installed in Server 2008:

- Terminal Services
- Fax Services
- Print Services
- File Services
- Hyper-V
- UDDI Services
- Web Server (IIS 7)
- Windows Deployment Services

Terminal Services   **Terminal Services** in Windows Server 2008 provides technologies that enable users to access Windows programs that are installed on a terminal server or to access the Windows desktop itself from almost any computing device. Originally designed as a **thin-client** terminal to present a working desktop to users, Terminal Services now delivers applications using this same technology, often referred to as remote desktop, remote desktop connection, or remote desktop protocol. Along with application and desktop presentation, Windows Server 2008 allows administrators to publish these services to the Internet using **Secure Sockets Layer**, or https. This is an excellent security alternative, as administrators have been wary for years of opening TCP port 3389, the Terminal Services default port assignment, to the Internet.

Fax Services   The Fax Services role in Windows Server 2008 allows administrators to create a fax gateway on their network. This gateway allows clients to send, receive, and manage faxes.

Print Services   The Print Services role in Windows Server 2008 allows you to create networked printer resources for clients. Also, it provides a central administrative point for printer management. You install the Print Services role in Activity 1-6. It is covered in depth in Chapter 8.

File Services   The File Services role allows you to share and manage file resources on a network. It includes technologies such as the distributed file system, EFS, and the core functionality of creating network file shares. You install the File Services role in Activity 1-5. It is covered in depth in Chapter 7.

Hyper-V   Discussed previously, Hyper-V is the newest virtualization technology from Microsoft. It allows you to deploy multiple virtual machine instances, or guests, within a single Windows Server 2008 server. Hyper-V uses hypervisor architecture. A hypervisor is a lightweight layer of software that separates hardware and the operating system. It performs simple partitioning tasks and maintains strong isolation between partitions. Within these partitions, the hypervisor hosts virtual machines. Microsoft's implementation is inherently secure, as it contains no third-party device drivers. This minimizes the attack surface of the host machines.

UDDI Services   Universal Description, Discovery, and Integration (UDDI) services are an industry specification for publishing and locating information about Web services. In Windows Server 2008, UDDI capabilities are provided for enterprise networks or between business partners. With UDDI, developers can publish and interact with Web services directly via their development tools and business applications.

Web Server/Internet Information Services 7.0   Internet Information Services 7.0 (IIS 7) is the latest version of a Web services platform from Microsoft. More than an ordinary Web server, the IIS 7 platform unifies a number of Web-based technologies including Windows Communication Foundation Web services and Windows SharePoint Services. With IIS 7, Microsoft has completely changed the way the product works, including new configuration, delegated administration, security enhancements, and real-time diagnostic and troubleshooting features.

Windows Deployment Services Windows Deployment Services (WDS) is the updated and reengineered implementation of Remote Installation Services. It is a suite of deployment tools managing your computer deployment processes. WDS assists with the deployment of Microsoft Windows operating systems, particularly Windows Server 2008 and Windows Vista. You can use WDS to set up new computers through a network-based installation without being physically present at each computer and without the use of CD or DVD media. WDS is discussed in more detail in Chapter 2.

Activity 1-4: Exploring the Available Roles in Server Manager

Time Required: 15 minutes

Objective: Identify the roles that can be installed in Server Manager using the Add Roles Wizard.

Description: As part of your company's evaluation of Windows Server 2008, your manager asks you to research the type of roles available on the Windows Server 2008 computer recently added into your test environment. You need to access the server and note the roles that are available through the Server Manager console.

1. Log onto your Windows Server 2008 Enterprise computer, if necessary.

2. If Server Manager does not start, click **Start** and then click **Server Manager**.

3. In the left pane of the Server Manager console, click **Roles** and then click **Add Roles** in the right pane. The Add Roles Wizard starts.

4. In the Before You Begin window, review the information, and then click **Next**. Click each role to read a description of each role.

5. Click **More about Server Roles** and read the Windows Help information on server roles. When you are finished reading, close the Help window.

6. If you are continuing to the next activity, leave Server Manager open. Otherwise, click **Cancel** and then click **Yes** to close the Add Roles Wizard.

New Features

Whereas a role is similar to a job role with a company, a **feature** is similar to a job responsibility performed by a specific role. Many of the features of Server 2008 are required for certain roles to function properly. When installing some roles, you may be prompted to include specific features during your installation. Following are the new features available in Server 2008:

- .NET 3.0 Framework
- Windows Desktop Experience
- Network Load Balancing
- Group Policy Management
- Remote Server Administration Tools
- Windows PowerShell
- Windows Server Backup Features

.NET Framework 3.0 This is the latest revision of the .NET Framework included in Windows Server 2008 and Windows Vista, though newer updates might be available by the time you read this. Formerly named WinFX and built on the 2.0 version, the 3.0 version includes new **managed code application programming interfaces** that provide the foundation for Windows Server 2008. The four components added to create the .NET Framework 3.0 include Windows Communication Foundation, Windows CardSpace, Windows Presentation Foundation, and Windows Workflow Foundation.

Windows Desktop Experience Not installed by default, the Windows Desktop Experience is available in Windows Server 2008. This includes many of the features of Windows Vista such as Aero Glass (with capable hardware), live thumbnails, and desktop themes. Although not important from the administrative standpoint of working on a Windows Server 2008, the Windows Desktop Experience allows you to provide these features in remote desktop connections users have established with a server. This feature lets you run remote Vista-like desktops and applications on servers for users. The Terminal Services role in Windows Server 2008 takes advantage of this feature.

Network Load Balancing Clusters Improved in Windows Server 2008, Network Load Balancing (NLB) clusters provide a cluster solution for implementing high TCP/IP availability for Web services and network-based applications. Traffic is balanced among servers using NLB so no one server receives all the traffic. A good example of where to use NLB is with multiple Web servers with static content. Through NLB, users and applications can see the multiple servers as a single server. Besides increasing availability and improving performance, NLB can help with performing maintenance on servers that must provide services around the clock. A server needing maintenance can be removed from the cluster, repaired, and returned to the cluster without loss of service.

Remote Server Administration Tools Remote Server Administration Tools (RSAT) allows you to remotely manage Windows Server 2008 and Windows Server 2003 from a computer running Windows Server 2008 or Windows Vista with SP1. It allows you to use management tools and snap-ins on remote machines. You can use RSAT to manage both the Full version and Server Core installation of Windows Server 2008. RSAT and other management tools are further discussed in Chapter 10.

Windows PowerShell Discussed previously, PowerShell is a CLI shell and scripting language that administrators can use in Windows Server 2008. Much like a UNIX/Linux shell, PowerShell provides administrators and developers greater flexibility and power within Windows Server 2008 and other operating systems that support PowerShell. Currently, PowerShell is available for Server 2003, Windows XP SP2, and Windows Vista, though all features and cmdlets may not be available.

PowerShell uses a verb–noun pairing syntax for its commands, which are called cmdlets (pronounced *commandlets*). An example of a common PowerShell cmdlet is get-service. The following code example retrieves all the services that are stopped on a server:

```
get-service | where-object { $_.status —eq "stopping"}
```

Figure 1-11 shows the output for the get-service cmdlet.

Windows Server Backup Features The backup tool has been updated in Windows Server 2008. The Windows Server Backup feature consists of a Microsoft Management Console (MMC) snap-in and command-line tools that provide a complete solution for your day-to-day backup and recovery needs. You can create backups from the GUI, the command line, scripts, or a regular schedule. Four wizards are available in the GUI to guide you through backing up and recovering data. Windows Server Backup can back up a full server (all volumes), selected volumes, or the system state. You can recover volumes, folders, files, certain applications, and the system state. More information on Windows Server Backup is provided in Chapter 11.

Roles and Features Management

Previous versions of Windows Server had a few options for installing roles and features other than the Manage Your Server Wizard. This provided a step-by-step installation process for specific server roles but did not allow for easy customization. Most administrators used the second choice of adding roles and features through the Add Windows Components tool in the Control Panel. In Windows Server 2008, you can use the Server Manager console and Server Manager command-line utility to manage roles and features. They are covered in more depth in Chapter 10.

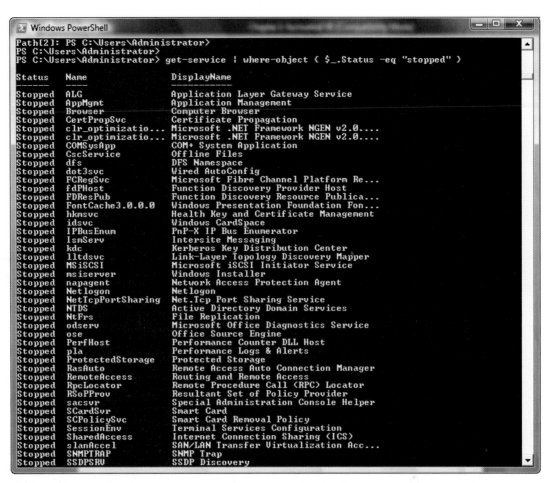

Figure 1-11   Output for the get-service cmdlet

Server Manager   As you've seen, Server Manager is the new management console for Windows Server 2008. Based on the MMC 3.0, it provides a single location for managing a local machine.

Following are all of the major areas of information within Server Manager:

- *Server Summary*—Displays system information when you start Server Manager

- *Roles*—Displays all installed roles and administrative consoles for installed roles and includes links to add and remove roles

- *Features*—Displays all installed features and includes links to add and remove features

- *Diagnostics*—Allows you to view and manage server status with built-in tools including Event Viewer, Reliability and Performance, and Device Manager

- *Configuration*—Allows you to manage system configurations with built-in tools including Windows Firewall with Advanced security, Services, and Local Users and Groups

- *Storage*—Allows you to manage storage on a server via Disk Management and manage backup and recovery via Windows Server Backup

You can manage system properties and computer information in the Server Summary window. Roles and features can be added, modified, or removed within their respective areas. Diagnostics, Configuration, and Storage provide many of the tools previously found in the Computer Management snap-in in Server 2000/2003 such as Event Viewer, Disk Management, and Local Users and Computers. Server Manager is covered more in depth in future chapters. Each of these areas is covered in depth in Chapter 10.

Activity 1-5: Adding the File Services Role and Windows Server Backup Feature

Time Required: 15 minutes

Objective: Install the File Services role and the Windows Server Backup feature using Server Manager.

Description: Your company has elected to use Windows Server 2008. You want to start by setting up a file server and installing Windows Server Backup on the new Windows Server 2008 server.

1. Log onto your Windows Server 2008 Enterprise computer, if necessary. If Server Manager does not start, click **Start** and then click **Server Manager**.

2. In the left pane of the Server Manager console, click **Roles** and then click **Add Roles** in the right pane. The Add Roles Wizard starts.

3. In the Before You Begin window, review the information and then click **Next**.

4. Click the **File Services** role and then click **Next** twice. Choose to install the default file server and do not add any role services at this time. Click **Next**, and then click **Install**.

5. Click **Close** when the File Services role is installed.

6. In the left pane of the Server Manager console, click **Features** and then click **Add Features** in the right pane. The Add Features Wizard starts.

7. Click the **Windows Server Backup** feature listed under Windows Server Backup Features and then click **Next** to review the features being installed on the next screen.

8. Click **Install** to install this feature. Click **Close** when the Windows Server Backup feature is installed.

9. In Server Manager, verify that the File Services role and Windows Server Backup feature are installed.

10. If you are continuing to the next activity, leave Server Manager open. Otherwise, close it.

Server Manager Command

While having a UI is great for new administrators and performing certain tasks, using the CLI in Windows Server 2008 can be quicker, easier, and necessary to complete certain tasks. Server Manager Command is a new CLI-based management tool that allows you to effectively install, configure, and remove roles and features in Server 2008. For example, to install the Print Services role, you enter the following command in the Command Prompt window:

```
servermanagercmd.exe –install print-server
```

Server Manager Command is useful if you want to create an unattended installation script for your servers. This is especially true in the Server Core environment, as this is the only way to install roles and features.

Activity 1-6: Adding the Print Services Role and PowerShell Feature using Server Manager Command

Time Required: 15 minutes

Objective: Install the Print Services role and the PowerShell feature using Server Manager Command.

Description: You have already installed the File Server role and the Windows Server Backup feature using the Server Manager console. Now you want to install a role and feature from the command prompt. This prepares you to install other roles and features without attending the installation.

1. Log onto your Windows Server 2008 Enterprise computer, if necessary.
2. Click **Start** and then type **cmd** in the Start Search text box.
3. In the list of search results, click **Cmd.exe** to open a Command Prompt window.
4. Type the following command and then press **Enter** to install the print Services:

```
Servermanagercmd.exe -install print-server
```

5. Type the following command and then press **Enter** to install PowerShell:

```
Servermanagercmd.exe -install PowerShell
```

6. Type the following command and then press **Enter** to verify the roles and features installed:

```
Servermanagercmd.exe -query
```

All installed features and roles are highlighted in green in the command prompt.

7. Type **Exit** and then press **Enter** to close the Command Prompt window.

Windows Server 2008 User Interface

If you have used Windows Vista, you will note some similarities between it and the Windows Server 2008 UI. When Microsoft began developing Windows Vista and Windows Server 2008, both were built on the same code base. It is estimated that the two OSs share 70 to 90 percent of their code. The following benefits are realized by sharing the code base:

- Because the OSs share the same management consoles, you can quickly learn to navigate the Windows Server 2008 UI if you have already worked with Windows Vista and vice versa.
- Through the Windows Desktop Experience and Terminal Services, Windows Server 2008 can deliver remote desktop experiences that come close to matching a user's desktop experience.
- Many applications and hardware drivers that work on Windows Vista also work on Windows Server 2008.
- Organizations that upgrade to Windows Vista and Windows Server 2008 have less administration costs in the long run because of the similarities between the operating systems.
- Shared code allows Microsoft to more quickly develop patches and updates. You are likely to see a benefit in quicker patch testing as well.
- With the release of SP1 for Windows Vista, Windows Server 2008 and Windows Vista have the same kernel code. Thus, performance between the two operating systems is similar.

Following are some new or improved features in Windows Server 2008:

- Start menu
- Network and Sharing Center
- Help and Support
- Windows Desktop Experience

Start Menu

Windows Server 2008 incorporates the redesigned Start menu into its UI. This Start menu was first introduced in Windows Vista. The most efficient way to use the Windows Server 2008 Start menu is to use the Start Search text box. When you open the Start menu, the insertion point appears in

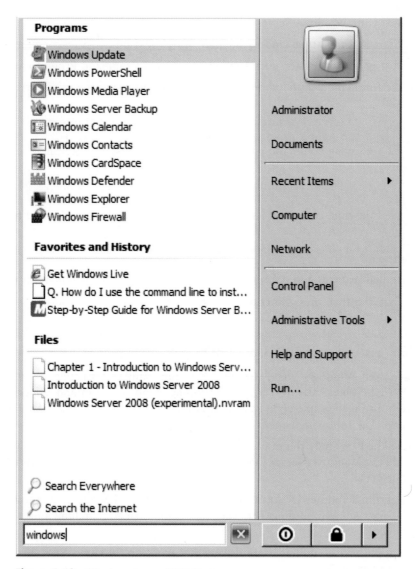

Figure 1-12 Windows Server 2008 Start menu

the Start Search text box. See Figure 1-12. You can begin typing the name of the application, console, or document you are looking for, and Windows Server 2008 begins displaying files whose names start with the characters you typed. In addition, instead of using cascading menus that take up a lot of desktop space, the Start menu is now more compact. The search results, for example, are displayed in a single vertical column. After searching for a program or navigating the Start menu, you can click the **Back** button to return to the previous view, such as the initial Start menu.

Activity 1-7: Using the Start Menu and Start Search Text Box

Time Required: 15 minutes

Objective: Use the Start Search text box to find and open a program.

Description: Your company has just upgraded to Windows Server 2008, and you want to start Notepad to create a text file. In this activity, you start Notepad using the Start Search text box on the Start menu.

1. Log onto your Windows Server 2008 Enterprise computer, if necessary.

2. Click **Start** or press the **Windows** key (lower-left corner of keyboard) or **Ctrl+Esc** to open the Start menu.

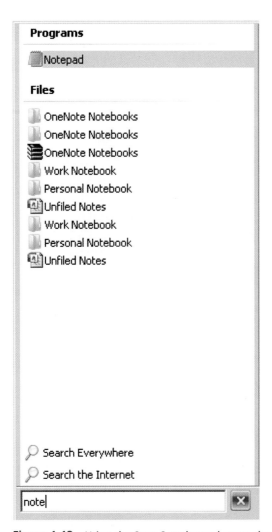

Figure 1-13   Using the Start Search text box on the Start menu

3. With the insertion point in the Start Search text box, type **note**. See Figure 1-13. The search results change with each letter you type.

4. When Notepad appears in the search results list, make sure it is selected and then press **Enter** to start the program. You can also click **Notepad** in the search results list. The Notepad window opens.

5. Close Notepad.

Network and Sharing Center

Another redesigned feature first introduced in Windows Vista is the Network and Sharing Center shown in Figure 1-14. This console provides a central location for administering many network tasks in Windows Server 2008 including network connections, sharing settings, and network discovery options. Like many of the new consoles, you will notice links to features that appear in multiple consoles. Instead of being in one location only, tools are available within the relevant area in which you are working. For example, you can access the Windows Firewall from the Network and Sharing window and the Security window. This makes sense since Windows Firewall affects both areas. As you explore Windows networking with Windows Server 2008, you will continue to use the Network and Sharing Center.

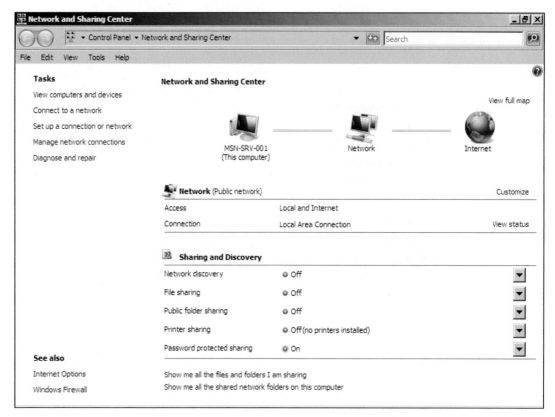

Figure 1-14   Network and Sharing Center

Windows Desktop Experience

The Desktop Experience is a new feature in Windows Server 2008. The Desktop Experience provides a number of applications that were introduced in Windows Vista such as Windows Media Player, Sync Center, and Disk Cleanup. This means that Windows Server 2008 feels more like your primary operating system, and provides less of a server-based desktop experience. Following are the applications Windows Desktop Experience makes available:

- Windows Mail
- Windows Media Player
- Windows Aero and other desktop themes
- Video for Windows (AVI support)
- Windows Photo Gallery
- Windows SideShow
- Windows Defender
- Disk Cleanup
- Sync Center
- Sound Recorder
- Character Map

For more information on the Windows Desktop Experience features, browse the Windows Vista product site at *www.microsoft.com*.

Chapter Summary

■ Over the years, network models have evolved, providing administrators with better ways to manage their networks. Most modern networks are based on client-server computing where one computer requests resources and another computer responds to those requests. Windows networks use two models: workgroup and domain. Current Windows Server 2008 networks have evolved from the Windows NT domain model, which is based on PDC/BDC domain security databases, to an AD domain model that uses multimaster replication of the domain security database between DCs.

■ Windows Server 2008 offers three general editions and two special-purpose editions: Windows Server 2008 Standard, Windows Server 2008 Enterprise, Windows Server 2008 Datacenter, Windows Web Server 2008, and Windows HPC Server 2008. Along with these new editions, you can install Windows Server 2008 as a Full installation or a limited functionality installation called Server Core.

■ Windows Server 2008 is available for both 32-bit and 64-bit hardware architectures. Like any OS, Windows Server 2008 has a minimum level of hardware requirements for its installation. Commonly, these requirements might not meet the functional needs of all environments, so you need to review the recommended and maximum hardware values when deploying Windows Server 2008.

■ New technologies in Windows Server 2008 focus on improving the performance, manageability, and security of networks. The improved installation process allows you to quickly deploy Windows Server 2008 servers with limited administrator input. Management tools such as Server Manager and WinRM help you easily manage network servers. Server Core provides a limited functionality server that improves network security by reducing the attack surface. Improvements to the TCP/IP implementation and the addition of NAP provide a number of performance, management, and security benefits to your networks.

■ Windows Server 2008 lets you organize server services into roles and features. Roles provide servers with a specific job that it provides to the network. Common roles include File services, Print services, and DNS services. The Full installation of Windows Server 2008 has 17 roles, and the Server Core installation has eight roles. Servers also provide features, or job duties, to networks. Common features include Windows Server Backup, PowerShell, and the .NET 3.0 Framework.

■ Server Manager provides administrators with a GUI console for managing roles and features, along with other aspects of the servers. Server Manager Command, or servermanagercmd.exe, is a CLI utility that allows for command line or scripted management of roles and features. This is helpful for automated installation of roles and features or for remote management of features and roles.

■ Windows Server 2008 has a look and feel similar to Windows Vista. They are similar because both OSs are built on the same secure code base. Sharing code helps you in many ways including patch deployment and application compatibility. Along with sharing code, many of the features are included in both OSs. The Start menu includes an integrated search tool for quickly finding information and applications. You can also apply the Windows Desktop Experience to Windows Server 2008 to make the OS seem more like Windows Vista, including features such as Windows Media Player and various desktop themes.

Key Terms

Active Directory (AD)   Represents the suite of roles in Windows Server 2008 domain networks for providing directory-based management, security, and authentication. Prior to Windows Server 2008, AD represented Microsoft's version of a directory services database that provided centralized security and object management.

Active Directory Domain Services (AD DS)   Stores information about objects such as users and groups on the network. This information is available so users can effectively access resources on the network and collaborate with other users. For network administrators, AD DS provides a framework for securing information and resources, along with facilitating the sharing of these resources to users.

application programming interface (API)   A set of rules and conditions created by the code writers of an operating system. Outside programmers use APIs so their applications can connect to a specific portion of the operating system. Companies such as Microsoft publish APIs for their operating systems to allow third parties to write complementary applications for their software.

attack surface   In computer networking, the available ports or services a network client or server makes available to other network clients. In network security, the goal is to reduce the attack surface to the minimum allowable level.

backup domain controller (BDC)   A domain controller in a Windows NT/pre-AD environment that is responsible for storing a read-only copy of the domain security database.

client   An entity that requests information or resources from another entity on a network. A client can be a computer, application, process, or hardware device.

client access licenses (CAL)   Software licenses that allow clients to access resources on a Microsoft network.

client-server computing   A network model that describes the relationship between two computer programs in which one program, the client, makes a service request from another program, the server, which fulfills the request.

command-line interface (CLI)   An administrative interface that requires the use of typed commands or scripted commands. After ending a command, a response is received from the system. The command prompt and Windows PowerShell are examples of CLIs in Windows Server 2008.

domain   In the client-server computing model, a group of users and computers that are managed by the same security database.

domain controller (DC)   A server responsible for holding a domain security database in an AD domain environment.

Domain Name System (DNS)   A system that matches a domain name to an Internet Protocol (IP) address based on a client query for information. Besides providing domain names, DNS provides information necessary for services such as e-mail to route mail to the proper destination. In an AD environment, DNS provides information to clients so they can connect with necessary network services.

feature   A function that enhances or supports a role or provides a stand-alone service.

forest   One or more domains with noncontiguous namespaces that are related to each other by trust relationships.

global catalog   A domain controller that holds a master searchable database of information about every object in every domain in a forest. The global catalog contains a complete replica of all objects in AD for its host domain and contains a partial replica of all objects in AD for every other domain in the forest.

Group Policy   A method for implementing specific configurations for users and computers within an AD domain. Group Policy settings are contained in Group Policy objects, which are linked to the following AD service containers: sites, domains, and organizational units.

high-performance computing (HPC)   The use of supercomputers and computer clusters, or computing systems made of multiple processors linked together in a single system, to perform computing tasks requiring large amounts of resources.

host-based stateful firewall   A local application that blocks incoming and outgoing connections based on its configuration.

mail exchanger (MX) record   A record containing DNS and IP information specifically designed to allow Internet mail servers to relay electronic messages.

managed code   Computer program code that executes under the management of a virtual machine, unlike unmanaged code, which is executed directly by the computer's central processing unit.

membership status   A setting indicating whether a network computer belongs to a workgroup or a domain.

multimaster replication   A form of replication used by domain controllers (DCs) that allows them to maintain the same read and write security databases. With multimaster replication, no DC is more authoritative than any other, and all DCs can respond to client requests.

.NET object   A data package containing information useable by applications and services that are compatible with .NET.

Network Access Protection (NAP)   A service that protects networks, both public and private, from malware such as viruses and spyware.

Network Access Control (NAC)   A computer networking concept and set of protocols used to explain how to secure network clients before the clients access the network.

Next-Generation TCP/IP stack   A new implementation of the Transmission Control Protocol (TCP)/IP protocol by Microsoft that contains full support for Internet Protocol version 4 (IPv4) and Internet Protocol version 6 (IPv6).

primary domain controller (PDC)   A central domain controller in a Windows NT/pre-AD environment that has a readable and writable copy of the domain security database. There can be only one PDC.

Receive Window Auto-tuning   A feature of TCP that allows the network interface receive window to be optimized based on the type of traffic that it is receiving.

role   A major function or service that a server performs.

Secure Sockets Layer (SSL)   An established industry standard that encrypts the channel between a Web browser and Web server to ensure the privacy and reliability of data transmitted over this channel. SSL does not, however, provide ways to validate the identities or banking accounts of the parties exchanging this data.

server   An entity that responds to requests for information and resources on a network. A server can be a computer, application, process, or hardware device.

Server Core   Available in Windows Server 2008, Server Core is a minimal server installation option designed to run a limited set of server roles and features and to provide a reduced attack surface.

Teredo   An IPv6 transition technology that provides address assignment and host-to-host automatic tunneling for unicast IPv6 traffic when IPv6/IPv4 hosts are located behind one or more IPv4 network address translators.

Terminal Services   A group of technologies that enable users to access Windows-based programs that are installed on a terminal server or to access the Windows desktop itself from almost any computing device.

thin client   A client computer or client software in a client-server network that depends primarily on a network server for processing activities and focuses mainly on conveying input and output between the user and the remote server.

tree   One or more domains related to each other by trust relationships and a shared namespace.

transitive trust   A trust between domains in a tree, which is automatically created during the domain creation process.

virtualization   A broad term that refers to presenting computing resources to users by hiding the physical characteristics of computing resources. This is done by providing an intermediary program responsible for managing communication between users and resources.

Web server   A network resource that hosts applications and information available through a Web browser or Web-based application.

Windows Remote Management (WinRM)   A new feature in Windows Server 2008 that provides administrators with remote system management capabilities. WinRM allows administrators to remotely run management scripts and manage data on remote machines. All connections are handled via the WS-Management protocol.

workgroup   A network model where each member has its own locally stored Security Account Manager database, which controls user and group membership and access to its local resources.

WS-Management protocol   A public standard for exchanging management data remotely by any device implementing the protocol, making it non–vendor specific.

Review Questions

1. The Server Core version of Windows Server 2008 Enterprise edition can be upgraded to the Full installation without a complete reinstallation of the OS. True or False?

2. _____ is Microsoft's newest server virtualization platform. It requires a(n) _____ version of Server 2008.

3. There is only one domain controller in an Active Directory domain that is writeable. The rest are read-only. True or False?

4. Which of the following Windows network models is a good choice for an environment with no IT staff, limited need for network-available resources, and a total of five computers?

   a. Domain

   b. Workgroup

   c. Ad hoc

   d. Mesh

5. You are an administrator for a small company running a Windows Web Server 2008 as a Full installation on your network. Your boss has asked you to add the following items to the Web server:

   • Simple company Web page

   • Financial application based on ASP.NET

   • Fax server

   However, you cannot complete all of your boss's requests. Why?

   a. Server Manager is not installed on Windows Web Server.

   b. Windows Web Server 2008 does not support ASP.NET.

   c. A fax server is not supported on Windows Web Server 2008.

   d. Windows Web Server 2008 requires PowerShell for Web pages to run.

6. All of the following Active Directory service containers can be linked to a Group Policy object except:

   a. Domains

   b. Organizational units

   c. Groups

   d. Sites

7. Hyper-V can be installed on which two of following editions of Windows Server 2008?

   a. Windows Server 2008 Standard, 64-bit

   b. Windows Web Server 2008, 64-bit

   c. Windows Server 2008 Enterprise, 32-bit

   d. Windows Server 2008 Datacenter, 64-bit

8. How do 64-bit versions of Windows Server 2008 differ from 32-bit versions?

   a. 64-bit versions do not support 16-bit drivers.

   b. 32-bit versions support twice the memory as 64-bit versions.

   c. 64-bit versions do not support 32-bit bit device drivers.

   d. All of the above

   e. None of the above

9. Which three of the following technologies are new to Windows Server 2008?

   a. Windows SkyDrive

   b. Hyper-V

   c. Server Hard Core

   d. PowerShell

   e. Windows FolderShare

   f. Network Access Protection

10. You must have a valid Windows Server 2008 product key to install Windows Server 2008 Datacenter. True or False?

11. Which one of the following technologies improves the installation process in Windows Server 2008?

    a. Windows Image Format (WIM)

    b. Active-X

    c. Windows ME

    d. Windows PE

12. _____ allows clients using computers with IPv6 to communicate over IPv4 networks. This is done by encapsulating the IPv__ packet inside of an IPv__ packet.

13. _____ is the new scripting and command-line interface for Windows Server 2008.

14. Group Policy preferences are enforced by computers and users, whereas Group Policy objects are not strictly enforced. True or False?

15. You are an administrator for a medium-sized business called Terrapin Technologies. Currently, you are running a Windows Server 2003 environment with Windows Server 2003 Active Directory. Your boss has asked you to look into using the Windows Server 2008 Standard edition with the Server Core installation as a solution for minimal attack surface computers at your remote locations. The following roles are required at the remote locations:

    • DNS for name resolution

    • Print Services for network printers

    • Web Server for a Web application based on ASP.NET

    • Active Directory Domain Services

    Based on what you know of Server Core, can you deploy all these roles to your remote locations? Why or why not?

    a. Yes, all of the roles can be installed on Server Core as long as you are running the 64-bit version of Windows Server 2008.

    b. No, Active Directory Domain Services and domain controllers are not supported on Server Core.

    c. No. Because of the command-line nature of Server Core, you cannot install print drivers for network printers.

    d. No, Server Core does not support ASP.NET.

16. Which one of the following commands installs the Terminal Services role on a Windows Server 2008 server?

   a. get-servermanager—install Terminal-Services

   b. servermanager.exe—install Terminal-Services

   c. servermanager.exe—installrole Terminal-Services

   d. get Servermanager—installrole Terminal-Services

17. _____ _____ _____ is a command-line interface (CLI) used to manage roles and features for the _____ _____ console.

18. The entire code base of Windows Server 2008 is based on the released version of Windows Vista. True or False?

19. Your manager has asked you to research options for deploying three Web-based applications to your network to MSN-WEB-001. Also, the applications need to use directory-based authentication without adding a domain controller to your network. Which two of the following steps meet the needs of your manager's request?

   a. Install Active Directory Federation Services on MSN-WEB-001.

   b. Install IIS 7 as a Web server on MSN-WEB-001.

   c. Install Active Directory Lightweight Directory Services on MSN-WEB-001.

   d. Install Active Directory Rights Management Services on MSN-WEB-001.

20. _____ _____ _____ has replaced the _____ _____ _____ in Windows Server 2008 as a method for deploying images across your network.

21. The Remote Server Administration Tools can be used to manage both Server Core and Full installations of Windows Server 2008. True or False?

22. Which one of the following applications is not included in the Windows Desktop Experience feature?

   a. Windows PowerShell

   b. Windows SlideShow

   c. Windows Media Player

   d. Disk Cleanup

23. What network protocol is responsible for providing IP addresses dynamically for clients that need them?

   a. DHCP

   b. DNS

   c. IPconfig

   d. IPSec

24. You have been given a server with the following hardware specifications:

   • Processor: Quad-Core Processor 64-bit

   • Memory: 8 GB

   • Available disk space: 135 GB

   • Drive: CD-ROM Drive

Given these specifications, can you install Windows Server 2008 Standard Edition as a 64-bit operating system? Why or why not?

a. No, the 64-bit version of Windows Server 2008 does not support 8 GB of memory.

b. No, Windows Server 2008 requires a DVD-ROM drive.

c. Yes, Windows Server 2008 can be installed from multiple CD-ROMs. Use setup.exe/unpackDVD to create the images needed for the install CDs.

d. No, quad-core processors are not currently supported by Microsoft for Windows Server 2008.

25. Active Directory Services domain controllers use which one of the following replication models?

a. Parent-child

b. Multihomed

c. Multimaster

d. Client-server

Case Projects

CASE PROJECTS

Case Project 1-1: Recommending Windows Server 2008 to an Organization

You are a consultant for Terrapin Technologies, a Microsoft-certified solutions provider. Terrapin Technologies has been asked by one of their clients, Vagabond Paper Products, for recommendations to meet their changing business needs. Currently, Vagabond Paper is running Server 2003 with Active Directory. They have five servers on Windows 2000 and 2003 running on old hardware. They want to maximize their future hardware investments through virtualization and clustering technology. What edition of Windows Server 2008 best suits their needs? Does Vagabond Paper need to purchase specific hardware to meet the requirements of the project?

Case Project 1-2: Creating a Batch File in Windows Server 2008

In preparation for installing new Windows Server 2008 servers into your environment, your manager has asked you to streamline the installation process by automating the setup of specific features and roles on the new servers. These servers will be Terminal Servers for your end users. You need to create a batch file that runs on each server. Research server-managercmd.exe and find the commands that will install the following roles and services:

- Fax Server
- Terminal Services
- Windows Desktop Experience
- Remote Server Administration Tools
- Network Load Balancing

Case Project 1-3: Recommending Roles and Services

Badger Iron Products is a large organization with 5,000 users spread across the Midwest. They have multiple office locations, along with a large contingent of traveling sales and marketing personnel. These remote employees need access to company applications and network file resources while working off site. The company president has also decided he wants to consolidate their server hardware as much as possible to save expenses. List several roles, features, and technologies in Windows Server 2008 that would assist Badger Iron in meeting their needs.

Case Project 1-4: Using Windows Server 2008 as a Desktop Replacement

After examining Windows Server 2008, you decide it would make a good desktop OS instead of your old Windows XP machine. It would also help increase your familiarity with the Windows Server 2008 UI. List several modifications you would make to the default installation of Windows Server 2008 so that is more like Windows Vista. If time and resources allow, configure your own Windows Server 2008 server with the modifications you devised.

chapter 2

Installing Windows Server 2008

After reading this chapter and completing the exercises, you will be able to:

- Describe the improvements and key technologies in deploying Windows Server 2008

- Prepare to install the Server Core version of Windows Server 2008

- Install a Server Core version of Windows Server 2008

- Configure Full and Server Core versions of Windows Server 2008

- Describe Windows Server 2008 with Server Core

Installing Windows Server 2008 is relatively easy because the installation media has been significantly improved and the steps are streamlined. The result is a quicker installation requiring less administrator input and more control for automation of the entire process.

In this chapter, you explore the deployment improvements and technologies such as **Windows Preinstallation Environment (Windows PE)** and **Windows Imaging Format (WIM)**. You install the Server Core version of Windows Server 2008 and examine the steps and options in depth. You also consider your options for installing and deploying Windows Server 2008 including unattended installations and Windows Deployment Services. Because no Windows installation would be complete without licensing, you explore the changes Microsoft made to the licensing and activation options in Windows Server 2008. Finally, you return your focus to Server Core to configure it for regular use.

Deployment Improvements in Windows Server 2008

All system administrators are looking for ways to work smarter, not harder. With the new deployment features of Windows Server 2008, Microsoft provides procedures, technologies, and tools to assist with achieving that goal. Improvements to the deployment process mean ease of administration and savings in dollars and time. An efficient deployment strategy decreases your time to deployment and reduces the long-term administrative costs for maintaining your systems.

Windows Server 2008 delivers new enhancements for easing deployment, which fall into the following two categories:

- Process improvements
- Tools and technologies improvements

Process Improvements

Windows Server 2008 introduces many new process improvements that ease both installation and deployment for any size organization. These improvements include the following features:

- Modularization
- WIM
- eXtensible Markup Language–based answer files
- Installation scripts

Modularization   In Windows 2008, Microsoft reengineered the basic architecture of the Windows operating system (OS) so that it uses independent units of programming logic called **modules**, meaning that you can customize Windows Server 2008 by using some modules and not others. To achieve this **modularization**, Microsoft separated parts of Windows Server 2008, such as system components, device drivers, language packs, and updates, into free-standing modules that the operating system links together. Separating the operating system into many modules allows you to do the following:

- Introduce new components, such as device drivers, language packs, and service packs easily because you are simply adding new modules to the system
- Update or remove an existing component and affect only the related module or modules for that component
- Install language packs quickly because language packs are modules

WIM   An **image file**, or disk **image**, contains all the information you need to make an exact copy of a storage device, including its structure and contents. System administrators use image files to quickly install operating systems on dozens of computers or more. You can use an image file to install Windows Server 2008 on the computers in your organization. All installations of Windows Server 2008 are based on a WIM image file. With this new format, you can modify an existing image and create new images with tools discussed later in the chapter.

The new WIM image file format is important because most legacy imaging tools did not allow you to modify an existing image. Instead, if you needed to add drivers or other files, they required you to rebuild the image in its entirety. Now, WIM allows you to mount your image files and add drivers, applications, or other files directly to your image through Windows Explorer. For example, you can add a security update or service pack directly to your image by copying it into the appropriate folder. Another benefit is that you can apply a single image file to different hardware platforms. In the past, you often had to create an image for each hardware platform. For example, suppose you purchased the same model of servers from a vendor at different times or updated the hardware profile of a specific model. Some imaging tools required you to create a different image for each model even if the change was as simple as updating a network adapter card. WIM allows you to add all the drivers you might need so the image file fits the hardware profiles in your organization. The only caveat is that you need different images for 32-bit and 64-bit versions of Windows Server 2008. WIM also lets Microsoft use a single binary format, or installation media, for each architecture type. Previous versions of Windows Server required you to have the media for the particular edition you were installing.

eXtensible Markup Language–Based Answer Files   As in other areas of Windows Server 2008, Microsoft has moved many of its processes to using **eXtensible Markup Language (XML)**, a standard for annotating and formatting data exchanged between applications. While previous versions of Windows required multiple answer files to perform **unattended installations** (an installation that does not require your input), Windows Server 2008 uses a single answer file using the XML format. An **answer file** is a text file that provides configuration settings during the installation of an operating system. Another improvement is that new files can be created only through the use of the **Windows System Image Manager (WSIM)**, a utility designed to create answer files for unattended installations. Although WSIM is the only tool that automates the creation of an answer file, you can still modify the files using a text editor or other tool.

Installation Scripts   For years, administrators have installed Windows servers by using **installation scripts**, which automate the installation of services and features that you would normally enter manually during installation. Using installation scripts can speed the deployment process, especially in remote locations where administrators might not be available to enter the necessary information. Scripts also remove human errors that can occur, especially when more than one administrator perform the installations. Windows Server 2008 includes extensive support for using the command line and scripting to enable remote, automated, and repeatable deployment solutions. Installation scripts are discussed in more depth later in this chapter in the section on unattended installation options for Windows Server 2008.

Tool and Technologies Improvements

Windows Server 2008 includes improvements to the following tools and technologies:

- Windows Deployment Services
- Multicast
- Trivial File Transfer Protocol

Windows Deployment Services

Windows Deployment Services (WDS) is a tool you use to manage the imaging process on a network. Imaging allows you to capture a customized Windows image that you can reuse throughout an organization. WDS includes multicast and Trivial File Transfer Protocol which are new features that improve deployment with Windows Server 2008 and are discussed in the following sections.

WDS provides the following benefits:

- Allows network-based installation of Windows operating systems, including Windows Vista and Windows Server 2008, reducing the complexity and cost when compared to manual installations
- Deploys Windows images to computers without operating systems.

- Supports mixed environments that include Windows Vista, Windows Server 2008, Windows XP, and Windows Server 2003
- Uses standard Windows Server 2008 setup technologies, including Windows PE, .wim files, and image-based setup

Because WDS is an enterprise deployment solution, your environment must meet the following requirements before you can install and use WDS:

- The computer must be a member of an Active Directory domain.
- Dynamic Host Configuration Protocol (DHCP) must be active and available on your network.
- Domain Name System (DNS) must be active and available on your network.
- A **New Technology File System (NTFS)** partition must be available for storing images.

Multicast   **Multicast** allows multiple computers to receive communication simultaneously. With multicast, you can efficiently build multiple workstations at the same time over the network. With traditional multicast implementations, the sender (such as the WDS server) broadcasts the information only once. Each client must then listen to the entire communication from end to end to receive it. This required all machines to begin the imaging process at the same time. With WDS, the server repeats the communication so that clients can begin installing an image at any time during the communication. This improvement to the multicast feature is due in part to the use of the WIM image format. It allows the server to continuously replay the image until all clients requesting an image are deployed. Other benefits from the new implementation of multicast include the following:

- Multicast works well on production networks without interfering with existing network communication because it controls congestion and data flow.
- Multicast is independent of WDS and Active Directory. This means you do not need to have Active Directory or an active WDS implementation to take advantage of it.

Trivial File Transfer Protocol   The **Trivial File Transfer Protocol (TFTP)** is the protocol used for transferring images across the network. It is a key component of the **Preboot eXecution Environment**, the backbone of WDS. Based on the **User Datagram Protocol (UDP)**, which is a core Internet Protocol (IP) suite protocol, TFTP traffic is connectionless in nature, meaning that the sequencing of data **packets**, or **datagrams**, is not guaranteed. UDP lends itself to applications that need efficiency and speed over guaranteed delivery. TFTP adds reliability checking to each packet to ensure that images are deployed correctly. This caused performance issues in WDS on Windows Server 2003. In Windows Server 2008, however, TFTP has been rewritten with new code to allow a server to send a series of packets, referred to as a window, before receiving an acknowledgment that the transfer was successful.

In Activity 2-1, you install the WDS role on Windows Server 2008. Because DHCP and Active Directory are not installed yet, you can only install the role and open the management console for WDS.

Activity 2-1: Installing the WDS Role

Time Required: 20 minutes

Objective: Install the WDS role in Windows Server 2008.

Description: As the systems administrator for your company, you want to install WDS so that you can centralize your installation processes and quickly deploy new systems. You are installing the WDS role on your server. However, you cannot use WDS until you install Active Directory and DHCP.

In all the activities, your instructor might give you additional steps to perform depending on your lab environment. All the activities in this chapter are appropriate for physical machines and virtual machine (VM) applications.

1. Log onto your server, if necessary. If Server Manager does not start, click **Start** and then click **Server Manager**.

2. Click **Roles** in the left pane of Server Manager and then click **Add Roles** in the right pane to start the Add Roles Wizard. Click **Next** in the Before You Begin dialog box.

3. In the Select Server Roles dialog box, click the **Windows Deployment Services** check box and then click **Next**.

4. Read the Introduction to Windows Deployment Services and then click **Next**.

5. Install the Deployment Server and the Transport Server by clicking **Next** and then clicking **Install**.

6. Click **Close**. A new role is installed on the server: Windows Deployment Services.

7. Reboot your computer so that the WDS service starts.

8. Log onto your server after the reboot.

9. In the left pane of Server Manager, click to expand **Roles**, the **Windows Deployment Services** role, and then **Servers**. Click **Servers** to display the servers (if any) in the right pane. Normally, a server is listed. However, your server cannot be added to WDS until it is a member of a domain.

Windows Automated Installation Kit

The **Windows Automated Installation Kit (WAIK)** for Windows Server 2008 is a suite of tools that helps **original equipment manufacturers (OEMs)**, system builders, and corporate IT professionals deploy Windows onto new hardware by automating the installation process. With WAIK version 1.1, you can configure and deploy the following operating systems:

- Windows Vista
- Windows Vista Service Pack 1 (SP1)
- Windows Server 2008

This version of WAIK includes new and improved tools and features including the following:

- WSIM
- ImageX
- Windows PE
- Windows Recovery Environment
- Sysprep

WAIK is a suite of tools that is not covered completely in this chapter. For more detailed information about WAIK and its tools, refer to the WAIK documentation provided as part of the WAIK installation.

Activity 2-2 Installing the Windows Automated Installation Kit

Time Required: 30 minutes

Objective: Install WAIK in Windows Server 2008 and become familiar with the WAIK user guide.

Description: One of your responsibilities is to manage the installation of your client machines. One tool for this is WAIK for Windows Server 2008. In this activity, you install WAIK on your Windows Server 2008 system and then review the tools it provides.

Before beginning this activity, you need a current copy of WAIK for Vista SP1 and Windows Server 2008. It is available as an ISO image, so you can burn it to a DVD for use with a physical machine, or you can mount it within a VM. If not provided by your instructor in your lab environment, you can download it from the Microsoft Web site. (Go to *www.microsoft.com* and search for WAIK.)

1. Log onto your server.

2. If the Welcome to Windows Automated Installation Kit window does not appear, browse to and open your optical drive and then double-click **startCD**.

3. In the Welcome to Windows Automated Installation Kit window, click **Windows AIK Setup** and then click **Next** to begin the installation.

4. Read the License Terms, select **I Agree**, and then click **Next**.

5. In the next dialog box, you choose the installation folder location and who can use the application once installed. Accept the default options by clicking **Next**.

6. Confirm the installation by clicking **Next**.

7. After Setup installs the WAIK components, click **Close** to exit.

8. To access all of the WAIK tools, click **Start**, point to **All Programs**, and then click **Microsoft Windows AIK**.

9. Click the **Documentation** folder and then click the **Windows Automated Installation Kit User's Guide** link. A window opens displaying the Windows help files for WAIK.

10. Browse through the help files to become familiar with the information they provide.

Windows System Image Manager

As mentioned earlier, WSIM is the recommended tool for creating your image distribution shares and the **unattend.xml** answer file, which Windows Server 2008 searches for during an unattended installation. Installed as part of WAIK, WSIM gives you access to all the configurable settings in Windows Server 2008. This includes modifying and saving your changes to unattend.xml. This file contains the information necessary for automating an installation, such as server name, workgroup, and roles to be installed. Figure 2-1 shows the WSIM console for performing management tasks including creating and modifying answer files.

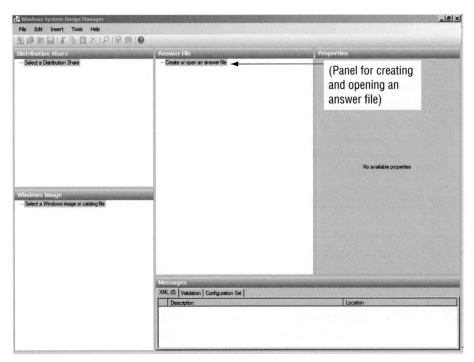

Figure 2-1   WSIM console in Windows Server 2008

Although the basic installation process for Windows Server 2008 has been simplified, creating and managing unattended installations is fairly complex. WSIM provides a friendly interface for managing the unattend.xml. However, with so many configuration settings, you might be overwhelmed by the possibilities. An easier way to create a unattend.xml is to find an existing file and customize it to your needs with a text editor. Figure 2-2 shows a sample unattend.xml file.

ImageX

ImageX is a new command-line tool that organizations can use to capture, modify, and apply file-based disk images for rapid deployment. ImageX works with Windows Imaging (.wim) files for copying to a network, or it can work with other technologies that use the WIM file format such as WDS. ImageX can capture an entire disk partition or a specific folder. This allows you to use ImageX as a backup utility as well as an imaging tool. ImageX is discussed in more depth later in this chapter.

Windows Preinstallation Environment

Windows PE is a limited 32-bit operating system based on the Windows Server 2008 and Windows Vista SP1 **kernel code**, which is the programmatic logic in the central components of Windows operating systems. Not to be used as a stand-alone operating system, Windows PE is designed for installing, troubleshooting, and recovering Windows Server 2008 and Windows Vista. With Windows PE, you can start a computer from network or removable media, which provides network resources and other resources necessary to install and troubleshoot Windows Vista. You can also use Windows PE to boot a server and create an image using ImageX. See Figure 2-3. This allows unrestricted access to all of the system files, necessary when imaging the entire operating system drive partition or disk.

Although Windows PE is a stable technology that has been used for years in different incarnations, Windows Server 2008 and Windows Vista are the first operating systems from Microsoft to use it during installation. It replaces MS-DOS-based boot disks and installers. Windows PE provides the following benefits over MS-DOS:

- Windows PE supports NTFS 5.x file systems.

- Windows PE natively supports TCP/IP network and file sharing.

```xml
<?xml version="1.0" encoding="utf-8" ?>
- <unattend xmlns="urn:schemas-microsoft-com:unattend">
  - <settings pass="windowsPE">
    + <component name="Microsoft-Windows-Setup"
        processorArchitecture="x86" publicKeyToken="31bf3856ad364e35"
        language="neutral" versionScope="nonSxS"
        xmlns:wcm="http://schemas.microsoft.com/WMIConfig/2002/State">
    + <component name="Microsoft-Windows-International-Core-WinPE"
        processorArchitecture="x86" publicKeyToken="31bf3856ad364e35"
        language="neutral" versionScope="nonSxS"
        xmlns:wcm="http://schemas.microsoft.com/WMIConfig/2002/State"
        xmlns:xsi="http://www.w3.org/2001/XMLSchema-instance">
    </settings>
  + <settings pass="specialize">
  + <settings pass="oobeSystem">
  + <settings pass="offlineServicing">
  + <settings pass="generalize">
    <cpi:offlineImage cpi:source="catalog://mniehaus-
      m400/distribution$/operating systems/windows vista
      5536/sources/install_windows vista ultimate.clg"
      xmlns:cpi="urn:schemas-microsoft-com:cpi" />
  </unattend>
```

Figure 2-2 Sample of unattend.xml

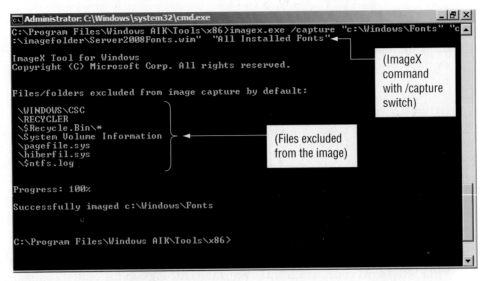

Figure 2-3   Using Windows PE to start ImageX

- Windows PE natively supports 32-bit and 64-bit Windows device drivers, which is especially important when it comes to network adapter drivers.
- Windows PE can be started with various media, including CDs, DVDs, USB flash drives, and WDS.

Windows Recovery Environment

Windows Recovery Environment (Windows RE) is a new recovery environment built into Windows Server 2008 and based on Windows PE 2.0. Windows RE is a complete diagnostic and recovery solution as well as a platform for building your own recovery solutions. For more information on building custom Windows RE solutions for recovery, search for the article "Walkthrough: Create a Bootable Windows PE RAM Disk on CD-ROM" at the Microsoft TechNet Web site. This article is based on Windows Vista but is applicable to Windows Server 2008 and Windows PE.

Activity 2-3: Launching Windows PE as a Recovery Tool

Time Required: 5 minutes

Objective: Start Windows PE and allow it to access your server's file system.

Description: You have heard that Windows PE is a helpful tool for performing system recovery tasks along with the normal installation tasks. In this activity, you boot your server from your Windows Server 2008 media to open Windows PE. Next, you access the recovery tools and open a command prompt for viewing the file directories on your server.

1. Insert your Windows Server 2008 media into your optical drive and then restart your computer.

2. When prompted, press any key to boot from the CD or DVD.

3. At the Install Windows screen, click **Next**.

4. Instead of choosing Install Now, click **Repair your computer** in the lower-left corner of the window.

5. In the System Recovery Options window, click **Next**. A window opens listing a number of recovery tools, including Windows Complete PC Restore, Windows Memory Diagnostic Tool, and Command Prompt.

6. Click **Command Prompt**.

```
Administrator: X:\windows\system32\cmd.exe                    _ □ X
Microsoft Windows [Version 6.0.6001]
Copyright (c) 2006 Microsoft Corporation.  All rights reserved.

X:\Sources>c:

C:\>dir
 Volume in drive C has no label.
 Volume Serial Number is F089-A453

 Directory of C:\

09/18/2006  01:43 PM                    24 autoexec.bat
09/18/2006  01:43 PM                    10 config.sys
05/19/2008  10:24 AM                 9,947 image.wim
05/18/2008  07:19 PM       <DIR>          imagefolder
05/18/2008  07:08 PM       <DIR>          images
05/18/2008  07:21 PM       <DIR>          myimage
01/19/2008  01:40 AM       <DIR>          PerfLogs
05/19/2008  05:57 AM       <DIR>          Program Files
05/19/2008  05:59 AM       <DIR>          Users
05/19/2008  05:55 AM       <DIR>          Windows
               3 File(s)          9,981 bytes
               7 Dir(s)  21,392,265,216 bytes free

C:\>
```

Figure 2-4   File directory listing from the command prompt in Windows PE

7. Type **c:** at the command prompt and then press **Enter**. This changes the command prompt so it accesses your C: drive.

8. Type **dir** and then press **Enter** to list the contents of the root directory of your C: drive, as shown in Figure 2-4.

9. Type **exit** and press **Enter** to close the Command Prompt window, and then click the **Restart** button to reboot your server.

Sysprep

Because even a basic installation of Windows Server 2008 contains unique information such as **security identifiers (SIDs)**, you might need to remove unique characteristics of an installation before creating an image. This task is called **generalization**. Without removing this information, each copy of an image that you deploy would have identical security information. This would cause difficulty when these servers try to communicate with each other. Basically, the machines would not be able to tell themselves apart from one another. To avoid this conflict, you can use the **System Preparation tool (Sysprep)**. Sysprep prepares an installation of Windows for imaging and deployment by modifying a system to create a new SID and other unique information the next time it starts. Sysprep also removes user and computer-specific information that should not be transferred to new images.

This section focuses on the **out-of-box experience (OOBE)** option with the /generalize switch to prepare an image for duplication and deployment. This option removes the unique characteristics of a server and prepares it for imaging.

Like many tools in Windows Server 2008, you can run Sysprep through the graphical user interface (GUI) or via the command line. Most administrators choose the GUI for Sysprep. To start Sysprep, type the following command in the Run dialog box or at the command prompt, as shown in Figure 2-5:

```
c:\windows\system32\sysprep\sysprep.exe
```

The command displayed in Figure 2-5 is being executed from the Run dialog box. Because c:\windows is the default system root directory, you might need to change your path if Windows Server 2008 was installed in a different directory or partition.

Figure 2-5 Starting the System Preparation Tool using the Run dialog box

Sysprep provides a set of system cleanup actions, as shown in Figure 2-6. You must choose Enter System Out-of-Box Experience (OOBE) or Enter System Audit Mode before you can generalize an image.

Out-of-Box Experience The most common cleanup action with Sysprep is to use the system OOBE when generalizing images. This combination will remove the computer security identifier (SID), reset the computer activation, and boot the computer into Windows Welcome.

Audit Mode The second system cleanup action is **Audit Mode**. This is an advanced generalization mode that allows you to apply additional application and driver modifications to a specific image. You can set the Windows Welcome window to open at the next boot. This allows you to verify that the drivers and applications are working properly before delivering them to your end users.

 You should only use Sysprep to configure new installations of Windows. You can run Sysprep as many times as required to build and configure your installation of Windows before imaging. Although Sysprep resets the activation of Windows Server 2008, you can only reactivate a Windows Server 2008 installation up to three times.

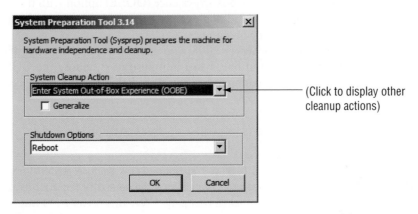

Figure 2-6 Selecting a cleanup action in the System Preparation Tool

Preparing to Install Windows Server 2008

Like most administrators, you are probably familiar with the traditional method of installing Windows:

1. Turn on the computer.
2. Insert the Windows installation media.
3. Answer questions and wait.

This is a great method when building one or two Windows systems, especially with the new installation process in Windows Server 2008. In environments that require building multiple systems simultaneously or customizing builds, this task can become time consuming for a single administrator to manage without assistance. In this section, you explore the types of installations you can perform with Windows Server 2008: Clean and Upgrade. Next, you focus on the methods available for completing an installation. Finally, you examine how to configure Windows Server 2008 after installation.

Installation Types

Depending on the state of your environment, existing servers, and data, you have two choices for the type of installation you can perform with Windows Server 2008:

- Clean (migrate) installation
- Upgrade installation

All installations can be performed as either an attended or an unattended installation. **Attended installations** require your input during installation, whereas an unattended installation uses answer files and scripts for automation and does not require you to be present. Figure 2-7 displays both installation options during the Windows PE portion of a Windows Server 2008 installation.

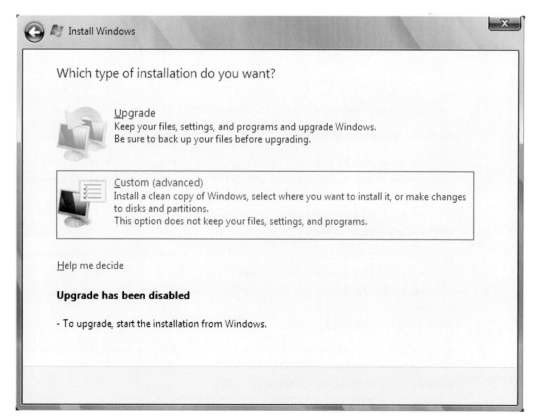

Figure 2-7   Installation options for Windows Server 2008

Clean/Migrate Installations   The preferred method of installing Windows Server 2008 is a **clean installation**, also called migrations. This method requires a complete installation of the operating system onto a new or a reformatted disk drive. Clean installations do not transfer settings from previous operating systems that might be installed on a server. For example, suppose you have a Windows Server 2003 file server storing company data. If you perform a clean installation of Windows Server 2008 on the file server, you will lose all your data unless you have backed it up to another location. In this case, you should perform an upgrade installation, covered next.

The following are good examples of when to use a clean installation:

- Your current server operating system is not Windows Server 2003 SP1 or greater.
- You cannot upgrade your current server operating system to Windows Server 2003 SP1.
- You have a third-party application installed that is not supported on Windows Server 2008.
- You do not have a driving business need that requires you to perform an upgrade.
- You have good backups and documentation.

Microsoft and most network administrators recommend performing a clean installation. Especially with a new operating system such as Windows Server 2008, you have few reasons to transfer the settings from a legacy installation. You performed a clean installation of Windows Server 2008 Enterprise (Full installation) in Activity 1-1 in Chapter 1, and you perform a clean installation of Windows Server 2008 Standard (Server Core) in Activity 2-8 in this chapter.

Upgrade Installations   **Upgrade installations** allow you to install Windows Server 2008 over an existing installation of Windows Server 2003. Upgrading means that you retain certain settings and applications on your system, which is often undesirable.

When you qualify for upgrading an operating system, you need to verify that the current server meets the installation requirements for Windows Server 2008. Besides the hardware requirements discussed in Chapter 1, Table 2-1 lists the Windows Server editions that can be upgraded.

Table 2-1   Supported upgrade paths to Windows Server 2008

Current Server Operating System	Upgrade to
Windows Server 2003 R2 Standard Edition	Full installation of Windows Server 2008 Standard
Windows Server 2003 Standard Edition with SP1	Full installation of Windows Server 2008 Enterprise
Windows Server 2003 Standard Edition with SP2	
Windows Server 2008 Standard RC0	
Windows Server 2008 Standard RC1	
Windows Server 2003 R2 Enterprise Edition	Full installation of Windows Server 2008 Enterprise
Windows Server 2003 Enterprise Edition with SP1	
Windows Server 2003 Enterprise Edition with SP2	
Windows Server 2008 Enterprise RC0	
Windows Server 2008 Enterprise RC1	
Windows Server 2003 R2 Datacenter Edition	Full installation of Windows Server 2008 Datacenter
Windows Server 2003 Datacenter Edition with SP1	
Windows Server 2003 Datacenter Edition with SP2	
Windows Server 2008 Datacenter RC0	
Windows Server 2008 Datacenter RC1	

Keep the following guidelines in mind as you consider upgrading instead of performing a clean installation:

- You cannot upgrade from Windows Server 2003 (any edition) to Windows Server 2008 with Server Core.

- You cannot upgrade from one hardware architecture to another, so you cannot upgrade from a 32-bit architecture to 64-bit or vice versa.

- Although you cannot uninstall Windows Server 2008 after performing an upgrade, you can revert to the previous state of your operating system if setup fails and the upgrade is unsuccessful.

- Verify that *all* of your third-party applications can run on Windows Server 2008 and are supported by the vendor.

- Before the installation begins, a compatibility check is performed to verify the computer you are upgrading is capable of being upgraded. This check produces a Compatibility Report, as shown in Figure 2-8.

Upgrading from previous Windows Server versions to Windows Server 2008 is *only* practical if the OS components are the only software installed on the server. Third-party applications and many installed roles in Active Directory probably cannot be upgraded successfully. Clean installations are the preferred installation choice when available. Considering the major changes in installation and the OS itself, upgrading is no longer a realistic installation option. For more information on known upgrade issues, search for the Upgrading to Windows Server 2008 document on the Microsoft Web site.

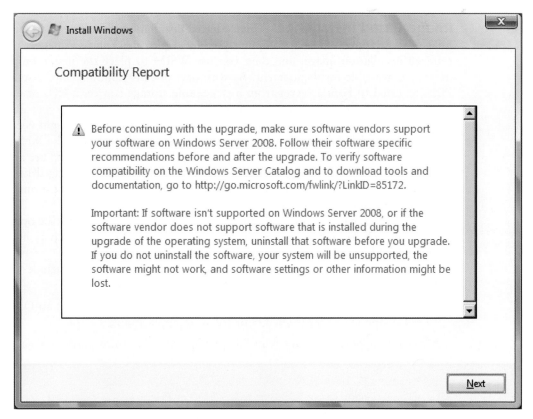

Figure 2-8 Compatibility Report produced during a Windows Server 2008 upgrade

Installing Windows Server 2008

This section explores the three installation methods available for Windows Server 2008. Each of the following methods has a purpose and place within a network:

- DVD/USB boot installation
- Network distribution share installation
- Image-based installation

DVD/USB Boot Installation   Probably the most familiar of the installation methods is using physical installation media. Windows Server 2008 can be installed via optical drive (that is a DVD drive) or via USB flash drive. This type of installation is called a **DVD boot installation** and is the most common media-based type. Installing with a USB flash drive is new and not yet as popular as using a DVD. However, with the advent of USB 2.0 and servers that can boot from the drives in their USB ports, USB flash drives are the perfect media for installing Windows Server 2008. Whether using optical or flash media, this installation method requires you to be present at the server. Activity 1-1, where you installed Windows Server 2008, is an example of a DVD installation.

Network Distribution Share Installation   Similar to the CD installation, **network distribution share installations** are installed from a drive location. However, this drive location is a network share, which is called a **network distribution share**, and is accessed over a **local area network**. To accomplish this, you boot a server from a removable storage source such as a CD or USB flash drive that contains Windows PE. The removable medium boots the server into Windows PE and then connects to the installation files located on the network. Because the installation takes place across the network, it is slower than the local media installations.

You have more options to customize installation when you use the network distribution share method. You can use tools such as WSIM and ImageX to customize the image with service packs, updates, or additional hardware drivers.

Image-Based Installation   **Image-based installations** require you to create a customized image that is applied to each computer you are deploying. You use ImageX to create this customized installation image, and then you use WSIM to place the image on a network share, making it available for deployment. As with network distribution share installation, Windows PE is required to boot a server from a removable storage source, a CD, or a USB flash drive. Because your image contains the complete installation of Windows Server 2008, image-based installations are the fastest installation type available. However, you might need to create multiple images to deploy different types of servers, such as a file server and a Web server.

Image-based installations give the highest level of customization and are an excellent choice for large enterprises deploying numerous systems. Along with including drivers, service packs, and updates, image-based installations can also include installed applications. This allows you to deploy fully functional systems right after deployment.

ImageX has many options that are covered next. Figure 2-9 lists all the options available for running ImageX from the command line. It shows the use of the /? switch along with the ImageX command in the command prompt.

Although ImageX provides benefits in the imaging process, it also includes the following limitations:

- ImageX can be used only for capturing and applying full images of an OS. It cannot be used to apply updates to the OS or software applications.
- ImageX supports only the .wim file type, unlike other third-party applications for imaging.

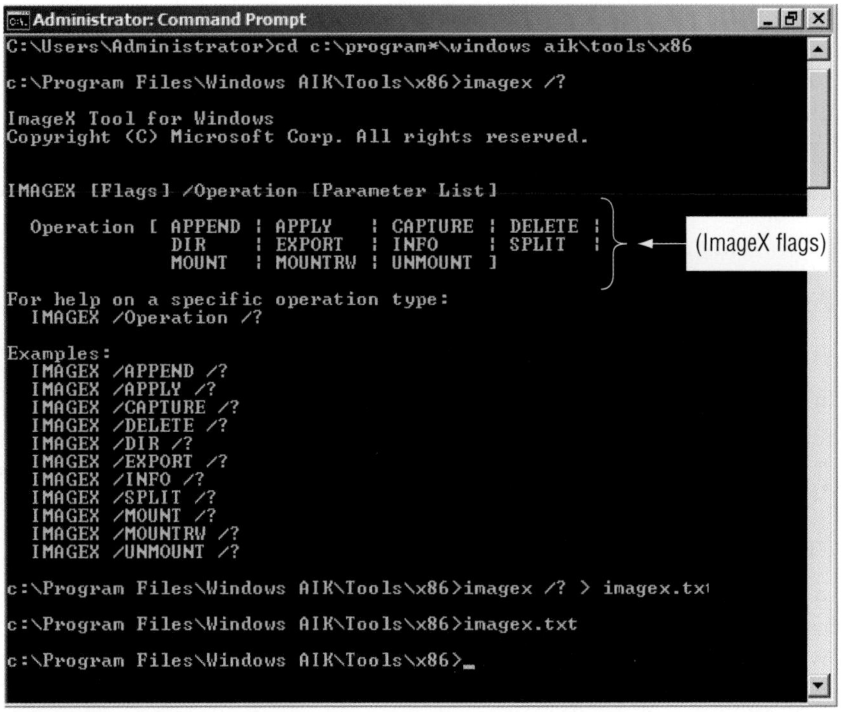

Figure 2-9 Command prompt listing of ImageX commands

- Mounting a .wim file as a read/write volume requires NTFS.
- ImageX images can be mounted only in Windows XP with SP2, Windows Vista, and Windows Server 2003 with SP1.

Imaging Options with ImageX

With ImageX, you can perform the following imaging tasks:

- Capture an image
- Append an image
- Modify an image
- Apply an image

Capturing an Image   The type of image you are creating (data or drive image) determines where the capturing begins. When imaging a drive that contains your running operating system, such as C:, you must boot into Windows PE and use ImageX. This ensures that you have unrestricted access to all file system files. For data file images not part of the operating system and closed at the time of imaging, you can run ImageX in Windows Server 2008. When you are in the proper capture environment, you can run ImageX to capture the image. The syntax for capturing an image is as follows:

```
imagex /capture image_path image_file "description"
```

Consider an example of this command:

```
imagex /capture "c:\*.*" "c:\images\Server2008.wim" "Server2008STD"
```

This example captures the source image, which is the C: drive. It places the image in c:\images\Server2008.wim and gives the image a description of Server2008STD. This is a unique identifier for the image you are creating.

ImageX can place multiple images within a single file. This provides an advantage for image storage when using **single-instance storage**. This means that if multiple images require the same file, such as different images of Windows Vista, that file is stored only once within the image. Imagine the amount of space you can save if you are creating an image file for operating systems such as Windows Vista or Windows Server 2008. Use the Append function in the ImageX command to add images or drive contents to an existing WIM file. The syntax for appending an image file is as follows:

```
imagex /append image_path image_file "description"
```

Consider an example of this command:

```
imagex /append d: c:\Server2008.wim "Server2008_W_DDrive"
```

In this example, you are adding the contents of the D: drive to the image, c:\Server2008.wim, and giving the new image a description of Server2008_W_DDrive.

Activity 2-4: Capturing an Image with ImageX

Time Required: 25 minutes

Objective: Create an image using ImageX.

Description: As the systems administrator for your company, you need to create images for deploying both Windows Server 2008 and Windows Vista SP1. To become familiar with ImageX, you want to create an image of part of your file system. You can then step through the imaging task without spending a considerable amount of time waiting for a full image to be created. In this activity, you create an image of the c:\windows\fonts folder.

1. Log onto your server.

2. Click **Start**, type **Windows PE Command Prompt** in the Start Search box. When it Windows PE Command Prompt appears, select it and press enter to launch.

3. Type **md c:\MCTS_70642\Ch2\ImageFolder** and then press **Enter** to create a new directory called ImageFolder in the folder created for this chapter. This represents a distribution point to contain the .wim file created with ImageX.

4. Change to the directory containing ImageX by using the following cd command:

```
cd \Program Files\Windows AIK\Tools\x86\
```

5. Next, run the following ImageX command to create an image of the c:\windows\fonts directory from the command prompt:

```
imagex /capture "c:\Windows\fonts"
"c:\MCTS_70642\Ch2\imagefolder\Server2008Fonts.wim" "All
Installed Fonts"
```

6. Leave the command prompt window open for the next exercise.

Modifying an Image

Using the WIM image format, you can modify images by adding or removing files. To accomplish this, you need to mount the image. This task connects an NTFS folder to the selected image. After mounting, you can use Windows Explorer or the command prompt to work with the files contained in the image. For example, suppose you create a folder located on your server in c:\ImageFolder. You can use ImageX to mount an image of Windows Server 2008 located in c:\Images\Server2008.wim. You can then open the c:\ImageFolder to access the files and folders contained in Server2008.wim.

The command you use for mounting an image is ImageX /mount. By default, /mount allows read access only to a mounted image. To have read/write access, you must use the /mountrw command with ImageX. The syntax for mounting an image as read only is as follows:

```
imagex /mount image_file [image_number | image_name] image_path
```

Consider an example of this command:

```
imagex /mount "c:\Images\Server2008.wim" "Standard"  c:\imagefolder\
```

In this command, you are using ImageX to mount the image named "Standard" from the Server2008.wim file to c:\imagefolder\. Remember that the image is read-only. If you want to write to this image, use /mountrw instead of /mount, as shown in the following command:

```
imagex /mountrw  "c:\Images\Server2008.wim" "Standard_RW"
c:\imagefolder\
```

After the image is mounted as a read/write file, you can modify it using Windows Explorer or the command line. You then need to remove the image from the local file system, a task called unmounting. To perform this task, use the /unmount option with the ImageX command. Any changes made need to be committed to the image. Otherwise, the image will be the same as it was prior to being mounted.

The syntax to unmount an image from the file system and commit the changes is the following:

```
imagex /unmount /commit image_path
```

Activity 2-5: Modifying an Image with ImageX

Time Required: 10 minutes

Objective: Mount and modify a WIM image.

Description: Along with being able to capture images, you have heard that ImageX allows you to access an image through the file system so that you can modify it. Because you anticipate adding new drivers and removing files from images, you want to explore ImageX. In this activity, you step through the tasks of mounting the WIM image, Server2008Fonts, and then adding a new font called Server2008SuperFont to the image.

1. Open the Windows PE Command Prompt from the start menu, if necessary.

2. Type **md c:\MCTS_70642\Ch2\ImageMountFolder** to create a new directory called ImageMountFolder. This is the mount point for your image within the file system.

3. Next, run the following ImageX command to mount the image Server2008Fonts.wim to the c:\MCTS_40642\Ch2\ImageMountFolder directory from the command prompt:

   **imagex /mount "c:\MCTS_70642\Ch2\imagefolder\Server2008fonts.wim"
   "All Installed Ionts" "c:\MCTS_70642\Ch2\imagemountfolder"**

4. Open Windows Explorer and browse to c:\MCTS_70642\Ch2\ImageMountFolder.5. Create a file named Server2008SuperFont.txt by right-clicking a blank spot in the folder window, pointing to New on the shortcut menu, and then clicking **Text Document**. Use **Server2008SuperFont.txt** as the file name. Note that access is denied because you did not mount the image as read/write.

5. Before mounting the image as read/write, unmount the current image as follows:

   imagex /unmount "c:\MCTS_70642\Ch2\imagemountfolder"

6. Rerun the ImageX command as follows using the /mountrw option:

   **imagex /mountrw "c:\MCTS_70642\Ch2\imagefolder\
   Server2008fonts.wim" "All Installed Fonts" "c:\MCTS_70642\Ch2\
   imagemountfolder"**

7. Create a file named **Server2008SuperFont.txt** and leave Windows Explorer open. This time you should be successful.

8. Commit and dismount the image using the following command:

```
imagex /unmount /commit "c:\MCTS_70642\Ch2\imagemountfolder"
```

9. In your Windows Explorer window, press F5 to refresh the screen. You should no longer have any files listed in c:\MCTS_70642\Ch2\ImageMountFolder.

10. Close the Command Prompt.

Applying an Image

After you create an image, you are ready to deploy it, which you can do with ImageX. You must apply an image to a disk drive or partition by booting from Windows PE. Before you begin to apply an image, verify that the target partition is created and has enough space to accommodate the image. Your disk partition should be equal to or greater than the image size. You can verify this from the command line in Windows PE. Next, in Windows PE, you connect to the distribution share containing the image you want to apply. Finally, you apply the image using ImageX. The syntax for applying an image file is the following:

```
imagex /apply image_file [image_number | image_name] image_path
```

Consider an example of this command:

```
imagex/ apply \\SRV-IMG-001\Images\Server2008.wim "Server2008STD" "c:"
```

In this example, you are applying the image you captured, Server2008.wim, with the description of Server2008STD to the local C: drive from a network distribution share. This process can be accomplished using Windows PE.

Configuring Windows Server 2008

This chapter has noted legacy installation practices and improvements in Windows Server 2008. Another noticeable change in Windows Server 2008 is to the initial configuration of an installation. In Chapter 1, you installed Windows Server 2008 and opened the new Initial Configuration Tasks window.

The introduction of the .wim image format and Windows PE paves the way for a new way to configure Windows. Instead of requiring configuration information during the installation, as in previous versions of Windows, you now add information such as name, domain/workgroup membership, and network information after the operating system is installed. The first time you log onto Windows Server 2008, you are greeted by the Initial Configuration Tasks Wizard.

The Initial Configuration Tasks Wizard includes the following configuration areas:

- *Provide Computer Information*—Change the time zone, networking, and computer name and domain information.

- *Update This Server*—Set up automatic update and feedback settings, along with downloading and installing updates.

- *Customize This Server*—Customize basic server settings, including adding roles and features, turning on Remote Desktop, and configuring Windows Firewall.

Figure 2-10 displays the Initial Configuration Tasks Wizard. You use the Initial Configuration Tasks Wizard in Activity 2-6.

To start the Initial Configuration Tasks Wizard, click **Start** and then click **Run**. Type **oobe** in the Open text box and then click **OK** or press **Enter**. You can also run this command from the command prompt.

Activity 2-6: Using the Initial Configuration Tasks Wizard

Time Required: 20 minutes

Objective: Configure Server 2008 using the Initial Configuration Tasks Wizard.
Description: You performed some initial configuration tasks when you installed Windows Server 2008 in Activity 1-1. Now you can complete additional configuration tasks including setting Windows updates, enabling Remote Desktop, and turning on Windows Firewall. You can use the Initial Configuration Tasks Wizard to do so.

1. Log onto your server and open a command prompt, if necessary.

2. Start the Initial Configuration Tasks Wizard by typing **oobe** at the command prompt and then pressing **Enter**.

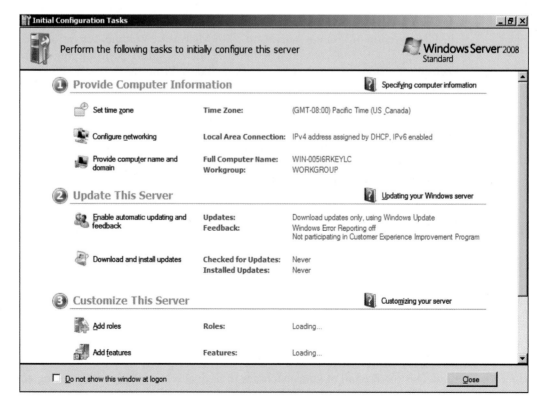

Figure 2-10   Initial Configuration Tasks Wizard

3. When the first dialog box in the Initial Configuration Tasks Wizard appears, click **Enable automatic updating and feedback** and then choose **Manually configure settings**.

4. In the Manually Configure Settings window, choose **Change Setting** under Windows automatic updating to manage this setting.

5. Choose **Download updates but let me choose whether to install them**.

6. Click **OK** to accept the new settings and then click **Close** to return to the Initial Configuration Tasks Wizard.

7. Click **Enable Remote Desktop** and then choose **Allow connections from computers running any version of Remote Desktop (less secure)**. This allows all computers running any version of Remote Desktop to connect to your server. Click **OK** in the Remote Desktop dialog box.

8. Click **OK** to accept the new settings.

9. Click **Configure Windows Firewall** to verify the firewall is turned on (which it should be, by default). If it is not, choose **Change settings** and then turn on the Windows Firewall.

10. Close the Windows Firewall window and then click **Close** to exit the Initial Configuration Tasks Wizard.

Product Activation and Licensing in Windows Server 2008

At its core, Microsoft is in the business of selling software. To do this effectively, Microsoft needs to have product activation processes and licensing models in place to protect their intellectual property. **Product activation** validates licensed software products by creating a unique installation ID based on a hashed hardware serial numbers and a product key. The installation ID is then sent to Microsoft to verify authenticity. For years, Microsoft has been refining its product activation process to deter software piracy and ensure customers are using genuine products. This section discusses product activation in Windows Server 2008 through the use of Volume Activation 2.0.

Product Activation   With Office 2000, Microsoft introduced product activation technologies that use either the Internet or the telephone. Windows Server 2008 and Windows Vista use the latest version of Volume Activation from Microsoft: **Volume Activation 2.0 (VA 2.0)**. VA 2.0 is included in all products sold whether they include **OEM licensing**, **retail licensing**, or **volume licensing**. Previous versions of Windows including Windows XP and Windows Server 2003 use VA 1.0. VA uses two types of keys for activating Windows:

- Multiple Activation Keys
- Key Management Services

You obtain your volume license product keys by visiting the Volume License Service Center and apply product keys for KMS and MAK to product key groups rather than to individual operating system editions. Product key groups are discussed in the following sections along with each type of key.

Multiple Activation Keys   With **Multiple Activation Keys (MAKs)**, you are provided with a key you can use to activate individual computers or a group of computers within your environment. Through the activation process, each computer communicates with special servers at Microsoft responsible for managing and maintaining activation records for its customers. By design, they can be activated only a limited number of times before activations are no longer allowed. When you purchase 20 licenses for Windows Server 2008, for example, you might be provided with a single MAK that can be activated up to 20 times. Activation fails when you attempt to activate a twenty-first computer. MAK allows for two types of activations: individual and proxy. With individual activations, each client is responsible for performing its own activation. This requires all of your machines to have access to the Internet during activation. Another type of activation is proxy. With proxy activation, administrators can activate a group of computers with a single connection to Microsoft. This requires the use of the **Volume Activation**

Management Tool (VAMT) from Microsoft. VAMT activates your MAK with Microsoft while it manages the activations of your network clients internally in its database.

Key Management Services

Key Management Services (KMS) provides an internal service for activating all computers in an enterprise network without requiring the computers to contact Microsoft. The KMS runs on a Windows 2003, Windows Vista, or Windows 2008 system on your network. After activating your KMS, a properly configured network requires no interaction from you or another administrator. This is a significant advantage if you are using automated deployment strategies. The downside is that KMS requires a minimum number of physical computers in a network environment, called the **activation threshold**, before it begins activating client machines. For Windows Server 2008, the threshold is five physical computers, and the activation threshold for Windows Vista is 25 physical computers.

KMS works by counting the number of physical client computers requesting activation and then storing information on these computers in a table based on **client machine identification (CMID)** numbers, which are unique client IDs stored in the KMS database. Each CMID is maintained in the table for 30 days. When renewing, a client overwrites the previous CMID with a new CMID. For each request made to a **KMS host**, which is a server or other computer hosting the KMS service and database, it returns the current count of activations to the **KMS client**, a computer that contacts the KMS host to determine whether it is eligible for activation. For example, when the first two computers on a network contact the KMS host, the first receives an activation count of one, and the second receives an activation count of two. This count includes both Windows Server 2008 clients and Windows Vista clients. If three Windows Vista clients and one Window Server 2008 client contact the KMS host, the next Windows Server 2008 client is activated because the threshold of five has been met. However, any additional Windows Vista clients need to wait until the threshold of 25 is exceeded before they begin activating.

KMS is installed by default in Windows Server 2008 and Windows Vista. It uses the Software License Manager script (slmgr.vbs) for activation. Figure 2-11 displays the options available for use with slmgr.vbs. The only requirement is that you must add your product key to the server hosting KMS with the following command:

```
slmgr.vbs /ipk
```

After installing the product key, ensure that the KMS auto-discovery Service Locator Record is published properly to your DNS server or servers. If Dynamic DNS is enabled, this is completed automatically through KMS auto-publishing.

 KMS activation is different depending on whether you are using physical or virtual instances of Windows Server 2008 and Windows Vista. At this time, KMS does not count VMs when calculating the activation threshold. However, it activates VMs when the threshold is exceeded.

 Product activation is a requirement for running a legal copy of Windows Server 2008 in a production environment. However, if you need to evaluate Windows Server 2008, you have up to 240 days to run Windows Server 2008 without activating. By default, Windows Server 2008 provides a 60-day grace period before you need to activate. You can restart this grace period by using the following command from a command prompt:

```
slmgr.vbs /rearm
```

This command works on Windows Vista as well. However, Windows Vista has a grace period of 30 days, and you must open the command prompt using the Run as Administrator command.

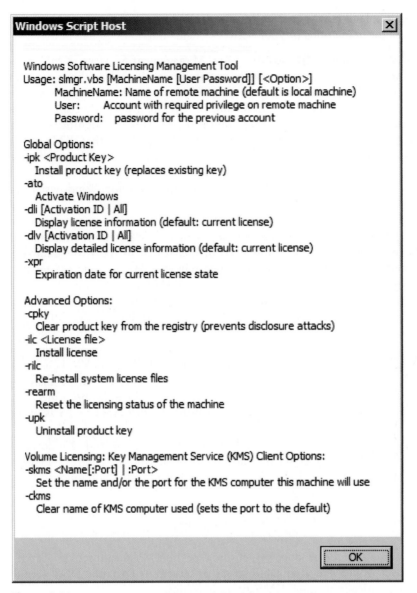

Figure 2-11   Command prompt listing of slmgr.vbs commands

Product Key Groups   A **product key group** is a collection of products used to identify the type of MAK or KMS key required to install specific operating system editions. Windows Server 2008 has three product key groups, and Windows Vista has one product key group. MAK keys function differently from KMS keys in regard to product groups. A MAK can activate the Windows editions only in its specific product group. This is referred to as a lateral association to the product group. In contrast, a KMS key can activate the Windows editions within its specific product group as well as editions in lower product key groups, acting in a hierarchical manner with regards to the product groups. Table 2-2 lists the Windows Server 2008 editions supported by each product group. As an example, a KMS host that is activated with a Server Group B KMS key can activate Windows Server 2008 Standard and Enterprise editions from Product Group B and Web, Storage, and Computer Cluster editions from Product Group A. If you are using MAK and have a Server Group B key, you can activate only Windows Server 2008 Standard and Enterprise editions.

Licensing   Another important aspect of the deployment process that must be managed is licensing. In this context, a **license** provides the right to install an instance of an operating system.

Table 2-2   Product groups by Windows Server 2008 editions

Product Group	Server Editions
A	Web Server
B	Standard
	Enterprise
C	Datacenter
	Itanium

For large environments, licensing and maintaining licensing compliance data can be a full-time responsibility. Unlike client operating systems such as Windows Vista, which requires a license only for itself, Windows Server 2008 requires the purchase of client access licenses along with the server license for the edition you have purchased. Server and client access licensing are discussed next.

Server Licensing   Each edition of Window Server 2008 you purchase requires a license to be installed. This license gives you the right to install an instance of Windows Server 2008 you purchased on a single physical computer. For Standard and Enterprise editions, one license is equal to one physical server no matter what type of hardware configuration the server has. This changes for Datacenter edition, as it is licensed per processor. If you deploy a server that has four processors and install Datacenter, you need four licenses, or one for each processor. Microsoft does not currently license by processor cores, only physical processors, or sockets. Therefore, a server running a quad-core processor requires one Datacenter license, whereas a server with two dual-core processors requires two Datacenter licenses. This information can be helpful when purchasing hardware and software licensing.

As mentioned previously, you can have a volume license key that covers multiple activations of installations. However, you still need a legal license for each installation. With the advent of virtualization in enterprise environments, licensing has become more complex. The number of virtual instances, or VM guests, you can run on a physical Windows Server 2008 server depends on the edition purchased and installed. You can run the following number of VMs by edition:

- Standard edition allows one VM guest to be hosted.

- Enterprise edition allows four VM guests to be hosted.

- Datacenter edition allows unlimited VMs to be hosted.

This means that a server running Windows Server 2008 Enterprise can run four additional instances of Windows Server 2008 Enterprise as **VM guests**, which are instances of an operating system running in a software-based workspace provided by a virtualization application such as Hyper-V.

Virtual licensing is not only for servers running Hyper-V. These **virtual licenses** can be used when running third-party virtualization software such as VMware ESX server, Virtual Iron, and XEN-based VMs. Also, consider the number of virtual licenses when planning for disaster recovery. If you need to migrate a VM guest to another **VM host,** which is a computer running a virtualization application for VM guests, you need to have available licenses on the target host. For example, suppose two servers are acting as VM hosts. One server has three VM guests, and the second server has two VM guests. In this configuration, neither server has enough licenses to host the other's VM guests in case of hardware failure or the need to migrate from a VM host. If the first VM host has two guests instead of three, both servers can provide enough licenses to support the other's VM guests.

Client Access Licenses   A **client access license (CAL)** is not a software product; rather, it is a license that grants to a user or computer device the right to access the server. You need a

CAL for each client connection to a Windows Server 2008 server with exception to the following instances:

- When the server is running Windows Web Server 2008
- When access is only via the Internet and no authentication or individual identification is being performed
- When up to two administrators are connecting locally or remotely to the server for management and administration

Windows Server 2008 has two types of CALs: device based and user based. As their names suggest, you purchase **device-based CALs** for each computer accessing server resources. Any number of users can use one device-based CAL, so this is the license of choice in situations where many users access resources from a few client computers. On the other hand, **user-based CALs** allow one user to access server resources from unknown or multiple devices. User-based CALs are popular in networks where users have a notebook computer, a desktop computer, or a mobile device and access the network remotely through a virtual private network.

After selecting the type of CAL for your environment, you have two options for CAL modes:

- *Per User/Per Device mode*—With **Per User** or **Per Device mode**, a separate Windows CAL is required for each device or user that accesses the resources on any of your network servers. The number of CALs required is determined by the total number of users or devices accessing your server resources. This is the most economical mode in environments with more than one Windows Server 2008 computer on the network because the Windows CALs are distributed for use across all the servers. For example, if you have 20 users accessing resources on two Windows Server 2008 servers, you need only 20 user CALs for your entire Windows Server 2008 infrastructure. If you switch to Per User/Per Device mode, it is a permanent choice, and you cannot modify the mode at a later date.

- *Per Server mode*—With **Per Server mode**, a separate Windows CAL is required for each device or user that accesses the resources on a specific server, not all your network servers. The number of CALs required is determined by the total number of users or devices that can simultaneously access a single server. Per Server is the most economical option in computing environments where a small number of servers have limited access requirements. It is the least economical mode in environments with more than one Windows Server 2008 computer on the network because the Windows CALs are not distributed for use across all the servers. Therefore, each server must have CALs equal to the number of users or devices that access their resources. For example, if you have 20 users accessing resources on two Windows Server 2008 servers, each server requires 20 user CALs, or a total of 40 user CALs.

Introduction to Windows Server 2008 Server Core

Recall that Windows Server 2008 includes a new type of Windows server installation called Server Core, which provides a reduced attack surface and limited role and feature hosting abilities. Server Core provides no GUI. You perform all configuration and administration tasks locally from the command prompt or remotely using tools such as WinRM. Because Server Core has a limited role and feature set, along with fewer installed services, it is a more secure server from the outset.

Basics of Server Core

The following are the basic features of Server Core:

- Windows Server 2008 system built on the same code base as the Full version but with a command-line interface, as shown in Figure 2-12
- Available in Standard, Enterprise, and Datacenter editions

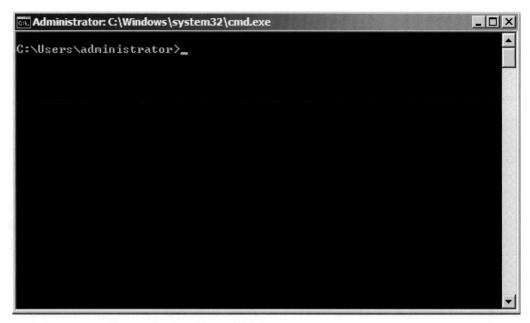

Figure 2-12   Server Core command prompt

- There is no way to upgrade from a previous version of the Windows Server operating system to a Server Core installation. Only a clean installation is supported.

- There is no way to upgrade from a full installation of Windows Server 2008 to a Server Core installation. Only a clean installation is supported.

- There is no way to upgrade from a Server Core installation to a full installation of Windows Server 2008. If you need the Windows® user interface or a server role that is not supported in a Server Core installation, you will need to install a full installation of Windows Server 2008.

As have mentioned earlier, Server Core has a limited set of roles and features, which were described in Chapter 1. For reference, Tables 2-3 and 2-4 list the roles and features that are available with Server Core along with the technical name for each. Given the list of available options, Server Core is a fully functional server. Whether deployed as a domain controller (DC),

Table 2-3   Server Core roles with technical names

Server Role Name	Server Core Role Technical Name
Active Directory Domain Services	DirectoryServices-DomainController-ServerFoundation
Active Directory Lightweight Directory Services	DirectoryServices-ADAM-ServerCore
DHCP Server	DHCPServerCore
DNS Server	DNS-Server-Core-Role
File Services	enabled by default
Hyper-V	Hyper-V **
Print Services	Printing-ServerCore-Role *
Web Services (IIS)	IIS-WebServerRole *
	WAS-WindowsActivationService *
Windows Media Services	MediaServer **

* Contains subroles that can be installed separately.

** Role components need to be downloaded first.

Table 2-4 Server Core features with technical names

Feature Name	Server Core Feature Technical Name
BitLocker	BitLocker
BitLocker Remote Admin Tool	BitLocker-RemoteAdminTool
Client for NFS	ClientForNFS-Base
Distributed File System Namespace Server	DFSN-Server
Distributed File System Replication	DFSR-Infrastructure-ServerEdition
File Replication Service	FRS-Infrastructure
Multipath IO	MultipathIo
Network Load Balancing (NLB)	NetworkLoadBalancingHeadlessServer
Quality of Service (QoS/qWAVE)	QWAVE
Removable Storage Management	Microsoft-Windows-RemovableStorageManagementCore
Server for NFS	ServerForNFS-Base
Simple Network Management Protocol	SNMP-SC
Subsystem for UNIX-based Applications	SUACore
Telnet Client	TelnetClient
Windows Internet Name Service	WINS-SC
Windows Server Backup	WindowsServerBackup

a DHCP server, or file server, Server Core provides the same functionality as the Full version of Windows Server 2008. The major differences are in configuration and administration. Without a GUI to rely on, you need to polish your command-line skills to work with Server Core. However, as noted earlier, Server Core offers notable advantages. For example, many of the available roles require little maintenance. The lack of a Web browser or other applications, which are often sources of security holes, means that you need to apply fewer updates and patches.

A DHCP server is a common deployment choice for Server Core. For the most part, DHCP requires little maintenance except for the occasional configuration of a new scope or modification to server and scope options. You can complete these tasks with Netsh or a remote management console. DHCP is covered in depth in Chapter 6. Another example uses new technologies in Windows Server 2008: **read-only domain controllers (RODCs)** and BitLocker Drive Encryption. For many years, administrators have worried about the security of their DC deployed to branch offices. Unlike the servers in their secured data centers, branch offices often place the server wherever it is most convenient, such as in the closet, under a desk, or next to the coffeemaker. With traditional DCs, this creates a security risk for your organization considering that the theft of this server would compromise all the accounts in your domain. RODCs allow you to deploy a DC that allows only specific account data to be read from the server. This, along with BitLocker Drive Encryption, provides a formidable obstacle if your server is removed or accessed without authorization. The following are some common deployment options for Server Core:

- Branch office server
- RODC or standard DC
- DNS
- DHCP
- File server
- Print server
- Hyper-V Host or Guest

Activity 2-7: Installing Windows Server 2008, Standard Edition with Server Core

2

Time Required: 30 minutes

Objective: Install Windows Server 2008 with Server Core.

Description: After verifying system requirements on the computers in your organization, you have decided to install Windows Server 2008, Standard edition, with Server Core. This option lets you make the most economical use of your network resources. However, before you deploy Server Core throughout the organization, you want to install it on a single server and become familiar with its installation steps. In this activity, you install Windows Server 2008 using the Standard edition with Server Core.

Before completing this activity, verify that your environment meets the hardware requirements listed in Table 1-2 in Chapter 1.

1. Place your Windows Server 2008 DVD in the DVD drive of your computer and then restart or power on your computer.

2. If prompted by the startup screen, press any key to boot from the DVD. You are prompted only if the computer has an existing operating system. The first portion of the installation program starts.

3. At the Install Windows initial screen, confirm your time and currency format and that the keyboard layout is correct and then click **Next**.

4. When the next window appears, click **Install now**.

5. If the next window requests a product key, enter your key in the product key in the text box if you have one or leave this text box blank for now. You can install Server 2008 without a product key. If you are not prompted for a product key, skip to Step 7.

Depending on the type of installation media and license model you are using, you might not be prompted for a product key.

6. Click to remove the checkmark from the **Automatically activate Windows when I'm online** box and then click **Next**.

   If you did not enter a product key, a message box opens asking whether you want to enter a key. Click **No** to continue installing without a product key.

7. When the next window appears, select the version of Server 2008 you are installing. For this activity, choose **Windows Server 2008 Enterprise (Server Core Installation)**, check the **I have selected the edition of Windows that I purchased** check box, and then click **Next**.

8. When the next window appears, read the Microsoft Software License Terms and then select the **I accept the license terms** check box. Click **Next**.

9. When the next window appears, click **Custom** to perform a custom installation, which is the appropriate option for performing a new installation. Notice that the choice to upgrade is not available.

10. If necessary when the next window appears, delete any existing partitions by completing the following steps:

    a. Click the partition you want to delete.

    b. Click the **Drive options (advanced)** link to display your partitioning options.

    c. Click **Delete**.

    d. Click **OK** to confirm you want to delete the partition and lose all of its data.

11. Click **Disk 0 Unallocated Space** and then click **Drive options (advanced)** to perform disk partitioning operations. Click **New**. Enter **10512** in the Size text box after ensuring you have at least 10 GB of unallocated disk space. Click **Apply**.

12. Select **Disk 0 Partition 1** and then click **Format**. Confirm that you understand all data will be lost when you format the partition by clicking **OK**.

13. Click **Next**. Windows begins performing tasks that do not require your input., including rebooting the computer. This portion of the installation takes approximately 5 to 10 minutes.

14. When Windows completes its tasks and reboots, press **Ctrl+Alt+Del** to pass the security key sequence to your server. Click the single user called **Other User**.

15. When asked to enter a user account name and password, type **Administrator** as the account name and leave the password blank. You change the password in the next step. Click the **arrow** button.

16. A warning reminds you that you need to change your password before logging on for the first time. Click **OK**. Use **P@ssw0rd** as your new password. Enter the password twice to ensure it is correct. Click the **arrow** button. Confirm that your password has been changed by clicking **OK**.

17. When the desktop is prepared, the Server Core command prompt appears, as shown in Figure 2-12.

Configuring Server Core

When configuring Windows Server 2008 with Server Core, you are limited to working with the command-line interface. From network adapter settings to roles and domain membership, you can set all the configurations for Server Core through the command prompt. For initial user configuration, you can use the net.exe utility. One of the first tasks to perform on a new Server Core machine is creating a user account. You can complete this task using net.exe with the following syntax:

```
net User YourLoginName YourPassword /add
```

For example, you can create a user account called ServerCoreAdmin with a password of P@ssw0rd. The net.exe command is as follows:

```
net User ServerCoreAdmin P@ssw0rd /add
```

This creates a user that is a member of the local Users group. To make the account a member of the local Administrators group, you need to use a different net.exe command, net.exe LocalGroup. The command for adding ServerCoreAdmin to the Administrators local group is as follows:

```
net LocalGroup "Administrators" ServerCoreAdmin /add
```

Next, you need to change the name of the current computer. When Windows Server 2008 computers are first built, they are given a computer-generated name. To change the computer name, you can use **Windows Management Instrumentation Command-line (WMIC)** commands. WMIC is a powerful configuration feature of Windows Server 2008. It simplifies many of the configuration tasks that otherwise require complex commands and utilities. You can use WMIC to change the server name, modify domain membership, and turn on a remote desktop.

Suppose you want to rename your server to MSN-SRVCR-001 and then change the workgroup name to ServerCoreWG. First, examine the syntax of the WMIC command for renaming the server:

```
wmic ComputerSystem Where name = "%computername%" Call Rename Name =
"New Name"
```

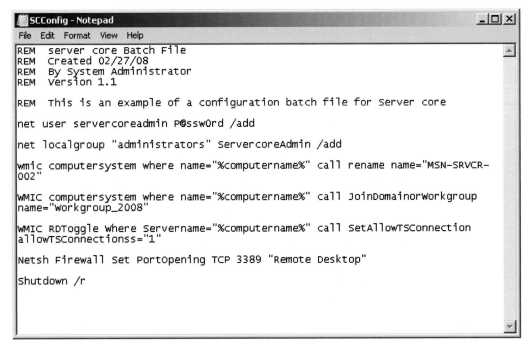

Figure 2-13 Sample batch file for configuring Server Core

%computername% is an environment variable, which is a variable that represents the name of the server. Windows has many environmental variables, such as %systemroot%, which represents the location where the Windows system files are installed. For a default installation of Windows Server 2008, %systemroot% is equal to the c:\Windows directory location.

The command to rename the server is as follows:

```
wmic ComputerSystem Where name = "%computername%" Call Rename Name =
"MSN-SRVCR-001"
```

Figure 2-13 shows an example of how you can store a number of Server Core commands into a batch file for ease of configuration. You can include this batch file with your image with ImageX, or you can call it as part of your automated installation process developed with WSIM, for example. You can also store the batch file on a USB flash drive as long as Group Policy and security settings allow the use of USB flash drives.

WMIC is a powerful tool and can be used in both Server Core and the Full version of Windows Server 2008. Like most Windows command-line utilities, you can append a command with /? to produce a listing of the associated help files, command usages, and available switches for the command.

Activity 2-8: Configuring a Server Core Computer

Time Required: 10 minutes

Objective: Configure a Windows Server 2008 system running as Server Core.

Description: Now that you have installed a server running Server Core, you need to configure it for use on your network. In this activity, you create a local administrative account, and then rename the computer.

1. Log onto your Windows Server 2008 Server Core computer. At the command prompt, type the following command and then press **Enter** to view the syntax of the net user command:

```
net user /?
```

2. Type the following command and then press **Enter** to create a user named CoreAdmin:

```
net user CoreAdmin P@ssw0rd /Add
```

3. Type the following command and then press **Enter** to add CoreAdmin to the local administrators group:

```
net LocalGroup "administrators" CoreAdmin /add
```

4. Type the following command and then press **Enter** to change the computer name to MSN-SC-001:

```
WMIC ComputerSystem Where name="%computername%" call Rename
Name="MSN-SC-0XX"
```

5. The system now requires a reboot so that the name change takes effect. Type the following command and then press **Enter** to reboot:

```
shutdown /r /f /t 0
```

6. After the system reboots, press **Ctrl+Alt+Del**.
7. When the logon screen appears, click **Switch User**.
8. On the next screen, click **Other User**. The Username and Password window opens.
9. Enter **CoreAdmin** as the username and **P@ssw0rd** as the password. Press **Enter** to log onto your server.
10. Verify the name has changed successfully by typing **whoami** at the command prompt and then pressing **Enter**. The response contains the server name and user account you are using.

Another CLI utility that is helpful is rmtshare.exe, which allows you to create and manage remote shared resources from the command line. Unlike net share, you run rmtshare from a management server to create and manage resources on a remote server. This utility also lets you create remote shares with a central script, such as when you deploy a group of Windows Server 2008 Server Core servers and want to configure them all at once.

For installing roles and features in Server Core, you can use the Optional Component Setup (OCSetup) tool. OCSetup is a CLI-based tool, which makes it an excellent choice for Server Core. This section covers OCSetup. OCSetup allows you to install components such as roles along with MSI-based applications. The syntax for installing a role or feature in Server Core is as follows:

```
start /w ocsetup
```

If you want to install the DHCP services role and the BitLocker Drive Encryption feature on a Server Core installation, use the following commands:

```
start /w ocsetup DHCPServerCore
start /w ocsetup BitLocker
start /w ocsetup BitLocker-RemoteAdminTool
```

To find a list of all the roles and features that you can install using OCSetup, execute the OClist.exe command. It lists the roles and features, as shown in Figure 2-14.

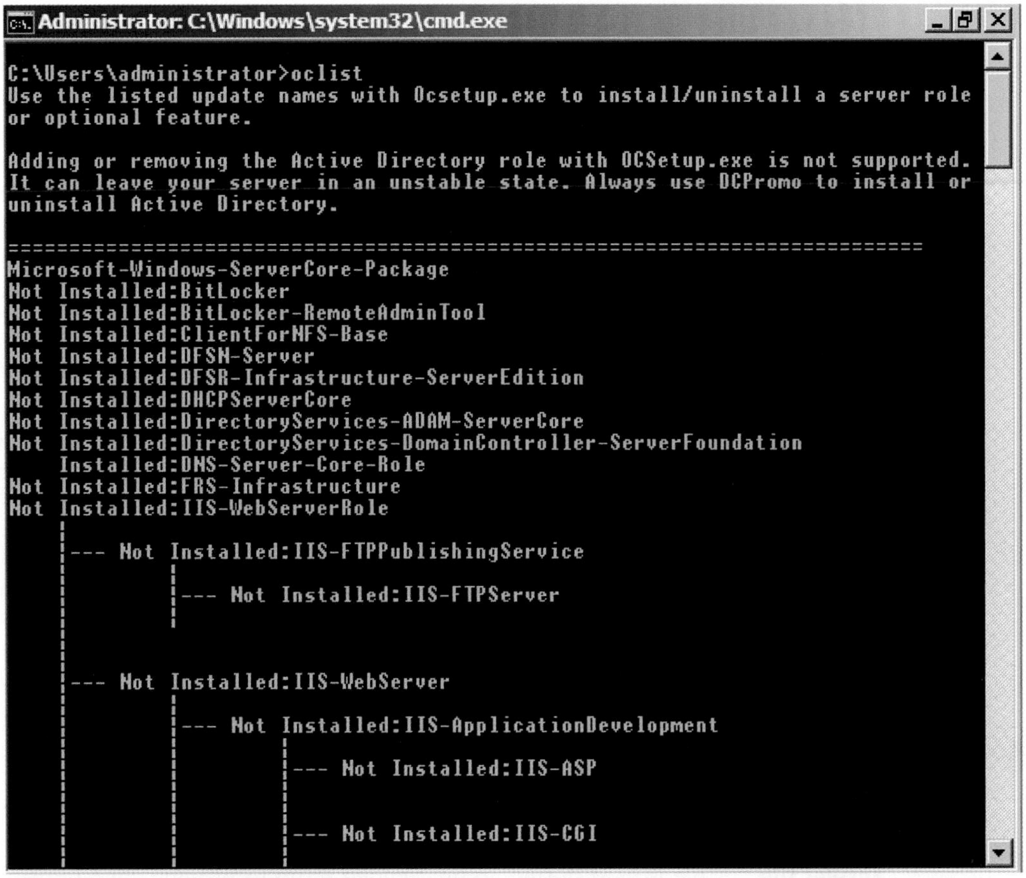

```
Administrator: C:\Windows\system32\cmd.exe                    _ |8| X

C:\Users\administrator>oclist
Use the listed update names with Ocsetup.exe to install/uninstall a server role
or optional feature.

Adding or removing the Active Directory role with OCSetup.exe is not supported.
It can leave your server in an unstable state. Always use DCPromo to install or
uninstall Active Directory.


================================================================================
Microsoft-Windows-ServerCore-Package
Not Installed:BitLocker
Not Installed:BitLocker-RemoteAdminTool
Not Installed:ClientForNFS-Base
Not Installed:DFSN-Server
Not Installed:DFSR-Infrastructure-ServerEdition
Not Installed:DHCPServerCore
Not Installed:DirectoryServices-ADAM-ServerCore
Not Installed:DirectoryServices-DomainController-ServerFoundation
    Installed:DNS-Server-Core-Role
Not Installed:FRS-Infrastructure
Not Installed:IIS-WebServerRole

    --- Not Installed:IIS-FTPPublishingService

            --- Not Installed:IIS-FTPServer


    --- Not Installed:IIS-WebServer

            --- Not Installed:IIS-ApplicationDevelopment

                    --- Not Installed:IIS-ASP

                    --- Not Installed:IIS-CGI
```

Figure 2-14   Output from oclist.exe in Server Core

You can use **Windows Remote Management (WinRM)** to configure and manage Server Core installations. As discussed in Chapter 1, WinRM is a suite of tools that allows you to remotely manage your servers. WinRM, rmtshare, and other management utilities are covered in depth in Chapter 11.

Chapter Summary

- Windows Server 2008 offers important enhancements to make deployment and installation easier. Modularization, WIM, and XML-based answer files are some of the process improvements in Windows Server 2008. With modularization, the operating system has been divided into modules that are easier to add, delete, and modify. Tools and technology improvements include WDS, WAIK, WSIM, ImageX, Windows PE, and Sysprep.

- You have two choices for installing Windows Server 2008. You can perform a clean installation, the preferred and recommended choice, that provides a fresh operating system installation without transferring data or settings. Another option is an upgrade installation on an existing system. This copies over existing settings and some applications and services. The choice depends on your hardware specifications, services provided by an existing server, and third-party application support for Windows Server 2008.

- You can install Windows Server 2008 using a number of installation methods: CD boot, Network Distribution Share, and image-based. CD boot installation is the most common yet provides the least opportunities for customization. A Network Distribution Share installation allows you to customize device drivers and packages. Image-based installations provide the most opportunities for customization by allowing you to include installed applications, device drivers, and packages.

■ ImageX is a new utility that allows you to create and manage images using a command-line interface.

■ Windows Server 2008 performs many tasks such as computer naming, network setup, and workgroup/domain membership after the application of the OS image. To complete these tasks, you use the Initial Configuration Tasks Wizard that starts when you first log onto a new Windows Server 2008 computer.

■ Product activation in Windows Server 2008 has been changed to use VA 2.0. With VA 2.0, you can purchase two types of keys for Windows Server 2008: MAKs and KMS keys. Both types use product key groups to determine which key should be purchased depending on the editions of Windows Server 2008 being deployed.

■ The new feature in licensing in Windows Server 2008 is the introduction of virtual licenses. Depending on the edition of Windows Server 2008 you purchase, you are allowed a specific number of VM guests to run on a VM host.

■ A new addition to Windows Server 2008 is Server Core, which is a command-line Windows Server 2008 installation that provides a reduced attack surface and limited role and feature hosting abilities. Because it lacks a GUI, you must configure Server Core from the command prompt using tools such as OCsetup, WMIC, and Net.exe or from remote systems using rmtshare.exe and WinRM.

Key Terms

activation threshold   The minimum number of physical computers in a network environment needed before a Key Management Services (KMS) server begins issuing activations.

answer file   A file is used during an unattended setup to provide configuration to Setup.exe. All answer files used by Windows Server 2008 are eXtensible Markup Language based and are created by using Windows System Image Manager (WSIM).

attended installation   An installation that requires a network administrator to be present to answer configuration questions presented during Windows Server 2008 installations.

Audit Mode   An advance generalization mode that allows administrators to perform additional application and driver modifications to a specific image. This is one of two options available when using System Preparation tool (Sysprep) on an operating system.

CD boot installation   An installation of Windows Server 2008 that initiates setup.exe by using a CD, DVD, or USB drive.

clean installation   A complete installation of the operating system onto a new or reformatted disk drive. By their nature, clean installations, or migrations, do not transfer any settings from previous operating systems installed on a server.

client access license (CAL)   A license that grants the right to access a server's resources to a user or computer device. You need a CAL for each client connection to a Windows Server 2008 server.

client machine identification (CMID)   A unique client ID stored in the KMS database as part of activation threshold enumeration.

datagram   A packet that is sent using a networking service, such as Internet Protocol (IP) or User Datagram Protocol (UDP). IP and UDP are unreliable services because they do not inform the sender of delivery failure. Reliable services such as TCP provide senders information on failure of delivery.

device-based CAL   A client access license (CAL) purchased for each computer accessing server resources. Because any number of users can use one device-based CAL, this is the license of choice in situations where many users access resources from a few client computers.

eXtensible Markup Language (XML)   A standard specification for annotating and formatting data exchanged between applications.

generalization   A process performed by Sysprep to prepare a computer running Windows Vista or Windows Server 2008 for imaging. The computer security identifier (SID), computer name, user profiles, and hardware information are removed during generalization.

image   A collection of files stored in a single file. Windows Server 2008 uses the .wim file format for images. Typically, an image represents a file that is used to deploy new operating systems to computers.

image file   A file that stores one or more images. In Windows Server 2008, the .wim file format is used. Windows Server 2008 uses single-instance storage to minimize the size of an image file containing multiple images.

ImageX   A command-line tool that enables organizations to capture, modify, and apply file-based disk images for rapid deployment.

image-based installation   An installation of Windows Server 2008 that requires you create a customized image and apply it to each computer you are deploying. You use ImageX to create this customized installation. The image can include applications as well as the operating system. You use Windows PE to initiate the connection with the remote share, often via an unattend.xml file.

installation script   A file that automates the installation of services and features that you would normally enter manually during the process.

kernel code   The programmatic logic, or code, that makes up the kernel.

Key Management Services (KMS)   An internal service for activating all computers within an enterprise network without the computers contacting Microsoft.

KMS host   A server or computer hosting the KMS service and database.

KMS client   A server or computer that contacts the KMS host for activation and assignment of a client machine ID.

license   The right to install an instance of Windows Server 2008 you purchased on a single physical computer.

local area network (LAN)   A computer network covering a small geographic area that has high data transfer speeds and does not require leased telecommunications lines such as T1 or ISDN lines. LANs are often installed in homes, offices, and groups of buildings that are interconnected via high-speed network connections.

Multiple Activation Key (MAK)   A key you can use to activate individual computers or a group of computers within your environment. Each computer communicates with special servers at Microsoft responsible for managing and maintaining activation records for its customers. By design, a computer can be activated only a limited number of times before activations are no longer allowed.

module   An independent unit of programming logic.

modularization   A design of the basic architecture of the Windows operating system so that it uses modules and provides a selective capability to customize Windows Server 2008 by swapping out modules.

multicast   A communications technology that allows multiple computers to receive a communication simultaneously.

New Technology File System (NTFS)   The file system of choice for current and legacy Windows operating systems in the Windows NT family.

network distribution share   A share configured through WSIM to store drivers and packages that can be added to Windows Vista during installation.

network distribution share installation   An installation of Windows Server 2008 that initiates setup.exe via a distribution share located on the network or network distribution share. Windows Preinstallation Environment (PE) is used to initiate the connection with the remote share often via an unattend.xml file.

original equipment manufacturer (OEM)   A company that originally produced a piece of hardware.

OEM licensing OEM copies of Windows are installed on a specific system, and the license is linked to that specific hardware. This means that OEM copies of Windows cannot be reinstalled on a new piece of hardware.

out-of-box experience (OOBE) A feature that removes the SIDs, unique characteristics, and applications from an OS. This allows it be more easily imaged and deployed to new clients. OOBE is one of two options available when performing Sysprep on an operating system.

packet A formatted block of data carried by a packet mode computer network.

Per Server mode The CAL type where a separate Windows CAL is required for each device or user that accesses the resources on specific server, not all network servers.

Per User or Per Device mode The CAL type where a separate Windows CAL is required for each device or user that accesses the resources on any network server.

Preboot eXecution Environment (PXE) An industry standard that allows PXE-compliant computers to boot the network using their network card, and install an operating system to facilitate processes such as imaging.

product key group A group of products that identify the type of MAK or KMS key required to install specific operating system editions.

product activation A process put in place by Microsoft to reduce piracy. Unique information about your computer is sent to Microsoft to ensure that operating systems such as Windows Server 2008 are installed on only the allowable number of systems. Activation is usually done over the Internet, but you can activate via a telephone connection if necessary.

read-only domain controller (RODC) A new type of domain controller in Windows Server 2008. Its main purpose is to improve security in branch office deployments that need additional physical security and on-site technical staff.

retail licensing OEM copies of Windows are installed on a specific system, and the license is linked to that specific hardware. This means OEM copies of Windows cannot be reinstalled on a new piece of hardware.

security identifier (SID) A unique name given to objects in a Windows environment. The SID is used for managing security and access in a Windows environment.

System Preparation tool (Sysprep) A tool that prepares an installation of Windows for imaging and deployment by modifying a system to create a new SID and other unique information the next time it starts. Sysprep also removes user and computer-specific information that should not be transferred to new images. Often, this process is referred to as generalization.

single-instance storage (SIS) A process that eliminates data duplication by allowing multiple users, computers, or processes to use the same files and data. A WIM image uses SIS to reduce its size by allowing multiple image instances within a single WIM file to share files.

Trivial File Transfer Protocol (TFTP) The protocol used for transferring images across the network. TFTP is a key component of the PXE, the backbone of Windows Deployment Services. Based on the UDP, TFTP traffic is connectionless in nature, meaning it does not guarantee sequencing or even arrival of data packets, or datagrams.

User Datagram Protocol (UDP) A core IP suite protocol that provides connectionless transport with no guarantees for delivery and no protection from duplication. Because UDP does not check for delivery success or failure, it is a faster and more efficient protocol for applications requiring speed instead of guarantee of delivery. Multicast and DNS are two services that use UDP.

unattend.xml An answer file used during the installation of Windows Server 2008. It is specifically sought out during installation phases to provide information for automating an installation.

unattended installation An installation that does not require an administrator's input because it uses answer files and scripts for automation.

upgrade installation An installation that migrates all of the settings from an existing operating system to Windows Server 2008.

user-based CAL   A CAL that allows one user to access server resources from unknown or multiple devices.

virtual license   A license to install an operating system within a virtual machine (VM) guest.

VM guest   An instance of an operating system like Windows Server 2008 that is running within a software-based workspace provided by a virtualization application such as Hyper-V.

VM host   A computer running a virtualization application that provides software-based workspaces for VM guests. Examples include Virtual Server 2005 R2 and Hyper-V.

Volume Activation 2.0 (VA 2.0)   The latest volume activation process used by Windows Server 2008 and Windows Vista.

Volume Activation Management Tool (VAMT)   A tool used for proxy activation of a MAK, allowing activation of a group of computers with a single connection to Microsoft. VAMT activates your MAK with Microsoft while it manages the activations of your network clients internally in its database.

volume licensing   A licensing model where you can use an individual key to license multiple installations of an operating system. Volume licensing is often used by business, government, and education institutions because it provides price discounts based on the application type, quantity, and applicable subscription term.

Windows Automated Installation Kit (WAIK)   A suite of tools that helps OEMs, system builders, and corporate IT professionals deploy Windows onto new hardware through automation of the installation process.

Windows Deployment Services (WDS)   A server-based framework used to automate the deployment of operating systems over the network from a centralized server.

Windows Imaging Format (WIM)   A file-based image format developed by Microsoft to create and manage WIM files using ImageX. WIM allows you to mount your image files and add drivers, applications, or files directly to your image through windows explorer.

Windows Management Instrumentation Command-line (WMIC)   An improved tool for managing WIM in Windows Server 2008.

Windows Preinstallation Environment (Windows PE)   A limited 32-bit operating system based on the Windows Server 2008 and Windows Vista SP1 kernel code. Not to be used as a stand-alone operating system, Windows PE is designed for installation, troubleshooting, and recovery of Windows Server 2008 and Windows Vista.

Windows Recovery Environment (Windows RE)   A new recovery environment built into Windows Server 2008 and based on Windows PE 2.0. Windows RE is a complete diagnostic and recovery solution as well as a platform for building your own recovery solutions.

Windows Remote Management (WinRM)   A new feature that provides administrators with remote system management capabilities. WinRM allows you to remotely run management scripts and manage data on remote machines. All connections are handled via the WS-Management protocol.

Windows System Image Manager (WSIM)   A utility used to create answer files for Windows Server 2008 unattended installations. WSIM can also create distribution shares and configuration sets.

Review Questions

1. The Server Core version of the Windows Server 2008 Enterprise edition can be upgraded to the Full version without completely reinstalling the OS. True or False?

2. You can use OCsetup.exe to install Active Directory Domain Services on a Server Core version of Windows Server 2008 Standard edition. True or False?

3. To capture a drive partition containing an operating system, you need run ImageX by booting from Windows PE. True or False?

4. You can use the same image file for 32-bit and 64-bit versions of Windows Server 2008. True or False?

5. TFTP and multicast are based on reliable network protocols and transport services. True or False?

6. The Windows Automated Installation Kit is installed by default as part of the Windows Deployment Services role installation. True or False?

7. ImageX automatically saves all changes you make to a mounted image. True or False?

8. By default, Windows Server 2008 has a grace period of 30 days in which to activate. True or False?

9. Which component would you install on a Windows Server 2008 server to manage the deployment of OS images over the network?

   a. ImageX

   b. Sysprep

   c. Windows PE

   d. Windows Deployment Services

   e. Windows System Image Manager

10. Which utility do you use to mount image files for adding device drivers and data?

    a. ImageX

    b. Sysprep

    c. Windows PE

    d. Windows Deployment Services

    e. Windows System Image Manager

11. Which utility do you use to create answer files for unattended installations?

    a. ImageX

    b. Sysprep

    c. Windows PE

    d. Windows Deployment Services

    e. Windows System Image Manager

12. Which utility do you use to generalize computers before imaging by removing specific information such as user settings and the security identifier?

    a. ImageX

    b. Sysprep

    c. Windows PE

    d. Windows Deployment Services

    e. Windows System Image Manager

13. Which Windows Server 2008 process improvement simplifies the development of service packs and updates?

    a. Modularization

    b. Windows Imaging Format

    c. XML-based answer files

    d. Installation scripts

    e. File and Registry redirection

14. Which extension is used for ImageX-based image files?

    a. .wmi

    b. .wim

    c. .iso

    d. .img

15. Which of the following are *not* requirements for running WDS?

    a. DHCP must be active and available on your network.

    b. DNS must be active and available on your network.

    c. An NTFS partition must be available for storing images.

    d. WDS must be running on a domain controller.

16. You have a Windows Server 2008 server named MSN-SRV001 that has been configured for company XYZ.com. Before imaging the machine for deployment, you need to generalize the image so that Windows Welcome runs on the next reboot of the server. Which of the following steps generalize your installation? (Choose three answers that together provide the complete solution.)

    a. Run ImageX /generalize:OOBE "c:*.*"

    b. Run Windows Deployment Services

    c. Choose Out-Of-Box Experience in Sysprep

    d. Choose Out-Of-Box Experience in Windows Deployment Services

    e. Run Sysprep.exe

    f. Choose the generalize check box in Windows Deployment Services

    g. Choose the generalize check box in Sysprep

17. Which command-line utility do you use to manage product activation and licensing in Windows Server 2008?

    a. ImageX

    b. Slmgr.vbs

    c. Servermanagercmd.exe

    d. WMIC

18. What type of media *cannot* be used to run Windows PE?

    a. CD

    b. DVD

    c. USB flash drive

    d. Distribution share

19. Which command can you use to mount an image using ImageX?

    a. ImageX /mount c:\imagefolder\ "Standard" "c:\Images\Server2008.img"

    b. ImageX /mnt c:\imagefolder\ "Standard" "c:\Images\Server2008.wim"

    c. ImageX /mount c:\imagefolder\ "Standard" "c:\Images\Server2008.wim"

    d. ImageX /mnt c:\imagefolder\ "Standard" "c:\Images\Server2008.img"

20. Retaining settings and applications is one reason for performing a(n) _____ installation instead of a(n) _____ installation.

21. _____ is a customizable 32-bit operating system that can be used for installation and recovery of Windows Server 2008.

22. _____ is the command-line tool for capturing a Windows image file.

23. _____ is an unreliable transport service used by Windows Deployment Service to install multiple images to clients across a network.

24. To use Windows System Image Manager and ImageX, you need to install the _____.

25. You have been asked to review the licensing for a future Windows Server 2008 deployment at Ditka's Coffee Traders (DCT). Based on the following information, recommend the

options that require the fewest CALs to be purchased by the client. Select two answers that together provide the complete solution.

- 5 Windows Server 2008 Standard edition servers will be deployed.
- 20 Windows Vista clients will be deployed.
- DCT has 20 employees who will need to access server resources.
- Each employee is provided a Windows Mobile 6.0 Smartphone for access to their server-based ordering application running in IIS 7.0.

    a. Use Per Server licensing mode

    b. Use Per User or Per Server licensing mode

    c. Use Per User or Per Device licensing mode

    d. Install 20 user-based CALs

    e. Install 40 device-based CALs

Case Projects

Case Project 2-1: Capturing an Image of Windows Server 2008 with ImageX

You are an administrator for Badger Novelties. The company is planning to introduce Windows Server 2008 Standard edition on 10 new servers to be installed in your data center. To ease the deployment burden, you want to create a custom image to deploy to all of the new servers. You've heard about ImageX and want to use it to create the image. Using ImageX, capture an image of a Windows Server 2008 installation and store it on an available network share. For this project, you can use your lab server for imaging or another server provided by your instructor.

Case Project 2-2: Creating a Batch File for Configuring Server Core Installations of Windows Server 2008

After researching Server Core and becoming familiar with it, you decided to create a batch script that will complete a default configuration of Server Core for you. The following is a list of settings you want to configure with your script:

- Rename the workgroup to SERVERCORE
- Add a local account named SAServerCoreAdmin with a password of P@ssw0rd
- Add SAServerCoreAdmin to the local Administrators group
- Install the Hyper-V role and the Telnet Client feature
- Activate Windows

With this information, create a batch script to configure the required settings.

Case Project 2-3: Building a Windows Server 2008 Standard Server for the Ongoing Case Study

In this project, you build an installation of Windows Server 2008 Standard (Full installation) for use in the ongoing case project. Install the default configuration with the following requirements:

- 20 GB system partition
- CS-SRV-001 as the server name
- Member of the CaseStudy workgroup
- Administrator account password set to P@ssw0rd

Case Project 2-4: Building a Server Core Server for the Ongoing Case Study

In this project, you build an installation of Windows Server 2008 Standard (Server Core installation) for use in the ongoing case project. Install the default configuration with the following requirements:

- 16 GB system partition
- CS-SCSRV-001 as the server name
- Member of the CaseStudy workgroup
- Administrator account password set to P@ssw0rd

For ongoing case projects, your instructor might give you additional steps to perform depending on your lab environment. All the activities in this chapter are appropriate for physical machines and VM applications.

chapter 3

Networking with Windows Server 2008

After reading this chapter and completing the exercises, you will be able to:

- Identify the basic components of a network

- Describe the features of Internet Protocol version 4 (IPv4) and Internet Protocol version 6 (IPv6)

- Configure clients for IPv4 and IPv6

- Upgrade a network from IPv4 to IPv6

- Troubleshoot Transmission Control Protocol/Internet Protocol on networks

Now that you are familiar with Windows Server 2008, you are ready to explore networking in a Windows environment. Just as a telephone does not reach its true potential and intended usage without a phone line, a Windows Server 2008 computer is not useful without a network. A network enables computers to communicate with and transfer data to one another. Without the network, a server is relegated to a stand-alone computer and must rely on obscure methods such as using removable media to transfer data and information from one machine to another.

This chapter begins by discussing the basics of networking and how networks function. Next, it provides details about two networking protocols: **Internet Protocol version 4 (IPv4)** and **Internet Protocol version 6 (IPv6)**. The chapter examines how these protocols work, what they are used for, and how to manage them within a Windows environment. Successful deployment and management of a Windows network requires a solid grasp of networking concepts including **Internet Protocol (IP)**. The chapter also provides an overview of specific network components and services available for Windows Server 2008. These topics are developed more thoroughly throughout the rest of the book. Finally, the chapter examines the tools available for troubleshooting networks in Windows Server 2008 and discusses troubleshooting methodology.

 This chapter includes network terminology that is important for you to know as you continue on to future chapters. Refer to the Key Terms section at the end of the chapter for specific definitions.

Introduction to Networking

Although introduced in previous chapters, this section thoroughly defines a network and examines its components.

Basics of Networking

In computer terms, a **network** is a group of two or more **nodes**, such as computers, printers, and other hardware devices, linked together for sharing data. Before the advent of the Internet, most networks were simply a group of computers connected together with access only to their own resources, as shown in Figure 3-1. Now, most private networks connect to the Internet to allow their clients and users to access public information networks, as shown in Figure 3-2.

As a network administrator, you become an expert in networking. **Networking** is the practice of designing, implementing, and managing a collection of computers and devices or a network. All IT professionals need to have a good grasp of networking, as it is the foundation of communication for computing systems.

Types of Networks

Similar to how you can categorize the many types of computers and devices, you can also classify computer networks according to the following characteristics:

- Network scale
- Connection methodology
- Network architecture
- Network topology
- Network protocol

Network Scale   Network scale refers to how networks occupy geographic space. A network can range from a small home network to one that covers multiple locations and continents. Table 3-1 lists the common networks by scale, along with a description and example of each.

The most common types of networks are **local area networks (LANs)** and **wide area networks (WANs)**. A LAN is a private network that interconnects one or more **subnets**—subnetworks, or smaller networks—using high-speed network connections.

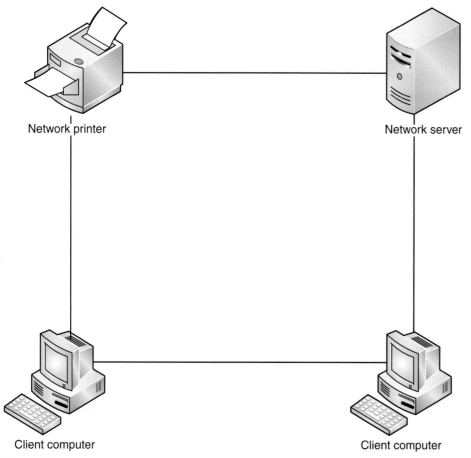

Figure 3-1   Basic network without Internet access

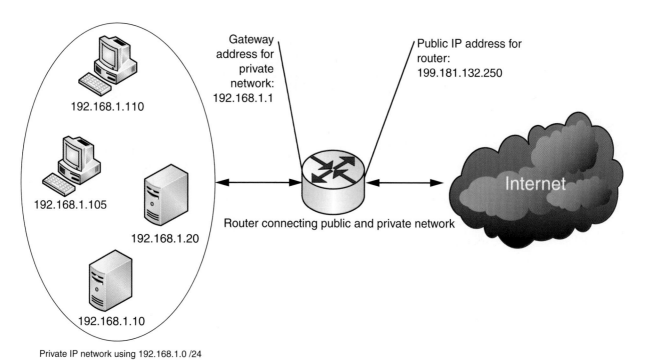

Figure 3-2   Basic network with Internet access

Table 3-1 Network descriptions based on scale

Scale type	Description	Example
Local area network (LAN)	Covers a small geographic area, such as a home, office, or building; current LANs are usually based on Ethernet technology	A business with only one building location has a wired or wireless LAN for users to interconnect local devices and to connect to the Internet.
Metropolitan area network (MAN)	Connects two or more LANs but does not extend beyond the boundaries of the immediate town, city, or metropolitan area	A business with two locations in the same city can use a MAN to connect locations and share information and network resources.
Wide area network (WAN)	Covers a relatively broad geographic area (i.e., one city to another or one country to another country) and often uses transmission facilities provided by common carriers, such as telephone companies	A company with offices in Chicago and New York City needs a WAN to connect the two offices.

A WAN is a group of networks spread across different geographic areas. WAN connections often use connections that have lower speeds than LAN connections. WAN connections commonly run through an **Internet service provider (ISP)**, which allocates WAN connections for private networks.

Figure 3-3 shows an example of a typical network using LAN and WAN connections.

Connection Methodology   How you connect networks is just as important as what type of devices you connect to it. **Connection methodology** defines the type of hardware technology used for connecting network nodes. The common technologies used today are **fiber optics**, which is a medium that uses glass fibers for transmitting data via light; **Ethernet**, which

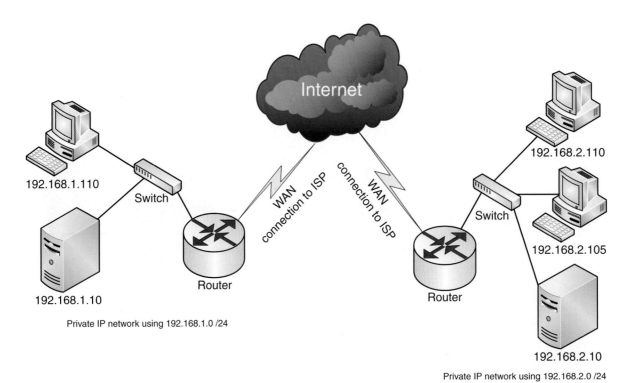

Figure 3-3 Example of a wide area network (WAN)

uses physical cables to connect network devices; and **wireless LAN**, which uses radio frequencies to transmit data between nodes.

Network Architectures   Chapter 1 describes the Windows network models you might encounter, such as client-server and workgroup, or peer-to-peer, architectures. **Network architectures** fall into the same categories and allow you to characterize needs based on the functional relationships between the nodes.

Network Topology   **Network topology** categorizes networks based on the physical and logical relationship among devices. A network's topology defines the physical placement of devices—the **physical layout**—the logical layout of networks, and protocol usage. (The **logical layout** defines how nodes communicate on the network.) Common network topologies include **star networks** and **mesh networks**, as shown in Figures 3-4 and 3-5.

Many factors determine which topology to use, including network speed, hardware deployed, fault tolerance, and cost of implementation.

Network Protocol   Just as two people need to share a common language to converse fully, computer networks require communication protocols to allow network nodes to communicate with each other called **network protocols**. A **protocol suite** is a group of protocols that work together to provide network services. The de facto network protocol suite used today is **Transmission Control Protocol/Internet Protocol (TCP/IP)**. TCP/IP is the basis for the Internet, the World Wide Web, and almost all networks. Implementing and configuring Windows networks with protocols from the TCP/IP suite are covered later in this chapter.

Basic Network Components

Now that you are aware of the different types of networks you can build, consider the basic components used to build those networks. These components are the hardware devices that provide

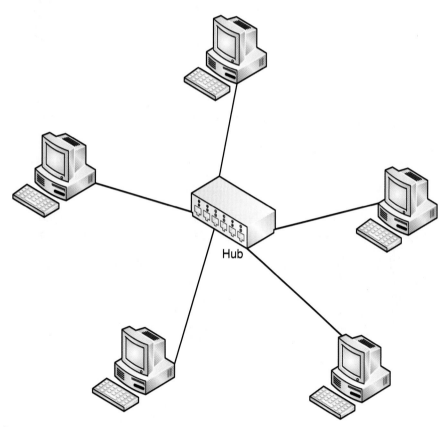

Figure 3-4   Example of a network using star topology

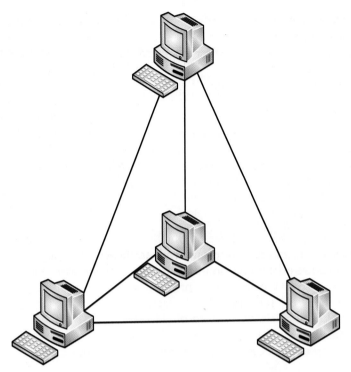

Figure 3-5   Example of a network using mesh topology

interconnections between computers and network resources such as printers. They include the following components:

- Network interface cards
- Repeaters
- Hubs
- Bridges
- Switches
- Routers

The roles of these devices are defined in the **Open Systems Interconnection (OSI) model**, a seven-layer reference model used to describe networks, the protocols they use, and applications running on them. The OSI model is discussed later in this chapter.

Network Interface Cards   **Network interface cards (NICs)** are hardware cards installed in computers so the computers can connect to a physical network. NICs can provide access to fiber-optic, wireless LAN, or Ethernet networks. Currently, Ethernet connections are the most common in enterprise environments. However, with the popularity of wireless and mobile devices such as notebooks, personal digital assistants, and smartphones, wireless LAN network adapters are becoming more popular. NICs use a low-level network addressing system based on **Media Access Control (MAC)** addresses. MAC addresses are designed to be globally unique and allow clients to communicate on certain networks. MAC addresses work on Layer 2 of the OSI model.

Repeaters   In Ethernet networks, signal strength degrades as the distance between devices increases. Most twisted-pair, or copper, Ethernet network configurations beyond 100 meters use a repeater to address this problem. A **repeater** is a hardware device that receives a signal and then resends it at a higher level or power so that it can travel longer distances between the start and end points of communication.

Hubs   A **hub** is the most basic of the hardware devices that interconnect multiple nodes. Hubs have multiple ports to which nodes connect. When a packet arrives at one port, it is sent to all the ports of the hub except for the port of entry. The bandwidth available for usage by all devices connected to a hub is equal to its total port speed. **Bandwidth** describes the amount of data that can travel from one network point to another within a specified time. For example, a five-port 10/100-megabit-per-second (Mbps) hub has five network ports that can transmit data at 10 Mbps or 100 Mbps, depending on the client NIC configuration. If five nodes are connected to this hub at 10 Mbps, those five nodes must share the 10 Mbps of bandwidth. If one node is sending large amounts of data, it decreases the available bandwidth for the other four nodes. Hubs work on the Physical layer (Layer 1) of the OSI model. Figure 3-6 displays how communication works among devices connected to a hub.

Network Bridges   Network bridges connect one or more networks segments. Like a **switch**, a bridge uses MAC addresses for managing traffic. A bridge learns from the traffic it processes, so it can associate a port with the specific MAC address to which it is connected. After the bridge associates a port and an address, it sends traffic for that address only to that port. This creates more efficient traffic on the network. Bridges work on the Layer 2 of the OSI model.

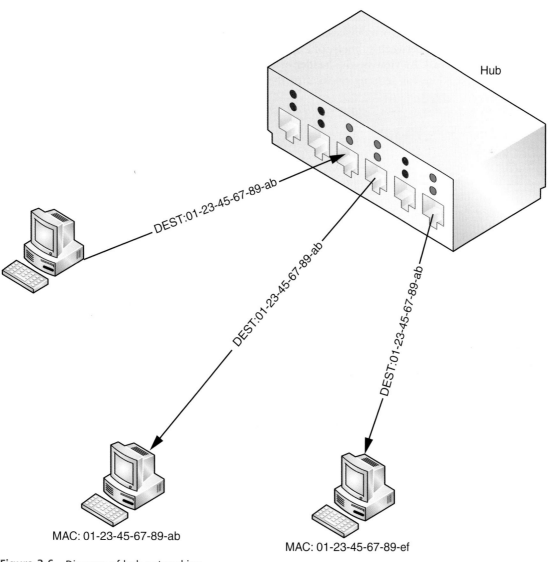

Figure 3-6   Diagram of hub networking

A bridge examines the source address of frames traveling across its ports. (A **frame** is a unit of data transferred between a sender and receiver on a network.) The bridge uses this information to associate bridge ports and MAC addresses and then stores it for future use. To process an unknown destination MAC address, the bridge forwards the traffic to all ports except for the arriving port. The bridge also stores this information for future reference.

Switches   Not to be confused with hubs, **switches** work at Layer 2 of the OSI model and forward frames between ports based on MAC addresses. However, switches are more intelligent Layer 2 devices because they forward only frames to the ports involved in sending and receiving the datagram. This gives switches an advantage over hubs because they can fully use the stated bandwidth of the switch on each port. Where a hub running at 100 Mbps must split bandwidth among all the ports, each port of a switch can use 100 Mbps. This makes switches a faster and more efficient way to move network traffic among nodes. Figure 3-7 displays how communication works between devices connected to a switch.

By design, switches cannot route traffic based on IP addresses. Although some switches are designated as Layer 3 switches, meaning that they can route by IP address, they are basically a router and switch combined into one device. These types of devices that span layers of the OSI model are referred to as **multilayer switches**. Within a normal network, all network nodes connect to one or more switches. For environments requiring connectivity to other subnets or the Internet, these switches are connected to a router for forwarding traffic to other subnets or public networks.

Routers   Among network devices, routers do the "heavy lifting." **Routers** are responsible for forwarding **packets** between subnets, or networks with differing IP addressing schemes. Routers accomplish this task by viewing the **header** of the data packet and using routing tables to determine the best route for sending packets to their destination. Working on Layer 3 of the OSI

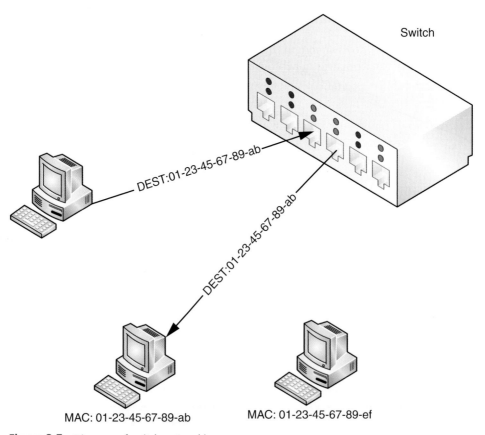

Figure 3-7   Diagram of switch networking

model, routers use dynamic routing protocols and preconfigured static routes to deliver packets using the best route possible between two subnets. Routers are always connected to at least two networks, such as two LANs or a **private network** connected to the Internet through an ISP. Figure 3-8 displays how communication works among devices connected to a router.

In Figure 3-8, the following five steps are performed:

1. The node at 192.168.1.10 sends a data packet destined for the node at 192.168.2.10.

2. The switch passes the data packet to the router.

3. The router receives the data and consults the Access Control List to determine where to route the packet. It identifies the interface at E2 as having the subnet 192.168.2.0.

4. The switch receives the packet from the router and sends the packet to the recipient.

5. The recipient receives the data packet.

The connection of two or more networks with Layer 3 devices is referred to as an internetwork. Routers interconnect subnets of differing types. You can build three distinct types of internetworks: extranets, intranets, and the **Internet**, a global network of networks.

Extranets are two or more networks connected to each other within the same organization. However, this connection cannot be from LAN to LAN. Extranets require a connection to a metropolitan area network (MAN) or WAN. Extranets do not require a connection to the Internet.

An intranet is a group of interconnected networks protected from external or public networks by hardware and software means. Intranets are typically used in private networks for organizations to provide resources such as Web-based applications and printers. Often, companies refer to their intranets as their internal Web presence for users.

The Internet is the globe-spanning IP network that links public resources such as Web sites, e-commerce applications, blogs, and more. Most importantly, it is home to the **World Wide**

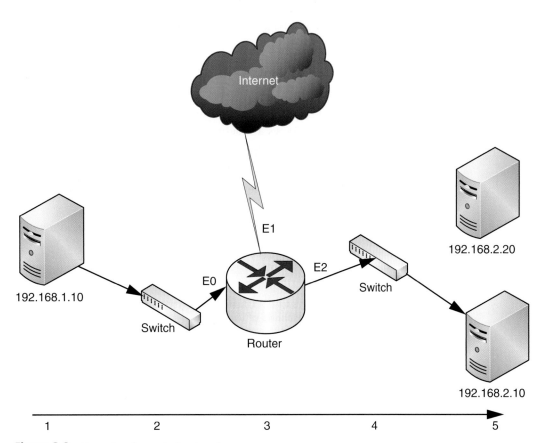

Figure 3-8 Example of a routed network

a system of hypertext documents linked by Universal Resource Locators (URLs) and accessed through the Internet. It is based on the network developed by the U.S. Department of Defense, called the **Advanced Research Projects Agency Network**.

Network Addressing with TCP/IP

Now that you've examined the basic components of networking and have an idea of what a network is, you are ready to explore network addressing and communication with TCP/IP. IP is currently available in version 4 and version 6. IPv4 is discussed in this section, and IPv6 is discussed in the next section.

IPv4

IPv4 is the industry standard for network addressing in public and private networks. Together, TCP and IP, referred to most commonly as TCP/IP, provide a suite of network protocols and services that are the basis for modern-day network communication. **Transmission Control Protocol (TCP)** is a set of rules to exchange messages with other Internet points at the information packet level, and guarantees the delivery of packets. Recall that IP is the basis for network addressing on the Internet. To understand IPv4, you need to be familiar with the following topics:

- Concepts of TCP/IP, including network layers, the OSI model, and the basics of IPv4
- Implementation of TCP/IP with IPv4
- Deployment considerations
- Troubleshooting TCP/IP networking
- Improvements to IPv4 in Windows Server 2008

Network Layers and the OSI Model   Network protocols are responsible for relaying communication on a network. These protocols are organized in a layered fashion with one protocol on top of another. With this design, protocols can communicate only with the protocol above it and below it, if applicable. The most common reference model depicting network layers is the OSI model, which is a seven-layer model responsible for end-to-end network traffic and communication. Table 3-2 shows the layers in the OSI model.

The layers in the OSI model are responsible for the following tasks:

- The **Physical layer** is responsible for bit-level transmission between network nodes. Cabling and connection types are defined at this layer.
- The **Data Link layer** is responsible for communications between adjacent network nodes. Bridges and switches operate at the Data Link layer.
- The **Network layer** is responsible for establishing paths for data transfer through the network. Routers operate at the Network layer.
- The **Transport layer** is responsible for delivering messages between networked hosts. User Datagram Protocol (UDP) and TCP function at this layer.

Table 3-2   OSI model

Layer	Examples of usage
1—Physical	Wired cabling and wireless frequency standards
2—Data Link	Ethernet and wireless LAN
3—Network	IPv4, IPv6, and Internet Control Message Protocol
4—Transport	TCP and User Datagram Protocol
5—Session	NetBIOS
6—Presentation	Encryption and Compression
7—Application	Simple Mail Transfer Protocol, Domain Name System, and Post Office Protocol

- The **Session layer** is responsible for establishing process-to-process communications between networked hosts.

- The **Presentation layer** is responsible for defining the syntax that two network hosts use to communicate.

- The **Application layer** is responsible for providing user services, such as file transfers, electronic messaging, e-mail, virtual terminal access, and network management. This is the layer with which the user interacts.

TCP/IP manages transmitted data in two layers of the OSI model: the Network layer for IP and the Transport layer for TCP. As the primary suite of protocols used by the Internet, TCP/IP encompasses application and transportation protocols such as File Transfer Protocol, Simple Mail Transfer Protocol, Telnet, and UDP.

Further discussion of the OSI model is outside the scope of this text and the 70-642 exam. For more information on the OSI model, refer to Microsoft Knowledge Base (KB) article ID 103884 at *www.microsoft.com*.

Anatomy of an IPv4 Address   IPv4 is based on an addressing scheme that uses unique 32-bit (4-byte) addresses. These addresses are used by network nodes for routing traffic between nodes, determining the senders of communication, and much more. Following are examples of typical IP addresses using dotted-decimal notation, which is the most common method for representing IP addresses:

```
192.168.115.100
10.10.1.15
```

Dotted-decimal notation uses four numbers known as octets that range from 0 to 255 and are separated by dots (.) or periods. They are called octets because the numbers in each range can be represented by 8 bits. Table 3-3 repeats these examples of IP addresses in dotted-decimal notation and provides their respective binary notation.

Although the decimal notation is more easily recognized by people, binary notation is important because all computers communicate in binary, a base-2 numbering system. **Binary numbers** are represented by either a 1 or a 0. 1 represents "on," or "true," and 0 represents "off," or "false." Computers use binary notation for communication because it is easier to implement with the current electronic technology than decimal. To give you an idea of counting in decimal and binary, consider what happens when you count from 0 to 10:

```
 0 = 0
 1 = 1
 2 = 10
 3 = 11
 4 = 100
 5 = 101
 6 = 110
 7 = 111
 8 = 1000
 9 = 1001
10 = 1010
```

Table 3-3   Examples of IP addresses

Dotted-Decimal IP	Octets Divided into Bits using Binary Numbering
192.168.115.100	11000000.10101000.01110011.01100100
10.10.1.15	00001010.00001010.00000001.00001111

The decimal number 10 is represented by 1010 as a binary number. How do you find this number? You begin by moving left to right.

Consider the first example of 192.168.115.100 from Table 3-3. You use binary math to determine the 8 bits represented by each octet in the address. Use Table 3-4 to complete binary math calculations for IP addresses.

Here's the basic formula to follow for binary conversion:

- Determine the greatest base-2 number that is no greater than your decimal number. For example, if your decimal number is 133, the greatest base-2 number is 128, or 2^7.

- Insert a 1 in the place of each base-2 number that fits and insert a 0 in the place of all base-2 numbers that remain.

- Subtract the base-2 number from your decimal number. Use this remainder as your next decimal starting point.

- Repeat these steps until you have a remainder of 0.

Using the third octet in the IP address 192.168.115.100, you can practice converting decimal notation into binary and reveal the 8-bit makeup of the number in the following activity.

Activity 3-1: Converting Decimal Numbers to Binary Numbers

Time Required: 15 minutes

Objective: Practice decimal-to-binary conversion.

Description: You want to practice your binary conversion skills. To do this, you start with an IP address of 192.168.115.100 and convert the third octet to binary using Table 3-4. Use the Bit row to complete this activity.

1. To convert the decimal number 115 to binary, answer the following questions. What is the greatest power of 2 that can be subtracted from 115 with a remainder of 0 or greater? In this example, it is 64 with a remainder of 51. Insert a 0 in the first column on the left because 128 is greater than 115 and insert a 1 in the second column because 115 can be divided by 2^6, or 64, one time. You will repeat this process until you have a remainder of 0.

2. Does the number 32 go into 51? Yes, so write a 1 as the next bit and subtract 32 from 51 for a remainder of 19.

3. Does the number 16 go into 19? Yes, so write a 1 as the next bit and subtract 16 from 19 for a remainder of 3.

4. Does the number 8 go into 3? It does not, so place a 0 as the next bit and continue.

5. Does the number 4 go into 3? It does not, so place a 0 as the next bit and continue.

6. Does the number 2 go into 3? Yes, so write a 1 as the next bit and subtract 2 from 3 for a remainder of 1.

Table 3-4 Base-2 numbering table for converting decimals to binary

	2^7	2^6	2^5	2^4	2^3	2^2	2^1	2^0
	128	64	32	16	8	4	2	1
Bit position	1	2	3	4	5	6	7	8
Bit								

7. Does 1 go into 1? Yes, so write a 1 as the next bit and you have completed the conversion from decimal to binary

8. Your binary number should be 01110011, as shown in Table 3-5.

Each IP address is made up of two parts: the network ID and the host ID. The network ID is used by routers to determine to which destination network a packet needs to be routed. The host ID is used by computers on the destination network to determine which packets are destined for them. The host and network ID portions are determined through use of a subnet mask, which is discussed in the following section.

Subnetting

Subnetting is the process of creating multiple smaller networks, or subnets, from an IP network address. Often, subnetting is used as a way to manage small groups of addresses within a single network. It is also used to work around the limited number of publicly available IP network addresses, a major reason for the present and future movement to IPv6 networks.

A **subnet mask** can determine the network and host ID portions of an IP address. Like an IP address, a subnet mask is represented by a four-octet dotted-decimal number. The following is an example of a network with an associated subnet mask:

IP address: 192.168.100.1

Subnet mask: 255.255.255.128

The network ID is 192.168.100 and the host ID is 1.

To determine the maximum number of hosts that can be used in a subnet mask, you raise the number 2 to the power of N, where N equals the number of bits allocated to the host portion of a subnet. N can be determined by converting the subnet mask to binary and counting the number of zeroes in number. Next, you subtract 2 from your total to remove the first and last values of an IP address range. The first value represents the address of the subnet itself, or the default route address. This address is often used by clients that have yet to receive an IP address such as those requesting an address via Dynamic Host Configuration Protocol (DHCP). The last value represents the subnet's broadcast address, or an IP address that allows information to be sent to all clients on particular subnet instead of a single client. Use the following equation to determine the maximum number of hosts:

$$\text{Maximum number of hosts} = 2^N - 2$$

Consider the following example of determining the number of hosts for a subnet. This example uses the IP address range of 192.168.100.0 with a subnet mask of 255.255.255.128.

First, you convert 255.255.255.128 to binary so you can determine the number of zeroes in the subnet mask.

255.255.255.128 = 11111111.11111111.11111111.10000000

Table 3-5   Base-2 numbering conversion for the decimal 115

	2^7	2^6	2^5	2^4	2^3	2^2	2^1	2^0
	128	64	32	16	8	4	2	1
Bit position	1	2	3	4	5	6	7	8
Bit	0	1	1	1	0	0	1	1

Next, you count the number of zeroes, which is seven in this example. Therefore, 7 becomes the value for N. Insert the value for N into the equation to determine the number of hosts on a network:

$$\text{Maximum number of hosts} = 2^N - 2 = 2^7 - 2 = 126$$

Based on these calculations, the subnet mask of 255.255.255.128 yields 126 usable host addresses that fall in the range of 192.168.100.1 to 192.168.100.126.

Activity 3-2: Using the Windows Calculator to Convert Decimal Numbers to Binary

Time Required: 5 minutes

Objective: Use the Windows Calculator to perform decimal-to-binary number conversions.

Description: When performing IP subnetting with IPv4, you often need to convert decimal numbers to binary and vice versa. In this activity, you use the Windows Calculator to perform the binary conversion of the last decimal number in the subnet mask of 255.255.255.192. This allows you to determine the number of bits available for host addresses.

Your instructor might give you additional steps to perform in all the activities depending on your lab environment. The activities are designed for running in virtual machine applications. However, they can also be performed in a physical machine environment by dual or multibooting your computer.

1. Log onto MSN-SRV-0XX (the Full version of Windows Server 2008 Enterprise edition you installed in Chapter 1).

2. Open the Run dialog box from the Start menu, type **calc**, and then press **Enter** to start the Windows Calculator.

3. Click **View** on the menu bar and then click **Scientific** to change to the scientific calculator.

4. Ensure that the Decimal option button is selected on the calculator.

5. Type the last octet of the subnet mask, **192**.

6. Click the **Bin** option button. Windows Calculator converts the number to 11000000.

7. Based on this binary number, determine the number of usable hosts on a network using the following equation:

Maximum number of hosts $= 2^N - 2$

8. Write the number of usable addresses in the following space:

When first implemented, network addressing used subnet network notation known as classful notation. Classful notation provides three classes of available public networks. Classful networks are no longer used on the Internet or in most medium-size to large private networks because the class model cannot provide enough useful network ranges and addresses. (In addition, they have other limitations that are outside the scope of this discussion.) Table 3-6 lists the three classes of available public networks.

Table 3-6   Classful IP address ranges

Class	Address Range	Default Subnet Mask	Number of Networks	Hosts per Network
Class A	0.0.0.0 to 127.255.255.255	255.0.0.0	127	16,777,214
Class B	128.0.0.0 to 191.255.255.255	255.255.0.0	16,384	65,534
Class C	192.0.0.0 to 223.255.255.255	255.255.255.0	2,097,152	254

Table 3-7 RFC 3330 special-use IPv4 addresses

Addresses	Purpose	Class	Total Number of Addresses (Including Broadcast and in Range Network Addresses)
0.0.0.0 to 0.255.255.255	Zero addresses	A	16,777,216
10.0.0.0 to 10.255.255.255	Private IP addresses	A	16,777,216
127.0.0.0 to 127.255.255.255	Local host loopback address	A	16,777,216
169.254.0.0 to 169.254.255.255	APIPA	B	65,536
172.16.0.0 to 172.31.255.255	Private IP addresses	B	1,048,576
192.0.2.0 to 192.0.2.255	Documentation and examples	C	256
192.88.99.0 to 192.88.99.255	IPv6-to-IPv4 relay	C	256
192.168.0.0 to 192.168.255.255	Private IP addresses	C	65,536
198.18.0.0 to 198.19.255.255	Network Device Benchmark	C	131,072
224.0.0.0 to 239.255.255.255	Multicast	D	268,435,456
240.0.0.0 to 255.255.255.255	Reserved	E	268,435,456

Certain ranges within the three classes are not usable because they fall into ranges defined and reserved for special uses. Special-use IPv4 addresses are defined by **Request for Comment (RFC)** 3330 and listed in Table 3-7. (An RFC is a document that describes the specifications for a recommended technology.)

The current method for IP address allocation is the **Classless Interdomain Routing (CIDR, pronounced "cider")** system. CIDR deals with the limitations of classful addressing by allowing the allocation of IP addresses based on need, not general classification. CIDR uses variable-length subnet masks to provide individualized network addressing.

Note that CIDR provides a different way of notating an address. For example, a network address of 192.168.100.0 with a subnet mask of 255.255.255.0 is a classic Class C address. In CIDR notation, the address would be listed as 192.168.100.0 /24. You use the "/" character followed by the number of bits allocated to the network portion of the address for CIDR notation.

Suppose you want to divide the 192.168.100.0 network address into eight smaller subnets. To do this, you would use a /27 subnet mask to create these smaller networks. Table 3-8 lists the commonly used **CIDR blocks**, each of which shows the number of bits used for the subnet mask.

With the /27 subnet mask, you now have the following subnets available for use, each with 32 host addresses:

192.168.100.0 /27

192.168.100.32 /27

192.168.100.64 /27

192.168.100.96 /27

Table 3-8 Common CIDR blocks (subnetting Class C addresses only)

CIDR Block	Subnet Mask	Hosts Per Network	Available Networks
/24	255.255.255.0	254	1
/25	255.255.255.128	126	2
/26	255.255.255.192	62	4
/27	255.255.255.224	30	8
/28	255.255.255.240	14	16

Table 3-9   Network addresses for common CIDR subnet masks

CIDR Notation	Subnet Mask	Available Networks	Hosts Per Network	Starting Network Addresses
/24	255.255.255.0	1	254	0
/25	255.255.255.128	2	126	0,128
/26	255.255.255.192	4	62	0,64,128,192
/27	255.255.255.224	8	30	0,32,64,96,128,160,192,224
/28	255.255.255.240	16	14	0,16,32,48,64,80,96,112,128, 144,160,176,192,208,224,240

192.168.100.128 /27

192.168.100.160 /27

192.168.100.192 /27

192.168.100.224 /27

You can use a table such as Table 3-9 or a CIDR calculator on the Internet, or you can determine the address ranges by hand.

Suppose you need to determine the address ranges for the 32 host addresses. The easiest way to do so is to follow these rules:

- The first network address is always 0 (zero). In the example, the first address is 192.168.100.0 /27.

- Add the number of hosts on each network, represented by N, to 0 to determine the next network address. In the example, the second network address is 192.168.100.32 /27.

- Continue adding the value of N to the previous network address until you have created the total number of available networks based on your CIDR block.

Although each provides 32 addresses, you have only 30 usable addresses because you need to reserve two for the network and broadcast addresses. Also, each subnet requires a router, so you truly have 29 addresses available for hosts, or $2^N - 3$.

In addition to subnetting, supernetting is related to CIDR because CIDR is simply the framework for performing subnetting or supernetting. Where subnetting splits a large network into smaller subnetworks, supernetting allows you to combine two or more subnetworks into a larger supernetwork, or supernet, when a smaller subnetwork cannot provide sufficient addresses for a particular need. In many references, CIDR and supernetting are synonymous. Supernetting is also often referred to as route aggregation.

Implementing supernets requires either creating static routes for all the networks or using a routing protocol such as the **Routing Information Protocol version 2 (RIPv2)**, which is available in Routing and Remote Access Service (RRAS) on Windows Server 2008. You create supernets and use RIPv2 in Chapter 9.

The MCTS 70-642 exam often includes questions on IP addressing, subnetting, and supernetting. Make sure you can determine the network range and available hosts based on the subnet mask. Although you should also understand classful addressing, CIDR notation and conversion is a requirement for success on the 70-642 exam.

Public and Private Addresses

Now that you understand the basics of IP addresses and how to create them, you can consider the addresses available for usage, which are public addresses and private addresses.

Public addresses are issued IP addresses that are available from the Internet. These addresses are centrally registered and maintained through the **Internet Corporation for Assigned Names**

and Numbers, ISPs, and domain registration organizations. Along with the distribution of public IP addresses, these organizations maintain domain name registrations and top-level domain name servers. Any resource or network that needs to be accessible from the Internet must have a public IP address. Examples include Web servers hosting public content and a router or firewall that provides Internet access to your network.

On the other hand, private IP addresses are not available or routable on the Internet. They are for use by administrators deploying internal networks. Private IP addresses are defined by RFC 1918. RFC 1918 can be viewed at *www.rfc.net*. Private IP addresses allow administrators to create workable internetworks for their internal network while needing only a small number of public addresses. While not externally routable, you can implement network address translation (NAT) so that your clients with private IP addresses can communicate. NAT is discussed in Chapter 9.

Introduction to IPv6

IPv6 is the future of IP on the Internet and on public and private networks. With an almost limitless address space and built-in security technologies, many organizations plan to migrate to the protocol in the next few years.

Why IPv6?   Because of the limitation of addressing in IPv4, an upgraded protocol was needed to allow for the ever-increasing demand for public IP addresses. IPv6 solves this problem by providing a 128-bit addressing space (compared to 32-bit with IPv4) that supports 2^{128} addresses, or 340,282,366,920,938,463,463,374,607,431,768,211,456 addresses. To put that in terms of the world's current population of 6.5 billion people, this means that each person on the planet could receive approximately 50 octillion IP addresses. Along with the increase in address space, IPv6 provides the following advantages:

- Improved security
- Improved autoconfiguration
- Simplified routing

For more information on the specifications of IPv6, refer to RFC 2460 at *www.rfc.net*.

Addressing with IPv6   IPv6 uses source and destination addresses that are 128 bits, or 16 bytes, in length. Typical IPv6 addresses contain 64 bits for the network portion and 64 bits for the host portion. The network portion is referred to as the prefix, and it represents the bits that are not under your control. The host portion is often referred to as the interface ID. Unlike IPv4, which uses dotted-decimal notation, IPv6 uses hexadecimal notation. An IPv6 address contains eight groups of four hexadecimal digits, as in the following examples:

```
1075:0:0:0:5:600:300c:422d
ff06::d5
```

As you can see from the examples, IPv6 addresses are more difficult to remember than IPv4 addresses. It is even more important with IPv6 that you implement name resolution properly.

Address Structure   IPv6 provides the following rules you can use for shortening addresses:

- Any leading digit of 0 (zero) can be dropped from any group.
- Two or more groups of zeroes can be replaced by two colons. However, this can be done only once per address.

Consider the following IPv6 address and then apply these rules to the address:

2008:0000:0000:0000:000b:2f36:0041:25ab

If you remove the leading zeroes from this example, you are left with the following address:

2008:0:0:0:b:2f36:41:25ab

If you replace groups of zeroes with two colons, you are left with the following address:

2008::b:2f36:41:25ab

As you can see, this is an easier number to read. If you were to receive the following address, you would know that three groups of zeroes have been replaced by double colons since all IPv6 addresses have eight groups.

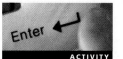

Activity 3-3: Simplifying IPv6 Addresses

Time Required: 10 minutes

Objective: Transcribe IPv6 addresses using rules for simplification.

Description: In this activity, you use the rules discussed earlier to simplify IP addresses by removing leading zeroes and multiple zero groups. You also convert simplified addresses to their original state. Use Table 3-10 to complete this activity.

Table 3-10   IPv6 address simplification

Full Address	Simplified Address
1075:0000:0000:0000:0005:0600:300c:422d	
	ff06::d5
1055:0000:0000:0000:000b:1bda:0041:25ab	
	abcd:12bc::34:1a
50ab:0353:2003:0001:0000:0000:abaf:0003	

Notation Usage   IPv6 addresses can be written with CIDR notation for subnetting an address. You no longer need subnet masks for this task in IPv6. For example, the following address represents a 48-bit network address:

1075:5:ab12::/48

This represents the addresses from 1075:5:ab12:0000:0000:0000:0000 to 1075:5:ab12:ffff:ffff:ffff:ffff:ffff.

Because IPv6 notation uses colons as separators, you have new standards when using addresses in URL and Universal Naming Convention (UNC) paths.

For UNC paths, all colons become hyphens, and ".ipv6-literal.net" is appended to the address. For example, connecting to the Users share on 2008::b:2f36:41:25ab results in the following UNC path:

\\2008-b-2f36-41-25ab.ipv6.literal.net\Users

For URLs, the IPv6 address must be enclosed in brackets. This allows the specification of a port number along with the address. For example, connecting to a Web page at ff06::d5 over port 443 results in the following URL:

https://[ff06::d5]:443/

IPv6 Address Types

IPv6 addresses fall into the following types:

- Link-local addresses
- Unique local addresses
- Global addresses
- Multicast addresses
- Special addresses

Link-Local Addresses Hosts use this type of address for communication with other hosts on the same network segment. Because all link-local addresses have the same network prefix, they cannot be routed between networks. All IPv6 interfaces have a link-local address. That means IPv6 interfaces can have multiple addresses; in contrast, IPv4 addresses typically have only one address. Link-local addresses are made up of the following:

- The first 10 bits are always 1111 1110 10.
- The next 54 bits are always zero. So the link-local address in CIDR notation is fe80::/64.
- The remaining 64 bits represent the interface ID, or host addresses on the network.

Not exclusive to link-local addresses, zone IDs are necessary when using link-local addresses. Zone IDs are used when a computer has multiple network adapters. To distinguish among the multiple networks, each IPv6 address is appended with a percent sign and a numeric zone ID. Following is an example of link-local addresses using zone IDs:

```
fe80::109f:7e16:d369:2d7c%12
fe80::a54d:d018:8f3d:5afd%13
```

Activity 3-4: Using IPconfig to Determine Link-Local Addresses

Time Required: 5 minutes

Objective: Use IPconfig to determine a link-local address.

Description: In this activity, you use the ipconfig /all command to determine the link-local IPv6 address on MSN-SRV-0XX, the Windows Server 2008 Enterprise computer.

1. On MSN-SRV-0XX, open a Command Prompt window from the Start menu. Type **ipconfig /all > ipv6LL.txt** and then press **Enter**.
2. Open the text file you created by typing **notepad ipv6LL.txt** at the command prompt and then pressing **Enter**.
3. Write the link-local address in the following space: _____

Unique Local Addresses This type of address can be routed on your internal network, or intranet. However, it cannot be routed to the Internet. These addresses are comparable to private IPv4 addresses because they allow you to create hidden networks. Unique local addresses are made up of the following:

- The first 8 bits are always 1111 1101, so the network prefix is fd00::/8.
- The next 40 bits represent the global ID, which identifies a specific site within an organization.
- The last 16 bits of the network address represent the subnet ID. This provides for the creation of 65,536 subnets within each site identified by a global ID.
- The remaining 64 bits represent the interface ID, or host addresses on the network.

Unlike link-local addresses, unique local addresses are not created automatically. To use them, a network must have a router or DHCP server that supplies the appropriate addresses.

Global Addresses   This type of address can be reached from the Internet, so it is similar to a public IPv4 address. All public IPv6 addresses have a 2000::/3 prefix. Global addresses are made up of the following:

- The first 3 bits are 001, so the network prefix always begins with 2 or 3.
- The next 45 bits are the global routing prefix, which identifies the destination network on the IPv6 Internet.
- The last 16 bits of the network address represent the subnet ID. This provides for the creation of 65,536 internal subnets for use on private networks.
- The remaining 64 bits represent the interface ID, or host addresses on the network.

Internet-connected IPv6-capable routers forward packets only with addresses starting with 2 or 3. They drop any other packets, which enhances security.

Multicast Addresses   These addresses are reserved for IPv6 to use for multicast communications. Recall that multicast allows a single node to send a single packet that multiple destinations can receive simultaneously. Voice over IP, streaming media, and computer imaging are a few of the applications that use multicast. Multicast addresses are made up of the following:

- The first 8 bits are 1111 1111, so the network prefix always begins with FF00::/8.
- The next 4 bits are flags that determine the state of the multicast address. Two states, permanent and temporary, are available.
- The next 4 bits define the scope of the multicast address. Two scopes, site local and link local, are available.
- The remaining 112 bits represent the group ID, which identifies the computer subscribed to a particular multicast.

Multicast communications require routers that support the forwarding of multicast traffic, so your network must be specifically configured to support multicast. Because of these limitations, multicast is not typically available on the Internet.

Special Addresses   As with IPv4 networks, IPv6 reserves addresses and networks for specific usage. Table 3-11 lists these special addresses.

Additional information on special addresses can be found in RFC 5156 at *www.rfc.net*.

Table 3-11   Special addresses

IPv6 Prefix	Usage
::1/128 or ::1	Loopback address
::ffff:0:0/96	Mapping IPv4 addresses
2002::/16	6to4 addressing
2001::/32	Teredo addresses
ff00::/8	Multicast addresses
2001:db8::/32	Reserved for documentation

Activity 3-5: Identifying Types of IPv6 Addresses

Time Required: 15 minutes

Objective: Identify different types of IPv6 addresses.

Description: In this activity, you determine the type of addresses each listed in Table 3-12. The first column lists each IPv6 address. In the next two columns, write what type of address it is and what it is used for.

Table 3-12   Identifying types of IPv6 addresses

IPv6 Address	Type of Address	Purpose
2020:ab10:5::a234		
ff00:cdc1:505:2234::1		
fd00:1223:455::3321		
fe80:22:ad32:3332::245		
2001:db8:2222:142a::3431		
::1		

Configuring Clients for IPv4 and IPv6

As a network administrator, you should also be familiar with configuring clients. Without properly configured clients, users and computers cannot access the network for resources. In this section, you learn about configuring Windows clients to use IPv4 and IPv6.

IPv4 Client Configuration

This section discusses setting up clients when deploying IPv4 addressing. Later chapters discuss the Dynamic Host Configuration Protocol (DHCP) and Dynamic Name System (DNS) in regard to deploying these services as network-based providers for your clients. You need to provide each client in your environment with an IP address that allows them to communicate with other clients on their subnet and other networks. You can use the following configurations on a client:

- DHCP configuration
- Manual configuration

DHCP   In cases where you cannot contact a DHCP server, even though the client is configured for dynamic addressing, Windows uses Automatic Private IP Addressing (APIPA) to assign a unique random IP address from the usable address range of 169.254.0.1 to 169.254.255.254

All Windows Server 2008 servers are set to use DHCP by default, as shown in Figure 3-9. If the server you are deploying uses DHCP, you don't need to configure anything else. You should have the DHCP service available for your clients or have a static IP address.

In cases where you cannot contact a DHCP server, even though the client is configured for dynamic addressing, Windows uses Automatic Private IP Addressing (APIPA) to assign a unique random IP address from the address range of 169.254.1.0 to 169.254.254.255. APIPA addresses allow clients on the same subnet to communicate without DHCP or manual configuration. However, APIPA addresses are not routable, so they cannot access resources on other networks.

Alternate configuration is an additional setting you can configure along with DHCP. With alternate configuration, you can set a static IP address in your IP configuration that will be used if DHCP is not available. To do so, you use the Alternate Configuration tab in the IPv4 Properties dialog box, shown in Figure 3-10. This is an excellent tool for mobile devices that work on DHCP networks but that require a static setting for a particular network.

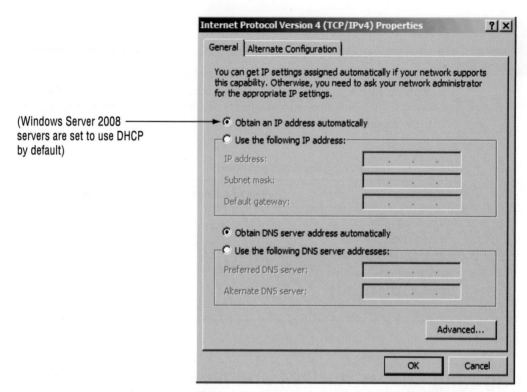

(Windows Server 2008 servers are set to use DHCP by default)

Figure 3-9   General tab in the IPv4 Properties dialog box

Activity 3-6: Manually Configuring DHCP with an Alternate IP Address Configuration

Time Required: 10 minutes

Objective: Configure a client to use DHCP and an alternate IP configuration.

Description: You are configuring your Windows Server 2008 server with a DHCP. Because you want to set up a static IP address in your IP configuration that the server can use if DHCP is not available, you plan to configure an alternate static IP as well.

1. On MSN-SRV-0XX, click **Start** and then click **Network**. In the Network window, click **Network and Sharing Center** on the Command bar. In the Network and Sharing Center window, click **Manage network connections** in the Tasks list in the left pane.

2. Right-click **Local Area Connection** and then click **Properties**. The Local Area Connection Properties dialog box opens.

3. Click **Internet Protocol Version 4 (TCP/IPv4)**, and then click **Properties**. The Internet Protocol Version 4 (TCP/IPv4) Properties dialog box opens.

4. Click the **General** tab if necessary and then verify that the "Obtain an IP address automatically" option button is selected.

5. Click the **Alternate Configuration** tab.

6. Click the **User configured** option button and then enter the following information or IP information provided by your instructor:

   - IP address: **192.168.100.10**

   - Subnet mask: **255.255.255.0**

   - Default gateway: **192.168.100.1**

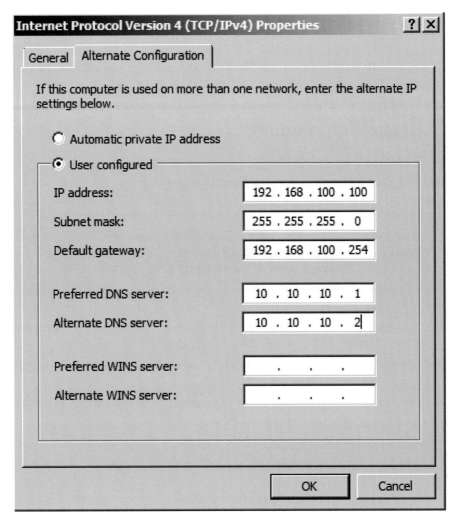

Figure 3-10   Alternate Configuration tab in the IPv4 Properties dialog box

7. If your environment has a DNS server available for use, enter its address under Preferred DNS Server. You will be installing your own DNS server in a later chapter.

8. Click **OK** to close the Internet Protocol Version 4 (TCP/IPv4) Properties dialog box and then click **Close** to close the Local Area Connection Properties dialog box and set new IP address information. Close all open windows.

Manual Configuration   Manually configuring IP addresses is often referred to as static configuration or a static IP address. In this case, you provide your clients with a predetermined IP address that is available for use on your network, and the client retains this IP address until it is changed on the client. You do this by manually entering the IP address, subnet mask, and any other network service information required on each client that will use a static IP address. You can use the following tools to perform this task:

- Initial Settings Wizard
- Server Manager
- Netsh

Static IP addresses are commonly used on servers where a dynamic IP address would affect network resources. For example, suppose your clients are set to use 192.168.100.100 for their DNS server, DNS1. DNS1 uses DHCP. If its IP address changes to 192.168.100.101, your clients do not have access to DNS. These types of servers include domain controllers and DHCP, DNS, and e-mail servers, to name a few. In Activity 3-7, you manually configure an IP address using the Network Connections window. Although you can open this window using Server Manager, the Initial Settings Wizard, or the Network and Sharing window, the process for configuring through the GUI is exactly the same for each.

Activity 3-7: Manually Configuring a Static IP Address Using Network Connections

Time Required: 10 minutes

Objective: Configure a client with manual IP addressing.

Description: You are configuring your Windows Server 2008 server with a static IP address. This is common practice for servers that run critical services that depend on an IP address.

1. On MSN-SRV-0XX, click **Start** and then click **Network**. In the Network window, click **Network and Sharing Center** on the Command bar. In the Network and Sharing Center window, click **Manage network connections** in the Tasks list in the left pane.

2. Right-click **Local Area Connection** and then click **Properties**. The Local Area Connection Properties dialog box opens.

3. Click **Internet Protocol Version 4 (TCP/IPv4)**, and then click **Properties**. The Internet Protocol Version 4 (TCP/IPv4) Properties dialog box opens.

4. Click the **General** tab if necessary and then click the **Use the following IP address:** option button.

5. Enter the following information or IP information provided by your instructor:
   - IP address: **192.168.100.10**
   - Subnet mask: **255.255.255.0**
   - Default gateway: **192.168.100.1**

6. If your environment has a DNS server available for use, enter the address under Use the following DNS server addresses. You install your own DNS server in a later chapter.

7. Click **OK** to close the Internet Protocol Version 4 (TCP/IPv4) Properties dialog box and then click **Close** to close the Local Area Connection Properties dialog box and set new IP address information. Close all open windows.

If you want to configure an IP address without using the GUI, you can use the netsh, or network shell, Windows utility. Recall that netsh performs local and remote network configuration tasks. You can run netsh from the command prompt, in scripts, or using the netsh prompt, as shown in Figure 3-11. The syntax for setting a static IP address for netsh is as follows:

```
netsh interface ip set address "NetworkAdapterName"
static ipaddr subnetmask gateway metric
```

Figure 3-11   Using netsh at the command prompt (command prompt only)

The following netsh command displays all the current network adapters on a system. This can be helpful to determine the network adapter name needed in the previous command:

```
netsh interface ip show config
```

Activity 3-8: Manually Configuring an IP Address Using netsh

Time Required: 10 minutes

Objective: Configure a client with manual IP addressing using netsh.

Description: You are configuring your Windows Server 2008 server running Server Core with a static IP address. You need to use netsh to complete this setup task.

1. Log onto MSN-SC-0XX (the Server Core version of Windows Server 2008 you set up in Chapter 2).

2. Use the following information or IP information provided by your instructor to configure networking on Server Core:

   - IP address: **192.168.100.20**
   - Subnet mask: **255.255.255.0**
   - Default gateway: **192.168.100.1**

3. At the command prompt, enter the following netsh command to set the IP address information mentioned previously:

```
netsh interface ip set address "local area connection"
static 192.168.100.20 255.255.255.0 192.168.100.1
```

4. Type **ipconfig /all** and then press **Enter** to verify that your IP address has changed successfully.

IPv6 Client Configuration   One of the benefits of IPv6 is the ease of configuration, especially when using autoconfiguration. Although manually configuring IP addresses is still an option, almost all computers automatically configure IPv6 settings. You will configure clients using autoconfiguration in the next section.

Autoconfiguration   When a Windows Server 2008 client connects to a network, it generates a link-local address for use in its local network and then begins acquiring configuration and address information from network services such as an IPv6 router or DHCP server. The configuration of your routers determines the way autoconfiguration takes place, which can be one of the following methods:

- *Stateless*—This type of configuration occurs when a client configures its own address based on an IPv6 router advertisement. In cases where DHCP is available, the client will retrieve DNS and other configuration information besides an IP address from the DHCP server. More information on stateless autoconfiguration can be found in RFC 2462 at *www.rfc.net*.

- *Stateful*—This type of configuration occurs when the client accepts configuration information, including an IPv6 address, from a DHCP server.

To maintain unique addresses, IPv6 uses Duplicate Address Detection (DAD) to avoid address duplication. The following summarizes the autoconfiguration process:

1. A Windows Server 2008 client generates a random 64-bit value, or interface ID, for creating a link-local address. Recall that the first 64 bits are predefined by the IPv6 standard.

2. The client registers the address as "tentative" until DAD determines its status.

3. Like APIPA in IPv4, the client checks the local network to determine if the address is in use. It uses the Neighbor Solicitation message, which contains the tentative address, for this task.

4. After determining that the address is valid, the server marks the address as "Preferred."

5. After assigning the link-local address, the client contacts a local router for configuration information.

6. Based on the router contact, the router provides the client network configuration information in the following ways:

   a. The router provides information to perform a stateful configuration via a DHCP server.

   b. The router provides information so that the client can generate its own global address using stateless configuration.

7. Based on the information from the router or the DHCP server, the client configures its global address.

8. If the router does not respond or no router is available, DHCP is used. If neither is available, the client will not configure a global address.

DHCPv6   With IPv6, DHCP's function on a network changes. On IPv4 networks, clients broadcast a request for an IP address, and DHCP responds. On IPv6 networks, client requests for IP addresses are directed to a router. Clients can request an IP address from a DHCP server only when instructed by the router to perform a stateful configuration or if a router never responds. DHCP's main function is to provide clients with secondary network configuration information such as DNS servers.

Neighbor Discovery   Based on RFC 4861, Neighbor Discovery (ND) is the protocol used by IPv6 clients for router discovery on a network. ND in IPv6 replaces Address Resolution Protocol in IPv4. Besides router discovery, the ND protocol performs the following tasks:

- *Prefix discovery*—Allows hosts to discover address prefixes for the link
- *Address autoconfiguration*—Configures addresses for an interface
- *Address resolution*—Maps IP addresses to link-layer addresses
- *Next-hop determination*—Determines the best path to route a packet based on information received from neighbors
- *Neighbor Unreachability Detection*—Determines that a neighbor is no longer reachable on the link
- *DAD*—Allows a node to check whether a proposed address is already in use
- *Redirect*—Allows routers to inform a node about better first-hop

The ND protocol uses the following Internet Control Message Protocol Version 6 (ICMPv6) messages for completing its tasks:

- *Router solicitation*—Request from client for router to advertise IPv6 configuration information
- *Router advertisement*—Message from router to clients with IPv6 configuration information
- *Neighbor solicitation*—Request from client to neighboring nodes for IPv6 link-layer address information
- *Neighbor advertisement*—Response from target to neighbor solicitation message, which provides the target's IPv6 link-layer information
- *Redirect*—Message sent to target informing them of better first hop router, a closer or more efficient router, for handling their request

For more information on Neighbor Discovery and ICMPv6, see RFC 4861 and RFC 1885 at *www.rfc.net*.

As discussed previously, IPv6 is enabled by default and automatically configures itself by working with IPv6 routers. Because of this, you normally do not need to perform additional configuration steps unless you need to statically assign an IP address or enable transition technologies between IPv4 and IPv6 such as ISATAP, Teredo, and 6to4.

Similar to IPv4, IPv6 can be configured through the GUI or from the command line. You can try both techniques for configuring IPv6 in Windows Server 2008 later in this section.

Manual Configuration Through the GUI

In the GUI, you manually configure IP addresses using the IPv6 Properties dialog box for the network adapter you want to change, as shown in Figure 3-12. In Activity 3-9, you manually configure IPv6 through the Network Connections window.

Activity 3-9: Manually Configure a Static IP Address Using Network Connections

Time Required: 10 minutes

Objective: Configure a client with manual IP addressing.
Description: You are configuring your Windows Server 2008 server with a static IPv6 address. This is common practice for servers that run critical services dependent on an IP address.

1. Log onto MSN-SRV-0XX.

2. Click **Start, Run** and enter **ncpa.cpl**. This will launch the Network Connections console from Control Panel.

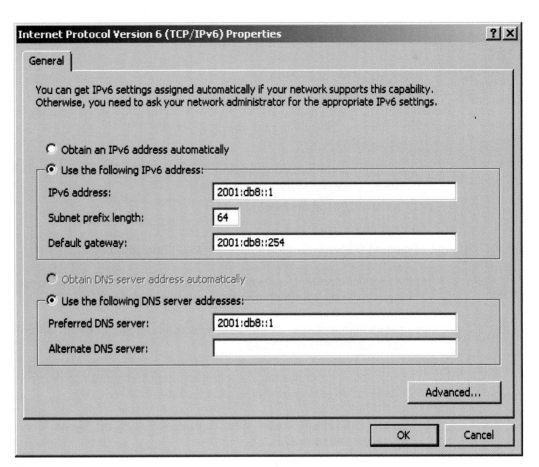

Figure 3-12   IPv6 Properties dialog box

3. Right-click **Local Area Connection** and then click **Properties**. The Local Area Connection Properties dialog box opens.

4. Click **Internet Protocol Version 6 (TCP/IPv6)**, and then click **Properties**. The Internet Protocol Version 6 (TCP/IPv6) Properties dialog box opens.

5. Click the **Use the following IPv6 address:** option button.

6. Enter the following information or IP information provided by your instructor:
   - IP address: **2001:db8:8765:4321::2**
   - Subnet prefix length: **64**
   - Default gateway: **2001:db8:8765:4321::1**
   - Preferred DNS server: **2001:db8:8765:4321::2**

7. Click **OK** to close the Internet Protocol Version 6 (TCP/IPv6) Properties dialog box and then click **Close** to close the Local Area Connection Properties dialog box and set new IP address information. Close all open windows.

8. Open a Command Prompt window from the Start menu.

9. Type **ipconfig /all** and then press **Enter** to verify that your IPv6 address is set correctly.

Manual Configuration with Netsh

You can use netsh to manually configure your Windows Server 2008 server with a static IP address. The syntax for using netsh to add an IPv6 address is:

```
netsh interface ipv6 add address "interface" address
```

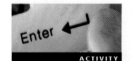

Activity 3-10: Manually Configuring an IP Address Using netsh

Time Required: 10 minutes

Objective: Configure a client with manual IP addressing using netsh.

Description: You are configuring your Windows Server 2008 server running Server Core with a static IPv6 address. This will require the use of netsh.

1. Log onto MSN-SC-0XX.

2. Use the following information or IP information provided by your instructor to configure networking on Server Core:
   - IP address: **2001:db8:8765:4321::3**
   - Subnet prefix length: **64**
   - Preferred DNS server: 2001:db8:8765:4321:2 (instead of ::3)

3. At the command prompt, enter the following netsh command and then press **Enter** to set the IP address from the information mentioned previously:

```
netsh interface ipv6 add address "local area connection"
2001:db8:8765:4321::3
```

4. At the command prompt, enter the following netsh command and then press **Enter** to set the DNS server address from the information mentioned previously:

```
Netsh interface ipv6 add dnsserver "local area connection"
2001:db8:8765:4321:2
```

5. Type **ipconfig /all** and then press **Enter** to verify that your IPv6 address has changed successfully. If changes do not appear promptly, wait about 30 seconds and rerun **ipconfig /all**.

Upgrading Your Network to IPv6

Moving to IPv6 is not a task you can accomplish overnight. With much of the world's networks entrenched in IPv4, you need capital expenditures and time to migrate to IPv6. To ease this transition, IPv6 has implemented the following transition technologies to work with IPv4:

- Dual-layer IP stack
- IPv6 over IPv4
- Intra-Site Automatic Tunnel Addressing Protocol
- 6to4
- Teredo

Dual-Layer IP Stack

The TCP/IP stack in Windows Server 2008 uses dual-layer architecture, as shown in Figure 3-13. As you can see, the Network layer is split into IPv4 and IPv6. This gives all Windows Server 2008 servers built-in IPv6 functionality and support. Also, it allows clients to participate on both IPv4 and IPv6 networks.

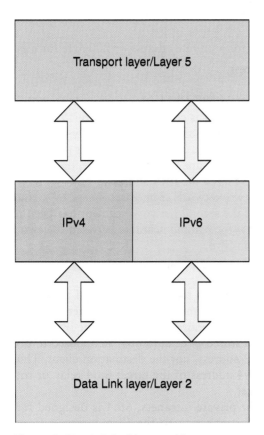

Figure 3-13   IPv6 dual-layer architecture

For more information about the dual-layer IP stack and other enhancements to Windows Server 2008 networking, read the Microsoft TechNet article "Next Generation TCP/IP Stack in Windows Vista and Windows Server 2008" at *http://technet.microsoft.com*.

IPv6 over IPv4

IPv6 over IPv4 is a transition technology where clients connected to an IPv4 network send IPv6 traffic over IPv4 by encapsulating the IPv6 traffic in an IPv4 packet. This is accomplished by adding an IPv4 header to the IPv6 packet. This works similar to virtual private network (VPN) tunneling. However, this technique provides you no additional authentication or encryption benefits, as with a VPN. The three IPv6 over IPv4 tunnels that can be created are the following:

- *Router-to-router*—This tunnel allows IPv6 networks to communicate when they are connected by an IPv4 network. For example, two companies with access to the IPv4 Internet could connect their IPv6 networks by tunneling between their routers. This technology can be used by 6to4 as well.

- *Host-to-router and router-to-host*—This tunnel allows an IPv6 host to connect with a remote IPv6 network even though it is connected to an IPv4 network. This technology can be used by Teredo and Intra-Site Automatic Tunnel Addressing Protocol (ISATAP).

- *Host-to-host*—This tunnel allows two IPv6 computers to communicate with one another when they are connected on the same IPv4 network. This technology can be used by Teredo and ISATAP.

ISATAP

Designed to connect intranets in heterogeneous IP environments, ISATAP allows IPv6 routers and hosts to communicate across IPv4 networks. ISATAP requires a router that supports ISATAP. Hosts at either end must also support IPv6, usually through a dual-layer IP stack. An ISATAP address has the IPv4 address of a host embedded in its address. The interface ID is separated into two parts as follows:

- The first 32 bits are either 0:5efe for a private address or 200:5efe for a public address.

- The last 32 bits are the IPv4 address.

For example, a public IPv4 address of 202.10.11.55 is converted to 200:5efe:202.10.11.55 in IPv6, and a private address of 192.168.1.1 is converted to 0:5efe:192.168.1.1.

Often, ISATAP is a transition technology for migrating from IPv4 to IPv6 on a private network while maintaining a period of coexistence. This is because of its ability to traverse IPv4 networks by tunneling the IPv6 traffic. On the same network segment, the ISATAP packet uses the destination IPv4 address as the last 32 bits of the IPv6 address.

For example, suppose you have two network segments connect by a router that supports ISATAP. One network runs IPv4, and the second network segment has been recently upgraded to IPv6. ISATAP-enabled routers allow for communications between the two networks as you work to migrate the first network from IPv4.

6to4

Similar to ISATAP, 6to4 uses tunneling of IPv6 packets over an IPv4 network. The technologies differ in how they store the IPv4 address in the IPv6 packet. Where ISATAP stores the IPv4 address as a decimal in the last 32 bits of the address, 6to4 stores the IPv4 address of the ISATAP router in bits 17 to 48. The address is stored in hexadecimal as opposed to decimal. Also, 6to4 encapsulates only the IPv4 router's IP address, not the destination client. Thus, no target IPv4 address is needed, only the public IPv4 address of the target 6to4 relay or router to determine the subnet in which to route the packet.

Although ISATAP is designed for private intranets, 6to4 is designed for communicating across the public IPv4 Internet and connecting to the IPv6 Internet. Connections to IPv6 Internet segments are completed through a 6to4 relay. 6to4 is a good option in a company that has migrated to IPv6 but is connected to the Internet by an ISP that does not support IPv6. 6to4 allows the network to communicate over the IPv4 network to reach the IPv6 Internet.

Teredo

The last IPv6 transition technology is called Teredo. Teredo allows IPv6 hosts to communicate over IPv4 networks that use NAT, which is a mechanism used in IPv4 networks for hiding a private IP network behind a public IP address. NAT acts as a translator for traffic between the public and private networks. Teredo works only with NAT implementations that support UDP port translation.

Similar to the other transition technologies, Teredo tunnels its IPv6 packets inside IPv4 packets. Common Teredo communications are between two IPv6 hosts or between an IPv6 host and a Teredo relay. The Teredo relay terminates the IPv6 over IPv4 tunnel, and it acts as a forwarder between IPv4 and IPv6 networks. To assist with Teredo communication, Teredo servers provide clients with configuration settings and initial communications between IPv6 hosts. Publicly available Teredo servers are hosted by many organizations, including Microsoft. Microsoft's Teredo servers use the DNS entry teredo.ipv6.microsoft.com.

Teredo's address is based on the 2001::/32 prefix. It is structured as follows:

- The first 32 bits of the address are 2001.
- The next 32 bits are the IPv4 address in hexadecimal to complete the network ID.
- The host ID begins with 16 bits used for Teredo flags.
- The next 16 bits represent the external UDP port number being used by the NAT.
- The remaining 32 bits are the IPv4 address of the NAT in hexadecimal.

Teredo is disabled by default in Windows Server 2008. Teredo should always be implemented with a client-based stateful firewall such as the Windows Firewall in Windows Server 2008. Application developers who decide to use IPv6 and users accessing those applications often use Teredo. For example, Windows Remote assistance uses IPv6 for end-to-end communication.

For more information on Teredo, read the Microsoft TechNet article "Teredo Overview" at *www.microsoft.com*.

Using Netsh to Configure Transition Technologies

All the transition technologies require specific configuration for implementation. In this section, you use netsh to configure transition technologies, including the following:

- ISATAP
- Teredo

ISATAP is disabled by default in Windows Server 2008. To determine the current state of ISATAP, you run the following command:

```
netsh interface isatap show state
```

Enable ISATAP by running the following command:

```
netsh interface isatap set state enabled
```

Conversely, if ISATAP is enabled and needs to be disabled, run the following command:

```
netsh interface isatap set state disabled
```

Activity 3-11: Manually Configuring Clients to Use ISATAP

Time Required: 10 minutes

Objective: Configure a Windows Server 2008 client.

Description: You are configuring your Windows Server 2008 server to use ISATAP and plan to use the netsh command-line utility for this task. After completing the configuration, you should return the computer to its original state by disabling ISATAP.

1. On MSN-SC-0XX, type the following netsh command and then press **Enter** to check the ISATAP status on the computer:

        netsh interface isatap show state

2. At the command prompt, enter the following netsh command and then press **Enter** to enable ISATAP on the computer:

        netsh interface isatap set state enabled

3. Type **ipconfig /all** and then press **Enter** to verify that an ISATAP address has been added to your network adapters. If changes do not appear promptly, wait about 30 seconds and rerun **ipconfig /all**.

4. At the command prompt, enter the following netsh command and then press **Enter** to disable ISATAP on the computer:

        netsh interface isatap set state disable

5. Type **ipconfig /all** and then press **Enter** to verify that ISATAP has been removed.

Enabling Teredo

Like ISATAP, Teredo is disabled by default. You need to enable Teredo on your computer to use it. To determine the current state of Teredo, you run the following command:

        netsh interface ipv6 show teredo

Whether your network is a workgroup or Active Directory domain, Teredo needs to be configured depending on your network model. Following are the commands for enabling Teredo in a workgroup environment using "client" in the command. Next is the command for enabling Teredo in an Active Directory environment using "enterpriseclient" in the command. The following command enables Teredo for workgroup clients:

        netsh interface ipv6 set teredo client

The following command enables Teredo for Active Directory clients:

        netsh interface ipv6 set teredo enterpriseclient

To view the Teredo status after enabling Teredo, use the following command:

        netsh interface teredo show state

Activity 3-12: Manually Configuring Clients to Use Teredo

Time Required: 10 minutes

Objective: Configure a Windows Server 2008 client to use Teredo.

Description: You are configuring your Windows Server 2008 server running Server Core to use Teredo. This requires the use of netsh.

1. Log onto MSN-SC-0XX.

2. At the command prompt, enter the following netsh command and then press **Enter** to check the Teredo status on the computer:

<code>netsh interface ipv6 show teredo</code>

3. At the command prompt, enter the following netsh command and then press **Enter** to set the network adapter to use Teredo on a workgroup computer:

<code>netsh interface ipv6 set teredo client</code>

4. Type **ipconfig /all** and then press **Enter** to verify that teredo has been added to your network adapters. If changes do not appear promptly, wait about 30 seconds and rerun **ipconfig /all**.

Disabling IPv6

If you are working on a network that does not require IPv6 and do not want to make it available to clients, you can disable IPv6 on specific network adapters or on a specific computer. For a specific network adapter, you can disable IPv6 using the Network Connections window and by editing the Registry. You cannot disable IPv6 using netsh, as you see later.

To use the Registry to disable all of IPv6 on a computer, you need to create the following Registry key:

```
HKEY_LOCAL_MACHINE\SYSTEM\CurrentControlSet\Services\TCPIP6\Parameters\
DisabledComponents
```

To create this key from command prompt, use the following reg add command:

```
reg add hklm\system\currentcontrolset\services\tcpip6\parameters
/v DisabledComponents /t REG_DWORD /d 255
```

The value of 255 disables all IPv6 network adapters, connections, and tunnel interfaces. Table 3-13 lists values you can use for disabling parts of IPv6 through the Registry.

Table 3-13 Registry values for disabling IPv6 components

Value (Hexadecimal/Decimal)	Component Disabled
0	Enables all IPv6 components
1	Disables Teredo and ISATAP adapters
4	Disables only ISATAP adapters
16	Disables only IPv6 and leaves Teredo and ISATAP adapters
255	Disables all IPv6 components

Troubleshooting TCP/IP Networking

In this section, you troubleshoot TCP/IP networking. Finding where a problem originates on a network can be a challenge, especially if the Internet is involved. First, you examine the tools available in Windows Server 2008 for diagnosing and resolving network problems. Next, you develop a core methodology for troubleshooting network issues.

Troubleshooting Tools in Windows Server 2008

In Windows Server 2008, you have many tools for troubleshooting network problems. You will look at some of the command-line utilities for troubleshooting networks. Additional tools are covered in later chapters. The following is a list of some tools you can use to troubleshoot from the command line:

- Ipconfig
- Ping
- Pathping
- Tracert
- Netstat

Ipconfig   Ipconfig.exe is one of the most widely used utilities in Windows. Short for Internet Protocol Configuration, ipconfig displays the current IP configuration on your local client. You can use a number of command-line switches to run ipconfig with settings other than the default behavior. A **command-line switch,** or option, indicates that the command should change its default behavior. Running ipconfig without any switches or options provides the following output, as shown in Figure 3-14.

Ipconfig provides basic IP information. However, you often want to examine more detailed information such as for DNS servers and DHCP servers. To do so, you use the ipconfig /all command, as shown in Figure 3-15.

Using Ipconfig /all is good way to start troubleshooting clients that have problems accessing network resources. You can use the command on both ends of the communication, that is, the client and the server, if applicable. Ipconfig /all also provides information such as the following:

- Whether a client is using DHCP
- The client's MAC address
- The interfaces installed on a client
- Which DNS servers a client is using

At this point, you want to verify that all the numbers are displayed correctly. Note the values for the subnet mask, default gateway, and the DNS servers. A common red flag is receiving an APIPA address (an IP address beginning with 169.254). This indicates a problem with DHCP.

You can use the Ipconfig command to release and renew a DHCP-assigned address. To do so, use the following commands:

```
ipconfig /release
ipconfig /renew
```

You explore ipconfig /release and /renew in more depth in Chapter 4.

Ping   Ping is a utility that determines whether a target host is on and responding to communication. Ping works by sending an ICMP echo request packet to the target. It then listens for an ICMP echo response reply. Through this communication, ping estimates the round-trip time for a particular target, and records any lost packets during the communication. Figure 3-16 displays the command syntax for ping and examples of the ping being executed:

```
ping targetHostnameorIPaddress
```

```
Administrator: Command Prompt                                        _ 8 X

C:\Users\mike>ipconfig

Windows IP Configuration

Wireless LAN adapter Wireless Network Connection:

    Connection-specific DNS Suffix  . :
    IPv4 Address. . . . . . . . . . . : 192.168.0.191
    Subnet Mask . . . . . . . . . . . : 255.255.255.0
    Default Gateway . . . . . . . . . : 192.168.0.1

Ethernet adapter Local Area Connection:

    Media State . . . . . . . . . . . : Media disconnected
    Connection-specific DNS Suffix  . :

Ethernet adapter Bluetooth Network Connection:

    Media State . . . . . . . . . . . : Media disconnected
    Connection-specific DNS Suffix  . :

Ethernet adapter VMware Network Adapter VMnet1:

    Connection-specific DNS Suffix  . :
    Link-local IPv6 Address . . . . . : fe80::8de9:9050:9559:6edf%15
    IPv4 Address. . . . . . . . . . . : 192.168.231.1
    Subnet Mask . . . . . . . . . . . : 255.255.255.0
    Default Gateway . . . . . . . . . :

Ethernet adapter VMware Network Adapter VMnet8:

    Connection-specific DNS Suffix  . :
    Link-local IPv6 Address . . . . . : fe80::a938:e918:4145:1143%17
    IPv4 Address. . . . . . . . . . . : 192.168.233.1
    Subnet Mask . . . . . . . . . . . : 255.255.255.0
    Default Gateway . . . . . . . . . :
```

Figure 3-14   Ipconfig command

By default, ping sends a 32-byte packet four times before exiting. This behavior can be modified through the use of switches. For a listing of the switches available with ping, type the following command:

ping /?

/? or ? is a common switch available for most Windows command-line executables. It displays a listing of the switches available for a command, the proper syntax, and often examples of usage.

Figure 3-16 shows a ping using the IP address because pinging the IP address indicates the target is available by IP address. Pinging a fully qualified domain name (FQDN) indicates whether the client is resolving the DNS name of the target. This is a quick way to test a DNS resolution without using another command-line tool called nslookup, which is discussed in Chapter 6.

Another helpful use for ping is to determine when a remote server is online after a reboot. For this, you can loop the ping utility. With the many remote utilities available with Windows Server 2008, you may need to reboot a server after performing a specific task. You can use the following command to send a continuous ping:

ping -t targethostname

See Figure 3-17. Note the lowercase "t" as this command does not work with a capital "T."

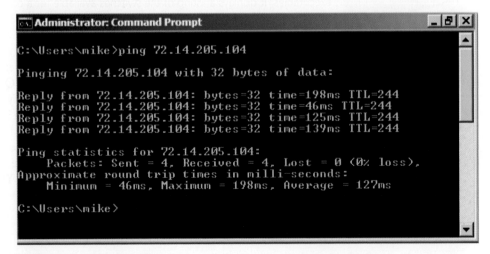

```
Administrator: Command Prompt                                        _ 8 X

C:\Users\mike>ipconfig /all

Windows IP Configuration

    Host Name . . . . . . . . . . . . : mike-PC
    Primary Dns Suffix . . . . . . . :
    Node Type . . . . . . . . . . . . : Hybrid
    IP Routing Enabled. . . . . . . . : No
    WINS Proxy Enabled. . . . . . . . : No

Wireless LAN adapter Wireless Network Connection:

    Connection-specific DNS Suffix  . :
    Description . . . . . . . . . . . : Intel(R) Wireless WiFi Link 4965AGN
    Physical Address. . . . . . . . . : 00-1F-3B-4A-D3-D5
    DHCP Enabled. . . . . . . . . . . : Yes
    Autoconfiguration Enabled . . . . : Yes
    IPv4 Address. . . . . . . . . . . : 192.168.0.191(Preferred)
    Subnet Mask . . . . . . . . . . . : 255.255.255.0
    Lease Obtained. . . . . . . . . . : Saturday, July 12, 2008 11:02:45 AM
    Lease Expires . . . . . . . . . . : Saturday, July 12, 2008 3:32:45 PM
    Default Gateway . . . . . . . . . : 192.168.0.1
    DHCP Server . . . . . . . . . . . : 192.168.0.1
    DNS Servers . . . . . . . . . . . : 192.168.0.1
    NetBIOS over Tcpip. . . . . . . . : Enabled

Ethernet adapter Local Area Connection:

    Media State . . . . . . . . . . . : Media disconnected
    Connection-specific DNS Suffix  . :
    Description . . . . . . . . . . . : Intel(R) 82566MM Gigabit Network Connecti
on
    Physical Address. . . . . . . . . : 00-1A-4B-7E-EB-7A
    DHCP Enabled. . . . . . . . . . . : Yes
    Autoconfiguration Enabled . . . . : Yes

Ethernet adapter Bluetooth Network Connection:

    Media State . . . . . . . . . . . : Media disconnected
    Connection-specific DNS Suffix  . :
    Description . . . . . . . . . . . : Bluetooth Device (Personal Area Network)
    Physical Address. . . . . . . . . : 00-1E-37-DD-25-6F
    DHCP Enabled. . . . . . . . . . . : Yes
    Autoconfiguration Enabled . . . . : Yes

Ethernet adapter VMware Network Adapter VMnet1:

    Connection-specific DNS Suffix  . :
    Description . . . . . . . . . . . : VMware Virtual Ethernet Adapter for VMnet
1
    Physical Address. . . . . . . . . : 00-50-56-C0-00-01
    DHCP Enabled. . . . . . . . . . . : No
    Autoconfiguration Enabled . . . . : Yes
    Link-local IPv6 Address . . . . . : fe80::8de9:9050:9559:6edf%15(Preferred)
    IPv4 Address. . . . . . . . . . . : 192.168.231.1(Preferred)
    Subnet Mask . . . . . . . . . . . : 255.255.255.0
    Default Gateway . . . . . . . . . :
    DNS Servers . . . . . . . . . . . : fec0:0:0:ffff::1%1
                                        fec0:0:0:ffff::2%1
                                        fec0:0:0:ffff::3%1
    NetBIOS over Tcpip. . . . . . . . : Enabled
```

Figure 3-15   Ipconfig /all command

```
Administrator: Command Prompt                                        _ 8 X

C:\Users\mike>ping 72.14.205.104

Pinging 72.14.205.104 with 32 bytes of data:

Reply from 72.14.205.104: bytes=32 time=198ms TTL=244
Reply from 72.14.205.104: bytes=32 time=46ms TTL=244
Reply from 72.14.205.104: bytes=32 time=125ms TTL=244
Reply from 72.14.205.104: bytes=32 time=139ms TTL=244

Ping statistics for 72.14.205.104:
    Packets: Sent = 4, Received = 4, Lost = 0 (0% loss),
Approximate round trip times in milli-seconds:
    Minimum = 46ms, Maximum = 198ms, Average = 127ms

C:\Users\mike>
```

Figure 3-16   Ping command

```
[C:.] Administrator: Command Prompt                              _ |8| X|

C:\Users\mike>ping -t 72.14.205.104

Pinging 72.14.205.104 with 32 bytes of data:

Reply from 72.14.205.104: bytes=32 time=83ms TTL=244
Reply from 72.14.205.104: bytes=32 time=104ms TTL=244
Reply from 72.14.205.104: bytes=32 time=29ms TTL=244
Reply from 72.14.205.104: bytes=32 time=29ms TTL=244
Reply from 72.14.205.104: bytes=32 time=27ms TTL=244
Reply from 72.14.205.104: bytes=32 time=27ms TTL=244
Reply from 72.14.205.104: bytes=32 time=28ms TTL=244
Reply from 72.14.205.104: bytes=32 time=30ms TTL=244
Reply from 72.14.205.104: bytes=32 time=27ms TTL=244
Reply from 72.14.205.104: bytes=32 time=30ms TTL=244
Reply from 72.14.205.104: bytes=32 time=28ms TTL=244
Reply from 72.14.205.104: bytes=32 time=30ms TTL=244
Reply from 72.14.205.104: bytes=32 time=30ms TTL=244
Reply from 72.14.205.104: bytes=32 time=30ms TTL=244
Reply from 72.14.205.104: bytes=32 time=28ms TTL=244
```

Figure 3-17   Ping -t command

NOTE   In many of today's firewall or device configurations (including Windows Firewall), ICMP replies are often denied by default for security purposes. This affects utilities such as ping, pathping, and tracert. Clients, routers, and other devices that you know to be working and communicating on your network might fail to respond. (You receive repeated "request timed out" replies.) To have these utilities work properly, allow ICMP replies in the device or software configurations.

Another test you can perform with the ping utility is to ping the localhost loopback addresses. In IPv4, 127.0.0.1 refers to the localhost loopback address of a computer. The loopback adapter is not associated with any hardware so the loopback is not physically connected to the computer's network. You use this address to test communication with the IP software, or IP stack, of the operating system without involving hardware or drivers. The following is the syntax for testing the loopback adapter:

```
ping 127.0.0.1
ping localhost
```

Additional uses for ping include the following:

- Determining the amount of time it requires to send a packet of data between two points. Ping allows you to modify the ICMP echo size using the -l switch.

- Determine causes of slowness to Web sites. Using ping allows you to see how many packets are lost on the way to a specific Web site. An increased number of lost, or dropped, packets might mean that the Web server you are connecting has a stressful load.

Pathping   Pathping is a utility you can use to map the hops a packet must make to reach a target. You can use the following command to execute pathping to a target:

```
pathping TargetFQDN
```

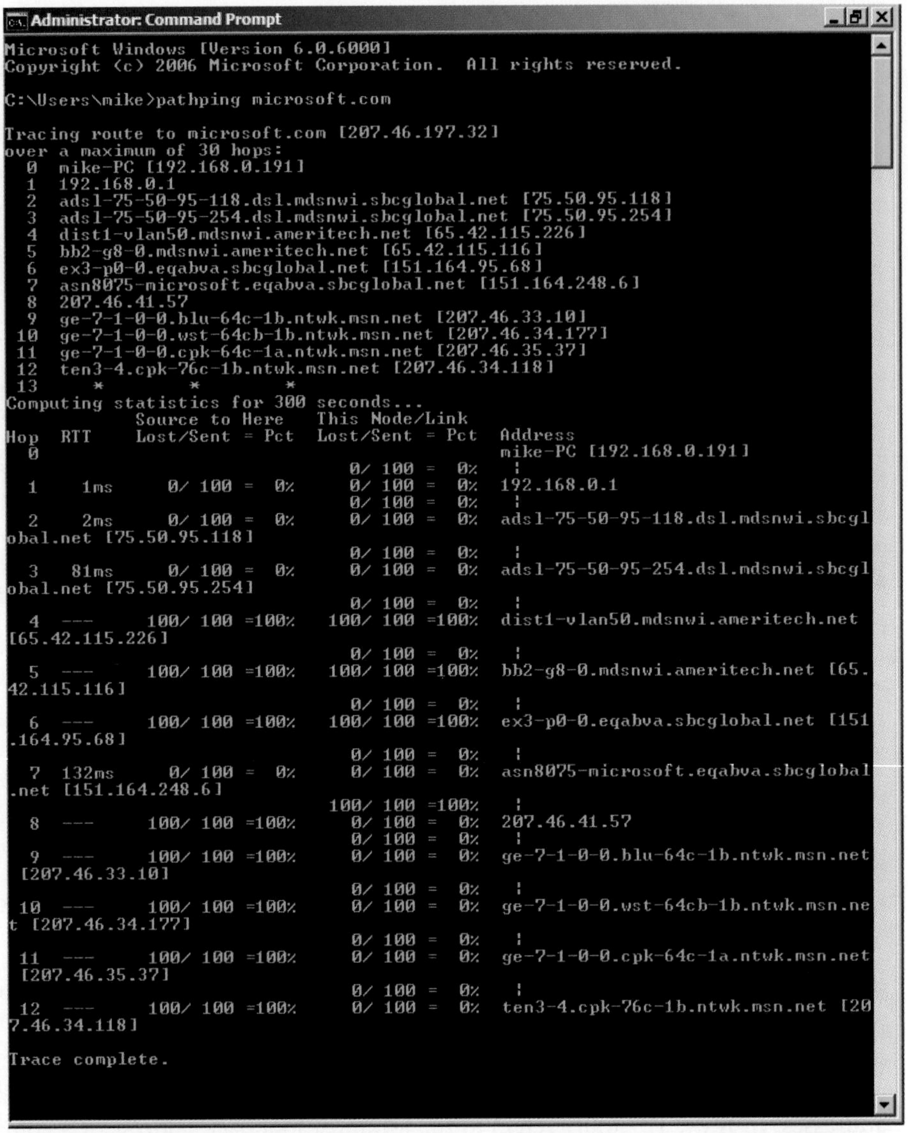

Figure 3-18   Pathping command

For example, suppose you want to know the hops from a client to microsoft.com. Use the following command to complete that task, as shown in Figure 3-18:

```
pathping microsoft.com
```

This is useful in determining where packets are being dropped before reaching a target. When troubleshooting Internet-based networking problems or problems outside your network, knowing the last hop that replied can be very helpful when working with your ISP or external companies. As the example shows, you might receive only an IP address in response, or you might receive a name of the router responding with the IP address. Also, line 13 at the beginning of the data includes three asterisks (*). This tells you that you did not receive ICMP replies after the twelfth hop. All this information is valuable when you are troubleshooting with an ISP or external company.

Tracert   Similar to pathping, tracert is another command-line tool for tracing the route between two nodes. Where pathping only provides information on whether a hop responds to a ICMP request, tracert displays the round-trip time for each packet sent to a hop. This can be

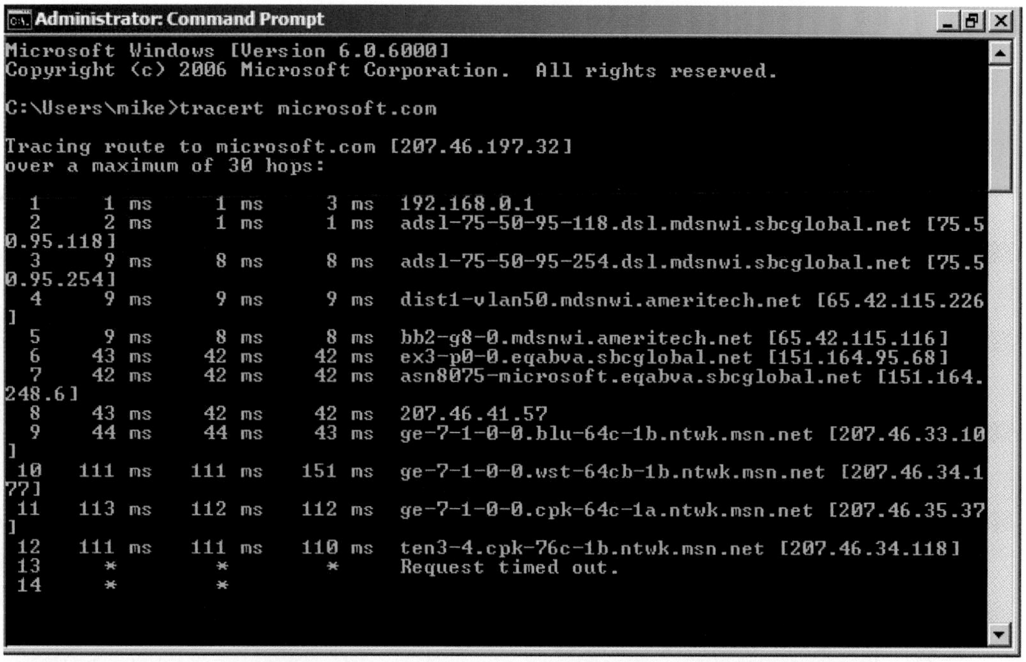

Figure 3-19 Tracert command

helpful in determining latency, or network slowness, along a route. Use the following syntax to use tracert, as shown in Figure 3-19.

```
tracert targethostname
```

Netstat   Netstat, short for network statistics, is command-line tool for displaying network connection information such as routing tables. Netstat is very helpful when troubleshooting network issues and determining network connections to and from a specific client. Like most Windows command-line utilities, netstat has a variety of switches available for modifying the base utility. Figure 3-20 displays the switches available in netstat from the command prompt using the netstat /? command.

Following is the syntax for using netstat and an example of netstat used to display statistics on all TCP port connections:

```
netstat [-a] [-b] [-e] [-n] [-o] [-p proto] [-r] [-s] [-v] [interval]
netstat -s -p TCP
```

Following are some common netstat commands you will use. To display the statistics for only the TCP or UDP protocols, type one of the following commands:

```
netstat -s -p tcp
netstat -s -p udp
```

Activity 3-13: Using Command-Line Utilities for Troubleshooting

Time Required: 20 minutes

Objective: Perform troubleshooting tasks using command-line utilities.

Description: All system administrators require a good understanding of the tools needed for troubleshooting. You run many of those tools from the command line. In this activity, you will use

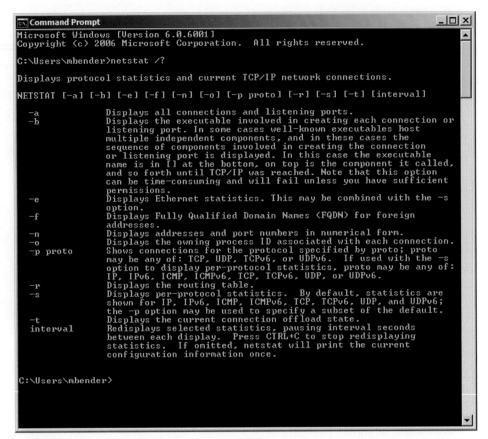

Figure 3-20   Netstat command

some of the common command-line tools for determining network information that can help you troubleshoot a network problem. Also, you send this information to a text file for viewing later.

1. At the command prompt of MSN-SRV-0XX, type **ipconfig /all** and then press **Enter** to verify the network adapter settings.

2. Verify that you can connect to your loopback adapter using ping. Here is the syntax for your command:

    ping 127.0.0.1 > CLI.txt

    This creates a new file called CLI.txt containing the results of the command.

3. Ping MSN-SC-0XX by IP address using the following command:

    ping 192.168.100.20 >> CLI.txt

    Adding >> CLI.txt appends the results of the command to CLI.txt.

4. Run tracert to view the route information between MSN-SRV-0XX and MSN-SC-0XX. Use the following command:

    tracert 192.168.100.10 >> CLI.txt

5. Run pathping to view the route information between MSN-SRV-0XX and MSN-SC-0XX. Use the following command:

    pathping 192.168.100.10 >> CLI.txt

6. Run netstat to gather network statistics on local network connections. Use the following commands:

```
netstat -s -p tcp >> CLI.txt
netstat -s -p udp >> CLI.txt
```

7. Type **notepad CLI.txt** and then press **Enter** to view the results of each command.

8. Close the Command Prompt window, and then close Notepad.

9. Log off your server.

Network Troubleshooting Methodology

Every good administrator has core methodologies they use for troubleshooting, and networking problems are no exception. Effective troubleshooting requires a logical and systematic approach that rules out possible areas of failure and allows you to narrow the search for the root cause of the failure. The following is a methodology you can use for troubleshooting networks:

1. On the client that is experiencing network issues, use the ipconfig /all command and verify the client settings. Troubleshoot based on results.

2. Ping the target by IP address to verify IP connectivity. Remember, some targets might block ICMP echo requests.

3. Ping the target by FQDN to verify name resolution and IP connectivity.

4. Ping the loopback adapter on your client: ping 127.0.0.1. This verifies that your TCP/IP stack is responding properly.

5. Ping a node on the client's subnet to verify that you can communicate with clients on your subnet.

6. Ping the default gateway of the client to verify that you can communicate with the router interface on your network.

7. Ping a node on a different subnet to verify that your router can forward your traffic properly. If this fails, perform Steps 8 and 9 to determine the last available hop in the route.

8. Use the tracert command to the target to verify the hops between two nodes.

9. Use the pathping command to the target to verify the hops between two nodes as well.

As you can see, this methodology moves from the client out to the network. This will help you isolate the network problem and put you on the road to resolution. Should any of the steps fail, begin your troubleshooting process at that point.

Chapter Summary

- A network can be described according to its scale, methodology, architecture, topology, and protocol.

- Networks have many components that are necessary for transmission of data including NICs, switches, and routers. Each work at different layers of the OSI model.

- Routers use IP addresses to route traffic between networks.

- IPv4 is the current industry standard for network addressing. It works with TCP, a connection-oriented Transport layer protocol, to create a suite of protocols and services for most modern networks including the Internet and World Wide Web.

- IPv4 IP addresses are 32-bit numbers split into four octets separated by decimal points. This notation is referred to as dotted-decimal notation and looks similar to 192.168.1.1.

- IPv6 is the future standard for network addressing. Like IPv4, it works with TCP to create a suite of protocols and services for networks. IPv6 solves the address shortage problem created by IPv4 by basing network addresses on 128 bits instead of 32 bits.

- IPv6 addresses are 128-bit numbers split into eight groups of four hexadecimal numbers. An IPv6 address looks similar to this: 1075:0000:0000:0000:0005:0600:300c:422d.

- Subnetting divides a larger network into smaller networks. It uses a number called the subnet mask that helps determine what portion of an IP address belongs to the network and what portion belongs to the host.

- You can use the equation $2^N - 2$ to determine the number of usable hosts on a network, where N is the number of bits used for host addresses in the subnet mask.

- Private IP addresses as defined by RFC 1918 include three IP ranges that are not publicly routable.

- Two types of IPv4 addressing exist: classful and classless. Classless, or CIDR, is most commonly used, as the classful addressing scheme has become outdated because of inefficient allocation of public IP addresses.

- When deploying IPv4 and IPv6 addresses, you can manually configure static IP addresses, or you can use automatic allocation. DHCP is the default in Windows Server 2008 for IPv4, and link-local is the default for IPv6.

- Windows Server 2008 provides built-in command-line tools for troubleshooting networking. They include ping, pathping, ipconfig, and netstat.

- A common practice for troubleshooting network issues works from the client out toward the Internet or other network. This helps determine specific points of failure.

Key Terms

Advanced Research Projects Agency Network (ARPANET)   The original network created by the U.S. Department of Defense that is the basis for the Internet.

Application layer   The Open Systems Interconnection (OSI) model layer responsible for providing user services, such as file transfers, electronic messaging, e-mail, virtual terminal access, and network management. This is the layer with which the user interacts.

bandwidth   The amount of data that can be carried from one point to another in a given time period. Bandwidth is normally measured in bits per second (bps).

binary number   A number represented by either 0 or 1. Binary numbers are used in subnetting and IP address range creation.

CIDR block   The number of bits used for the subnet mask when using classless networks.

Classless Interdomain Routing (CIDR)   A method for assigning IP addresses without using the standard IP address classes such as Class A, Class B, or Class C. CIDR allows for the more efficient usage and distribution of public IP addresses.

command-line switch   An indication by a user that a computer program should change its default behavior. Also known as a flag, an option, or a command-line parameter.

connection methodology   A network characteristic that defines the type of hardware technology used for connecting network nodes.

Data Link layer   The OSI model layer responsible for communications between adjacent network nodes. Hubs and switches operate at the Data Link layer.

Ethernet   A protocol and set of cabling specifications for local area networks (LANs) based on the IEEE 802.3 standard.

fiber optics   A form of telecommunication media that uses glass fibers for transmitting data via light.

frame   A unit of data transferred between a sender and a receiver on a network. Frames are Data Link layer data units.

header   Information appended to the beginning of a packet that specifies information about a packet, including protocol, destination address, and origin address.

hub   The most basic of the hardware devices that interconnect multiple nodes. Hubs have multiple ports to which nodes connect. When a packet arrives at one port, it is broadcast to all the ports of the hub.

Internet   A global network of networks used to exchange information using Transmission Control Protocol/Internet Protocol (TCP/IP). It allows for electronic mail and the accessing and retrieval of information from remote sources.

Internet Corporation for Assigned Names and Numbers (ICANN)   The organization that oversees the distribution of public IP addresses, along with the maintenance of Domain Name System and domain name registrations.

Internet Protocol (IP)   A set of rules to send and receive messages at the Internet address level. IP is the basis for network addressing on the Internet, the World Wide Web, and almost every network around the world.

Internet Protocol version 4 (IPv4)   A version of IP whose address scheme is based on 32-bit addresses. IPv4 is the current standard, though available public addresses are becoming limited.

Internet Protocol version 6 (IPv6)   A version of IP whose address scheme is based on 128-bit addresses.

Internet service provider (ISP)   A company that provides public network access to the Internet for private networks.

local area network (LAN)   A network covering a small geographic area, such as a home, office, or building. Current LANs are usually based on Ethernet technology.

logical layout   Defines how nodes communicate over a network.

Media Access Control (MAC)   A low-level network addressing system designed to be globally unique and allow clients to communicate on certain networks. MAC addresses work on Layer 2 of the OSI model.

mesh network   A LAN in which each node has a direct network connection to every other node on the network or at least two routes of travel from a single node to other nodes.

multilayer switch (MLS)   A computer networking device that switches on OSI Layer 2 like an ordinary network switch and provides extra functions on higher OSI layers. A common usage is a Layer 3 switch, which allows routing based on IP address as well as Layer 2 switch functionality.

network   A group of two or more network nodes or computers and hardware devices linked together for sharing data.

network architecture   A characteristic of networks that categorizes needs on the basis of the functional relationships between the nodes.

network interface card (NIC)   A hardware card installed in a computer so that it can connect to a physical network.

Network layer   The OSI model layer responsible for establishing paths for data transfer through the network. Routers operate at the Network layer.

network protocol   The special set of rules that end points in a telecommunication connection use when they communicate.

network scale   A characteristic of networks that defines how they occupy geographic space.

network topology   A characteristic of networks that describes the physical and logical relationship that devices have to one another.

networking   The practice of designing, implementing, and managing a collection of computers and devices, or a network.

node   A computer or hardware device that participates in a network.

Open Systems Interconnection (OSI) model   A seven-layer model responsible for detailing end-to-end network traffic and communication.

packet   A unit of data routed between a sender and a receiver on the Internet or any other packet-switched network. Packets are Network layer data units.

physical layout   In a network, defines how the cables are arranged and how the computers are connected.

Physical layer   The OSI model layer responsible for bit-level transmission between network nodes. Cabling and connection types are defined at this layer.

Presentation layer   The OSI model layer responsible for defining the syntax that two network hosts use to communicate.

private network   A network with an address range that is not routable on the Internet.

protocol suite   A group of interconnected network protocols from different layers of the OSI model that work together to provide network services. An example of a protocol suite is TCP/IP.

repeater   A hardware device that receives a signal and resends the signal at a higher level or higher power so that it can go longer distances between the start and end points of communication.

Request for Comment (RFC)   A document that describes the specifications for a recommended technology. RFCs are used by the Internet Engineering Task Force and other standards bodies.

router   A device responsible for forwarding packets between subnets, or networks with differing IP addressing schemes. Routers work on Layer 3 of the OSI model.

Routing Information Protocol (RIP) version 2   A routing protocol that uses hop count to determine which path to use for sending packets so that they reach their destination.

Session layer   An OSI model layer responsible for establishing process-to-process communications between networked hosts.

star network   LAN topology in which each node on a network is connected directly to a central network hub or switch.

subnet   A subnetwork; a separate part of an organization's network.

subnet mask   A 32-bit number used to determine the host and network portions of an IP address.

subnetting   The process of creating multiple smaller networks, or subnets, from the network address of an IP network.

switch   A network device that works at Layer 2 of the OSI model and forwards frames between ports based on MAC address. However, a switch is a more intelligent Layer 2 device because it forwards frames only to the ports involved in sending and receiving a datagram.

Transmission Control Protocol (TCP)   A set of rules to exchange messages with other Internet points at the information packet level. TCP guarantees the delivery of packets. This is the reason it is paired with IP for the basis of modern network communications.

Transmission Control Protocol/Internet Protocol (TCP/IP)   A suite of protocols that provides the backbone for the Internet and most modern networks. TCP/IP is made up of protocols from the Network and Transport layers of the OSI model.

Transport layer   The OSI model layer responsible for delivering messages between networked hosts. User Datagram Protocol and TCP function at this layer.

wide area network (WAN)   A network connecting computers within very large areas, such as states, countries, and the world.

wireless LAN   A network that uses radio frequencies to transmit data between nodes. Wireless networks do not use cables except for their connections to wired networks.

World Wide Web (WWW)   A part of the Internet designed to allow easier navigation of the network through the use of graphical user interfaces and hypertext links between different Universal Resource Locators. Also called the Web. Often mistaken for the Internet, the WWW is actually a service of the Internet, like e-mail.

Review Questions

1. Classful network addressing has replaced classless network addressing because of a shortage of public IP addresses. True or False?

2. Base-2 numbering is used instead of Base-10 numbering in IP addressing. True or False?

3. Internet Protocol (IP) is the primary protocol used on the World Wide Web. True or False?

4. On a 100-Mbps hub, each port can use the full bandwidth (100 Mbps) without affecting other ports. True or False?

5. As a best practice, switches are used to connect clients on a subnet, and routers are used to connect subnets to other subnets. True or False?

6. The subnet mask helps determine what portion of an IP address belongs to the network and what portion belongs to the host. True or False?

7. Which of the following network protocols is *not* supported in Windows Server 2008?

    a. IPX

    b. IP

    c. TCP

    d. UDP

8. You are responsible for deploying clients to a new four-story office building in Chicago. You are deploying 500 Windows Vista workstations, 30 network printers, and five Windows Server 2008 servers to this building. Your network administrator has provided you with the following private network address: 192.168.200.0 /23. Based on the information provided, will you be able to deploy as planned? (Choose the best two answers.)

    a. Yes, this solution has 768 usable addresses.

    b. No, this solution has only 256 usable addresses.

    c. No, this solution has only 254 usable addresses.

    d. You should request a network address range of 192.168.200.0 /24.

    e. You should request a network address range of 192.168.200.0 /22.

9. Which of the following is *not* a commonly used network topology?

    a. Star network

    b. Ring network

    c. Local area network

    d. Mesh network

10. Which of the following network scales is used for highly connected private networks, such as a single office building or a home network?

    a. Metropolitan area network

    b. Private area network

    c. Local area network

    d. Wide area network

11. Which of the following two statements are true about network interface cards? Choose two answers.

    a. They are assigned a unique MAC address by the manufacturer.

    b. They are assigned a unique static IP address by the manufacturer.

    c. They allow devices to connect to a physical network.

    d. Multiple network interface cards cannot be used on a single device.

12. You need to create a CIDR addressing scheme that meets the following criteria:

    • You have a minimum of eight network address ranges.

    • Each network address range supports at least 25 hosts.

    • The address scheme is based on a private IP addressing scheme.

    Which of the following solutions meet this criteria?

    a. Use 192.168.100.0 /27

    b. Use 192.168.100.0 /28

    c. Use 192.165.100.0 /27

    d. Use 192.165.100.0 /28

    e. Use 192.165.100.0 /21

13. Choose the binary conversion that best matches the following IP address: 192.168.100.212

    a.   11000000.10101000.0011010.11010100

    b.   11000001.10010001.0011010.11010100

    c.   11000000.10101000.01100100.11010100

    d.   11000000.10101001.0011010.11010100

14. IP addresses are represented by _____-bit numbers that are separated into _____ octets using dotted-decimal notation.

15. IPv6 addresses are represented by _____-bit numbers that are separated into _____ groups of hexadecimal numbers.

16. Which IPv6 transition technology is used on IPv4 networks currently using NAT?

    a.   ISATAP

    b.   6to4

    c.   Teredo

    d.   IPv6overNAT

17. _____ configuration is often used for devices that need a static IP address available in case DHCP is not available.

18. Receiving the IP address of 169.254.100.1 is a good indication that your client cannot contact a(n) _____ server.

19. _____ servers and _____ are server roles that are good candidates for using a manually configured IP address.

20. CIDR notation of _____ will divide the IP address 192.168.100.0 into 16 networks with 16 hosts.

21. Use _____ from the command line to view a client's detailed IP information.

22. _____ uses ICMP requests to determine whether a target host is available.

23. Name two command-line utilities that can be used to map the network route between two hosts:

    a.   netstat

    b.   tracert

    c.   pingAll

    d.   pathping

    e.   ipconfig /route

24. What is the proper syntax for initiating a looping ping to the IP address of 192.168.100.100?

    a.   ping -T 192.168.100.100

    b.   ping -L 192.168.100.100

    c.   ping -t 192.168.100.100

    d.   ping -l 192.168.100.100

25. When using the ping utility, how do you use ping for testing name resolution to the target of Server01.abc.com at 192.168.100.100?

    a.   ping 192.168.100.100 /hostname

    b.   ping 192.168.100.100 /h

    c.   ping server01.abc.com /hostname

    d.   ping 192.168.100.100

Case Projects

Case Project 3-1: Creating a Batch File for Logging Networking Information

To assist with troubleshooting network systems, you want to create a batch file that automatically runs common command-line tools and logs that information to a text file for review. Include four commands from this chapter and send the output to a text file called caseproject31.txt. The batch file should run with a parameter of an IP address or host name. For example, if you named your batch file case31.bat and you wanted to input 192.168.100.2, you would enter the following command:

```
Case31.bat 192.168.100.2
```

You need to research running batch files with variables to complete this task.

Case Project 3-2: Developing a Network Address Scheme

You are an administrator for a company called Badger Novelties. You are considering whether to revise your network address scheme to meet the current and future growth demands of your company. Currently, your company has a Class C address range of 192.168.150.0 for its internal network layout. You need to develop a network address scheme that will accommodate a minimum of four subnets and 35 hosts per subnet. Use 192.168.175.0 for your new address scheme.

Case Project 3-3: Setting IP Address Information on CS-SRV-001

In this activity, you will be manually configuring the IP address information on CS-SRV-001 (which you set up in Chapter 2). You may use the GUI or the command line to complete this project. Use the following information or information provided by your instructor for configuring the network properties:

- IP address: 192.168.100.10
- Subnet mask: 255.255.255.0
- Default gateway: 192.168.200.1

Case Project 3-4: Setting IP Address Information on CS-SCSRV-001

In this activity, you will be manually configuring the IP address information on CS-SCSRV-001 (which you set up in Chapter 2). You will need to use the command line to complete this activity. Use the following information or information provided by your instructor for configuring the network properties:

- IP address: 192.168.100.20
- Subnet mask: 255.255.255.0
- Default gateway: 192.168.200.1

After completing Case Projects 3-3 and 3-4, verify that you have network connectivity between CS-SRV-001 and CS-SCSRV-001.

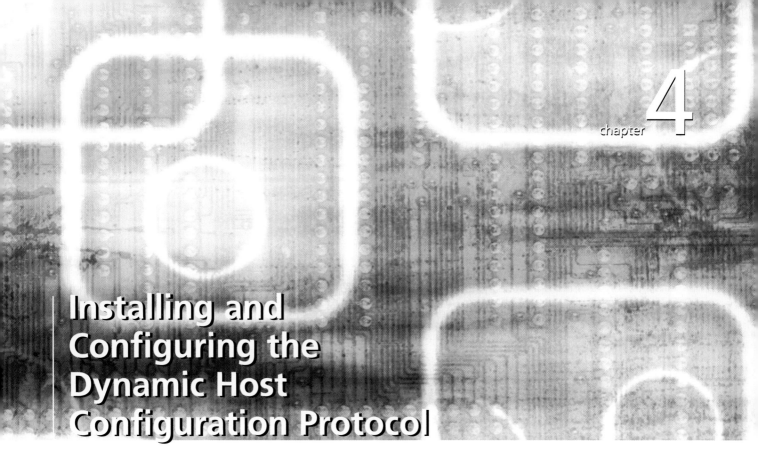

chapter 4

Installing and Configuring the Dynamic Host Configuration Protocol

After reading this chapter and completing the exercises, you will be able to:

- Discuss the basics of Dynamic Host Configuration Protocol (DHCP)
- Describe the components and processes of DHCP
- Install DHCP in a Windows Server 2008 environment
- Configure the DHCP server
- Administer DHCP on clients and servers
- Troubleshoot DHCP

Whether you oversee a small or large network, managing Internet Protocol (IP) addresses and allocating them to your clients can be a daunting task if not done properly. The wrong subnet mask, default gateway, or Domain Name System (DNS) server can wreak havoc on your network, causing access issues or even preventing clients from joining your domain. Except for critical systems within environments that require statically assigned IP addresses, most of your clients need only a temporary IP address that provides them access to resources and the network. Dynamic Host Configuration Protocol (DHCP) provides this service. DHCP manages the automatic allocation of IP addresses and other client configuration settings for network clients.

Previous chapters introduced you to DHCP as it pertains to network clients. This chapter examines DHCP more closely and discusses how to implement DHCP on a Windows Server 2008 computer. You start by learning the basics of DHCP, characteristics of the protocol, and how it works. Then you install and configure DHCP on a Windows Server 2008 network. Next, you examine administrative tasks to keep your DHCP servers running efficiently. Finally, you explore the tools needed for troubleshooting DHCP client and server issues in a Windows Server 2008 environment.

Basics of DHCP

Dynamic Host Configuration Protocol provides automatic IP addressing for Windows clients. An industry-standard protocol, you use DHCP to ease the burden of maintaining IP addresses on small and large networks. DHCP allows you to create pools of IP addresses, called **scopes**, from which clients can request a temporary IP address, or lease.

By exchanging messages when a client powers on or connects to a network, DHCP automatically configures the client's IP address information on the basis of administrator-defined configurations on a DHCP server.

This section presents the basics of DHCP, including the following topics:

- DHCP protocol basics
- DHCP address assignment process
- DHCP for Internet Protocol version 4 (IPv4) and Internet Protocol version 6 (IPv6)

DHCP Protocol Basics

DHCP is a Layer 4 protocol that uses User Datagram Protocol (UDP) datagrams for communication, as shown in Figure 4-1. As an industry-standard protocol, it is defined by Request for Comment (RFC) 2131. DHCP clients use UDP port 68 to send and receive DHCP broadcast communication. DHCP servers use UDP port 67 to send and receive DHCP broadcast communication. Through these communications, a DHCP client and a DHCP server can provide each other with the information necessary for allocating an IP address and configuration information to the client.

Most current and legacy Windows clients support DHCP. Along with Windows clients, non-Microsoft operating systems and devices such as Linux, Macintosh, and many network-capable

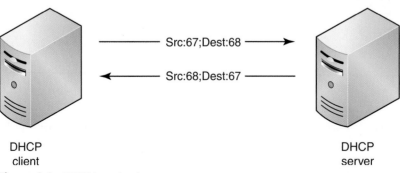

DHCP
client

DHCP
server

Figure 4-1 DHCP broadcasts

printers can use DHCP from a Windows Server 2008 DHCP server. This is ideal for heterogeneous networks running multiple operating system platforms.

In addition to industry standardization and usage on multiple operating system platforms, DHCP offers the following benefits for managing a Transmission Control Protocol/Internet Protocol (TCP/IP) network:

- *Flexible configuration*—DHCP allows you to implement IP address changes easily. For example, in a non-DHCP environment, you have to manually change every network client when a new DNS server is added to the network. With DHCP, this information is propagated to clients as they acquire new IP addresses or renew their existing address.

- *Scalable design*—Small and large networks can benefit from DHCP. Whether you have 10 clients or 1000 clients, DHCP manages IP addressing.

- *Centralized administration*—DHCP allows you to store IP address and configuration information in a single, central location. The DHCP server stores all IP addresses, leased or reserved, in its database. You can use the DHCP console to view this information. Along with tracking IP addresses, you can add or change information in one place instead of making the change on every client.

- *Automatic host configuration*—As discussed previously, DHCP automates the distribution of IP address information to DHCP clients on a network. This allows computers to be deployed without manual IP configuration.

Exploring DHCP Components and Processes

DHCP uses a number of components to automate IP addressing and follows standard processes to send and receive messages. These components and processes are discussed in the following sections.

Components of DHCP

To understand DHCP, you need a good understanding of the components necessary for implementing DHCP, including the following:

- DHCP leases
- DHCP scopes
- DHCP reservations
- DHCP options
- DHCP relay agents

DHCP Leases   A DHCP lease defines the amount of time, or the duration, that an IP address is loaned to a DHCP client. DHCP clients and DHCP servers use leases to manage DHCP.

A client uses a lease to determine when lease renewals are attempted and when it must relinquish its temporary IP address.

For a server, a lease acts a placeholder in the DHCP database. When a lease is issued, the IP address is removed from the available pool of IP addresses. This prevents the same IP address from being issued to multiple clients. As shown in Figure 4-2, a DHCP lease displays information, including the following:

- DHCP client name
- IP address
- Media Access Control (MAC) address of the client (or unique ID)
- Lease expiration time and date

A **lease duration** is the amount of time a client keeps an IP address before releasing it. Default lease durations for Windows Server 2008 are 8 days for wired clients and 6 hours for wireless clients. The option for setting a default for wireless clients is a new addition to DHCP in Windows Server 2008.

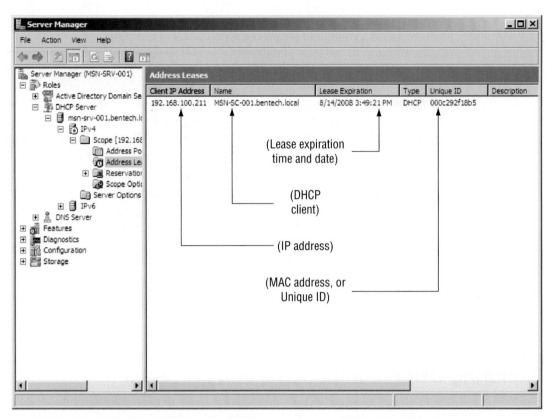

Figure 4-2   DHCP lease in the DHCP server console

Determining the duration for a lease requires considering the following factors:

- *Client type*—Identify the type of clients on your network, such as desktop computers, mobile notebooks, and servers. As the mix of mobile computers increases in an environment, the lease duration should decrease.

- *Connection time*—Estimate the length of time clients remain connected to the network. If the average client connection time is low, such as 2 to 4 hours, decrease the lease duration to prevent exhaustion of IP addresses.

- *Number of IP addresses*—Evaluate the size of your internal IP address ranges in relation to the number of clients requiring DHCP addresses. A low number of available addresses in an IP range suggests a need to decrease the lease duration or increase the IP range.

The default settings are appropriate for most networks with desktop computers that are always connected, a few mobile workstations, and a few wireless devices.

Shorter lease times are necessary in networks with many clients that connect to the network for less than one day. For example, a college campus that provides wireless access to its students requires a short lease period, such as 2 to 4 hours. Even the default setting of 6 hours might be too long, depending on the amount of new connections per hour and the length of time students remain connected.

Another option is to use a private IP address scheme that allows for larger address pools. Using network address translation and a private Class A or B network as you learned in Chapter 3, you could deploy large subnets to network segments with a high turnover rate.

Originally, the convention was to issue longer leases to lessen the burden of DHCP communication on a network. With today's higher-speed local area network environments, even large DHCP deployments should have little effect on bandwidth when their lease duration is decreased.

DHCP Scope   A DHCP scope is a range of IP addresses and related configuration information available by request from a DHCP client. DHCP scopes most often represent a single subnet.

Each scope is defined on a DHCP server by a starting IP address and an ending IP address. A DHCP scope range must be a continuous range of numbers. If you need to exclude one or more IP addresses within a range, you are required to create **exclusions** for those IP addresses. You often need to create exclusions for existing hardware devices with static IP addresses that cannot be changed. When the DHCP server creates the address pool for a scope, it does not include exclusions in the available address pool. Figure 4-3 depicts the DHCP address pool as displayed in the DHCP console.

DHCP Options   Besides an IP address, DHCP address assignments contain basic settings, or **DHCP options**, that a client needs for proper network communication. For basic networking needs, the following options are usually specified to a DHCP client via the address assignment:

- IP address
- Subnet mask
- Default gateway
- Primary and secondary DNS servers
- Primary and secondary Windows Internet Name Service (WINS) servers (if applicable)
- DHCP lease expiration

Figure 4-4 displays the IP address information for a Windows Vista client using the ipconfig/all command from the command prompt.

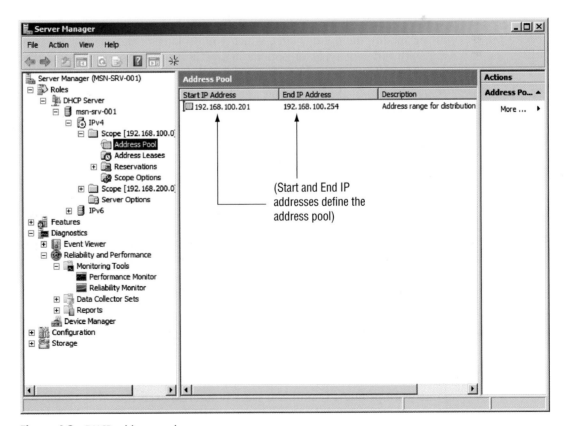

Figure 4-3   DHCP address pool

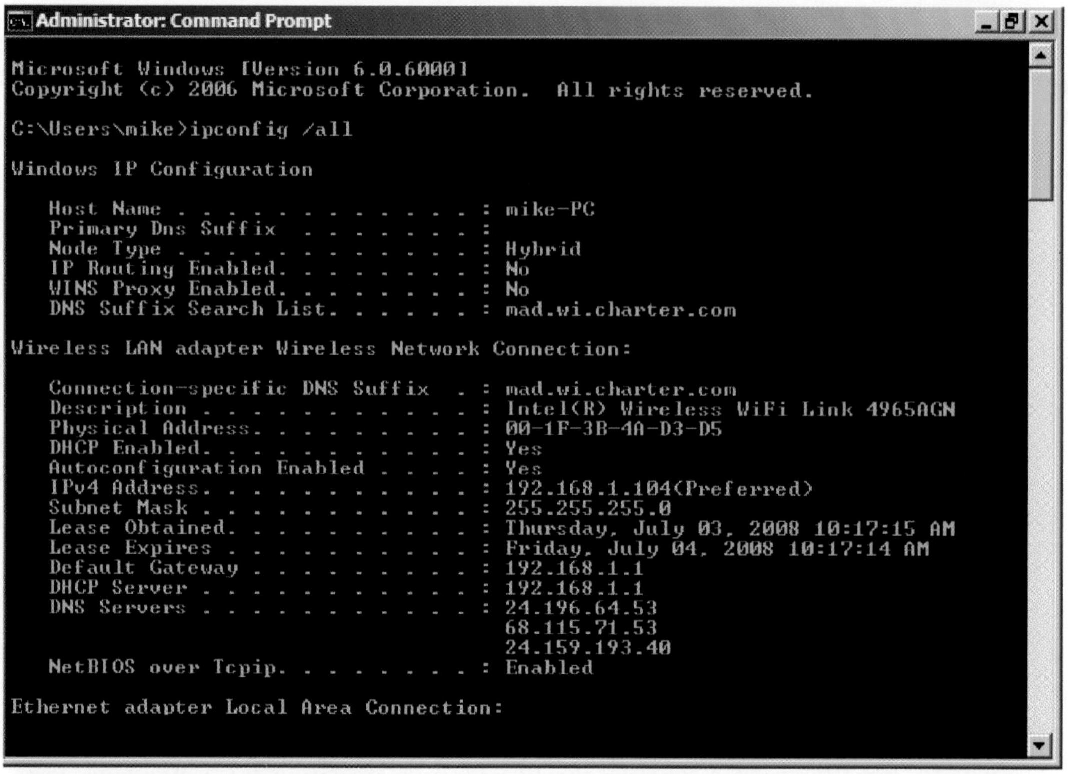

```
Administrator: Command Prompt                                          _ | 8 | X

Microsoft Windows [Version 6.0.6000]
Copyright (c) 2006 Microsoft Corporation.  All rights reserved.

C:\Users\mike>ipconfig /all

Windows IP Configuration

    Host Name . . . . . . . . . . . . : mike-PC
    Primary Dns Suffix  . . . . . . . :
    Node Type . . . . . . . . . . . . : Hybrid
    IP Routing Enabled. . . . . . . . : No
    WINS Proxy Enabled. . . . . . . . : No
    DNS Suffix Search List. . . . . . : mad.wi.charter.com

Wireless LAN adapter Wireless Network Connection:

    Connection-specific DNS Suffix  . : mad.wi.charter.com
    Description . . . . . . . . . . . : Intel(R) Wireless WiFi Link 4965AGN
    Physical Address. . . . . . . . . : 00-1F-3B-4A-D3-D5
    DHCP Enabled. . . . . . . . . . . : Yes
    Autoconfiguration Enabled . . . . : Yes
    IPv4 Address. . . . . . . . . . . : 192.168.1.104(Preferred)
    Subnet Mask . . . . . . . . . . . : 255.255.255.0
    Lease Obtained. . . . . . . . . . : Thursday, July 03, 2008 10:17:15 AM
    Lease Expires . . . . . . . . . . : Friday, July 04, 2008 10:17:14 AM
    Default Gateway . . . . . . . . . : 192.168.1.1
    DHCP Server . . . . . . . . . . . : 192.168.1.1
    DNS Servers . . . . . . . . . . . : 24.196.64.53
                                        68.115.71.53
                                        24.159.193.40
    NetBIOS over Tcpip. . . . . . . . : Enabled

Ethernet adapter Local Area Connection:
```

Figure 4-4   IP address information

You can define options when you are creating the scope (which is the preferred method), or you can modify the options later, which you do later in the chapter. As an administrator, you work with different types of options in DHCP. Each option type has a specific purpose and usage. The following are option types you will use most often:

- *Server options*—**Server options** are settings defined per server that apply to all scopes on a specific DHCP server.

- *Scope options*—**Scope options** are settings defined per scope that apply only to the scope to which they are added.

Whether to create a server option or a scope option depends on how each client uses the setting. Server options are often used for options such as DNS, WINS, or other network resources whose IP addresses are the same for all scopes. Table 4-1 lists some of the common DHCP options.

You use scope options for router options because each scope represents a subnet or part of a subnet, and each scope often has a unique router IP address. Scope options override server options, so in any conflicts between option settings such as DNS servers, the scope option values take precedence.

DHCP Reservations   In some situations, you might want to assign an address to a device using DHCP but a network device or server requires that same IP address. **DHCP reservations** allow you to assign a specific IP address to a DHCP client without statically configuring the device with IP information. DHCP uses the client's MAC address to determine the IP address a client receives. Servers, such as DNS, and domain controllers and devices, such as routers and network printers, require the same IP address each time they connect to a network. For these computers and devices, you create DHCP reservations in the DHCP role console, as shown in Figure 4-5.

Table 4-1   Common DHCP options

Code	Option Name
3	Router
6	DNS server
15	DNS domain name
42	NTP server
44	WINS server (NetBIOS name server)
45	NetBIOS datagram distribution server (NBDD)
46	WINS/NetBIOS node type
47	NetBIOS scope ID
51	Lease time
53	DHCP message type
55	Special option type used to communicate a parameter request list to the DHCP server
58	Renewal time value (T1)
59	Rebind time value (T2)

Network printers are good candidates for using reservations. A common printer connectivity problem occurs when a printer loses power and returns to its factory-default settings. This often changes the IP address on the physical printer so that it no longer matches the logical printer on the print server. By creating a reservation, your printers always receive the same IP addresses.

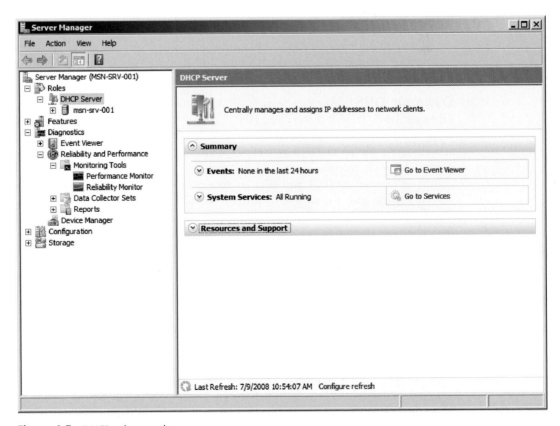

Figure 4-5   DHCP role console

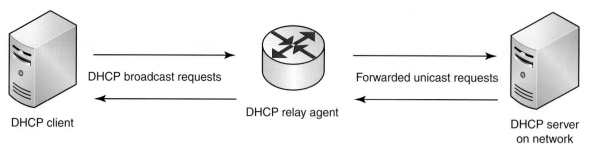

Figure 4-6   DHCP relay agent

DHCP Relay Agent   As mentioned earlier, DHCP requests are broadcast messages. You learned in Chapter 3 that broadcasts cannot be routed, so they are limited to the subnet of the client requesting an IP address. A DHCP server must therefore be available on each subnet requiring DHCP service. Because it is not necessarily appropriate or plausible to have a DHCP server on each subnet, you can use a **DHCP relay agent** to forward DHCP requests from DHCP clients to a DHCP server on the network, as shown in Figure 4-6. The DHCP relay agent accepts the broadcast packets from the client and converts them to unicast packets that can traverse a routed network and vice versa when the DHCP server responds to the client.

Most modern routers support the passing of DHCP requests, often referred to as a **BOOTP relay agent. BOOTP** refers to the former dynamic IP allocation standard that DHCP replaced. Each subnet that needs DHCP should have a DHCP relay agent configured unless the subnet has a DHCP server.

   DHCP relay agents are defined in RFC 1542. For more information about DHCP relay agents, see *www.rfc.net*.

If you do not have an RFC-1542 compliant router, you can set Windows Server 2008 to act as a DHCP relay agent using the Routing and Remote Access Service Setup Wizard. You learn about the process for configuring a DHCP relay agent in Chapter 9.

Dynamic DNS   Another feature of Windows Server 2008 DHCP is Dynamic DNS. With **Dynamic DNS**, DHCP servers and DHCP clients work with DNS servers to create, modify, and delete DNS name records for DHCP clients. When a DHCP client receives a new IP address, its records are updated in DNS as well. Dynamic DNS updates A and AAAA records for clients along with PTR records. A and AAAA records are responsible for resolving host names, or a computer's name, to IPv4 and IPv6 addresses, respectively. PTR records, often referred to as reverse lookup records, resolve IP address (both IPv4 and IPv6) to host names.

By default, Windows Server 2008 supports dynamic updates for clients that can update their own records. These clients include the following:

- Windows 2000 clients
- Windows XP clients
- Windows Vista clients
- Windows Server 2008 clients

The default setup of DHCP in Windows Server 2008 enables Dynamic DNS for these clients, so most installations do not require changes to support Dynamic DNS on the DHCP server. Along with the default DHCP settings, Dynamic DNS requires you to configure a DNS server to accept dynamic updates. You learn more about Dynamic DNS in Chapter 6. Clients prior to Windows 2000 (including Windows NT 4.0 and earlier clients) and clients that are members of a different Active Directory domain cannot update their own records. They rely on the DHCP server to perform this task for them. In this case, the DHCP server updates all the DNS records for the DHCP client. To support legacy clients, you open the IPv4 Properties dialog box to the DNS tab and then set the option to dynamically update DNS A and PTR records for DHCP clients that do not request them (for example, clients running Windows NT 4.0), as shown in Figure 4-7.

DHCP Communication Processes

In this section, you examine the message types that DHCP clients and DHCP servers use to perform their duties. You also explore the communication processes to make initial lease requests, renew leases, and change subnets.

DHCP Message Types   DHCP uses a standard set of messages for its communication between DHCP clients and DHCP servers. These messages are defined in RFC 2131 and are described in the following list:

- *DHCPDiscover*—A DHCP client broadcasts a **DHCPDiscover** message to locate a DHCP server. The message often includes suggested values for the network address and lease duration.

- *DHCPOffer*—One or more DHCP servers responds to a DHCPDiscover message from a DHCP client with a **DHCPOffer** message, which offers configuration information.

- *DHCPRequest*—A DHCP client broadcasts a **DHCPRequest** message to a DHCP server to accept a DHCPOffer. The message contains the accepted IP address and the server it is accepting the address from. Because it is a broadcast message, it is heard by the server whose offer was accepted and the server(s) whose offers were not accepted, if applicable.

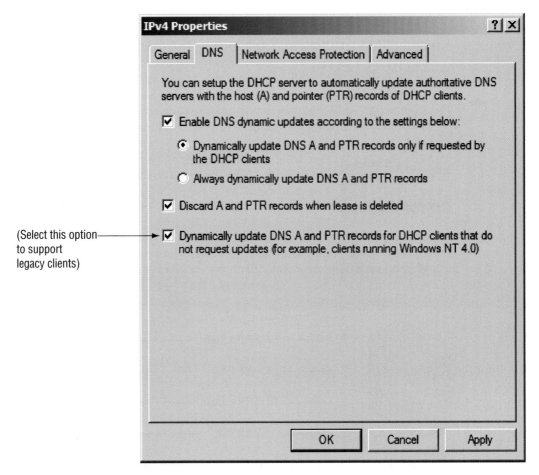

Figure 4-7   Dynamic DNS example

- *DHCPAck*—A **DHCPAck** message is a response from the DHCP server that confirms a DHCP client's IP address. It includes configuration information and the confirmed IP address.

- *DHCPNack*—This response from the DHCP server declines the DHCP client's request.

- *DHCPDecline*—A DHCP client sends this type of message to a DHCP server that declines an offered IP address. It sends the message when a DHCP client determines that the offered address is already in use. When an address is declined, the DHCP client must restart the IP request process.

- *DHCPRelease*—A DHCP client sends this type of message to a DHCP server to relinquish its IP address and end its lease. The message is sent to the DHCP server that issued the DHCP client's address.

- *DHCPInform*—If a DHCP **client** already has an IP address, it sends this type of message to a DHCP server requesting local configuration information only.

As previously noted, the DHCP protocol is defined in RFC 2131. For more information on Windows Server 2008 DHCP standards, see *www.rfc.net*.

Initial Lease Request   By default, all Windows clients are initially configured to use DHCP for IP address allocation. Clients make initial lease requests if they do not have a current lease on a scope. They can be clients that are new to a network (or, more specifically, to a subnet), or they can be clients whose lease expired after being unable to renew. Initial DHCP lease requests are assigned to clients on the basis of the process shown in Figure 4-8.

Based on Figure 4-8, when a DHCP client connects to a network and needs an IP address, it performs the following tasks:

- *Step 1*—The DHCP client seeks a DHCP server through a DHCPDiscover message. The client waits 1 second for a response. If it receives no response, it rebroadcasts the request at intervals of 9, 13, and 16 seconds plus a time variable between 0 milliseconds and 1 second. If these attempts fail, the client begins assigning an Automatic Private IP Addressing (APIPA) address for temporary connectivity while it continues to retry broadcasts every 5 minutes. APIPA addresses are IP addresses starting with 169.254.

Remember that APIPA addresses are only assigned to a local machine if the alternative configuration option for adding a static IP address has not been configured.

- *Step 2*—One or more DHCP servers responsible for the client's subnet answers the request by sending an IP address offer, or a DHCPOffer message. Each offering server temporarily reserves an IP address in anticipation of an acceptance by the client.

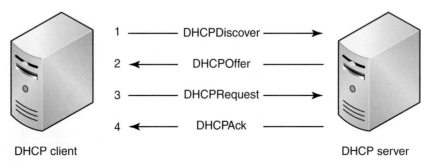

Figure 4-8   Initial DHCP lease request process

- *Step 3*—Although each subnet typically has only one DHCP server, if the client receives multiple offers, it chooses one of them and accepts the server's offer. The client responds with a DHCPRequest asking for the appropriate DHCP server to assign it an IP address. This packet is broadcast to all listening devices so that any other listening DHCP servers that also made a DHCPOffer can be informed that the client accepted an offer from a different DHCP server and free their own temporarily reserved address.

- *Step 4*—On receiving the client's acceptance, the DHCP server creates a lease for the address it offered and confirms the IP address assignment with a DHCPAck message.

Why do you need all the messages if you have only one DHCP server in your environment? First, that's the way the protocol works. In addition, DHCP servers and clients are not as aware of their surroundings or other DHCP servers as some applications. Clients and servers therefore follow the protocol standards when communicating.

Lease Renewals   DHCP clients attempt lease renewals in different ways. When a DHCP client powers on or connects to the network, it confirms that it can continue to use its currently assigned address; if so, the lease is renewed and the expiration date extended. If not, they attempt to renew their lease at the following intervals:

- *Renewal time value*—After 50 percent of the lease time has expired, the DHCP client attempts to renew its lease with the DHCP server that issued the IP address. This **renewal time value** is referred to as T1.

- *Binding time value*—After 87.5 percent of the lease time has expired, the DHCP client attempts to renew its lease again. If unsuccessful, it initiates a DHCPDiscover broadcast request to receive an IP address from any DHCP server on its network. This **binding time value** is referred to as T2.

DHCP renewals use a two-message communication process, as shown in Figure 4-9. Based on the Figure 4-9, a DHCP client makes a request to renew its current DHCP lease using the following steps:

- *Step 1*—When a client needs to renew its DHCP address, it sends a DHCPRequest asking for the renewal of the lease it currently holds.

- *Step 2*—When it receives the client's renewal request, the DHCP server confirms the renewal request with a DHCPAck message that includes an updated DHCP lease and any updated DHCP options. The updated lease includes a new expiration date for the lease.

If a client cannot contact a DHCP server through these actions, it maintains its current IP address until its lease expires. At that time, it attempts to acquire a new IP address through the Initial Release process.

Changing Subnets   With the proliferation of mobile devices requiring IP addresses, you often need to accommodate DHCP clients that move among subnets. When a client moves to a

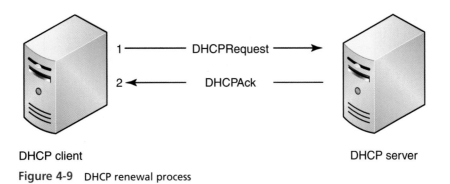

DHCP client   DHCP server

Figure 4-9 DHCP renewal process

new subnet, it cannot use its current lease because the IP information does match the new network configuration.

The process of moving to a new subnet is not always automatic, depending on how a computer is being used. In a well-designed network, wireless access points are placed on a single subnet throughout an organization, though that is not always the case. For example, if a mobile user accesses the network with a laptop through wireless access points that are connected to different subnets, the user would lose connectivity until either the lease was scheduled for renewal or the user manually forced a request for a new address (by executing the ipconfig /renew command). However, the client does not detect that it needs a new address until it finds out for itself or you force it to check again. There are now mechanisms that wireless access points can use to force clients to connect to new subnets more seamlessly, but those technologies fall outside the scope of this book.

A more common example, however, is when the mobile device is turned off, moved to a new location, and then rebooted. Because the DHCP process is carried out every time the computer is started (regardless of whether it has a current lease), the client on the new subnet uses the following steps to acquire a new IP address configuration.

DHCP clients that move to a different subnet follow the process shown in Figure 4-10 to request a new IP address.

A DHCP client that moves to a new subnet performs the following steps to acquire a new IP address configuration:

- *Step 1*—When a client moves to a new subnet, it sends a DHCPRequest asking for the renewal of the lease it currently holds.

- *Step 2*—When it receives the client's renewal request, the DHCP server determines that the renewal request is asking for an IP address configuration it cannot provide, so it issues a DHCPNack message.

- *Step 3*—When it receives the DHCPNack message from the DHCP server, the DHCP client seeks an IP address on the new network through a DHCPDiscover message.

- *Step 4*—The DHCP server responsible for the client's subnet answers the request by sending an IP address offer, or DHCPOffer message.

- *Step 5*—If the client wants to accept the server's offer, it responds with a DHCPRequest asking for the IP address to assign.

- *Step 6*—When it receives the client's acceptance, the DHCP server confirms the IP address assignment with a DHCPAck message.

When a client starts up but cannot contact a DHCP server, the client uses APIPA addressing and creates a unique IP address for communicating with other clients on its subnet. APIPA addresses begin with 169.254 as discussed in Chapter 3. APIPA addresses cannot be routed and allow clients to communicate only with other APIPA-configured clients on their subnet. The DHCP client rebroadcasts a request every 5 minutes attempting to solicit a valid IP address from a DHCP server.

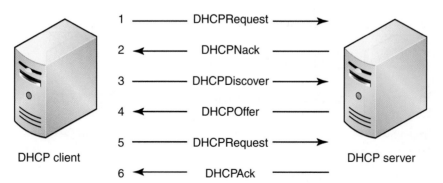

Figure 4-10   DHCP renewal when a client changes subnets

Using DHCPv6

Most of the discussion on DHCP involves IPv4. IPv4 clients using DHCP retrieve all the information you need for IP addressing from a DHCP server. This differs from IPv6. By default, IPv6 clients use DHCP (often referred to as DHCPv6) to receive IP address and configuration information from an IPv6 router on their network. This is referred to as stateless mode. Implementing DHCPv6 requires configuring your router to forward all autoconfiguration requests to an available DHCPv6 server and disabling stateless mode on your Windows Server 2008 DHCP servers. Configuring DHCPv6 scopes in Windows Server 2008 is covered later in this chapter. For more information on DHCP for IPv6, see RFC 3315 at *www.rfc.net*.

4

Installing DHCP in a Windows Server 2008 Environment

Now that you are familiar with the DHCP protocol and how it works, you can focus on the DHCP Server role in Windows Server 2008. By default, the DHCP Server role is not installed on Windows Server 2008. You must install and configure DHCP before your DHCP clients can use it. This section explains how to install and configure the DHCP server, including the components discussed earlier in this chapter. You also learn how to configure DHCP clients.

You use Windows Server 2008 to install the DHCP Server role. The DHCP Server role requires minimal server resources, so it can be run on a server that meets the minimum requirements for Windows Server 2008. The DHCP Server role starts the DHCP Server service, installs the files needed for the DHCP database, and initializes the DHCP console on the local system. In Activity 4-1, you install the DHCP Server role using Server Manager.

Activity 4-1: Installing the DHCP Server Role

Time Required: 15 minutes

Objective: Install the DHCP server role.

Description: After installing Windows Server 2008 successfully and completing the immediate postinstallation tasks for your organization, you decide to install the DHCP Server role so that your server can automatically assign IP addressing information to clients.

This activity and the remaining activities require that the network adapters of each machine mapping to Local Area Connection are on the same network segment, or subnet. (This should already be completed as part of the setup for this book.) Your instructor might give you additional steps to perform depending on your lab environment. All the activities in this chapter are appropriate for physical machines and virtual machine applications.

1. Log on to MSN-SRV-0XX.

2. If Server Manager does not appear, click **Start** and then click **Server Manager**.

3. In the right pane, expand the **Roles** section and then click **Add Roles**. The Add Roles Wizard starts. Click **Next**.

4. In the first Select Server Roles Wizard dialog box, check the **DHCP Server** box and then click **Next**.

5. Review the information in the DHCP Server window and then click **Next** to begin installing the server role.

6. Verify that the network adapter with the IP address 192.168.100.10 is checked and then click **Next**.

7. In the Specify IPv4 DNS Server Settings dialog box, enter the following information and then click **Next**:

   - Parent Domain: **BenTech.local**
   - Preferred DNS Server IPv4 Address: **192.168.100.10**

Because DNS is not set up on the server at 192.168.100.10, attempts to validate the DNS server will fail.

8. In the Specify IPv4 WINS Server Settings dialog box, click **Next**. This installs DHCP without requiring support for WINS.

9. In the Add or Edit DHCP Scopes dialog box, click **Next**. You add a DHCP scope in a later activity.

10. In the Configure DHCPv6 Stateless Mode dialog box, choose **Disable DHCPv6 stateless mode for this server** and then click **Next**. You configure DHCPv6 in a later activity.

11. Review the settings in the Confirm Installation Settings dialog box and then click **Install** to begin the installation process.

12. When the installation is complete, click **Close** to exit the wizard.

13. Close Server Manager.

You can also install DHCP using servermangercmd.exe on a Full version of Windows Server 2008 or using ocsetup.exe on Server Core. This allows you to install DHCP from the command prompt or script. Figure 4-11 shows the ocsetup.exe command used to install the DHCP role on Server Core.

DHCP Database　The DHCP server provides its services by maintaining a database of client IP addresses. This database is constantly updated as new requests for IP addresses are fulfilled and as clients release old addresses into the address pool. Unlike DNS, which distributes its database across multiple servers, DHCP maintains a single database on each DHCP server installation.

The DHCP database is based on the Joint Engine Technology (JET) storage engine. Several Microsoft products use the JET storage engine, including Microsoft Office Access 2000/2002/2003 and the WINS database. The default location for the installation of the DHCP database files is the %systemroot%\system32\DHCP directory.

DHCP has no theoretical limit to the number of records it can store or the size of its database. The database size is based on the number of client requests it receives. The database grows as new records are created and deleted, though it does not shrink when records are deleted.

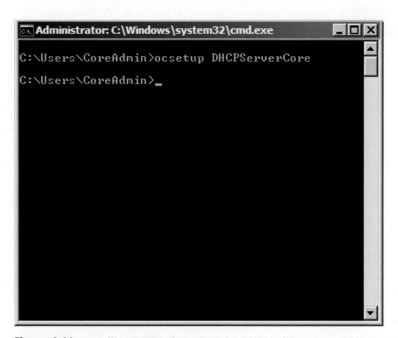

Figure 4-11 Installing DHCP role on Server Core

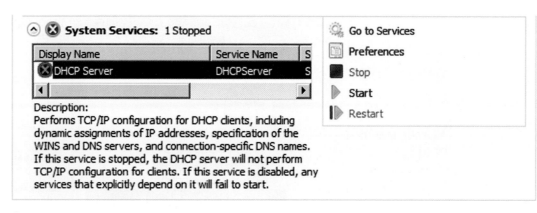

Figure 4-12   DHCP Server service stopped

To recover space allocated previously, you need to compact the DHCP database. DHCP automatically compacts the database as a background process during system idle periods.

DHCP Server Service   The DHCP Server service is installed with the DHCP Server role. This service runs the processes the DHCP server uses. If the service is not running, DHCP clients cannot receive IP addresses and configuration information from the DHCP server. The DHCP Server role displays an error message that the service is stopped, similar to the message in Figure 4-12.

DHCP Server Console   After the DHCP Server role is installed, the DHCP Server console is available in both Server Manager and under Administrative Tools. These tools are stored in the Administrative Tools folder on the Windows Server 2008 Start menu, as shown in Figure 4-13.

The DHCP Server console is the GUI tool for managing DHCP on Windows Server 2008. It provides tools for configuring both IPv6 and IPv4 DHCP implementations. You use the Server console in many of the activities in this chapter. In the next activity, you review the Server console prior to performing configuration activities.

The default installation of the DHCP console in Administrative Tools does not display the Actions pane. To view the Actions pane, click the **Show/Hide Action Pane** icon on the toolbar or click View on the menu bar, click Customize, click the **Action pane** check box, and then click OK.

Activity 4-2: Reviewing the DHCP Server Console

Time Required: 5 minutes

Objective: Explore the DHCP Server console.

Description: Now that you've installed the DHCP Server role, you want to spend some time exploring the DHCP Server console to prepare for performing configuration tasks with it.

1. Open Server Manager.

2. In the right pane of Server Manager, expand the **Roles** section and then click **DHCP Server**.

3. In the DHCP Server summary pane, review the Events summary. You can view any Event Viewer messages related to DHCP in the Events summary.

4. In the DHCP Server summary pane, review the System Services summary. You can view the status of the DHCP Server service in the System Services summary.

5. In the DHCP Server summary pane, review the Resources and Support summary. Click each recommendation to view its description.

(Administrative Tools folder)

Figure 4-13 DHCP console in Administrative Tools

6. In the left pane, click to expand **DHCP Server** and then expand **MSN-SRV-0XX**. Click **MSN-SRV-0XX** to expand the DHCP Server. The IPv4 and IPv6 areas for your DHCP server are also displayed.

7. Close Server Manager.

Authorizing DHCP

In Active Directory domains, DHCP servers must be authorized before they can begin supplying IP addresses. This prevents unauthorized or rogue Windows DHCP servers from being deployed on your domain clients. Rogue servers that are improperly or mischievously configured can cause communication problems for clients because of incorrect configurations or IP address conflicts.

In Windows Server 2008, you are prompted for credentials during installation if your server is a member of a domain. This is different from previous versions of Windows Server.

Workgroup DHCP servers do not require authorization because they do not have an Active Directory in which to list them. To prevent unauthorized client connections to your network on workgroup DHCP servers, you use Network Address Protection, which is discussed in Chapter 9.

Configuring the DHCP Server

To configure the DHCP server, you set up scopes, exclusions, and options; create reservations; and configure the DHCP clients.

Configuring Scopes

After installing the DHCP role, you need to configure DHCP for its initial use. DHCP requires at least one DHCP scope to issue IP addresses for network clients. Like many of the upcoming configuration activities, you can create the initial DHCP scope when you install roles. In Activity 4-3, you configure a DHCP server with an IPv4 scope.

Activity 4-3: Creating a Scope for the 192.168.100.0 Subnet

Time Required: 10 minutes

Objective: Create scopes in the DHCP console.

Description: Now that you are familiar with the DHCP Server console, you are ready to create your first scope on your server. You start with an IPv4 scope for a single client on your network.

1. Open Server Manager.

2. In the left pane of Server Manager, expand the **Roles** section and the **DHCP Server** role and then click **MSN-SRV-0XX**. The DHCP Server administration console opens.

3. In the left pane, click **IPv4**. Add a Scope is displayed in the middle pane of the console.

4. Click **More Actions** and then click **New Scope**. The New Scope Wizard starts.

The More Actions options are also available in the Action pane.

5. Click **Next** in the Welcome to the New Scope Wizard dialog box.

6. In the Scope Name dialog box, enter the following information and then click **Next**:

   • Name: **Partner Local Scope – IPv4**

   • Description: **This is the IPv4 scope for the partner machine, MSN-SC-0XX.**

7. In the IP Address Range dialog box, enter the following information and then click **Next**:

   • Start IP address: **192.168.100.201**

   • End IP address: **192.168.100.201**

8. In the Add Exclusions dialog box, click **Next**. You add DHCP exclusions in a future activity.

9. In the Lease Duration dialog box, click **Next** to accept the default of 8 days.

10. In the Configure DHCP Options dialog box, click **No, I will configure these options** later and then click **Next**.

11. Click **Finish** to complete the DHCP scope creation. In the IPv4 console pane, the scope is displayed with a down-pointing red arrow. This denotes the scope is created but is not active.

12. Close Server Manager.

Creating IPv6 scopes is similar to creating them for IPv4, as you see in Activity 4-4. The major difference is that you add in the IPv6 prefix for the network you want to use instead of a starting and ending IP address.

Activity 4-4: Creating a Scope for an IPv6 Subnet

Time Required: 10 minutes

Objective: Create an IPv6 scope in the DHCP console.

Description: In this activity, you create a second scope, this time for an IPv6 client.

1. Start Server Manager.

2. In the left pane of Server Manager, expand the **Roles** section and the **DHCP Server** role and then click **MSN-SRV-0XX**. The DHCP Server administration console opens.

3. In the left pane, click **IPv6**. Add a Scope is displayed in the middle pane of the console.

4. Click **More Actions** and then click **New Scope**. The New Scope Wizard starts.

5. In the Welcome to the New Scope Wizard dialog box, click **Next**.

6. In the Scope Name dialog box, enter the following information and then click **Next**:

   - Name: **Partner Scope – IPv6**

   - Description: **This is the IPv6 scope for the partner machine, MSN-SC-0XX.**

7. In the Scope Prefix dialog box, enter **2250::** as the prefix and then click **Next**.

8. In the Add Exclusions dialog box, click **Next**.

9. In the Scope Lease dialog box, click **Next** to accept the defaults.

 The default setting activates the DHCPv6 scope.

10. In the Completing the New Scope dialog box, click **Finish** to complete the scope creation. The scope is displayed in the DHCP Server console pane.

11. Close Server Manager.

When you do not want to use the GUI such as with a Server Core installation or a scripted installation, you can use netsh. Using the netsh command to configure the DHCP server is covered at the end of this section.

If you choose to not configure the DHCP options as in Activity 4-3, the scope you create is not active. All scopes must be active before the DHCP server can allocate addresses from the scope. Activity 4-5 steps you through activating a scope.

 Deactivated scopes are often used when administrators introduce a new DHCP server or reconfigure the current DHCP server. This prevents current DHCP clients from errantly obtaining IP addresses from new scopes that might not be ready for usage.

Activity 4-5: Activating an IPv4 DHCP Scope

Time Required: 5 minutes

Objective: Activate a DHCP scope.

Description: In a previous activity, you created an IPv4 DHCP scope. Now you can activate the IPv4 scope so that clients can begin using your DHCP server.

1. Start Server Manager.

2. In the left pane of Server Manager, expand the **Roles** section and the **DHCP Server** role and then click **MSN-SRV-0XX**. The DHCP Server administration console opens.

3. In the left pane, click **IPv4**. The scope you created earlier is displayed.

4. In the left pane, click **Scope [192.168.100.0] Partner Scope**.

5. Click **More Actions** and then click **Activate**.

6. Verify that the red arrow is removed from the scope name. This denotes that the scope is now active and makes the DHCP address available in the scope.

7. Leave MSN-SRV-0XX running and log onto MSN-SC-0XX.

8. Type the following commands to set the network adapter on MSN-SC-0XX to using DHCP:

```
netsh int ip set addr "local area connection" DHCP
netsh int ip set dns "local area connection" DHCP
```

9. Type **ipconfig /all** and verify that the server receives the IP address of 192.168.100.201. If it does not, type **ipconfig /release** and **ipconfig /renew** to refresh the IP address.

10. Return to MSN-SRV-0XX, expand **Scope [192.168.100.0] Partner Scope**, and click **Address Leases**. Verify that you see a lease for **msn-sc-0XX.bentech.local** of **192.168.100.201**.

11. Close Server Manager.

After a scope is created, you can modify certain properties of the scope using the DHCP console. Right-click the **IPv4 scope** and then click Properties to open the Properties dialog box for that scope. On the General tab, you can perform the following tasks:

• Increase (if there are available addresses) or decrease the address pool

• Change the scope name and description

• Adjust the lease duration as well as set as unlimited (not recommended)

The only value you cannot change is the subnet mask. To modify the subnet mask, you need to re-create the scope.

Activity 4-6: Expanding an IPv4 Address Pool

Time Required: 5 minutes

Objective: Modify an IPv4 address pool.

Description: Your organization has been using the scope you created for a few days but now needs additional IP addresses to accommodate users in a new department. You need to modify the scope's address pool by expanding the scope.

1. Start Server Manager.

2. In the left pane of Server Manager, expand the **Roles** section and the **DHCP Server** role and then click **MSN-SRV-0XX**. The DHCP Server administration console opens.

3. Expand **IPv4** and then click **Scope [192.168.100.0] Partner Scope**.

4. In the Actions pane, click **More Actions** and then click **Properties**.

5. In the Scope Properties dialog box, change the end IP address to **192.168.100.254** and then click **OK** to save the change.

6. With Address Pool selected in the left pane of the Server administration console, press **F5** to refresh the console information. The address pool range is now 192.168.100.201 to 192.168.100.254, as shown in Figure 4-14.

F5 is the standard keystroke to refresh administrative consoles in Windows Server 2008. Because many Windows consoles do not automatically refresh their contents, you should press F5 to refresh the display after making changes. In this and future activities, use F5 whenever you want to see the latest information in a console window.

7. Close Server Manager.

Configuring Exclusions

As discussed earlier, you create exclusions so that static IP addresses for devices such as routers, printers, or other network devices are not assigned. A common practice is to create exclusionary

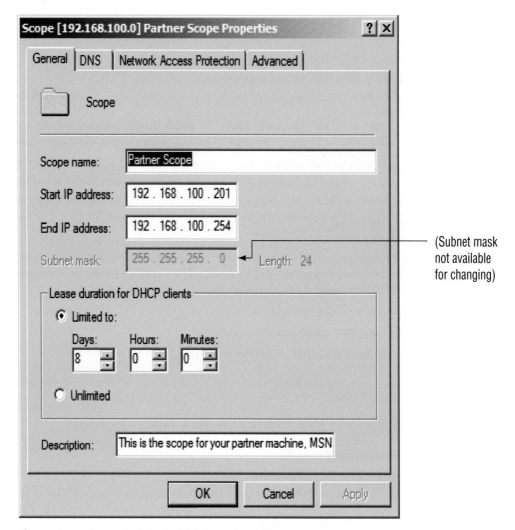

Figure 4-14   General tab in the IPv4 Scope Properties dialog box

ranges at the beginning and end of a scope range. For example, suppose you create a scope for the 192.168.200.0 /24 subnet. To account for network devices and static IP addresses, you could create two exclusionary ranges: 192.168.200.1 to 192.168.200.50 and 192.168.200.201 to 192.168.200.254. This leaves an address pool with 150 addresses for DHCP clients.

Activity 4-7: Adding IPv4 Exclusion

Time Required: 10 minutes

Objective: Create IPv4 exclusionary ranges.

Description: Because your organization has existing devices with static IP addresses, you need to create exclusions so that their IP addresses are not assigned to clients. In this activity, you configure exclusions for the IPv4 scope you created previously.

1. Start Server Manager.

2. In the left pane of Server Manager, expand the **Roles** section and the **DHCP Server** role and then click **MSN-SRV-0XX**. The DHCP Server administration console opens.

3. In the left pane, expand **IPv4**, expand **Scope [192.168.100.0] Partner Scope**, and then click **Address Pool**.

4. In the Actions pane, click **More Actions** and then click **New Exclusion Range**.

5. Type an exclusionary range beginning with **192.168.100.201** and ending with **192.168.100.210**.

6. Click **Add** and then click **Close** in the Add Exclusion dialog box.

7. Log onto MSN-SC-0XX, if necessary.

8. In the Command Prompt, type **ipconfig /release**. When the command finishes running, type **ipconfig /renew**.

9. Type **ipconfig /all** to verify the new settings. You should now receive a new IP address of 192.168.100.211.

10. Return to MSN-SRV-0XX, expand Scope [192.168.100.0] Partner Scope, and then click Address Leases. Verify that you see a lease for msn-sc-0XX.bentech.local of 192.168.100.211. (Press F5 to update the display.)

11. Close Server Manager.

Configuring Options

Options allow you to quickly and easily provide DHCP clients with updated configuration information, such as new DNS servers or additional domain prefixes. After you add the new option to DHCP, clients update their configuration information at their next renewal interval or when new IP addresses are issued.

NOTE If you are using the default lease duration of 8 days, it could take up to 4 days before clients receive the new DHCP options you deploy. To have them update more frequently, you can reduce the lease duration prior to your update. When all DHCP clients are using the shorter lease duration, apply the updates to your DHCP server and return the lease duration setting to its normal value. Remember to always perform activities like this in a test environment.

Previously, you learned the difference between server options and scope options. Basically, you should apply server options for values that affect all scopes on a DHCP server. Apply scope options for values that affect a single scope. Remember that scope options override server options if there is a conflict. You modify server and scope options in the next activities.

Activity 4-8: Modifying the Server Options

Time Required: 10 minutes

Objective: Modify the DHCP server options.

Description: Your organization has decided to implement a DNS server on your network. This server will provide updated name resolution for your clients. In this activity, you modify the server scope so all scopes in your environment use the DNS server, 192.168.100.10.

1. Start Server Manager on the MSN-SRV-0XX computer.

2. In the left pane of Server Manager, expand the **Roles** section and the **DHCP Server** role and then click **MSN-SRV-0XX**. The DHCP Server administration console opens.

3. In the left pane, expand **IPv4** and then click **Server Options**.

4. Click **More Actions** and then click **Configure Options**.

5. In the Server Options dialog box, click **006 DNS Servers** and then enter 192.168.100.10 in the String Value text box.

6. Click **OK** to close the Server Options dialog box.

7. Verify that the server option for DNS Servers appears in the Server Options pane.

8. Log onto MSN-SC-0XX, if necessary.

9. In the Command Prompt, type **ipconfig /renew**.

10. Type **ipconfig /all** to verify the new settings. You should now receive a new DNS server of 192.168.100.10.

11. Leave the DHCP console open for the next activity.

Activity 4-9: Modifying the Scope Options

Time Required: 10 minutes

Objective: Modify the DHCP scope options.

Description: You have been informed that the IP address of your router on the 192.168.100.0 subnet is incorrect in the DHCP scope. You need to modify this property so that DHCP clients can communicate properly. In this activity, you modify the DHCP options on a scope.

1. In the left pane of the DHCP console, expand **IPv4** and then click **Scope [192.168.100.0] Partner Scope.**

2. Click **Scope Options.**

3. Click **More Actions** and then click **Configure Options.**

4. In the Scope Options dialog box, click the **003 Router** check box.

5. Enter **192.168.100.1** as the IP address and then click **Add.**

6. Click **OK** to close the Scope Options dialog box.

7. Verify that the server option for Router is added in the Scope Options pane.

8. Log onto MSN-SC-0XX, if necessary.

9. At the command prompt, type **ipconfig /renew.**

10. Type **ipconfig /all** to verify the new settings. You should now receive a new Default Gateway of 192.168.100.1.

11. Leave the DHCP console open for the next activity.

Creating Reservations

Reservations are used in DHCP to give a DHCP client a static IP address without manually configuring the address on the client. As mentioned previously, network printers are good candidates for reservations. In Activity 4-10, you create a reservation for a client.

> The only requirement of reservations is that a DHCP server must be available to provide the reservation information. If you plan to use reservations, make sure you have redundancy in your DHCP infrastructure. If you are using more than one DHCP server, each reservation needs to be created on every DHCP server. This is another opportunity to automate configuration by using a netsh batch file or script.

Activity 4-10: Adding a Reservation for 192.168.100.225

Time Required: 5 minutes

Objective: Add a reservation for a new network printer.

Description: You are deploying a new network printer and you want to create a reservation for it in DHCP so that it receives the same IP address even if it loses its settings. In this activity, you add a reservation to the scope you created previously.

1. In the left pane of the DHCP console, expand **IPv4** and then expand **Scope [192.168.100.0] Partner Scope** to display the Reservations folder.

2. Click the **Reservations** folder. In the Actions pane, click **More Actions** and then click **New Reservation.** This opens the New Reservation window. In the New Reservation window, enter the following information:

   • Reservation name: **Network Printer 1**

   • IP address: **192.168.100.225**

   • MAC address: **12-12-34-34-12-12**

   • Description: **Network Printer Deployed by Administrator**

4. Click **Add** and then click **Close**. Your reservation appears in the Reservations pane in the DHCP console.

5. Close the DHCP console.

Using netsh

As discussed in Chapter 3, netsh is a powerful command-line tool for working with network settings in Windows Server 2008. Many of the tasks you performed earlier can be completed using netsh. This section guides you through the netsh commands commonly used for configuring DHCP.

The netsh examples are based on the following variables:

- DHCPScopeName = "Primary Scope"
- DHCPScopeDescription = "Primary Scope for Netsh Example"
- DHCPServerIP = 192.168.100.10
- TargetDHCPScope = 192.168.150.0
- ReservedIP = 192.168.150.20
- ReservationIP = 192.168.150.20
- MACAddress = 03043c40fb6a
- ReservationName = MSN-SRV-150

In this example, the first line of code creates the scope, and the second line of code defines the IP range of the scope. The syntax for creating a DHCP scope with netsh is the following:

```
netsh Dhcp Server 192.168.100.10 add scope 192.168.150.0
255.255.255.0 "Primary Scope" "Primary Scope for Netsh Example"

netsh Dhcp Server 192.168.100.10 Scope 192.168.150.0 add iprange
192.168.150.1 192.168.150.254
```

The syntax for creating a DHCP reservation with netsh is the following:

```
netsh Dhcp Server 192.168.100.10 Scope 192.168.150.0 add
reservedip 192.168.150.20 03043c40fb6a MSN-SRV-150
```

The syntax for creating a DHCP exclusionary range with netsh is the following:

```
netsh Dhcp Server 192.168.100.10 Scope 192.168.150.0 add
excluderange 192.168.150.1 192.168.150.10
```

The syntax for configuring a DHCP option with netsh is the following:

```
netsh Dhcp Server 192.168.100.10 Scope 192.168.150.0 set
optionvalue 6 IPADDRESS "192.168.100.10" "192.168.100.20"
```

The syntax for deactivating a DHCP scope is the following:

```
netsh Dhcp Server 192.168.100.10 Scope 192.168.150.0 set state 0
```

Figure 4-15 shows all the netsh commands run from the command prompt.

DHCP Client Configuration

By default, Windows Server 2008 installations and most other operating systems (client and server) are configured to use DHCP for addressing. Thus, you do not need to configure a client unless a static IP address must be applied to it.

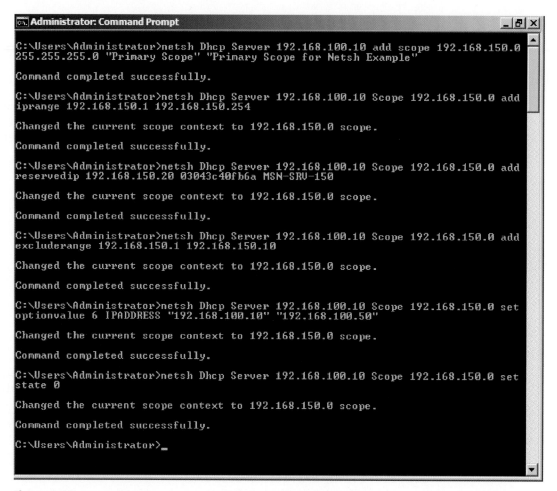

```
C:\Users\Administrator>netsh Dhcp Server 192.168.100.10 add scope 192.168.150.0
255.255.255.0 "Primary Scope" "Primary Scope for Netsh Example"

Command completed successfully.

C:\Users\Administrator>netsh Dhcp Server 192.168.100.10 Scope 192.168.150.0 add
iprange 192.168.150.1 192.168.150.254

Changed the current scope context to 192.168.150.0 scope.

Command completed successfully.

C:\Users\Administrator>netsh Dhcp Server 192.168.100.10 Scope 192.168.150.0 add
reservedip 192.168.150.20 03043c40fb6a MSN-SRU-150

Changed the current scope context to 192.168.150.0 scope.

Command completed successfully.

C:\Users\Administrator>netsh Dhcp Server 192.168.100.10 Scope 192.168.150.0 add
excluderange 192.168.150.1 192.168.150.10

Changed the current scope context to 192.168.150.0 scope.

Command completed successfully.

C:\Users\Administrator>netsh Dhcp Server 192.168.100.10 Scope 192.168.150.0 set
optionvalue 6 IPADDRESS "192.168.100.10" "192.168.100.50"

Changed the current scope context to 192.168.150.0 scope.

Command completed successfully.

C:\Users\Administrator>netsh Dhcp Server 192.168.100.10 Scope 192.168.150.0 set
state 0

Changed the current scope context to 192.168.150.0 scope.

Command completed successfully.

C:\Users\Administrator>_
```

Figure 4-15 Netsh example

The DHCP Client service is responsible for the DHCP configuration process on a client machine. The service initiates DHCP messaging while Windows Server 2008 is running. The DHCP Client service also initiates the T1 and T2 lease renewals. You can access this service in the Services console in Server Manager, as shown in Figure 4-16.

Fault Tolerance and DHCP

As with any critical service on the network, fault tolerance is an important part of deploying DHCP. Because many organizations can effectively use only one or two DHCP servers, you do not need to deploy several DHCP servers. You should deploy enough to handle the load of your DHCP clients and provide backup DHCP services in case of a server failure.

Microsoft recommends using an 80/20 rule for splitting scopes between two servers for fault tolerance. With the 80/20 rule, 80 percent of a scope's total IP range is hosted on your primary DHCP server, while the remaining 20 percent is hosted on your secondary DHCP server. In case the primary server fails, you have IP addresses for new DHCP client requests and renewals. The 80/20 rule assumes that you can return the primary DHCP server to service within 1 or 2 days.

Although the 80/20 rule is helpful, another recommendation is to split your scopes 50/50. This provides true fault tolerance, unlike the 80/20 method. If you lose your primary server for longer than 4 days, the secondary server can handle the load. The important caveat is that you are using an entire IP space that supports this model. You need a private IP addressing scheme that leaves at least 50 percent (70 to 80 percent is recommended) of your available address pool free. You view the available address space on a DHCP scope later in this chapter.

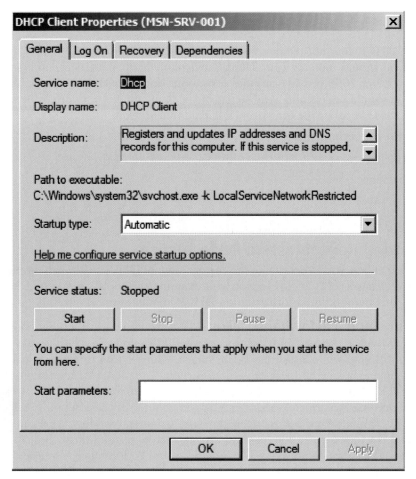

Figure 4-16   DHCP Client service in Server Manager

In case you cannot return the primary DHCP server to service within a short period of time, you have the following options:

- You can expand the scope ranges on the secondary server so that it can handle the load for your network.

- You can temporarily install the DHCP service on another server in your environment. This option requires that you modify your DHCP relay agents with the IP address of the new DHCP servers.

DHCP is a good candidate for using the following features that are built into Windows Server 2008:

- *Hyper-V*—Because of the minimal resource requirements of DHCP, it is a perfect candidate for running as virtual machine guest.

- *Failover clustering*—If your environment meets the hardware requirements of clustering, DHCP works well as a clustered service. Failover clustering allows you to set up an additional server to act as a stand in if your primary server fails. Windows Server 2008 manages the transfer of services between the two servers, so the changes are transparent to the DHCP clients. Moreover, you can skip the 80/20 rule when clustering and keep all IP addresses in a single scope because a cluster shifts the entire scope to a failover system if the primary server fails.

DHCP Administration

Although DHCP does not require much maintenance or administration after it is properly configured, you should monitor your DHCP environment for bottlenecks and sources of failure. Windows Server 2008 provides utilities for monitoring your DHCP servers. Along with monitoring, you should understand and use regular backup and recovery procedures for DHCP. This section covers the following topics on DHCP administration:

- Monitoring performance
- Backup and recovery
- Maintenance
- Troubleshooting
- DHCP clients

Monitoring Reliability and Performance

Monitoring allows you to determine the current state of DHCP. Although monitoring is covered in detail in Chapter 11, in this section you examine the tools specific to DHCP and explore examples of where to find information on DHCP in Windows Server 2008.

Reliability and Performance Monitor   You can use the new Reliability and Performance Monitor console in Windows Server 2008 to identify bottlenecks on your DHCP server. Specifically, you can use the Performance Monitor tool to create a real-time picture of what is happening on the local or remote servers. By adding data counters to Performance Monitor, you begin to develop a picture of your DHCP environment.

After opening Performance Monitor, you add counters by clicking the green plus sign on the Performance Monitor toolbar to open the Add Counters window. You can then review the DHCP and DHCPv6 Server objects, double-click each to expand them, and choose the counters you want to track. See Figure 4-17. The Reliability and Performance Monitor is covered in more depth in Chapter 11.

Activity 4-11: Adding Counters to Performance Monitor

Time Required: 10 minutes

Objective: Configure Performance Monitor by adding DHCP Server counters.

Description: Now that your organization has been using DHCP for a few months, you want to see how DHCP is performing on your server. Using Performance Monitor, you add counters for measuring the performance of DHCP.

1. Open Server Manager.
2. In the left pane of Server Manager, double-click **Diagnostics**, then **Reliability and Performance**, and then **Monitoring Tools**.
3. In the left pane, click **Performance Monitor**. The current performance activity is displayed in the right pane.
4. Click the **Add** button (the green plus sign) to open the Add Counters window.
5. Scroll through the available counters, click **DHCP Server**, and then click the **Add** button to select all of the DHCP counters.
6. Click **OK** to close the Add Counters window.
7. At the bottom of the Performance Monitor window, scroll through the listed counters to verify that all the DHCP counters have been added.
8. Let the counter run for approximately 2 minutes to view activity based on the counters you added.
9. Return to MSN-SC-0XX, type **ipconfig /renew** at the command prompt, and then press **Enter**. When the command completes, press the up arrow to add the ipconfig /renew

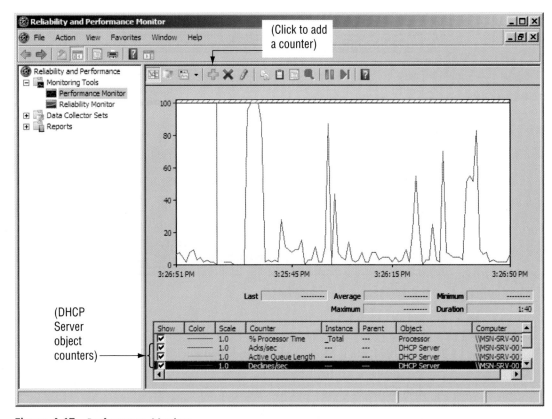

Figure 4-17   Performance Monitor

command to the command line and then press **Enter**. Repeat this step for about 1 minute or 10 times to generate performance events.

10. Return to MSN-SRV-0XX. View the Performance Monitor graph. Small peaks appear at the bottom of the Performance Monitor graph for DHCPRequests DHCP Server: Packets Received/sec from MSN-SC-0XX.

11. Close the Performance Monitor window.

DHCP Console Statistics   Within the DHCP console, you can view two types of statistics: server and scope. Server statistics are broader and provide a more comprehensive picture of the status of your DHCP server, as shown in Figure 4-18. To open this window, click IPv4 or IPv6 in the DHCP console, click Action on the menu bar, and then click Display Statistics.

Scope statistics display information about each scope, including total addresses, number and percentage in use, and number and percentage available in the address pool. You can view the scope statistics by selecting a scope name in the DHCP console, clicking Action on the menu bar, and then clicking Display Statistics.

Activity 4-12: Viewing Statistics

Time Required: 5 minutes

Objective: View server and scope statistics.

Description: From time to time, you should check a server to determine if it has enough addresses available for clients or to see the amount of activity on the server based on DHCP messages being sent and received. In this activity, you work with the statistics monitors built into the DHCP console.

1. In the left pane of Server Manager, expand the **Roles** section and the **DHCP Server** role and then click **MSN-SRV-0XX**. The DHCP Server administration console opens.

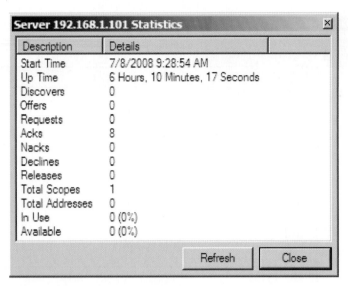

Figure 4-18   DHCP server statistics

2. Click **IPv4**, click **More Actions**, and then click **Display Statistics**. The Statistics window for the DHCP server opens.

3. Click **Close** to close the window.

4. Expand **IPv4** and then click **Scope [192.168.100.0] Partner Scope**.

5. Click **More Actions** and then click **Display Statistics**. The Statistics window for the Partner Scope opens.

6. Click **Close** to close the window.

DHCP Audit Log   DHCP maintains a detailed record of the transactions it performs through the DHCP audit log. Enabled by default in Windows Server 2008, DHCP audit logs are created only on a daily basis. The last seven audit logs are saved in the %systemroot%\system32\dhcp directory for default installations of DHCP. You can change the default path using the DHCP console.

Each audit log follows the naming convention of DhcpSrvLog-XXX for IPv4 and DhcpV6SrvLog-XXX for IPv6 where XXX represents the day of the week when the log is created. For example, the logs for Tuesday are stored in DhcpSrvLog-Tue.txt and DhcpV6SrvLog-Tue.txt, as shown in Figure 4-19.

Because they are text documents, you can open DHCP audit logs in Notepad. The audit log lists detailed information about events occurring on a specific day, including the following:

- Event ID
- Date and time
- Event description
- IP address
- Host name
- MAC address

You can use the Event ID to determine what type of event occurred. Examples of Event IDs include the following:

- *10*—A new IP address was leased to a DHCP client.
- *11*—A lease was renewed by a DHCP client.
- *12*—A lease was released by a DHCP client.

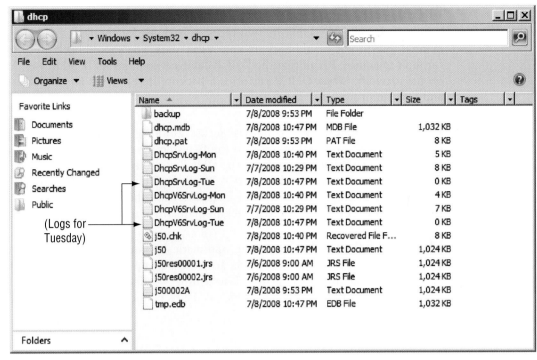

Figure 4-19 DHCP audit logs

All the Event IDs used in the audit log can viewed at the beginning of each audit log file.

NOTE

Reviewing the audit logs can help you determine whether messages from a specific DHCP client are being received. It is also a good security measure to check these logs regularly. Other network security measures for Windows Server 2008 are discussed in Chapter 10.

Activity 4-13: Viewing Audit Logs

Time Required: 10 minutes

Objective: View audit logs.

Description: DHCP produces daily audit logs of the events and transactions on the server. In this activity, you view the IPv4 and IPv6 logs.

1. On MSN-SRV-0XX, click **Start**, type **c:\windows\system32\dhcp** in the Start Search box, and then press **Enter**. The dhcp folder opens in Windows Explorer.

2. Double-click a text document whose name starts with DhcpSrvLog- to open the document in Notepad.

3. Review the events in the audit file. Note that all of the Event IDs are displayed at the top of the window.

4. Close Notepad.

5. Double-click a text document whose name starts with DhcpV6SrvLog- to open the document in Notepad.

6. Review the events in the audit file.

7. Close Notepad.

8. Close the dhcp folder.

Backup and Recovery

Windows Server 2008 supports two types of backups for the DHCP database: automatic and manual. Just as you would back up your users' data, you should back up your DHCP database for fault tolerance. Recall that the DHCP database contains all IP addresses, leased or reserved, on the network. When DHCP performs a backup, it also saves DHCP leases, options, scopes, and reservations.

Automatic Backup

Windows Server 2008 performs an automated backup of the DHCP database every 60 minutes to the %systemroot%\ dhcp\backup directory by default. You can change this location using the DHCP console to open the Properties dialog box for the DHCP server, as shown in Figure 4-20. If the DHCP database is unavailable or does not load, DHCP attempts to recover the database from the latest backup file. In the case of full system failure, you must create a backup manually and then restore from that backup.

Manual Backup

In addition to automatic backups, you can perform manual backups. This is a good idea, as it allows you to store backup files offline. Like automatic backups, manual backups are stored in the %systemroot%\ dhcp\backup folder by default. You can change this to a different location, which is the recommended best practice for manual backups of DHCP databases.

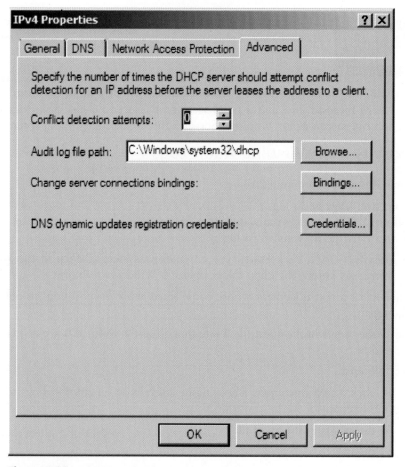

Figure 4-20   DHCP Server Properties dialog box

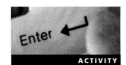

Activity 4-14: Performing a Manual Backup

Time Required: 10 minutes

Objective: Back up the DHCP database.

Description: You want to create a backup of the DHCP database so that you can store the current configuration offline. In this activity, you create a manual DHCP database backup and store it in a location other than the default folder.

1. In the left pane of Server Manager, expand the **Roles** section and the **DHCP Server** role and then click **MSN-SRV-0XX**. The DHCP Server administration console opens.

2. Click **More Actions** and then click **Backup**. The Browse For Folder dialog box opens to the default backup location.

3. Browse to **c:\70642\Ch4** and then click **Make New Folder** to create a folder named **ManualBackup**. (This folder should have been created when the files were prepared for this book.)

4. Click **OK** to back up the DHCP database.

5. Click **Start**, type **c:\70642\Ch4\ManualBackup** in the Start Search box, and then press **Enter**. The ManualBackup folder opens in Windows Explorer.

6. The ManualBackup folder contains a file named DhcpCfg and a folder named new. These are the files necessary to restore a DHCP database from an offline backup.

7. Double-click the **new** folder to view the DHCP database files.

8. Close the folder window. Leave the DHCP Server administration console open for the next activity.

After performing a manual backup of the DHCP database, you should create an offline backup for safekeeping. Windows Server 2008 backup technologies and disaster recovery practices are discussed in Chapter 11.

Restoring the DHCP Database from a Backup   Servers fail. It is a fact of life on a network. Having a backup is worthwhile only if you can restore it. You can restore a DHCP database from an offline backup when you are building a new DHCP server or replacing the data in your current DHCP database. In Activity 4-15, you restore the DHCP database backup you just performed.

Activity 4-15: Restoring a DHCP Database

Time Required: 10 minutes

Objective: Restoring the DHCP database.

Description: Now that you've created a backup of the DHCP database and stored it offline, you can restore the data to become familiar with the process. In this activity, you restore a manual DHCP database backup.

1. In the DHCP Server administration console, click **More Actions** and then click **Restore**. The Browse For Folder dialog box opens to the default backup location.

2. Browse to the **c:\70642\Ch4\ManualBackup** folder.

3. Click **OK** to restore the files.

4. When the message box shown in Figure 4-21 appears, click **Yes** to stop the services while the database is being restored and then restart them at completion.

5. Wait about 30 seconds and then press **F5** to refresh the DHCP console.

6. Verify that your scopes are still present and that your DHCP server is available by browsing the DHCP console.

7. Leave the DHCP Server administration console open for the next activity.

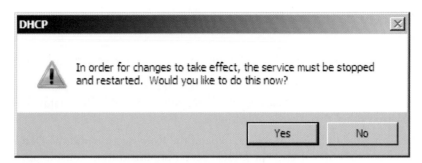

Figure 4-21   DHCP Server services informational message

DHCP Relay Agent   In most environments, you don't need to configure a DHCP relay agent because most modern routers support passing DHCP requests. If you are working in an environment that requires a DHCP relay agent, you should know how to configure Windows Server 2008 as a DHCP relay agent.

Because you need to use the Routing and Remote Access tool to configure Windows Server 2008 as a DHCP relay agent, you perform this task in Chapter 9.

Troubleshooting DHCP

Along with monitoring and recovery tools, you need to be familiar with resources for troubleshooting typical problems. This section covers some of the tools used to troubleshoot DHCP.

Reconciling the Database

One maintenance and troubleshooting task you should perform regularly is reconciling the DHCP database. Reconciling validates the DHCP database by comparing it with the Registry values of the operating system to verify that the database contains the most current data. The DHCP database stores detailed information, and the Registry contains summary information of IP address lease information. If the values in the DHCP database do not appear to be correct (the dates or IP addresses are incorrect, for example), you need to reconcile the database. You can perform this task on all the scopes on a DHCP server or only on individual scopes. You can reconcile the DHCP database in one of the following ways:

- To reconcile all the scopes, select IPv4 in the DHCP console, click Action on the menu bar, and then click Reconcile All Scopes.
- To reconcile an individual scope, select the scope that needs reconciliation, click Action on the menu bar, and then click Reconcile.

Activity 4-16: Reconciling the DHCP Database

Time Required: 10 minutes

Objective: Reconcile individual and all scopes in the DHCP console.

Description: You had a power outage last evening, and your DHCP server was powered off when you arrived this morning. You have since powered it back on. While doing a general review of your DHCP server, you notice that some of the values listed do not appear correct, so you decide to reconcile the database with the Registry on your DHCP server. In this activity, you reconcile the IPv4 scope you created in an earlier activity and then reconcile all the scopes on a DHCP server.

1. In the DHCP Server administration console, expand **IPv4** and then click **Scope [192.168.100.0] Partner Scope.**

2. In the Actions pane, click **More Actions** and then click **Reconcile.** The Reconcile dialog box opens.

3. Click **Verify.** A message indicates that the database is consistent. Click **OK** to close the informational message box.

4. Click **Cancel** to close the Reconcile dialog box.

5. Click **IPv4**.

6. In the Actions pane, click **More Actions** and then click **Reconcile All Scopes**. The Reconcile All Scopes dialog box opens.

7. Click **Verify**. A message indicates that the database is consistent. Click **OK** to close the informational message box.

8. Click **Cancel** to close the Reconcile All Scopes dialog box.

9. Verify that your scopes are still present and that your DHCP server is available by browsing the DHCP console.

10. Log off MSN-SRV-0XX.

Verifying DHCP Services

As with many Windows roles, running services are crucial for DHCP to work correctly. Some of the first areas to check when your network experiences DHCP problems are the DHCP service lists on the client and the server. Although you can manage these services in the Server Manager console, you can easily determine the running services on a system by entering the net start command at a command prompt. This displays the services currently running. Use the net stop command to stop a running service, as in the following examples:

```
net stop "DHCP Server" or "DHCP Client"
net start "DHCP Server" or "DHCP Client"
```

Troubleshooting DHCP Clients: IPconfig

Using the ipconfig command-line utility is one of the best options for troubleshooting DHCP clients. You can use ipconfig to renew the current IP address and configuration information and to release the current IP address.

Entering the ipconfig /release command issues the DHCPRelease message to the server currently holding the IP address lease for a client, as shown in Figure 4-22. This clears all DHCP information on the client.

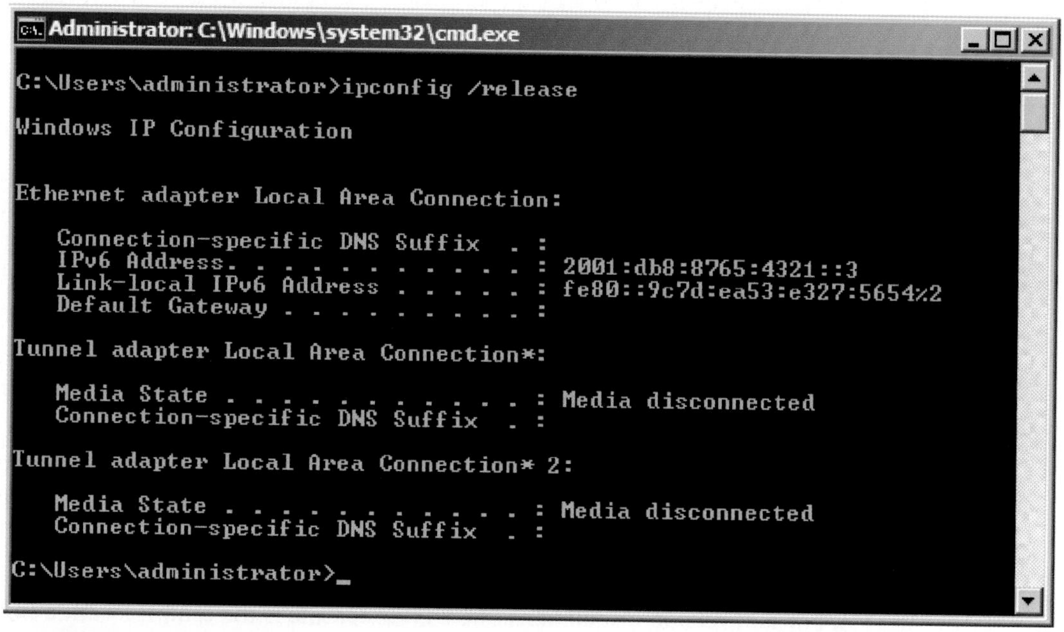

```
Administrator: C:\Windows\system32\cmd.exe

C:\Users\administrator>ipconfig /release

Windows IP Configuration


Ethernet adapter Local Area Connection:

   Connection-specific DNS Suffix  . :
   IPv6 Address. . . . . . . . . . . : 2001:db8:8765:4321::3
   Link-local IPv6 Address . . . . . : fe80::9c7d:ea53:e327:5654%2
   Default Gateway . . . . . . . . . :

Tunnel adapter Local Area Connection*:

   Media State . . . . . . . . . . . : Media disconnected
   Connection-specific DNS Suffix  . :

Tunnel adapter Local Area Connection* 2:

   Media State . . . . . . . . . . . : Media disconnected
   Connection-specific DNS Suffix  . :

C:\Users\administrator>_
```

Figure 4-22   Ipconfig /release

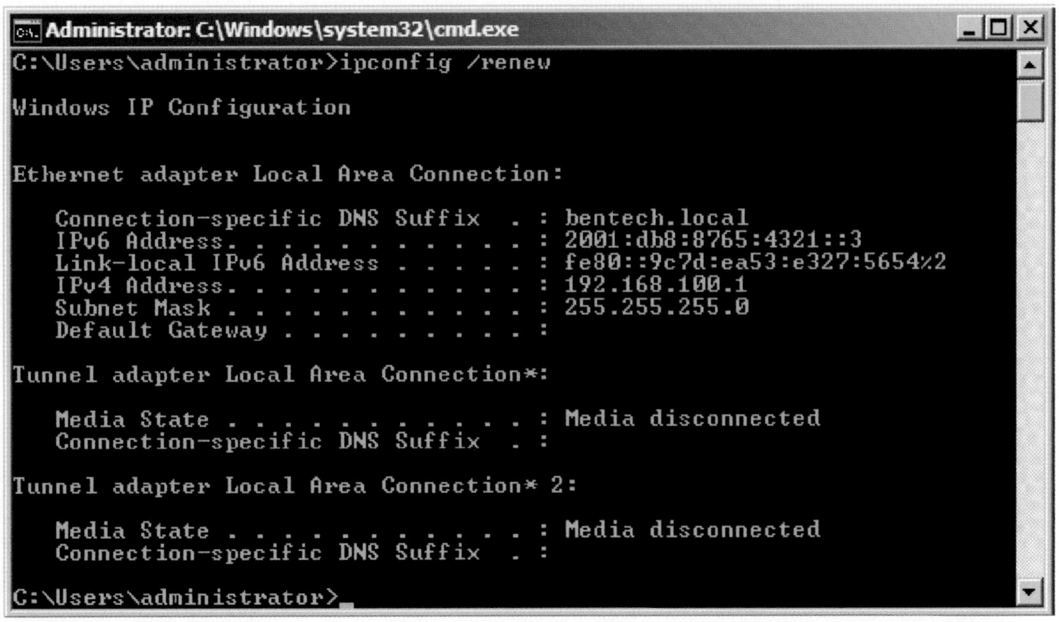

```
Administrator: C:\Windows\system32\cmd.exe                              _ □ X
C:\Users\administrator>ipconfig /renew

Windows IP Configuration


Ethernet adapter Local Area Connection:

   Connection-specific DNS Suffix  . : bentech.local
   IPv6 Address. . . . . . . . . . . : 2001:db8:8765:4321::3
   Link-local IPv6 Address . . . . . : fe80::9c7d:ea53:e327:5654%2
   IPv4 Address. . . . . . . . . . . : 192.168.100.1
   Subnet Mask . . . . . . . . . . . : 255.255.255.0
   Default Gateway . . . . . . . . . :

Tunnel adapter Local Area Connection*:

   Media State . . . . . . . . . . . : Media disconnected
   Connection-specific DNS Suffix  . :

Tunnel adapter Local Area Connection* 2:

   Media State . . . . . . . . . . . : Media disconnected
   Connection-specific DNS Suffix  . :

C:\Users\administrator>
```

Figure 4-23 Ipconfig /renew

At the command prompt of a client, entering the ipconfig /renew command initiates the DHCP renewal process discussed earlier. Any changes to DHCP options are relayed to the client. Figure 4-23 shows ipconfig /renew being run from the command prompt and its results.

If you receive a 169.254 address, or APIPA, you cannot contact a DHCP server. This is a red flag indicating network trouble or a problem on the DHCP server. When you see an APIPA address, you should first look at DHCP.

Troubleshooting the version of IP that your network uses determines how much or how little you use DHCP within your environment. Both IPv4 and IPv6 receive benefits from the use of a properly configured DHCP server.

Chapter Summary

- DHCP is an industry-standard protocol for automatically allocating IP addresses and configuration information. Windows Server 2008 supports DHCP and can be installed with the DHCP server role.

- The information provided by a DHCP server includes leases, scopes, and options.

- For DHCP to function properly in a routed network, a DHCP relay agent or an RFC 1542–compliant router needs to be in place to pass along DHCP messages. Most modern routers can perform this task. Otherwise, a DHCP relay can be installed using the Routing and Remote Access tool in Windows Server 2008.

- DHCP uses a standard set of messages for communicating between DHCP clients and DHCP servers.

- Common communication processes include initial lease requests, lease renewals, and changing subnet renewals.

- You can install DHCP in Server Manager on Full versions of Windows Server 2008. You can also install it using command-line utilities in Full and Server Core versions of Windows Server 2008.

- All data in DHCP is stored in the DHCP database.

- For Full version installations, the DHCP console is the central location for managing DHCP. In Server Core and from the command line, netsh is the utility of choice.

- Only DHCP servers in an Active Directory domain need to be authorized.

- After DHCP is installed, you must configure scopes for DHCP clients to receive addresses. Scopes contain IP address pools and configuration information that DHCP clients can use to access the network.

- You can perform all configuration tasks using the DHCP console or netsh.

- DHCP uses exclusions to prevent making the IP addresses of statically assigned devices available in an IP scope range.

- You use DHCP options to provide configuration information such as routers and DNS servers to DHCP clients. You can configure options at the server and scope level.

- You monitor DHCP using Performance Monitor, DHCP statistics, and the DHCP audit log.

- DHCP allows for two types of backups: automatic and manual. Automatic backups are performed every 60 minutes. You should set up and use a manual backup routine for creating offline backups in case of server hardware failure or local backups not being available.

- Along with monitoring and maintenance utilities, DHCP has troubleshooting tools including reconciling the database, ipconfig, and DHCP services.

Key Terms

binding time value   Equal to 87.5 percent of the Dynamic Host Configuration Protocol (DHCP) lease duration, the binding time value is the number of seconds before a DHCP client attempts to renew its address lease with the DHCP server. If unsuccessful, it initiates a DHCPDiscover request to receive an IP address from any DHCP server on its network.

BOOTP   An industry-standard protocol used for dynamic Internet Protocol (IP) allocation for clients prior to the proliferation of DHCP.

BOOTP relay agent   Another name for a DHCP relay agent.

DHCP lease   A placeholder in the DHCP database for an IP address. When a lease is issued, the IP address is removed from the available pool of IP addresses.

DHCP option   A setting provided by a DHCP server to clients. Domain Name System (DNS) servers, router address, and domain name are some of the values for DHCP options.

DHCP relay agent   A Windows Server 2008 server or hardware device configured to pass DHCP/BOOTP requests between clients and DHCP servers.

DHCP reservation   A record on a DHCP server that provides a client with a static IP address based on the client's Media Access Control address.

DHCPAck   A response from the DHCP server that confirms a DHCP client's IP address and includes configuration information and the confirmed IP address.

DHCPDiscover   A broadcast message a client sends requesting an IP address from a DHCP server.

DHCPOffer   A response message from a server that provides a client with an offer of an IP address.

DHCPRequest   A broadcast message from a client that acknowledges the acceptance of an offered IP address from a specific DHCP server.

Dynamic DNS   A feature of DHCP and DNS where DHCP servers work with DNS servers to create, modify, and delete DNS name records for clients in its environment.

Dynamic Host Configuration Protocol (DHCP)   An industry-standard communications protocol that provides automatic IP addressing for Windows clients. Administrators use DHCP to ease the burden of maintaining IP addresses on small and large networks.

exclusion   An IP address or range of addresses that are reserved for routers, printers, or other network devices.

lease duration   The amount of time the client keeps an IP address before releasing it.

renewal time value   Equal to 50 percent of the DHCP lease duration, the renewal time value is the number of seconds before a DHCP client attempts to renew its lease with the DHCP server that issued its current IP address.

scope   A pool of IP addresses created on a DHCP server from which the server responds to requests for addresses.

scope option   A setting defined per scope that applies only to the scope to which it is added.

server option   A setting defined per server that applies to all scopes on a specific DHCP server.

Review Questions

1. Workgroup and domain installations of DHCP require the authorization of the DHCP server before IP addresses can be allocated. True or False?

2. As with the Active Directory database, the DHCP database is replicated among all DHCP servers in a domain. True or False?

3. What is the default location for DHCP backups?

   a. %systemroot%\windows\dhcp

   b. %systemroot%\system\dhcp\backup

   c. %systemroot%\system32\dhcp\backup

   d. %systemroot%\system32\dhcp\

4. What is the default directory for the DHCP database files?

   a. %systemroot%\windows\dhcp

   b. %systemroot%\system\dhcp\backup

   c. %systemroot%\system32\dhcp\backup

   d. %systemroot%\system32\dhcp\

5. What command-line utility can you use to configure DHCP options?

   a. Netsh

   b. Ipconfig

   c. DHCPconfig

   d. Oclist

6. Which of the following are required to propagate DHCP messages between routed subnets? (Choose all that apply.)

   a. DHCP-compliant switch

   b. DHCP relay agent

   c. RFC 1542–compliant router

   d. RFC 1512–compliant router

7. DHCP can be installed on Server Core using the following command: `servermanagercmd.exe - install DHCP`. True or False?

8. What is the default lease length used by a scope in Windows Server 2008? (Choose all that apply.)

   a. 6 days (wired)

   b. 1 day (wired)

   c. 1 day (wireless)

   d. 8 days (wired)

   e. 12 hours (wireless)

   f. 6 hours (wireless)

9. What are the benefits of using DHCP? (Choose all that apply.)

    a. Flexibility

    b. Centralized administration

    c. Multimaster replication

    d. Scalability

    e. Ease of use

10. Server options take precedence over scope options if they conflict. True or False?

11. Which of the following intervals do DHCP clients use to perform lease renewals? (Choose all that apply.)

    a. 50% of lease duration

    b. 75% of lease duration

    c. 87.5% of lease duration

    d. 65% of lease duration

12. Which of the following do DHCP servers use to determine if a DHCP client has an IP reservation?

    a. NIC number

    b. MAC address

    c. Default gateway

    d. IP address

13. Your company has introduced wireless connectivity for your network. Most of your users have wireless devices along with their desktop computers. Your help desk analysts report that they are responding to many calls from users receiving APIPA addresses—IP addresses starting with 169.254. DHCP was implemented using the default settings for Windows Server 2008. Also, wireless and wired clients use the same scopes. Which of the following actions will resolve your problem? (Choose all that apply.)

    a. Check DHCP scope statistics for scopes that have 0 available addresses.

    b. Check DHCP server statistics for scopes that have 0 available addresses.

    c. Decrease the lease duration to 1 day for wired clients.

    d. Increase the lease duration to 2 days for wireless clients.

14. Which type of options can be set in the DHCP console? (Choose all that apply.)

    a. Scope

    b. Domain

    c. Client

    d. Server

15. Which type of message tells a client that its lease renewal request has been refused?

    a. DHCPNack

    b. DHCPDecline

    c. DHCPRefuse

    d. DHCPReject

16. Which type of message is sent from a DHCP client to a DHCP server? (Choose all that apply.)

    a. DHCPAck

    b. DHCPRequest

    c. DHCPRelease

    d. DHCPDiscover

17. What types of messages are used during an initial lease request? (Choose all that apply.)

    a. DHCPAck

    b. DHCPNack

    c. DHCPRelease

    d. DHCPRequest

    e. DHCPDiscover

    f. DHCPOffer

    g. DHCPInform

18. What types of messages are used when a DHCP client moves to another subnet? (Choose all that apply.)

    a. DHCPAck

    b. DHCPNack

    c. DHCPRelease

    d. DHCPRequest

    e. DHCPDiscover

    f. DHCPOffer

    g. DHCPInform

19. What types of messages are used when a DHCP client renews its lease? (Choose all that apply.)

    a. DHCPAck

    b. DHCPNack

    c. DHCPRelease

    d. DHCPRequest

    e. DHCPDiscover

    f. DHCPOffer

    g. DHCPInform

20. You have just changed your DHCP options to include a new DNS server. Your clients have a lease duration of five days. If all of your clients can successfully renew their lease, what is the longest you have to wait for clients to have the new DHCP option?

    a. 60 hours

    b. 72 hours

    c. 105 hour

    d. 140 hours

21. What is the default location for DHCP audit logs?

    a. %systemroot%\windows\dhcp

    b. %systemroot%\system\dhcp\backup

    c. %systemroot%\system32\dhcp\backup

    d. %systemroot%\system32\dhcp\

22. How often do automatic backups of the DHCP database occur?

    a. Never

    b. Every 4 hours

    c. Every day

    d. Every 1 hour

23. For disaster recovery, manual DHCP backups should be stored _____.

24. After DHCP is installed, you must configure _____ for DHCP clients to receive addresses.

25. What is the syntax used to stop the DHCP Server service?

    a. ipconfig /stopdhcp

    b. net stop dhcpserver

    c. net stop dhcp

    d. netsh dhcpserver -stop

Case Projects

CASE PROJECTS

Case Project 4-1: Load Balancing a DHCP Server

You have two DHCP servers on your network, and you need to split the scopes to maintain fault tolerance. Given the following information and using Table 4-2, split the scopes using the 80/20 rule and the 50/50 rule:

- Scope 1 (Server1 is primary server): 192.168.175.0 /24

- Scope 2 (Server2 is primary server): 192.168.180.0 /24

Table 4-2   Case Project 4-1

IP Ranges	DHCPServer1 Enter Scope Ranges:	DHCPServer2 Enter Scope Ranges:
192.168.175.0 /24		
192.168.180.0 /24		

Case Project 4-2: Installing a DHCP Server on CS-SRV-001 Using Server Manager

For your project network, install DHCP on CS-SRV-001 using Server Manager.

Case Project 4-3: Creating a Batch File to Create a Scope

On CS-SRV-001, use netsh to write a batch file named scope.bat that performs the following configuration tasks:

- Create a scope for 192.168.150.0 /24 using all the addresses

- Use 192.168.150.1 as the subnet's gateway

- Add an exclusionary range of 192.168.150.1 to 192.168.150.50

- Add DNS server of 192.168.100.20

- Set the default lease duration to one day

- Activate Scope

Once the batch file is completed, run the batch file on CS-SRV-001 and verify that the scope is added correctly to the DHCP server.

chapter 5

Introduction to DNS in Windows Server 2008

After reading this chapter and completing the exercises, you will be able to:

- Discuss the basics of the Domain Name System (DNS) and its terminology

- Configure DNS clients

- Install a standard DNS server on Windows Server 2008

- Create standard DNS zones

The Domain Name System (DNS) is one of the most important protocols used in Windows and non-Windows environments. DNS provides name resolution for all Internet communications and many private networks, including all Windows Active Directory domains.

You should have a thorough understanding of DNS to successfully run a Windows Server 2008 network. Whether your network uses Active Directory or simply runs as a workgroup, all clients on your network use DNS in some way. Without DNS, it would be very difficult to visit your favorite Web site, shop online, or even receive e-mail from friends.

In the next two chapters, you will learn about DNS along with its relationship to Active Directory, including Active Directory Domain Services–integrated DNS and Dynamic DNS (DDNS). You will also cover **Windows Internet Name Service**, the precursor to DNS used in older Windows environments and by applications that don't support DNS.

In this chapter, you will learn about DNS and the concepts supporting it. You will review DNS terminology and examine the different implementations of DNS. You will also install DNS in Windows Server 2008 and create standard DNS zones.

Domain Name System

At its core, DNS provides **name resolution**. In other words, the primary function of DNS is to translate human-readable host names, such as microsoft.com, to network-required Internet Protocol (IP) addresses. This translation makes it possible for you to open Internet Explorer and browse the World Wide Web using Universal Resource Locators (URLs) such as *www.microsoft.com* or *www.google.com*. Without this translation, you would need to remember and use an address such as 207.246.19.190 every time you wanted to visit any Web site. DNS also assists the flow of e-mail by providing mail exchanger records that tell a Simple Mail Transfer Protocol (SMTP) server where to send an e-mail message.

DNS is supported on the Internet by thousands of distributed servers, or **DNS servers**, that maintain all the records necessary for name resolution. These servers use a client-server model of networking where the DNS server provides information to the DNS clients, or DNS resolvers, who request name resolution information. Many of these servers host zones that include records for specific domains or subdomains they are responsible for maintaining. The type of zones that a DNS server hosts determines the type of server it is. As you learn later in this chapter, DNS servers can host several types of zones.

Like most industry standards, DNS is defined by a Request for Comment (RFC). RFC 882 is the base RFC for DNS. For more information on DNS and the information contained in RFC 882, see *www.ietf.org/rfc*.

Activity 5-1: Resetting Network Adapters and Disabling DHCP

Time Required: 20 minutes

Objective: Reset the network adapters on lab servers.

Description: Before you perform the other activities in this chapter, you need to reset the IP addresses on your network adapters and deactivate any DHCP scopes that might be active on MSN-SRV-0XX. You complete these tasks in this activity.

This activity requires a computer with two network adapters. Your instructor may give you additional steps to perform depending on your lab environment. This activity is designed for running in virtual machine applications. However, this can be performed in a physical machine environment by dual or multi-booting your computer.

1. Log onto MSN-SRV-0XX, if necessary.

2. If Server Manager is not open, open Server Manager from the Start menu.

3. In Server Manager, click **Roles** in the left pane and then click **Remove Roles** in the right pane.

4. When the Before You Begin window appears, click **Next**, In the Remove Server Roles window, click **DHCP Server** to remove the checkmark and then click **Next**.

5. In the Confirm Removal Selections window, verify that DHCP Server is listed and then click **Remove**. The DHCP Server role is removed from Windows Server 2008.

6. In the Removal Results window, click **Close**. You need to restart your machine for the changes to finish the removal process.

7. When a Remove Roles Wizard dialog box appears, click **Yes** to restart your computer.

8. After your computer restarts and the Resume Configuration Wizard completes the removal of DHCP, click **Close** to exit the wizard.

9. Under Roles Summary in Server Manager, verify that DHCP is not listed.

10. Open a command prompt from the Start menu and then enter the following command to change the IP address and DNS information:

```
netsh int ip set address name = "Local Area Connection" static
192.168.100.10 255.255.255.0
netsh int ip set dns "Local Area Connection" static
192.168.100.10
```

11. Open a command prompt from the Start menu and then enter the following command to change the IP address and DNS information:

```
netsh int ip set address name="Local Area Connection" static
192.168.100.10 255.255.255.0
```

12. Log onto MSN-SC-0XX, your Server Core computer.

13. At the command prompt, enter the following command to change the Internet Protocol version 4 (IPv4) address:

```
netsh int ip set address name="Local Area Connection" static
192.168.100.20 255.255.255.0
```

14. Log off your Server Core computer by typing **logoff** at the command prompt and then pressing **Enter**.

DNS Terminology

DNS has been used for over 25 years and therefore has a set of well-established terms. You must have a good understanding of these terms and what they represent in relation to DNS. Some terms have multiple meanings depending on their context. This is especially true when you are discussing Active Directory and NT domains. For example, when Microsoft began developing network operating systems, they chose "domain" as the name for their administrative structure. As you know, DNS uses a different type of domain. The following terms are important to know before beginning a study of DNS:

- DNS namespace
- DNS domain
- Fully qualified domain name
- Hosts
- Host name
- DNS record
- DNS zone

DNS Namespace   The backbone of the DNS structure is the concept of **DNS namespace**. The DNS namespace is a top-down hierarchical structure based on domain names. As you move down the branches of the hierarchy, one or more nodes, or hosts, hold **resource records** that contain details about a specific portion of the domain name. Figure 5-1 depicts the hierarchical structure of part of the DNS namespace for the Internet.

The DNS namespace is organized into the following domains:

- *Root domain (.)*—Often represented by an implied decimal point, or dot, at the end of a domain name, the root domain is currently made up of 13 servers that provide referrals to all the top-level domains. Although all domain namespaces must start with a root domain, most software today assumes this is the case, which is why you do not have to enter the last dot when entering URLs.

- *Top-level domain (TLD)*—One in a group of centrally managed domains created to differentiate the types of Internet domains, these domains are managed by organizations called domain name registrars. Examples of top-level public Internet domains include .com, .net, and .gov. Nonstandard top-level domains can be used when creating a domain, but they are generally for internal use only because they are not accessible on the public Internet.

- *Second-level domain*—This level most often denotes the company or organization name associated with the domain. For example, in *www.bentech.net*, bentech is the second-level domain registered with a domain registrar in the .net top-level domain.

- *Subdomain*—This facilitates the distribution of DNS databases and records across thousands of servers.

Activity 5-2: Using Whois

Time Required: 5 minutes

Objective: Research domain names.

Description: As the systems administrator for your company, you want to make sure the bentech.net domain is registered correctly. In this activity, you research a registered domain using

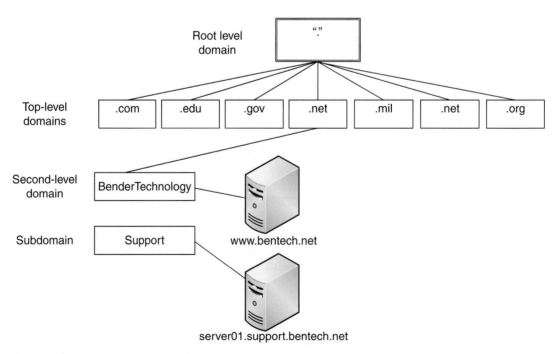

Figure 5-1   DNS namespace example

the whois utility. Whois provides information such as name servers and other details about registered domain names.

For this activity, your server needs to have access to the Internet and be able to resolve Internet-based DNS zones.

1. Log onto MSN-SRV-0XX.

2. In Server Manager, scroll down to Security Information and click **Configure IE ESC**, which allows you to enable or disable the Internet Explorer Enhanced Security Configuration, and then turn off **IE ESC**.

3. Start Internet Explorer as you usually do.

4. Browse to **http://www.internic.net/whois.html**. This Web page allows you to perform a DNS domain name registration of a domain.

5. Type **bentech.net** into the text box on the Whois page and then click **Submit**.

6. Review the records and record the names of the name servers in the following space:

_____

_____

7. Close Internet Explorer.

DNS Domains A **DNS domain** represents the portion of the namespace to the right of the host name. For example, server01.bentech.net is a fully qualified domain name for a host called Server01 in the bentech.net DNS domain. It is made up of two parts. The first part is the top-level domain, such as .com or .net. The next part is the second-level domain, such as bentech. Together, they represent bentech's public domain name—bentech.net—which can be used for connecting with public resources attached to the domain name. See Figure 5-2.

In Windows networking, a domain represents an administrative structure used to logically represent and manage a network of computing devices. It uses a similar hierarchical structure as DNS in organizing its resources. You learn more about Active Directory and its relationship with DNS in Chapter 6.

Fully Qualified Domain Names Server01.bentech.net, www.bentech.net, and remote. bentech.net are all **fully qualified domain names (FQDNs)**. An FQDN represents the entire name for a specific host, or the DNS name, that needs to have a DNS record created. Users can then use the FQDN to get the host's IP address. Each part of the domain name, referred to as a **label**, is separated by a decimal point (.). FQDNs are created by appending the host name label of a computer to the DNS domain name, sometimes referred to as the DNS suffix, that contains the computer. For example, suppose you have a server called webserver01 that needs to be available from the Internet so your users can access the corporate Web site. You have purchased the domain name mycorporation.net as your public domain name. When users need to access your Web server from the Internet, they type **webserver01.mycorporation.net** into their Web browser, and your Web site is then displayed to them.

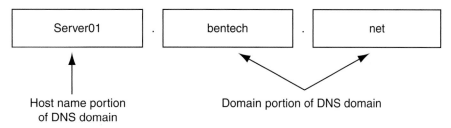

Figure 5-2   DNS domain example

The current DNS system does not support every character on a modern keyboard. DNS has a particular naming convention that must be followed. When creating a new public domain, you can use any of the following characters to create your name:

- Uppercase letters (A to Z)
- Lowercase letters (a to z)
- Numbers
- Hyphen (-)

In addition to these characters, Microsoft DNS reserves the underscore (_) for its Active Directory services. As mentioned previously, Active Directory and its relation to DNS are discussed later in Chapter 6.

Hosts   A computer on the Internet that provides a specific resource is called a **host**. This host is most often a Web server responsible for supplying Web-based information or applications. Hosts can also be network entry points for a company's network such as a firewall or a router. In DNS, hosts are identified by the creation of an A record.

Prior to the implementation of DNS, computers used a file called Hosts for name resolution. On Windows Server 2008, the Hosts file is located in the %systemroot%\System32\drivers\etc folder. Although rarely used, the Hosts file is a good option when nothing else works in resolving a host name to an IP address.

Activity 5-3: Configuring the Hosts File

Time Required: 10 minutes

Objective: Modifying the local Hosts file.

Description: Your company is deploying a new application that requires connecting to a server named host.bentobox.net. After installing the application, you cannot contact the application server. When you talk to the administrators at bentobox.net, you learn that they are experiencing DNS record issues for their domain. They instruct you to create a temporary host record that resolves host.bentobox.net to 192.168.201.102 on each client using the application. To provide a fix, you will use the local Hosts file to create host record until bentobox.net resolves its DNS record problems.

1. On the MSN-SRV-0XX computer, open a command prompt from the Start menu and then type **ipconfig /flushdns** and press **Enter** to clear the local DNS resolver cache.

2. Type **ipconfig /displaydns** and then press **Enter** to display the contents of the DNS resolver cache on the local system. You should not see any records relating to host.bentobox.net.

3. Click **Start** and then type **%systemroot%\System32\drivers\etc** in the Start Search box. Press **Enter**. The folder containing the Hosts file opens in Windows Explorer.

4. Right-click the **Hosts** file and then click **Open** on the shortcut menu. The Open with dialog box appears so you can choose an application for opening the Hosts file.

5. Click **Notepad** and then click **OK**. Notepad starts and opens the Hosts file.

6. Review the documentation contained in the Hosts file. Notice that it provides you with examples of how to format your entries.

7. Scroll to the first blank line in the Hosts file and then enter **192.168.201.102 host. bentobox.net**.

8. Save the Hosts file by pressing **Ctrl+S**, and then close Notepad.

9. Open a command prompt from the Start menu and then type **ipconfig /flushdns** and press **Enter** to clear the local DNS resolver cache.

10. Type **ipconfig /displaydns** and then press **Enter** to display the contents of the DNS resolver cache on the local system.

11. Verify that a Host record for **host.bentobox.net** is displayed in the cache. The Time to Live is listed as 86400, or 24 hours. This is the default setting for Hosts file entries. As you will learn later, most DNS servers have a default Time to Live of 1 hour.

12. Close the Command Prompt window.

Host Name   A **host name** is a name given to a computer, or host, to make connecting to it easier. Instead of typing a long IP address, you can enter the host name followed by the domain name, such as myhost name.no-ip.com. Host names are recorded in DNS through the creation of an A record that maps the host name to an IP address.

DNS Zones   A **DNS zone** consists of a collection of connected nodes served by an authoritative DNS name server. A zone can be a single domain namespace such as badgerironman.com, or it could be multiple domains in a contiguous namespace, as shown in Figure 5-3 with bentech.net and NA.bentech.net. In the last example, the bentech.net zone is authoritative for all the domain namespaces it contains. A contiguous namespace is a requirement for having multiple domains in one zone.

Although you might have multiple domains within a single zone, you often need to split a large zone into two administrative units. Delegation is the process by which part of a domain namespace is placed (or delegated) into its own DNS zone. The new zone has its own authoritative DNS server responsible for its records only. For example, when a large multidomain company splits up its namespace for easier management by administrators in a different location, it

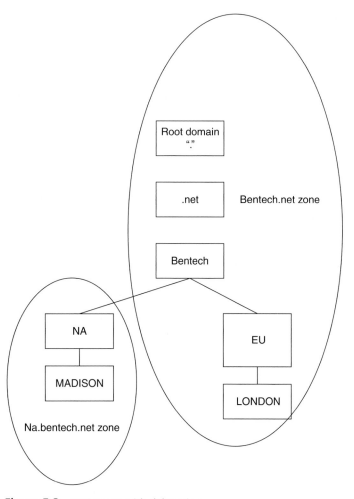

Figure 5-3   DNS zones with delegation

can use delegation. Large companies with separate IT staffs for different parts of the domain can use multiple zones as well. DNS zones are stored on DNS servers. That makes a DNS server authoritative for the zones it hosts. In Figure 5-3, the bentech.net namespace has been split into two zones: bentech.net and NA.bentech.net.

DNS Records   DNS uses records to provide the information it stores in its database. A and AAAA records are the main records stored in a DNS database. Additional records containing information about directory services and e-mail are also configured in DNS records. You learn about DNS records later in this chapter.

Activity 5-4: Resolving DNS Records with NSLookup

Time Required: 10 minutes

Objective: Query a DNS server with nslookup.

Description: You are still troubleshooting DNS on your network and want to query DNS servers to see what records they have for a domain and whether they can resolve your queries. In this activity, you will use nslookup to perform queries against DNS servers.

For this activity, your server needs to have access to the Internet. You will not have name resolution, but you need connectivity. Also, ensure that your preferred DNS server is listed as 127.0.0.1.

1. On the MSN-SRV-0XX computer, open a command prompt form the Start menu, type **ncpa.cpl** and then press **Enter** to open the Network Properties windows.

2. In the Network Properties window, right-click **Local Area Connection 2**, and then click **Properties.**

3. In the Local Area Connection 2 Properties dialog box, click **Internet Protocol Version 4 (TCP/IPv4)**, and then click **Properties.**

4. In the Internet Protocol Version 4 (TCP/IPv4) Properties dialog box, click **Use the following DNS Server addresses**, and then enter **192.168.100.10.**

5. Click **OK** to close the dialog box, and then click **Close** to close the Network Properties window.

6. At the command prompt, type **ipconfig /flushdns** and then press **Enter** to clear the local DNS resolver cache.

7. At the command prompt, type **nslookup cengage.com** and then press **Enter.** You should receive an error message because you do not have DNS name resolution from 192.168.100.10.

8. At the command prompt, type **nslookup cengage.com 4.2.2.1** and then press **Enter.** This forces nslookup to query the name server at 4.2.2.1 instead of your preferred DNS server. This time, you should receive a nonauthoritative answer for cengage.com of 69.32.133.79. If the IP address is different, it simply means that the record for cengage.com has been changed.

9. Close the Command Prompt window.

DNS Queries in Windows Server 2008

At the heart of the name resolution is the **DNS query process.** In order for DNS clients and DNS servers to interact, they need to be able to query for, or request, information from each other. Two types of queries are used in the DNS query process:

- Iterative queries
- Recursive queries

Iterative Queries   With an **iterative query**, a DNS client requests the best answer that its DNS server can provide. This means that if the DNS server has the answer cached, it provides the address. If the DNS server does not have the answer cached or is not authoritative for the zone, it provides the host client with a referral. The **referral** is an answer provided to the client of a different DNS server that can provide a better answer. When it receives a referral, the client contacts the referred DNS server for the same information.

Recursive Queries   **Recursive queries** are queries where the client requires an answer from its DNS server. In this case, it receives a positive or a negative answer. The client either receives the resolved address or is told that it cannot be resolved, and no answer is given to the client.

Most environments use a combination of iterative and recursive queries in the DNS process. Often, desktop clients and non-DNS servers perform recursive queries of their preferred or alternate DNS servers. The DNS servers then perform iterative queries to get the information they need to provide to the clients.

In Figure 5-4, Client1.widgets.local needs the IP address of www.bentech.net, which is hosted on web1.bentech.net.

The following events take place:

1. Client1.widgets.local contacts its preferred DNS server, NS1.widgets.local, with a recursive query for www.bentech.net. The server is required to return an answer or an error message if no answer is available.

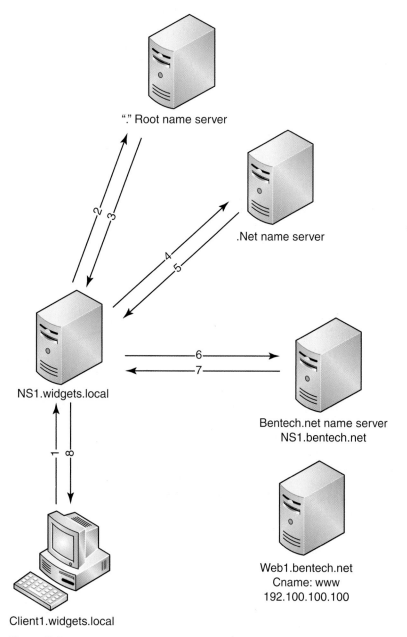

Figure 5-4 Iterative and recursive query process

2. NS1.widgets.local checks its cache and zones for the answer but does not find it. NameServer1 contacts an Internet root server—a server that is authoritative for the Internet—with an iterative query for www.bentech.net.

3. The Internet root server does not know the answer, so it responds with a referral to a server authoritative for the .net domain.

4. NS1.widgets.local contacts a server authoritative for the .net domain with an iterative query for www.bentech.net.

5. The .net domain server does not know the exact answer, so it responds with a referral to a server authoritative for the bentech.net domain.

6. NS1.widgets.local contacts the server authoritative for the bentech.net domain with an iterative query for web1.bentech.net.

7. Because the bentech.net domain server is authoritative for the zone, it responds with the requested IP address.

8. On receiving a final response for its query, NS1.widgets.local responds by sending the IP address for www.bentech.net to Client1.widgets.local.

NOTE   Although you should know the query types in this example, a properly configured DNS server performs both types of queries to acquire the information it needs for its clients. You learn about forwarders and root hints, two important tools for resolving nonauthoritative zone queries, later in this chapter.

Configuring DNS Clients

Now that you have learned the terminology, you are ready to explore DNS from the client side before proceeding to DNS servers. All clients, whether they are Windows Vista desktop or Windows Server 2008 domain controllers, act as **DNS clients**. DNS clients often are referred to as DNS resolvers. Any computer that requires host name–to–IP address resolution is a DNS client. Windows Server 2008 uses the **DNS Client service** to perform DNS queries on behalf of the client. In this section, you learn how to configure DNS clients and examine the important configuration settings on the client side.

DNS Client Settings

When configuring a DNS client, you can use the following settings, which provide the DNS client with access to DNS servers, and provide information used by the DNS client to properly perform DNS queries:

- DNS servers
- DNS suffix

DNS Servers   For a client to resolve DNS queries, it needs to know which server to contact. That's where the preferred and **alternate DNS servers** come in. Your Windows DNS client can be set to use one or more DNS servers for name resolution. The first DNS server in the list is called the **preferred DNS server**. It is the first DNS server your client attempts to query. If preferred DNS server does not respond, the DNS client refers to its list of alternate DNS servers one at a time. However, if the preferred DNS server responds without being able to resolve the name request, clients do not query the alternate DNS servers. They simply fail in their query. As shown in Figure 5-5, you can now enter only two DNS servers (one preferred and one alternate) on the General tab of a dialog box for network adapters IP properties.

Configuring the preferred DNS server using netsh is fairly straightforward. At the command prompt, enter the netsh command using the following syntax:

```
netsh int ip set dns adaptername static ipaddress
```

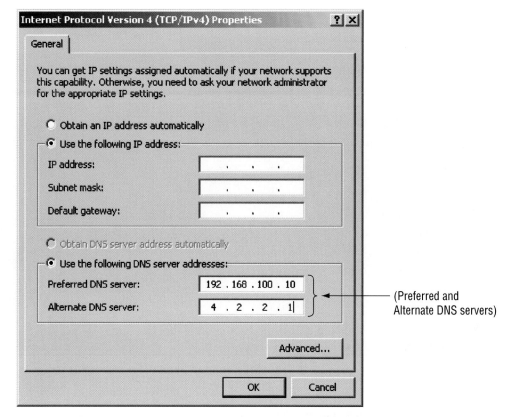

Figure 5-5 DNS servers in the Internet Protocol Version 4 (TCP/IPv4) Properties dialog box

As an example, suppose you want to set the preferred DNS server on the local area connection network adapter to 192.168.100.30. The syntax for that command is shown in Figure 5-6.

You can set additional DNS servers using the Advanced TCP/IP Settings dialog box, as shown in Figure 5-7, or by using netsh from the command line.

If you want to add other DNS servers, use the following netsh command:

```
netsh int ip add dns "adaptername" index=indexnumber ipaddress
```

For this command, the *indexnumber* is the number 2 or greater since any primary or initial DNS server you specify will be an index of 1.

If you want to add the DNS servers 192.168.100.40 and 192.168.100.50 (in this order) as alternate DNS servers, use the following commands:

```
netsh int ip add dns "local area connection" index=2
192.168.100.40
netsh int ip add dns "local area connection" index=3
192.168.100.50
```

Figure 5-8 shows each command being executed. Both servers have also been added in order as alternate DNS servers.

Activity 5-5: Adding an Alternate DNS server

Time Required: 10 minutes

Objective: Add an alternate DNS server.

Description: Your company is adding a DNS server to your environment for redundancy. In this activity, you add the IP address of a DNS server that will be deployed in the future.

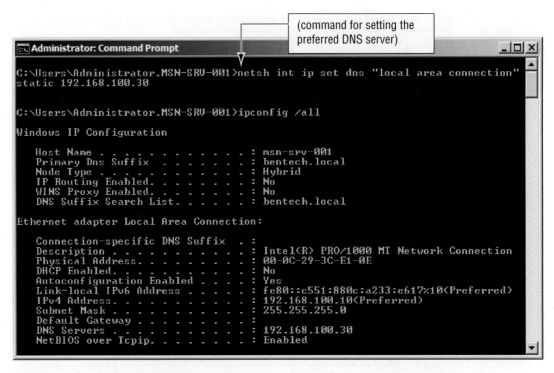

(command for setting the preferred DNS server)

Figure 5-6 Adding a DNS server with netsh

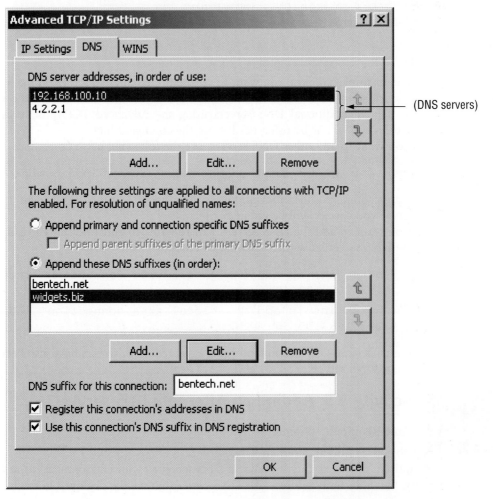

(DNS servers)

Figure 5-7 DNS servers listed in the Advanced TCP/IP Settings dialog box

```
Administrator: Command Prompt                                              _ □ X

C:\Users\Administrator.MSN-SRV-001>netsh int ip add dns "local area connection"
192.168.100.40 index=2

C:\Users\Administrator.MSN-SRV-001>netsh int ip add dns "local area connection"
192.168.100.50 index=3

C:\Users\Administrator.MSN-SRV-001>ipconfig /all

Windows IP Configuration

    Host Name . . . . . . . . . . . . : msn-srv-001
    Primary Dns Suffix  . . . . . . . : bentech.local
    Node Type . . . . . . . . . . . . : Hybrid
    IP Routing Enabled. . . . . . . . : No
    WINS Proxy Enabled. . . . . . . . : No
    DNS Suffix Search List. . . . . . : bentech.local

Ethernet adapter Local Area Connection:

    Connection-specific DNS Suffix  . :
    Description . . . . . . . . . . . : Intel(R) PRO/1000 MT Network Connection
    Physical Address. . . . . . . . . : 00-0C-29-3C-E1-0E
    DHCP Enabled. . . . . . . . . . . : No
    Autoconfiguration Enabled . . . . : Yes
    Link-local IPv6 Address . . . . . : fe80::c551:880c:a233:e617%10(Preferred)
    IPv4 Address. . . . . . . . . . . : 192.168.100.10(Preferred)
    Subnet Mask . . . . . . . . . . . : 255.255.255.0
    Default Gateway . . . . . . . . . :
    DNS Servers . . . . . . . . . . . : 192.168.100.30
                                        192.168.100.40
                                        192.168.100.50
    NetBIOS over Tcpip. . . . . . . . : Enabled
```

Figure 5-8   Adding alternate DNS servers with netsh

 For this activity, your server needs to have access to the Internet. You will not have name resolution, but you need connectivity.

NOTE

1. On the MSN-SRV-0XX computer, open a command prompt from the Start menu and then enter the following commands at the command prompt to add the alternate DNS server on local area connection and local area connection 2:

   ```
   netsh int ip add dns "local area connection" index=2
   192.168.100.20

   netsh int ip add dns "local area connection 2" index=2
   192.168.100.20
   ```

2. At the command prompt, type **ipconfig /all** and press **Enter**. Verify that the alternate DNS servers have been added to the adapters.

3. Close the Command Prompt window.

DNS Suffix   The **DNS suffix** is the DNS domain that is appended to all unqualified name queries, or a query that contains only a host name. For example, suppose you have a server called server02.bentech.local on your network. You could use a ping server02 command to perform name resolution by appending the domain suffix bentech.local. Why is this important? Especially in environments with multiple domains, adding domain suffixes can ease the burden of communicating with clients in other domains without fully qualifying the name. For example, suppose bentech.net purchases a company called widgets.biz. Both network structures are connected. However, you are going to maintain both domain names. So that clients in the bentech.net domain can more easily resolve widgets.biz hosts, you can add widgets.biz to the domain suffixes settings on your clients. Then your client can use widgets.biz as a DNS domain for your request when the request using bentech.net fails.

NOTE   DNS suffixes are very helpful for resolving FQDNs when only a host name is specified. However, if you perform an nslookup query, the Windows DNS client will append the current DNS suffix to the action. For example, if you had a DNS suffix setup for bentech.local and you performed nslookup server01.bentech.net, you will receive results for server01.bentech.net and server01.bentech.net.bentech.local. To prevent this, you should "dot terminate" your FQDNs, or add a dot to the end of the FQDN. For example, nslookup server01.bentech.net. is the dot-terminated version of the nslookup query. Dot termination is not necessary if you are resolving unqualified names for domains with DNS suffixes.

To change the DNS suffix, open the TCP/IP Properties dialog box, click Advanced to display the Advanced TCP/IP Settings dialog box, click the DNS tab in the Advanced TCP/IP Settings dialog box, and then click the appropriate Add button to open the DNS Suffix and NetBIOS Computer Name dialog box, shown in Figure 5-9.

Following are the options you can use to manage on the DNS tab of the Advanced TCP/IP Settings dialog box:

- *Append primary and connection specific DNS suffixes*—When this option is selected, all queries use the primary DNS suffix and the connection specific DNS suffix. You configure the primary DNS suffix by clicking Change on the Computer Name tab of the System Properties dialog box, and then click More on the Computer Name/Domain Changes dialog box.

- *Append these DNS suffixes (in order)*—When this option is selected, all queries use the DNS suffixes as listed. Remember that the suffixes are used in order and that you can change them using the up and down arrow buttons.

- *DNS suffix for this connection*—When this option is filled in, it is used in addition to the two previous options. This value can be assigned via DHCP, set manually on the local machine, or it can be defined via group policy. The local machine setting and group policy override any value delivered via DHCP.

- *Register this connection's addresses in DNS*—After checking this option, the computer attempts dynamic DNS registration with the full computer name and IP addresses. The full computer name is specified on the Computer Name tab of the System Properties dialog box.

DNS Suffix and NetBIOS Computer Name   ☒

Primary DNS suffix of this computer:

bentech.local

☑ Change primary DNS suffix when domain membership changes

NetBIOS computer name:

MSN-SRV-001

This name is used for interoperability with older computers and services.

OK   Cancel

Figure 5-9   DNS search suffixes

• *Use this connection's DNS suffix in DNS registration*—After checking this option, the computer uses DNS dynamic update to register the connection-specific domain name and the IP addresses. The connection-specific DNS name is created by appending the computer name and the DNS suffix for the connection. The computer name is the first portion of the full computer name specified on the computer name tab. When the Register this connection's addresses in DNS check box is selected as well, this registration is performed in addition to the registration of the full computer name.

Computer Name and other properties are managed through the System applet in Control Panel. An easier way to access the System applet is to type sysdm.cpl in the Start Search box on the Start menu.

Activity 5-6: Adding a Domain Suffix to IP Properties

Time Required: 10 minutes

Objective: Configure a client with an additional DNS suffix.

Description: You need to add a DNS suffix to your server so that you can resolve host names from widgets.biz without entering the domain information. In this activity, you will add widgets.biz to your DNS suffix search list.

1. On the MSN-SRV-0XX computer, open Server Manager, if necessary, by entering **servermanager.msc** in the Start menu search box.

2. In Server Manager, click **View Network Connections**.

3. Right-click **Local Area Connection 2** and then click **Properties**. The Local Area Connection 2 Properties dialog box opens.

4. Click the **Networking** tab if necessary, click **Internet Protocol Version 4 (TCP/IPv4)**, and then click **Properties**. The Internet Protocol Version 4 (TCP/IPv4) Properties dialog box opens.

5. Click **Advanced**.

6. In the Advanced TCP/IP Settings dialog box, click the **DNS** tab and then enter **widgets.biz** in the DNS suffix for this connection: text box.

7. Click **OK** to close this dialog box. Click **OK** to close the Internet Protocol Version 4 (TCP/IPv4) Properties dialog box and then click **Close** to close the Local Area Connection 2 Properties dialog box.

8. Open a command prompt, type **ipconfig /all**, and then press **Enter**. Verify that widgets.biz is listed under DNS Suffix Search List.

9. Close the Command Prompt window.

Activity 5-7: Creating a Full Computer Name

Time Required: 10 minutes

Objective: Change the computer name.

Description: In this activity, you add a DNS suffix using the DNS Suffix and NetBIOS Computer Name dialog box so that your server will use the suffix when performing unqualified name resolution requests.

1. In Server Manager on the MSN-SRV-0XX computer, click **Change System Properties**.

2. In the System Properties window, click **Change** on the Computer Name tab.

3. On the Computer Name/Domain Changes tab, click **More**.

4. On the DNS Suffix and NetBIOS Computer Name tab, enter **bentech.local** in the Primary DNS suffix of this computer: text box and then click **OK**.

5. In the Computer Name/Domain Changes dialog box, verify that the Full computer name is listed as msn-srv-0xx.bentech.local and then click **OK** to accept the changes. Click **OK** and then click **Close**. You are prompted to restart.

6. Click **Restart Now**.

7. When the server reboots, log onto MSN-SRV-0XX.

8. Open a command prompt from the Start menu, type **ping msn-srv-0XX**, and then press **Enter**. Notice that the ping command uses msn-srv-0xx.bentech.local to resolve the IP address for the command.

9. Close the Command Prompt window.

For Server Core versions of Windows Server 2008, changing the DNS suffix is more complicated. Unlike the other properties for a network adapter, Server Core does not support changing the DNS suffix with netsh. You have two options. If your Server Core installation is a member of a domain, you can use Group Policy to apply the DNS suffix. The next option is to edit the Registry using regedit.exe, another GUI tool that is available in Server Core. You need to change the following key:

```
Hkey_Local_Machine\SYSTEM\CurrentControlSet\Services\Tcpip\
Parameters\Domain
```

The parameter you specify in regedit is the domain suffix. For example, to add the bentech.local DNS suffix to a Server Core machine, you specify bentech.local as the value for the Domain Registry key, as shown in Figure 5-10.

 Because changing the Registry causes immediate changes, it can be hazardous to your computer configuration. Prior to making any changes to the Registry, verify that you have a good system backup and create a backup of any Registry keys you are deleting or changing. For more information on the Registry, search for Knowledge Base article 256986 at *http://support.microsoft.com*.

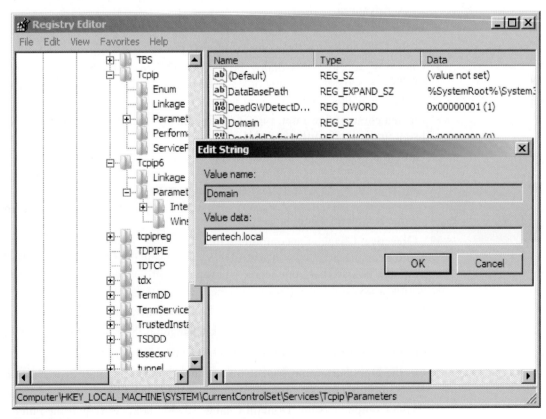

Figure 5-10   Adding a DNS suffix through the Registry

Dynamic Updates

Windows clients that support Dynamic updates will automatically create host and reverse-lookup records for themselves on DNS servers supporting Dynamic updates. Windows Server 2008 supports dynamic updates with both standard and Active Directory Domain Services–integrated domains. Dynamic updates are sometimes referred to as DDNS. Dynamic updates and DDNS will be discussed in more depth in Chapter 6 when you learn about Active Directory Domain Services and Windows Server 2008 DNS.

Installing DNS in Windows Server 2008

DNS is a role that can be installed on Windows Server 2008 Full and Server Core versions. Often, DNS is combined with other services such as DHCP, or, in the case of **Active Directory–integrated DNS**, it is combined with a domain controller. In this section, you learn to install the DNS Server role and build standard DNS servers. In Chapter 6, you learn about Active Directory along with the installation and configuration of Active Directory–integrated DNS. Chapter 6 also covers advanced configuration settings for DNS on Windows Server 2008.

Installing Cache-only DNS servers

A **cache-only DNS server** is a server that has the DNS role installed. However, it does not hold a DNS zone so it is not authoritative for any DNS zones, nor does it maintain any DNS records. It simply acts as an intermediary for DNS clients in resolving DNS queries. Using the caching functionality of DNS, a cache-only server provides clients with query answers and stores the answers in case other clients request the same information. Cache-only DNS servers are a good option for workgroup environments that want to centralize DNS requests through a single server. This optimizes the usage of an organization's wide area network (WAN) connection.

In the following activity, you install the DNS role and set up your server as a cache-only DNS server for your current workgroup.

Activity 5-8: Installing DNS on MSN-SRV-0XX

Time Required: 10 minutes

Objective: Install the DNS Server role.

Description: You need to install the first DNS server in your environment. In this activity, you add the DNS Server role to MSN-SRV-0XX through Server Manager.

1. In Server Manager on the MSN-SRV-0XX computer, click **Roles** in the left pane and then click **Add Roles** in the right pane. When the Before you Begin window appears, click **Next**.

2. In the Select Server Roles window, click the **DNS Server** check box and then click **Next**.

3. Review the information in the Introduction to DNS Server window and then click **Next**.

4. In the Confirm Installation Selections window, verify Domain Name Server is listed and then click **Install** to start the DNS installation.

5. In the Installation Results window, verify DNS has been installed successfully and then click **Close** to exit the Add Roles Wizard.

6. Under Roles Summary in Server Manager, verify that DNS Server is listed.

7. Click **DNS Server** to open the DNS Summary pane.

8. At the command prompt, type **nslookup bentech.net** and then press **Enter**. You should receive a nonauthoritative response because your server is now acting as a cache-only DNS server and queries external servers for your DNS client.

9. Close the Command Prompt window.

Besides the GUI, you can use the command-line interface to install the DNS role. For Full versions of Windows Server 2008, you can use the servermanagercmd.exe command to install the DNS role. The syntax for this command is the following:

```
servermanagercmd.exe -install DNS
```

For Server Core, you use the ocsetup command to install the DNS role. As you learned in previous chapters, ocsetup is a command-line tool for installing roles on Windows Server 2008 running Server Core. You install the DNS role on a Server Core installation in a later activity in this chapter.

When DNS is installed on Full versions of Windows Server 2008, the DNS console is available through Server Manager and as a standalone in the Microsoft Management Console. The DNS console allows you to create DNS zones and manage the DNS server settings, as shown in Figure 5-11.

For configuring DNS from the command line in both versions of Windows Server 2008, you can use the dnscmd utility. Dnscmd allows you to manage all the DNS server configuration and management settings from the command prompt or a script. This is perfect for Server Core installations. You can configure DNS using netsh, which is available on the Full version of Windows Server 2008 as well. You use dnscmd along with the DNS console throughout the activities in this chapter and future chapters.

When the DNS role is installed on an Internet-connected server, it configures the IP addresses for referral servers for the root domain. These servers are known as **root hints**. Root hints provide IP address pointers to top-level DNS servers and are kept current on the computer via Microsoft Update. With root hints configured, a DNS server can perform queries when it receives domain name requests for zones in which it is not authoritative. Root hints provide referral answers to queries in a DNS server's quest to resolve an unknown domain name request. Figure 5-12 shows the Root Hints tab in the Properties dialog box for a DNS server and the IP addresses of the root domain servers.

Because the purpose of the root hints servers is to resolve the common top-level domains such as .net, .com, and .gov, access to the Internet is required when you use root hints. The root hints installed on a Windows Server 2008 DNS server is based on a list of common root domain

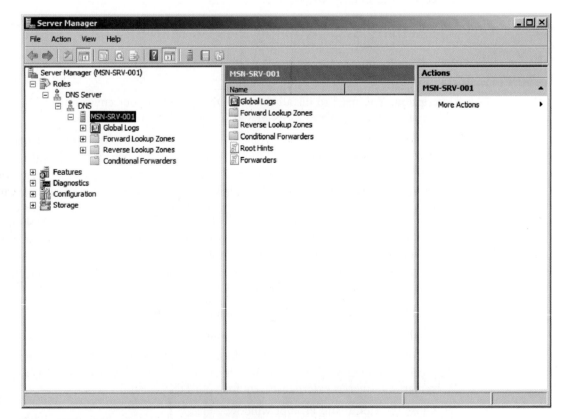

Figure 5-11   DNS console

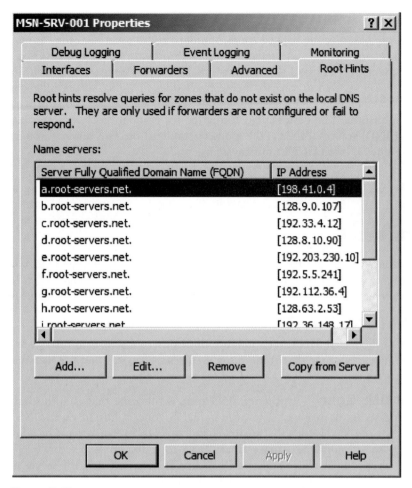

Figure 5-12   Root domain servers on the Root Hints tab of the server's Properties dialog box

DNS servers. This list is defined in a file called cache.dns, which is located by default in the %systemroot%\windows32\dns\samples folder when the DNS role is installed.

Another option for querying is to use **forwarders**. Forwarders are servers used to resolve names. They have the addresses of one or more DNS servers that a DNS server queries when it receives domain name requests for zones in which it is not authoritative. Other servers can be configured to use forwarders to increase security or efficiency when resolving names. For example, companies often set up forwarders to the DNS servers of their Internet service providers (ISPs). Contrast this with root hints, which provide a referral so a DNS server can perform the iterative query process. The DNS server requests that the forwarder provide recursion, or the best answer for its request. This allows you to offload a large amount of DNS query tasks to a server designed specifically for the purpose of providing DNS information and shift the additional workload of iterative queries from your WAN connection, preserving valuable bandwidth.

Forwarders are defined per server and can be added through the DNS console. As with most DNS configurations, you can also use dnscmd to configure forwarders. You learn more about forwarders and using them in deploying DNS across a network in Chapter 6.

DNS Zones

Zones are the building blocks for creating your DNS infrastructure. DNS zones are classified in three ways: the information they store, where they are stored, and their read/write status. DNS zones fall into two categories: standard and Active Directory. The environment you are deploying to and the features you need from DNS determine which type of zone you will use. In this section, you will learn about standard DNS zones.

Standard Zones

Known as file-based or file-backed zones, standard zones use a file called zone.dns to store all of their DNS records where zone refers to the DNS domain being stored. On a Windows Server 2008 computer, you can find the zone.dns file in the %systemroot%\system32\DNS folder. For example, if you created a zone for bentech.net on your DNS server, all records for this zone would be stored in a file called bentech.net.dns. This is a text-based document that can be viewed in Notepad or other text editors. It is formatted for compatibility with **Berkeley Internet Name Domain (BIND) servers**. BIND is the industry standard of DNS servers on the Internet and networks running DNS on UNIX/Linux systems.

Active Directory supports the use of BIND for DNS in BIND versions 8.2.2 and later. This allows for the usage of SRV records and Dynamic updates. For more information on BIND, search for BIND at *www.isc.org*.

DNS zones can be created after the DNS role is installed using the DNS console or from the command line. In the next section, you learn about the type of standard DNS zones available on Windows Server 2008 DNS servers. You also use the different methods available for creating zones.

Standard DNS Zone Types

Standard, or file-based, DNS zones fall into three different scopes: primary, secondary, and stub. The scope of a DNS zone determines how it stores its records and provides name resolution to DNS client requests.

Primary DNS Zone   A **primary DNS zone** is the zone that is authoritative for a specific domain and its name records. The primary DNS zone is hosted on a DNS server hosting a writable copy of the zone.dns file, so any changes to DNS records must be completed at the primary zone. You can only have one primary DNS zone in a DNS structure even if you have multiple DNS servers. If there are multiple DNS servers on a network, the server holding a primary DNS zone acts as a master server for replicating changes via zone transfers.

Activity 5-9: Installing a Primary DNS Zone for bentech.local

Time Required: 10 minutes

Objective: Create a primary DNS zone.

Description: Now that DNS is installed, you need to configure a zone for bentech.local. In this activity, you create your first DNS zone on MSN-SRV-0XX through the DNS console.

1. Close Server Manager on the MSN-SRV-0XX computer, and then reopen it. If necessary, expand **Roles** and then expand the **DNS Server** role until the Forward Lookup Zones folder is available. See Figure 5-13.

2. Click **Forward Lookup Zones** in the left pane.

3. Click the **server name** under DNS to open the Actions pane. In the Actions pane, click **More Actions** and then click **New Zone** to start the New Zone Wizard. Click **Next**.

4. In the Zone Type dialog box, accept the default selection of a Primary zone by clicking **Next**. Note that the Active Directory–integrated option is not available, as the wizard will detect whether this action is being performed on a domain controller.

5. Accept the Forward lookup zone option by clicking **Next**.

6. In the Zone Name dialog box, type **bentech.local** and then click **Next**.

7. In the Zone File dialog box, accept the default zone file name by clicking **Next**. Notice you can add existing files in this dialog box.

8. In the Dynamic Update dialog box, choose **Allow both nonsecure and secure dynamic updates** and then click **Next**. This displays Dynamic Updates in action.

9. Click **Finish** in the final dialog box to create your new zone for bentech.local.

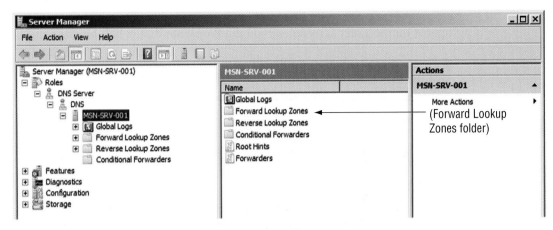

Figure 5-13 Forward Lookup Zones folder in DNS console

10. Minimize the Server Manager window and then open a command prompt. Type **ipconfig /registerdns** and press **Enter** to register the DNS record for MSN-SRV-0XX. This process may take a few minutes for the changes to be reflected in the DNS console.

11. In the command prompt, enter the following commands. You will need to wait for each to complete before entering the next.

    Net stop DNS
    Net start DNS

12. Return to Server Manager, and then expand the **bentech.local** folder within the Forward Lookup Zones folder in the DNS console to view the records in the zone.

13. At the command prompt, enter the following command to set the primary DNS zone, bentech.local, to accept zone transfer requests from any Name servers:

    dnscmd /zoneresetsecondaries bentech.local /nonsecure

14. Log onto MSN-SC-0XX. From the command prompt, type **regedit** and then press **Enter** to open the Registry Editor.

15. Expand the DNS tree by clicking the following key:

    Computer\HKey_Local_Machine\SYSTEM\CurrentControlSet\Services\Tcpip\Parameters

    Click **Domain** in the right pane. (Editing the Registry is currently the only way to manually update the DNS suffix on a Server Core machine.)

16. Click **Edit** on the menu bar, click **Modify**, and then enter **bentech.local** in the Value data text box.

17. Click **OK** and close Registry Editor.

18. At the command prompt, **ipconfig /registerdns**, and then press **Enter** to register the server's information with its preferred DNS server, 192.168.100.10

19. Log off server MSN-SC-0XX.

When the primary zone is installed on a DNS server, it is available for DNS clients to use for querying name information about the newly installed zone. When the zone is created, Start of Authority and name server records are added to the zone.

Secondary DNS zones   A **secondary DNS zone** is a read-only version of the DNS records for a zone. For improving performance, balancing load, and redundancy, you might need to deploy multiple DNS servers within your organization. Secondary zones allow you to do this. You can implement as many secondary DNS zone servers as you need to provide effective name resolution on your network. Servers holding a secondary zone point to a master server (either a primary or another secondary server) for requesting updates.

In order for a secondary DNS zone to become active, it must have access to the master records so it can perform zone transfers. By default, DNS servers in Windows Server 2008 allow zone transfers only to servers that are specified as name servers for the zones either by being listed on the zone's Name Servers tab or by having a name server record created for it. Along with the default setting, you can deny all zone transfers, allow zone transfers to all servers (not recommended), or specify IP addresses of servers needing zone transfers. These options are configured on the Zone Transfers tab on the Properties dialog box for the zone. See Figure 5-14.

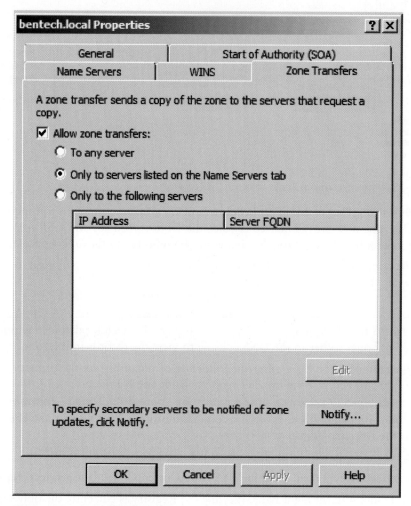

Figure 5-14   Zone Transfers tab

Activity 5-10: Installing a Secondary DNS Zone on MSN-SC-0XX

Time Required: 15 minutes

Objective: Install DNS on Server Core.

Description: Your company is adding a DNS server to your environment for redundancy. In this activity, you add the IP address of another DNS server that will be deployed in the future.

For this activity, your server needs to have access to the Internet. You will not have name resolution, but you need connectivity.

1. Log onto MSN-SC-0XX.

2. From the command prompt, type **start /w ocsetup DNS-Server-Core-Role** and then press **Enter**. This command is case sensitive, so if you do not type the command with the proper case, you receive an error message.

3. On MSN-SC-0XX, type **netsh int ip set dns "local area connection" static 192.168.100.20** at the command prompt and then press **Enter**. MSN-SC-0XX points to itself for DNS.

4. Type **dnscmd /zoneadd bentech.local /secondary 192.168.100.10** and then press **Enter** to add a secondary zone for bentech.local to MSN-SC-0XX. Figure 5-15 displays both the ocsetup and dnscmd commands.

5. Without logging off MSN-SC-0XX, log onto MSN-SRV-0XX.

6. If Server Manager is not open, open Server Manager from the Start menu.

7. In the left pane of Server Manager, expand **Roles** and then expand the **DNS** role until the bentech.local folder is displayed.

8. Click **bentech.local**, click **More Actions** in the Actions pane and then click **Properties** to open the bentech.local Properties dialog box.

9. Click the **Name Servers** tab, click **Add** and then type **msn-sc-0xx** in the "Server fully qualified domain name (FQDN)" text box.

10. Click **Resolve** to add msn-sc-0xx to the list of new name servers. Click **OK** to close the dialog box.

11. In the bentech.local Properties dialog box, click **Apply** to save the changes and then click **OK** to close the bentech.local Properties dialog box.

12. Switch to MSN-SC-0XX. At the command prompt, type **dnscmd /clearcache** and then press **Enter** to clear the DNS server cache on MSN-SC-0XX.

13. Type **dnscmd /zonerefresh bentech.local** and then press **Enter** to refresh the zone file on MSN-SC-0XX.

14. Type **dnscmd /enumzones** and then press **Enter** to list the DNS zones on MSN-SC-0XX.

15. Type **dnscmd /zoneprint bentech.local** and then press **Enter** to list all the zone records on MSN-SC-0XX.

16. Type **nslookup msn-srv-0xx** and then press **Enter** to verify you get a response back with an IP address of 192.168.100.10.

17. Log off MSN-SC-0XX.

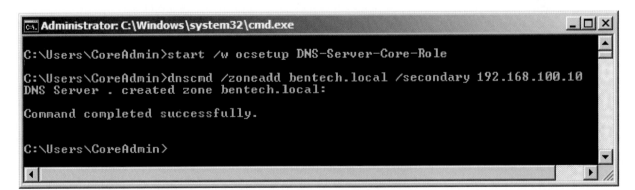

```
C:\Users\CoreAdmin>start /w ocsetup DNS-Server-Core-Role

C:\Users\CoreAdmin>dnscmd /zoneadd bentech.local /secondary 192.168.100.10
DNS Server . created zone bentech.local:

Command completed successfully.

C:\Users\CoreAdmin>
```

Figure 5-15   Installing a DNS role and creating a secondary zone for bentech.local

Stub Zones   A **stub zone** is a read-only copy of a zone that obtains its resource records from the name servers that are authoritative for a particular zone. Unlike a secondary zone, a stub zone contains only the following resource records for a zone:

- Start of Authority record for the zone

- Name server (NS) records for all name servers authoritative for the zone

- Host (A) records for all name servers authoritative for the zone

This reduces the size of the stub zone's database, which is the major advantage of using stub zones. Stub zones can help reduce the amount of DNS traffic on your network by streamlining name resolution and zone replication. Instead of a master server having to replicate all its records to a secondary server across a WAN link, you can set up a stub zone. When it needs to resolve DNS information from the zone represented by the stub zone, it queries the NS servers listed in its zone. Like all DNS servers, this information is cached for future queries.

For example, suppose you have two companies that you want to share DNS information between, bentech.net and widgets.biz. These companies are connected over a WAN connection, so you need to minimize the traffic that flows between the two servers. The administrator in bentech.net can create a stub zone that points to the name servers in widgets.biz. This allows DNS clients in bentech.local to easily resolve DNS names for widgets.biz without having to resort to iterative queries.

Another advantage to stub zones is that they can be integrated into Active Directory and be replicated as part of Active Directory replication. Standard secondary servers cannot. You learn more about creating stub zones in an Active Directory environment in Chapter 6.

Direction of DNS Zones

DNS zones can perform two types of name resolution in two directions: forward lookups and reverse lookups.

Forward Lookup Zones
Forward lookup DNS zones allow a DNS client to resolve an FQDN to an IP address. Forward lookups are the most commonly used DNS records on the Internet and within private networks using DNS for name resolution. Communicating on the Internet would be almost impossible without forward lookup zones.

How does a forward lookup zone work? First, you create a forward lookup zone to hold the records. Next, you create the records needed for resolution. Consider the example of bentech.net. To allow DNS clients to resolve resources for bentech.net, you need to create a zone and records for the domain.

Reverse Lookup Zones
A **reverse lookup DNS zone** performs the opposite action of a forward lookup zone. It maps IP addresses to host names. For example, a server might receive a malicious packet from an unidentified source. With a reverse lookup query, the server requests the host name of the sender based on the source IP address in the packet. Reverse lookup zones are less commonly used. Uses for reverse lookup zones include verification of an SMTP server's name.

Reverse lookup zones are contained within a special domain called the in-addr.arpa domain for IPv4 and ip6.arpa in Internet Protocol version 6 (IPv6). Subdomains in the in-addr.arpa zone are configured using the octets in the dotted quads of each network ID. Each octet is reversed in the naming of each zone.

Within the in-addr.arpa domain, zones are created that are represented by the network ID of a subnet range in reverse. For example, if you have a network ID of 192.168.100.0, the reverse lookup zone for this domain is 100.168.192.in-addr.arpa.

After a reverse lookup zone is created, **pointer records (PTRs)** are created to map IP addresses to the host name of a node. These records can be created manually through the DNS console or from the command line, or you can have the record created automatically when a forward lookup record, or an A record, is created. Unlike forward lookup zones, reverse lookup zones are not required for Active Directory functionality or even name resolution in workgroup environments. You need reverse lookups in cases where applications or nodes require the host name for known IP addresses.

Activity 5-11: Creating a Reverse Lookup Zone

Time Required: 15 minutes

Objective: Create a reverse lookup zone.

Description: You have just been informed that a third-party application installed on the network requires the ability to resolve IP addresses to host names, or reverse lookup name resolution. In this activity, you configure MSN-SRV-0XX with a reverse lookup zone for the 192.168.100.0 subnet.

1. Log onto MSN-SRV-0XX if necessary.

2. If Server Manager is not open, open Server Manager from the Start menu.

3. In the left pane of Server Manager, expand **Roles** and then expand the **DNS Server** role until the Reverse Lookup Zones folder is available. Click **Reverse Lookup Zones** in the left pane.

4. In the Actions pane, click **More Actions** and then click **New Zone** to start the New Zone Wizard. Click **Next**.

5. In the Zone Type dialog box, accept the default selection of a Primary zone by clicking **Next**. Note that the Active Directory–integrated option is not available because the wizard will detect whether this action is being performed on a domain controller.

6. In the Reverse Lookup Zone Name dialog box, accept the default of an IPv4 Reverse Lookup Zone by clicking **Next**.

7. In the next dialog box, enter **192.168.100** as the Network ID, as shown in Figure 5-16, and then click **Next**.

8. In the Zone File dialog box, accept the default zone file name by clicking **Next**. Notice you can add existing files in this dialog box as well.

9. In the Dynamic Update dialog box, choose **Allow both nonsecure and secure dynamic updates** and then click **Next**. This displays Dynamic Updates in action.

10. Click **Finish** in the final dialog box to create your new zone 100.168.192.in-addr.arpa.

11. Browse to the bentech.local forward lookup zone and then click the **A record** for MSN-SRV-0XX.

12. In the Actions pane, click **More Actions** and then click **Properties** under msn-srv-001. The Properties dialog box for the server opens.

13. In the Properties dialog box for your server, check the **Update associated pointer (PTR) record** box. This creates an associated PTR record in the newly created reverse lookup zone. Click **OK**.

14. Browse to the 100.168.192.in-addr.arpa zone folder and verify that a PTR record is created for 192.168.100.10 and points to MSN-SRV-0XX.

DNS Resource Records

As mentioned earlier, the DNS database uses DNS resource records to store information about hosts, host names, and other information that DNS provides to DNS clients. Besides A records, many other resource records are used on networks for providing information to its clients.

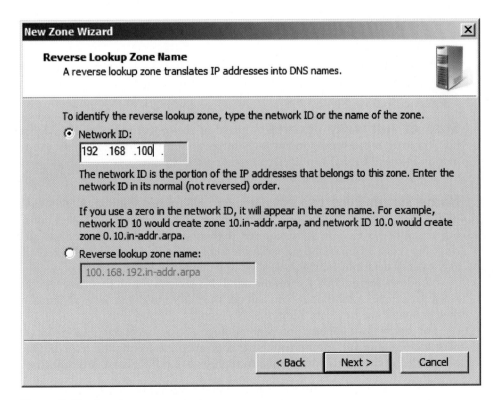

Figure 5-16 Creating a reverse lookup zone

DNS records are stored as text-based information in the database that contains them. Commonly, a DNS record contains the following pieces of information:

- *Owner*—This value defines the host or domain to which a resource record belongs.
- *Time-to-Live (TTL)*—This is the amount of time (in seconds) that a resource record is cached by a DNS client before it is discarded. If this value is not specified, the record uses the default TTL for the zone as specified in the Start of Authority record.
- *Class*—This value defines the protocol family the record uses. In most instances, this value is IN to represent the Internet system.
- *Type*—This value defines the type of resource record.
- *Resource Record Data (RDATA)*—This field contains information provided by the resource record or its data.

A typical DNS record uses the following syntax:

`Owner [TTL] Class Type RDATA`

In the DNS record syntax, TTL is in brackets because it is an optional value. Brackets are usually used to denote optional items in scripts, command-line executables, and other applications.

Using this syntax, a DNS record for server01.bentech.local is the following:

`server01.bentech.local. IN A 192.168.100.175`

From this record, you can determine that the zone, bentech.local, has a record for a host name (A) record for server01 that points to the IP address of 192.168.100.175.

The next section covers the following types of DNS records:

- Start of Authority
- Name Server
- IPv4 Hosts (A)
- IPv6 Hosts (AAAA)
- Alias (CNAME)
- Mail exchanger (MX)
- Reverse host (PTR)
- Service locator (SRV)

Start of Authority Records   Listed at the top of the zone file, the **Start of Authority (SOA) record** is the starting point for information related to a zone. Table 5-1 shows the information in the SOA that is needed to maintain a DNS zone.

Figure 5-17 shows the output of the SOA record for bentech.net.

Name Server Records   A **name server (NS) record** identifies a DNS server that is authoritative for a zone. Depending on the number of DNS servers that host a zone, you might have one or more NS records. It is required that each authoritative server has an NS record in its respective zone. Primary and secondary servers are both identified by NS records. NS records are also used to determine name servers for any delegated zones.

Windows Server 2008 creates the initial NS records for all the name servers currently recognized for a zone. Additionally, you can use the DNS console in Server Manager or dnscmd from the command line to create additional NS records.

For example, suppose you are adding a new secondary DNS server, NS2, for the bentech.local domain. After creating the zone and transferring the records, the following record is recorded in the bentech.local zone to represent that NS2 is an authoritative name server:

`bentech.local. IN NS ns2.bentech.local.`

Table 5-1 Resource record data (RData) for SOA resource records

RDATA Field Name	Description
Serial Number	A number that increments by 1 for every change occurring in a DNS zone. This is used during the zone transfer process. Secondary servers for a zone compare the master SOA serial number with their own SOA serial number to determine if updates are necessary.
Responsible Person	The e-mail address of the person responsible for a domain
Primary Server	Contains the name of the primary DNS server that is authoritative for the zone
Refresh Interval	The interval in which secondary servers check for updates to the zone
Retry Interval	The amount of time (in seconds) that a secondary server will wait after submitting a zone transfer request before it sends another request
Expires After	The amount of time (in seconds) that a secondary server responds to queries before it discards its own zone. This time value restarts at zero after each zone transfer is completed.
Minimum (Default) TTL	The minimum amount of time (in seconds) that a resource record is considered valid. Unless explicitly set at the resource record level, this applies to all zone records in a particular zone. This time is used by DNS clients in determining how long a query answer they have received is valid.
TTL for this Record	The time-to-live value used by the SOA record

An associated host record is needed so clients using the NS record can resolve the name contained in the RData. Host records are discussed next.

Host (A) Records for IPv4   The **host (A) record** provides host name–to–IP address resolution for DNS clients. Each node on a network that requires DNS name resolution needs an A record to point clients to the appropriate IP address of the target machine.

The following is the A record that would be created for NS2.bentech.local:

```
ns2.bentech.local. IN A 192.168.100.100
```

```
C:\Users\mike>nslookup -type=SOA bentech.net
Server:  vip1ftbgwi.ftbg.wi.charter.com
Address:  24.196.64.53:53

bentech.net
        primary name server = ns49.domaincontrol.com
        responsible mail addr = dns.jomax.net
        serial  = 2008071500
        refresh = 28800 (8 hours)
        retry   = 7200 (2 hours)
        expire  = 604800 (7 days)
        default TTL = 86400 (1 day)

C:\Users\mike>
```

Figure 5-17   SOA record output

A records contain many of the same fields described earlier, including the Owner, TTL, Class, and Type fields. Because A records resolve host names to IP addresses, the RData contained in an A record is the IP address of the host.

Host (AAAA) Records for IPv6

Similar to A records for IPv4, AAAA, or quad-A, records map a host name to an IPv6 address. This lets IPv6 clients and applications that support IPv6 resolve IPv6 names from a DNS server.

The following is the AAAA record that would be created for NS2.bentech.local:

```
ns2.bentech.local. IN AAAA 2001:23::fe01:fda:1001
```

During the discussion of DDNS later in this chapter, deployment of IPv6 DNS in coexistence with IPv4 will be discussed.

Mail Exchanger Records

The **mail exchanger (MX)** record specifies the server that is responsible for handling e-mail and acting as a mail server for a particular domain. Depending on the configuration of a target domain, the MX record might represent the destination e-mail server, or more likely it will represent an intermediary firewall or SMTP responsible for passing the mail along to its destination. E-mail traffic is sent using SMTP. This is the industry standard for transporting Internet mail between e-mail servers. When a mail server receives a piece of e-mail bound for a domain, it queries the MX and A records of the domain so that it can route the mail appropriately. Like NS records, MX records record the FQDN in its RData. In addition, the RData includes the **mail server preference value**. MX records use preference values, starting with the number 0, to designate the order in which mail servers should be attempted. It also contains the Owner, TTL, Class, and Type fields.

Because e-mail is one of the most important services within an organization, additional servers are often responsible for receiving e-mail in case your primary server is unavailable.

If you perform an nslookup on bentech.net from the command prompt, the output shown in Figure 5-18 appears.

Figure 5-19 lists two servers with differing preferences. This means that the server smtp.secureserver.net is the primary mail target, and mailstore1.secureserver.net is its backup.

A good tool for checking that your external MX records are set up properly to route mail is located at *mxtoolbox.com*. This Web site allows you to enter the domain name you want to test. It then queries for the MX records of the domain's mail servers.

If you created mail records for bentech.net, they might look like this:

```
bentech.net. 14400  IN MX 10 mail1.bentech.net.
bentech.net. 14400  IN MX 20 mail2.bentech.net.
bentech.net. 14400  IN MX 30 mail3.bentech.net.
```

```
Command Prompt                                                    _ |□| x|
Microsoft Windows [Version 6.0.6001]
Copyright (c) 2006 Microsoft Corporation.  All rights reserved.

C:\Users\mike>NSLOOKUP BENTECH.NET
Server:  vip1ftbgwi.ftbg.wi.charter.com
Address:  24.196.64.53

Non-authoritative answer:
Name:    BENTECH.NET
Address:  68.178.232.100
```

Figure 5-18   nslookup output for bentech.net

```
Command Prompt                                                    _|□|×|

C:\Users\mike>nslookup -type=mx bentech.net ns49.domaincontrol.com
Server:  UnKnown
Address:  208.109.14.200:53

bentech.net.bentech.net MX preference = 0, mail exchanger = smtp.secureserver.ne
t
bentech.net.bentech.net MX preference = 10, mail exchanger = mailstore1.securese
rver.net
bentech.net        nameserver = ns49.domaincontrol.com
bentech.net        nameserver = ns50.domaincontrol.com

C:\Users\mike>_
```

Figure 5-19   MX record output

Figure 5-19 shows the output of an MX record.

Alias Records   The **alias**, or canonical name (CNAME), record is used to create an alias for a specific host. This is often used for security purposes, or, if your naming convention is too complex, and a more user-friendly name is needed. For example, suppose you have a Web application server that has been deployed named MSN-SRVWeb-005.bentech.net. To make it easier for your users to remember the FQDN for the Web server, you can create the CNAME of webapp.bentech.net and point it to MSN-SRVWeb-005.bentech.net. Your record would look like this:

```
webapp.bentech.net.  IN CNAME msn-srvweb-005.bentech.net
```

CNAMEs also allow you to make background name changes without affecting the FQDNs that users and applications are using. This might be a good option if your network might experience growth or major upgrades in the near future.

Pointer Records   The pointer (PTR), or reverse lookup, record resolves IP address to host names for DNS clients. Basically, it performs the function of an A record, but in reverse. PTR records are often used when setting up an e-mail server. Most public SMTP servers do not accept mail unless they can perform a reverse lookup on the IP address of the e-mail server to determine the host that sent it. The RDATA field for a PTR record contains the host name, and the Owner field contains the IP address of the host. Like most DNS records, it also contains the TTL, Class, and Type fields.

If you created a PTR record for NS2.bentech.net, it would look like this:

```
100.100.168.192.in-addr.arpa.  IN PTR ns2.bentech.net.
```

 Unless you host your own external DNS zone for your domain, a PTR record needs to be created with your ISP or whoever provides public IP addresses. As they hold the address space for your server's IP address, they
NOTE   need to place a PTR record in their public reverse lookup zone.

IPv6 has changed to support reverse lookup records for IPv6 hosts and addresses. PTR records for IPv6 hosts are stored in IP6.ARPA domains. Unlike the IPv4 PTR records, where the address is simply reversed, IPv6 addresses must be split into separate hexadecimal numbers. Along with this, double-colon compression notation and zero compression in IPv6 addresses cannot be used for reverse lookups. The reverse lookup record for the example IPv6 address of 2001:23::1111:2222:1001 for NS3.bentech.local is the following:

```
1.0.0.1.2.2.2.2.1.1.1.1.0.0.0.0.0.0.0.0.0.0.0.0.3.2.0.0.1.0.0.2.IP6.
INT IN PTR ns3.bentech.local.
```

Because of the complexity of these records, Microsoft recommends not implementing IPv6 PTR records.

Service Locator Records   DNS servers use the **service locator (SRV) record** to provide important service information to DNS clients. SRV records provide a DNS client with the following specific information:

- Location of services it needs
- Network protocol needed to access the previously mentioned services
- Domain services it provides

Like all DNS records, SRV records contain information that DNS clients require for one purpose or another. SRV records use the following fields to record the information:

- *Service*—This entry shows the name of the desired service. Applications use this name when requesting information about a specific service.
- *Protocol*—This value is the protocol of the service, either TCP or UDP.
- *Name*—This value is the domain name to which the record relates.
- *TTL*—This is the time-to-live value for the record. This value is optional; the record uses the SOA TTL in cases where it is not specified.
- *Class*—This value defines the protocol family the record uses. In most instances, this value is IN to represent the Internet system.
- *Priority*—This value is the priority of the target host. The lower values have the first priority.
- *Weight*—This value determines the host preference when priorities are the same. When two or more records have the same priority, hosts with larger weights are used more often than hosts with lower weights.
- *Port*—This value specifies the port the service uses.
- *Target*—This is the FQDN of the host providing the service.

Similar to MX records, SRV records have a priority field that allows you to map multiple resources to a service. DNS uses the priority to determine the next host to try if the first priority host is unavailable. SRV records also include a Weight field that allows you to perform load balancing. The total weights of all records with the same priority must equal 100.

For example, suppose you have three servers that provide the FTP service for bentech.local. The following are the SRV records for the three servers:

```
_ftp_tcp.bentech.net IN SRV 10 35 21 server01.bentech.net.
_ftp_tcp.bentech.net IN SRV 10 35 21 server02.bentech.net.
_ftp_tcp.bentech.net IN SRV 10 30 21 server03.bentech.net.
```

In this example, server01 and server02 are used for 70 percent of the requests (35×2), and server03 is used for the other 30 percent of the requests.

SRV records are very important when you are working on a Windows network that uses Active Directory. You learn more about how SRV records work with Active Directory in Chapter 6.

Activity 5-12: Creating DNS Records in the DNS Console

Time Required: 10 minutes

Objective: Create DNS records.

Description: You plan to add an e-mail server to the network, but it does not support DDNS. This means you need to create the records for the e-mail server manually. In this activity, you use the DNS console to create DNS records for your new e-mail server.

1. In the left pane of Server Manager on the MSN-SRV-0XX computer, expand **Roles** and then expand the **DNS Server** role until the bentech.local DNS zone folder is displayed. Click **bentech.local.**

2. Click **More Actions** in the Actions pane and then click **New Host (A or AAAA)**. The New Host window opens.

3. Type **MSN-MSG-001** as the host name and **192.168.100.50** as the IP address. Click **Add Host,** and then click **OK**. Click **Done.**

4. Click **More Actions** in the Actions pane and then click **New Alias (CNAME)**. The New Resource Record window opens.

5. Type **mail** as the alias name. This allows your internal clients to connect with the mail server by using a user-friendly name, mail.bentech.local.

 Bentech.local is not a valid public domain name. The .local domain name is often used to differentiate internal domains from external domains.

6. Type **MSN-MSG-001** as the FQDN. This matches the alias with the appropriate A record. You can also browse to find the appropriate A record that matches the alias. Click **OK**.

7. Click **More Actions** in the Actions pane and then click **New Mail Exchanger (MX)**. The New Resource Record window opens.

8. In the "Fully qualified domain name (FQDN) of mail server" text box, type **mail.bentech.local** for the FQDN of the mail server and then click **OK** to save the record. This is the name SMTP servers use when sending mail to bentech.local.

9. Log onto MSN-SC-0XX.

10. At the command prompt, type **nslookup -type=all bentech.local** and then press **Enter**.

You can also create the records using dnscmd. Table 5-2 lists commonly used dnscmd commands with syntax and examples.

Table 5-2 Common dnscmd commands

DNS administrative tasks	Syntax of dnscmd	Example of dnscmd
Creating a primary zone	dnscmd /zoneadd zonename / primary	dnscmd /zoneadd widgets.local /primary
Creating a secondary zone	dnscmd /zoneadd zonename / secondary *master IP address*	dnscmd /zoneadd widgets.local / secondary 192.168.100.10
Adding A records	dnscmd /recordadd zonename hostname A ipaddress	dnscmd /recordadd widgets.local SRV1 A 192.168.100.155
Adding NS records	dnscmd /recordadd zonename @ NS servername	dnscmd /recordadd bigfirm.com @ A NS2.widgets.local
Adding MX records	dnscmd /recordadd zonename @ MX priority servername	dnscmd /recordadd bigfirm.com @ MX 10 mail.widgets.biz
Adding PTR records	dnscmd /recordadd zonename lowIP PTR FQDN	dnscmd /recordadd 100.168.192. in-addr.arpa 155 PTR srv1.widgets.local
Adding AAAA records	dnscmd /recordadd zonename hostname AAAA ipaddress	dnscmd /recordadd widgets.local SRV1 AAAA 2001:45ab::1
Clearing the DNS server cache	dnscmd /clearcache	dnscmd /clearcache
Reloading a zone file on a standard DNS server (from %systemroot%\ system32\dns)	dnscmd /zonereload zonename	dnscmd /zonereload widgets.local

Standard DNS Zone Transfers

Replicating record changes is necessary so that secondary servers are updated with the most current DNS information to provide to its clients. Standard DNS zones perform **zone transfers** to replicate these changes. DNS servers can host one of the following two roles in the replication process:

- *Master server*—The **master server** provides updated DNS record information to secondary servers. The primary and secondary zones can act as secondary zone transfer partners.

- *Slave (Secondary) server*—The **slave server** gets its updates from the master zone transfer partner specified on the Zone Transfer tab in DNS.

Both partners work in tandem to provide DNS clients the most current DNS information it has available. Standard DNS servers use the SOA record for a zone to determine when updates are needed. Contained in the SOA record is a **serial number** that increments each time a DNS zone is changed. Secondary partners use this serial number in determining whether a master has any changes for it. The process of updating zone files is always initiated by the secondary server through the following process. See Figure 5-20.

Figure 5-20 illustrates the following steps in a zone transfer:

1. The secondary server requests a copy of the current SOA record from the master/primary server. The SOA includes a serial number that increments for each change written to the zone file.

2. When the secondary server receives the SOA record, it compares it against its current record. If the serial numbers are different, the secondary server requests a zone transfer.

3. Upon receiving the request from the secondary server, the master initiates the zone transfer to the secondary.

The zone transfers from the master to the secondary server come in two varieties: **incremental zone transfers (IXFRs)** and **full zone transfers (AXFRs)**. Incremental zone transfers send updates of the DNS zone only to the secondary server. This is determined by the SOA record and its serial number. IXFRs reduce the amount of replicated data. Full zone transfers send the entire zone data file to the secondary server. After the first successful full zone transfer to a secondary server or if the information is reloaded from the master server, a request for an AXFR is initiated, and the action is performed on the secondary server. By default, Windows Server 2008 DNS servers request IXFRs from its master server. Secondary servers also request an AXFR if the difference between serial numbers (thus the number of updates needed) is too great for an incremental transfer.

NOTE What defines "too great for an incremental transfer"? Microsoft defines that as when the number of changes or updates is greater than the size of the zone. If the difference between the SOA serial numbers is greater than the secondary server's current serial number, secondary servers request AXFRs.

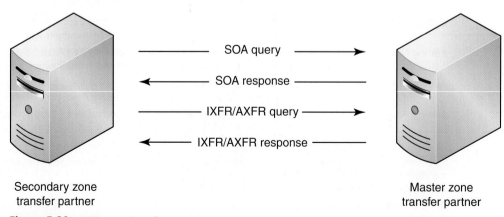

Secondary zone
transfer partner

SOA query →
← SOA response
IXFR/AXFR query →
← IXFR/AXFR response

Master zone
transfer partner

Figure 5-20 DNS zone transfer process

Master zones can be set to notify their secondary servers when any changes are made so that it knows to perform an update. (You set this on the Zone Transfer tab for the DNS server.) Remember that even when a master server is set to notify a slave server of changes, the slave always initiates the zone transfer process by requesting the SOA record from the master server.

Chapter Summary

- DNS is responsible for providing name resolution for clients on public and private networks. The Internet is supported by thousands of distributed DNS servers that hold records and information that clients need to communicate.

- The core functionality of DNS is to provide host name–to–IP address resolution, or forward lookups.

- Windows Server 2008 can host both standard, or file-based, DNS zones or Active Directory–integrated DNS zones. Zones can be either forward lookup (host name–to–IP address resolution) or reverse lookup (IP address–to–host name resolution). Forward lookups are the most used, but some applications such as e-mail use reverse lookups to verify the name based on an IP address.

- Standard zones are classified as primary, secondary, and stub zones. Primary zones are authoritative for a zone and contain a writable copy of the zone file. Only one primary server per zone may exist. Secondary zones are read-only, and stub zones are used to provide name server information about a remote DNS zone.

- When more than one standard DNS server hosts a DNS zone, those servers use zone transfers keep records updated. They use a master/slave (secondary) arrangement where the secondary server always initiates the zone transfer process.

- DNS uses many types of records to store information in its zones. A records map hosts names to IP addresses, NS records record the names of zones name servers, and MX records are used to determine the servers responsible for receiving a domain's e-mail.

- Installing the DNS role can be done through the GUI using Server Manager, or you can use servermanagercmd.exe (on Full versions) or ocsetup (on Server Core versions) for command-line installations.

- The DNS console is the main GUI tool responsible for managing DNS. It allows you to add, delete, and modify all aspects of DNS including zones, records, and server configurations. Dnscmd is a command-line utility that allows you to perform most of the same actions as the DNS console.

Key Terms

Active Directory–integrated DNS   A type of Domain Name System (DNS) available in Windows Server 2008 where the DNS database is stored within Active Directory. DNS replication occurs through the normal Active Directory replication process.

alias   A record used to create an alias for an existing host name. Also called a canonical (CNAME) record.

alternate DNS server   A DNS server that a client attempts to contact should their preferred DNS server be unavailable or unresponsive.

Berkeley Internet Name Domain (BIND) server   The industry standard for DNS servers on the Internet and networks running DNS on Linux/UNIX systems.

cache-only DNS server   A DNS server that does not host any zone but is set up to perform DNS queries based on client requests. On receiving its query answers, the answers are stored on the server for a specific time period in case other DNS clients request the same information.

Domain Name System (DNS)   The system that resolves human-readable host names to network-required Internet Protocol (IP) addresses.

DNS client   Any computing device that requests DNS information via DNS queries. Also known as a DNS resolver.

DNS Client service   The service that Windows Server 2008 uses to manage DNS client processes.

DNS domain   The portion of the DNS namespace to the right of the host name.

DNS namespace   A top-down hierarchical structure based on domain names.

DNS query process   The process that DNS resolvers and DNS servers perform when they request information from each other.

DNS server   A server that hosts one or more DNS domains.

DNS suffix   The portion of the DNS namespace to the right of the host name. It is used by DNS clients to resolve unqualified DNS queries, or those that only contain a host name.

DNS zone   A group of one or more DNS domains that contain the authoritative records for the member domains.

forward lookup DNS zones   A DNS zone that performs host name–to–IP address resolution.

forwarder   An IP address of a server that a DNS server queries when it receives domain name requests for zones in which it is not authoritative.

full zone transfer (AXFR)   A zone transfer request where the slave is requesting the entire zone be reloaded.

fully qualified domain name (FQDN)   The entire name for a specific host, or the DNS name, that needs to have a DNS record created so that users can use the FQDN to get the host's IP address.

host   A computer on the Internet that provides a specific resource is called a host. This host is most often a Web server responsible for supplying Web-based information or applications. Hosts can also be network entry points for a company's network such as a firewall or a router.

host (A) record   A record that is used to map a host name to an IP address.

host name   A name given to a computer, or host, to make connecting to it easier.

incremental zone transfer (IXFR)   A zone transfer request where the slave is requesting only the updates since its last successful update.

iterative query   When a DNS client requests the best answer that its DNS server can provide. If the DNS server has the answer cached, it will provide it with the address. If the DNS Server does not have it cached or it is not authoritative for the zone, it will provide a referral.

label   Each part of a fully qualified domain name.

mail exchanger (MX) record   A record used by e-mail servers for determining the host names of servers responsible for handling a domain's incoming e-mail.

mail server preference value   A value starting from 0 that designates the order in which mail servers should be attempted. The lowest number has first priority and so on.

master server   A server responsible for providing DNS database updates and responding to Start of Authority (SOA) queries and IXFR/AXFR queries.

name resolution   The process of resolving a host name to an IP address or some other piece of information stored in a DNS database.

name server (NS) record   A record that denotes a DNS name server that is authoritative for a particular zone.

pointer record (PTR)   A record used by reverse lookup zones. It maps an IP address to a host name.

preferred DNS server   The first DNS server listed in the DNS search order. It is the first server that a client will use in performing a DNS query.

primary DNS zone   The zone that is authoritative for a domain and its records.

recursive query   A query where the client requires an answer from its DNS server. In this case, it receives a positive or a negative answer. It either receives an answer or is told it cannot be resolved, and no answer will be given to the client.

referral   An answer provided to the client of the DNS server that can provide a better answer than it can provide. Also, a pointer to a DNS server authoritative for a lower level of the domain namespace.

resource record   A record that contains details about a specific portion of the domain name.

reverse lookup DNS (rDNS) zone   A DNS zone that performs IP address–to–host name resolution.

root hint   A referral server for the root domain. Root hints provide IP address pointers to top-level DNS servers and are kept current on the computer via Microsoft Update.

secondary DNS zone   A read-only version of the DNS records for a zone.

serial number   A number stored in the SOA record that increments by 1 for every change occurring in a DNS zone. This is used during the zone transfer process.

service locator (SRV) record   A record used to resolve the location of specific services available within a DNS zone. SRV records are used by DNS clients to find resources in an Active Directory environment.

slave server   A server responsible for requesting DNS database updates and initiating SOA queries and IXFR/AXFR queries. Also called a secondary server.

Start of Authority (SOA) record   A DNS record that contains important zone information including the serial number, default TTL value, and authoritative name servers for the zone.

stub zone   A read-only copy of a zone that obtains its resource records from the name servers that are authoritative for a particular zone. Unlike a secondary zone, a stub zone only contains only SOA, NS, and A records for a zone.

Windows Internet Name Service (WINS)   A Microsoft-developed name server that resolves Windows network computer names (also known as NetBIOS names) to Internet IP addresses, allowing Windows computers on a network to easily find and communicate with each other. WINS has been replaced by DNS for most name resolution since Windows 2000. However, some legacy computers and application that do not support DNS require WINS to function mostly in older NT networks.

zone transfer   A process used by standard DNS servers to replicate changes in the DNS database.

Review Questions

1. Which DNS record determines the destination mail server for a domain?

    a. A

    b. MX

    c. CNAME

    d. SRV

    e. NS

2. What is the name of the text file used on a local machine to perform host name–to–IP address resolutions?

    a. LMHosts

    b. Hosts.sam

    c. Host

    d. Hosts

3. Which of the following commands installs the DNS Server role on a Windows Server 2008 server running Server Core?

    a. Start w/ ocsetup DNS

    b. Start w/ocsetup DNS-Server-Core-Role

    c. Servermanagercmd.exe -DNS

    d. Servermanagercmd.exe -DNS-Server-Core-Role

4. Which of the following directories contains the text file used for mapping host names to IP addresses?

    a.   %systemroot%\system\drivers\etc

    b.   %systemroot%\system32\dns\

    c.   %systemroot%\system32\drivers\etc

    d.   %systemroot%\system\dns

5. What type of DNS record do slave/secondary servers use to determine whether a request for a zone transfer is necessary?

    a.   NS

    b.   SerialNumber

    c.   SOA

    d.   TXT

    e.   SRV

6. What type of DNS record do DNS clients use to locate domain controllers in an Active Directory domain?

    a.   NS

    b.   SOA

    c.   MX

    d.   A

    e.   SRV

7. What type of zone responds to queries for resolving IP addresses to host names?

    a.   Forward lookup zone

    b.   Reverse lookup zone

    c.   Primary zone

    d.   Secondary zone

    e.   Stub zone

8. Your company has just opened a remote office with 10 workstations at the site. Unfortunately, the site is connected by a slow WAN link. You need to deploy a DNS solution to the site that minimizes the amount of network traffic while improving DNS name resolution response for the local clients. Which of the following servers is the best solution for your company?

    a.   Active Directory integrated

    b.   Primary

    c.   Secondary

    d.   Cache-only

9. Which of the following is *not* a supported DNS domain name?

    a.   Microsoft.com

    b.   Ben-tech.com

    c.   High$jobs.com

    d.   NA.bentech.com

10. Which of the following commands can you use to display the DNS cache on a Windows DNS client?

   a. ipconfig /showdns

   b. ipconfig /flushdns

   c. netsh -showdns

   d. ipconfig /displaydns

   e. nbtstat -localdns

11. Which of the following commands can you use to add 192.168.100.100 and 192.168.200.100 as alternate DNS name servers on a network adapter? (Choose all that apply.)

   a. netsh int ip set dns "local area connection" index=2 192.168.100.100

   b. netsh int ip add dns "local area connection" index=2 192.168.100.100

   c. netsh int ip add dns "local area connection" static index=3 192.168.200.100

   d. netsh int ip add dns "local area connection" static 192.168.200.100

   e. netsh int ip add dns "local area connection" index=3 192.168.200.100

   f. netsh int ip set dns "local area connection" static 192.168.100.100

12. Like alternate name servers, netsh can be used to add a DNS suffix from the command line. True or False?

13. Which of the following records creates an alias for a host record?

   a. SRV

   b. SOA

   c. ALS

   d. CNAME

   e. MX

14. You installed a standard primary DNS server on your network. It will host the bentech.local, widgets.local, and nushooz.biz domains. You want to verify that all of the DNS zone files are created. What folder contains the zone files you want to verify?

   a. %systemroot%\system\drivers\etc

   b. %systemroot%\system32\dns\

   c. %systemroot%\system32\drivers\etc

   d. %systemroot%\system\dns

   e. %systemroot%\system32\dhcp

15. Which of the following commands can be used on Windows Server 2008 running Server Core to determine whether DNS is installed?

   a. ocsetup -displayroles

   b. oclist

   c. servermanagercmd.exe -showroles

   d. ipconfig /showroles

16. Which of the following records are not included in a stub zone? (Choose all that apply.)

   a. A

   b. NS

   c. SOA

   d. SRV

   e. MX

   f. CNAME

   g. TXT

17. Which of the following contains the information being provided by a DNS record?

    a. Owner

    b. Class

    c. RData

    d. Value

    e. Type

18. Primary, secondary, and stub zones are all authoritative for the zones stored on them. True or False?

19. A new e-mail server is being deployed for the public domain widgets.biz. All Internet-based e-mail for widgets.biz needs to go to a server called SMTP1.widgets.biz at the IP address of 66.12.3.4. Your manager asks you to work with your ISP to create the DNS records necessary for mail to flow properly. Which of the following records need to be created to complete the task? (Choose the two best answers.)

    a. smtp1.widgets.biz. IN A 66.12.3.4.

    b. mail.widgets.biz. IN CNAME 66.12.3.4.

    c. widgets.biz. 14400 IN MX 10 66.12.3.4.

    d. widgets.biz. 14400 IN MX smtp1.widgets.biz.

    e. widgets.biz. 14400 IN MX mail.widgets.biz.

    f. smtp1.widgets.biz IN A mail.widgets.biz

20. Which of the following DNS server types initiates the zone transfer process?

    a. Primary

    b. Master

    c. Secondary

    d. Cache-only

21. Widgets.local is a standard DNS zone. DNS1.widgets.local is the primary for the zone, and DN2.widgets.local is the secondary for the zone. Currently the serial number in DNS1's SOA record is 51, and the serial number in DNS2's SOA record is 26. At the next zone transfer, which of the following will be attempted?

    a. IXFR from DNS2 to DNS1

    b. AXFR from DNS2 to DNS1

    c. IXFR from DNS1 to DNS2

    d. AXFR from DNS1 to DNS2

22. Which of the following does *not* store any DNS zone files?

    a. Active Directory–integrated DNS

    b. Standard primary DNS

    c. Secondary DNS

    d. Cache-only DNS

    e. Stub zone

23. Which of the following tools *cannot* be used to manage DNS records?

    a. dnscmd

    b. ocsetup

    c. netsh

    d. DNS console

    e. Hosts

24. Server05.widgets.local is an example of which of the following:

    a. DNS zone

    b. FQDN

    c. Host name

    d. Domain name

    e. CNAME

25. When entering MX records, you should always map them to an IP address for proper resolution and mail flow. True or False?

Case Projects

Case Project 5-1: Researching DNS Names

Using tools you learned about in this chapter and other tools available, research sun.com, whois.net, and icann.org. Your goal is to find out all the publicly available information about each domain, including domain registration information, DNS records, and IP addresses. At a minimum, you will submit the following for each domain:

- Domain admin e-mail address

- Domain expiration date

- All name servers for the domain

- All available A records

- All available MX records

Case Project 5-2: Installing a Primary DNS Zone

You need to install DNS on your company's server. Create a primary DNS zone on CS-SRV-001 for the following domains:

- badgertools.local

- buckyutilities.local

Add DNS suffixes to CS-SRV-001 and CS-SCSRV-001 for the domains so that they can update their records in DNS. After adding the suffixes, verify that each server has A records listed in each DNS zone. Once the A records are available in each domain, create CNAME records in each domain so the alias "Primary" refers to CS-SRV-001 and "Secondary" refers to CS-SCSRV-001.

Case Project 5-3: Installing a Secondary DNS Zone

Now that you have a primary DNS zone for badgertools.local and buckyutilities.local, you need some redundancy. Create secondary DNS zones for each domain on CS-SRV-001. After the zone is created, verify that you can resolve names from the server by pointing CS-SCSRV-001 toward itself for DNS.

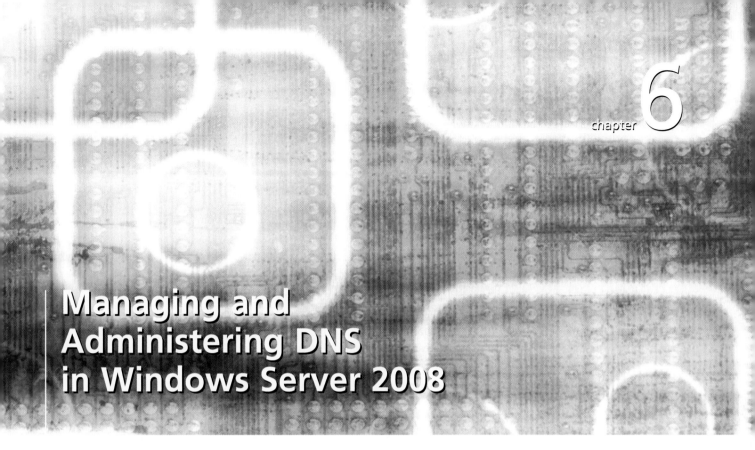

chapter 6

Managing and Administering DNS in Windows Server 2008

After reading this chapter and completing the exercises, you will be able to:

- Describe and install Active Directory Domain Services
- Manage your Domain Name System (DNS) environment
- Troubleshoot your DNS environment
- Manage Windows Internet Name Service
- Describe the new features of DNS in Windows Server 2008

Many networks use Active Directory to implement a domain networking model. Active Directory Domain Services is the latest version of Microsoft's centralized directory services application. Among other features, it provides user and object management, Group Policy distribution, and networkwide security. Active Directory Domain Services is built on and relies on Domain Name System (DNS) to function properly in a Windows Server 2008 domain environment.

This chapter introduces you to Active Directory Domain Services so that you can better understand how it integrates with DNS. You also learn about different deployment scenarios for DNS. Along the way, you examine a number of tools, those based on both the graphical user interface (GUI) and the command line, that you can use to manage your DNS environments and to troubleshoot DNS environments when problems occur.

Introduction to Active Directory Domain Services

As mentioned previously, **Active Directory Domain Services (AD DS)** is directly tied to and requires the installation of a DNS server to function properly. Active Directory (AD) clients use DNS to locate all the resources available on the network. In an AD DS environment, you can run two types of DNS servers:

- *Standard DNS servers*—These servers use file-based DNS zone files for storing their zone information.

- *AD DS–integrated DNS servers*—These servers use the AD DS database and replication structure for storing and maintaining their zone information.

Although standard DNS servers are supported in an AD domain, it is highly recommended and considered a best practice to implement AD DS–integrated DNS in AD domain environments. (In **Active Directory–integrated DNS [AD DS DNS]**, the DNS database is stored in AD, and DNS replication occurs through the normal AD replication process.) You will learn more about AD DS–integrated DNS throughout this chapter. In the next section, you learn about AD DS and its relationship with DNS.

In preparation for the activities in this chapter, you need to modify the network adapter configurations on your lab servers. In Activity 6-1, you reset your network adapters.

Activity 6-1: Resetting Network Adapters

Time Required: 15 minutes

Objective: Reset the network adapters on lab servers.

Description: Before you perform the other activities in this chapter, you need to verify the Internet Protocol (IP) addresses on your network adapters on MSN-SRV-0XX and MSN-SC-0XX and then reset the network adapters.

1. Log onto MSN-SRV-0XX, if necessary.

2. Open a command prompt from the Start menu, type **ipconfig /all**, and then press **Enter** to list the network adapter settings. They should be similar to those shown in Figure 6-1, which shows the final IP address settings for MSN-SRV-0XX.

Your IP address settings might differ depending on your lab and network setup. See your instructor for details about setting up your network adapters if necessary.

3. At the command prompt, enter the following commands to change the network adapter names and reset the network adapter configuration:

```
Netsh interface set interface name="local area connection"
newname="Internet"
```

```
Administrator: Command Prompt                                            _ □ ×
Ethernet adapter Internet Connection:

   Connection-specific DNS Suffix   . : localdomain
   Description . . . . . . . . . . . : Intel(R) PRO/1000 MT Network Connection #
2
   Physical Address. . . . . . . . . : 00-0C-29-3C-E1-18
   DHCP Enabled. . . . . . . . . . . : Yes
   Autoconfiguration Enabled . . . . : Yes
   Link-local IPv6 Address . . . . . : fe80::91f5:f64:f999:6de%12(Preferred)
   IPv4 Address. . . . . . . . . . . : 192.168.189.128(Preferred)
   Subnet Mask . . . . . . . . . . . : 255.255.255.0
   Lease Obtained. . . . . . . . . . : Wednesday, August 20, 2008 10:13:12 AM
   Lease Expires . . . . . . . . . . : Wednesday, August 20, 2008 10:43:12 AM
   Default Gateway . . . . . . . . . : 192.168.189.2
   DHCP Server . . . . . . . . . . . : 192.168.189.254
   DNS Servers . . . . . . . . . . . : 192.168.1.100
   Primary WINS Server . . . . . . . : 192.168.189.2
   NetBIOS over Tcpip. . . . . . . . : Enabled

Ethernet adapter bentech.local Connection:

   Connection-specific DNS Suffix   . :
   Description . . . . . . . . . . . : Intel(R) PRO/1000 MT Network Connection
   Physical Address. . . . . . . . . : 00-0C-29-3C-E1-0E
   DHCP Enabled. . . . . . . . . . . : No
   Autoconfiguration Enabled . . . . : Yes
   Link-local IPv6 Address . . . . . : fe80::c551:880c:a233:e617%10(Preferred)
   IPv4 Address. . . . . . . . . . . : 192.168.100.10(Preferred)
   Subnet Mask . . . . . . . . . . . : 255.255.255.0
   Default Gateway . . . . . . . . . :
   DNS Servers . . . . . . . . . . . : 192.168.100.10
   NetBIOS over Tcpip. . . . . . . . : Enabled
```

Figure 6-1   IP address settings for MSN-SRV-0XX

```
netsh interface set interface name="local area connection 2"
newname="bentech.local"

nets int ipv4 set address name="bentech.local" static ......

nets int ipv4 set dns "bentech.local" static
```

Your instructor will provide you with the proper IP address information for your "internet" connection. When setting up this connection, ensure that it points to 192.168.100.10 for DNS.

4. Enter the following command at the command prompt to set your DNS server to forward all external zone DNS requests to an Internet DNS server:

DNScmd MSN-SRV-0XX /resetforwarders 4.2.2.1 4.2.2.2

4.2.2.1 and 4.2.2.2 are publicly available DNS servers. If necessary, your instructor might provide you with a different DNS server for name resolution.

5. Enter the following command to verify you have name resolution. You should receive a nonauthoritative response similar to the one shown in Figure 6-2.

nslookup microsoft.com

6. Log off MSN-SRV-0XX.

7. Log onto MSN-SC-0XX, your Server Core computer.

Figure 6-2   Nslookup nonauthoritative response

8. At the command prompt, enter the following command to change the Internet Protocol version 4 (IPv4) address:

```
netsh interface set interface name="local area connection"
newname="bentech.local"
netsh int ip set address name="bentech.local" static
192.168.100.20 255.255.255.0
netsh int ip set dns "bentech.local" static 192.168.100.10
```

9. Enter the following command to verify you have name resolution. After

```
nslookup microsoft.com
```

10. Log off your Server Core computer by typing **logoff** at the command prompt and then pressing **Enter**.

Using AD DS

AD DS is Microsoft's implementation of a directory services infrastructure. Similar to how a phone book stores information about a person or business, AD DS stores attributes, or specific information, for objects within a network. Objects can include computers, users, and groups. For example, suppose you create a user object for John Reynolds in AD. Through utilities available for managing AD DS, you can enter attributes for John, such as his phone number, office location, or mailing address. Because AD DS stores its information in a database, it can be queried. In fact, any attributes you specify within AD DS can be queried.

AD DS in a Windows Server 2008 environment is a wide-ranging topic. For more detailed information on AD, see *MCTS Guide to Configuring Microsoft Windows Server 2008 Active Directory (Exam #70-640)* by Greg Tomsho from Cengage Learning, or visit *www.microsoft.com* and search for information on "Active Directory" in Windows Server 2008.

Activity 6-2: Installing the AD DS Role on MSN-SRV-0XX

Time Required: 10 minutes

Objective: Install the AD DS server role.

Description: In preparation for creating your first domain controller (DC) to manage AD DS, you need to install the AD DS role. You should also remove the current DNS zone for bentech.local so that you can re-create it during the dcpromo process in Activity 6-3. In this activity, you add the AD DS role to MSN-SRV-0XX through Server Manager.

1. Prior to beginning Activity 6-5, run the following command on MSN-SRV-0XX:

```
DNSCMD /CONFIG  BENTECH.LOCAL /ALLOWUPDATE 1
```

2. If Server Manager is not open, open Server Manager from the Start menu.

3. In the left pane, expand **Roles, DNS Server, DNS,** and **MSN-SRV-0XX** to display bentech.local under the Forward Lookup zone folder. Select **bentech.local**, click **Action**, and then click **Delete**. Click **Yes** to confirm the deletion.

4. In Server Manager, right-click **Roles** and then click **Add Roles**.

5. If the Before You Begin page opens, click **Next**.

6. Click **Active Directory Domain Services** and then click **Next**. Review the Introduction to Active Directory Domain Services and then click **Next**.

7. In the Confirm Installation Selections window, review the selections and then click **Install** to begin installing the AD DS role. To install a fully functional DC, you need to run the AD DS Installation Wizard, or dcpromo.exe, after the role is installed.

8. In the Installation Results window, click **Close**. The new role appears in the Server Manager window.

9. Click the **Active Directory Domain Services** role to view the AD DS summary pane.

10. Leave Server Manager open for the next activity.

A DC is used by AD DS for storing all of the AD objects and information about your network environment. Unlike DCs in Windows NT environments, AD DS DCs use multimaster replication to keep their data updated. In addition, writable changes to AD can be made on any DC.

When installing AD DS and creating the first DC in a forest, it is considered a best practice to install the DNS Server role when you run the **Active Directory Domain Services Installation Wizard**, or dcpromo.exe. Dcpromo.exe automatically creates and delegates the forest root domain DNS zone, or the first domain in your forest. It also creates the **_msdcs.forestname zone**, where *forestname* is the name of the first domain created in the forest, sometimes referred to as the **root domain**. The _msdcs.*forestname* zone contains the AD forestwide locator, or service (SRV), records needed by clients to find AD DS resources, such as DCs and global catalog servers. A **global catalog (GC) server** is similar to a DC in that it holds a directory services database. However, the database on the GC contains objects from the entire forest, not only a specific domain as with a DC.

For example, suppose you run dcpromo.exe and create a new domain for widgets.local. Along with creating an AD DS database, DNS zones are created for widgets.local, the forest root domain, and _msdcs.widgets.local. The _msdcs.widgets.local zone will hold all the SRV records necessary for clients to find a DC or a GC server for the widgets.local domain. These SRV records are created automatically when the domain is created and the first DC is installed into the forest.

Activity 6-3: Promoting MSN-SRV-0XX to a DC

Time Required: 40 minutes

Objective: Build the first DC in a domain.

Description: You need to install the first DNS server in your environment. In this activity, you add the DNS role to MSN-SRV-0XX through Server Manager.

1. If Server Manager is not open, open Server Manager.

2. In Server Manager, click the **Active Directory Domain Services** role to view the AD DS summary pane.

3. In the AD DS summary pane, click **Run the Active Directory Domain Services Installation Wizard (dcpromo.exe)** to make MSN-SRV-0XX a DC and install the first DC in the forest.

4. When the Active Directory Domain Services Installation Wizard starts, click **Next** to begin the installation. In the Operating System Compatibility dialog box, click **Next** to accept the defaults.

5. Click the **Create a new domain in a new forest** option button and then click **Next**.

6. In the Name the Forest Root Domain dialog box, enter **bentech.local** as the fully qualified domain name (FQDN) of the forest root domain and then click **Next**.

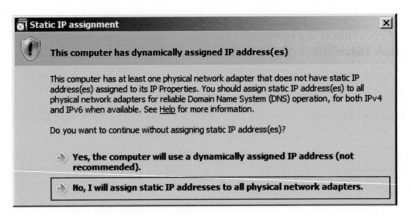

Figure 6-3 Static IP address assignment warning

7. In the Set Forest Functional Level dialog box, choose **Windows Server 2008** in the Forest functional level text box and then click **Next**. In the Additional Domain Controller Options dialog box, click **Next** without adding controller options.

8. If a Static IP assignment warning appears as shown in Figure 6-3, choose **Yes, the computer will use a dynamically assigned IP address (not recommended)**. This dialog box appears if you are using virtualization software, running Windows Server 2008 on a computer with multiple network adapters that are not all statically assigned, or using Dynamic Host Configuration Protocol (DHCP) reservations for IP address assignment to your DCs.

9. If a delegation credentials message appears as shown in Figure 6-4, click **Yes**.

10. Click **Next** to accept the default locations for the database, log files, and SYSVOL folder. Normally, the database and the log files are split between two separate physical drives for performance.

11. Type **P@ssw0rd** as the Directory Services Restore Mode Administrator Password and then click Next. This password is crucial to restoring an AD database from backup files.

12. In the Summary dialog box, click **Next**. The installation wizard begins.

13. In the Completing the Active Directory Domain Services Installation Wizard dialog box, click **Finish**. To reboot your computer to finish the installation, click **Restart Now** in the message box.

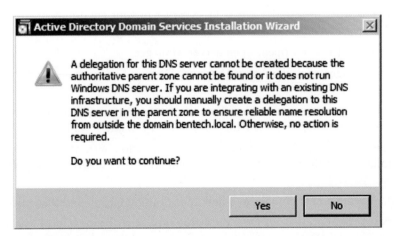

Figure 6-4 Delegation credentials message box

14. When the server reboots, wait 15 minutes before proceeding to the next activity. This allows AD DS to complete its postinstallation routine.

After installing AD DS and building a DC, you will see some changes in DNS. You now have a zone for your domain and a new zone called _msdcs.*forestname*. (Recall that this new zone enables clients to locate DCs and GC servers for a domain through the use of SRV records.) The AD DS–integrated DNS zone for your domain now stores more records than DNS zones for non–AD DS networks. Figure 6-5 shows all the new partitions within each DNS zone. Note that widgets.local, a standard primary DNS zone, contains none of the partitions that are available under bentech.local.

Table 6-1 lists the additions to DNS when AD DS is installed. Included are the zones that hold SRV records responsible for providing DNS clients' access to AD DS hosts. In addition, the new SRV records of _ldap and _kerberos are defined.

Activity 6-4: Reviewing the New DNS Zone Additions

Time Required: 10 minutes

Objective: Review new zones and records created by the AD DS installation process.

Description: Now that you have installed AD DS and created the first DC on your network, you are interested in the changes that have taken place on your DNS server. In this activity, you review the new zones and records created during the AD DS installation.

1. If Server Manager is not open, open Server Manager.

2. Expand the **DNS** role until you display the two new forward lookup zones: _msdcs.bentech.local and bentech.local.

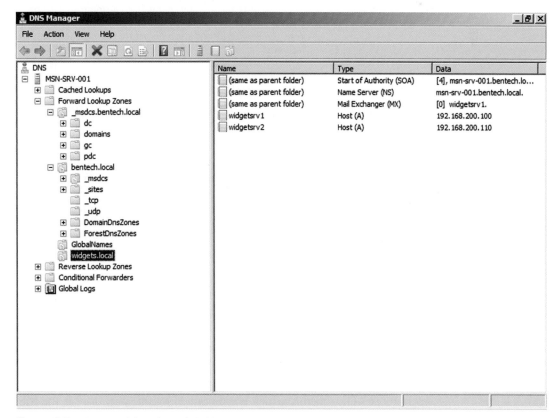

Figure 6-5   New partitions in each DNS zone

Table 6-1 DNS zone additions after running AD DS Installation Wizard

New DNS Zones	Description
_msdcs.forestname	This Microsoft-specific subdomain specifies DCs that have Windows Server 2008–specific roles in the domain or forest Windows Server 2008–based DCs register SRV records in the following form: _Service._Protocol.DcType._**msdcs**.DnsDomainName
DomainDNSZones partition	This DNS zone partition stores domain information that is shared by all DCs. Information includes records for DCs for the domain.
ForestDNSZones partition	This DNS zone partition stores forest information that is shared by all of the DCs. Information includes records for GC servers for the forest.
dc subdomain	This DNS zone stores the SRV records needed to respond to client requests for a DC.
gc subdomain	This DNS zone stores the SRV records needed to respond to client requests for a GC server.
pdc subdomain	This DNS zone stores the SRV records needed to respond to Windows NT client requests for a primary DC.
dc._sites	This zone includes all the AD DS sites for the domain, including records for DCs in each site.
dc._tcp	This zone includes all the _ldap SRV records for the DCs in the domain.
_ldap SRV records	These records are used by AD DS clients to find IP information about the computer or computers on the network that provide access to directory services, specifically AD DS.
_kerberos SRV records	These records are used by clients to determine the **Kerberos Key Distribution Center (KDC)**, the security accounts database in the AD DS database, for an AD DS environment. **Kerberos** (the security protocol used by AD DS clients and servers for secure communications) and the KDC servers are used by AD DS clients and servers for secure communications through mutual authentication. The KDC uses the AD DS database to store security account information.
_kpasswd SRV records	These records are used by clients to determine where the password change service is located for an AD DS environment. Clients are provided with the service information necessary to manage password change requests.

3. Select **_msdcs.bentech.local**, the DNS zone folder responsible for hosting the SRV records needed for DNS clients to access AD DS resources. Also notice four subdomain folders: dc, gc, pdc, and domains.

4. Expand the dc subdomain and the _sites subdomain and **default First Site** and then click _tcp. Note a new zone folder called **_msdcs** is listed under the bentech.local zone. It is grayed out and represents the delegation of the _msdcs zone. It contains the NS records point-ing to the server or servers responsible for hosting the _msdcs.bentech.local zone.

5. Leave Server Manager open for the next activity.

AD DS uses a database structure to maintain its objects. This structure is based on the DNS domain-naming hierarchy. The AD DS database is built on stores, or partitions, responsible for maintaining particular pieces of the AD DS database. (A **partition** in this case is a storage area in AD that holds parts of the AD DS database.) These partitions include the following:

- *Domain partition*—This partition stores all the objects, such as users and groups, in a particular domain. Each domain in an AD DS forest maintains its domain partition.

- *Schema partition*—This partition stores all the classes and attributes for objects across the entire forest. The schema, which is maintained by this partition, is the framework for all the objects within a forest. It also contains rules defining properties that are required by specific objects.

- *Configuration partition*—This partition maintains configuration data for the entire forest. Included are items such as the domains and DCs in a forest, AD DS site and replication settings, and application information for products, such as Microsoft Exchange Server 2007. Exchange Server 2007 stores its entire configuration in the Configuration partition.

- *Application partition*—This partition is a customized partition that is used to store information about specific applications available in an environment. Each application determines what is stored within this partition. However, application partitions cannot store security principal objects, such as user accounts. Examples of application partitions include ForestDNSZones and DomainDNSZones.

AD requires DNS for locating DCs. This client process is referred to as the DC locator function. Along with resolving DCs, AD uses DNS naming conventions in the architecture of its domains. AD's dependence on DNS is based on the following components:

- Domain controller locator

- AD domain names

- AD DNS objects

Domain Controller Locator
Part of the **netlogon service** used by every client logging onto an Active Directory domain, the **domain controller locator** runs at logon to provide the client with the location of a DC that can authenticate its requests. Without the proper DNS records, clients cannot access domain resources. The records that the service looks for include the SRV records for a DC and a GC server. These records are located in the _msdcs.*forestdomainname* zone created during the installation of AD DS.

AD Domain Names
Every AD domain in Windows Server 2008 has a naming convention based on a DNS domain name. For example, you create a domain for bentech.local in the next activity. Each Windows Server 2008 computer has an FQDN such as Server01.bentech.local. In AD, domains and computers are represented as objects, while they are represented as nodes in DNS. This can cause some confusion in regard to their roles because they have identical domain names. Table 6-2 differentiates between AD roles and DNS roles.

DNS Requirements for AD
A DNS server must support the SRV record type and dynamic update protocol, or Request for Comment (RFC) 2136, to support an AD environment properly. When a DC is added to a domain, SRV and A records are created to allow clients to find a DC during logon. Although they can be created manually, it is simpler to use dynamic update and automatically create the necessary records.

Table 6-2   Differentiating DNS and AD roles

	AD Role	DNS Role
Data stored in database	Stores domains and domain objects including users, computers, and groups	Stores DNS zones and resource records
Name resolution	Resolves domain object names to object records in the AD database	Resolves domain and computer names to resource records stored in a DNS database

AD-Integrated DNS

In the previous activity, you installed AD and created the DNS zone for bentech.local. Most often, you use AD DNS because of the following benefits it provides:

- *Faster and more efficient replication*—By integrating DNS into AD, you take advantage of the replication process used by AD and DCs. AD compresses intersite, or site-to-site, replication traffic so its updates are not as large as updates from file-based, or standard, DNS servers.

- *Database security*—DNS data is encrypted when it resides in the AD database; in contrast, standard zones maintain their data in an unencrypted DNS zone file by default.

- *Multimaster support for updates and replication*—Unlike standard DNS zones that run a **single-master environment**, AD DS DNS zones support multiple primary DNS zones. This is known as a **multimaster environment**. This allows a client to update its DNS records through dynamic update to any AD DS DNS DC, and that update is replicated to the other DCs on the network.

With AD DS DNS, all the zone records are stored in the AD DS database within a domain or application partition. This database is replicated between DCs on a network. Depending on the availability needed for a specific zone, administrators can choose one of the following zone replication options for AD DS DNS zones:

- *To all DNS servers in this forest*—This option replicates a zone to all AD DS DNS servers in a forest. This is helpful in environments with multiple domains that often need to perform **cross-domain name resolution**, which resolves hosts from another domain. Although it provides more availability for the zone, this option also increases the amount of replication between domains and across the forest.

- *To all DNS servers in this domain*—This option replicates a zone to all AD DS DNS servers in a domain. This is helpful in environments where DNS zones need to be available only within the domain boundaries and there is little cross-domain name resolution. This has less of an impact on replication, as it is confined to the DCs within its domain. This is the default option on Windows Server 2008 DNS servers.

- *To all domain controllers in this domain (for Windows 2000 compatibility)*—This option replicates a zone to all AD DS DCs, Windows Server 2003 DCs, and Windows 2000 server DCs. This is the only option available to you if you are running any Windows 2000 server DCs.

Activity 6-5: Changing the Zone Replication Settings for bentech.local

Time Required: 10 minutes

Objective: Change replication options for AD DS–integrated zone.

Description: Currently, the DNS zone for bentech.local is replicated to all DNS servers in the domain, bentech.local. In preparation for future expansion and cross-domain name resolution needs, you have decided to change the replication options so the bentech.local zone is available on all DNS servers in the forest. In this activity, you change the zone replication options for bentech.local.

1. In Server Manager, expand **DNS Server** under Roles until you display the bentech.local zone. Select **bentech.local**, click **More Actions** in the Actions pane, and then click **Properties**. The Properties dialog box for the zone opens.

2. On the General tab, click **Change** to the right of Replication: All DNS servers in this domain. The Change Zone Replication Scope dialog box opens.

3. Click the **To all DNS servers in this forest** option button and then click **OK**.

4. Click **OK** again to apply the settings and return to the DNS console. Your zone information is replicated to all the DNS servers during the next AD DS replication cycle.

DNS Zone Layout

A DNS server can host a single DNS zone, or it can host multiple DNS zones. Determining how to best deploy your zones requires some analysis of your environment. The following factors determine how DNS zones are deployed:

- AD DS site structure
- Distribution of your IT department
- Security needs

AD DS Site Structure   When you deploy a large AD DS environment that spans a number of geographic locations, you use sites to manage the replication of traffic between these locations. **AD DS sites** are designed to limit the replication traffic across wide area network (WAN) links, as this traffic can affect performance for clients and users. Although multiple AD DS sites might not require multiple domains, each site has at least one DC for managing requests from local clients. In these scenarios, you could use AD DS DNS to respond to client requests.

Distribution of an IT Department   How your network is administered helps determine the layout for your DNS zones and servers. In a company with a centralized IT management structure, maintaining fewer DNS zones is easier because one group has the responsibility over the infrastructure. In a decentralized IT management structure where multiple IT departments are responsible for different parts of the network, delegating zones to these departments can alleviate management issues by assigning DNS record management to the people responsible for each particular area.

For example, consider the company bentech.net in Figure 6-6. Bentech.net is global company with offices in the European Union and North America and headquarters in North America. Its AD structure has been designed with a root domain of bentech.net and two subdomains for each geographic region: eu.bentech.net and na.bentech.net. Bentech has an IT organization in each location. To ease the administrative burden, the DNS zone, eu.bentech.net, has been delegated to a server in the eu.bentech.net domain, NS1.eu.bentech.net. NS1.eu.bentech.net is the primary DNS server for eu.bentech.net. This removes the maintenance burden of eu.bentech.net from the IT administrators in the North American offices. The DNS zone of bentech.net, hosted on NS2.bentech.net and NS1.na.bentech.net, maintains all DNS records for both bentech.net and na.bentech.net. The **delegation** process creates a pointer in the parent domain, bentech.net, that points to eu.bentech.net.

Delegation requires two steps. First, you must create the delegated zone on the server that will host the domain. In the case of bentech.net, you create a primary DNS zone for eu.bentech.net on NS1.eu.bentech.net. Next, you create a delegation for eu.bentech.net on the server that holds the primary zone for bentech.net. The delegation in the parent domain stores the NS record of the server now hosting eu.bentech.net and acts as a point for any requests for eu.bentech.net.

Activity 6-6: Delegating a DNS Zone to MSN-SC-0XX

Time Required: 20 minutes

Objective: Delegate control of a DNS zone for a subdomain to another server.

Description: Your company is expanding to a location in the European Union. Because of this move, you need to assist with the delegation of the new zone and subdomain, eu.bentech.local, to MSN-SC-0XX.

1. On the MSN-SRV-00X server, open the DNS console by clicking **Start** and then entering **DNS** in the Start Search box.

2. In the DNS console, select **DNS**, click **Action**, and then click **Connect to DNS server**.

3. In the Connect to DNS Server window, click **The following computer** and then type **MSN-SC-0XX**. This allows you to remotely manage the DNS server role on MSN-SC-0XX.

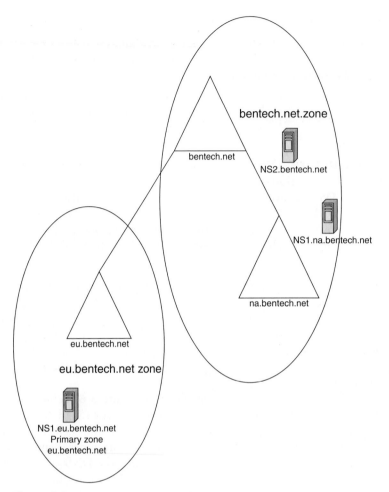

Figure 6-6   Example of delegated domain: bentech.net

Make sure the **Connect to the specified computer now** box is checked and then click **OK**.

4. Expand **MSN-SC-0XX** in the DNS console until you display the Forward Lookup Zones folder. Right-click **Forward Lookup Zones** and then click **New Zone** on the shortcut menu.

5. In the Welcome to the New Zone Wizard dialog box, click **Next**. In the Zone Type dialog box, accept the default selection of a Primary zone by clicking **Next**. Note that the AD-integrated option is not available because the wizard detects whether this action is being performed on a DC.

6. In the Zone Name dialog box, type **eu.bentech.local** and then click **Next**.

7. In the Zone File dialog box, accept the default zone file name by clicking **Next**. Notice that you can add existing files in this dialog box.

8. In the Dynamic Update dialog box, choose **Allow both nonsecure and secure dynamic updates** and then click **Next**.

9. Click **Finish** in the final dialog box to create your new zone for eu.bentech.local.

10. Minimize the DNS Manager window and then open a command prompt. Type **ipconfig /registerdns** and press **Enter** to register the DNS record for MSN-SRV-0XX. This process may take a few minutes for the changes to be reflected in the DNS console.

11. Restore the DNS Manager window and then expand **MSN-SRV-0XX** console until you display the DNS zone, bentech.local.

12. Right-click **bentech.local** and then click **New Delegation** on the shortcut menu.

13. In the New Delegation Wizard dialog box, click **Next**. In the Delegated Domain Name dialog box, enter **eu** in the text box. Note that the FQDN automatically resolves to eu.bentech.local based on the parent zone in which the delegation is created. Click **Next**.

14. In the Name Servers dialog box, click **Add**. This opens the new name server window for you to add the IP address or FQDN of the delegated name server. Enter **MSN-SC-0XX** in the text box and then click **Resolve**. Note that OK appears in the Validated column, indicating that the address has been resolved.

15. Click **OK**. In the Name Servers window, click **Next**, and then click **Finish** to create the delegation.

Forwarding Windows Server 2008 DNS implementations support two types of forwarding: standard and conditional. Standard forwarding instructs a DNS server to forward all queries for DNS domains not hosted on a server to another server or servers, as shown in Figure 6-7. Conditional forwarding instructs a DNS server to forward nonauthoritative queries for a specific nonhosted domain, such as widgetsbiz.net, to a specific DNS server or servers. This is often used in cases in which a partner company hosts its own DNS. With conditional forwarding, you can specify that all queries go to the partner's DNS server automatically. This reduces DNS queries by nonauthoritative servers, such as that of your Internet service provider (ISP). In cases where standard and conditional forwarders are created, the conditional forwarder for a specific domain is used instead of any server-based standard forwarders.

Another use for forwarding is in creating your internal DNS hierarchy. Services you deploy affect your WAN connection. The WAN connection, for the most part, is the slowest segment of

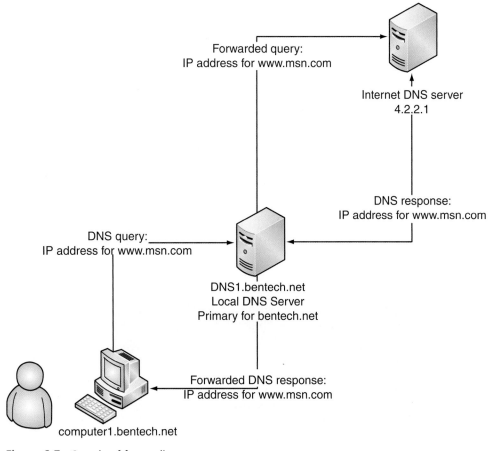

Figure 6-7 Sample of forwarding

your network. Optimizing this link is an important responsibility. By setting up your DNS infrastructure correctly, you can have a robust and efficient DNS environment and minimize the effects of querying on your WAN connection.

This is accomplished by centralizing your DNS through forwarding. At the top of your hierarchy, you can deploy two DNS servers that forward all queries to your ISP or another Internet-based DNS server. You could use one, but two gives you fault tolerance in case of a server failure. Moving down your DNS structure, the rest of your DNS servers point to either the external-forwarding DNS servers or another internal server. This keeps all external query traffic limited to your two top-tier servers, and caching temporarily stores responses on each server.

Forwarders are an excellent way to protect your internal DNS servers. By forcing your internal DNS servers to forward Internet name requests to another server, you prevent them from performing recursive queries against Internet DNS servers along with shielding them from direct Internet communication.

Dynamic DNS

As you have learned previously, Dynamic DNS allows supported DNS clients to dynamically update their DNS records on a DNS server. Dynamic DNS is often used along with DHCP in environments where clients and servers can use dynamic IP addresses. Dynamic DNS allows DNS clients to update their A, AAAA, and PTR records.

Dynamic updates and Dynamic DNS are often thought to perform the same tasks. Although both technologies provide much of the functionality, they are technically different. Dynamic DNS is not explicitly a Microsoft concept. Dynamic DNS can refer to the common practice of assigning an FQDN to a computer or device whose IP address changes from time to time. Through different software processes, such a device updates its Host record with a new IP address when it changes. On the other hand, Windows computers use dynamic updates to update their DNS records through processes built into each client, specifically the DNS client service working with the netlogon process. In Windows Server 2008, Dynamic DNS is part of dynamic updates. The netlogon process works with DHCP and DNS to update information regarding a specific client. In the case of clients that use static IP addressing, the DNS client service contacts its preferred DNS server during netlogon. It provides the DNS server with information necessary to process to DNS records. This process can be initiated by issuing the ipconfig /registerdns command, as shown in Figure 6-8.

Along with registering the DNS records for a client again, ipconfig /registerdns refreshes clients currently holding a lease from a DHCP server.

In addition to creating new records and modifying existing records, Dynamic DNS deletes the records of clients removed from the domain or whose DHCP leases expire. This feature helps administrators maintain an up-to-date DNS database. From time to time, records might not be deleted properly, maintaining host names that are no longer valid or correct. These types of records are called **stale records**. To remove stale records, you can manually delete records you know to be stale, or you can start scavenging the records. **Scavenging** is a process within a DNS

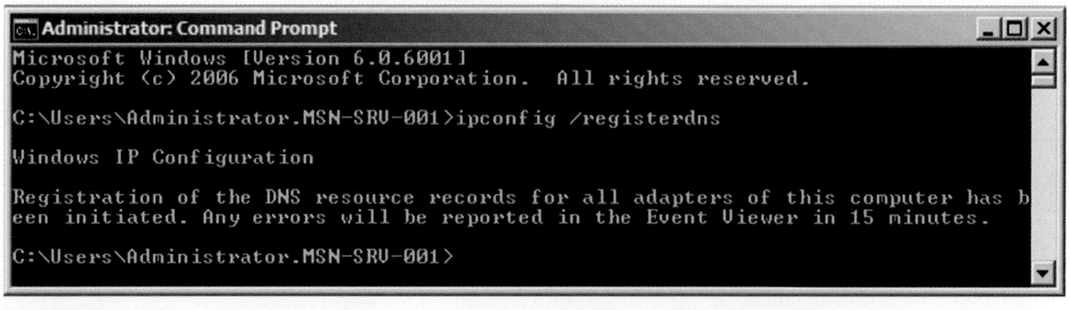

```
Administrator: Command Prompt                                        _ |□| x|
Microsoft Windows [Version 6.0.6001]
Copyright (c) 2006 Microsoft Corporation.  All rights reserved.

C:\Users\Administrator.MSN-SRV-001>ipconfig /registerdns

Windows IP Configuration

Registration of the DNS resource records for all adapters of this computer has b
een initiated. Any errors will be reported in the Event Viewer in 15 minutes.

C:\Users\Administrator.MSN-SRV-001>
```

Figure 6-8 Ipconfig /registerdns

database that uses time stamps to determine when records can update themselves and whether a record has exceeded the length of time records can exist without an update. You can scavenge records in Windows Server 2008 manually or automatically. You learn about both types later in this chapter.

DHCP Configuration

By default, DHCP is configured to provide dynamic updates to clients that support this feature. As you have learned, clients running older operating systems such as Windows NT 4.0 cannot update their records on their own. They require the assistance of DHCP server to act as a registrar for their records in DNS. To set up Windows NT 4.0 support, you use the DHCP console as shown in Figure 6-9, where DHCP has been configured to support Windows NT 4.0 clients.

DNS Configuration

When DHCP is in place and ready to support dynamic updates, you also need a DNS server hosting zones that support dynamic updates. By default, Windows Server 2008 DNS servers support dynamic updates through the dynamic update protocol as defined by RFC 2136.

For more information on the dynamic update protocol, visit *www.ietf.org/rfc* and refer to RFC 2136. Chapter 4 in this book also covers DHCP.

Dynamic updates are configured at the DNS zone level. This can be done during the creation process as in Figure 6-10, which shows the Dynamic Updates dialog box in the New Zone Wizard.

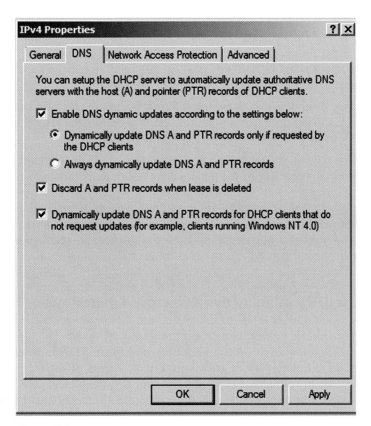

Figure 6-9 Dynamic update settings in the IPv4 Properties dialog box

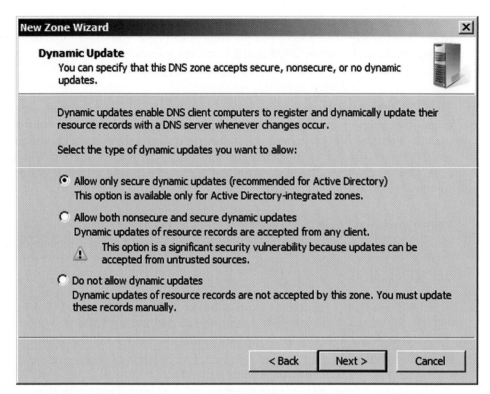

Figure 6-10   Configuring dynamic updates in the New Zone Wizard

If you choose to not support dynamic updates when you create the zone or you change from a standard to an AD DS–integrated zone, you can modify the configuration either through the GUI, as shown in Figure 6-11, or from the command line using DNScmd, as shown in Figure 6-12.

Secure and Nonsecure Updates

As an administrator, you need to choose how dynamic updates are performed by clients. You have two choices:

- *Secure*—This type of update can be performed only by an authenticated client. An authenticated client (1) is joined to a domain and (2) is the owner of the record being changed. Secure updates can be performed only in AD DS–integrated zones.
- *Nonsecure*—This type of update can be performed by any client. Domain membership is not required, and the requester of the update does not require authentication.

In cases where you are using AD DS–integrated zones, it is a best practice to use secure updates when working with newer Windows clients. If your network includes domains and work groups, secure and nonsecure updates should be allowed. Allowing nonsecured updates in your environment can leave a network susceptible to unauthorized changes to DNS records.

How Clients Use DNS in an Active Directory Environment

To find DCs in a domain or forest, a client queries DNS for the SRV and A DNS resource records of the DC. The resource records provide the client with the names and IP addresses of the DCs. In this context, the SRV and A resource records are referred to as **locator DNS resource records**. DNS must be configured appropriately along with setting your clients to use internal DNS servers. Failure to point your client to internal DNS servers can cause problems, such as slow logon or the inability to add a client to a domain. Because of this, all clients and member servers in domain environments need to point to an internal DNS server that hosts the zone records for the domains.

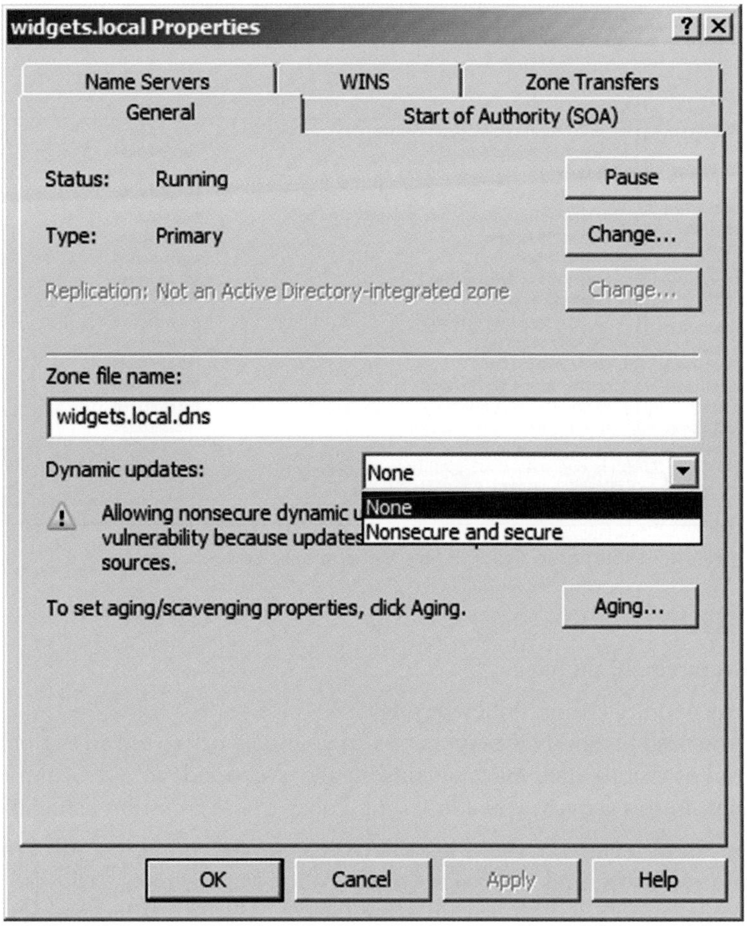

6

Figure 6-11 Configuring a DNS zone for dynamic updates in the GUI

DNS Client Group Policy Settings   Many of the DNS settings you have learned about can be distributed to clients via Group Policy. For environments that do not use DHCP or have statically assigned IP addresses, this is a good option for defining DNS suffixes and search orders, along with deploying new DNS server settings. Figure 6-13 displays the settings that can be configured for the DNS client.

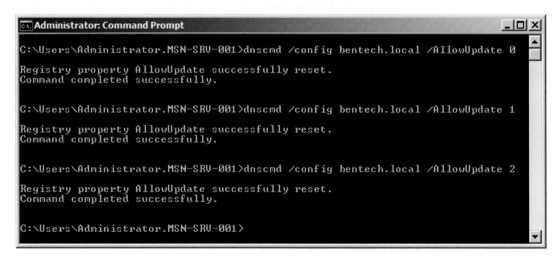

Figure 6-12 Configuring a DNS zone for dynamic updates with DNScmd

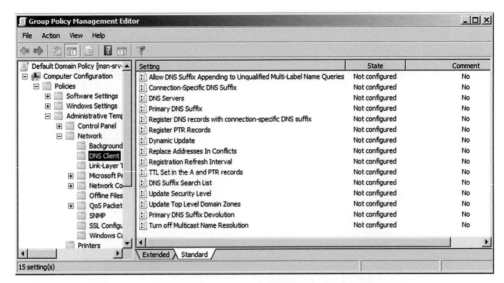

Figure 6-13 DNS client settings in Group Policy Management Editor

Activity 6-7: Changing Group Policy Settings

Time Required: 20 minutes

Objective: Modify Group Policy settings.

Description: You need to modify the computers on your network to use an expanded listing of DNS suffixes. Instead of visiting each machine individually, you decide to use Group Policy to send out the new settings. In this activity, you edit Group Policy to use a custom listing of DNS suffixes.

1. Open the Start menu on the MSN-SRV-0XX server, point to **All Programs**, point to **Administrative Tools**, and then click **Group Policy Management**. You use the Group Policy Management console (GPMC) to manage Group Policy in Windows Server 2008 AD DS environments.

2. In the GPMC, expand each level, starting with Forest: bentech.local, and working your way down to Default Domain Policy, as shown in Figure 6-14.

3. In the left pane, click **Default Domain Policy**, click **Action** on the menu bar, and then click **Edit** to open the Group Policy Management Editor.

4. In the left pane of the Group Policy Management Editor, expand the **Computer Configuration** folders (expand Administrative Templates) until you display the DNS Client folder and then click the **DNS Client** folder. The DNS client Group Policy settings are displayed in the right pane.

5. Double-click **DNS Suffix Search List**. This allows you to modify the Group Policy setting.

6. In the DNS Suffix Search List, click the **Explain** tab and read the description for the DNS Suffix Search List. All Group Policy settings include an Explain tab that provides usage guidelines for each policy.

7. Click the **Setting** tab. Click the **Enabled** option button and then enter **bentech.local,widgets-biz.local** in the DNS Suffixes text box. You can enter multiple DNS suffixes as long as they are comma-separated values.

    If you get an error in step 7, then skip steps 7 through 9. There is a bug in Server 2008 and the current hotfix from Microsoft does not resolve it. To add these suffixes within the GUI, use the procedure in Activity 5-6 on page 179. Then continue with step 10. To add these suffixes in Server Core, start the Registry Editor(regedit) and add the list as the value for **SearchList** located in *HKLM\System\CurrentControlSet\Services\Tcpip\Parameters*. A Reboot is required after this registry change.

8. Click **Apply** to add the policy. Click **OK** to close the DNS Suffix Search List Properties dialog box. Close the Group Policy Management Editor. Close the GPMC.

9. Open a command prompt. Type **gpupdate /force** and then press **Enter**. This command forces Group Policy to update on your computer. Normally, computer configuration Group Policy settings will update the next time a system is rebooted.

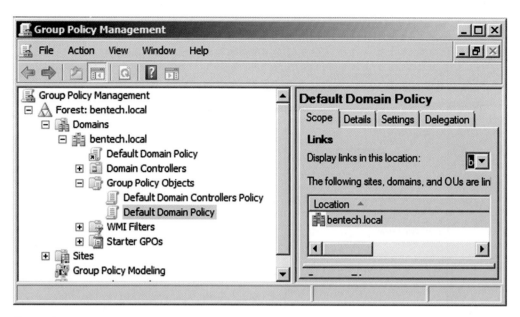

Figure 6-14   Group Policy Management console

10. Type **ipconfig /all** and then press **Enter**. Review the results, noting that you now have three DNS suffixes.

11. Close the command prompt and logoff MSN-SRV-0XX.

12. Log onto MSN-SC-0XX and type **shutdown –r** at the command prompt to reboot the server.

13. After the reboot is completed, log onto MSN-SC-0XX and type **ipconfig /all** at the command prompt to verify MSN-SRV-0XX has three DNS suffixes.

Managing DNS

In Chapter 5, you learned how to install DNS and perform basic configurations. In this section, you learn about advanced DNS configurations, such as round-robin DNS and conditional forwarders. You also learn about the tools built into Windows Server 2008 for managing the DNS role, including the DNS console and DNScmd.

Using the DNS Console

As you've seen, the DNS console is the main GUI tool used for configuring DNS. It provides access to all the DNS zones available on a server, along with configuration settings for the DNS role. As shown in Figure 6-15, the DNS console displays a number of areas for you to work with on each DNS server in your environment.

Another version of the DNS console is called the DNS Manager. It is available through Administrative Tools, or you can add it to a Microsoft Management Console shell. Although similar in the information they display, they are different in one major way. DNS Manager allows you to add DNS servers so that you can view all your DNS servers in the same interface, as shown in Figure 6-16.

Configuration Settings in the DNS Console

Depending on the settings you want to put into place, you can configure DNS in the following levels:

- *DNS server level*—Settings at this level apply to the DNS server role and impact all zones hosted on the server. Server-specific maintenance tasks are performed at this level as well.

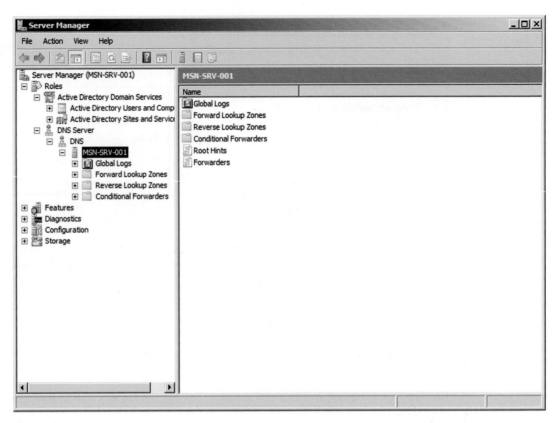

Figure 6-15   DNS console

- *DNS zone level*—Settings at this level apply to a specific DNS zone and affect all the records included in the zone.
- *DNS record level*—Settings at this level affect only a single record.

DNS Server Level

At the DNS server level, you make configuration changes that are server specific along with performing maintenance tasks for a specific server. The following are configuration and maintenance tasks you can perform:

- *Configure a DNS server*—This is a wizard-based process that allows you to manage a server by creating new forward and reverse lookup zones, along with specifying root hints and forwarders on a server.

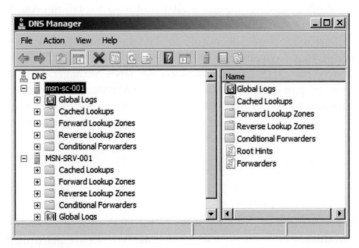

Figure 6-16   DNS Manager with DNS server

- *Create the default application (Directory Partitions)*—This process will create default partitions for the Application Directory within DNS. Most often, administrators will choose to have these created during the AD DS creation process. However, there may be instances where it was not performed during the initial process, so it can be performed after the installation of AD DS.

- *Create a zone*—This launches the New Zone Wizard for creating new forward or reverse lookup zones on a server.

- *Set aging/scavenging for all zones*—This defines the aging and scavenging process settings. Scavenging is the process DNS uses to find and remove stale records. These settings define the **No-refresh interval**, the length of time records wait before they can refresh their time stamp, and **Refresh interval**, the length of time after a record can refresh that it is determined to be stale and scavenging can begin. Setting these allows the DNS to perform scavenging as part of its background maintenance processes.

- *Scavenge stale resource records*—This allows an administrator to force the scavenging of stale records. If auto-scavenging is not configured on your DNS servers, this is a good option for routinely cleaning up DNS.

- *Update server data files*—This forces a DNS server to update its data files.

- *Clear cache*—This clears the DNS cache on the DNS server. All cached entries from recursive queries are removed.

- *Launch nslookup*—This allows you to launch an interactive nslookup shell in a separate window without using the command prompt.

In addition to these tasks, you can modify the DNS server's properties by accessing the DNS server's Properties dialog box through the DNS console. The Properties dialog box includes eight tabs, as shown in Figure 6-17.

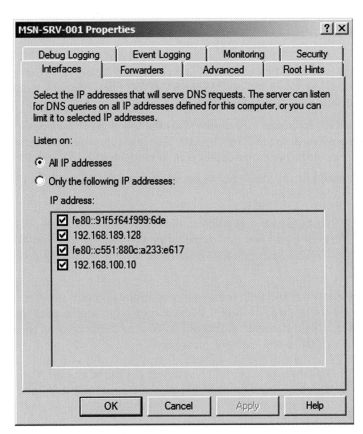

Figure 6-17   DNS Server Properties dialog box

Each of the following tabs has its own group of settings for the DNS server:

- *Interfaces*—This tab defines the interfaces, or IP addresses, on which the DNS server listens for DNS requests. The default configuration is to listen to All IP addresses. However, in some cases, such as a multihomed server or a server with multiple IP addresses on different subnets, you might want to limit DNS responses to a particular subnet.

- *Forwarders*—This tab defines the IP addresses that are used when the DNS server has to forward DNS requests. You can also define whether the server uses root hints when none of the defined forwarders are available.

- *Advanced*—This tab allows you to determine server options, such as enabling round-robin, using BIND secondary DNS servers, and disabling recursion. You define automatic scavenging on this tab as well.

- *Root Hints*—This tab allows you to add or modify the root hints defined on a server. This can be done manually through the GUI using Add, Edit, or Remove. Another option is to use Copy from Server, which allows you to copy the root hints from another name server.

- *Debug Logging*—This tab is used to turn on and modify the settings of the debug logger.

- *Event Logging*—This tab is used to specify the type of events that appear in the DNS event log.

- *Monitoring*—This tab allows you to perform configuration verification tests on your server. This can be for one-time testing, or you can set up automatic testing. You can perform two types of test queries: simple queries and recursive queries against other DNS servers.

- *Security*—This tab defines the permissions that users and groups have to the DNS server.

Activity 6-8: Configuring DNS at the Server Level

Time Required: 15 minutes

Objective: Setting server-level properties.

Description: You need to make some modifications to your DNS server for better performance, maintenance, and reporting. In this activity, you explore and configure the DNS server properties.

1. In Server Manager of the MSN-SRV-0XX server, expand **Roles**, **DNS Server**, and **DNS** until MSN-SRV-0XX is displayed. Select **MSN-SRV-0XX**, click **More Actions**, and then click **Properties**. This opens the MSN-SRV-0XX Properties dialog box.

2. If necessary, click the **Interfaces** tab, choose **Only the following IP addresses**, and then uncheck all the IP addresses except for 192.168.100.10. This instructs your DNS server to listen only to requests that arrive at the network adapter configured with 192.168.100.10 as its IP address.

3. Click the **Advanced** tab and then choose **Enable automatic scavenging of stale records** with the default period of 7 days.

For automatic scavenging to function in Windows Server 2008, it needs to be configured at both the server level and the zone level. In addition, individual records can be selected for scavenging, but this optional.

4. Click the **Root Hints** tab and then remove any root hints servers you have listed by clicking **Remove** until all are deleted. To add a backup root hints server, click **Add** and then type **a.public-root.net**. Click **Resolve**, and a.public-root.net will resolve to an IP address of 84.22.106.2. Click **OK** to add the root hints server.

Currently, 13 public root hint servers service the Internet. They are maintained by a not-for-profit organization called the Public-Root. For more information on Public-Root and the servers they maintain, visit their Web site at *http://public-root.com*.

5. Click the **Event Logging** tab and then choose **Errors and warnings**. This keeps your DNS event logs clear of informational messages so that you can focus on errors and warning messages.

6. Click the **Monitoring** tab and select **A simple query against this DNS server** and **A recursive query to other DNS servers**. This allows you to verify that your server is properly responding to queries it receives and has an upstream DNS server responding to its recursive queries. Click **Test Now**. If your DNS server service is running and DNS is set up correctly with an upstream server, you receive Pass responses in the Test Results box.

7. Click **OK** to apply all the changes you have made at the server level.

8. In Server Manager, click **View** and then click **Advanced**. This opens the Advanced view of the DNS console. You can now see a folder called Cached Lookups that contains all the currently cached DNS query results.

9. Double-click **Cached Lookups** in the middle pane and expand folders to review any cache results on your server.

10. In Server Manager, click **MSN-SRV-0XX** in the left pane, click **More Actions**, and then click **Set Aging/Scavenging for All Zones**. Select the **Scavenge stale resource records** check box and then click **OK**. In the confirmation dialog box, click **OK**. This sets up aging/scavenging for all new AD DS–integrated zones.

11. Click **More Actions** and then click **Clear Cache**. This clears all records in the DNS cache. Open **Cached Lookups** and verify that any records that previously existed have been removed.

12. Leave Server Manager open for the next activity.

DNS Zone Level   The DNS zone level is the level where all the DNS zones exist, such as bentech.local and _msdcs.bentech.local. From here, you can perform the following activities that affect a specific zone:

- Creating and deleting DNS zones
- Creating new DNS records
- Creating new DNS domains and delegations
- Reloading the DNS zone
- Setting the DNS record level

The Zone Properties dialog box contains the following tabs that you use to configure and modify a DNS zone, as shown in Figure 6-18:

- *General*—This tab provides information about the zone, including status, type, replication, and whether dynamic updates are configured. These may be modified at this level. In addition, you configure zone aging on the General tab.

- *Start of Authority (SOA)*—This tab allows you to view and modify the information contained with the start of authority record for the current zone.

- *Name Servers*—This tab allows you to view and modify the name servers responsible for the current zone.

- *WINS*—This tab allows you to configure the current zone to use Windows Internet Name Service (WINS) hosted on a specific WINS server in cases where names cannot be resolved by querying DNS.

- *Zone Transfers*—This tab is used to allow zone transfers and determines who should receive them. Another option on this tab is to configure notification settings for secondary servers.

- *Security*—This tab defines the permissions that users and groups have to the DNS zone.

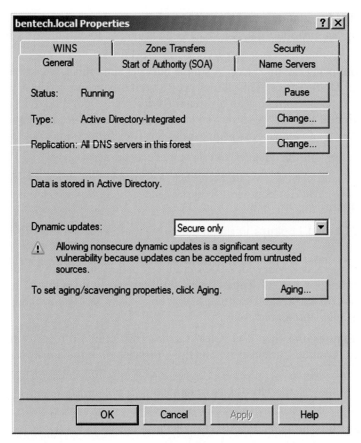

Figure 6-18   DNS Zone Properties dialog box

Activity 6-9: Configuring DNS at the Zone Level

Time Required: 15 minutes

Objective: Configuring and maintaining a DNS zone.

Description: You need to modify the settings for the bentech.local zone. Along with the modifications, you will perform routine maintenance on the zone. In this activity, you explore and configure the bentech.local zone.

1. In Server Manager, click **bentech.local,** click **More Actions** and then click **Reload.** Click **Yes** in the message box to confirm that you want to reload the zone. For an AD DS–integrated zone, this refreshes the DNS zone by requesting the current zone files from the AD DS database. Standard zones are reloaded from the associated zone file on the server.

2. Click **bentech.local** in the left pane, click **More Actions,** and then click **New Host (A or AAAA).** In the New Host dialog box, type **NewA** in the Name field and **192.168.100.225** in the IP address field and then click **Add Host** to create the record. Choose **OK** in the confirmation dialog box and then click **Done** to close the New Host dialog box.

3. Click **More Actions** and then click **Properties** to open the bentech.local Properties dialog box. On the General tab, click **Aging.** In the Zone Aging/Scavenging Properties dialog box, choose **Scavenge stale resource records** to complete the second part of configuring scavenging. Click **OK** to close the Properties dialog box.

4. Click the **Start of Authority (SOA)** tab. Click **Increment** twice to increase the serial number.

5. Click the **Name Servers** tab. Click **Edit** to modify the current name servers. If necessary, remove all name servers in the Edit Name Server Record dialog box except for 192.168.100.10 by selecting each IP address and then clicking **Delete.** Click **OK** when you

are finished deleting name servers. This aligns your zone with the server-level change to only accept DNS queries at 192.168.100.10 in the previous activity.

6. Click **OK** to apply the changes you have made. Click **Yes** if you receive a warning message about removing any name servers.

7. Leave Server Manager open for the next activity.

DNS Record Level   At the DNS record level, you perform the following activities directly related to a specific record:

- Modifying and deleting records
- Defining security settings on a DNS record
- Managing scavenging settings for a record
- Setting record Time to Live

Figure 6-19 shows the Properties dialog box for an individual A record.

Activity 6-10: Modifying a DNS Record

Time Required: 5 minutes

Objective: Modify properties of a DNS record.

Description: You have learned that the properties for a DNS record you just created are incorrect, so you need to modify them. In this activity, you modify the NewA host record.

1. In Server Manager, select the **NewA** host record under the bentech.local zone. Click **More Actions** and then click **Properties** under NewA in the Actions menu.

2. In the NewA Properties dialog box, change the IP address to **192.168.100.175**, check **Delete this record when it becomes stale**, and change the Time to live (TTL) to **30 minutes**. Click **OK**.

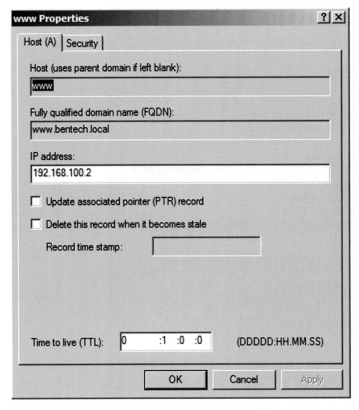

Figure 6-19   Example of an A record Properties dialog box

3. Press **F5** to refresh the DNS console and verify that the IP address for NewA has been updated.

4. Leave Server Manager open for the next activity.

Round-Robin DNS

Round-robin DNS allows an administrator to configure load balancing of servers based on DNS name resolution information. This works by creating Host records with the same host name but that point to different IP addresses. This is an excellent solution if you have multiple Web servers hosting static, or unchanging, content and you want users to be able to connect with any of the servers with a single Web address. For example, you have three Web servers in your domain called web1.bentech.net, web2.bentech.net, and web3.bentech.net. In this example, you set up round-robin load balancing by creating three Host records called www with each record pointing to a different IP address representing one of the three Web servers. When a user requests the resolution of www.bentech.net, the DNS server starts by issuing the first IP address in the list. The next request is sent to the second IP address. This continues as requests are fulfilled by looping through the host records on the DNS server. Windows Server 2008 DNS servers are configured to support round-robin DNS by default. If you do not want to make this feature available, you can remove the functionality by modifying the advanced properties for the DNS server as shown in Figure 6-20.

DNScmd can be used to disable or enable round-robin DNS along with other DNS features. The command for disabling round robin is as follows for MSN-SRV-0XX:

```
DNScmd MSN-SRV-0XX /config /roundrobin 0
```

where the last variable can be either 1 to enable or 0 to disable.

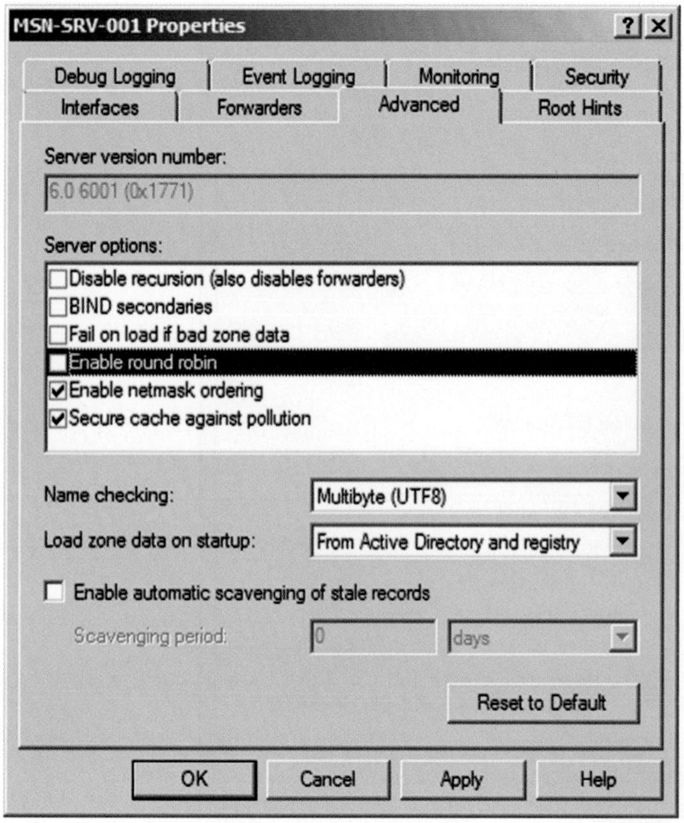

Figure 6-20   Disabling round-robin DNS

ACTIVITY

Activity 6-11: Setting Up Round-Robin DNS and Creating Records

Time Required: 15 minutes

Objective: Setting up DNS records for load balancing using round-robin DNS.

Description: Your company is deploying two identical Web servers with static content. You need to implement a low-cost load balancing solution that distributes Web server usage between both systems. In researching Windows Server 2008 DNS features, you decide that round-robin DNS is a great choice for load balancing your Web servers cost effectively. In this activity, you verify your DNS server is ready to use round-robin DNS records, create records for your Web servers, and verify that name requests are being balanced between the two servers.

1. In Server Manager, expand **Roles**, **DNS Server**, and **DNS** until you display MSN-SRV-0XX. Select **MSN-SRV-0XX**, click **Action**, and then click **Properties**.

2. In the MSN-SRV-0XX Properties dialog box, click the **Advanced** tab and verify that the Enable round robin box is checked. If not, click the **Enable round robin** check box and then click **OK**.

3. Expand the DNS console until you reach the bentech.local forward lookup zone folder. Select the zone folder, click **Action** on the menu bar, and then click **New Host (A or AAAA)**.

4. In the New Host dialog box, type **www** for the host name and enter **192.168.100.1** for the IP address. Click **Add Host**. Click **OK** on the informational message stating that the record was created.

5. Create a second record for **www** with an IP address of **192.168.100.2**. Click **Add Host**, click **OK**, and then click **Done** to close the New Host dialog box.

6. Verify that two records for "www" now appear in the center pane of the DNS console.

7. Open a command prompt from the Start menu. Type **ipconfig /flushdns** and then press **Enter** to clear the client cache.

8. Type **ping www.bentech.local** and then press **Enter**. You should receive a response back of 192.168.100.2 or 192.168.100.1.

9. Type **ipconfig /flushdns** and then press **Enter** to clear the client cache.

10. Type **ping www.bentech.local** and then press **Enter**. You should receive a response back resolving to 192.168.100.1 or 192.168.100.2, depending on what IP was received in Step 8; it will be the opposite IP address.

11. Repeat Steps 8 and 9 two more times. Verify that the IP addresses resolved continue to switch between 192.168.100.1 and 192.168.100.2.

12. Type **ping www.bentech.local** and then press **Enter** without flushing the DNS cache. Note that the IP address does not change on subsequent pings because of client-side caching of the host record.

13. Type **ipconfig /displaydns** and then press **Enter**. Scroll through the listing to find the records for www.bentech.local. Both IP addresses are listed including information such as the Time to Live value for the record.

14. Close the command prompt.

While this provides a form of load balancing, it does not provide fault tolerance because no current process ensures that a list server is available. It is up to the administrator to remove a DNS record that points to a failed server. In the previous example, if one of the three servers fails, every third query fails. A better solution is to use Windows Server 2008 network load balancing. Network load balancing routes traffic accordingly based on server availability at the time of the service request.

For more information about network load balancing in Windows Server 2008, see the "Network Load Balance Overview" in the Microsoft Technet library at *http://technet.microsoft.com/en-us/library*. Another good article is "Network Load Balancing (NLB) in Windows Server 2008" from Technet Edge at *http://edge.technet.com*.

Conditional Forwarding

In Chapter 5, you learned about forwarding, which involves a DNS server sending to another DNS server queries made for DNS zones that do not match its own zone and cache information. This server can be an internal or an external DNS server. Traditionally, forwarding is set up so that all nonmatching queries are sent to one or more servers. This is referred to as standard forwarding.

Another form of forwarding is **conditional forwarding**, or forwarding based on a specific domain name. For example, you could set up a conditional forwarder for your sister company, fun-widgets.biz, so that all queries go directly to the DNS server authoritative for the zone. In previous versions of Windows Server, conditional forwarding was set up on the same tab (the Forwarders tab) as standard forwarding settings. In Windows Server 2008, conditional forwarders are created in their own location under your server in the DNS console as shown in Figure 6-21.

Activity 6-12: Creating a Conditional Forwarder for badgerironman.com

Time Required: 15 minutes

Objective: Create a conditional forwarder in the DNS console.

Description: Your partner company, badgerironman.com, has a number of network resources, including Web applications and file shares, that your users need to access. To ease the burden of

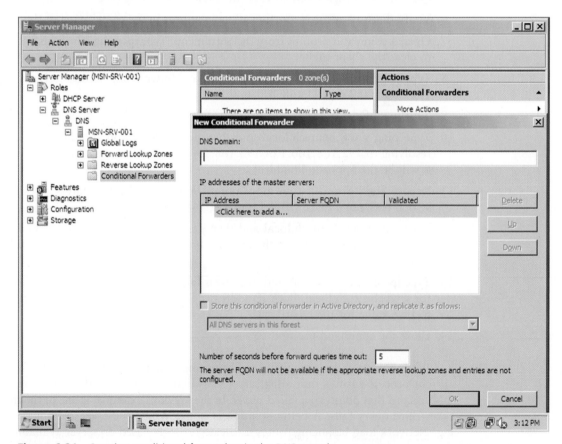

Figure 6-21   Creating conditional forwarders in the DNS console

resolving the host names of resources on the badgerironman.com network, you want to deploy a conditional forwarder that sends all badgerironman.com host name requests to a DNS server that is authoritative for the zone. In this activity, create a conditional forwarder for badgerironman.com that points to the authoritative server.

1. At the command prompt on your MSN-SRV-0XX server, type **nslookup -type = NS badgerironman.com** and then press **Enter**. Note the NS records for badgerironman.com so that you can use them when creating your conditional forwarder in a later step.

2. Enter the following commands to remove all forwarders and clear the DNS cache on MSN-SRV-0XX:

```
dnscmd MSN-SRV-0xx /resetforwarders
dnscmd MSN-SRV-0xx /clearcache
```

3. In Server Manager, expand **Roles**, **DNS Server**, and **DNS** until you display MSN-SRV-0XX. Select **MSN-SRV-0XX**, click **More Actions**, and then click **Properties**. Click the **Root Hints** tab and delete any listings by selecting the IP address and then clicking **Remove**. Click **OK**.

4. In Server Manager, expand **MSN-SRV-0XX** until you display the Conditional Forwarders folder. Select **Conditional Forwarders**. In the Actions pane, click **More Actions** and then click **New Conditional Forwarder**.

5. In the New Conditional Forwarder dialog box, enter **badgerironman.com** in the DNS Domain text box.

6. Click the text in the IP addresses of the master servers text box and type **4.2.2.1**. Press **Enter**. This causes the DNS server to attempt IPv4 and Internet Protocol version 6 (IPv6) name resolution against the record you have added.

7. You will receive a green checkmark and OK under validated for the IPv4 Address lookup. However, you will receive an error that an IPv6 address was not available. This means that the name server does not have an associated IPv6 address.

8. Click the **IPv6 error message** and choose **Delete**. This allows you to click **OK** in the New Conditional Forwarder dialog box to add the forwarder to your server.

9. At the command prompt, type **ping www.badgerironman.com** and then press **Enter**. You should receive a reply back including the domain name and IP address. However, the ping will time out.

Using DNScmd   DNScmd, as you learned through activities in the previous chapter, is an excellent command-line tool for performing configuration and maintenance tasks on a DNS server. It performs most of the tasks available through the GUI, such as creating new zones, creating DNS records, and updating zone files. Use DNScmd to perform the following tasks:

- Create and delete DNS zones
- Add and delete
- View information about DNS zones and records
- Change the zone type

Activity 6-13: Performing Management Tasks with DNScmd

Time Required: 15 minutes

Objective: Managing DNS zones with DNScmd.

Description: You need to create a new DNS zone, widgetsbiz.local, and then manage some of the records within it. Normally, you would do this through the DNS console, but you have heard that the same tasks can be easily performed using DNScmd. In this activity, you use DNScmd to create a new DNS zone and records for widgetsbiz.local.

1. At the command prompt on the MSN-SRV-0XX server, type **dnscmd /zoneadd widgetsbiz.local /primary** and then press **Enter**. This adds the widgetsbiz.local zone as a Standard Primary DNS zone on MSN-SRV-0XX.

2. Enter the following commands to create two A records and an MX record in widgetsbiz.local:

```
dnscmd /recordadd widgetsbiz.local WidgetSRV1 A 192.168.200.100
dnscmd /recordadd widgetsbiz.local WidgetSRV2 A 192.168.200.110
dnscmd /recordadd widgetsbiz.local @ MX priority WidgetSRV1
```

3. Type **dnscmd /enumzones** and then press **Enter**. This lists all the zones stored on MSN-SRV-0XX.

4. Type **dnscmd /zoneprint widgetsbiz.local** and then press **Enter**. This lists all the zone records for widgetsbiz.local.

5. Close the command prompt.

Troubleshooting DNS

Whether your network is running AD or is set up as a work group, if your clients are having difficulties connecting to applications or resources, DNS is likely the problem. Without a properly implemented DNS infrastructure, your clients will have problems logging onto the network, finding other clients and resources, and connecting to the Internet, to name only a few problems. Learning to troubleshoot DNS and solve name resolution problems is a critical skill every administrator needs. In this section, you learn how to troubleshoot DNS using the tools available in Windows Server 2008.

DNS Server Logs

The DNS console lists the **Global Logs folder**, which contains a subset of the event logs relating specifically to DNS called DNS Events. DNS Events, the display name for the DNS Server log, contains all the DNS-related events that have occurred on a specific server. Event logs are one of the first areas to check when you are having DNS problems. Common events displayed include the status of zone transfers, the DNS Server service, and the loading of DNS zones. The DNS Events log is displayed in Figure 6-22.

Like all event logs in Windows Server 2008, you can manage the type of events displayed and how Windows Server 2008 manages the log files related to the DNS Server logs. When viewing the properties of the DNS Server logs, you can configure the following two tabs:

- *General*—This tab allows you to set the name of the event log, the size of the associated log file, and how log events will be retained.

- *Filter*—This tab allows you to manipulate the view of the event log to your needs.

 The DNS Server log in the DNS console uses the older Microsoft Management Console (MMC) interface instead of the new MMC 3.0 interface used in Event Viewer.

General Tab   By default, the DNS Server Log Properties dialog box opens to the General tab. As shown in Figure 6-23, you use the first text box to change the name of the log. The default name of DNS Events can be changed if you want to use a more appropriate name. Most often, you can accept the default setting to avoid confusion among administrators.

The DNS Events log file is set to a default size of 16,384 KB, though you can increase the size in increments of 64 KB. On average, each event logged in the Event Viewer is approximately 500 bytes in size. A general guideline for setting the size of your Events log involves multiplying

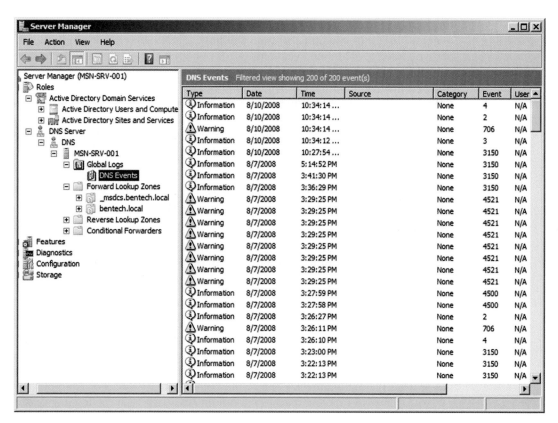

Figure 6-22   DNS Events log

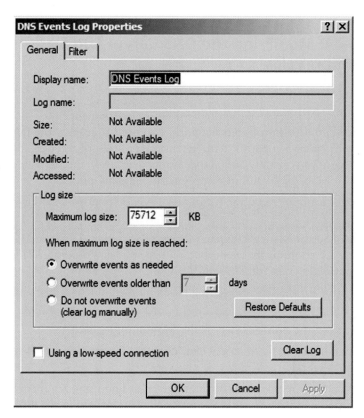

Figure 6-23   DNS Events Log Properties dialog box

the event size by the average number of events per day and the number of days that you need to maintain logs. For example, suppose you have a DNS server that produces 5000 events per day and you need to maintain events for 31 days before they are overwritten. Based on the general guideline, you should set your maximum log size to approximately 75,684 KB (500 bytes × 5000 events/day × 31 days = 77,500,000 bytes). Round up this number to the next multiple of 64 KB, which is 75,712. (Windows Server 2008 performs this task automatically.) Before modifying the log size, you should verify that the drive maintaining the log files has adequate space. By default, the DNS Server log is located at %SystemRoot%\System32\Winevt\Logs\DNS Server.evtx.

Although the technical limit for the maximum log size is 4 GB for each log, Microsoft has determined the practical limit as 300 MB for all logs combined.

After setting the maximum log size, determine the log's retention settings. Retention settings determine what happens to old events within the DNS Server log file when the maximum file size for the log is reached. You have the following three options for retention:

- *Overwrite events as needed*—This option clears the oldest events in the log file when the maximum size is reached. This is the default setting for the DNS Server log.

- *Overwrite events older than X days*—This option clears only events that are older than the number of days you have specified. The default value is 7 days. When using this setting, you must set the size of the log file appropriately; otherwise, logging ceases if the log reaches the maximum size before the "older than" value. For example, if you set the value to 21 days and the log reaches maximum size after 18 days, logging ceases until you clear the log manually.

- *Do not overwrite events (clear logs manually)*—This option does not overwrite the log files and ceases logging when the log reaches maximum size. If you choose this option, you must manually clear or archive the existing events in the log file.

Activity 6-14: Modifying the DNS Server Log Size and Retention Value

Time Required: 10 minutes

Objective: Modify the DNS Server log settings for your environment.

Description: As the administrator of your network, you need to modify the DNS Server log settings to comply with your company's data retention policies of keeping data for 21 days. Currently, you receive approximately 3000 DNS events per day. In this activity, you modify DNS Server log settings on MSN-SRV-0XX to comply with company policy.

1. If Server Manager is not open on the MSN-SRV-0XX server, open Server Manager from the Start menu.

2. In the left pane of Server Manager, expand **Roles**, **DNS Server**, **DNS**, and **Global Logs**. Click **DNS Events**, click **Action** on the menu bar, and then click **Properties**. This opens the DNS Events Properties dialog box for MSN-SRV-0XX.

3. Determine the value for the DNS Server log based on the guidelines discussed previously and the information provided earlier: _____

4. Enter the value from the previous step as the Maximum log size.

5. Under When maximum log size is reached, click the **Overwrite events older than** option button and then enter **21**.

6. Click **Apply**. When you receive an error message regarding using numbers that are multiples of 64K, choose **OK**, and the log size is automatically rounded up to the nearest 64K multiple.

7. What is the new maximum size of the log? _____

8. Click **OK** to close the Properties dialog box.

9. Leave Server Manager open for the next activity.

Filter Tab   The Filter tab allows you to modify the view of the DNS Server log for better analysis of the events it contains. On the Filter tab, you have of the following options for filtering events:

- *Event types*—This option allows you to choose which type of events appear in the log. By default, all types of events are available.

- *Event source*—This option allows you to choose which events appear based on the source of the event. By default, all source types are displayed.

- *Category*—This option allows you to choose which events appear based on the category classifying the event. By default, all categories are displayed.

- *Event ID*—This option allows you to view specific events that have a particular Event ID. Windows Server 2008 uses default Event IDs for all events. By default, this is blank.

- *User*—This option allows you to view specific events that are linked to a particular user. By default, this is blank.

- *Computer*—This option allows you to view specific events that are linked to a particular computer. By default, this is blank.

- *From and To*—This option allows you to define a time and date range of events. By default, all events (first event to last event) are displayed.

Based on the information you need from the DNS server log, filtering can help narrow the search for possible problems. For example, suppose you are receiving errors from one of your applications stating that it cannot contact a particular DNS server, NS1.bentech.local, every day around 1 pm. Using the Filter tab, you can modify the log view so that you see only events occurring from 12:30 pm to 1:30 pm on the day of the last error as shown in Figure 6-24.

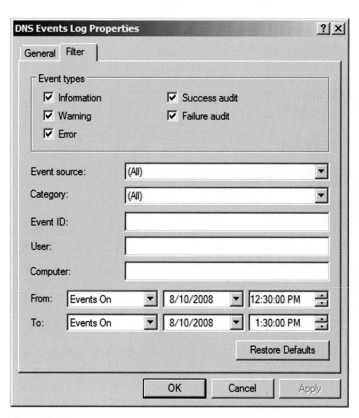

Figure 6-24   Filter tab in the DNS Events Log Properties dialog box

Only events falling in the specified time frame appear in the event log. From here, you can more easily view the events happening around the time of the outage by double-clicking each event. This displays the event properties including all the pertinent information on the event as shown in Figure 6-25.

Activity 6-15: Modifying the DNS Server Log View

Time Required: 10 minutes

Objective: Modify the DNS Server log view to find the root cause of a network issue.

Description: As the administrator of your network, you have just received a trouble ticket indicating that one of your DNS servers is currently unavailable. In this activity, you use filtering to narrow the scope of your event logs to find the cause of the outage.

1. Open a command prompt on the MSN-SRV-0XX server, type **net stop dns**, and then press **Enter**. This simulates suspending your DNS server for the activity by stopping the DNS Server service. Minimize the command prompt window.

2. If Server Manager is not open, open Server Manager from the Start menu.

3. In the left pane of Server Manager, expand **Roles, DNS Server, DNS**, and **Global Logs**. Click **DNS Events**, click **Action** on the menu bar, and then click **Properties**. This opens the DNS Event Log Properties dialog box for MSN-SRV-0XX.

4. Click the **Filter** tab.

5. Edit the From setting by selecting **Events On** in the list box next to From and then entering the date and time so that the value is the current system time and date minus 60 minutes. Use the same technique to edit the To setting so that the value is the current system time and date plus 60 minutes. This gives you 2 hours to see the event that might relate to the outage.

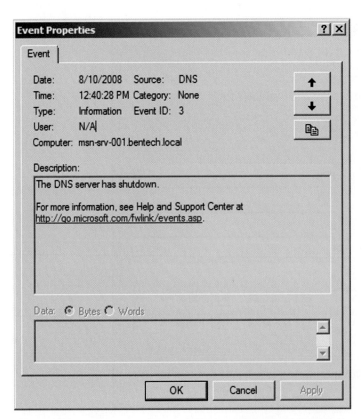

Figure 6-25   DNS event properties for an informational message

6. Click **OK** to filter the event log view similar to Figure 6-26. A message is displayed in the DNS Events Log pane indicating the number of filtered events being shown out of the total number of events.

7. Double-click the **newest event** in the Events Log, which is labeled with an Event ID of 3.

8. Read the Description of the event. It tells you that the DNS server was shut down at a certain time.

9. Click **OK** to close the event.

10. Maximize your command prompt window, type **net start DNS**, and then press **Enter**. This starts the DNS Server service.

11. Close the command prompt window.

Command-Line Utilities

You can use many command-line utilities for troubleshooting DNS in Windows Server 2008, including those discussed in the following sections.

Ping   As discussed in Chapter 3, you can use the ping utility for testing name resolution. Instead of using ping on an IP address, you can ping a server by host name or FQDN. If it responds when pinging by host name, your DNS suffixes are resolving properly, you can query the proper DNS zone, and the DNS zone has an A record created for it. Failure to resolve the host name or FQDN could be caused by any of the following issues:

- *Improperly configured client*—The client does not have the correct DNS servers or domain suffixes.

- *Network failure*—The client cannot route queries to the DNS server because of a network-related failure, such as a bad switch port or powered-off router.

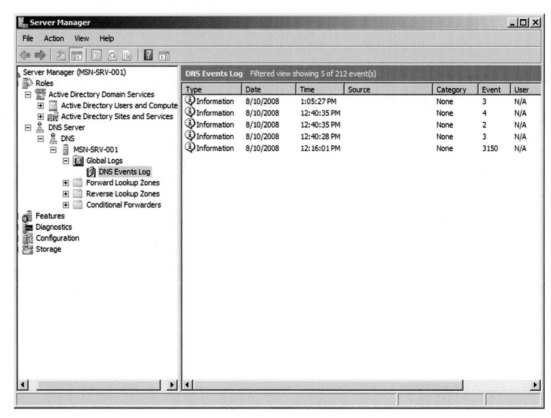

Figure 6-26 DNS Events Log with filter applied

- *DNS server failure*—The server is not available for the client, such as when a hardware failure occurs or the DNS server service is not running.
- *Improperly configured DNS server*—The DNS server is available. However, the necessary records (A) are not configured for the zone being requested.

Ipconfig   You can use the ipconfig utility for a number of activities while working with DNS clients. The following commands and switches are helpful in troubleshooting issues with DNS:

- *ipconfig /all*—As discussed previously, this command lists all the vital information about the network connections on a client, including the DNS servers and suffixes.
- *ipconfig /flushdns*—This command deletes all DNS query responses that have been cached on the local DNS client. This does not affect the cache of a DNS server running on Windows Server 2008.
- *ipconfig /displaydns*—This command displays all the currently cached query responses on a DNS client. This is helpful in determining if stale, or old, DNS information is cached and being used by the client.
- *ipconfig /registerdns*—In environments where Dynamic DNS updates are configured, this command forces registration or refresh of a DNS client's DNS records on the server specified as the Preferred DNS server.

DCDiag   Another utility for DNS troubleshooting comes as part of the DCDiag utility. **DCDiag,** short for "Domain controller diagnostic," allows you to perform diagnostic queries of your DCs. For testing the general health of your DNS settings in relation to your DC, you can run the following DCDiag command:

```
dcdiag /test:DNS /e /v >dns.txt
```

This command queries all of the DNS servers (/e), and you receive a verbose, or detailed response (/v). This information is sent to a text file called dns.txt that you can review for any errors or possible DNS issues.

This detailed diagnostic provides test results relating to services and configurations that should be present on a DC in an AD DS environment. The following is a list of some of the information the /test:DNS switch provides:

- Status of networking services on network adapters including netlogon and the DNS service
- IP address information for each network adapter
- Status of forwarders and root hints
- Listing of DNS records for each IP address (both IPv4 and IPv6) specified on network adapters

Figure 6-27 shows a portion of the DCDiag report when run using the preceding detailed command.

Windows 2000 Server and Server 2003 included another tool often used for checking network diagnostics along with DCDiag. This tool was called netdiag. It is no longer supported by Microsoft in Windows Server 2008 and has been deprecated in the Server operating system platform.

Nslookup   Nslookup is the tool you use most often when working with DNS. Nslookup allows you to perform detailed queries for DNS information from the command line. When using nslookup, you are sending a DNS query directly to the DNS server. It can be used for querying specific records such as SOA or MX. You can also attempt zone transfers using nslookup. It can be used in two ways:

- *Noninteractive*—This allows you to perform a single query from the command line by entering all of the query parameters at once.

```
dns - Notepad
File  Edit  Format  View  Help

                    TEST: Records registration (RReg)
                      Network Adapter
                      [00000006] Intel(R) PRO/1000 MT Network Connection:
                          Matching CNAME record found at DNS server 192.168.100.10:
                          b142183d-0769-441b-b91b-f45ed1aace25._msdcs.bentech.local

                          Matching A record found at DNS server 192.168.100.10:
                          msn-srv-001.bentech.local

                          Warning:
                          Missing AAAA record at DNS server 192.168.100.10:
                          msn-srv-001.bentech.local
                          [Error details: 9501 (Type: Win32 - Description: No records found for given
DNS query.)]

                          Matching  SRV record found at DNS server 192.168.100.10:
                          _ldap._tcp.bentech.local

                          Matching  SRV record found at DNS server 192.168.100.10:
                          _ldap._tcp.e66a86a3-055d-4c79-8c65-144fe354ccd9.domains._msdcs.bentech.local

                          Matching  SRV record found at DNS server 192.168.100.10:
                          _kerberos._tcp.dc._msdcs.bentech.local

                          Matching  SRV record found at DNS server 192.168.100.10:
                          _ldap._tcp.dc._msdcs.bentech.local

                          Matching  SRV record found at DNS server 192.168.100.10:
                          _kerberos._tcp.bentech.local

                          Matching  SRV record found at DNS server 192.168.100.10:
                          _kerberos._udp.bentech.local

                          Matching  SRV record found at DNS server 192.168.100.10:
                          _kpasswd._tcp.bentech.local

                          Matching  SRV record found at DNS server 192.168.100.10:
                          _ldap._tcp.Default-First-Site-Name._sites.bentech.local
```

Figure 6-27   Excerpts from the DCDiag summary

- *Interactive*—This allows you to launch nslookup in a command-line shell where you can define parameters one by one for more complex query types or when looking for multiple pieces of DNS information.

Performing a noninteractive query provides excellent information from a single command. For example, you can query the domain requesting all the IP addresses associated with a domain. The syntax for querying the cengage.com domain is the following:

```
nslookup cengage.com
```

This command produces the output shown in Figure 6-28.

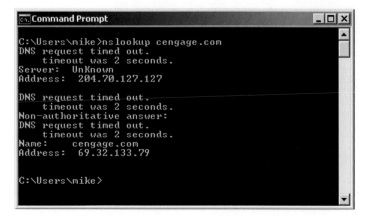

```
Command Prompt

C:\Users\mike>nslookup cengage.com
DNS request timed out.
    timeout was 2 seconds.
Server:  UnKnown
Address:  204.70.127.127

DNS request timed out.
    timeout was 2 seconds.
Non-authoritative answer:
DNS request timed out.
    timeout was 2 seconds.
Name:     cengage.com
Address:  69.32.133.79


C:\Users\mike>
```

Figure 6-28   Simple nslookup query of cengage.com

```
Command Prompt                                          _ □ ×

C:\Users\mike>nslookup -type=SOA cengage.com
Server:  resolver1.savvis.net
Address:  204.70.127.127

DNS request timed out.
    timeout was 2 seconds.
Non-authoritative answer:
cengage.com
        primary name server = tlauns3.ohcinmason.com
        responsible mail addr = hostmaster.ohcinmason.com
        serial  = 2008081203
        refresh = 7200 (2 hours)
        retry   = 3600 (1 hour)
        expire  = 86400 (1 day)
        default TTL = 3600 (1 hour)

cengage.com        nameserver = dns3.gale.com
cengage.com        nameserver = dns4.gale.com
cengage.com        nameserver = tlauns4.ohcinmason.com
cengage.com        nameserver = tlauns3.ohcinmason.com
cengage.com        nameserver = tlauns5.ohcinmason.com

C:\Users\mike>
```

Figure 6-29   Nslookup queries of SOA records at cengage.com

This query tells you that the client contacted the default DNS server at 204.70.127.127. In response to the query, the DNS server provides the client with the IP address of 69.32.133.79.

NOTE   Microsoft's implementation of nslookup uses the default behavior of appending the dns suffix to all queries it performs. This means that entering an FQDN of server1.bentech.net on a client with the dns suffix bentech.local results in the nslookup first querying server1.bentech.net.bentech.local. This allows for the use of unqualified query requests with nslookup. To prevent the appending of the dns suffix, dot-terminate your FQDN queries by ending the FQDN with a decimal point (.).

You can use noninteractive mode for querying specific records as well by adding the - type = *RecordType* parameter. For example, you want to see the SOA records for cengage.com. Using a record type of SOA produces the results shown in Figure 6-29.

Another helpful parameter is specifying a different DNS server that the preferred server uses by default. This is used when you troubleshoot problems with records on a DNS server. It is also a good way to determine if two DNS servers provide the same results when queried. Figure 6-30 shows the nslookup command performed with a public DNS server at 4.2.2.1.

```
Command Prompt                                          _ □ ×

C:\Users\mike>nslookup cengage.com 4.2.2.1
Server:  vnsc-pri.sys.gtei.net
Address:  4.2.2.1

DNS request timed out.
    timeout was 2 seconds.
DNS request timed out.
    timeout was 2 seconds.
Non-authoritative answer:
DNS request timed out.
    timeout was 2 seconds.
Name:    cengage.com
Address:  69.32.133.79

C:\Users\mike>
```

Figure 6-30   Nslookup query using a specific DNS server

For more detailed information, you can use the debug parameter with the nslookup command. This includes detailed information about the query process and the specific syntax of the query being sent to the DNS server by the client. Figure 6-31 shows the use of -debug when querying cengage.com.

In Figure 6-31, the server name is listed as Unknown for the IP address of 4.2.2.1. The reason for this is that nslookup performs a reverse lookup query when it launches. If a PTR record is unavailable for the DNS server being queried, you receive the name as Unknown. This does not mean that your nslookup query failed; rather, it means that a host name for your DNS server is unavailable through reverse lookup. This can be resolved by ensuring that reverse lookup zones are set up properly.

All the commands used earlier and many more are also available in interactive mode. Interactive mode provides a command prompt that responds only to nslookup commands. You launch nslookup in this mode by typing nslookup at the command prompt and pressing Enter. Another option is to type nslookup.exe in the Start menu search box or from the Run line to launch nslookup in its own window. Using the ? parameter lists the available nslookup commands and parameters you can use in interactive mode, as shown in Figure 6-32.

This provides the same functionality as noninteractive mode with greater flexibility. Using the server DnsServerIP command allows you to change the default DNS server in nslookup to one of your choice. This setting is temporary and is discarded when you close the nslookup shell by typing exit. Figure 6-33 shows the use of multiple commands in the nslookup.exe shell.

In Figure 6-33, you see that the default DNS server is set to 4.2.2.1, a query of cengage.com is performed, and the SOA records for cengage.com is performed.

An important command in nslookup is ls, or list. This lists all the host records on a remote domain and requests a zone transfer to a DNS server. For the most part, you use this command internally with your DNS servers because most public DNS servers refuse direct requests to transfer records for security reasons.

```
Command Prompt
C:\Users\mike>nslookup -debug cengage.com 4.2.2.1
------------
Got answer:
    HEADER:
        opcode = QUERY, id = 1, rcode = NOERROR
        header flags:  response, want recursion, recursion avail.
        questions = 1,  answers = 1,  authority records = 0,  additional = 0

    QUESTIONS:
        1.2.2.4.in-addr.arpa, type = PTR, class = IN
    ANSWERS:
    ->  1.2.2.4.in-addr.arpa
        name = vnsc-pri.sys.gtei.net
        ttl = 23265 (6 hours 27 mins 45 secs)

------------
Server:  vnsc-pri.sys.gtei.net
Address:  4.2.2.1

------------
Got answer:
    HEADER:
        opcode = QUERY, id = 2, rcode = NXDOMAIN
        header flags:  response, want recursion, recursion avail.
        questions = 1,  answers = 0,  authority records = 1,  additional = 0

    QUESTIONS:
        cengage.com.mcallenit.local, type = A, class = IN
    AUTHORITY RECORDS:
    ->  (root)
        ttl = 900 (15 mins)
        primary name server = a.root-servers.net
        responsible mail addr = nstld.verisign-grs.com
        serial  = 2008090600
        refresh = 1800 (30 mins)
        retry   = 900 (15 mins)
        expire  = 604800 (7 days)
        default TTL = 86400 (1 day)
```

Figure 6-31 Nslookup query using the –debug parameter

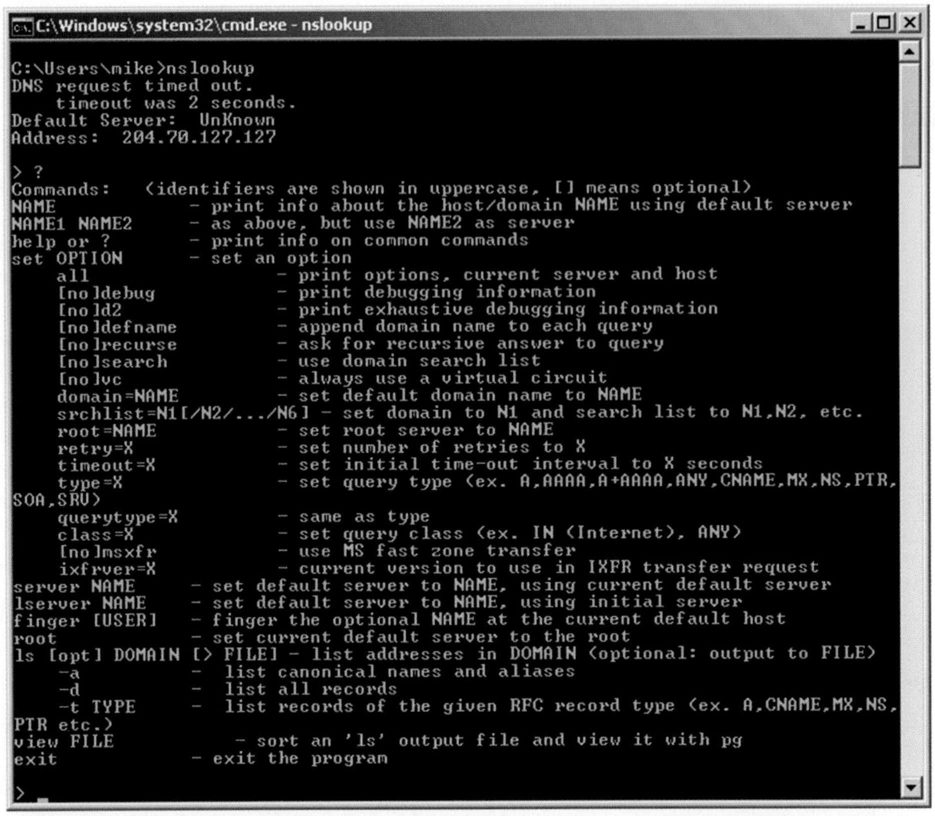

```
C:\Windows\system32\cmd.exe - nslookup                                  _ □ X

C:\Users\mike>nslookup
DNS request timed out.
    timeout was 2 seconds.
Default Server:  UnKnown
Address:  204.70.127.127

> ?
Commands:   (identifiers are shown in uppercase, [] means optional)
NAME          - print info about the host/domain NAME using default server
NAME1 NAME2   - as above, but use NAME2 as server
help or ?     - print info on common commands
set OPTION    - set an option
    all                  - print options, current server and host
    [no]debug            - print debugging information
    [no]d2               - print exhaustive debugging information
    [no]defname          - append domain name to each query
    [no]recurse          - ask for recursive answer to query
    [no]search           - use domain search list
    [no]vc               - always use a virtual circuit
    domain=NAME          - set default domain name to NAME
    srchlist=N1[/N2/.../N6] - set domain to N1 and search list to N1,N2, etc.
    root=NAME            - set root server to NAME
    retry=X              - set number of retries to X
    timeout=X            - set initial time-out interval to X seconds
    type=X               - set query type (ex. A,AAAA,A+AAAA,ANY,CNAME,MX,NS,PTR,
SOA,SRV)
    querytype=X          - same as type
    class=X              - set query class (ex. IN (Internet), ANY)
    [no]msxfr            - use MS fast zone transfer
    ixfrver=X            - current version to use in IXFR transfer request
server NAME    - set default server to NAME, using current default server
lserver NAME   - set default server to NAME, using initial server
finger [USER]  - finger the optional NAME at the current default host
root           - set current default server to the root
ls [opt] DOMAIN [> FILE] - list addresses in DOMAIN (optional: output to FILE)
    -a           - list canonical names and aliases
    -d           - list all records
    -t TYPE      - list records of the given RFC record type (ex. A,CNAME,MX,NS,
PTR etc.)
view FILE          - sort an 'ls' output file and view it with pg
exit           - exit the program

>
```

Figure 6-32   Commands and parameters for using nslookup in interactive mode

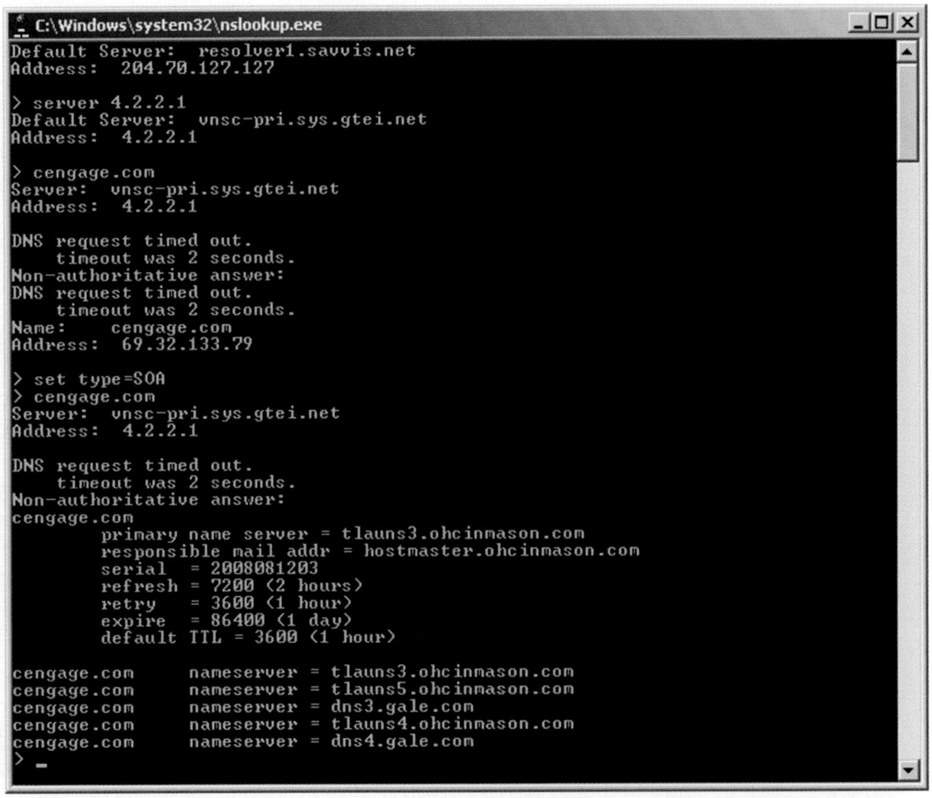

```
C:\Windows\system32\nslookup.exe                                        _ □ X
Default Server:  resolver1.savvis.net
Address:  204.70.127.127

> server 4.2.2.1
Default Server:  vnsc-pri.sys.gtei.net
Address:  4.2.2.1

> cengage.com
Server:  vnsc-pri.sys.gtei.net
Address:  4.2.2.1

DNS request timed out.
    timeout was 2 seconds.
Non-authoritative answer:
DNS request timed out.
    timeout was 2 seconds.
Name:    cengage.com
Address: 69.32.133.79

> set type=SOA
> cengage.com
Server:  vnsc-pri.sys.gtei.net
Address:  4.2.2.1

DNS request timed out.
    timeout was 2 seconds.
Non-authoritative answer:
cengage.com
    primary name server = tlauns3.ohcinmason.com
    responsible mail addr = hostmaster.ohcinmason.com
    serial  = 2008081203
    refresh = 7200 (2 hours)
    retry   = 3600 (1 hour)
    expire  = 86400 (1 day)
    default TTL = 3600 (1 hour)

cengage.com    nameserver = tlauns3.ohcinmason.com
cengage.com    nameserver = tlauns5.ohcinmason.com
cengage.com    nameserver = dns3.gale.com
cengage.com    nameserver = tlauns4.ohcinmason.com
cengage.com    nameserver = dns4.gale.com
> _
```

Figure 6-33   Using nslookup in interactive mode

Activity 6-16: Using Nslookup in Interactive Mode

Time Required: 15 minutes

Objective: Perform DNS queries with nslookup.

Description: Nslookup is a powerful tool for troubleshooting DNS issues and finding DNS information quickly. Every system administrator should have a good understanding of using nslookup in interactive mode. In this activity, you execute many commands while learning about nslookup.

1. In Server Manager on the MSN-SRV-0XX server, expand **Roles, DNS Server,** and **DNS** until you display the bentech.local forward lookup zone folder. Select the folder, click **More Actions,** and then click **Properties.**

2. In the bentech.local Properties dialog box, click the **Zone Transfers** tab. Click the **Allow zone transfers** check box. Accept the default of allowing transfers to any server. Click **OK.**

3. Open the command prompt, type **nslookup,** and then press **Enter** to enter interactive mode.

4. Type **bentech.local** and then press **Enter** to view the IP addresses associated with the zone.

5. Type **set type=NS** and then press **Enter.** This tells nslookup to query only for NS records.

6. Type **bentech.local** and then press **Enter.** Note that the query response gives you detailed information about the NS records for the zone.

7. Type **set type=all** and then press **Enter.** This tells nslookup to query for all DNS records.

8. Type **bentech.local** and then press **Enter.** Note that the query response provides a larger set of DNS records.

9. Type **ls bentech.local** and then press **Enter.** The `ls` command lists all the DNS records in a zone.

10. Type **server 4.2.2.1** and then press **Enter.** This tells nslookup to use a specific name server for any query commands that follow.

11. Type **ls bentech.local** and then press **Enter.** You receive an error because you do not have permissions to transfer zone records from 4.2.2.1. This is most likely because 4.2.2.1 is not authoritative for the zone. This error could also appear if a zone did not have zone transfer settings set properly.

12. Type **set debug** and then press **Enter.** This provides detailed information about the queries you are performing.

13. Type **bentech.local** and then press **Enter.** This displays the results of the queries along with all the detailed information, including query questions and answers.

14. Leave the command prompt open for the next activity.

Besides positive responses, you might receive error messages while using nslookup. Errors may range from negative responses that the domain or records you are requesting do not exist to refusal of a DNS server to transfer records. Table 6-3 lists some of the common nslookup errors you may receive.

Debug Log   Windows Server 2008 allows you to turn on debug logging for a DNS server. This is helpful when other troubleshooting tools, such as Event Viewer or nslookup, are not providing the information you need. To configure the DNS debug log, use the Debug Logging tab located in the Properties dialog box for a specific DNS server, as shown in Figure 6-34.

With the Debug log, you can capture packet data related to the DNS server functionality. Similar to the data you receive when using nslookup with the debug switch, the Debug log gives detailed information about the communications with a DNS server. This is helpful when troubleshooting a specific DNS server. For example, suppose you have a client computer that is having trouble resolving DNS names from your DNS server. You can turn on debug logging and re-create the issue by initiating queries from the client so that you can capture data about the

Table 6-3   Nslookup errors

Nslookup Response	Description
*** resolver1.savvis.net can't find bentech.local: Nonexistent domain	This indicates that the DNS server you are querying cannot find an answer.
DNS request timed out. time-out was 2 seconds.	This indicates that the DNS server is not responding in a timely manner.
*** Can't list domain *example.com*.: Query refused or Unspecified Error	This indicates that the DNS server hosting the DNS zone being queried refuses to transfer the domain records. In addition, you can receive this error if you are attempting to transfer the zone from a DNS server that is not authoritative for a zone.
*** Can't find server name for address w.x.y.z: Timed out	This indicates that the DNS server cannot be reached or that the service is not running on that computer.
*** Can't find server name for address w.x.y.z: Nonexistent domain	This error occurs when there is no PTR record for the name server's IP address. When nslookup.exe starts, it does a reverse lookup to get the name of the default server.

transaction. You then can open the Debug log in a text editor such as Notepad. The Debug log will list all the data packets to help you determine a possible cause. For the contents of each packet and more detailed information, you can choose Details on the Debug Logging tab. If you do not see any packets from the client, you know that there is a network connectivity problem between the client and the DNS server. Figure 6-35 shows an example of a Debug log depicting MSN-SRV-0XX's response for the NS records for bentech.local.

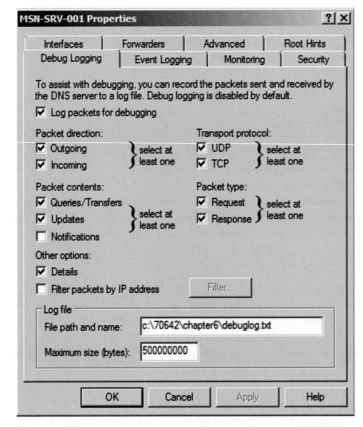

Figure 6-34   Debug Logging tab in the server Properties dialog box

```
debuglogSOAv3.txt - Notepad                              _ |□| X|
File  Edit  Format  View  Help
8/14/2008 10:54:46 AM 0E24 PACKET  UDP Snd 192.168.100.20  0003 R Q [8085 A DR
NOERROR] NS   (7)bentech(5)local(0)
UDP response info at 00C6A6B0
    Socket = 380
    Remote addr 192.168.100.20, port 50197
    Time Query=68071, Queued=0, Expire=0
    Buf length = 0x0200 (512)
    Msg length = 0x0059 (89)
    Message:
      XID         0x0003
      Flags       0x8580
        QR          1  (RESPONSE)
        OPCODE      0  (QUERY)
        AA          1
        TC          0
        RD          1
        RA          1
        Z           0
        RCODE       0  (NOERROR)
      QCOUNT    1
      ACOUNT    1
      NSCOUNT   0
      ARCOUNT   2
      QUESTION SECTION:
      Offset = 0x000c, RR count = 0
      Name        "(7)bentech(5)local(0)"
        QTYPE    NS (2)
        QCLASS   1
      ANSWER SECTION:
      Offset = 0x001f, RR count = 0
      Name        "[C00C](7)bentech(5)local(0)"
        TYPE     NS  (2)
        CLASS    1
        TTL      3600
        DLEN     14
        DATA     (11)msn-srv-001[C00C](7)bentech(5)local(0)
      AUTHORITY SECTION:
        empty
      ADDITIONAL SECTION:
      Offset = 0x0039, RR count = 0
      Name        "[C02B](11)msn-srv-001[C00C](7)bentech(5)local(0)"
        TYPE     A  (1)
        CLASS    1
        TTL      3600
        DLEN     4
        DATA     192.168.100.10
      Offset = 0x0049, RR count = 1
      Name        "[C02B](11)msn-srv-001[C00C](7)bentech(5)local(0)"
        TYPE     A  (1)
        CLASS    1
        TTL      3600
        DLEN     4
        DATA     10.0.10.33
```

Figure 6-35   Debug log

WINS

Prior to the proliferation of DNS usage with Windows 2000, **NetBIOS** was the naming convention of choice for Windows nodes. Every node on a Windows Server 2008 network is assigned a NetBIOS name at installation. This name is normally the same as the computer name, but it does not have to be. NetBIOS names are limited to 15 characters. Furthermore, NetBIOS names can be almost any combination of alphanumeric characters with the following exceptions:

• Spaces are not allowed in NetBIOS names.

• Names cannot use the following symbols—; : * ? " | ? / \.

As you have learned, all clients require IP addressing in some form to communicate with other clients. Before DNS was used in internal networks, NetBIOS names were resolved to IP addresses either by broadcast messages between clients or by using a **NetBIOS Name Server (NBNS)**. In Windows environments, the NBNS function is handled by **Windows Internet Name Service (WINS)**. WINS is Microsoft's technology for resolving NetBIOS names to IP addresses. Similar to DNS, WINS is based on two important pieces: the Server service and the Client service. The WINS server service is responsible for maintaining the WINS database and responding to WINS requests. The WINS client service is responsible for initiating WINS queries, client registration, and name renewal.

WINS is part of Windows Server 2008. However, it has been demoted from a role to a feature, which might indicate its future as part of Windows Server. No Windows Server 2008 components require WINS, and most new services—such as Exchange 2007—don't require it. There remains some need for flat name resolution (i.e., with clustered Exchange), but that can also be accomplished through the DNS search suffix list or by using the new Windows Server 2008 global names zone.

Activity 6-17: Installing WINS

Time Required: 15 minutes

Objective: Install a WINS server on your network.

Description: To support legacy applications and Exchange 2003, you have decided to install a WINS server on your network. It is decided that MSN-SRV-0XX will host WINS for your environment. In this activity, you add the WINS feature to MSN-SRV-0XX and create initial WINS records.

1. From the command prompt on the MSN-SRV-0XX server, type the following command and then press **Enter**:

   ```
   servermanagercmd.exe -install WINS-Server
   ```

2. From the command prompt, enter the following commands:

   ```
   netsh int ip set wins "bentech.local" static 192.168.100.10
   netsh
   ```

3. Log onto MSN-SC-0XX. Enter the following command at the command prompt:

   ```
   netsh int ip set wins "bentech.local" static 192.168.100.10
   ```

4. Type **shutdown /r** and then press **Enter** to reboot MSN-SC-0XX.

5. Switch back to MSN-SRV-0XX, and then open the WINS console. In the WINS console, right-click **Active Registrations**, and then click **Display Records**.

6. In the Display Records dialog box, click **Find Now**. This should display WINS records for MSN-SC-0XX and MSN-SRV-0XX.

7. Close the WINS console.

The Windows LMHOSTS file provides a NetBIOS name resolution method that can be used for small networks that do not use a WINS server. This is similar to the hosts file used by DNS for local name resolution. The LMHOSTS file is located in the %systemroot%\system32\drivers\etc directory. Using a text editor such as Notepad, you can open the LMHOSTS file for editing.

Activity 6-18: Editing the LMHOSTS File

Time Required: 15 minutes

Objective: Edit a user's LMHOSTS file.

Description: One of your users has a legacy application that does not support DNS names, only NetBIOS host names. You need a quick fix for that user that doesn't require you to make changes to your name resolution servers. You decide that editing the user's LMHOSTS file is the best solution for the problem.

1. From the command prompt on the MSN-SRV-0XX server, type **ping appserver** and then press **Enter**. This should fail because no name resolution record has been created for appserver.

2. In the Start Search box on the Start menu, type **c:\windows\system32\drivers\etc** and then press **Enter** to open the folder containing the LMHOSTS file.

3. Double-click the **lmhosts.sam** file.

4. Click the **Select a program from a list of installed programs** option button and then click **OK** to select the program you want to use to open the file.

5. In the list of applications, click **Notepad** and then click **OK**.

6. In Notepad, scroll down the LMHOSTS file until your reach the line, #The following example illustrates all of these extensions:. Click after that line and press **Enter** to insert a blank line.

7. Enter **192.168.225.125 AppServer #PRE #sample LMhosts entry for application server** on the new line.

8. Click **File** on the menu bar and then click **Save As**. Type the name as "**lmhosts**" including the quotation marks, change the Save as type to **All Files**, and then click **Save**.

9. If necessary, click **Yes** to confirm that you want to overwrite the existing file name lmhosts. Close Notepad.

10. Open the command prompt. Type **nbtstat -R** and press **Enter** to clear and preload the NBT remote name cache.

11. Type **nbtstat -c** and press **Enter** to verify that the computer name is loaded in the cache. (The "computer name" here refers to the AppServer computer.)

12. Type **ping appserver** and press **Enter** to verify that the IP address is being resolved.

13. Leave the command prompt open for the next activity.

WINS

In Windows Server 2008, DNS is the preferred option and is required if running AD DS. Theoretically, WINS should be required only on a network that has pre–Windows 2000 clients and servers that need name resolution. However, some applications, such as Microsoft Exchange, often require WINS to function fully. Exchange Server 2000 and 2003 still require WINS for full functionality.

Windows Server 2008 has no components that require WINS, and most new applications, such as Microsoft Exchange Server 2007, do not require WINS because they are fully supported by DNS. For applications that require NetBIOS name resolution, the DNS search suffix list can provide the same outcome (of providing an IP address) for clients. Another feature is the **global name zones (GNZs)**, a new feature in Windows Server 2008. GNZs provide single name–to–IP address resolution by creating CNAME records in a special GNZ. If a GNZ is created, a DNS server looks to the GNZ first and then to WINS.

Prior to creating a GNZ, you need to enable the functionality on your Windows Server 2008. You can do so from the command line. The following syntax enables global name support on a DNS server using the command-line utility DNScmd:

```
DNScmd ServerName /config /EnableGlobalNamesSupport 1
```

Creating a GNZ can be done through the DNS console like any other DNS zone, or it can be completed from the command line. To create the zone through the DNS console, you must create a new zone called GlobalNames. The name is not case sensitive, but the spelling must be exactly as shown. Another requirement is that all DNS servers in the forest must be enable to use global name zones.

The following command creates a GNZ on a DNS server:

```
dnscmd ServerName /ZoneAdd GlobalNames /DsPrimary /DP /forest
```

After you create the GNZ, you create CNAME records for each node requiring a NetBIOS name. Like CNAMES in forward lookup zones, these records map to the A records of each node.

Activity 6-19: Creating the GNZ

Time Required: 15 minutes

Objective: Create the GNZ and associated alias records.

Description: You are receiving reports from users having difficulties running an application that accesses data on widgetSRV1. After reviewing the application, you notice that the application uses NetBIOS, not DNS names, for connection with widgetSRV1. Instead of installing a WINS server in your environment, you decide to create a GNZ record for widgetSRV1 that points clients to widgetSRV1.widgets.local. In this activity, you enable the GNZ support on MSN-SRV-0XX, create the GNZ, and create an alias record for widgetSRV1.

1. At the command prompt on the MSN-SRV-0XX server, type **DNScmd msn-srv-0xx /config /EnableGlobalNamesSupport 1** and then press **Enter**. This allows the creation and use of the GNZ.

2. Type **DNScmd /ZoneAdd GlobalNames /DSPrimary /DP /Forest** and press **Enter**.

3. Type **ping widgetsrv1** and press **Enter**. You receive an error that the host could not be found because widgetsrv1 is a host in widgets.local. However, MSN-SRV-0XX has only bentech.local as a dns suffix.

4. In Server Manager, expand **Roles**, **DNS Server**, and **DNS** until you display the Forward Lookup Zones folder. Click the **GlobalNames** folder, choose **More Actions**, and then choose **New Alias (CNAME)**.

5. In the New Resource Record dialog box, type **widgetSRV1** as the Alias name and type **widgetSRV1** as the FQDN of the target host. Click **OK** to create the record.

6. At the command prompt, type **ping widgetSRV1** and press **Enter**. This time you receive a reply with the FQDN and IP address of 192.168.200.100. (Although the FQDN and IP address are returned, the pings will time out.)

7. Close the command prompt.

New DNS Features

Windows Server 2008 includes new DNS features. In this section, you will learn about the new features, how they are used, and how to implement them in Windows Server 2008. The features covered will include the following:

- Server Core and DNS
- Support for IPv6
- Primary read-only zones
- Link-local multicast name resolution
- Dynamic updates
- Background zone loading
- Global name zones and WINS

DNS on Server Core

With the introduction of Server Core, you can deploy a single or multirole server running DNS and other services without the increased footprint and resources required by the Windows GUI. Considering that services such as DHCP, DNS, and WINS often require little maintenance after they are initially created, Server Core is an excellent solution for deploying these roles on a hardened and secure server. Recall that Server Core also provides a low-maintenance, secure server in branch office locations where physical security is an issue and on-site administrators are not available or needed.

Support for IPv6

Windows Server 2008 DNS is ready for IPv6 by default. It supports the IPv6 address numbering scheme along with the AAAA resource records that are used for forward name resolution. Reverse lookup zones are supported by using the new IP6.ARPA domain. For clients using IPv6 and IPv4, dynamic updates update both the AAAA and the A records for the clients, respectively.

Primary Read-Only Zone

Windows Server 2008 AD DS introduces you to a new type of DC called a **read-only domain controller (RODC)**. RODCs are like any other DC; they contain a copy of the AD DS database and can answer client requests. However, all the information on the RODC is read-only. Changes cannot be made to AD DS via the RODC. This provides more secure options for providing DCs in locations that may not be entirely secure such as branch offices. Another feature of RODC is that you can define the accounts that will be stored on it. Instead of having the entire AD DS database, you can choose to have only the security accounts of the local users to a branch office located on the server. Requests for security accounts not held by the RODC are passed to the nearest standard, or writable, DC. That way, if the server is compromised, it has limited exposure.

If you are implementing RODCs, you should know how DNS changes when installed on a RODC. Unlike standard DCs that act in a multimaster updatable configuration, RODCs running AD-integrated DNS hold a **primary read-only zone** for the forestDNSzones and DomainDNSzones. This means clients do not update their records via an RODC. Requests for updating DNS records are passed to a standard DC for processing via dynamic updates. Again, this provides improved security in cases where an unauthorized person gains physical access to a remote machine. They cannot compromise the local machine and propagate malicious DNS entries to the other DCs.

Activity 6-20: Creating an RODC

Time Required: 20 minutes

Objective: Create an RODC.

Description: As part of the deployment of the network for bentech.local, you need to implement an RODC on MSN-SC-0XX because it will be placed where physical security cannot be guaranteed. In this activity, you will create an RODC on MSN-SC-0XX. The MSN-SC-0XX server will become a primary read-only DNS server for the bentech.local zone because DNS is installed on the server.

1. Log onto MSN-SC-0XX using the domain.

2. At the command prompt, enter the following command to add MSN-SC-0XX into the bentech.local domain:

```
netdom join \\MSN-SC-0XX /domain:bentech.local
/UserD:bentech.local\administrator /PasswordD:P@ssw0rd

shutdown /r /t 0
```

After the computer reboots, you should log onto the MSN-SC-0XX server.

3. At the command prompt, start Notepad by typing **notepad** and pressing **Enter**. In Notepad, enter the following information:

```
[DCINSTALL]

InstallDNS=Yes

ConfirmGc=No

CriticalReplicationOnly=No
```

```
DisableCancelForDnsInstall=No
Password=P@ssw0rd
RebootOnCompletion=No
ReplicaDomainDNSName=bentech.local
ReplicaOrNewDomain=ReadOnlyReplica
SafeModeAdminPassword=P@ssw0rd
SiteName=Default-First-Site-Name
UserDomain=bentech.local
Username=administrator
```

4. Save the file in its current location as **rodcpromo.txt**. Now when you run the dcpromo command in Server Core, it will use the answer file for the installation.

5. Close Notepad.

6. At the command prompt, type **dcpromo /answer:rodcpromo.txt** and then press **Enter**. This process will take 5 to 10 minutes and will require a reboot once completed.

7. Type **shutdown /r** to reboot MSN-SC-0XX.

8. Log onto MSN-SRV-0XX. In Server Manager, expand **ADDs** and expand the AD hierarchy to display Domain Controllers OU. Verify that an object exists for MSN-SC-0XX.

Link-Local Multicast Name Resolution

Link-local multicast name resolution (LLMNR) is a new protocol whereby Windows 2008 member servers, Vista clients, and Windows 2003 member servers can resolve names on the local subnet even when the DNS server is down. Usable by IPv4 and IPv6 clients, LLMNR clients exchange simple messages to verify that they have a unique name on the local subnet and to determine the names of their neighbors so that they may communicate with them. These messages have a format similar to DNS queries but use different ports.

A good example of where you might want to use LLMNR is when you have a small network where installing a DNS server is not feasible, such as a work group environment. Another option would be when creating an **ad-hoc wireless** connection to privately connect two or more clients. LLMNR allows clients on the wireless network to communicate with each other without having to install DNS on one of the machines.

Link-local multicast name resolution is defined by RFC 4795. For more information, review RFC 4795 at *www.ietf.org/rfc*. Also, visit the November 2006 article by The Cable Guy at *http://technet.microsoft.com*.

DNS Client Changes

The DNS client service in Windows Server 2008 and Windows Vista includes the following changes to provide better performance:

- Clients periodically perform a check to ensure that they are authenticating with a local DC. Previously, a client would fall back to the closest DC only when forced. This setting is configured through the use of Group Policy.

- Clients use AD DS site link costs to determine the nearest DC instead of randomly searching for a DC. You assign costs to site links so that clients can determine the lowest-cost path. This is a good option to enable if you have sites connected by slow WAN links. (It is disabled by default.)

- Clients use LLMNR to resolve names on a local network segment when a DNS server is not available.

Background Zone Loading

DNS servers that host a large number of zones and DNS records can take a long time to load all the records if the server or DNS service is restarted. New in Windows Server 2008, AD DS DNS servers load their records as a background process known as **background zone loading**. This allows the DNS server to handle client requests immediately instead of waiting until the entire DNS zone is loaded. If a DNS client requests data in a zone that has already been loaded, the DNS server responds to the request. If the DNS server receives a client request for information that has yet to be loaded, the DNS server retrieves the information directly from AD. Mostly, this benefits large organizations with huge DNS zones.

GNZ

GNZ, as discussed in the earlier section on WINS, allows you to host computer name–to–IP address resolution records in their Windows Server 2008 DNS zone instead of using WINS or some other method.

Chapter Summary

- In an AD DS environment, you can run two types of DNS servers: standard DNS servers and AD DS DNS–integrated servers.

- AD DS uses DCs to store all the AD objects and information about an environment. AD DS DCs use multimaster replication to keep their data updated. All DCs are writable, so changes to AD can be made on any DC, not just the primary DC.

- AD DS uses a database structure to maintain its objects. This structure is based on the DNS domain naming hierarchy. The AD DS database is built on three stores, or partitions.

- AD requires DNS for locating DCs, or the DC locator function. Along with resolving DCs, AD uses DNS naming conventions in the architecture of its domains.

- Every AD domain in Windows Server 2008 has a naming convention based on a DNS domain name. In AD, domains and computers are represented as objects, while they are represented as nodes in DNS.

- Determining whether to have a DNS server host a single DNS zone or multiple DNS zones depends on factors such as the AD DS site structure, the distribution of your IT department, and your security needs.

- Windows Server 2008 DNS implementations support two types of forwarding: standard and conditional. Standard forwarding instructs a DNS server to forward all nonauthoritative queries, or queries for DNS zones not hosted on a server, to another server or servers. Conditional forwarding instructs a DNS server to forward nonauthoritative queries for a specific domain to a specific DNS server or servers.

- Dynamic DNS allows supported DNS clients to dynamically update their DNS records on a DNS server. Dynamic DNS is often used along with DHCP in environments where clients and servers may use dynamic IP addresses. Dynamic DNS will update the A, AAAA, and PTR records for DNS clients.

- As an administrator, you choose how clients perform dynamic updates—as a secure update or nonsecure update. Only authenticated clients can perform secure updates, while any client can perform a nonsecure update.

- The DNS console is the main GUI tool used for managing DNS. It provides access to all the DNS zones available on a server, along with configuration settings for the DNS role.

- You can configure DNS at the DNS server, zone, or record level.

- If you have multiple Web servers hosting static content and you want users to be able to connect with any of the servers with a single Web address, set up round-robin DNS, which allows you to configure load balancing of servers based on DNS name resolution information.

- During forwarding, a DNS server sends queries made for DNS zones that do not match its own zone and cache information to another internal or external DNS server. In standard forwarding, all nonmatching queries are sent to one or more servers. In conditional forwarding, forwarding is based on a specific domain name.

- Troubleshoot DNS when your clients are having difficulties connecting to applications or resources, logging onto the network, finding other clients and resources, and accessing the Internet.

Key Terms

_msdcs.*forestname* zone   The Domain Name System (DNS) zone created in an Active Directory Domain Services (AD DS)–integrated zone that is responsible for maintaining the records of the servers responsible for the forest services.

Active Directory–integrated DNS (AD DS DNS)   A type of DNS available in Windows Server 2008 where the DNS database is stored within Active Directory (AD). DNS replication occurs through the normal AD replication process.

Active Directory Domain Services (AD DS)   Microsoft's implementation of a directory services infrastructure.

Active Directory Domain Services Installation Wizard   The second stage of the AD DS installation process where a Windows Server 2008 server is promoted to a domain controller (DC). This process is often referred to as dcpromo, which is the name of the executable for the process.

AD DS sites   Sites designed to limit the replication traffic across wide area network links as this traffic may affect the performance on client and user computers. Although multiple AD DS sites might not require multiple domains, each site has at least one DC for managing requests from local clients.

ad-hoc wireless   A method for wireless devices to directly communicate with each other. Operating in ad-hoc mode allows all wireless devices within range of each other to discover and communicate in peer-to-peer fashion without involving central access points.

background zone loading   A new feature of AD DS–integrated DNS servers that loads DNS records as a background process to allow the server to respond more quickly to client requests after restarting the server of the DNS service.

conditional forwarding   Forwarding based on a specific domain name.

cross-domain name resolution   The process where a client in a domain seeks to resolve the host name for target computer in another domain.

DCDiag   A Windows Server 2008 utility that allows administrators to perform diagnostic queries of your DCs.

delegation   The process by which a DNS namespace is split so that a child, or subdomain, is stored in a different zone outside the parent, or root, domain.

domain controller locator   A service that runs at logon to provide the client with the location of a DC that can authenticate its requests.

global catalog (GC) server   A DC in an AD DS forest that maintains a database containing objects from the entire forest, not just specific domains along with the directory services database.

Global Logs folder   The folder located in the DNS console that stores a subset of Windows Events encompassing events based on DNS.

global name zone (GNZ)   A feature of Windows Server 2008 DNS that provides single name–to–Internet Protocol (IP) address resolution by creating CNAME records in a special DNS zone. If a global name zone is created, a DNS server looks to the global name zone prior to failing over to Windows Internet Name Service.

Kerberos   The computer security protocol used by AD DS clients and servers for secure communications. It is based on mutual authentication. The name comes from the three-headed dog that guarded the gates of Hades in Greek mythology.

Kerberos Key Distribution Center (KDC)   The security accounts database stored within the AD DS database responsible for managing and storing security account information.

link-local multicast name resolution (LLMNR)   A new protocol whereby Windows 2008 member servers, Vista clients, and Window 2003 member servers can resolve names on the local subnet even when the DNS server is down.

locator DNS resource records   To find DCs in a domain or forest, a client queries DNS for the SRV and A DNS resource records of the DC. The resource records provide the client with the names and IP addresses of the DCs.

multimaster environment   An environment where more than one server is responsible for providing current information and changing information. In an AD DS environment, DCs are multimaster and AD DS-integrated DNS servers are multimaster.

NetBIOS   The naming convention of choice for Windows nodes prior to the use of DNS. Every node on a Windows Server 2008 network is assigned a NetBIOS name at installation. This name is normally the same as the computer name, but it does not have to be. NetBIOS names are limited to 15 characters.

NetBIOS Name Server (NBNS)   A server responsible for providing NetBIOS name–to–IP resolution for network clients.

netlogon service   The client service responsible for finding AD DS resources such as DCs and GC servers.

No-refresh interval   The time between the most recent refresh of a record time stamp and the moment when the time stamp may be refreshed again.

partition   A storage area within AD where parts of the AD DS database are stored.

primary domain controller (PDC)   A single-master domain controller from a Windows NT domain.

primary read-only zone   Read-only domain controllers running AD-integrated DNS only hold a primary read-only zone only for the forestDNSzones and DomainDNSzones.

read-only domain controller (RODC)   An AD DS domain controller that contains a read-only copy of the AD DS database and can answer client requests. Changes cannot be made to AD DS via the RODC.

Refresh interval   The interval from the point that the No-refresh interval expires. It is number of days Dynamic DNS waits for the client to refresh its record before it becomes stale.

root domain   The first domain created when AD DS is installed and configured on the first domain controller on the network.

round-robin DNS   A feature of Windows Server 2008 DNS that allows multiple IP addresses to be assigned to a single host name.

scavenge   To use time stamps to determine when DNS records can update themselves and whether a record has exceeded the length of time records can exist without an update. You can scavenge manually or automatically in Windows Server 2008.

single-master environment   An environment where one server holds the writable copy of a database such as the DNS database. Standard Primary DNS zones are single master.

stale record   A DNS record that is out of date or no longer valid. These can occur when the Dynamic DNS process does not delete records out of DNS properly.

Windows Internet Name Service (WINS)   A Microsoft-developed name server that resolves Windows network computer names (also known as NetBIOS names) to Internet IP addresses, allowing Windows computers on a network to easily find and communicate with each other. WINS has been replaced by DNS for most name resolution since Windows 2000. However, some legacy computers and application that do not support DNS require WINS to function.

Review Questions

1. Which two network services are required for dynamic updates to function properly in a Windows 2008 environment? (Choose two answers.)

   a. POP3

   b. HOSTS

   c. SMTP

   d. DNS

   e. WINS

   f. DHCP

2. Which one of the following types of DNS records does a domain client use to find a DC?

   a. DC

   b. SRV

   c. CNAME

   d. A

   e. MX

3. What responsibility does the DC locator function perform on an AD client?

   a. Starting the netlogon service

   b. Locating the names of local domain controllers from the HOSTS file

   c. Querying DNS for the location of local DCs and GC servers

   d. Querying WINS for the location of local DCs and GC servers

4. Name two advantages of using AD DS–integrated DNS zones over standard DNS zones. (Choose two answers.)

   a. All AD DS–integrated DNS zone records are stored in a flat file that is easily backed up.

   b. AD DS–integrated DNS uses the multimaster replication process of AD.

   c. Standard DNS zones are more secure.

   d. All AD DS–integrated DNS zone records are stored in the AD database.

   e. AD DS–integrated DNS will resolve NetBIOS names by default using Global Name Zones.

5. For clients that support Dynamic DNS, what records are updated in a DNS zone? (Choose two answers.)

   a. MX

   b. CNAME

   c. A/AAAA

   d. SRV

   e. PTR

6. Which one of the following clients do not support dynamic updates natively?

   a. Windows 2000

   b. Windows 2008

   c. Windows NT 4.0

   d. Windows 2003

7. Clients are sporadically having trouble connecting to your internal Web site at intranet. widgets.local. Round-robin DNS is used to load balance your Web site on three servers: web1.widgets.local, web2.widgets.local, and web3.widgets.local. You suspect that one of the Web servers has failed but are not sure which one. What steps would you perform to resolve this issue and maintain load balancing of your Web site? (Choose two answers.)

   a. Set round-robin DNS to "Discard Hosts that are not available"

   b. Turn off round-robin DNS

   c. Ping each of the Web servers individually

   d. Delete the A record for the failed server

   e. Delete the CNAME for intranet.widgets.local that points to the failed server

   f. Instruct your end users to use the two functional Web servers

8. Calls to the help desk are reporting that users are receiving incorrect host name requests for your internal file server, files.widgets.local. It appears that the users with 10.1.1.10, or NS1.widgets.local, as their preferred DNS server are having trouble, while 10.1.1.20, or ns2.widgets.local, is resolving properly. Which of the following commands would verify what ns1.widgets.local resolves for files.widgets.local?

   a. nslookup -type = SRV files.widgets.local 10.1.1.10

   b. nslookup -type = A files.widgets.local 10.1.1.20

   c. nslookup -type = A 10.1.1.10 files.widgets.local

   d. nslookup -type = A files.widgets.local ns1.widgets.local

9. Which of the following is *not* a valid NetBIOS name in Windows Server 2008?

   a. NS1-Server

   b. NS1 Server

   c. NS1_Server

   d. NS1Server

   e. NameServer1Server

10. What new feature of Windows Server 2008 DNS is a viable replacement for WINS in some situations?

   a. Primary read-only zone

   b. Global names zone

   c. Link-local multimaster name resolution

   d. Stub zone

11. You need to edit the LMHOSTS file on server FS1.widgets.local. In what directory is the LMHOSTS file located?

   a. %systemroot%\system\drivers\etc

   b. %systemroot%\system32\wins\

   c. %systemroot%\system32\drivers\etc

   d. %systemroot%\system32\lmhosts

   e. %systemroot%\system32\

12. Which of the following is used to add WINS to Windows Server 2008?

   a. In Server Manager, click Add Roles to add WINS

   b. In Server Manager, click Add Features to add WINS

   c. Use DNScmd from the command line

   d. Use Add/Remove Windows Components in the Control Panel

13. Which one of the following does WINS resolve?

    a. NetBIOS names to IP addresses

    b. Global names to IP addresses

    c. Host names to IP addresses

    d. Computer names to IP addresses

14. Which of the following can be used in place of WINS on networks that require the resolution of NetBIOS names? (Choose two answers.)

    a. LMHOSTS file

    b. HOSTS file

    c. Global names zone

    d. Stub zone

15. Using nslookup in interactive mode, which of the following commands let you view all the MX records for widgets.net stored on the DNS server, NS1.widgets.net? (Choose three commands.)

    a. >set type=MX

    b. >NS1.widgets.net

    c. >widgets.net

    d. >server NS1.widgets.net

    e. >server widgets.net

    f. >ls NS1.widgets.net

    g. >set type=A

16. Which tools in Windows Server 2008 can be used to enable global name zones? (Choose two answers.)

    a. Registry editor

    b. Nslookup

    c. DNS console

    d. DNScmd

    e. Server Manager

17. What tool can you use to view the data packets related to DNS activity?

    a. Event Viewer

    b. Debug Log

    c. nslookup -verbose

    d. DCDiag

    e. Netdiag

    f. DNS Network Monitor

18. What tool do you use to view messages, warnings, or errors specific to the DNS Server role in Windows Server 2008?

    a. Event Viewer

    b. Debug Log

    c. nslookup -verbose

    d. DCDiag

    e. Netdiag

    f. DNS Network Monitor

19. Which of the following commands will flush the DNS client cache?

    a. DNScmd /flushcache

    b. Ipconfig /flushcache

    c. Ipconfig /registerdns

    d. Ipconfig /flushcache

    e. Ipconfig /flushdns

20. Which of the following commands will clear the DNS server cache?

    a. DNScmd /clearcache

    b. Ipconfig /flushcache

    c. Ipconfig /registerdns

    d. Ipconfig /flushcache

21. You have just added new DNS servers to the server options on your DHCP server. Generally, what is the quickest way for your clients to receive the new settings?

    a. Run ipconfig /registerDNS on the client

    b. Reboot the workstation twice

    c. Wait for the DHCP client to renew its lease

    d. Run ipconfig /renew on the client

    e. Clear the DNS server cache

22. You have been asked to reconfigure the size of the DNS event log based on new information about your network environment. You have determined that your DNS servers handle 10,000 events per day and you need to keep 14 days of information. Which of the following sizes would best meet the needs of your environment?

    a. 70,000 KB

    b. 67,392 KB

    c. 54,700 KB

    d. 70,016 KB

    e. 70,048 KB

23. Which of the following commands starts the process of creating a DC on a Windows Server 2008 computer with AD DS already instead?

    a. dcadd.exe

    b. servermanagercmd.exe -install DC

    c. dcpromo.exe

    d. servermanagercmd.exe -install AD-DSRole

    e. ipconfig /showroles

Case Projects

Case Project 6-1: Troubleshooting DNS Records

You have been hired to determine the cause of e-mail and Web site outages at a local company, Bender Technology. Bender Technology owns the public domain of bentech.net, which it uses to receive e-mail and host its Web site. Bender Technology's network is connected to the Internet by a router and firewall with the FQDN of FW.bentech.net. Use the utilities for troubleshooting DNS to determine why mail destined for bentech.net is not arriving at the network. Your answer should include the DNS errors and issues that you find along with the changes necessary to route mail properly.

Case Project 6-2: Resolving NetBIOS Name Resolution Problems

Badger Technology, a local company, has recently upgraded its network from Windows 2000 Server to Windows Server 2008. Since the upgrade, 10 Badger users have been unable to use an important line-of-business application. This desktop application uses name resolution to connect to a central database on the network. The database server is called DB1.badgertech.priv and has an IP address of 10.10.10.50. Unfortunately, it is an older application and does not support the use of DNS. Based on your study of name resolution, list the options available for resolving this issue. Your answer should include at least two technologies that would resolve this problem, along with details on how each technology would be implemented.

Case Project 6-3: Installing AD

You need to add AD DS to your case project server, CS-SRV-001. Using the tools available in Windows Server 2008, install AD DS and promote CS-SRV-001 to be the first DC for badgertech.local. You need to remove all of the currently hosted DNS zones prior to beginning this activity. See Case Projects 5-2 and 5-3 if necessary.

Case Project 6-4: Installing a Read-Only DC

You need to install a read-only DC on CS-SCSRV-001. Along with creating the RODC, CS-SCSRV-001 should host a primary read-only zone for badgertech.local.

chapter 7

Configuring File Services in Windows Server 2008

After reading this chapter and completing the exercises, you will be able to:

- Discuss File Services in Windows Server 2008
- Install the Distributed File System in Windows Server 2008
- Discuss and create shared file resources in Windows Server 2008

At its core, a server is responsible for providing access to resources used by client computers. Clients connect to a server over the network to gain access to a shared file or to store data from an application. Handling these types of requests for file resources is the focus of this chapter.

Similar to Windows Server 2003, Windows Server 2008 provides clients access to files and folders across the network. However, Windows Server 2008 uses new or improved technologies, such as an improved Distributed File Services (DFS) feature and the improved File Sharing Wizard.

In this chapter, you will learn about File Services in Windows Server 2008. You will start by examining the components of the File Services role. Next, you will begin working with permissions and learn how they are used for sharing files and folders. You also explore how to configure hard disks and allocate disk space. Finally, you will be introduced to DFS and learn how it can be incorporated into a Windows Server 2008 network.

Introduction to File Services

One of the fundamental roles of a server is to act as an electronic filing cabinet. Depending only on the space available on your servers and the needs of your clients, your ability to store data electronically is otherwise limitless.

The Windows Server 2008 File Services role contains many functions for providing access to and storage of electronic data. Each function includes a specific service for network clients. These functions include the following:

- *File Server*—The most basic of the File Services functions, the **file server** is responsible for sharing and managing data resources on a Windows Server 2008 computer.

- *Distributed File System*—This function is improved in Windows Server 2008. DFS provides a framework for creating a centralized point of entry for accessing network data. DFS uses a common namespace as the entry point for all clients to access data on one or more servers.

- *File Server Resource Manager*—This console provides you with a number of tools for managing and reporting on file server resources, including folder and files. Using the console, you can understand, control, and manage the quantity and type of data stored on your servers. By using the File Server Resource Manager (FSRM), you can place quotas on folders and volumes, actively screen files, and generate comprehensive storage reports.

- *Services for Network File System*—Services for Network File System (NFS) provide a file-sharing solution for enterprises that have a mixed Windows and UNIX environment. With Services for NFS, you can transfer files between computers running Windows Server 2008 and UNIX operating systems using the NFS protocol.

- *Windows Server 2003 File Services*—This function provides backward compatibility for Windows Server 2003 computers by providing access to two Windows Server 2003 features: the File Replication Service and the Indexing Service.

Along with the File Services role, you can add to Windows Server 2008 a number of other features that support file services. These features include the following:

- *Windows Backup*—This feature is Microsoft's improved backup utility for Windows Server 2008. Windows Backup and other disaster recovery features are covered in Chapter 10.

- *Storage Manager for SANS*—This feature allows you to manage the disk subsystems for the storage area networks (SANS) on their network.

- *Failover Clustering*—This feature allows administrators to implement fault tolerance of service applications through the use of server clustering. With failover clustering, one active node has a corresponding passive node that will step in to service clients should the active node fail.

Installing the File Server Role

Using a Windows Server 2008 Server as a file server is easy because all versions of Windows Server 2008 support the File Server role by default. You install the File Server role by activating File Services if necessary. The File Server role, its role services, and other features can be installed through the graphical user interface (GUI) via the Server Manager console. To work from the command line, you can use servermanagercmd.exe (Full versions of Windows Server 2008) and ocsetup.exe (Server Core versions of Windows Server 2008).

Creating a single, stand-alone file server is satisfactory for small environments that have basic file server needs. However, larger networks have different requirements. Instead of a single file server, larger networks often need multiple file servers in the same location and additional file servers distributed across the network. If your file services infrastructure spreads to multiple locations, you should consider the effect this has on wide area network (WAN) connections and users at remote sites. Technologies such as DFS help you manage such a configuration. DFS allows you to create a centralized entry point for accessing data stores on the network. It also distributes that data across multiple servers for higher availability. You will learn more about DFS later in this chapter.

File and Folder Sharing

One of the basic ways of making resources available on a network is through file and folder sharing. Sharing creates a **network access point** for clients to access data across the network. This access point is referred to as a share. Clients use **Server Message Block (SMB)** connections to access shared resources. The SMB protocol can be used on private networks and the Internet by communicating over TCP/IP.

Public and Standard Sharing

Windows Server 2008 supports two types of file sharing: public folder sharing and standard file sharing. Public folder sharing is a new feature first introduced in Windows Vista, whereas standard file sharing is traditional file sharing, which makes files and folders available from a network location.

Public Folder Sharing   Public folder sharing allows users to share files with all the users logged on locally or on the network, if that feature is enabled. Public folders are located in the %systemdrive%\Users\Public directory or c:\Users\Public in a default Windows Server 2008 installation. In workgroup environments, access to public folders is controlled through password protection. Network access can be restricted to either read and execute permissions or read, write, create, and delete permissions. You manage public folder sharing in the Network and Sharing Center, as shown in Figure 7-1.

Activity 7-1: Using Public Folder Sharing

Time Required: 10 minutes.

Objective: Learn how to use public folder sharing.

Description: You have two documents that you plan to store on MSN-SRV-0XX so that they are available to local and network users. Users need only read access to the files. In this activity, you will create two text files and share them on the network using public folder sharing.

1. On the MSN-SRV-0XX computer, open Windows Explorer and browse to **C:\Users\ Public\Public Documents**.

2. In the Public Documents folder, create two text documents named **Public1.txt** and **Public2.txt**.

3. In the Start Search box on the Start menu, type **Network and Sharing Center** and then press **Enter**.

4. In the Network and Sharing Center, click the **down arrow** button to the right of Public folder sharing. This exposes three options for Public folder sharing.

5. Click **Turn on sharing so anyone with network access can open files** and then click **Apply**. Notice that Public folder sharing is now labeled On (read only) with a green light.

6. In the Start Search box on the Start menu, type **\\msn-srv-0xx\public\documents** and then press **Enter**. This will open the Documents folder in the Public folder.

7. Log onto MSN-SC-0XX, open a command prompt, type **net use x: \\msn-srv-0xx\public**, and then press **Enter**. This maps a drive to the Public folder.

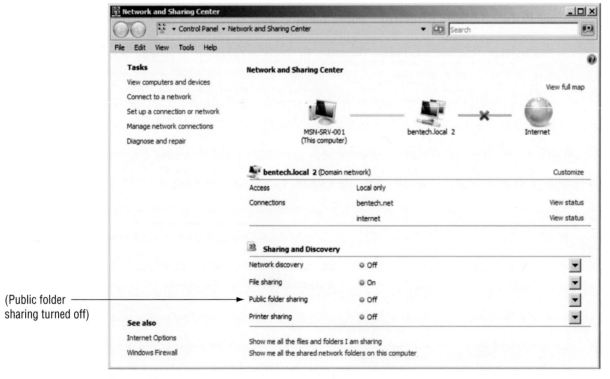

(Public folder sharing turned off)

Figure 7-1   Network and Sharing Center

8. Type **x:** and then press **Enter** to change your command prompt to the Public folder Type **cd documents** and then press **Enter** to switch to the documents folder.

9. Type **dir** and then press **Enter** to view the folder's contents.

10. On MSN-SRV-0XX, turn off Public folder sharing in the Network and Sharing Center.

11. Switch back to the command prompt on MSN-SC-0XX, type **dir**, and then press **Enter**. You will receive an error message stating "The network name cannot be found" because you turned off the share you mapped the x drive.

12. Log off MSN-SC-0XX.

Although public folder sharing may have some administrative uses, such as providing a central location on a server for administrative scripts and documents, the number of times different users log onto a server locally should be low. Even with the proper security, this will increase the attack surface of your server and make it more at risk. Public folder sharing usage on Windows Server 2008 servers should be carefully thought out prior to deploying.

Standard File Sharing   **Standard file sharing** makes files and folders accessible from a network location. In Windows Server 2008, standard file sharing is permitted on New Technology File System (NTFS) volumes and partitions and File Allocation Table 32 (FAT32) volumes. NTFS is the preferred format in Windows Server 2008 due to its more robust features and file-level security. Access to resources contained on shares on NTFS volumes is determined by combining NTFS, or user-level, file and folder permissions and share permissions, both of which are discussed later in this chapter. Shares on FAT32 volumes can only use share permissions; they do not have the ability to use file or folder-level security as NTFS does.

While Windows Server 2008 supports FAT32 volumes on all drives except the system partition, it is highly recommended not to use FAT32 on Windows Servers. FAT32 lacks the level of security required by current networks.

Access Control

In order for a client to access shared resources, it needs to have permissions to access those resources. On Windows Server 2008, these permissions are split into two categories: share-level permissions and user-level permissions.

Share-Level Permissions   **Share-level permissions**, or **share permissions**, are defined at the shared resource level and allow clients access to a network share. For file resources, share permissions have three different levels, which are described in Table 7-1.

Share-level permissions apply only when a file or folder is being accessed via the network and do not apply to a user logged into the machine locally. NTFS permissions are retained when a file or folder is backed up, while share permissions are not. As a result, the security and record details of NTFS permissions can be retained for disaster recovery.

Table 7-1   Shared folder permissions

Permission	Description
Read	Allows you to view files and subdirectories and execute applications but not make any changes
Change	Includes read permissions and the ability to add, delete, or change files or subdirectories
Full Control	Allows you to perform all functions on all files and folders within the share
Deny	Denies access to the files and folders

As a best practice, it is most efficient to configure share permissions with authenticated users having Full Control access. Then, the NTFS permissions should configure each group with standard permissions. This provides excellent security for local and network access to the resource. It also provides excellent protection of the resource when it is backed up and when the resource name is changed or relocated. Recall that the NTFS permissions will protect the resource even if the share permissions are set to Full Control access. On FAT partitions, however, that share permissions are the only permissions available, so you need to manage them more carefully.

Default and Administrative Shares

When Windows Server 2008 is installed, some default shares are created. These shares are mostly administrative shares, or shares hidden from regular users. **Administrative shares** can be identified by name because they always end with a dollar sign ($). For example, C$ is an administrative share used to access the C: drive of a computer. Administrative shares give access to specific resources and perform different functions. Figure 7-2 shows the default shares displayed on the Shares tab in the Share and Storage Management console.

The default shares include the following information:

- *Drive Letter Shares*—Known as administrative shares, these shares provide you with quick over-the-network access to the drives on a remote system. By default, all hard disk drives created on a Windows Server 2008 computer are assigned an associated administrative share.

- *Admin$*—This share provides you with network access to the Windows Server 2008 system files on a remote computer. By default, the system files, also known by the environmental variable of %systemroot%, are located in the c:\Windows directory.

- *IPC$*—This share is used by Windows Server 2008 for sharing resources, not files or folders, and facilitating communication between processes and computers. IPC$ is used for

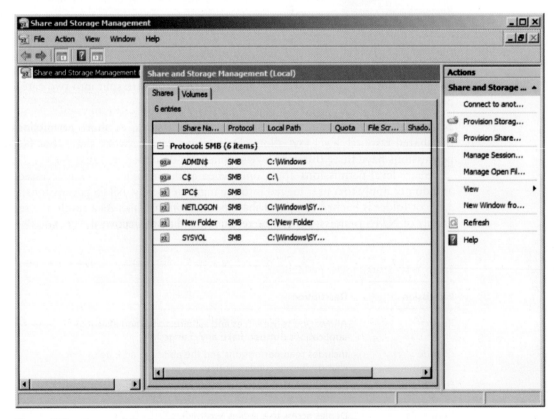

Figure 7-2   Shares tab in the Share and Storage Management console

any remote management function not related to the sharing of files. For example, IPC$ is used to exchange authentication data between computers wanting to communicate.

- *NETLOGON*—This share appears on all domain controllers (DCs) in an Active Directory Domain Services (AD DS) environment. The NETLOGON share is used to store information users read and access as part of network logon and logoff processes. Items such as logon scripts, installation programs, and profile information are often stored in the NETLOGON share. By default, it is located in the %systemroot%\sysvol*domainname*\SCRIPTS directory on every DC.

- *PRINT$*—This share is used by Windows Server 2008 for storing print drivers that are provided to clients when they install a network printer from the server. By default, this share maps to the %systemroot%\Windows32\spool\drivers directory

- *SYSVOL*—This share is used by DCs for internal operations. By default, it is located in the %systemroot%\SYSVOL\sysvol directory on every DC.

Another use of the NETLOGON and SYSVOL directories is to test AD DS replication. As part of AD DS replication between DCs, all the contents of both shares are replicated throughout the domain. If you want to test that all your DCs are replicating properly, place a test file in the NETLOGON or SYSVOL folder and wait for it to propagate to the other DCs.

Besides the default administrative shares, you can create other shares that are hidden from the view of users by appending a dollar sign ($) to the name of the share. For example, suppose you want to create a hidden share on your servers that will store log files that are used by a third-party application. You could accomplish this by walking through the share process and naming your share AppLog$. This share is not visible through network browsing but is available with the right permissions by using a UNC path similar to \\MSN-SRV-0XX\AppLog$.

Activity 7-2: Creating and Verifying Administrative Shares

Time Required: 15 minutes.

Objective: Create and verify administrative shares.

Description: You have been asked by your manager to create two folders on each of your servers, MSN-SRV-0XX and MSN-SC-0XX, which will be used for storing administrative documents and scripts. The folders need to be invisible to network browsing and only available when the folder's full UNC path is entered. In this activity, you will create administrative shares on both of your servers. Then you will verify that they are available for you to access via a UNC path.

1. At a command prompt on MSN-SRV-0XX, enter the following commands:

```
md "c:\70642\Chapter 7\Admin Share"
net share AdminShare$= "c:\70642\Chapter 7\Admin Share"
```

2. Open c:\70642\Chapter 7\Admin Share in Windows Explorer. Create a new text file named **NewTextFile.txt**.

3. Log onto MSN-SC-0XX.

4. At the command prompt, enter the following commands to create and share a new folder called SCAdminShare, and map the drive to the letter z:.

```
md "c:\70642\Chapter 7\SCAdminShare"
net share SCAdmin$= "c:\70642\Chapter 7\SCAdminShare"
net use z: \\MSN-SRV-0XX\adminshare$
```

5. At the command prompt, type **Z:** and then press **Enter** to open the network drive you created.

6. Type **dir** and then press **Enter** to list the files included in the share, including NewTextFile.txt.

User-Level Permissions   **User-level permissions** are defined at the folder or file level. On Windows Server 2008 computers, user-level permissions are based on the **New Technology File System (NTFS)**. NTFS is the preferred file system used in Windows networks for its increased security and detailed configuration settings. NTFS permissions apply anytime that a file or folder resource is accessed. This includes access from a network share or on a local drive. NTFS permissions are divided into two types: file permissions and folder permissions.

You use folder and file permissions to manage access by users. To do so, you place users in groups and then assign permissions to the groups. In this way, each user inherits the permissions assigned to the group. Inheritance in general can come from any parent object, such as a folder, partition, or disk.

File permissions are applied to a specific file on a Windows Server 2008 server. You can create them as necessary, or they can be inherited from a folder that contains the permissions. Table 7-2 describes the NTFS file permissions.

Folder permissions are applied to a specific folder on a Windows Server 2008 server. They define access through the folder and to documents contained within a folder. Folders also are responsible for providing permissions to new or existing files or folders it contains through the process of inheritance. Table 7-3 describes each of the NTFS folder permissions.

When resources are accessed via a network share, both the share permissions and NTFS permissions are used. When these permissions are combined, the most restrictive permissions of the two prevail. This is one of the more confusing areas for administrators when managing Windows Server 2008 file resources. If you fail to properly set the permissions levels in both places, you might grant unwanted access to a resource or incorrectly restrict the access of users.

Table 7-2   NTFS file permissions

NTFS Permission	Description
Full Control	Read, write, modify, execute, change attributes and permissions, and take ownership of the file
Modify	Read, write, modify, execute, and change the file's attributes
Read & Execute	Display the file's data, attributes, owner, and permissions and run the file (if it's a program or has a program associated with it for which you have the necessary permissions)
Read	Display the file's data, attributes, owner, and permissions
Write	Write to the file, append to the file, and read or change its attributes

Table 7-3   NTFS folder permissions

NTFS Permission	Description
Full Control	Read, write, modify, and execute files in the folder; change attributes and permissions; and take ownership of the folder or files it contains
Modify	Read, write, modify, and execute files in the folder and change attributes of the folder or files it contains
Read & Execute	Display the folder's contents and the data, attributes, owner, and permissions for files within the folder; also run files within the folder (if they're programs or have a program associated with them for which you have the necessary permissions)
List Folder	Display all files and subfolders contained within a folder
Read	Display the file's data, attributes, owner, and permissions
Write	Write to the file, append to the file, and read or change its attributes

For example, suppose you create a new shared resource called NewShare on a server called FS1. NewShare maps to a location on the server of f:\data\NewShare. When you access the share using a UNC pathname of \\FS1\NewShare, your access to resources will be determined by the share-level permissions along with the user-level permissions, or NTFS permissions, for Windows Server 2008 computers.

You can use GUI-based tools such as Windows Explorer and the File Services console to manage the NTFS permissions on share files and folders. In the next activity, you will use both tools to modify NTFS permissions on shared resources.

Activity 7-3: Modifying NTFS Permissions Using Windows Explorer

Time Required: 15 minutes.

Objective: Modify NTFS permissions.

Description: You need to change some permissions for shared resources you deployed earlier. Because modifying NTFS permissions provides more detailed control when securing your data, you need to modify the NTFS permissions on two folders by removing permissions for the Everyone group in the Public share and the Domain Users group in the Shared Data folder. In this activity, you will use Windows Explorer and the File Services console to modify NTFS permissions.

1. In the Start Search box on the Start menu of MSN-SRV-0XX, type **Network and Sharing Center** and then press **Enter**.

2. In the Network and Sharing Center, click the **down arrow** button to the right of Public folder sharing. This exposes three options for Public folder sharing.

3. Click **Turn on sharing so anyone with network access can open files** and then click **Apply**. Notice that Public folder sharing is now labeled On (read only) with a green light.

4. At a command prompt, enter the following commands:

```
md "c:\70642\Chapter 7\NTFS Data"
```

5. Open Server Manager, if necessary.

6. Expand **Roles**, expand **File Services**, and then click **Share and Storage Management**. The local shares are displayed in the Summary pane.

7. Click the **Public** share and then click **Properties** in the Actions pane.

8. In the Properties dialog box, click the **Permissions** tab and then click **NTFS Permissions**.

9. Select **Everyone** and then click **Remove**. Click **OK** to save the changes.

10. Click **OK** to close the Properties dialog box.

11. Open Windows Explorer and browse to c:\70642\Chapter 7\NTFS Data.

12. Click **Organize** on the command bar and then click **Properties**.

13. In the Properties dialog box, click the **Security** tab.

14. Select the **Domain Users** group and then click **Edit** to open the Permissions dialog box for the Domain Users group.

15. Select the **Domain Users** group and then click **Remove**.

16. Click **OK** to close the Permissions dialog box. Click **OK** to close the Properties dialog box.

17. Close Windows Explorer.

When modifying permissions through the GUI is not an option, you need to use a command-line utility. Built into Windows Server 2008 is a utility called the Change Access Control List (CACLS). You can use CACLS to view and manage NTFS permissions on local and remote servers.

7

Activity 7-4: Modifying NTFS Permissions Using the CACLS Command

Time Required: 5 minutes.

Objective: Modify NTFS permissions with CACLS.

Description: You need to modify permissions on your Server Core computer. Specifically, you need to revoke the Users group because your users do not require access to the folder. In this activity, you will use the CACLS utility to make these changes.

1. Log onto MSN-SC-0XX.

2. At the command prompt, type **net use** and then press **Enter**. This displays all the mapped drives on MSN-SC-0XX. If z: is not listed, type **net use z: \\msn-srv-0xx\adminshare$** and then press **Enter** to re-create the mapped drive.

3. Type **cacls z:** and then press **Enter**. This displays the contents for the adminshare$ folder on MSN-SRV-0XX. You will notice that the Users group has permissions on this folder.

4. Type **cacls z: /E /R Users** and then press **Enter**. This instructs CACLS that you want to edit (/E) the ACL and revoke (/R) the Users group.

5. Type **cacls z:** and then press **Enter**. This displays the contents for the adminshare$ folder on MSN-SRV-0XX. You will notice that the Users group is no longer listed.

CACLS has many variables and switches that you can display by typing cacls /?. Another utility, ICACLS, allows you to perform tasks similar to CACLS while adding the ability to back up and restore access control lists. For more information on CACLS and ICACLS, search for each utility in the alphabetic list for Windows Server 2008 at *http://technet.microsoft.com*.

Access Control Lists NTFS uses **access control lists** (ACLs) to define permissions to resources. Each file and folder object on a Windows Server 2008 computer maintains an ACL. Each ACL contains **access control entries** (ACEs), which are the individual permissions assigned to a specific user or group on an object. Figure 7-3 shows the ACL for a folder called SharedFolder.

Authentication When a user connects to a network resource, that user must have permission or rights to access the resource. In Windows environments, rights and permissions are associated with a user's account through the use of tokens. A **token** is an object attached to a user's account that validates the user's identity and privileges they have to resources. Windows uses **security identifiers** (SIDs) to make every user, computer, and resource on a network unique. You can think of SIDs as being similar to your Social Security number: although your name and other attributes can change, your Social Security number is always identified with you.

SIDs from a user's token are matched against the SIDs on a resource to determine what privileges that specific user has. Security objects, such as users, computers, and groups, have a unique SID assigned to them. The user's token includes an SID and the SIDs of the groups to which the user belongs. When Windows Server 2008 needs to determine whether access is allowed to a file or folder, Windows evaluates all these SIDs.

Deploying Shares

Once you have determined the data you want to share on the network and the server that will host the data, it is time to deploy your shared resources. File and folder sharing can be implemented through the following tools installed in Windows Server 2008:

- Shared Folders console
- Windows Explorer
- Net share command
- Share and Storage Management console

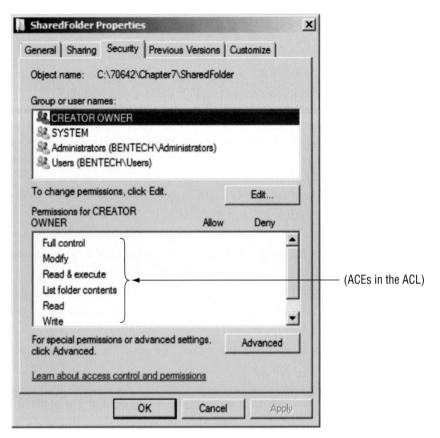

Figure 7-3 Folder permissions in the ACL

Deploying Shares with the Shared Folders Console The Shared Folders console is available through the Computer Management console or as a stand-alone MMC snap-in. It provides a GUI-based tool for managing shares and the connections to them. Figure 7-4 shows the Shared Folders console as accessed through Computer Management. Besides allowing you to create and modify existing shares, it allows you to view the users connected to local shares by double-clicking Sessions. You can also view files being accessed within the shares by double-clicking Open Files. This can be helpful when you are performing maintenance on a server. If the server requires a reboot or needs to restart services, which could affect a remote user, you can view open files or sessions, close them, or alert connected users of an impending restart using network messaging—all through the console.

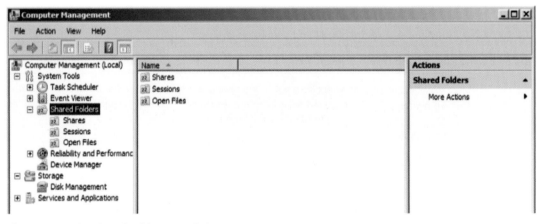

Figure 7-4 The Shared Folders console in Computer Management

Activity 7-5: Managing Shared Folders through the Shared Folders Console

Time Required: 10 minutes.

Objective: Explore the Shared Folders console and close open sessions.

Description: You have just found out that you need to perform an emergency reboot of MSN-SRV-0XX. Before rebooting the server, you want to determine if any users are accessing shared folder resources. If they are, you will close their session and perform the reboot. In this activity, you will explore the Shared Folder console. You will learn how to manage open files and sessions with the console as well.

1. At the command prompt on MSN-SC-0XX, type **z:\NewTextFile.txt** and then press **Enter**. This opens the file, which you created earlier on MSN-SRV-0XX.

2. Switch to MSN-SRV-0XX and open the Computer Management console.

3. Expand the objects in the left pane to display the Shared Folders object under System Tools. Click **Shared Folders**.

4. In the middle pane, open the **Shares** folder and review all the shared folders on MSN-SRV-0XX.

5. Open the **Sessions** folder. This allows you to see if anyone is accessing shares on MSN-SRV-0XX. You should see one connection from administrator on MSN-SC-0XX.

6. Open the **Open Files** folder. This allows you to see all the files opened through shares on MSN-SRV-0XX.

7. Return to the **Sessions** folder, select **administrator**, click **Action** on the menu bar, and then click **Close Session**. Click **Yes** to confirm you want to close the session.

8. Open the **Open Files** folder one last time. Notice that there are no longer any files listed as open.

9. Close the Computer Management console.

Deploying Shares with Windows Explorer   Another GUI-based tool you can use for creating and managing shares is Windows Explorer. By browsing the file system on a local computer, you can create new folders for sharing, as you will do in the next activity, or you can choose existing folders and share them. When sharing through Windows Explorer, Windows Server 2008 allows you to configure shares in two ways: network file and folder sharing and advanced sharing. Network file and folder sharing, or sharing, is performed when using the **File Sharing Wizard**. The File Sharing Wizard helps solve a problem in previous versions of Windows Server—needing to combine shared and NTFS permissions. With the File Sharing Wizard, Windows Server 2008 configures the NTFS permissions and the shared permissions simultaneously, depending on the type of access you give users or groups. Although advanced sharing is more common, the File Sharing Wizard allows you to initially set up a share quickly. You can grant four types of access through the File Sharing Wizard, listed in Table 7-4.

Table 7-4   File Sharing Wizard permission levels

Permission Level	Description	NTFS Permissions	Share Permissions
Owner	Assigned to the user creating the share	Full Control	Full Control
Co-owner	Assigned to users or groups that require full control of the file share	Full Control	Full Control
Contributor	Assigned to users or groups that require the permissions to modify resources within a shared folder	Modify	Change
Reader	Assigned to users or groups that require the ability to read and execute shared resources, along with viewing the available resources in a share	Read & Execute List Folder contents (folders only)	Read

Activity 7-6: Creating a Shared Folder through Windows Explorer

Time Required: 15 minutes.

Objective: Create a shared folder in Windows Explorer.

Description: You just received a help desk request for a shared folder to be created on MSN-SRV-0XX. The user, Bob, has requested that a folder called Shared Data be available to all domain users. Users need to be able to read any documents stored in the Shared Data folder. In this activity, you will use Windows Explorer to create a shared folder for Bob. On creating the folder, you will verify that it is visible in the Share and Storage Management console on MSN-SRV-0XX.

1. On MSN-SRV-0XX, open Windows Explorer and browse to c:\70642\Chapter 7.

2. Create a folder named **Shared Data** in the c:\70642\Chapter 7 folder by clicking **Organize** on the command bar and then clicking **New Folder**. Use **Shared Data** as the name of the new folder.

3. Click **Shared Data** and then click the **Share** icon on the command bar.

4. In the **File Sharing** dialog box, type **Domain Users** in the text box and then click **Add**. This adds Domain Users to the access control list for the share you are creating.

5. Click **Share** to create the new share.

6. In the following space, write the UNC path that users will use to connect to the new share:

   _____

7. Click **Done** to close the File Sharing dialog box.

8. In Server Manager, open the Share and Storage Management console and then press **F5** to verify that the Shared Data share is listed in the Summary pane.

9. Select **Shared Data** and then click **Properties** in the Actions pane.

10. In the Shared Data Properties dialog box, type **This is a shared folder** in the Description text box.

11. Click the **Permissions** tab. This opens the Permissions dialog box, where you can modify either NTFS or Share permissions.

12. Click **OK** to save the changes and close the dialog box.

To create shared folders using Advanced Sharing, you use the Properties dialog box for a folder. This dialog box also includes the Sharing tab. On the Sharing tab, you can choose Sharing to start the File Sharing Wizard, or you can choose Advanced Sharing to open the Advanced Sharing dialog box, as shown in Figure 7-5.

The Advanced Sharing options allow you to perform more advanced tasks with a shared folder, such as adding shares to a folder, caching offline files, and limiting the number of simultaneous connections to a shared folder.

Activity 7-7: Modifying the Advanced Sharing Properties on a Share through Windows Explorer

Time Required: 10 minutes.

Objective: Modify a share using Advanced Sharing properties.

Description: Previously, you created a text file called NewTextFile.txt in the adminshare$ shared folder. Your manager wants you to limit the folder to 10 users and set the caching on the folder so that the text file is not available offline. In this activity, you will use Windows Explorer and Advanced Sharing to modify an existing share.

1. On MSN-SRV-0XX, open Windows Explorer and browse to c:\70642\Chapter 7.

2. Right-click the **Admin Share** folder and then click **Properties** on the shortcut menu. The Properties dialog box for the folder opens.

Figure 7-5   Advanced Sharing dialog box for the Shared Data folder

3. Click the **Sharing** tab in the Properties dialog box.

4. Click the **Advanced Sharing** button.

5. In the Advanced Sharing dialog box, select the value in the Limit the number of simultaneous users to box and then type **10**.

6. In the Comments box, type **This share was modified by administrator on** *DD/MM/YY*, where DD, MM, and YY are the current day, month, and year.

7. Click the **Permissions** button.

8. In the Permissions dialog box, click **Add**. Type **administrators** in the Enter object names to select (examples) text box and then click **OK**.

9. In the Permissions dialog box, click **Administrators** and then click the **Full Control** check box under Allow.

10. Click **Everyone** and then click **Remove**. Click **OK** to close the Permissions dialog box.

11. Click the **Caching** button. Choose **Files or programs from the share will not be available offline** and then click **OK**.

12. Click **OK** in the Advanced Sharing dialog box to save the changes and close the dialog box. Click **Close** to close the Properties dialog box for the Admin Share folder.

13. Open a command prompt, type **net share adminshare$** and then press **Enter**. This displays the properties of adminshare$, as shown in Figure 7-6.

14. Close the command prompt.

Deploying Shares with Net Share   **Net share** is a CLI utility provided with Windows. This utility allows you to create and manage shared folder resources. It contains many switches for assigning permissions, which are listed in Table 7-5. Note that "Examples" is the name of the share in Table 7-5.

Figure 7-6 Displaying share properties with the net share command

Table 7-5 Net share variables and switches

Variable/Switch	Description	Example
sharename	Displays all the properties for the specified share.	Net share "Shared Data"*
Sharename=folderpath	Creates a share on the local server that points to the specified folder path.	Net share Examples="C:\70642\Chapter 7 \Shared Data\Examples"
/GRANT:user,[Read | Change | Full Control]	When used during the creation of a share, allows you to specify users or groups and their permissions to the share. If skipped, default share permissions of Everyone – Read and Administrators – Full Control are applied.	Net share Examples="C:\70642\Chapter 7 \Shared Data\Examples" /Grant:Users, Change
/USERS:*number* or /UNLIMITED	When specified along with a share name, sets the user limit to a specific number or unlimited. If omitted, UNLIMITED is applied.	Net share Examples="C:\70642\Chapter 7 \Shared Data\Examples"/USERS:100 Net share Examples="C:\70642\Chapter 7 \Shared Data\Examples" /UNLIMITED
/REMARK: "*Text*"	When specified along with a share name, defines the comments or description field of a share. If omitted, this is left blank.	Net Share Examples="C:\70642\Chapter 7 \Shared Data\Examples" /Remark: "This is a share for Examples"
/CACHE: Manual | Documents | Programs | None	When specified along with a share name, defines the type of caching the share allows for clients. If omitted, the default is Manual.	Net share Examples="C:\70642\Chapter 7 \Shared Data\Examples" /CACHING:None
Sharename /DELETE	Deletes an existing local share. You can specify a computer name or path to delete shares on a remote system.	Net share Examples /Delete Net share Examples\\MSN-SRV-0XX Examples /Delete

*All CLI utility variables and switches that have spaces need to be enclosed in quotation marks (" ").

Activity 7-8: Creating a Shared Folder Using the CLI

Time Required: 15 minutes.

Objective: Use the CLI to create shared folders.

Description: You are working on your Server Core server and need to create and share some folders for your users. In this activity, you will create new folders and share them using the command prompt and the net share utility.

1. Open the command prompt on the MSN-SRV-0XX computer.

2. At the command prompt, enter the following commands to create and share a new folder called CLI_Share:

```
md "c:\70642\Chapter 7\CLI_Share"
net share CLIShare="c:\70642\Chapter 7\CLI_Share"
```

3. At the command prompt, type **net share** and then press **Enter**. This lists all the shares on MSN-SRV-0XX, including CLIShare.

4. Close the command prompt window.

5. Log onto MSN-SC-0XX. Type **net share** and then press **Enter**. How many shares are available on MSN-SC-0XX? _____.

6. At the command prompt, enter the following commands to create and share a new folder called **NewData**:

```
md "c:\70642\chapter 7\NewData"
Net share NewData="c:\70642\chapter 7\NewData" /Users:1
/Remark:"this is the NewData Share"
```

 Users:<number> is used to specify the number of connections that can be made the share. /Remark: "text" applies a description to the share.

7. Log off MSN-SC-0XX.

8. On the MSN-SRV-0XX computer, click **Start** and then type **\\MSN-SC-0XX** in the Start Search text box and press **Enter**. This displays the shares available on MSN-SC-0XX. If you are prompted for credentials, enter the administrator account name and pass-word for MSN-SC-0XX.

9. Double-click **NewData** to open the Data share in Windows Explorer.

10. Leave Windows Explorer open for the next exercise.

All the commands you have learned for setting properties on a share must be completed when the share is first created. Otherwise, net share will produce an error that the share already exists. Only the /delete command can be performed on an existing share. To modify the share permissions of an existing share, you need to use one of the GUI utilities or you can re-create the share with the new settings.

Offline Files   An additional feature of shared folder resources is offline file availability. Offline files allow shared file resources to be available to clients when they are not connected to the network. Storing offline files is also called caching. Similar to how DNS caches name reso-lution requests, Windows Server 2008 clients can cache copies of network resources on their local system for use when they are offline. Caching is defined by administrators at the shared resource level. Table 7-6 describes the three options for caching of offline folders in Windows Server 2008.

When a file is cached on a local system, users can access the file when they are offline. This functionality is helpful for mobile users who need to take work with them on a notebook com-puter, for example. Users can modify the cached document as necessary. On reconnecting to the network, the cached copy is synchronized with the original shared resource. Changes made since the original version are added.

Table 7-6 Options for defining client options for caching offline folders

Client Option	Description
Only the files and programs that users specify will be available offline	This is the default option when creating a new share. It allows users to define which shared resources they want to have available offline. This is the best choice for allowing clients to using caching while reducing the network and client-side impact of caching.
All files and programs that users open from the share will be automatically available offline	This option automatically creates offline copies of all shared programs and documents that a user can access. This makes the process of caching easier for users because they do not need to define the items to cache. However, this can affect both the network and the client depending on the number and size of the files being cached.
Files or programs from the share will not be available offline	This option prohibits the use of client-side caching. This prevents users from creating a cached copy of a shared document or program on their client machine. However, it does not prevent the user from copying the file locally to their computer.

Offline files present a serious security risk depending on the sensitivity of the files being cached. You should allow offline files only for shares that do not contain data that might compromise company secrets or other confidential information.

Figure 7-7 depicts the four settings that can be used for offline files when creating a new share through the New Share Wizard.

Activity 7-9: Creating a Document on a Remote Server and Setting Up Offline Availability

Time Required: 15 minutes.

Objective: Set caching requirements for offline files.

Description: You need to deploy a share on MSN-SRV-0XX that will automatically make documents in the share available offline when a user accesses the document. In this activity, you will create a share with the caching properties set so that users automatically cache documents they open.

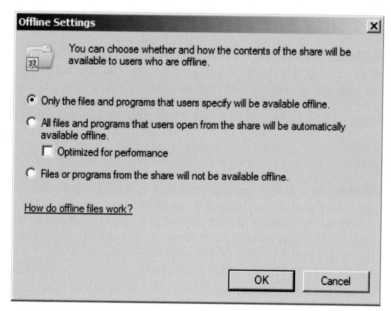

Figure 7-7 Offline folder options for a shared file resource

1. On MSN-SRV-0XX, open the Control Panel, switch to Classic view, and then double-click **Offline Files**.

2. In the Offline Files dialog box, click the **Enable Offline Files** button and then click **OK**. A message box indicates that you need to restart your server.

3. Click **Yes** to restart the server.

4. While the server is rebooting, log onto MSN-SC-0XX.

5. At the command prompt, type **net share offline=c:\data 70642\Chapter 7\scadminshare /CACHE: Documents** and then press **Enter**. This creates a new share named offline with the default permissions and caching set to automatically cache accessed documents.

6. At the command prompt, type **net share offline** and then press **Enter**. Verify that the caching setting for Offline is set to **Automatic caching of documents**.

7. At the command prompt, type **notepad** and then press **Enter** to start Notepad.

8. In Notepad, type **This is a test document on MSN-SC-0XX**.

9. Click **File** on the menu bar and then click **Save**. In the Save As dialog box, type **c:\70642\chapter 7\scadminshare\Test.txt** as the name of the file and then click **OK**.

10. Close Notepad and log off MSN-SC-0XX.

11. Log onto MSN-SRV-0XX.

12. In the Start Search box, type **\\MSN-SC-0XX\offline** and then press **Enter**. You will see Test.txt listed in the folder.

13. Click the **Work offline** button on the command bar. This temporarily disconnects you from the remote share. Notice that an X appears over the document icon for Test.txt. This signifies the file is not available offline.

14. Click the **Work online** button on the command bar and then open **Test.txt** in Notepad. Close Notepad.

15. Click the **Work offline** button and open **Test.txt** in Notepad. Now it is available because you accessed the file previously.

16. Close Notepad and Windows Explorer.

Distributed File System

Introduction to DFS

Distributed File System (DFS) is a set of client and server services that allows companies to deploy their shared file resources, known as targets, as a single file structure while distributing the resources across multiple servers and network locations. By distributing the load across servers and locations, networks gain data redundancy, fault tolerance, and improved availability. This concept is known as a DFS. In Windows Server 2008, DFS is comprised of two technologies:

- DFS namespace
- DFS replication

DFS Namespace   Microsoft's implementation of DFS allows you to create an entry point for shared file resources using a naming convention of your choice. This is referred to as the **DFS namespace**, the first of two technologies that make up DFS. This central namespace makes the distributed nature of the file resources transparent to the user. To them, it appears as a single shared folder that may contain a series of subfolders and files.

DFS namespaces use two types of implementations:

- *Domain-based*—A **domain-based namespace** is stored on one or more servers as part of AD DS. Because of its integration with AD DS, this namespace provides increased scalability and availability because it can be spread across multiple servers.

- *Stand-alone*—This type of namespace is stored on a single server so that it is restricted to the space and availability of the server on which it is stored. Stand-alone namespace servers can use increased availability if they are hosted on a failover cluster.

For example, suppose you have three file servers that contain data for various departments. It can be confusing for users to remember which server contains a particular shared file resource, and mapping drive letters for each of the shares is cumbersome. With domain-based DFS, you create a namespace of \\bentech.local\ and place all the shared resources under the root namespace. This allows users to more easily find data. From an administrative standpoint, it allows you to easily add disk storage or provide fault tolerance without affecting the user.

Domain-based namespaces can be implemented in the following two modes depending on the resources being used:

- *Windows Server 2008 Mode*—The **Windows Server 2008 mode** requires a domain to be running in Windows Server 2008 AD DS functional mode, and all namespace servers are running Windows Server 2008. This mode allows for access-based enumeration (ABE) of your DFS root and for multiple servers to host the namespace. With ABE enabled, users do not have access to or cannot view files or folders to which they do not have access. Without ABE, you can allow users to see a file or folder but deny access when they attempt access.

- *Windows Server 2000 mode*—The **Windows Server 2000 mode** requires a domain to be running in Windows 2000 mixed AD DS functional mode or higher, and all namespace servers are running at least Windows 2000 Server. This mode allows the use of multiple namespace servers and supports the use of DFS replication to target folders.

The type of namespace you deploy depends on factors within your network. The following questions will help you determine how to deploy DFS:

- Are you running an AD DS domain?
- Do you need support for DFS servers not running Windows Server 2008?
- Do you need multiple DFS servers or just one?
- Will your environment support moving to Windows Server 2008 functional mode on all your DCs?
- Does your solution require scalability?
- Do you need to replicate across LAN or WAN connections?

Using these questions and Table 7-7, you should have a better idea of the solutions DFS supports and the situations to deploy the various types and modes.

Activity 7-10: Adding DFS Role Services

Time Required: 15 minutes.

Objective: Install the DFS Role services.

Description: Your manager is looking for a way to organize data stored in the server and allow for future expansion. Based on your knowledge of Windows Server 2008, you decide that implementing DFS would provide a centralized organizational structure for the data and provide you with room to grow without affecting users. In this activity, you install the DFS Role services on your MSN-SRV-0XX server.

1. On MSN-SRV-0XX, open Server Manager, if necessary.

2. In the left pane of Server Manager, expand the **Roles** node, right-click the **Files Services** node, and then click **Add Role Services**.

3. Click the **Distributed File System** check box. This selects both DFS Namespaces and DFS Replication. Click **Next**.

Table 7-7 Comparing DFS namespace types and modes

Characteristic	Domain-Based Namespace (Windows Server 2008 Mode)	Domain-Based Namespace (Windows 2000 Server Mode)	Standalone Namespace Server
Client access path	\\DomainName\ DFSRootname	\\DomainName\ DFSRootname	
	\\NetBIOSName\ DFSRootname	\\NetBIOSName\ DFSRootname	\\Servername\ DFSRootname
Minimum supported operating system	Windows Server 2008	Windows 2000 Server	Windows 2000 Server
Requires AD DS	Yes	Yes	No
AD DS functional level	Windows Server 2008*	Windows 2000 Mixed	N/A
Support for ABE	Yes	No	Yes**
High availability options	Use of multiple namespace servers hosting the namespace***	Use of multiple namespace servers hosting the namespace***	Use of failover cluster.
Supports DFS replication	Yes	Yes	Yes****

*Server Core editions of Windows Server 2008 are limited to acting as a single stand-alone DFS namespace server. However, they can participate in DFS replication.

**Requires that the stand-alone namespace server is running on Windows Server 2008.

***All namespace servers must be in the same domain.

****Stand-alone namespace server must be joined to a domain.

4. In the Create a DFS Namespace dialog box, type **Data** in the text box for your namespace and then click **Next**.

5. Accept the default of a Domain-based namespace in Windows Server 2008 mode by clicking **Next**.

6. In the Configure Namespace dialog box, click **Next**. You will add target folders later.

7. In the Confirm Installation Selections dialog box, click **Install**.

8. Once the installation has completed successfully, click **Close**.

9. Close Server Manager and then reopen it to refresh the view so that you can see the DFS Management console.

10. Expand **Roles**, **File Services**, and **DFS Management**, and then click **DFS Management** to open the DFS Management console.

11. Expand **Namespaces** and verify that \\bentech.local\Data is an available namespace.

12. Close Server Manager.

DFS Replication   **DFS replication** is responsible for synchronizing all the data within a DFS structure. Using a multimaster replication engine (such as AD), DFS replication allows servers connected across WAN or limited bandwidth network connections to stay current. This replaces the File Replication Service (FRS), which was used in previous versions of Windows Server, for replicating the DFS namespace. If the servers are located in different AD DS sites, clients using DFS will be automatically referred to shared folders located within the same AD DS site, when available. This helps prevent routing file resource requests across WAN links unless a local copy of a file is unavailable.

If your environment is running the Windows Server 2008 domain functional level, DFS replication will be responsible for replicating the SYSVOL folder between DCs.

DFS replication can be used on its own for replicating data, or it can be combined with the DFS namespace. When used along with the DFS namespace, you receive the following advantages:

- *Data collection*—This allows you to take data from multiple servers and collect it in a central location on one server. Data collection is helpful if you need to perform local server backups from a single server.

- *Data distribution*—DFS allows you to distribute data across multiple locations so that users can use a copy of a resource located in their geographic location. AD DS sites are used to determine which DFS resources are local to the user.

- *Load balancing*—This allows you to deploy multiple servers that hold copies of your data. When users attempt to access a document stored in DFS, they will be directed to a DFS server in their AD DS site or the closest AD DS site.

Load Balancing   DFS can be used to provide load balancing for your shared file services. By replicating your file resources across multiple servers, you can spread the usage load to multiple sources. DFS assists this process by pointing client requests to resources that are located close to them. This is determined through AD DS sites. Figure 7-8 shows how different users can access the same DFS namespace but be sent to different servers.

Fault Tolerance   By replicating your data across multiple servers, you will have a copy of your data on a separate system should you experience a failure. This failure does not affect users because they will be directed to available servers in the DFS server hierarchy. Figure 7-9 shows an example of how a DFS namespace with a server failure still allows users to transparently use copies of a file stored on other servers.

Backup Centralization   DFS can facilitate centralized backups. By replicating data spread across multiple servers to a single server, a backup can be performed on the single server that

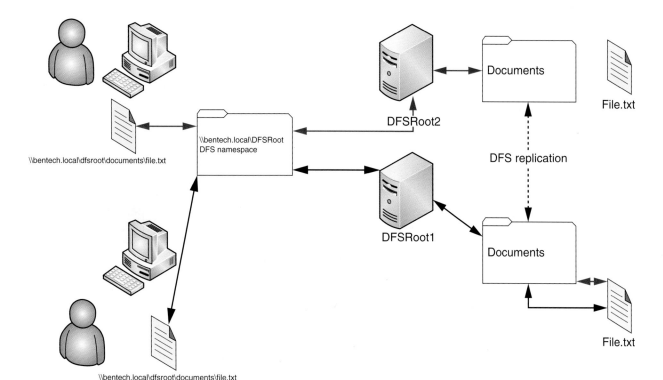

Figure 7-8   Load balancing with DFS

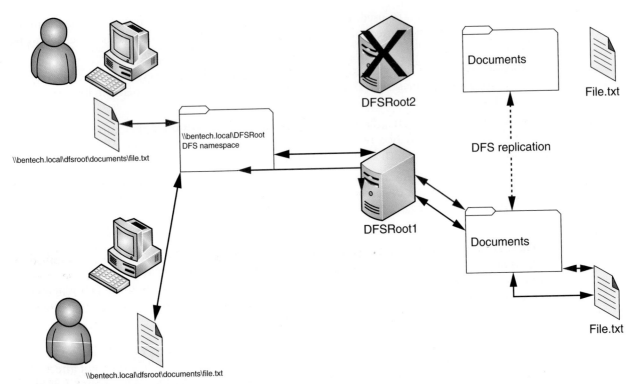

Figure 7-9   Fault tolerance with DFS

captures all the necessary files. Figure 7-10 shows you how data on network servers can be replicated to a central DFS server using DFS replication. Once all the data is replicated, an off-site backup can be taken from the central DFS server.

Once deployed, DFS has a hierarchical namespace structure that allows users to locate information using a UNC path location.

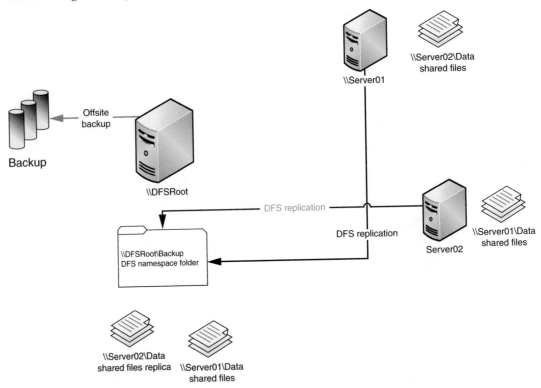

Figure 7-10   Backup centralization with DFS

Configuring DFS

To get DFS up and running on your network, you need to complete some configuration tasks in addition to installing the necessary roles. The tasks you complete depend on the type of DFS implementation you want to deploy in your environment. Configuration of DFS is performed through the DFS Management console, as shown in Figure 7-11.

The steps for deploying DFS are as follows:

- Install the File Services role and the Distributed File System role services

- Create a namespace

- Add folders to the namespace

- Configure the DFS referral order

- Create a DFS replication group

File Services and Distributed File System Roles   By default, DFS is not installed in Windows Server 2008. You need to install the File Services role along with the DFS services of your choosing. By choosing the DFS Namespace service, you can create a centralized namespace for file resources that are spread across more than one server. This does not provide any form of replication. It simply provides a central share point for accessing resources.

Namespaces   After installing the DFS roles and role services, you should create a DFS namespace to act as the central point for clients to access network shared data. If you are using a stand-alone DFS root, the namespace is \\<*servername*>\<*namespace*> similar to \\Server01\data. For domain-based implementation, the namespace is \\<*domainname*>\<*namespace*> similar to \\bentech.local\data.

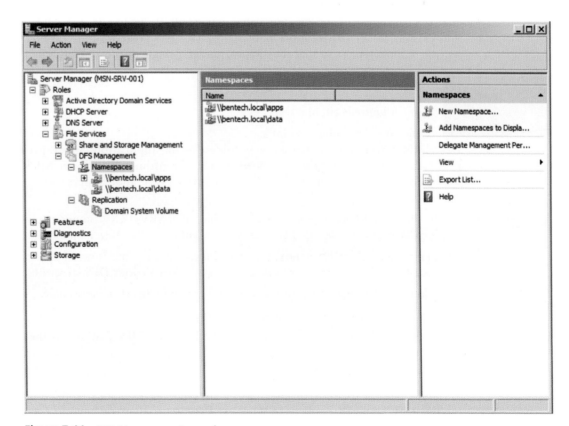

Figure 7-11   DFS Management console

Activity 7-11: Creating a Namespace for the Applications Folder

Time Required: 10 minutes.

Objective: Create a new DFS namespace.

Description: Your manager has requested that you create a centralized access point for all company applications. Since you have recently configured DFS on your network, you decide to create a DFS namespace for the MSN-SRV-0XX server.

1. On the MSN-SRV-0XX computer, open the DFS Management console. Select **Namespaces** and then click **New Namespace** in the Actions pane.

2. In the Namespace Server dialog box, type **MSN-SRV-0XX** in the text box. Click **Next**.

3. In the Namespace Name and Settings dialog box, type **Apps** in the Name text box and then click **Edit Settings**.

4. In the Edit Settings dialog box, choose **Administrators have full access; other users have read-only permissions** and then click **OK**.

5. Click **Next**.

6. In the Namespace Type dialog box, accept the default settings by clicking **Next**.

7. In the Review Settings and Create Namespace dialog box, choose **Create**.

8. In the Confirmation dialog box, click **Close**.

9. In the DFS Management console, verify that a new namespace for \\bentech.local\Apps has been created.

10. In the Start Search text box on the Start menu, type **\\bentech.local\apps** and then press **Enter**.

11. In Windows Explorer, create two text documents named **DFStext1.txt** and **DFStext2.txt**.

Namespace Folders   After you create your namespace, you can populate the folder. You can create new folders in a DFS namespace to provide folder locations for your users. Through the DFS Management console, you can complete all of this in one step. DFS also allows you to add existing folder shares into a namespace. This is a great way to consolidate shares spread across multiple servers so that they appear under a single directory hierarchy.

Activity 7-12: Adding Folders to the DFS Namespace

Time Required: 10 minutes.

Objective: Add folders to DFS.

Description: You need to create a new folder for the application, SuperSpreadsheet, in \\bentech.local\apps. In addition, you need to add the offline share from MSN-SC-0XX to the \\bentech.local\apps namespace. In this activity, you add folders into an existing DFS namespace.

1. In the DFS Management console on the MSN-SRV-0XX computer, click the **\\bentech.local\Apps** namespace and then click **New Folder** in the Actions pane.

2. In the New Folder dialog box, type **SuperSpreadsheet** as the name of the new folder and then click **OK**. This verifies that you can create a folder in your DFS structure.

3. Select the **\\bentech.local\Apps** namespace again and then click **New Folder** in the Actions pane.

4. In the New Folder dialog box, click the **Add** button.

5. In the Add Folder Target dialog box, type **\\MSN-SC-0XX\offline** as the target folder and then click **OK**.

6. In the New Folder dialog box, type **offline** as the name of the folder and then click **OK**.

7. In the Start Search box on the Start menu, type **\\bentech.local\apps\offline** and then press **Enter**. SCAdminShare opens in Windows Explorer so that you have access to the Test.txt file.

8. Close Windows Explorer.

Adding Servers to DFS Namespace For higher availability and ease of access for remote users, you will often add DFS servers to a DFS namespace. Once added to the DFS namespace, the new server creates the file system hierarchy for the namespace in its DFS root located at c:\DFSRoot, by default.

Activity 7-13: Adding Servers to a DFS Namespace

Time Required: 5 minutes.

Objective: Add servers to the DFS namespace.

Description: As you build your DFS namespace, you want to have multiple servers participating. In this activity, you will add MSN-SRV-0XX so that it is participating in the DFS namespace for \\bentech.local\apps.

1. In the DFS Management console for MSN-SRV-0XX, expand **Namespaces**, click **\\bentech.local\Apps**, and then click **Add Namespace Server** in the Actions pane.
2. In the Add Namespace Server dialog box, type **MSN-SC-0XX** in the text box and then click **Edit Settings**.
3. In the Edit Settings window, choose **Administrators have full access; other users have read-only permissions** and click **OK**.
4. Click **OK**. The changes begin to be committed. If necessary, click the **Details** button to view the progress of the changes.
5. In the DFS Management console, verify that MSN-SC-0XX is listed as a namespace server for \\bentech.local\apps.
6. Click **MSN-SC-0XX**. Choose **Open in Explorer** under Actions to open the Apps folder on MSN-SC-0XX so that you can verify that MSN-SC-0XX is added properly as a DFS namespace server.
7. Close Windows Explorer.

Creating a DFS Replication Group DFS replication is not created in Windows Server 2008 by default. You create replication groups that will be responsible for updating each other. Before creating the replication group, you need to have two or more servers configured as target folders. You can set up DFS topology as a hub or as a full mesh.

Activity 7-14: Creating a DFS Replication Group

Time Required: 20 minutes.

Objective: Configure DFS replication between DFS namespace servers.

Description: Now that both servers are participating in your DFS namespace, it is time to configure replication so that each server has copies of the shared data. In this activity, you configure a replication group between MSN-SRV-0XX and MSN-SC-0XX.

1. At the command prompt, enter the following commands to create and share a new folder called SCAdmin:

```
md "c:\70642\Chapter 7\SCAdmin"
Net share SCAdminShare="c:\70642\Chapter 7\SCAdmin"
```

Also, if replication does not take place, you may need to add Administrator with Full Control permissions to the offline folder on MSN-SC-0XX.
2. In the DFS Management console for MSN-SRV-0XX, expand the DFS namespace until you can click the offline folder target.
3. In the Actions pane, click **Add Folder Target**.
4. In the Add Folder Target dialog box, type **\\MSN-SRV-0XX\scadmin**.
5. When a message box appears warning that the share, offline, does not exist, click **Yes** to create the shared folder.
6. In the Create Share dialog box, type **c:\70642\Chapter 7\offline** for the local destination and click **OK**.
7. When a message box appears indicating that the folder does not exist, click **Yes** to create the folder.
8. When a message box appears asking if you want to create a replication group, click **Yes** to begin the creating the replication group.

9. In the Replication Folder Wizard's initial dialog box, click **Next.**

10. In the Replication Eligibility dialog box, click **Next.**

11. Click the **Primary Member** list arrow and then click **MSN-SC-0XX** as the primary member from which content will be initially copied.

12. In the Topology dialog box, accept the default of Full mesh by clicking **Next.**

13. In the Replication dialog box, accept the default of replicating continuously by clicking **Next.**

14. In the final dialog box, click **Create** to begin creating the replication group.

15. Click **Close** in the Replication Wizard dialog box. Click **OK** in the Replication Delay dialog box and then wait approximately 10 minutes for replication to occur.

16. Open Windows Explorer, browse to **c:\70642\Chapter 7\offline** and verify the files from \\MSN-SC-0XX\offline have replicated to MSN-SRV-0XX. Close Windows Explorer.

Configuring the DFS Referral Order DFS namespaces use a referral order to determine the DFS server that will provide shared resources to client requests. The referral order, by default, uses AD DS sites to determine the closest DFS server to a client. In AD DS, sites are groups of computers separated by a low-bandwidth connection, such as two branch offices connected to a central office across WAN links.

During the client connection process, DFS does not directly connect clients to a target server. The DFS infrastructure provides the client with a referral that contains the name of server for the client to use for connecting to resources. In organizations with multiple DFS servers as targets, clients receive a referral with their targets in the following order:

- DFS targets in the same site as the client. This order is randomized by DFS.

- DFS targets from external sites. This order is determined by the AD DS site costs. The higher the cost of connecting to a target server, the lower it appears on the referral list.

These referrals are cached by the client for a default of 300 seconds, or 5 minutes. This default is configured at the namespace level. You can override this setting for individual folders by viewing the folder's properties and changing settings on the Referrals tab as shown in Figure 7-12.

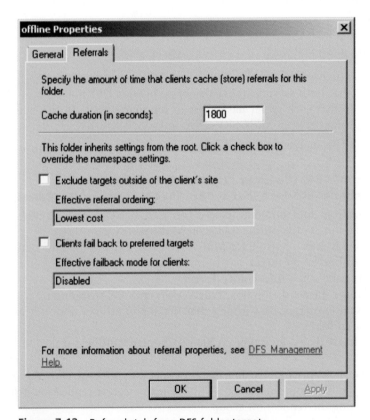

Figure 7-12 Referrals tab for a DFS folder target

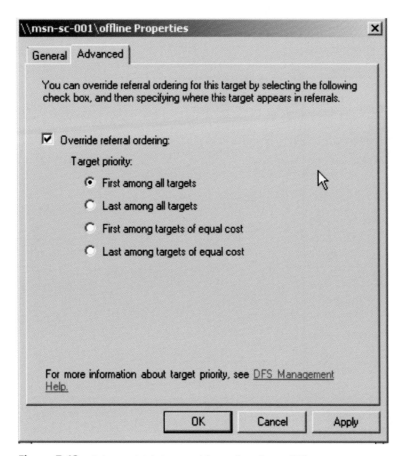

Figure 7-13 Advanced tab to override a referral on a DFS server

In addition to referrals caching, you can manage two additional settings:

- *Exclude clients outside of client's site*—This setting prevents clients from looking outside their current site for DFS targets. Use this setting when connections between sites are very slow and accessing data across WAN connections would provide a poor user experience.

- *Clients fail back to preferred targets*—When enabled, this setting causes users to fail back to using a preferred, or lower-cost, target. This happens when a target server is unavailable as a client initially connects, but comes back online later.

In certain cases, you might want to override the default referral behavior. Use the Properties dialog box of each DFS namespace server in the DFS console to override the referral settings, as shown in Figure 7-13.

Managing Windows Server 2008 with FSRM

FSRM allows administrators to perform various tasks in managing files and disk volumes through the FSRM console, as shown in Figure 7-14. These tasks include the following:

- Managing file and disk quotas
- Screening files using built-in and custom templates
- Creating reports on storage resources

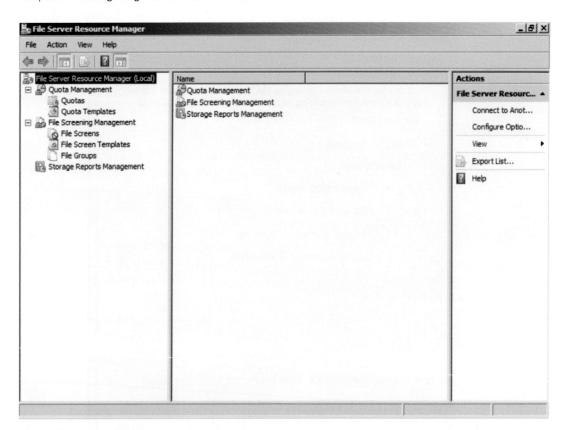

Figure 7-14   File Server Resource Manager console

Activity 7-15: Installing FSRM

Time Required: 10 minutes.

Objective: Install the FSRM role service.

Description: Your manager has asked you to find resources for managing user disk space and filter files stored on the server. She would like to create reports on file usage as well. You decide that implementing FSRM would accomplish these tasks. In this activity, you install the FSRM role service for use in future activities.

1. Start and log onto MSN-SC-0XX before beginning this lab.

   Servermanagercmd.exe -install FS-Resource-Manager

2. Open the command prompt on the MSN-SRV-0XX computer, type **servermanagercmd.exe -install FS-Resource-Manager**, and then press **Enter**.

3. In the Administrative Tools window, open the **File Server Resource Manager** console.

4. In the Actions pane, click **Connect to Another Computer**.

5. In the Connect to Another Computer dialog box, enter **MSN-SC-0XX** in the text box and then click **OK**. After about 30 seconds, you will receive an error warning. This warning states that you are unable to connect to the selected computer. This is due to FSRM not being supported on Server Core.

6. Click **OK** and then click **Cancel** to return to the FSRM console.

7. Leave the FSRM console open for future activities.

Managing File and Disk Quotas   In previous and current versions of Windows Server, NTFS-formatted drives offered disk quotas based on user usage per volume. With FSRM, you can now work with quotas at the file level as well. Use quotas for both monitoring space usage and enforcing space usage limits. FSRM quotas use actual file size instead of the logical file size. This means that a 10-MB file compressed to 1 MB on a disk appears as 1 MB with FSRM quotas. Quotas are divided into two types: hard and soft. Hard quotas do not allow users to exceed the set limit. This type is used to enforce storage limits. Soft quotas allow users to exceed the set limit and should be used only for monitoring purposes.

Activity 7-16: Creating Quotas

Time Required: 15 minutes.

Objective: Create a custom file quota.

Description: Before implementing file quotas, you want to learn how the technology works. In this activity, you learn how to create a custom quota and apply it to a folder on server MSN-SRV-0XX.

1. Open the command prompt on the MSN-SRV-0XX computer, type **md "c:\70642\ Chapter 7\Quotas"** and then press **Enter.**

2. In the Start Search box on the Start menu, type **paint** and press **Enter** to start the Paint program.

3. In Paint, click **File** on the menu bar and then click **Save.** In the Save As dialog box, type **c:\70642\Chapter 7\Quotas\quota** as the file name and select **24-bit Bitmap** as the type. Minimize the Paint window.

4. In the File Server Resource Manager console, expand the objects in the left pane to display Quotas under Quota Management.

5. Click **Quotas** and then click **Create Quota** in the Actions pane.

6. In the Create Quota dialog box, type **c:\70642\Chapter 7\Quotas** as the quota path.

7. Choose the **Define custom quota properties** and click the **Custom Properties** button.

8. In the Quota Properties dialog box, enter **500 KB** as the limit under Space Limit, click the **Hard Quota** option button, and then click **Add** under Notification thresholds.

9. In the Add Threshold dialog box, enter **50** in the Generate notifications when usage reaches text box.

10. Click the **Event Log** tab and then click the **Send warning to event log** check box.

11. Click the **Report** tab, click **Generate reports** and then click **Quota Usage** under Select the reports to generate.

12. Click **OK** to close the Add Threshold dialog box and apply settings. Click **OK** and then click **Create** to add the quota.

13. In the Save Custom Properties as a Template dialog box, enter **Chapter 7 Quota** as the template name and then click **OK.**

14. In the FSRM center pane, the new quota is displayed with its percentage of usage. Restore the Paint window, click **File** on the menu bar, click **Save As**, enter **Quota2** as the file name, and then click **Save.** You will receive an error message similar to that shown in Figure 7-15. This is due to the hard quota limit.

15. Click **OK** to close the message. Close Paint.

Figure 7-15 Disk quota error message

Screening Files Using Built-In and Custom Templates   Another new feature of FSRM is filter screening. **Filter screening** allows administrators to block specific types of files from being stored in Windows Server 2008 file directories. Filters can be defined by using built-in templates or custom-created templates or by specific file type. Filter screening is available through the FSRM console.

Activity 7-17: Creating a File Screen

Time Required: 10 minutes.

Objective: Create a file screen to block files.

Description: Your manager asked you to find a way to prevent users from storing image files to the offline directory on MSN-SRV-0XX. You can use filter screening to accomplish this. In this activity, you apply the built-in template for blocking image files to the offline folder.

1. On the MSN-SRV-0XX computer, open the **File Server Resource Manager** from Administrative Tools, if necessary, and browse to the **File Screen Templates** section of the FSRM console.

2. Click **Block Image Files** in the Templates pane and then click **Create File Screen from Template** in the Actions pane.

3. In the Create File Screen dialog box, type **c:\70642\chapter 7\offline** as the file screen path and then click **Create**.

4. Browse to **c:\70642\chapter 7\offline** and try to create a new bitmap image in the folder. To do so, right-click a blank spot in the folder window, point to **New**, and then click **Bitmap Image**. You receive an error message as shown in Figure 7-16.

5. Click **Cancel**.

6. Open Event Viewer from the Administrative Tools and browse to the Application Event logs under Windows logs.

7. In the Application Event logs, look for error 8215 in the logs, as shown in Figure 7-17.

8. Close Event Viewer and the FSRM console.

Creating Reports on Storage Resources   One of the responsibilities of managing a Windows network is forecasting drive space usage. Without data to support how much space users and applications use, it is very difficult to determine when you might run out of storage. Using the reporting features in FSRM can help you forecast space needs and plan for deploying additional storage. FSRM reporting can also identify the types of data being stored by users.

Figure 7-16   Destination Folder Access Denied dialog box

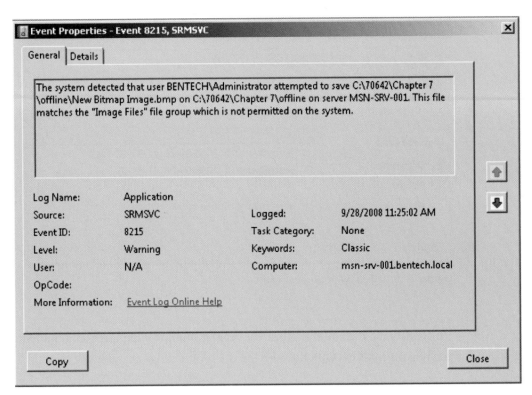

Figure 7-17 Event Viewer error message

Activity 7-18: Running a Storage Report

Time Required: 15 minutes.

Objective: Create a storage report.

Description: Your manager has asked you to create a report of the file usage on the C: drive of MSN-SRV-0XX. The report needs to include all the files on C: by owner. In this activity, you will create a report task to generate a report on files.

1. On the MSN-SRV-0XX computer, open the command prompt, type **servermanagercmd.exe -install FS-Resource-Manager**, and then press **Enter**.

2. From Administrative Tools, open the File Server Resource Manager console and browse to **Storage Reports Management**.

3. Click **Storage Reports Management** and then click **Generate Reports Now** in the Actions pane.

4. In the Storage Reports Tasks Properties dialog box, click **Add**, click **C:** in the **Browse for Folder** dialog box, and then click **OK**. This adds the C: drive to the report.

5. Click the **Files by Owner** check box in the Report data section. Click **OK** to create the report.

6. In the Generate Storage Reports dialog box, click **Generate reports in the background** and then click **OK**.

   The task appears in the Report Task pane. It will take approximately 5 minutes for the report to run. When it is complete, the task will no longer be displayed.

7. Browse to **c:\StorageReports\Interactive**. This is the default location for interactive reports.

8. Select the .html file that begins with FilesbyOwner and the current date and time, as shown in Figure 7-18.

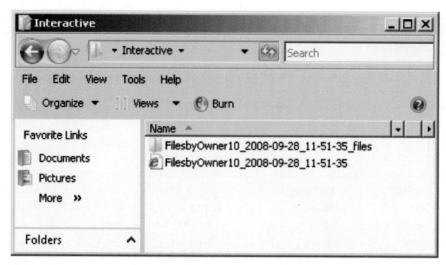

Figure 7-18   Folder with storage report

9. Review the file and then close the report, Windows Explorer, and the FSRM console.

10. Log off MSN-SRV-0XX.

Chapter Summary

- The Windows Server 2008 File Services role provides access to and storage of electronic data through functions such as File Server and DFS. DFS provides a framework for creating a centralized point of entry for accessing network data. DFS uses a common namespace as the entry point for all clients.

- File and folder sharing creates a network access point, or share, for clients to access data across the network. Windows Server 2008 supports public folder sharing and standard file sharing. Public folder sharing allows users to share files with all the users logged on locally or on the network. Network access can be restricted to either read and execute permissions or read, write, create, and delete permissions. On NTFS volumes and partitions, standard file sharing makes files and folders accessible from a network location. Security is provided through the combination of user-level file and folder permissions and share permissions.

- On Windows Server 2008, a client must have the necessary share-level and user-level permissions to access shared resources. Share permissions can be read, change, or full control. Share permissions provide access only to the shared resource when a file or folder is accessed via the network, not when a user connects to the resources while logged on locally to a computer.

- User permissions are based on NTFS settings and are defined at the file level. NTFS permissions apply when a file or folder is accessed, including access from a network share or when accessed locally on a computer. Folder permissions are applied to a specific folder. Through inheritance, they define access through the folder and to documents contained within a folder. Folders also are responsible for providing permissions sets to new or existing files or folders they contain.

- NTFS uses ACLs to define permissions to resources. Each ACL contains ACEs, which are the individual permissions assigned to a specific user or group on an object. When a user connects to a network resource, Windows Server 2008 authenticates the user by examining the token attached to the user's account and comparing the SIDs from the token to the SIDs on the resource to determine the privileges a specific user has.

- You can implement file and folder sharing using the Shared Folders console, Windows Explorer, the net share command, and the Share and Storage Management console.

- DFS is a set of client and server services that allows companies to deploy shared file resources, or targets, as a single file structure. At the same time, they can distribute the resources across multiple servers and network locations. Networks then gain data redundancy, fault tolerance, and improved availability. DFS technologies include the DFS namespace and replication.

- In Windows Server 2008, DFS allows you to create an entry point for shared file resources using your preferred naming convention. This entry point is the DFS namespace, which appears to users as a single shared folder that may contain subfolders and files. DFS can be domain based, where it is stored on one or more servers as part of AD DS, or stand-alone.

- DFS replication is responsible for synchronizing all of the data within a DFS structure. DFS replication uses a multimaster replication engine to keep servers current when they are connected across WAN or limited bandwidth network connections. If the servers are located in different AD DS sites, clients using DFS are referred to shared folders located within the same AD DS site to prevent routing file resource requests across WAN links unless a local copy of a file is unavailable.

- DFS can be used to provide load balancing for shared file services so that they spread the usage load to multiple sources. DFS assists this process by pointing client requests to resources that are located close to them through AD DS sites. DFS also helps maintain fault tolerance to centralize backups.

- You use the DFS Management console to configure DFS by installing the File Services role and the DFS role services, creating a namespace, adding folders to the namespace, configuring the DFS referral order, and creating a DFS replication group.

Key Terms

access control entry (ACE)   An individual permission assigned to a specific user or group on an object.

access control list (ACL)   A list that defines permissions to resources. Each file and folder object on a Windows Server 2008 computer maintains an ACL.

administrative share   A share hidden from regular users and identified by a name ending with a dollar sign ($). For example, C$ is an administrative share used to access the C: drive of a computer.

DFS namespace   A File Services role service that creates a shared file resources entry point using a single naming convention. It is the first of two technologies that make up the Distributed File System (DFS). This central namespace makes the distributed nature of the file resources transparent to the user.

DFS replication   A File Services role service that is responsible for synchronizing all the data within a DFS structure. Using a multimaster replication engine, DFS replication allows servers connected across wide area network or limited bandwidth network connections to stay current.

Distributed File System (DFS)   A set of client and server services that allows companies to deploy their shared file resources, known as targets, as a single file structure, while distributing the resources across multiple servers and multiple network locations.

domain-based namespace   A namespace stored on one or more servers as part of Active Directory Domain Services (AD DS). Because of its integration with AD DS, this namespace provides increased scalability and availability, as it can be spread across multiple servers.

filter screening   A feature that allows administrators to block specific types of files from being stored in Windows Server 2008 file directories. Filters can be defined by using built-in templates or custom-created templates or by specific file type.

file server   The server responsible for sharing and managing data resources on a Windows Server 2008 computer.

File Sharing Wizard   A wizard in Windows Server 2008 you use to configure both the New Technology File System (NTFS) permissions and the shared permissions simultaneously, depending on the type of access you give users or groups.

net share   A Windows utility that allows you to create and manage shared folder resources and that contains many switches for assigning permissions.

network access point   A private point of access to shared network resources.

New Technology File System (NTFS)   The default file system used by Windows Server 2008. NTFS provides file-level security for its resources along with other features, such as file compression and file and folder encryption.

Offline Files   A feature in Windows Server 2008 that makes shared file resources available to clients when they are not connected to the network.

Public folder sharing   When enabled, a feature that allows users to share files with all the users logged on locally or on the network.

security identifier (SID)   An identifier that makes every user, computer, and resource on a network unique.

Server Message Block (SMB)   A protocol that clients use to access shared resources.

share-level permission   A permission defined at the shared resource level that allows clients access to network shares. Also called a **share permission**.

stand-alone namespace   A namespace stored on a single server and restricted to the space and availability of that server.

standard file sharing   A type of file sharing that makes files and folders accessible from a network location. In Windows Server 2008, standard file sharing is permitted only on NTFS volumes and partitions.

token   An object attached to a user's account that validates the user's identity and privileges they have to resources.

user-level permission   A permission defined at the file level. On Windows Server 2008 computers, user-level permissions are based on NTFS.

Windows 2000 Server mode   A domain-based namespace that requires a domain to be running in Windows 2000 mixed AD DS functional mode and all namespace servers are running at least Windows 2000 Server.

Windows Server 2008 mode   A domain-based namespace that requires a domain to be running in Windows Server 2008 AD DS functional mode, and all namespace servers are running at least Windows Server 2008.

Review Questions

1. What protocol is used by Windows clients for accessing shared resources in Windows Server 2008?

   a.   NTP

   b.   SMTP

   c.   SMB

   d.   FTP

   e.   NFS

2. User-level permissions in Windows Server 2008 are based on _____, or the _____ _____ _____ _____.

3. Which of the following are not share-level permissions in Windows Server 2008?

   a. Read

   b. Execute

   c. Write

   d. Change

   e. Modify

   f. Full Control

4. A user is accessing a file called bentechacctg.xls. It is in the DATA share located at \\Server01\Data\bentechacctg.xls. The DATA share was created with the default share permissions from the command line using net share. The NTFS permissions on the file, located at d:\Data\bentechacctg.xls, provide the following permissions: Administrators - Allow full control, Domain Users - Allow Modify, and Authenticated Users - Allow Read & Execute. The user can read the spreadsheet but cannot make any changes. Which of the following tasks will allow the user to change the file from the share?

   a. Add the user to the Domain administrators group

   b. Add authenticated users to the DATA share with Modify permissions

   c. Add authenticated users to the DATA share with Change permissions

   d. Re-create the share through Windows Explorer with the default settings

   e. Change NTFS permissions for Authenticated Users to modify

5. When share-level permissions and user-level (NTFS) permissions are combined, what is the net effect as users access a file through a shared resource?

   a. The least restrictive permission applies.

   b. NTFS permissions always override share permissions.

   c. The most restrictive permission applies.

   d. Share permissions always override NTFS permissions.

6. Which of the following are *not* NTFS file permissions? (Choose two answers.)

   a. Full Control

   b. Modify

   c. Change

   d. Read & Execute

   e. List Folder Contents

   f. Read

   g. Write

7. On a file or folder, access control _____ contain access control _____ for assigning users and groups permission to resources.

8. In a Windows Server 2008 DFS implementation, which service replaces the FRS used in Windows Server 2003?

   a. DFS namespace

   b. AD DS replication

   c. DNS replication

   d. DFS replication

   e. DFSsync.exe

9. Before you can create a single DFS namespace on Windows Server 2008, you need to install which two of the following? (Choose two answers.)

    a. File Services role

    b. FSRM role service

    c. DFS role service

    d. Windows Server 2003 File Services including the FRS

10. DFS replication is based on what type of replication?

    a. Single-master replication

    b. Multimaster replication

    c. Multiserver replication

    d. Single-server replication

11. The FSRM allows administrators to perform which of the following duties?

    a. Report on storage data on a server

    b. Configure DFS servers

    c. Create a Shared folder

    d. Configure disk quotas for end users

    e. Auto-allocate storage based on administrator-defined policies

12. You are trying to edit a script that a fellow administrator wrote. You are accessing the file locally on Server01 at D:\Data\Admins\UserScript.ps1. The script is inheriting permissions from the Admins folder, which has the following permissions: Domain Admins - Allow Full Control, Everyone - Deny Write and Allow Read & Execute, Administrators - Allow Modify. You are a member of the Domain Admins group. What are your effective NTFS permissions on the file userScript.ps1?

    a. Full control

    b. Modify

    c. Read & Execute

    d. No permissions

    e. Read

13. You have been called in to assist with a small business client who is running Windows Server 2003 on their DCs, DC1 and DC2, and has a Windows Server 2008 member server, SRV3. The client tried to install domain-based DFS in Windows Server 2008 mode without success on SRV3. What needs to be performed so that the client is able to use domain-based DFS in Windows Server 2008 mode? Choose the two answers that will act as part of the solution.

    a. Add a Windows Server 2008 DC to the current environment as an RODC

    b. Replace all Windows Server 2003 DCs with Windows Server 2008 DCs

    c. Upgrade the Domain functional level to Windows Server 2003/2008

    d. Apply the Microsoft hotfix to support DFS in Windows Server 2003 AD domains

    e. Upgrade the Domain functional level to Windows Server 2008

    f. On SRV3, install DFS with the following: *servermanagercmd.exe -install DFSR-Infrastructure-ServerEdition2008*

14. Which of the following commands can be used to install DFS Replication on the Windows Server 2008 running Server Core?

    a. servermanagercmd.exe -install DFSR-Infrastructure-ServerEdition2008

    b. OCSetup DFSR-Infrastructure-ServerEdition

    c. ServerManagerCmd -install FS-DFS-Replication

    d. OCSetup FS-DFS-Replication

    e. Start /w OCSetup FS-DFS-Replication

15. Which Windows Server 2008 technology allows users to work with shared network documents when they are not connected to the network?

    a. FolderShare

    b. Offline Files

    c. Briefcase

    d. DFS

16. You receive a help request from a user that is having trouble accessing files using the recently installed DFS namespace. They are using \\widgets.priv\DFS to access the DFS folder. The DFS server, DFS1, is a member of the widgets.priv domain and is running on a Windows Server 2008, Standard edition server. The DFS namespace is installed as a stand-alone server with a root folder of DFS. What should you do to resolve this issue?

    a. Restart the DFS server

    b. Install DFS replication on DFS1

    c. Use \\DFS1\DFS to access the share

    d. Note that stand-alone implementations of DFS cannot be members of a domain

    e. Install the DFS client on the user's machine

17. Which service is installed by default in Windows Server 2008 running Server Core?

    a. DFS

    b. File Services

    c. DHCP

    d. DNS

    e. Print Server

18. Which of the following is *not* an appropriate use of DFS?

    a. Provide automated recovery of end user documents

    b. Collect data in a central location for backup tasks

    c. Provide high availability by deploying multiple servers with replication

    d. Creating a single point of access for end users to share documents

19. Stand-alone DFS namespaces are based on the name of the _____ hosting DFS.

20. Domain-based DFS namespaces are based on the name of the _____ the server is a member of.

21. What is the DFS namespace for a folder called DATA on server called SRV01.widgets.local if DFS is installed as a standalone implementation?

    a. \\widgets.local\DATA

    b. \\widgets.local\DFSroot\DATA

    c. \\SRV01\DFRroot\DATA

    d. \\SRV01\DATA

22. What feature of Windows Server 2008 provides support for environments running Windows and UNIX clients?

    a. UNIX client for Windows Server 2008

    b. Services for Network File System

    c. Client Services for UNIX

    d. Services for New Technology File System

    e. Windows Server 2003 Files services

23. Which of the following is *not* a default share on a Windows Server 2008 server running as a workgroup server?

    a. C$

    b. Admin$

    c. Netlogon

    d. IPC$

24. Which of the following is *not* an administrative share?

    a. Admin$

    b. IPC$

    c. $IPC

    d. C$

25. Which of the following CLI utilities can be used to change the NTFS permissions on an existing folder?

    a. Net share

    b. CACLS

    c. Net use

    d. Dsmod

    e. Netsh

Case Projects

Case Project 7-1: Configuring File Screening

Bentech.local is discovering that many employees are storing personal files on their corporate servers. Most of these files use .mp3 and .wmv formats. To reduce the storage space for unwanted user data, the company asks you how they can manage this issue. Describe what technologies you would use to prevent audio and video files from being saved on corporate servers. Also suggest how you would implement file screening on their file server with the following characteristics:

- The name of the file server is FS-SRV-005

- The shared folders on the server available to all users are \\fs-srv-005\SharedData and \\fs-srv-005\Users\<username>\

Case Project 7-2: Selecting File Service Technologies

Bentech.local has two remote sites in Chicago and Indianapolis. They want the data stored in each location to be available to users in the Minneapolis corporate headquarters. They also want to minimize the effect storing these files has on the corporate network. In addition, they want to centrally back up all the file resources from each location. What File Service technologies can be used as possible solutions to these needs?

Case Project 7-3: Setting Up Shared Folder Resources with Offline Capability on CS-SC-001

In this project, you will be creating two shared folder resources, OfflineApps and OfflineFiles, for users. These folders need to be set up so that users can automatically have their files and applications available offline after they access them. Set up the shared folder resources with offline capability on CS-SC-001.

7

chapter 8

Introduction to Printers in a Windows Server 2008 Network

After reading this chapter and completing the exercises, you can:

- Discuss the Windows Printer Model and how it is implemented in Windows Server 2008

- Install the Print Services components of Windows Server 2008

- Deploy printers with Windows Server 2008

- Configure printers on a Windows Server 2008 network

Printers, like shared files and folders, are a staple of any Windows network because they allow users to print documents on paper. With Windows Server 2008, Microsoft delivers a strong platform for deploying and managing printers and print services. Besides the basic services of network printing and administration, Windows Server 2008 provides an improved management interface with the Print Management Console (PMC) and enhances deployment with the Active Directory Group Policy Objects.

This chapter introduces you to the Windows Printer Model (WPM). WPM defines basic components and methods for deploying printers and print services on a Windows network. Along with WPM, you will learn how to install Print Services such as the Print Server role service, which includes the PMC, and the Line Printer Daemon for supporting UNIX-based clients. Next, you will learn how to deploy Print Services using both graphical user interface (GUI) and command-line interface (CLI) tools in Windows Server 2008. Once you have deployed your printers, the discussion turns to configuring and managing printers and print services on a Windows network.

Windows Printer Model for Windows Server 2008

Windows Server 2008, like its predecessor, provides robust print services for centrally managing your printing infrastructure. By using Windows Server 2008 print services, printers are made available to the local server hosting the printers along with users on other client platforms, such as Windows Vista, Windows XP, UNIX, and Mac operating system (OS).

To better understand the Windows Server 2008 printing model, you need to be familiar with the components involved in the printing process. The following components are most often found in Windows printing environments:

- *Print device*—The **print device** is the physical printer hardware that is connected either locally or on the network.

- *Printer driver*—The **printer driver** is the software provided by the printer's manufacturer that allows clients to prepare a document for printing.

- *Printer*—A **printer** is a logical device created on a computer to allow output to physical media, such as paper. In the Windows Server 2008 printing model, this is the logical device you create on a Windows Server 2008 printer, which is simply a logical link between clients and a physical printer.

- *Print server*—The **print server** is the computer that hosts one or more printers for use by network clients. The print server is responsible for the queuing and submitting print jobs to the print device.

By using these four components, client applications that support Windows printing can send their digital output to a print device and produce physical documents. Figure 8-1 depicts all the components in the print process in action.

As shown in Figure 8-1, the printing components perform the following steps to turn data from an application into a printed document:

1. The application transfers the data to the printer for processing.

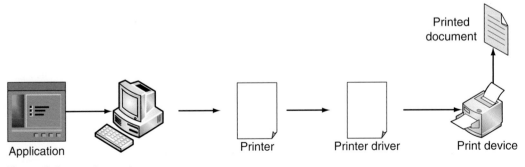

Printed document

Application   Printer   Printer driver   Print device

Figure 8-1 Windows print process

2. When the printer receives data in the form of a print job, it uses the printer driver to render the print job so that it can be processed by the print device. The processing order for print jobs by default is the order received, though you can change this order.

3. After formatting and processing, the print job is transferred to the print server, where the job enters the print queue.

4. The print server then processes the jobs in the order they are queued by sending them to the print device.

5. On receiving the formatted print job, the print device transfers the data to a physical medium. This medium is most often paper, but it could be other forms of physical material.

In Windows Server 2008 and Windows Vista, the printer driver can render the print job in the following formats:

- *Enhanced metafile*—The **enhanced metafile (EMF)** format is a standardized format and the default print job format for use with Windows 2000, Windows XP, and Windows Server 2003 clients. With this format, application data is converted into an EMF file using the printer driver assigned to the printer. When completed, the printer sends the job file to the print server, where the job is stored in the spooler. Once again, the printer driver is used. This time, the spooler uses the printer driver to render the job file into its final format so that the print device can process the job. The format used by Windows-based printers is PCL. This process is also known as graphics device interface (GDI)–based printing.

- *XML paper specification*—The **XML paper specification (XPS)** format is new to Windows Server 2008 and Windows Vista. XPS is a platform-independent document format that does not require the job file to be converted at different steps of the process like EMF jobs. XPS requires the use of print devices that support XPS.

Windows Printer Types

Windows Server 2008 supports printing using two types of printers:

- *Locally attached printers*—A **locally attached printer** is connected directly to a physical computer port. Typical ports include universal serial bus (USB) and parallel port.

- *Network attached printers*—A **network attached printer** is connected directly to the network, not to a physical port on a computer.

Locally Attached Printers   By installing a locally attached printer, you provide the hosting system with the ability to process print jobs through its logical printer. A **print job** is a document submitted by a client computer for processing through the logical printer. Like folders, local printers can be shared with other users on the network. This process turns the local system into a print server. As noted earlier, the print server is any computer that processes print jobs using its hardware resources to connect to a remote computer. The print server directs the print jobs to the printer that is attached locally.

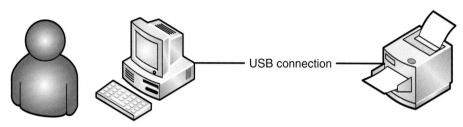

Figure 8-2 Locally attached printer

Activity 8-1: Installing a Local Printer

Time Required: 10 minutes.

Objective: Install a locally attached printer.

Description: For various small print jobs, you have decided to add a locally attached printer to MSN-SRV-0XX. In this activity, you add a local printer. You also install the .NET 3.0 Framework software for later activities.

1. Log onto MSN-SRV-0XX, if necessary.

2. Open a command prompt, type **servermanagercmd.exe -install net-xps-viewer**, and then press **Enter**. This installs the .NET 3.0 Framework feature service that supports XPS documents. You need this functionality for creating printers later in the chapter.

3. Open **Control Panel** and then, in Classic view, double-click **Printers**.

4. Click the **Add a printer** icon in the toolbar to start the Add Printer Wizard.

5. In the first Add Printer Wizard dialog box, click **Add a local printer**.

6. In the Choose a printer port dialog box, click **LPT1: (Printer Port)** in the list box of existing ports and then click **Next**.

7. In the Install the printer driver dialog box, browse for and then select the **Generic/Text Only** driver listed under Generic.

8. Click **Next** to use the currently installed driver.

9. In the Type a printer name dialog box, type **Printer01** as the printer name and then click **Next**.

10. In the Printer Sharing dialog box, click **Do not share this printer** and then click **Next**.

11. In the summary dialog box, click **Finish**.

12. Verify that Printer01 is available in the Printers window. Leave the Printers windows open for the next activity.

Network Attached Printers   Network attached printers contain a network adapter or connect to a hardware print server that manages it. A common device for connecting parallel port printers to a network is an HP Jet Direct print server. Numerous types of print servers are available for wired and wireless networks. Most current models support USB, but devices for supporting parallel port connections are available as well.

Network attached printers can be deployed using the following two network printing models:

- Using a logical printer on every client
- Using a Windows Server 2008 print server

Using a Logical Printer on Every Client   In small environments or other environments where a server is not available to host a logical printer, you create a logical printer on each computer that needs to connect to a printer on the network. Each computer acts as its own print server by maintaining the printer settings and drivers, queuing and processing jobs, and sending the processed jobs to the printer. Figure 8-3 shows an example of how clients using local logical printers use a network printer.

While this model provides an easy setup for small environments, larger environments find its decentralized nature to be a disadvantage. For example, it does not provide a centralized location for maintaining printer drivers and monitoring print queues. It might also require you to visit multiple workstations when you deploy new printers.

Using a Windows Server 2008 Print Server   For most environments, running the Print Server role service is the suggested method for managing multiple printers attached to the

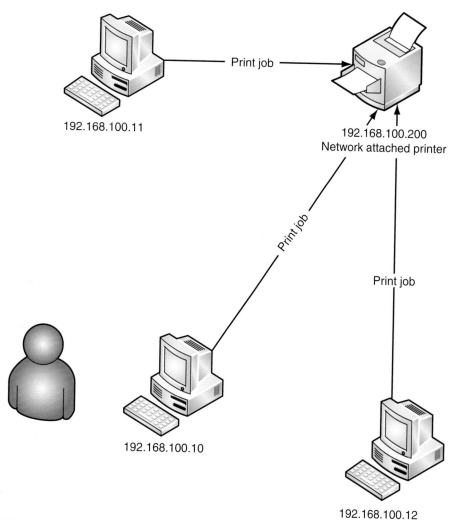

Figure 8-3   Network attached printer: Using a logical printer on each client

network. By using Windows Server 2008 as a print server, you create a central location for managing and monitoring your printer resources. With a print server, all network clients can print through the server when they are connected to it, as shown in Figure 8-4.

Although the Print Server role service is not extremely resource intensive, you need to be aware of the resource usage on your server and other roles that may be deployed on the server. Often, File Services and Print Services are deployed on the same machine because both perform short transactions that work well together. Database applications such as Microsoft Structured Query Language Server and Microsoft Exchange or Active Directory Domain Services (AD DS) domain controllers are not good options for sharing the Print Services role.

Deploying Printers and Print Services

After exploring the types of printers available for use in a Windows network, you can begin deploying printers and print services. You can add local printers through the Printers window, available in Control Panel. However, you need to install specific print service roles and role

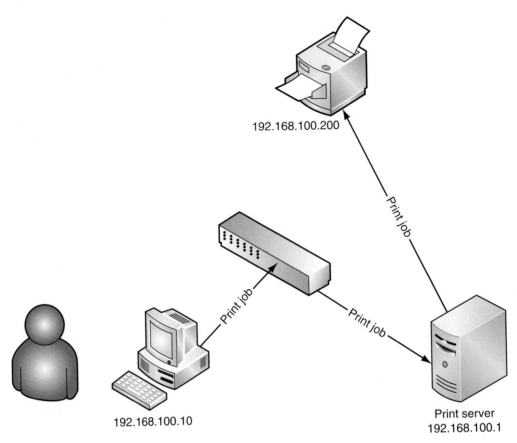

192.168.100.200

Print job

Print job

Print job

192.168.100.10

Print server
192.168.100.1

Figure 8-4   Network attached printer: Using a print server

services if you want to host the Print Services role. In this section, you learn how to install different Print Services and deploy printers to client computers.

Installing the Print Services Role

Installing the Print Services role and the associated role services is similar to the other roles you have installed. You can install the role through Server Manager or from the command line. Like File Services, Print Services is supported on both the Full version and the Server Core version of Windows Server 2008. The Print Services role in Windows Server 2008 includes three role services:

- Print Server service
- Line Printer Daemon service
- Internet printing service

These three roles are the basis for all the functions performed by a Windows Server 2008 print server.

Print Server   Of the three role services, Print Server is the only required service when installing the Print Services role. The PMC is also installed on Full versions of Windows Server 2008. The PMC allows you to manage local and remote print servers. After you share a printer or a file, Windows enables the File and Printer Sharing exception in Windows Firewall with Advanced Security.

Activity 8-2: Adding a network printer

Time Required: 15 minutes.

Objective: Adding a printer through the Print Management console.

Description: Your company decided it needs to centralize its printing administration. To facilitate this, you need to configure a printer using previously implemented print services on MSN-SRV-0XX. In this activity, you will create a new network printer, Printer02.

Print Services were installed previously in Activity 1-6.

1. Open Server Manager, if necessary.

2. Expand **Roles** and then click **Print Services** to view the Print Services Summary pane.

3. In the Start Search box on the Start menu, type **printmanagement.msc** and press **Enter** to open the Print Management console.

4. In the Print Management console, expand **Print Servers** and **MSN-SRV-0XX** until you display Printers. Click **Printers**. This displays all the printers installed and managed on MSN-SRV-0XX. Printer01 is listed in the center pane.

5. Right-click a blank spot in the centers pane and then click **Add Printer**.

6. In the Network Printer Installation Wizard, click **Add a new printer using an existing port:** and then click **LPT2: (Printer Port)**. Click **Next**.

7. In the Printer Driver dialog box, click **Use an existing printer driver on the computer** and then click **Next**.

8. On the Printer Name and Sharing Settings dialog box, enter following information and then click **Next**:

   Printer Name: **Printer02**   Location: **Room 11**
   Share Name: **Printer02**   Comment: **This is a generic printer**

9. In the Printer Found dialog box, click **Next**.

10. In the final dialog box, click **Finish** when the printer is installed successfully.

11. In the Print Management Console, select **Printer02**, click **More Actions**, and then click **List in Directory** under the Actions pane for Printer02.

12. Close the Print Management console.

Line Printer Daemon Service   Not all networks you work with use only Windows-based clients. Often, you have UNIX-based client computers that require access to printers through a Windows Server 2008 print server. The **Line Printer Daemon (LPD) service** allows access to shared printers from computers that use the Line Printer Remote (LPR) service. When the LPD service is installed, the Transmission Control Protocol/Internet Protocol (TCP/IP) Print Server (LPDSVC) service is started, and a Windows Firewall exception is created for port 515.

Your Windows clients might also need to print to a UNIX print server that uses the LPD protocol. To support this from Windows Server 2008 clients, you need to install the **Line Printer Remote (LPR) Port Monitor** on the client. You can enable the LPR Port Monitor feature through the Add Features menu or from the command line using the following:

```
servermanagercmd.exe -install start LPR-Port-Monitor
```

Internet Printing   The **Internet printing** role service in Windows Server 2008 creates a Web site that hosts printers. This Web site is built on the Internet Information Services (IIS) 7.0 platform. From this Web site, users can add printers to their clients and manage the printers on the print server, as shown in Figure 8-5.

The default Web site location is *http://servername/printers*, where servername is the name of the server. For example, if Internet printing is deployed to MSN-SRV-001, you can manage the printers through a Web browser pointing to *http://MSN-SRV-001/printers*. Clients who are adding new network printers can use the Uniform Resource Locater (URL) to add printers that their local machine can use. To support this feature on clients, they must install the Internet printing client.

Because of its reliance on IIS 7.0 components, Internet printing cannot be installed on Windows Server 2008 computers running Server Core. If the IIS roles you need are not installed currently, you will be prompted to install them with the role service.

Activity 8-3: Connecting to a Network Printer Using a Web Browser

Time Required: 15 minutes

Objective: Install the Internet printing role service.

Description: Your fellow administrators have mentioned that they want to manage network printers through a Web browser. They say it is easier and more convenient given the mobile nature of the company. To accomplish this, you need to install the Internet printing role service. In this activity, you will install the Internet printing role service and connect to network printers using Internet Explorer 7.0.

1. On MSN-SRV-0XX, open Server Manager, if necessary, and browse to the Print Services console.

2. In the Print Services Summary pane, scroll down and then click **Add Role Services**.

3. In the Select Role Services dialog box, click the **Internet Printing** check box. The Add Role Services message appears, as shown in Figure 8-6.

4. Click the **Add Required Role Services** button and then click **Next** to continue the installation.

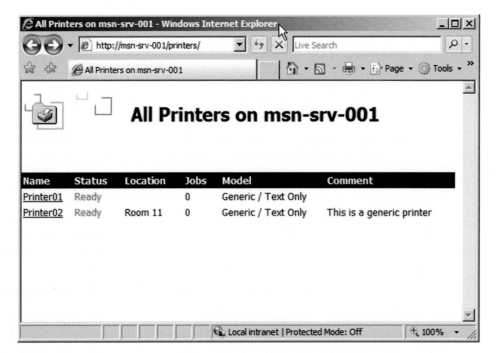

Figure 8-5 Internet printing Web site on print server

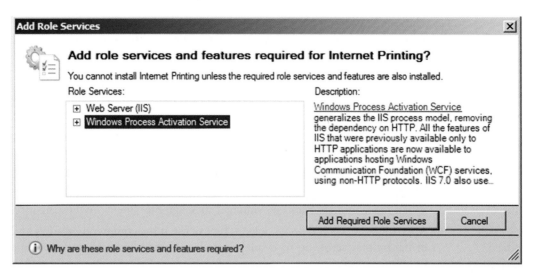

Figure 8-6 Adding role services and features

5. Click **Next** in the Web Server (IIS) dialog box.

6. Click **Next** in the Select Role Services dialog box.

7. Click **Install** in the Confirm Installation Selections dialog box.

8. Click **Close** when the installation is completed.

9. Start Internet Explorer and then enter **msn-srv-0xx/printers** in the Address bar to open the All Printers Web page on MSN-SRV-0XX.

10. In the browser, click the link to **Printer02**. Review the actions on the left side of the window. Note that these are the same actions that can be performed through the printer console for each printer.

11. Close Internet Explorer and then close Server Manager.

Installing Print Services and Printers on Server Core   Similar to the Full version of Windows Server 2008, Server Core can be used as a print server. Server Core supports the Print Server role service and the LPD service for UNIX role.

To install Print Services and the related role services, you use ocsetup. Figure 8-7 displays the commands that can be used for installing Print Services on Server Core.

Activity 8-4: Installing the Print Services Role on Server Core

Time Required: 15 minutes.

Objective: Configure Server Core as a print server.

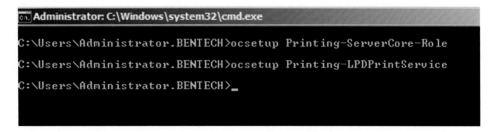

Figure 8-7 Installing Print Services in Server Core

Description: Your manager has decided that along with using Server Core as an RODC and a file server, future deployments will support printers for Windows and UNIX clients. In this activity, you deploy Print Services and the LPD Print Service role to MSN-SC-0XX.

1. Log onto MSN-SC-0XX.

2. At the command prompt, type **start /w ocsetup Printing-ServerCore-Role** and then press **Enter**. This installs the Print Services role along with the print server role service.

3. When the Windows Package Manager message box opens, requesting a restart, click **No**. You will restart MSN-SC-0XX after installing the remaining print server role.

4. Type **start /w ocsetup Printing-LPDPrintService** and then press **Enter** to install the LPD Print Service role.

5. When the Windows Package Manager message box opens, requesting a restart, click **Yes**.

6. After MSN-SC-0XX reboots, log on, type **oclist** at the command prompt, and then press **Enter**. In the output, scroll up to display Installed:Printing-ServerCore-Role and Installed:Printing-LPDPrintService.

After Server Core is set up as a print server, you can deploy printers to it. With no GUI, printers can be deployed in two ways. The first option is through the command line using built-in scripts, which are discussed later in the chapter. The second option is to remotely install the printers on the Server Core computer using a Windows Server 2008 computer that has the PMC installed.

Activity 8-5: Installing a Printer on Server Core

Time Required: 15 minutes.

Objective: Install a network printer on Server Core.

Description: Now that you have deployed print services to a Server Core computer, you need to configure a network printer to use it. In this activity, you use the PMC to add a printer remotely to MSN-SC-0XX, and you use the built-in printing scripts to verify the printers from the console of MSN-SC-0XX.

1. Log onto MSN-SC-0XX as a domain administrator.

2. At the command prompt of the MSN-SC-0XX computer, type **cd %systemroot%\system32\ printing_admin_scripts\en-us** and then press **Enter** to change to the Printing Scripts directory.

3. Type **cscript //H:Cscript //S** and then press **Enter**. This sets cscript as the default scripting host.

4. Type **prnmngr –l** (lowercase l) and then press **Enter** to display the printers on the server.

5. Switch to MSN-SRV-0XX.

6. From the Administrative Tools menu, open **Print Management**.

7. Expand the PMC until Print Servers is selected. Click **More Actions** and then click **Add/Remove Servers** in the Actions pane.

8. In the Add servers text box under Specify print server, type **MSN-SC-0XX** and then click **Add to List**.

9. Click **OK** to close the dialog box. MSN-SC-0XX is now listed as a print server in the PMC.

10. In the left pane, click **MSN-SC-0XX**, click **More Actions** in the Actions pane, and then click **Add Printer**.

11. In the first dialog box of the Network Printer Installation Wizard, click **Add a new printer using an existing port** and then click **FILE: (Print to File)**. Click **Next**.

12. Click **Use an existing printer driver on the computer**, click **Next**, click **Generic/Text Only** and then click **Next**. (If no printers have been installed on the computer, click **Install a new driver**, and then click **Generic/Text Only**.)

13. In the Printer Name and Sharing Settings dialog box, type **PrinterSC01** as the printer name and the share name and specify **MSN-SC-0XX** as the location. Click **Next** to continue.

14. In the Printer Found dialog box, click **Next** to continue.

15. On the Completing the Network Printer Installation Wizard page, click **Finish**.

16. Verify the new printer appears in the PMC by clicking the **Printers** node below MSN-SC-0XX in the left pane. Close the PMC.

Deploying Printers to Clients

As an administrator, one of the complex tasks you will perform is deploying printers. While the concept is straightforward, the execution can be complex as the number of users and printers increases. Windows Server 2008 allows you to deploy printer connections to clients in the following ways:

- Selecting the Add Printer Wizard in Control Panel
- Browsing the shared printer resources with Windows Explorer
- Adding printers with Group Policy

Add Printer Wizard in Control Panel   After you assign the proper permissions to a shared printer, users who have permissions can use the Add Printer Wizard on their client computer. When they run the wizard, they have the choice of installing a local printer (if they have permission) or installing a network printer. They should choose a network printer. When doing so, Windows Server 2008 attempts to discover network printers. If Windows does not discover the printer you want to connect to, you can choose to search for an unlisted printer. When searching for unlisted printers, you can search using the following methods, as shown in Figure 8-8:

- Search the directory, based on location or feature
- Select a shared printer by either Uniform Naming Convention (UNC) pathname or URL
- Select a printer based on TCP/IP address or a host name

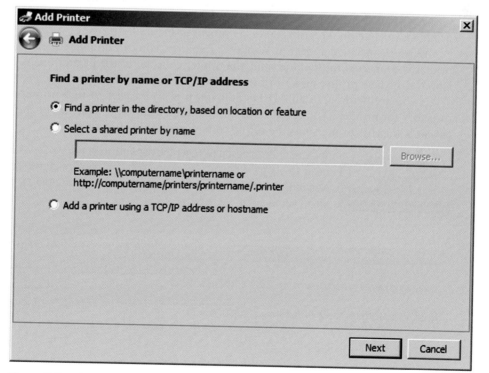

Figure 8-8   Find a printer by name or TCP/IP address dialog box in Add Printer Wizard

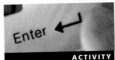

Activity 8-6: Adding a Network Printer

Time Required: 5 minutes.

Objective: Add a network printer to use an LPR port.

Description: Your company has deployed a new application that supports only LPD printers. This requires installing the LPR monitor on clients and configuring a network printer to use an LPR port. In this activity, you install the LPR Monitor on MSN-SRV-0XX and an LPR printer pointing to the LPD Daemon service on MSN-SC-0XX.

1. On the MSN-SRV-0XX server, open the command prompt, type **servermanagercmd.exe -install lpr-port-monitor**, and then press **Enter**. This installs the LPR Client feature.

2. Close the command prompt and open the **Printers** console under Control Panel.

3. Click the **Add a printer** icon on the toolbar.

4. In the Add Printer Wizard, click **Add a local printer**.

5. In the Choose a printer port dialog box, click **Create a new port**, select **LPR Port** as the type, and then click **Next**.

6. In the Add LPR compatible printer dialog box, type **192.168.100.20** as the address of the server and **SCPrinter01** as the name of the printer or print queue, as shown in Figure 8-9. Click **OK**.

7. In the Install the printer driver dialog box, accept the default selection of Generic/ Text Only by clicking **Next**.

8. Click **Next** to use the current driver.

9. Type **Printer03** in the text box for the printer name and then click **Next**.

10. In Printer Sharing dialog box, accept the default of "Do not share this printer" by clicking **Next**.

11. Click **Finish** to install the printer.

Adding Shared Printer Resources with Windows Explorer

With Windows Explorer, you can search your local network to find printers. By using the name of the print server, browse the network to navigate to the Printers share. The Printers share contains all the printers available on the print server, as shown in Figure 8-10.

When the printers appear in Windows Explorer, you can double-click the printer. When the printer is connected for the first time, the printer console for the printer opens. You also have an icon for the new printer under Printers in Control Panel.

If you are working in an AD DS domain, it is even easier to find printers by searching the directory for printers. You can do this based on the location or features of the printer. The only caveat is that the printer must be set up to be listed in the directory.

To access shared resources over the network in Windows Server 2008, you need to enable Network Discovery. This can be configured through the Network and Sharing Center. You will also be prompted to turn it on when you browse the network.

Add LPR compatible printer		
Name or address of server providing lpd:	192.168.100.20	OK
Name of printer or print queue on that server:	SCPrinter01	Cancel

Figure 8-9 Add LPR compatible printer dialog box

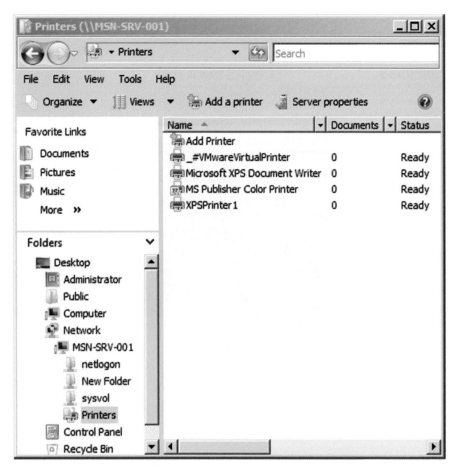

Figure 8-10   Browsing a print server with Windows Explorer

Activity 8-7: Finding a Network Printer Using Active Directory

Time Required: 5 minutes.

Objective: Use the Active Directory search window.

Description: One of the benefits of Active Directory is the ability to search for resources that you have listed in the directory, such as printers. In this activity, you use the AD search window to find any printers described as being located in Room 11. This can be very helpful for users when they are searching for a printer close to their office location.

1. On the MSN-SRV-0XX server, click **Start** and then click **Network**.

2. Click the **Search Active Directory** button on the toolbar.

3. In the Find Users, Contacts, and Groups window, select **Printers** in the Find list box and then type **Room 11** in the Location text box.

4. Click **Find Now**. Printer02 should be displayed as shown in Figure 8-11.

5. Close the Find Printers window and then close the Network window.

Adding a Printer with a UNC Path
Like any shared resource in a Windows environment, you can add printers by using the UNC path to the printer. To do so, you enter the path in the Start Search box on the Start menu or in the Run command window.

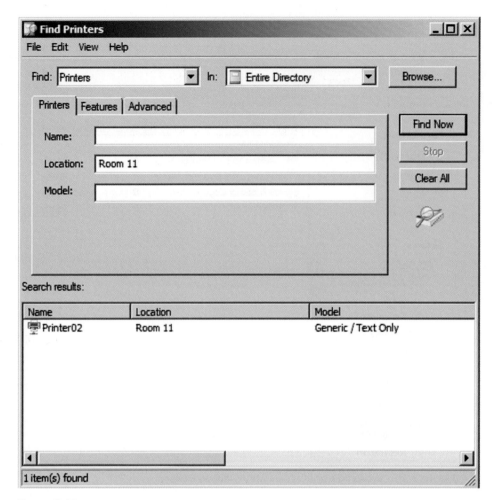

Figure 8-11   Searching for printers in Active Directory

Activity 8-8: Connecting to a Network Printer Using a UNC Path

Time Required: 5 minutes.

Objective: Add a network printer.

Description: A typical administration task is adding a network printer to a client. Before providing the UNC path for the new printer, PrinterSC01, to your users, you need to make sure that the printer will connect properly with clients. In this activity, you use the UNC path of \\MSN-SC-0XX to add the network printer, PrinterSC01.

1. In the Start Search box on the Start menu of the MSN-SRV-0XX server, type **\\msn-sc-0xx\ printersc01**, and press **Enter**. MSN-SRV-0XX connects to MSN-SC-0XX to add the printer.

2. When completed, the printer console for PrinterSC01 on MSN-SC-0XX appears.

3. Close the printer console on MSN-SRV-0XX.

Adding Printers Using Group Policy

As you have seen, you can add a single shared printer by browsing the network or searching Active Directory. However, deploying many printers using these methods would be time consuming. A better way is to use Active Directory and Group Policy objects.

First introduced in Windows Server 2003 R2, you can now deploy printers using Group Policy. This means that you can include printer assignments into your Group Policy structure in

AD DS. You can then deploy printers to both users and computers via Group Policy. You can use both Computer configuration and User configuration policies. This is important, as access to specific printers may be determined on the basis of a user's job role or a computer's location in a building. For example, suppose your marketing department has a color LaserJet printer for creating marketing materials. The cost of maintenance is high, so you want to limit its usage to users in the marketing department.

Policy-based printer deployments are supported only with Windows Vista and Windows Server 2008. For previous versions of Windows, you can configure them to use the Group Policy objects by running a utility called PushPrinter Connections.exe. For more information about this utility and how to deploy it, visit the "Deploy printers by Group Policy and Deploy the PushPrinterConnections.exe utility" articles at *http:// technet.microsoft.com/en-us/library*.

Activity 8-9: Adding a Printer to a Group Policy Object

Time Required: 10 minutes.

Objective: Add a printer to a Group Policy object.

Description: You need to deploy PrinterSC01 to users in the bentech.local domain. You decide that deploying the printer to the domain users with Active Directory is the easiest solution. In this activity, you configure a Group Policy object to deploy a printer to users in the bentech.local domain.

1. On the MSN-SRV-0XX server, open the Printers window from Control Panel. Click **PrinterSC01 on MSN-SC-0XX** and then click the **Delete this printer** button on the toolbar.

2. Click **Yes** in the Printers message box.

3. Close the Printers window.

4. Open the Print Management Console from Administrative Tools.

5. Expand **Print Servers**, and then expand **MSN-SC-0XX**. Click **Printers**, and then click **PrinterSC01** under Print Server MSN-SC-0XX.

6. In the Actions pane, click **More Actions** under PrinterSC01, and then click **Deploy with Group Policy**. This opens the Deploy with Group Policy window as shown in Figure 8-12.

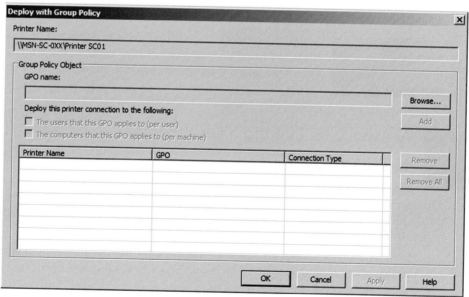

Figure 8-12   Deploy with Group Policy window

7. Click the **Browse** button.

8. In the Browse for a Group Policy Object window, click the **Default Domain Policy** Group Policy object and then click **OK**.

9. In the Deploy with Group Policy window, click **The users that this GPO applies to (per user)** check box and then click **Add**.

10. Click **OK** to deploy the policy.

11. Click **OK** in the Print Management message box confirming the success of the policy deployment, and then click **OK** to close the Deploy with Group Policy dialog box.

12. Browse to **Deployed Printers** in the PMC and verify that PrinterSC01 is listed as a deployed printer.

13. Close the PMC.

Configuring Printer Resources

After deploying new printer resources, you may need to reconfigure them to meet the changing needs of your business. One of the benefits of running a Windows Server 2008 print server is that it allows you to centralize your printers and update drivers and configurations in a single location. In this section, you learn to configure a printer based on the following types of tasks:

- Sharing a stand-alone printer
- Changing permissions on a printer
- Managing printer ports
- Creating a printer pool
- Creating multiple printers for a single print device
- Setting printer priorities and scheduling

Sharing a Stand-Alone Printer

When you have a single locally attached printer, you can share the resource for others to use. This does not require installing any of the print services you have learned about. The only requirement is that your computer has Network Discovery turned on so that others in your network can see your printer. Note that shared printers are not available in Active Directory by default. To list your shared printer in the directory, you can choose to list it on the Sharing tab.

 Turning on Network Discovery on Windows Server 2008 increases the attack surface of your computer. If you choose to make this change, be diligent in keeping the computer patched with the latest OS updates and use the Windows Firewall.

Activity 8-10: Sharing a Local Printer

Time Required: 5 minutes.

Objective: Set up a local printer for sharing.

Description: One of your coworkers needs to use the Printer01 printer that you installed on MSN-SRV-0XX. A good way for them to access the printer is by sharing it from the local computer. In this activity, you set up printer sharing for a locally attached printer.

1. On MSN-SRV-0XX, open the Printers window from Control Panel, click **Printer01** and then click the **Share** button on the toolbar. The Printer Properties dialog box opens to the Sharing tab.

2. On the Sharing tab, click the **Share this printer** check box to use the default share name of Printer01.

3. Click the **List in the directory** check box and then click **OK** to save the changes and close the Printer Properties dialog box.

4. Open a command prompt, type **net share** and then press **Enter** to verify that Printer01 is listed as a shared printer resource. Close the command prompt.

5. Close the Printers window.

Changing Permissions on a Printer

Similar to shared files and folders, printers use permissions based on Access Control Lists to manage access and control usage. Printer permissions in Windows Server 2008 fall into three categories of permissions as shown in Table 8-1.

By using these permissions effectively, you can allow users to print to specific printers and allow certain users or groups to manage the print queues of a printer. This means that users can solve some printing problems independently, such as when documents stall in the printer queue or big print jobs need to be removed.

Activity 8-11: Setting Permissions on a Shared Printer

Time Required: 5 minutes.

Objective: Manage printer share permissions.

Description: Your company just performed a security review. You received low marks on your printer security because the Everyone group is listed in the permissions. You need to modify the permissions on Printer02 so that all domain users can print to the printer and then remove the Everyone group. In this activity, you modify the permissions on a shared printer.

1. On MSN-SRV-0XX, open the Printers window from Control Panel and then click **Printer02**.

2. Click the **Set printer properties** button on the toolbar.

3. In the Printer02 Properties dialog box, click the **Security** tab.

4. Click the **Everyone** group and then click **Remove**.

5. Click the **Add** button.

6. In the Select Users, Computers, or Groups message box, type **domain users** in the Enter the object names to select text box and click **OK**.

7. In the Printer02 Properties dialog box, click **OK** to apply the changes and close the window.

Changing the Printer Port

A printer port is the connection that printers use to send print jobs to a print device. These can be based on TCP/IP ports, USB connections, or other types of printer connections. As an administrator, you might need to change printer ports for the following reasons:

- Replacing a new print device
- Changing the IP address of a network print device
- Migrating the jobs on a printer to a different print device when a print device fails
- Creating a printer pool

Table 8-1   Printer permissions

Print	This permission allows users to add a network printer, print documents, and manage their own documents.
Manage Documents	This permission includes the Print permissions along with giving users the ability to manage all documents on a printer.
Manage Printers	This permission includes the Manage Documents permissions along with giving users the ability to manage all settings and configuration information on a printer.

Activity 8-12: Manually Creating a Printer Port (TCP/IP)

Time Required: 10 minutes.

Objective: Manually create printer ports.

Description: You plan to deploy two new print devices in the near future. Your network administrator has given you the IP addresses to use for the new printers. To save yourself some time when the printers arrive, you want to create the ports now. In this activity, you create the Standard TCP/IP ports in the PMC.

If your lab environment has physical print devices available, you can use them in place of the TCP/IP addresses given here. Ask your instructor for more details on whether this is available.

1. On MSN-SRV-0XX, open the PMC and expand **MSN-SRV-0XX** until you display Ports and then click **Ports**.

2. In the Actions pane, click **More Actions** and then click **Add Port**.

3. In the Printer Ports dialog box, click **Standard TCP/IP Port** and then click **New Port**.

4. When the Welcome to the Add Standard TCP/IP Printer Port Wizard dialog box opens, click **Next**.

5. In the Add Port dialog box, enter **192.168.100.200** as the IP address and then click **Next**. There will be a short search for the TCP/IP port. Unless you are using real addresses, this will fail.

6. In the Additional Port Information Required dialog box, click **Next** to accept the default selections. Click **Finish** to add the port and return to the Printer Ports dialog box.

7. Repeat Steps 3 through 6 using the IP address of **192.168.100.201**.

8. Click **Close** in the Printer Ports dialog box to return to the PMC.

9. Verify that both ports have been added to the PMC.

Activity 8-13: Changing the Port on a Printer

Time Required: 5 minutes.

Objective: Manage printer ports.

Description: You just received a call from the Help Desk. The print device used by Printer02 is out of toner and a replacement cannot be found. Many print jobs are waiting in the Printer02 queue and you need to migrate them to another print device. In this activity, you move the printer port on a printer.

1. On MSN-SRV-0XX, open the PMC and expand **MSN-SRV-0XX** until you display Printers. Click **Printers**.

2. Click **Printer02**.

3. In the Actions pane below Printer02, click **More Actions** and then click **Properties**. The Printer02 Properties dialog box opens.

4. On the Ports tab, switch the port from LPT2 to 192.168.100.200 by clicking the **192.168.100.200** check box.

5. Click **OK** to apply changes and close the Printer02 Properties dialog box.

As you learned, printer ports are managed through the printer properties on the Ports tab, as shown in Figure 8-13. On this tab, you can add, delete, or configure new and existing ports for use by your printer.

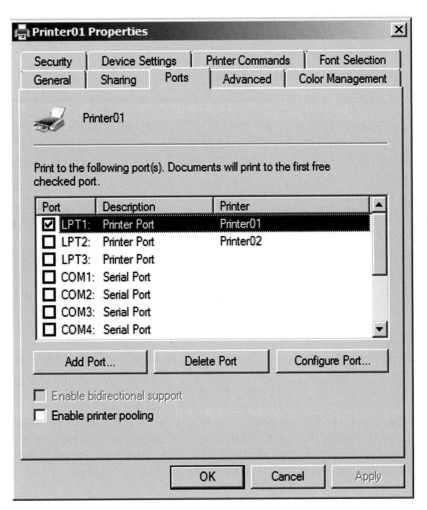

Figure 8-13   Ports tab in the Printer Properties dialog box

Creating a Printer Pool

Occasionally, a single print device does not meet the needs of your users. In these situations, you could deploy an additional printer to your print server. However, this requires users to add and remember to use the new printer. A better solution is to create a printer pool. A **printer pool** is a single printer that sends jobs to multiple print devices. This allows you to print more documents and balance the load across multiple print devices. With a printer pool, the printer on Windows Server 2008 determines which printer is available and then sends the current print job to that printer. It switches among the print devices to manage the load.

For example, suppose a user prints a 200-page document to a normal printer. Without a printer pool, other users must wait for this document to finish printing before they can print their documents. With a printer pool, jobs queued after the large job are sent to the other available printers in the pool.

The requirements for a printer pool are minimal yet important. You need to have two or more printers that can use the same printer driver. This means you can use two different HP printers, for example, as long as both support jobs formatted with the same printer driver. The reason for this is that you cannot create a printer in Windows Server 2008 that uses multiple printer drivers. The second requirement is that the printers are located in the same general vicinity. If you pooled two printers on opposite sides of an office floor, for example, users would not know which printer is completing their print job.

Activity 8-14: Creating a Printer Pool

Time Required: 5 minutes.

Objective: Create a printer pool using an existing printer.

Description: Because many users complained about print performance, management has decided to deploy an additional print device to ease the printing burden on Printer02. You decide that it is more effective to create a printer pool than to deploy an additional network printer. In this activity, you create a printer pool using Printer02 by adding another printer port.

1. On MSN-SRV-0XX, expand **MSN-SRV-0XX** in the PMC until you display Printers. Click **Printers**.

2. Click **Printer02**.

3. In the Actions pane, click **More Actions** under Printer02, and then click **Properties**. The Printer02 Properties dialog box opens.

4. Click the **Ports** tab, click **Enable printer pooling**, and then click the **192.168.100.201** check box.

5. Click **OK** to apply changes and close the Printer02 Properties dialog box.

Creating Multiple Printers for a Single Print Device

Although printer pools are an excellent configuration option, you usually need to create multiple printers for a single print device. Doing so allows you to control document printing priority, scheduling, and access to functionality on a print device.

For example, suppose that all employees use a central printer on an office floor. Among them are two executives who require priority in completing their print jobs. By creating two separate printers, one for the regular users and one for executives, you can assign access to each user on the basis of their job status, and then you can assign a higher priority to the executive printer. Jobs with a higher priority move forward in the print device's queue.

While priority will place jobs ahead of other jobs, it will not skip over a currently printing job. If someone is printing a large job, the higher priority jobs will have to wait. A better option would be to combine this functionality with a printer pool.

Activity 8-15: Creating an Additional Printer for the Exec Printers Group

Time Required: 20 minutes.

Objective: Add a printer that prints to a single print device.

Description: Your manager reports that some executives indicate that their print jobs to Printer02 take too long to print, even with the new printer pool. She asks you to create a printer for the executives that prints to the print device at 192.168.100.200. In this activity, you create a new printer that will be configured in a later activity and then assign it a higher priority than other printers.

1. On MSN-SRV-0XX, expand **MSN-SRV-0XX** in the PMC until you display Printers.

2. Click **Printers**, click **More Actions** under Printers in the Actions pane and then click **Add Printer**.

3. In the Network Printer Installation Wizard, click **Add a new printer using an existing port**, click **192.168.100.200 (Standard TCP/IP Port)**, and then click **Next**.

4. In the Printer Driver dialog box, click the **Use an existing printer driver on the computer** option button, and then click **Next** to select the current printer driver of Generic/Text Only.

5. In the Printer Name and Sharing Settings dialog box, enter following information and then click **Next**:

   Printer Name: **EXPrinter02**

   Share Name: **EXPrinter02**

   Location: **Room 11**

   Comment: **This printer is for use by members of the executive staff only.**

6. In the Printer Found dialog box, click **Next**.

7. In the final dialog box, click **Finish** when the printer is installed successfully.

8. In the Printer Console, click **EXPrinter02**, click **More Actions** in the Actions pane for EXPrinter02, and then click **List in Directory**.

9. Open Active Directory Users and Computers (ADUC) from the Administrative Tools menu.

10. In ADUC, expand the domain tree and then click the **Builtin** container.

11. Click **Action** on the menu bar, point to **New**, and then click **Group**.

12. In the New Object – Group dialog box, type **Exec Printers** for the group name and set the group as a **Domain local Security Group** as shown in Figure 8-14. Click **OK** to create group.

13. Close Active Directory Users and Computers and leave the PMC open for the next activity.

Printer priorities and scheduling options are managed on the Advanced tab of a printer's Properties dialog box as shown in Figure 8-15. Priority is set by choosing a number between 1 and 99, where 1 is lowest priority and 99 is the highest priority. For the executives in the preceding example, you would create one printer for the users and set the priority as 1. Create the next printer with a priority of 99 and assign permissions to allow only the executives to print to the printer.

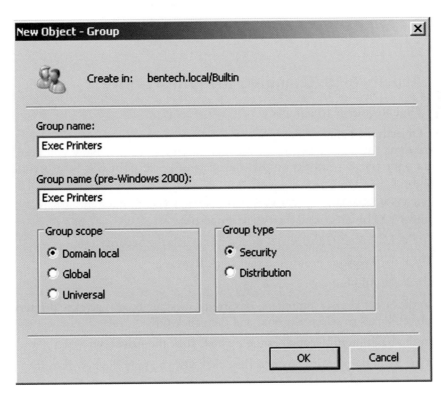

Figure 8-14   Creating Exec Printers security group

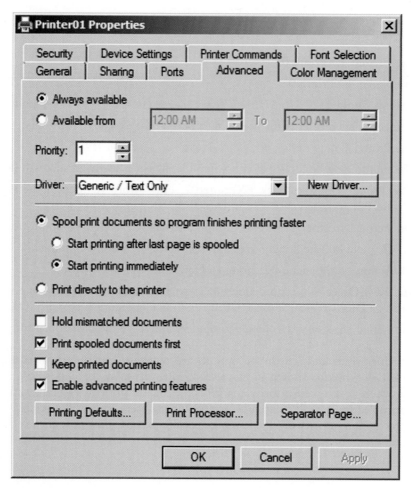

Figure 8-15   Advanced tab in the Printer Properties dialog box

Activity 8-16: Changing the Print Priority

Time Required: 10 minutes.

Objective: Change printer priority.

Description: You have created a printer for executives to use. Now you need to configure the printer with a higher priority so that the executive print jobs will be processed first within the print queue.

1. On MSN-SRV-0XX, click **EXPrinter02** in the PMC. In the Actions pane, click **More Actions** under EXPrinter02, and then click **Properties**.

2. In the EXPrinter02 Properties dialog box, click the **Security** tab.

3. Click the **Everyone** group and then click **Remove**.

4. Click the **Add** button.

5. In the Select Users, Computers, or Groups message box, type **exec printers** in the Enter the object names to select text box, and then click **OK**.

6. In the EXPrinter02 Properties dialog box, click the **Advanced** tab.

7. Type **99** in the Priority box and then click **OK** to apply the new priority.

8. Close the PMC.

When this printer is configured, you need to assign executive users permissions by adding their accounts to the Executive Printers group. Deploying the printers can be done manually or you could use Group Policy.

Although not used as much as priorities, you can create a printer that prints jobs only during a scheduled period. This would be a good solution for an application that prints long daily reports. In this instance, you would create a printer for use by the application and set the scheduling so that jobs are only printed after 6:00 pm, for example. This printer can point to a print device used by your normal users. However, the large jobs will not affect them, as they are completed during off hours and will be available for the parties needing them the next day. Although jobs will be printed only after 6:00 pm, the jobs will be accepted by the printer at anytime. They are queued in order of receipt and priority until the scheduled start time is reached.

Activity 8-17: Scheduling Printers

Time Required: 10 minutes.

Objective: Create a printer schedule.

Description: Your company has rolled out a new accounting system that creates large reports and statements that need to be printed for the accounting staff to review. These reports are not time sensitive, so they do not need to be printed as soon as they are generated. However, they can contain up to 300 pages. You decide that the best solution is to deploy a printer for the application to use and then set it to print during off hours. In this activity, you create a new printer, AcctPrinter01, and schedule it to print during the period of 6:00 pm to 5:00 am.

1. On MSN-SRV-0XX, open the PMC and expand **MSN-SRV-0XX** until you display Printers.

2. Click **Printers**, click **More Actions** in the Actions pane, and then click **Add Printer**.

3. In the Network Printer Installation Wizard, click **Add a new printer using an existing port**, click **192.168.100.201 (Standard TCP/IP Port)**, and then click **Next**.

4. In the Printer Driver dialog box, choose **Next** to select the current printer driver of Generic/Text Only.

5. In the Printer Name and Sharing Settings dialog box, enter following information and then click **Next**:

   Printer Name: **AcctPrinter01**

   Share Name: **AcctPrinter01**

   Location: **Room 22**

   Comment: **This printer is for use by the Very Large Accounting application and only prints from 6 pm to 5 am daily.**

6. In the Printer Found dialog box, click **Next**.

7. In the final dialog box, click **Finish** when the printer is installed successfully.

8. In the PMC, click **AcctPrinter01**, click **More Actions** under AcctPrinter01 in the Actions pane, and then click **Properties**. The AcctPrinter01 Properties dialog box opens.

9. Click the **Advanced** tab.

10. Click the **Available from** option button and then set the times from **6:00 PM** to **5:00 AM** or a time suggested by your instructor. The time period should not overlap the time period in which this lab activity is being completed.

11. Click **OK** to apply the configuration changes and close the Properties dialog box.

12. In the PMC, click **AcctPrinter01**, click **More Actions** under AcctPrinter01 in the Actions pane, and then click **Print Test Page**. Click **Close** in message box stating that the test print has been submitted.

13. In the PMC, click **More Actions** under AcctPrinter01 in the Actions pane and then **Open Printer Queue**. Verify that the Test Page print job is listed in the print queue and has no status, as shown in Figure 8-16.

14. Close the print queue and the PMC.

To verify that your printer is working properly, you could change the system time on your server to 6:30 pm and wait a few minutes. The Test Page will attempt to print as its scheduled time has been exceeded.

Updating a Printer Driver

You occasionally need to update printer drivers as manufacturers provide new ones. Whether it is to fix a hardware issue or to provide new features and functionality, changing a printer driver is a straightforward process. You manage drivers on the Advanced tab of a printer's Properties dialog box by clicking the New Driver button, which starts the Add Printer Driver Wizard, as shown in Figure 8-17.

Activity 8-18: Updating a Printer Driver

Time Required: 10 minutes.

Objective: Update printer drivers.

Description: You have just learned that the driver for one of your network printers, Printer02, has been updated to allow for improved performance and functionality. Your new driver has already been downloaded and is available for installation. In this activity, you install a new driver for a network printer.

1. On MSN-SRV-0XX, open the Print Management Console.

2. Expand the PMC and then click **Printer02**.

3. In the Actions pane, click **More Actions** and then click **Properties** under Printer02.

4. In the Printer02 Properties dialog box, click the **Advanced** tab. This tab displays the current driver.

5. Click the **New Driver** button to start the Add Printer Driver Wizard. Click **Next** to continue.

6. In the Printer Driver Selection list, click **Generic** as the Manufacturer. Click **MS Publisher Color Printer** in the Printers list. Click **Next** to continue.

7. Click **Finish** to complete the driver change.

8. Click **OK** to apply the changes and close the Printer02 Properties dialog box.

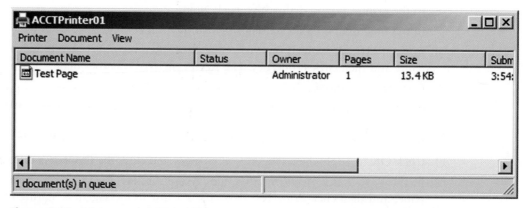

Figure 8-16 Printer queue with held job

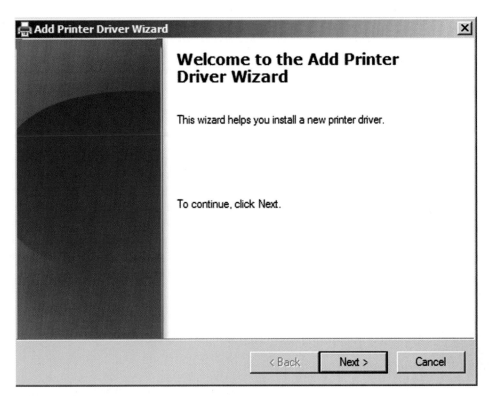

Figure 8-17   Add Printer Driver Wizard

9. In the PMC, click **View** and then click **Add/Remove Columns** to open the Add/Remove Columns dialog box. Click **Driver Name** and then click the **Add** button to place "Driver Name" in the Displayed columns list.

10. Click **OK** to add the new column.

11. In the PMC, expand the Summary pane, if necessary, to view the names of the drivers for each printer on MSN-SRV-0XX. Verify that the driver for Printer02 is MS Publisher Color Printer.

12. Close the PMC.

Managing Printers and Print Services

Printers and print services in Windows Server 2008 are managed through a number of different tools. For GUI-based systems and remote computers, you can use the PMC. For Server Core installation or CLI configuration options, you can use a built-in set of commands and scripts for managing the printers and print services. In this section, you learn to manage a Windows Server 2008 print server using the available tools.

Using the PMC

The PMC is installed on Full versions of Windows Server 2008 when the Print Server role service is installed. This does not mean that you have to be running a print server to manage your printers. Like many of the services in Windows Server 2008, you can manage print services from a Windows Server 2008 or certain Windows Vista clients that have the Remote Server Administration Tools (RSAT) installed. For printer management, you can choose the Print Services Tools from the RSAT menu under Features on Windows Server 2008.

For more information on the RSAT tools for Windows Vista, visit *http://support.microsoft.com* and search for knowledge base article 941314, or KB941314.

The PMC is available as a stand-alone Microsoft Management Console (MMC) or through the Server Manager console. Similar to many of the Server Manager consoles, you can use the PMC to manage the local server only when accessed through Server Manager. If you need to work with remote printers or multiple printers, you need to use the PMC available through Administrative Tools, or you can add Printer Management to a custom MMC console.

Working with Print Queues

As you have learned, jobs that are submitted to a printer sit in the print queue until they are sent and processed by the print device. On some occasions, you might need to allow the print queue on a printer to be submitted to a different print device. This is often the case when a print device fails during business hours and a large amount of print jobs still need to be completed. To use a different print device, you need to change the printer port to the new print device. Similar to printer pools, the new target print device must support the printer driver that the printer is currently using. Another important note is that only queued jobs will be transferred. If a job is currently being printed to a print device when it fails, the job must be resent by the user.

Activity 8-19: Migrating a Print Queue

Time Required: 10 minutes

Objective: Migrate a print queue from a failed print device.

Description: Users are reporting that Printer01 has a number of print jobs stuck in the queue. After some investigating, you determine that the print device Printer01 uses is damaged. Until you can replace the print device, you will migrate the print queue from the current port on Printer01 to 192.168.100.205. This port maps to another print device near Printer01. In this activity, you change the printer port on a printer so that it uses a different port/print device combination.

1. On MSN-SRV-0XX, open the PMC and expand **MSN-SRV-0XX** until you display Ports. Click **Ports**.

2. In the Actions pane, click **More Actions** and then click **Add Port**.

3. In the Printer Ports dialog box, click **Standard TCP/IP Port** and then click **New Port**.

4. In the Welcome dialog box of the wizard, click **Next**. In the Add Port dialog box, enter **192.168.100.205** as the IP address and then click **Next**. There will be a short search for the TCP/IP port. Unless you are using real addresses, this will fail.

5. In the Additional Port Information Required dialog box, click **Next** to choose the default selections. Click **Finish** to add the port and return to the Printer Ports dialog box.

6. In the Printer Ports dialog box, click **Close**.

Managing Server Core Print Services

Print Servers installed on Server Core can be managed in two ways. From the Server Core console, you can use a combination of CLI utilities and built-in print scripts. The scripts are stored in a default directory location of %systemroot%\System32\Printing_Admin_Scripts\en-US. Table 8-2 lists the scripts and commands that can be used from the console.

The second option, which is probably easier for most administrators, is to use the PMC from a computer running the Full version of Windows Server 2008. By adding your Server Core print server to the PMC, you can perform all the necessary management tasks, such as adding printers, deleting printers, and modifying printer properties.

Table 8-2 CLI printer commands

CLI Utility	Description
Lpq	This command will display the status of a print queue on a computer running LPD.
Lpr	This command will send a file to a computer or printer-sharing device running the LPD service in preparation for printing.
Net print	This command will display information about a specified printer queue, display information about a specified print job, or control a specified print job.
Print	This command will send a text file to a printer.
Prncnfg.vbs	This command will configure or display configuration information about a printer.
Prndrvr.vbs	This command will add, delete, and list printer drivers.
Prnjobs.vbs	This command will pause, resume, cancel, and list print jobs.
Prnmngr.vbs	This command will add, delete, and list printers or printer connections in addition to setting and displaying the default printer.
Prnport.vbs	This command will create, delete, and list standard TCP/IP printer ports in addition to displaying and changing port configuration.
Prnqctl.vbs	This command will print a test page, pause or resume a printer, and clear a printer queue.
Pubprn.vbs	This command will publish a printer to the AD DS database.

Activity 8-20: Managing a Printer on Server Core using PMC

Time Required: 10 minutes.

Objective: Remotely manage a printer using the PMC.

Description: You need to make some changes to PrinterSC01. You've been asked to create a printer pool on the printer, remove the Everyone group, and add domain users with Print permissions. In this activity, you remotely configure PrinterSC01 from MSN-SRV-0XX using the PMC.

1. On MSN-SRV-0XX, open the PMC and expand **MSN-SC-0XX** until you display **Ports**.

2. Click **More Actions** in the Actions pane, and then click **Add Port**.

3. In the Printer Ports dialog box, click **Standard TCP/IP Port** and then click **New Port**.

4. Click **Next** in the Add Standard TCP/IP Printer Port Wizard dialog box.

5. Enter **192.168.200.200** in the Printer Name or IP Address text box and then click **Next**.

6. In the Additional Port Information Required dialog box, click **Next** to choose the default selections. Click **Finish** to add the port and return to the Printer Ports dialog box.

7. Repeat Steps 3 through 6 using the IP address of **192.168.200.201**. Click **Close** when the second port is created.

8. Click **Printers** in the left pane, click **PrinterSC01** in the middle pane, click **More Actions** under PrinterSC01 in the Actions pane, and then click **Properties**.

9. Click the **Ports** tab and then click **Enable printer pooling**.

10. In the Port list, click **FILE:** to remove the checkmark. Click the **192.168.200.200** and **192.168.200.201** check boxes to select them.

11. Click the **Security** tab.

12. Click the **Everyone** group and then click **Remove**.

13. Click the **Add** button.

14. In the Select Users, Computers, or Groups message box, type **domain users** in the Enter the object names to select text box and then click **OK**.

15. In the PrinterSC01 Properties dialog box, click **OK** to apply the changes and close the window.

16. Close the PMC.

Chapter Summary

- The four components involved in the printing process are the print device, which is the physical printer hardware that is connected either locally or on the network; the printer driver, which is the software provided by the printer's manufacturer that allows clients to prepare a document for printing; the printer, which you create on a Windows Server 2008 printer; and the print server, which is the computer that hosts one or more printers for use by network clients. The print server is responsible for queuing and submitting print jobs to the print device. Note that the printer here is not a physical entity but a logical link between clients and a physical printer.

- In Windows Server 2008 and Windows Vista, the printer driver can render the print job in the EMF format, a standardized format, and is the default print job format for use with Windows 2000, Windows XP, and Windows Server 2003 clients. It can also render the print job in the XPS format, a new format in Windows Server 2008 and Windows Vista. XPS is a platform-independent document format that does not require the job file to be converted at different steps of the process like EMF jobs. XPS requires the use of print devices that support XPS.

- Windows Server 2008 supports printing using locally attached printers, which are connected directly to a physical computer port, and network attached printers, which are connected directly to the network, not to a physical port on a computer.

- In small environments or other environments where a server is not available to host a logical printer, you create a logical printer on each computer that needs to connect to a printer on the network. Each computer acts as its own print server by maintaining the printer settings and drivers, queuing and processing jobs, and sending the processed jobs to the printer.

- For most environments, running the Print Server role service is the suggested method for managing multiple printers attached to the network. By using Windows Server 2008 as a print server, you create a central location for managing and monitoring your printer resources. With a print server, all network clients can print through the server when they are connected to it.

- To install the Print Services role and the associated role services, you can use Server Manager or from the command line. Like File Services, Print Services is supported on both the Full version and the Server Core version of Windows Server 2008.

- Deploying printers is a typical administrative task. Windows Server 2008 allows you to deploy printer connections to clients by selecting the Add Printer Wizard in Control Panel, browsing the shared printer resources with Windows Explorer, or adding printers with Group Policy.

- After deploying new printer resources, you may need to reconfigure them to meet the changing needs of your business. Windows Server 2008 print servers allow you to centralize your printers and update drivers and configurations in a single location. You can configure a printer by sharing a stand-alone printer, changing permissions on a printer, managing printer ports, creating a printer pool, creating multiple printers for a single print device, and setting printer priorities and scheduling.

Key Terms

enhanced metafile (EMF)   The default print job format for use with Windows 2000, Windows XP, and Windows Server 2003 clients. With this format, application data is converted into an EMF file using the printer driver assigned to the printer.

Internet printing   Windows service based on Internet Information Services 7.0 where users can add printers to their client as well as manage the printers on the print server through a Web browser.

Line Printer Daemon (LPD) service   The server-based service that allows access to shared printers from computers that use the Line Printer Remote (LPR) service. This is often used for UNIX-based clients.

Line Printer Remote (LPR) port monitor   A feature needed by your Windows Clients to print to a print server that uses the LPD protocol.

locally attached printers   This type of printer is connected directly to a physical computer port. Typical port examples include universal serial bus (USB) and parallel port.

network attached printers   A printer that is attached to the network by either a network adapter or a hardware print server. This type of printer is connected directly to the network, not to a physical port on a computer.

print device   This is the physical printer hardware that is connected either locally or on the network.

print job   A document that is prepared and submitted by a client computer to a logical printer for process to a physical printer.

print server   This is the computer that hosts one or more printers for use by network clients. The print server is responsible for the queuing and submitting print jobs to the print device.

printer   A logical device created on a computer to allow output to physical media, such as paper.

printer driver   This is the software provided by the printer's manufacturer that allows clients to prepare a document for printing.

printer pool   A single printer that sends jobs to multiple print devices.

XML paper specification (XPS)   This format is a new format in Windows Server 2008 and Windows Vista. XPS is a platform-independent document format does not require the job file to be converted at different steps of the process like EMF jobs.

Review Questions

1. Which of the following is *not* a standard permission that can be assigned to a printer Access Control List?

    a. Manage Printers

    b. Manage Properties

    c. Print

    d. Manage Documents

    e. Print Documents

2. When viewing the properties of a printer, which tab will be used to configure printer pooling?

    a. Device Settings

    b. Configuration

    c. Pooling

    d. Ports

3. A printer that is available from 5:00 pm to 5:00 am can accept print jobs in the print queue at 4:45 pm. True or False?

4. Which of the following Windows Server 2008 services helps support UNIX-based clients?

    a. Line Printer Remote Port Monitor

    b. Line Printer Daemon Server Service

    c. XML Paper Specification

    d. Print Services for Unix

5. A _____ device represents the printer hardware used on a Windows network.

6. ___ LPR Port Monitor_____ must be installed on a Windows client in order to print to an LPD print server.

7. You are deploying Windows Server 2008 Standard edition running Server Core on your network. You decide to install Internet Printing along with the Print Server role service. Which of the following is true about the solution?

    a. This is supported only on Server Core versions running Enterprise and Datacenter editions of Windows Server 2008.

    b. This requires the installation of Windows PowerShell on Server Core.

    c. This is supported only on Full versions of Windows Server 2008.

    d. This requires an AD DS domain environment.

8. You are deploying Windows Server 2008 Standard edition running Server Core on your network. Your network includes Windows XP clients, Windows Vista clients, Windows Server 2008 servers, and Ubuntu Linux clients. All clients require access to network printers and print services. Which of the following are required on your Windows Server 2008 server?

    a. Print Services role and print server role services

    b. Print Services for UNIX/Linux

    c. LPD Server services

    d. Internet Printing role service

    e. LPR Port Monitor

9. Which of the following commands installs the Internet Printing role service on Windows Server 2008?

    a. servermanagercmd.exe Print-Internet

    b. ocsetup.exe Printing-Internet

    c. servermanagercmd.exe –install Print-Internet

    d. ocsetup.exe –install Printing-Internet

10. Which of the following commands can be run from the command line to display the all printers installed on a Windows Server 2008 computer called PRNTSRV001?

    a. oclist.exe–query Printing-ServerCore-Role

    b. prnmngr.vbs –l PRNTSRV001

    c. net share

    d. prncfg.vbs –l PRNTSRV001

11. Which of the following are required for a printer pool on Windows Server 2008 when using differing models of print devices?

    a. Two or more printer ports pointing at the same print device

    b. Two or more printers pointing at the same print device

    c. Two or more print devices using the same printer driver

    d. Two or more printer drivers

12. Which of the following commands verify that a printer has been shared on a Windows Server 2008 computer?

    a. oclist.exe–query Printing-ServerCore-Role

    b. netsh show share printer

    c. net share

    d. prncfg.vbs –l PRNTSRV001

13. Which of the following permissions give a user or group the ability to change a printer driver?

    a. Printer Full Control

    b. Modify Printer

    c. Manage Printer

    d. Manage Documents

    e. Modify Documents

14. Which tab on the Printer Properties dialog box would you use to change a printer port?

    a. Ports

    b. General

    c. Advanced

    d. Security

    e. Sharing

15. Which tab on the Printer Properties dialog box would you use to change a printer driver?

    a. Ports

    b. General

    c. Advanced

    d. Security

16. Which tab on the Printer Properties dialog box would you use to add drivers for x64 and Itanium computers?

    a. Ports

    b. General

    c. Advanced

    d. Security

    e. Sharing

17. All shared printers are listed in Active Directory in AD DS domain networks. True or False?

18. When you change the port on a printer in Windows Server 2008, which documents currently in the print queue will print?

    a. All documents including the currently printing document.

    b. All documents you select to be transferred to the new port.

    c. All documents except the currently printing document.

    d. No documents. Changing the printer port cancels all print jobs.

Case Projects

Case Project 8-1: Researching the XML Paper Specification

You learned that Windows Server 2008 uses the new printing format XPS for formatting print jobs. There may be instances where a printer uses the new drivers for the XPS format, but the print device does not support XPS. Research how Windows Server 2008 deals with legacy print devices with XPS. In addition, list the benefits of using XPS over GDI-based printing.

Case Project 8-2: Installing the PMC

For this project, you need to install the PMC on CS-SRV-001 so that you can manage any printers you deploy in the future. Research how to install the PMC without installing any additional printer role services.

Case Project 8-3: Installing Print Services and Printers in Server Core

Install the Print Services Role on CS-SC-001 and create the following printers using Table 8-3.

Table 8-3 Printers for Case Project 8-3

Printer Name	Server Core Printer01	Server Core Printer02
Share Name	SCPrnt01	SCPrnt02
Driver	Generic/Text Only	Generic/Text Only
Port	Standard TCP/IP	Standard TCP/IP
IP	192.168.200.201	192.168.200.202

Network Policy and Access Services in Windows Server 2008

After reading this chapter and completing the exercises, you will be able to:

- Configure routing in Windows Server 2008
- Configure Routing and Remote Access Services in Windows Server 2008
- Describe Network Policy Server
- Discuss wireless networking with Windows Server 2008

Windows Server 2008 provides a new role for supporting management of your network. The Network Policy and Access Services let you manage remote access connections for your remote users along with managing the client health of your network computers.

In this chapter, you will be introduced to the Routing and Remote Access console. This console allows you to use Windows Server 2008 as a router for small networks along with providing other network services. Next, you will discover the different types of remote access connections that can be used with Windows Server 2008. You will also examine the Network Policy Server, its related console, and wireless networking.

Configuring Routing in Windows Server 2008

Routing and Remote Access Services (RRAS) is a role service used to configure and manage network routing in Windows Server 2008. As a software-based router, RRAS is recommended for use in small networks that require simple routing directions but is not recommended for large and complex environments. Along with routing, RRAS provides Dynamic Host Configuration Protocol (DHCP) relay agent functionality for networks.

Networking in general and Transmission Control Protocol/Internet Protocol (TCP/IP) were discussed in Chapter 3. You should ensure that you have a good understanding of those concepts before proceeding with this section on routing.

To prepare for the activities in this chapter, you need to use an additional Windows Server 2008 computer that has at least two network adapters. If you have already added another Windows Server 2008 computer, you can skip Activity 9-1.

Activity 9-1: Installing a Windows Server 2008 Member Server

Time Required: 75 minutes.

Objective: Install a Windows Server 2008 member server.

Description: You need to deploy another server for a test subnet you are adding to the network. In this activity, you will build another Windows Server 2008 computer for working with RRAS and other roles and services.

Your instructor may give you additional steps to perform depending on your lab environment. This activity is compatible for labs with physical machines and within virtual machine applications.

1. Place your Windows Server 2008 DVD in the DVD drive of your computer, and then restart or power on your computer.

2. If prompted by the startup screen, press any key to boot from the DVD.

3. At the Install Windows window, confirm your time and currency format and that keyboard layout is correct, and then click **Next**. Click **Install now**.

4. If you have a product key, enter it in the product key box. Otherwise, you can install Server 2008 without a product key. Uncheck the **Automatically activate Windows when I'm online** check box and then click **Next**.

5. If you did not enter a product key, you will receive a message box asking whether you want to enter a key. Click **No** to continue installing without a product key.

6. Select the version of Server 2008 you are installing. For this exercise, choose **Windows Server 2008 Enterprise (Full Installation)**, check the **I have selected the edition of Windows that I purchased** check box, and then click **Next**.

7. Select the **I accept the license terms** check box and then click **Next**.

8. Click **Custom**.

9. On the Where do you want to install Windows? window, delete any existing partitions using the following steps:

   a.   Click the partition you want to delete.

   b.   Click **Delete**.

   c.   Click **OK** to confirm that you want to delete the partition and that all data will be lost.

10. Select **Disk 0 Unallocated Space** and then click **Drive options** (**advanced**) to perform disk partitioning operations.

11. Click **New**. Enter **30000** in the Size text box, ensuring that you have at least 10 GB of extra unallocated disk space (after creating the 30 GB partition), and then click **Apply**.

12. Select **Disk 0 Partition 1** and then click **Format**.

13. Confirm that all data will be lost when formatting the partition by clicking **OK**.

14. Wait a few moments for the partition to be created, and then click **Next**. If you are prompted to press a key to start from DVD, ignore the message.

15. The installation process will proceed for at least a few minutes. You will receive a warning that you need to change your password before logging on for the first time. Click **OK**.

16. Use **P@ssw0rd** as your new password. You will need to enter the password twice to ensure that it is correct. Click **OK** to accept your new password, and then click **OK** again after verifying it.

17. When Windows Server 2008 displays the Initial Configuration Tasks window, click **Set time zone** and change the time zone to your current location. Also change the time, if necessary. Ask your instructor if you are not sure of the proper time zone for your location.

18. Open the command prompt and enter the following commands to set the network adapters:

```
netsh interface set interface name="local area connection"
newname="bentech.local"
netsh interface set interface name="local area connection 2"
newname="Test Subnet"
netsh int ipv4 set address name="bentech.local" static
192.168.100.110 255.255.255.0 192.168.100.10
netsh int ipv4 set address name="test subnet" static
192.168.175.110 255.255.255.0
netsh int ip set dns "bentech.local" static 192.168.100.10
```

19. Open Server Manager and change the computer name to MSN-SRV-1XX, where XX is a number supplied by your instructor. Reboot the server, and then log onto MSN-SRV-1XX.

20. On MSN-SRV-1xx, open the command prompt, and enter the following command to add MSN-SRV-1XX to the domain, bentech.local:

```
NETDOM join MSN-SRV-1XX /Domain:bentech.local /userD:administrator
                    /passwordD:P@ssw0rd
```

21. Reboot the server, and then log onto MSN-SRV-1XX as administrator@bentech.local.

22. In the Initial Configuration Tasks window, click the **Do not show this window at logon** check box and then click **Close**.

23. Make sure the MSN-SRV-0XX computer is running. Open the command prompt, type **ping 192.168.100.10**, and then press **Enter**. Verify that you receive a successful reply back before beginning the next activities.

24. Open the command prompt, type **ping msn-srv-0XX**, and then press **Enter**. Verify that you receive a successful reply before beginning the next activities.

Configuring RRAS as a Router

As discussed in Chapter 3, **routers** are responsible for forwarding packets between subnets, or networks with differing IP addressing schemes. Routers accomplish this task by viewing the **header** of the data packet and using routing tables for determining the best route for sending packets to their destination. Because of the nature of information packets, this process requires an intelligent networking device, or router, to evaluate and forward this traffic to its destination.

Figure 9-1 shows a simple routing example where Windows Server 2008 acts as a router.

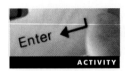

Activity 9-2: Installing RRAS on MSN-SRV-0XX and MSN-SRV-1XX

Time Required: 15 minutes.

Objective: Install RRAS.

Description: With a new subnet in place and the need to provide Internet connectivity to those clients, you have decided to implement RRAS in your environment. In this activity, you will install RRAS on two Windows Server 2008 computers and test connectivity to the Internet. One of the benefits of using RRAS is that simply installing the service allows connectivity between two subnets linked by an RRAS-enabled Windows Server 2008 server.

1. Log onto MSN-SRV-0XX, if necessary. Close Server Manager, if necessary.

2. Open the command prompt, and type **servermanagercmd.exe –install NPAS-RRAS-Services**. Once the command is completed, close the command prompt.

3. On MSN-SRV-0XX, open Server Manager and expand the Network Policy and Access Services console under Roles to view the Routing and Remote Access console.

4. Click the **RRAS** node to select it. Click **More Actions** and then click **Configure and Enable Routing and Remote Access** to start the Routing and Remote Access Server Setup Wizard.

5. Click **Next** in the first RRAS Wizard dialog box.

6. Click **Custom configuration** and then click **Next**.

7. In the Custom Configuration dialog box, click **NAT** and **LAN routing**, and then click **Next**. If a message appears regarding a default connection request policy, click **OK**.

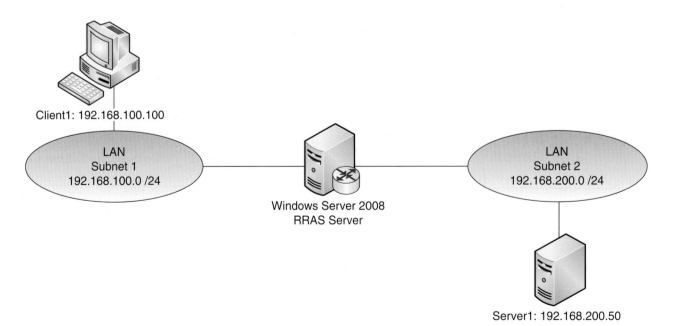

Figure 9-1 Routing two subnets

8. Click **Finish** to close the wizard. In the message window, click **Start service** to start the RRAS service.

9. Close the Server Manager console and open the RRAS console from Administrative Tools.

10. In the RRAS console, verify that the console icon includes a green arrow and is expanded to reveal a number of sections, as shown in Figure 9-2.

11. Open a command prompt and enter the following command to set up MSN-SRV-0XX for routing:

```
netsh routing ip nat add interface "internet" full
netsh routing ip nat add interface "bentech.local" private
```

The netsh routing ip nat command was necessary so that the Internet facing network adapter would route traffic out to the Internet. Normally, two connected subnets do not require additional configuration once RRAS is installed.

12. Log onto MSN-SC-0XX and enter the following command to set MSN-SC-0XX to use MSN-SRV-0XX as a default gateway:

```
netsh int ipv4 set address name = "bentech.net" static
192.168.100.20 255.255.255.0 192.168.100.10
```

13. Ping **192.168.100.10**. This should return a successful response.

14. Ping the IP address of the external network adapter on MSN-SRV-0XX. This should return a successful response and verify that RRAS is routing traffic without needing to configure any routes.

15. Ping an external Internet IP address provided by your instructor.

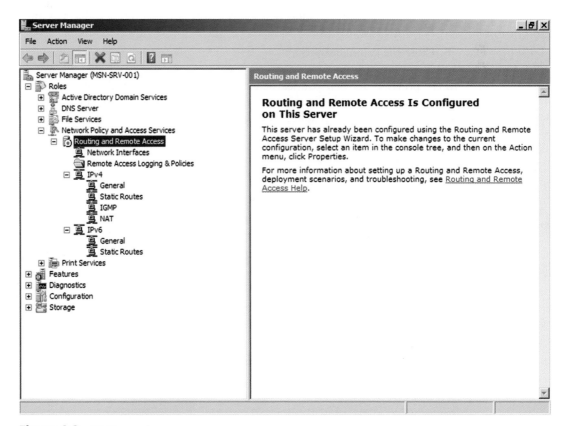

Figure 9-2   RRAS console

16. Log onto MSN-SRV-1XX. At the command prompt, enter the following command:

start /w servermanagercmd.exe –install NPAS-RRAS-Services

17. Type **logoff** at the command prompt and then press **Enter** to log out of MSN-SC-0XX.

Working with Routing Tables

To process traffic, a router uses routing tables to determine where to send traffic. **Routing tables** are composed of routes. The operating system creates the routes based on the interfaces configured in the server. Routes direct data traffic to its destination based on the information it contains. Routing tables can be managed in the RRAS console or from the command line using the route command. As administrator, you can create, change, or delete routes as necessary.

In the RRAS console, the routing table is displayed, as shown in Figure 9-3.

Activity 9-3: Viewing the Routing Table in RRAS

Time Required: 5 minutes.

Objective: View the routing table in RRAS.

Description: Routing tables are the simplest way for you to determine the routes stored in a routing table. In this activity, you view the routing table on MSN-SRV-0XX using the graphical user interface (GUI) and the command line.

1. On MSN-SRV-0XX, open the Routing and Remote Access console from Administrative Tools.

2. In the RRAS console, expand **MSN-SRV-0xx** and **IPv4**. Click **IPv4** to select it.

3. Click **Static Routes**, click **Action** on the menu bar, and then click **Show IP Routing Table**.

4. According to the dialog box that opens, what is the gateway used by default on MSN-SRV-0XX?

_____

5. Open a command prompt, type **route print**, and then press **Enter**. A table is displayed similar to the one in Figure 9-4.

6. Close the command prompt.

In the previous activity, you learned the route print command. Route is the second option for managing routing tables in the command line. Windows Server 2008 and RRAS use the route command to view and manage routing tables. The syntax for the route command is shown in Figure 9-5.

Route uses four commands to perform its duties. Those commands, including descriptions and examples, are included in Table 9-1.

You can display the routing table shown in Figure 9-4 by entering the following command:

```
route print
```

MSN-SRV-001 - IP Routing Table						
Destination	Network mask	Gateway	Interface	Metric	Protocol	
0.0.0.0	0.0.0.0	172.18.255.254	internet	10	Network management	
127.0.0.0	255.0.0.0	127.0.0.1	Loopback	51	Local	
127.0.0.1	255.255.255.255	127.0.0.1	Loopback	306	Local	
172.18.0.0	255.255.0.0	0.0.0.0	internet	266	Network management	
172.18.0.65	255.255.255.255	0.0.0.0	internet	266	Network management	
172.18.255.255	255.255.255.255	0.0.0.0	internet	266	Network management	
192.168.100.0	255.255.255.0	0.0.0.0	bentech.local	266	Network management	
192.168.100.10	255.255.255.255	0.0.0.0	bentech.local	266	Network management	
192.168.100.255	255.255.255.255	0.0.0.0	bentech.local	266	Network management	
224.0.0.0	240.0.0.0	0.0.0.0	bentech.local	266	Network management	
255.255.255.255	255.255.255.255	0.0.0.0	bentech.local	266	Network management	

Figure 9-3   Example of a routing table in the RRAS console

```
[□.] Administrator: Command Prompt                                         _□×
C:\Users\Administrator>route print
===========================================================================
Interface List
 10 ...00 0c 29 31 42 9d ...... Intel(R) PRO/1000 MT Network Connection
  1 ...........................  Software Loopback Interface 1
 11 ...00 00 00 00 00 00 00 e0  isatap.{7AA35AF1-02E6-48F8-889A-71B495025374}
===========================================================================

IPv4 Route Table
===========================================================================
Active Routes:
Network Destination        Netmask          Gateway      Interface  Metric
         10.1.1.0    255.255.255.0         On-link      10.1.1.1    266
         10.1.1.1  255.255.255.255         On-link      10.1.1.1    266
       10.1.1.255  255.255.255.255         On-link      10.1.1.1    266
        127.0.0.0        255.0.0.0         On-link     127.0.0.1    306
        127.0.0.1  255.255.255.255         On-link     127.0.0.1    306
  127.255.255.255  255.255.255.255         On-link     127.0.0.1    306
        224.0.0.0        240.0.0.0         On-link     127.0.0.1    306
        224.0.0.0        240.0.0.0         On-link      10.1.1.1    266
  255.255.255.255  255.255.255.255         On-link     127.0.0.1    306
  255.255.255.255  255.255.255.255         On-link      10.1.1.1    266
===========================================================================
Persistent Routes:
  None

IPv6 Route Table
===========================================================================
Active Routes:
 If Metric Network Destination      Gateway
  1    306 ::1/128                  On-link
 10    266 fe80::/64                On-link
 10    266 fe80::9401:f88e:9f97:2041/128
                                    On-link
  1    306 ff00::/8                 On-link
 10    266 ff00::/8                 On-link
===========================================================================
Persistent Routes:
  None

C:\Users\Administrator>
```

Figure 9-4 Displaying a routing table using the route print command

Both of the preceding routing tables provide similar information. The routing table displays the following columns with information used to determine how packets are routed:

- *Network Destination*—This column displays the destination network address that will be used by the routing table entry. These entries are compared to the packet's destination, and the IP address that most specifically describes the destination is used.

```
[□.] Administrator: Command Prompt                                         _□

C:\Users\Administrator.MSN-SRV-001>route /?

Manipulates network routing tables.

ROUTE [-f] [-p] [-4|-6] command [destination]
              [MASK netmask] [gateway] [METRIC metric]  [IF interface]

  -f            Clears the routing tables of all gateway entries.  If this is
                used in conjunction with one of the commands, the tables are
                cleared prior to running the command.

  -p            When used with the ADD command, makes a route persistent across
                boots of the system. By default, routes are not preserved
                when the system is restarted. Ignored for all other commands,
                which always affect the appropriate persistent routes. This
                option is not supported in Windows 95.

  -4            Force using IPv4.

  -6            Force using IPv6.

  command       One of these:
                  PRINT     Prints   a route
                  ADD       Adds     a route
                  DELETE    Deletes  a route
                  CHANGE    Modifies an existing route
  destination   Specifies the host.
  MASK          Specifies that the next parameter is the 'netmask' value.
  netmask       Specifies a subnet mask value for this route entry.
                If not specified, it defaults to 255.255.255.255.
  gateway       Specifies gateway.
  interface     the interface number for the specified route.
  METRIC        specifies the metric, ie. cost for the destination.
```

Figure 9-5 Syntax for the route command

Table 9-1   Route command options

Command	Description	Example
Print	Prints the current routing table.	Route print
Add	Adds a route to a routing table for a RRAS server. -p can be used with the command to add a persistent route so that it will be available after a reboot.	Route -p add 192.168.200.0 mask 255.255.255.0 192.168.200.1
Change	Modifies an existing route in a routing table.	Route change 192.168.200.0 mask 255.255.255.0 192.168.200.254
Delete	Deletes an existing route from a routing table.	Route delete 192.168.200.0

- *Netmask*—This column displays the subnet mask of the destination network. The router uses this value to determine the routing table entry to apply to a packet. The largest match will be applied when there are multiple matches.
- *Gateway*—This column displays the address of the gateway computer.
- *Interface*—This column displays the IP address of the local network interface that will be used to forward a packet using a specific route.
- *Metric*—This column displays the metric, or cost, of using a specific route. In determining routes to use, a router will take routes with lower metrics before higher metrics when there are matching destination entries.
- *Protocol* (GUI only)—This column displays the protocol the router will use.

For example, suppose a router receives two packets bound for destination IP addresses 192.168.100.10 and 192.168.100.20. On a router with a single route entry with a destination of 192.168.100.0 and a subnet mask of 255.255.255.0, both packets match the route entry for 192.168.100.0 and will be sent to the same interface. If you add a route entry with a destination of 192.168.100.10 with a netmask of 255.255.255.255, this will match the first packet of 192.168.100.10 and route it to the interface specified. The reason for this is that the entry for 192.168.100.10 is the most specific in terms of directing the traffic, and it is a direct match to the packets' destination. The second packet will be routed using the first entry as it is the most specific destination on the routing table.

Another twist to this example would be if another entry was added for 192.168.100.0, but a different gateway was specified. How would the router determine which rule to follow? That is where the metric for each route comes into play. The route with the lower metric will be used first.

Configuring Routes

Routers use dynamic routing protocols and preconfigured static routes to deliver packets using the best route possible between two subnets. Static routes are used on simple network implementations where manually configuring a route is not an administrative burden. Static routing is limited for the following reasons:

- It requires manual creation and management.
- It should not be used on networks with more than 10 subnets.
- All affected routers require reconfiguration if the network changes.

Activity 9-4: Creating a Static Route

Time Required: 15 minutes.

Objective: Create a static route from the command line.

Description: You need to create a static route on MSN-SRV-0XX. The static route will map 4.2.2.1 through the gateway 192.168.100.10. In this activity, you will create a static route using the route command.

1. On MSN-SRV-1XX, open a command prompt, type **ping 4.2.2.1 -t**, and then press **Enter**. Verify that you receive a continuous successful reply.

2. Type **ping 4.2.2.1 –t > ping.txt** and then press **Enter**. This will send the results of the ping command to a text file for future review.

3. Leave the command prompt open and switch to MSN-SRV-0XX.

4. Open a command prompt, type **route add 4.2.2.1 mask 255.255.255.255 192.168.100.10**, and then press **Enter**.

5. Switch back to MSN-SRV-1XX. In the open command prompt, press **Ctrl+C** to break the continuous reply of the ping command.

6. Type **ping.txt** and then press **Enter**. This will open the results of the ping command in Notepad. Review the Notepad file and verify that there is a brief stoppage of pings, as shown in Figure 9-6. This is due to the temporary dropping of packets while the router on MSN-SRV-0XX calculates the new routing table route and how to forward the packets of data.

7. Close Notepad and close the command prompt.

8. Log off MSN-SRV-1XX and then switch back to MSN-SRV-0XX.

9. Open a command prompt, type **route print**, and then press **Enter** to verify the route for **4.2.2.1** is listed.

As networks grow in size, it becomes more difficult to manually configure routes. This is when dynamic routing protocols can be helpful. Unlike static routes, **dynamic protocols** route traffic based on information they discover about remote networks from other routers. In Windows Server 2008, you can configure the **Routing Information Protocol version 2 (RIPv2)**. RIPv2 uses partner routers, or RIP neighbors, in determining the dynamic routes it can use for forwarding packets of data. As routes are added to RIP-enabled routers, neighbors will share the information about remote networks.

In addition to RIPv2, RRAS supports following routing protocols:

- *DHCP Relay Agent*—As discussed in Chapter 4, a **DHCP relay agent** forwards DHCPDiscover messages for subnets that do not have a DHCP server and that are not connected to a router that supports passing DHCP broadcast messages.

- *IGMP router and proxy*—The **IGMP router and proxy** component of RRAS provides support for multicast network traffic by routing multicast traffic to networks that host these services.

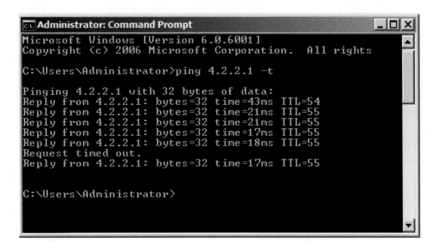

Figure 9-6 Displaying stoppage of ping responses

Configuring a DHCP Relay Agent

Most networks you work on probably have modern network routers. Most of these support the passing of DHCP broadcast messages between subnets without a DHCP server to subnets that contain a DHCP server. These routers are known as RFC 1542–compliant routers. In situations where you do not have a RFC 1542-compliant router, you can create a DHCP relay agent using RRAS. A DHCP relay agent manages the communication between a network's DHCP server and clients on subnets without a DHCP server.

With RRAS, network adapters are added and configured to listen for DHCP broadcast messages. When a broadcast message is received, the communication will be forwarded to the DHCP server on the network.

Activity 9-5: Configuring MSN-SRV-0XX as a DHCP Relay Agent

Time Required: 15 minutes.

Objective: Install a DHCP relay agent.

Description: As plans for your new test subnet continue, you learn you need to be able to support DHCP on the new subnet. You decide that installing a DHCP relay agent using RRAS will be a good solution. In this activity, you will install the DHCP relay agent protocol and configure it.

1. On MSN-SRV-0XX, open the command prompt and enter the following commands to add a default gateway to a scope:

   ```
   Servermanagercmd.exe -install DHCP
   sc config dhcpserver start= auto
   net start dhcpserver
   netsh dhcp server 192.168.100.10 scope 192.168.100.0
   netsh dhcp add iprange 192.168.100.201 192.168.100.250 set
   optionvalue
   003 IPADDRESS "192.168.100.10"
   ```

2. Open the DHCP console, expand the IPv4 scopes, and verify that a scope exists for 192.168.100.0.

3. Open the RRAS console, expand **IPv4**, and then click **General**.

4. In the Actions pane, click **More Actions** under General and then click **New Routing Protocol**. Select **DHCP Relay Agent** and then click **OK**.

5. Click **DHCP Relay Agent** to select it.

6. In the Actions pane, click **More Actions** under DHCP Relay Agent and then click **New Interface**. Select **bentech.local** and then click **OK**.

7. On the DHCP Relay Properties - bentech.net page, click **OK**.

8. With DHCP Relay Agent selected, click **More Actions** and then click **Properties**.

9. On the DHCP Relay Agent Properties page, type **192.168.100.10**, click **Add**, and then click **OK** to add MSN-SRV-0XX as the DHCP server used by the DHCP relay agent, as shown in Figure 9-7. This is also known as the DHCP helper address.

10. Switch to MSN-SRV-1XX, open a command prompt and then enter the following command to set the bentech.local network adapter to use DHCP:

    ```
    netsh int ip set addr "bentech.local" dhcp
    ```

11. Enter the following command to display the configurations of the installed network adapters, as shown in Figure 9-8:

    ```
    netsh int ip show config
    ```

12. Verify that bentech.local is using an IP address of 192.168.100.211. If you do not see the change, you may have to issue **ipconfig /release** followed by **ipconfig/renew** or reboot the server. If you required a server reboot, you will need to logon to **MSN-SRV-1xx** to complete the next step.

13. Ping **4.2.2.1**. You will receive a positive response, which verifies that you have Internet access with your DHCP-addressed computer.

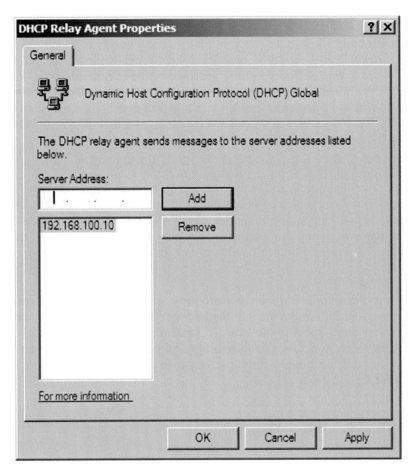

Figure 9-7   Adding a DHCP helper address

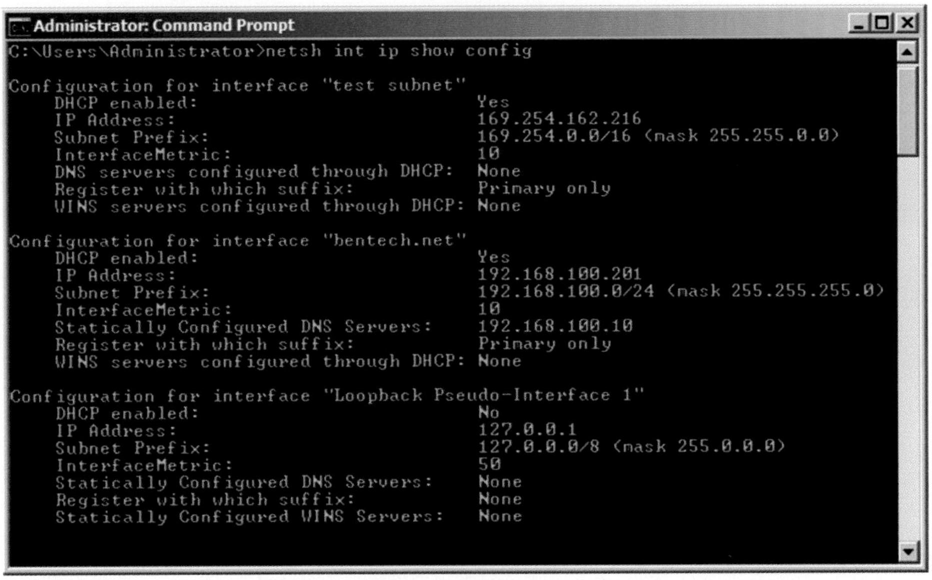

Figure 9-8   Viewing network configurations using netsh

9

Configuring Dial-on-Demand Routing

Demand-dial routing allows a server to initiate a connection only when it receives data traffic bound for a remote network. The connection is kept active while traffic is flowing. When traffic stops, the connection is dropped after a specified period of time. Demand-dial routing can use dial-up networks instead of more expensive leased lines, such as digital subscriber line (DSL), cable, or T1. This can offer a significant cost savings in situations where network traffic is low. Using RRAS, Windows Server 2008 can be configured as a dial-on-demand connector.

Configuring Remote Access Services in Windows Server 2008

With a server running routing and remote access role service, Windows Server 2008 can provide different options for connecting a remote client's networks to your network. This includes traditional dial-up networking and virtual private network access. Remote Access Services (RAS) is not just for connecting users and clients to your network. RAS can be used to securely connect remote networks, such as a branch office network, to its central corporate network.

Dial-Up Networking

Prior to the proliferation of broadband Internet connections, **dial-up networking (DUN)** was common for connecting remote users to their networks using a standard phone line. For administrators, this required banks of modems, or modem pools, and dedicated phone lines to be in place. For companies that have this technology and need to use dial-up connections, Windows Server 2008 has this functionality built in. As shown in Figure 9-9, a number of settings can be configured for dial-up access.

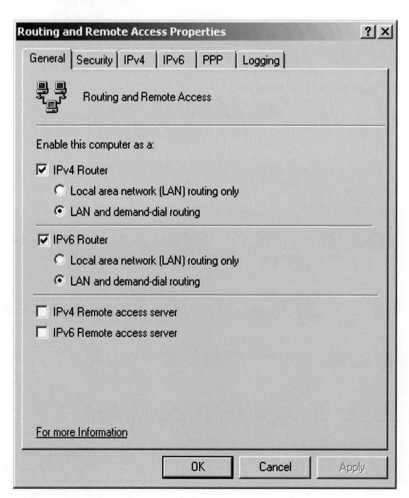

Figure 9-9 Property settings for dial-up network connections

Using Virtual Private Networks

Like dial-up connections, **virtual private networks** (VPNs) allow client connections to your network from remote locations. A VPN provides secure network access for remote clients over the Internet through the use of tunneling protocols. This means that your clients can securely access your network resources as if they were on the network from any Internet-connected location, such as a user's home, a coffee shop with wireless services, or another company's network. The only caveat for VPN connections is that both ends of the connection must be connected to the Internet and be properly configured to communicate with one another.

A VPN works by creating a secure tunnel for transmitting data packets between two points. The intent is that the client's network connection behaves as if it is directly connected to your private network. This is accomplished through the use of tunneling protocols. Tunneling protocols encapsulate data packets inside a new packet header. This header allows the packet to traverse public networks to its destination while keeping its contents, or payload, safe through the use of packet encryption technology. Windows Server 2008 supports three type of VPN tunneling protocols:

- *Point-to-Point Tunneling Protocol*—Based on the Point-to-Point Protocol (PPP), the Point-to-Point Tunneling Protocol (PPTP) is widely used for remote access and site-to-site VPN connections. The protocol was developed by a group of vendors including Microsoft, Lucent, 3COM, and others. PPTP supports securing VPNs using 128-bit RC4 encryption. Despite its popularity, best security practices currently recommend that this type of connection is used only for temporary or occasional connections because of potential security weaknesses in the RC4 algorithm. It should not be used for long-term VPN connections between branch offices, for example.

- *Layer 2 Tunneling Protocol*—The **Layer 2 Tunneling Protocol** (L2TP) is an industry-standard, recommended protocol for securing VPN connections. L2TP works by encapsulating PPP frames before they are transmitted across a network. It is a combination of PPTP, developed by Microsoft, and Layer 2 Forwarding, developed by Cisco Systems. L2TP is most often implementing Internet Protocol Security (IPSec) to provide a secure, encrypted VPN solution. Unlike PPTP, L2TP supports a number of encryption methods including Advanced Encryption Standard in 256-bit, 192-bit, and 128-bit flavors, along with Triple Data Encryption Standard.

- *Secure Socket Tunneling Protocol*—The **Secure Socket Tunneling Protocol** (SSTP) is a new tunneling protocol in Windows Server 2008. SSTP uses PPP to encapsulate traffic for transmission across network using a secure socket layer (SSL) connection. SSL, which is HTTP with SSL, or HTTPS, provides authentication and encryption of its traffic across public and private networks. An advantage of SSTP is that SSL uses TCP port 443, a commonly allowed traffic port on most firewalls and proxy servers.

Activity 9-6: Installing Remote Access Support for VPNs in RRAS

Time Required: 15 minutes.

Objective: Install Remote Access Support with VPN in RRAS.

Description: Your boss has asked you to prepare the network for the addition of VPN connectivity for remote clients. In this activity, you reconfigure the RRAS service with remote access for VPN clients.

Logon to MSN-SRV-0XX for this activity.

1. In the Routing and Remote Access console, click **More Actions** and then click **Configure and Enable Routing and Remote Access**.

2. In the RRAS Setup Wizard dialog box, click **Next**.

3. In the Configuration dialog box, click **Next** to choose the default of Remote access (dial-up or VPN).

4. In the Remote Access dialog box, click the **VPN** check box to select it and then click **Next**.

5. In the VPN Connection dialog box, click **bentech.local** and then click **Next**.

6. In the IP Address Assignment dialog box, click the **From a specified range of addresses** option button and then click **Next**.

In steps 6 and 7, RAS is providing an IP address to the remote client, which will already have an IP address as assigned by its ISP. In addition, it will now have a virtual adapter created with an IP address consistent with the network it's accessing via RAS. An internal DHCP server or the RAS can assign this address from a block of reserved addresses.

7. In the Address Range Assignment dialog box, click **New**, enter the following information, and then click **OK**, as shown in Figure 9-10:

Start IP address: **192.168.100.150**
Number of IP addresses: **2**

8. In the Address Range Assignment dialog box, click **Next**.

9. Click **Next** again and then click **Finish** to close the wizard.

10. Click **OK** to respond to the message about configuring a DHCP relay agent.

11. Expand Routing and Remote Access and verify that Ports and Remote Access Clients (0) appear below it.

When VPN support is installed in RRAS, you will have ports created for use by remote access clients. By default, Windows Server 2008 will install 128 ports for each of the three VPN protocols, including SSTP, PPTP, and L2TP. This can be configured through the Ports Properties dialog box, as shown in Figure 9-11.

VPNs require access to ports through your corporate firewall. This means you should be familiar with the ports necessary to allow traffic for each of the protocols the VPN uses. Table 9-2 lists each protocol and the ports they use.

Activity 9-7: Configuring VPN Ports

Time Required: 15 minutes.

Objective: Configure VPN ports.

Description: You need to configure your newly created VPN so that the number of available ports for PPTP and SSTP connections is limited to five. In addition, you will not be allowing

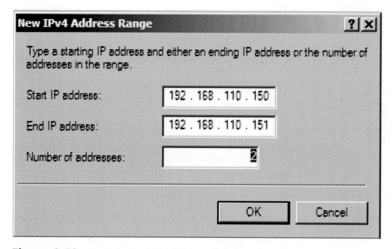

Figure 9-10   New IPv4 Address Range dialog box

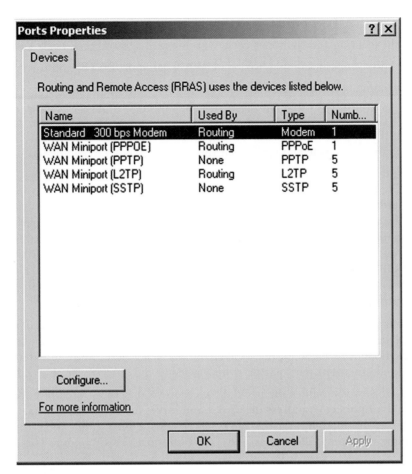

Figure 9-11 Ports Properties dialog box

L2TP connections, so you will set the connection limit to zero. In this activity, you reconfigure the VPN ports on MSN-SRV-0XX.

1. On MSN-SRV-0XX, open the Routing and Remote Access console, click **Ports**, click **Action**, and then click **Properties**.

2. In the Ports Properties dialog box, click **WAN Miniport (PPTP)** and then click **Configure**.

3. In the Configure Device dialog box, enter **5** for the Maximum ports value and then click **OK**.

4. Read the Routing and Remote Access warning message and then click **Yes** to continue.

5. In the Ports Properties dialog box, click **WAN Miniport (L2TP)** and then click **Configure**.

Table 9-2 VPN firewall ports

Protocol	VPN Ports - Outbound	VPN Ports - Inbound
PPTP	TCP 1723 for PPTP traffic	TCP 1723 for PPTP traffic
	IP Type 47 for generic routing encapsulation (GRE) packets	IP Type 47 for generic routing encapsulation (GRE) packets
L2TP	UDP 500 for IKE traffic	UDP 500 for IKE traffic
	UPD 4500 for IPsec NAT-T	UPD 4500 for IPsec NAT-T
	IP Protocol ID of 50 for IPSec ESP traffic	IP Protocol ID of 50 for IPsec ESP traffic
	UDP 1701 for L2TP traffic	UDP 1701 for L2TP traffic
SSTP	Port 443 for SSL traffic	Port 443 for SSL traffic

6. In the Configure Device dialog box, enter **0** for the Maximum ports value and then click **OK**.

7. Read the Routing and Remote Access warning message and then click **Yes** to continue.

8. In the Ports Properties dialog box, click **WAN Miniport (SSTP)** and then click **Configure**.

9. In the Configure Device dialog box, enter **5** for the Maximum ports value and then click **OK**.

10. Read the Routing and Remote Access warning message and then click **Yes** to continue.

11. In the Ports Properties dialog box, click **OK**.

12. Refresh the Ports pane and verify that the number of ports available has been reduced.

Network Address Translation

Network address translation (NAT) allows you to shield internal IP address ranges from public networks by allowing internal clients to access the Internet through a shared IP address. This allows organizations to minimize the number of public IP addresses required for their network, thus reducing networking costs. NAT performs this function by keeping a table listing the source computer's IP address and TCP/UDP port, and the NAT router's IP address. Figure 9-12 depicts how NAT works when an internal client requests information from *www.microsoft.com*.

NAT performs the following tasks, as shown in Figure 9-12:

1. The internal client makes a request for information at *www.microsoft.com* in the form of a TCP/IP data packet. The packet sent by the client contains header information including the client's IP address (source), the TCP/UDP port being used, and the external Web site's IP address (destination). This packet is forwarded to the NAT server at 192.168.100.1.

2. The NAT server modifies the packet it receives so that the source IP address becomes the external, or public, IP address of 1.2.3.4 and leaves the destination the same. The packet is sent to its destination, and the NAT server adds a NAT table entry for the transaction including the source IP address and TCP/UDP port. This mapping is stored in the NAT table.

3. The Web server receives the packet and sends a response back to the NAT server.

4. The NAT server receives the packet. On receipt, it checks the packet information against its NAT table to determine the destination client on the private network. The NAT server changes the packet header so the destination matches the client IP of 192.168.100.100.

NOTE   You may hear network administrators refer to Port Address Translation, or PAT. PAT involves address translation which includes port information as well as IP. Windows Server 2008's implementation of NAT utilizes port translation by default.

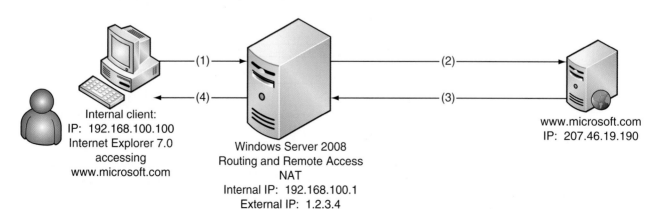

Figure 9-12   Diagram of how NAT works

Introduction to Network Policy Server

The **Network Policy Server (NPS)** is a role service that provides you with a framework for creating and enforcing network access policies for client health, along with policies for authentication and authorization of connection requests. It is the replacement for Internet Authentication Services (IAS) in Windows Server 2003. On Windows Server 2008, you can perform the following using NPS:

- Configure a RADIUS server
- Configure a RADIUS proxy
- Configure and implement Network Access Protection (NAP)

In this section, you will learn about using NPS to manage authorization and authentication. In Chapter 10, you will cover NAP and client health in more depth as you learn about Windows Server 2008 security.

Windows Server 2008 Editions and the NPS Console

NPS can be installed on all three general editions of Windows Server 2008. However, each edition has different levels of supported functionality. Enterprise and Datacenter editions support the configuration of an unlimited number of Remote Authentication Dial-In User Service (RADIUS) clients and RADIUS server groups. (RADIUS is covered in depth in the following section.) Standard edition supports 50 RADIUS clients and two remote RADIUS server groups. NPS is not supported on Windows Server 2008, Web edition, and is not supported on Windows Server 2008 running Server Core.

NPS Console The NPS console is the central utility for managing RADIUS clients and remote RADIUS servers, network health and access policies, NAP settings for NAP scenarios, and logging settings. The console is divided into four nodes, as shown in Figure 9-13:

- *RADIUS Clients and Servers*—This section allows you to configure RADIUS clients and RADIUS servers on your network.

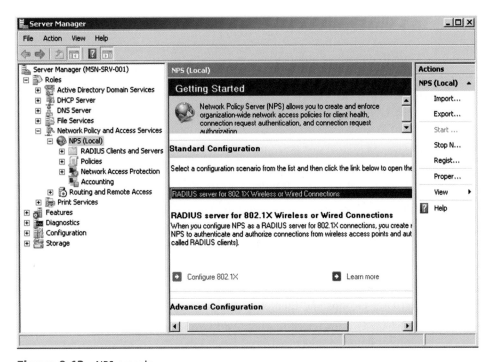

Figure 9-13 NPS console

- *Policies*—This section allows you to manage and configure policies based on health, network, and access requests.
- *Network Access Protection*—NAP provides a framework for protecting your networks, both public and private, from malware such as viruses and spyware.
- *Accounting*—This section allows you to manage how data is collected and logged for remote access connection.

Activity 9-8: Installing NPS

Time Required: 15 minutes

Objective: Install the NPS role service.

Description: Your company is considering whether to use NPS to manage access and client health on your network. In this activity, you will install NPS.

1. On MSN-SRV-0XX, open Server Manager, expand **Roles**, and then click **Network Policy and Access Services**.

2. Under Role Services, click the **Add Role Services** link. This starts the Add Role Services Wizard.

3. In the Select Role Services dialog box, click the **Network Policy Server** check box to select it and click **Next**.

4. In the next dialog box, click **Install** to begin installing the role service.

5. On the Installation Results page, click **Close**.

6. In Server Manager, expand Network Policy and Access Services and then verify that the NPS console is available. (You might need to close and then reopen Server Manager.)

7. Leave Server Manager open for the next activity.

After installing NPS, you can configure it to manage your remote access and other policies. As stated previously, you configure RADIUS, policies, and NAP settings through the NPS console. From here, you can create user, group, or computer-specific policies for allowing or denying remote access using VPN.

Activity 9-9: Creating a Network Access Policy for VPN Connections

Time Required: 15 minutes.

Objective: Create a network access policy.

Description: Now that NPS is installed, you need to configure a network policy that allows members of the Domain Admins group to use your company's VPN. You need to configure the idle time-out so that sessions do not remain open longer than 30 minutes when idle.

1. In Server Manager on MSN-SRV-0XX, expand **NPS (Local)**, expand Policies, and then click **Network Policies**.

2. Click **New** under Network Policies to open the New Network Policy window.

3. In the New Network Policy window, enter **Allow VPN access - Server Operators** in the Policy name text box.

4. Select **Remote Access Server (VPN-Dial up)** from the Type of network access server list box and then click **Next** to continue.

5. In the Specify Conditions dialog box, click **Add** to open the Select Condition window.

6. Select **User Groups** and then click **Add**.

7. In the User Groups window, click **Add Groups** and then type **Domain Admins** in the Enter the object name to select text box. Click **OK**.

8. Click **OK** to close the User Groups window.

9. Click **Next** in the Specify Conditions dialog box.

10. Accept the default of Access granted in the Specify Access Permission dialog box by clicking **Next**.

11. Click **Next** to accept the default authentication methods of MS-CHAP-v2 and MS-CHAP.

12. In the Configure Constraints window, click **Idle Timeout**, click the **Disconnect after the maximum idle time** check box, and then enter **30** minutes in the number box.

13. Click **Next** to access the Configure Settings window, and then click **Next**.

14. Click **Finish** in the Completing New Network Policy window.

Introduction to RADIUS

RADIUS is an industry-standard protocol that provides centralized authentication, authorization, and accounting for network access devices such as wireless access points and remote access servers. RADIUS has been in use for many years, in particular by Internet service providers. Microsoft introduced a RADIUS server in Windows 2000 Server and later renamed it IAS. Recall that NPS is the Windows Server 2008 implementation of RADIUS.

While the term "RADIUS" is often used to represent the server hosting it, RADIUS is a framework made up of a number of components, each with a specific purpose within the RADIUS process. The following are the components of RADIUS:

- *RADIUS clients*—A **RADIUS client** is any device such as a remote access server, wireless access point, or VPN concentrator, that accepts remote connections from remote access clients. Note that a RADIUS client (the device that conveys authentication requests to a RADIUS server) is not a remote access client (a computer or other device attempting to authenticate to the network via the RADIUS client).

- *Network access servers*—A **network access server** is responsible for providing network access to remote access clients such as users needing VPN or dial-in network access. This server can also act as the RADIUS client.

- *RADIUS proxy*—A **RADIUS proxy** is a setting used to route RADIUS messages between the access client and the appropriate RADIUS server.

- *RADIUS server*—**RADIUS servers** are used on networks to perform authentication, authorization, and accounting for RADIUS clients, or convey authentication requests to other centralized authenticating systems (such as Active Directory or Novell eDirectory).

- *User account database*—A **user account database** is the database used by a RADIUS server to authenticate users. This can be either a directory-based database or a local Security Accounts Manager database.

Depending on your network setup, you may implement RADIUS in different ways. Two common implementations of RADIUS include environments with RADIUS proxy servers. These are environments that use a RADIUS proxy server for routing traffic such as the network in Figure 9-14.

The other common type of implementation is an environment without RADIUS proxy servers. This environment does not use or require a RADIUS proxy and traffic is routed directly to the RADIUS servers as shown in Figure 9-15.

RADIUS is in place to allow remote clients, or RADIUS clients, a means to access network resources. The following steps outline the typical end-to-end process used by RADIUS:

1. A remote access client connects to a private network through a RADIUS client.

2. On receiving a client connection, the RADIUS client will request authentication information from the remote access client.

3. When the client information is received, the RADIUS client forwards the information to either a RADIUS proxy for further forwarding or directly to a RADIUS server via an Access-Request message.

4. The RADIUS server first authenticates the user against a user account database, such as Active Directory or the Security Access Manager. This encompasses the authentication portion of RADIUS.

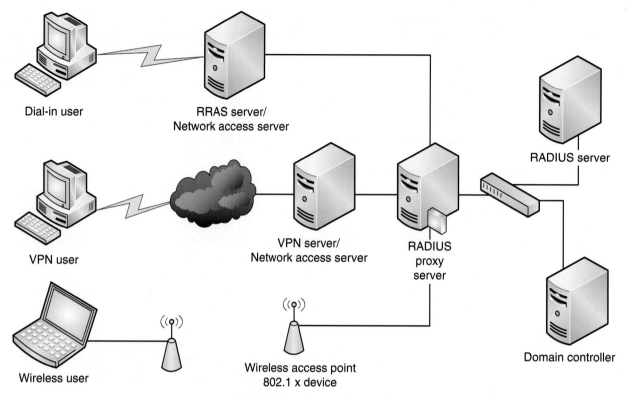

Figure 9-14   Example of RADIUS network with RADIUS proxy server

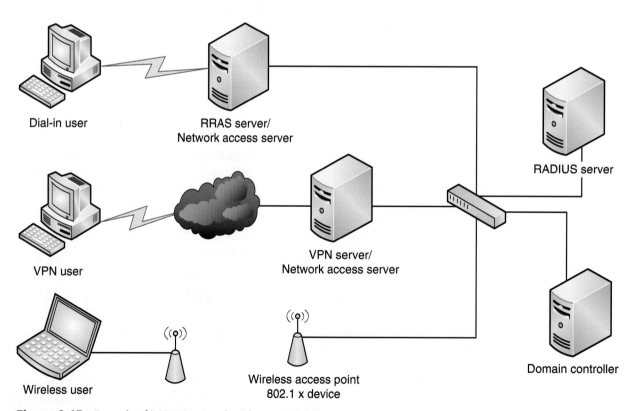

Figure 9-15   Example of RADIUS network without a RADIUS proxy server

5. After authenticating the request, the RADIUS server processes the client request against its defined policies. Based on the policies, an Access-Accept or Access-Reject message is sent to the RADIUS client along with any restrictions that might be defined by the policies. This encompasses the authorization portion of RADIUS.

6. After authentication, the RADIUS server forwards the access information to RADIUS clients who determine what actions to take for the remote access client.

7. If the RADIUS infrastructure is set to use accounting, as most are, the RADIUS client sends an Accounting-Request message to the RADIUS server, including information about the remote access client that will be added to the accounting logs.

8. On receipt of the Accounting-Request message, the RADIUS server logs the information and acknowledges the completion of the accounting process with an Accounting-Response message to the RADIUS client. This encompasses the authorization portion of RADIUS.

Table 9-3 lists the types of messages used by RADIUS for communication.

Each message type contains RADIUS attributes, such as user name, password, types of services requested, and other information used in the RADIUS process. These attributes provide information that RADIUS clients, RADIUS proxies, and RADIUS servers use. For example, the Access-Accept message includes attributes that define the type of connection a client can make, any connection restrictions, and other attributes necessary for managing access to the network. The message flow of a typical RADIUS transaction is displayed in Figure 9-16.

For more information about these attributes, refer to RFC[†] 2865-Remote Authentication Dial-In User Service (RADIUS) and RFC[†] 2548-Microsoft Vendor-Specific RADIUS Attributes at *http://www.ietf.org*.

RADIUS Server

Windows Server 2008 can be used as a RADIUS server. RADIUS servers are used on networks to perform authentication, authorization, and accounting for RADIUS clients. A RADIUS client can be an NPS, which replaces the IAS from previous versions of Windows Server. RADIUS is a standardized network protocol that centralizes the following process for user connections:

- *Authentication*—**Authentication** is the first component of the RADIUS process in which the identity of a user connecting to a resource is verified.

Table 9-3   RADIUS message types

RADIUS Message	Description
Access-Request	Sent by a RADIUS client to request authentication and authorization for a network access connection attempt.
Access-Accept	Sent by a RADIUS server in response to an Access-Request message. This message informs the RADIUS client that the connection attempt is authenticated and authorized.
Access-Reject	Sent by a RADIUS server in response to an Access-Request message. This message informs the RADIUS client that the connection attempt is rejected. A RADIUS server sends this message if either the credentials are not authentic or the connection attempt is not authorized.
Access-Challenge	Sent by a RADIUS server in response to an Access-Request message. This message is a challenge to the RADIUS client that requires a response.
Accounting-Request	Sent by a RADIUS client to specify accounting information for a connection that was accepted.
Accounting-Response	Sent by the RADIUS server in response to the Accounting-Request message. This message acknowledges the successful receipt and processing of the Accounting-Request message.

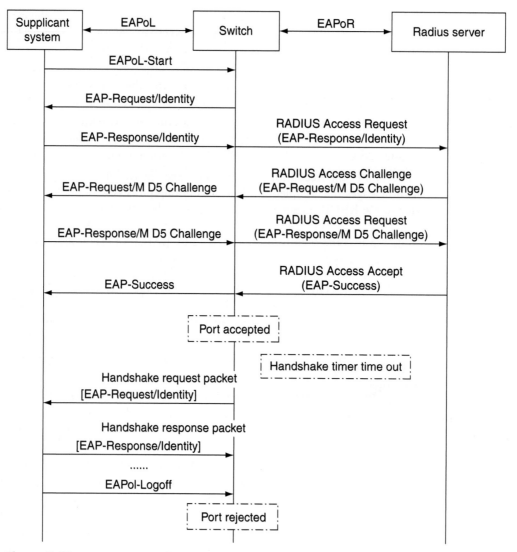

Figure 9-16   RADIUS message flow

- *Authorization*—Completed after authentication, the **authorization** component is used to determine what a user is allowed to do on a network or with resources.

- *Accounting*—Often used along with authorization, the **accounting** component logs the RADIUS processes so that access to resources can be reviewed at a later date.

This sequence of authentication, authorization, and accounting is referred to as the AAA (triple A) process.

In Windows Server 2008, remote access connection properties are defined for users on the Dial-In tab of the user's Properties dialog box.

RADIUS Proxy

NPS can be configured as a RADIUS proxy. RADIUS proxies route RADIUS messages between RADIUS clients and RADIUS servers. When used as a RADIUS proxy, NPS is a central switching or routing point through which RADIUS access and accounting messages flow. As part of the accounting function of RADIUS, NPS records information about forwarded messages in an accounting log for future review.

NAP

For years, viruses and malware have caused havoc with networks. In response, most networks use client and sometimes server-based antivirus or antimalware solutions for protection. Although this is a good short-term solution, a better answer is to allow only clients access to a network that do not allow the threat on the network in the first place.

This is the role of **Network Access Protection (NAP)**. In Windows Server 2008, NAP provides a tool for you to block external and internal network threats. NAP works by measuring network clients against specified health requirements, or policies. If clients do not meet the network health standards, such as out-of-date antivirus or missing security updates, the client is prevented from accessing the network. NAP can be broken into three parts:

- *Health policy validation*—This process involves a health examination of clients attempting to access the network. Network policies you create are used for this examination. Common policies include minimum levels of antivirus, OS updates, and more.

- *Health policy compliance*—This process provides mechanisms that allow clients to become "compliant" by updating their antivirus or applying need updates.

- *Limited access*—This process allows administrators to limit or deny clients access to network resources depending on their compliance with defined health policies.

As the majority of NAP's functionality is security related, you will learn more about NAP in Chapter 10.

Authentication Protocol

Remote access connections require authentication of the remote client by the remote server. To perform this, each party (client and server) must negotiate the use of a common authentication protocol. While most protocols offer some level of security, some protocols are better than others. The following are the supported authentication protocols in Windows Server 2008:

- *Extensible Authentication Protocol–Transport Layer Security (EAP-TLS)*—An Internet Engineering Task Force (IETF)-accepted standard, RFC 2716, EAP-TLS was created by Microsoft. It combines EAP, which supports additional authentication methods for PPP, and TLS. TLS provides enhanced security through the use of mutual authentication, or authentication between both parties. In addition, it uses integrity-protected negotiation of cryptographic service providers and a secret key exchange between two systems that use public key cryptography. EAP-TLS is supported only on computers in a Windows Server 2008 domain. EAP-TLS requires a public key infrastructure (PKI) and uses certificates for authentication. Certificates may be stored as certificate files on a computer or on smart cards.

- *Protected Extensible Authentication Protocol–Transport Layer Security PEAP-TLS*—This protocol provides the same protection and functionality as EAP-TLS with the exception of how it is deployed. Unlike EAP-TLS, clients connecting to an authenticating server do not require a certificate; they require only user credentials that allow them access. These credentials are passed via TLS. In the case of PEAP-TLS, you are relying on the strength of the NPS's certificate.

- *Protected PEAP–Microsoft Challenge Handshake Authentication Protocol version 2 (PEAP-MSCHAPv2)*—Unlike the previous protocols, PEAP-MSCHAPv2 does not require a PKI for authentication on wired or wireless networks. It uses PEAP to create an encrypted communication session, using TLS, prior to initiating password-based authentication. This helps protect authentication communication from outside sources. Although not as secure because of the use of passwords, it is a good solution for small organizations that cannot implement a PKI infrastructure.

EAP-TLS and PEAP-TLS require the implementation of a PKI. For more information on PKI, search for PKI at *http://technet.microsoft.com*.

Wireless Access Configuration in Windows Server 2008

With the proliferation of wireless networks, you need to secure network access for wireless and wired network connections, or **network access control**. To meet this need, the **802.1x standard** was developed by the Institute of Electrical and Electronics Engineers (IEEE). On 802.1x networks, network access control provides an authentication mechanism to allow or deny network access based on port connection. It is used for most wireless 802.11 access points and is based on the Extensible Authentication Protocol (EAP), an industry-standard protocol for authentication. EAP implementations fall into two categories:

- *EAP over local area network (LAN)*—Known by the acronym EAPOL, **EAP over LAN** refers to 802.1x implementations in which clients make physical Ethernet connections over Ethernet cable.

- *EAP over wireless*—Known by the acronym EAPOW, **EAP over wireless** refers to 802.1x implementations in which clients make wireless Ethernet connections.

For more information on the IEEE and the 802.1x protocol, visit *http://www.ieee.org*.

802.1x uses a three-component model for authenticating access to networks. The three components include the following:

- *Supplicant*—A **supplicant** is the client or device attempting to gain access to an 802.1x network.

- *Authenticator*—An **authenticator** is a device, such as a wireless access point or a network switch, that receives a supplicant's initial connection and requests authentication information from them. On receiving authentication information, the authenticator forwards the information to an authentication server; it does not process authentications itself. Per RFC 2865, the authenticator in 802.1x acts as the network access server.

- *Authentication server*—An **authentication server (AS)** is the server responsible for authenticating a supplicant's request for network access. It will inform the authenticator whether to allow or disallow the supplicant access to the 802.1x network. In Windows Server 2008, the AS function can be performed by a server running the Network Policy Server role. This replaces the Internet Authentication Service from previous versions of Windows Server. In addition to a Windows-based AS, a third-party RADIUS server can serve this function.

The 802.1x authentication process is described in the following section and depicted in Figure 9-17.

1. A supplicant tries to connect to an authenticator on an 802.1x network.

2. The authenticator detects the client and enables the client's port but sets the port state to Unauthorized. In this state, all client traffic is blocked except 802.1x messages. The authenticator requests the supplicant's identity information via an EAP-Request packet.

3. The supplicant provides its identity response to the authenticator via an EAP-Response packet.

4. The authenticator forwards the supplicant's EAP responses to the AS.

5. The AS determines whether to accept or deny the EAP response. On accepting the response, the AS informs the authenticator to set the port state to Authorized.

6. The authenticator allows client traffic to pass through to the destination network or resources.

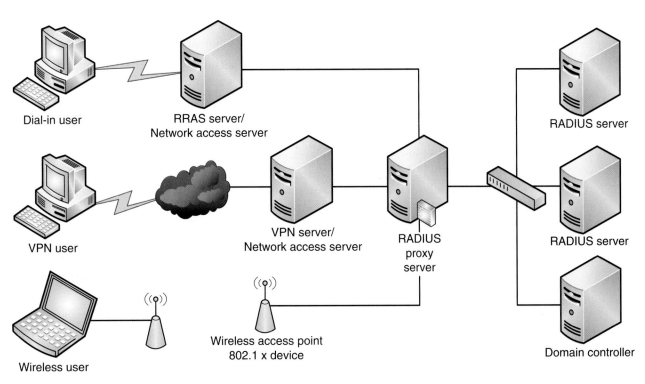

Figure 9-17 802.1x authentication process

Chapter Summary

- RRAS is a role service used to configure and manage network routing in Windows Server 2008. As a software-based router, RRAS is recommended for use in small networks requiring simple routing directions, so it is not recommended for large and complex environments. Along with routing functionality, RRAS provides DHCP Relay Agent functionality for networks.

- Routers are responsible for forwarding packets between subnets, or networks with differing IP addressing schemes. Routers accomplish this task by viewing the header of the data packet and using routing tables for determining the best route for sending packets to their destination. Because of the nature of information packets, this process requires an intelligent networking device, or router, to forward this traffic to its destination.

- To process traffic, a router uses routing tables to determine where to send traffic. Routing tables are based on routes. Routes direct data traffic to its destination based on the information they contain. Routing tables can be managed by the GUI in the RRAS console or from the command line using the route command.

- Routers use dynamic routing protocols and preconfigured static routes to deliver packets using the best route possible between two subnets. Static routes are used on simple network implementations where manually configuring a route is not an administrative burden.

- Most modern networks support the passing of DHCP broadcast messages between subnets without a DHCP server to subnets that contain a DHCP server. These routers are known as RFC-1542–compliant routers. In situations where you do not have an RFC-1542–compliant router, you can create a DHCP-Relay agent using RRAS. A DHCP relay agent manages the communication between clients on subnets without a DHCP server and a network's DHCP server.

- Demand-dial routing allows a server to initiate a connection only when it receives data traffic bound for a remote network. The connection is kept active while traffic is flowing. When traffic stops, the connection is discontinued after a specified period of time. Demand-dial routing can use dial-up networks instead of using leased lines, such as DSL, cable, or

T1, which offers a significant cost savings in situations where network traffic is low. Using RRAS, Windows Server 2008 can be configured as a dial-on-demand connector.

■ VPNs provide secure network access for remote clients over the Internet through the use of tunneling protocols. The only caveat for VPN connections is that both ends of the connection must be connected to the Internet.

■ NAT allows you to shield internal IP address ranges from public networks by allowing internal clients to access the Internet through a shared IP address. This allows organizations to minimize the number of public IP addresses required for their network, thus reducing networking costs.

■ NPS is a role service that provides administrators with a framework for creating and enforcing network access policies for client health along with policies for authentication and authorization of connection requests. It is the replacement for IAS in Windows Server 2003.

■ RADIUS is an industry-standard protocol which provides centralized authentication, authorization, and accounting for network access devices, such as wireless access points and remote access servers.

■ In Windows Server 2008, NAP provides a framework for you to block external and internal network threats. NAP works by measuring network clients against specified health requirements, or policies. If clients do not meet the network health standards, such as out-of-date antivirus or missing security updates, the client is prevented from accessing the network.

■ To provide network access control, the 802.1x standard was developed by the IEEE. On 802.1x networks, it provides an authentication mechanism to allow or deny network access based on port connection. It is used for most wireless 802.11 access points and is based on the EAP, an industry-standard protocol for authentication.

Key Terms

802.1x standard   A standard that provides an authentication mechanism to allow or deny network access based on port connection. It is used for most wireless 802.11 access points and is based on the Extensible Authentication Protocol (EAP), an industry-standard protocol for authentication.

accounting   Often used along with authorization, this component logs the RADIUS processes so that access to resources can be reviewed at a later date.

authentication   The first component of the RADIUS process in which the identity of a user connecting to a resource is verified.

authentication server (AS)   The server responsible for authenticating a supplicant's request for network access.

authenticator   A device, such as a wireless access point or a network switch, that receives a supplicant's initial connection and requests authentication information from them.

authorization   Completed after authentication, this component determines what a user is allowed to do on a network or with resources.

demand-dial routing   A type of routing that allows a server to initiate a connection only when it receives data traffic bound for a remote network.

DHCP relay agent   An agent that forwards DHCPDiscover messages for subnets that do not have a DHCP server and are not connected to a router that supports passing DHCP broadcast messages.

dial-up networking (DUN)   A form of remote access that uses modems for connecting remote clients over telephone networks.

dynamic protocol   A protocol that routes traffic based on information it discovers about remote networks from other routers.

EAP over local area network (LAN)   Known by the acronym EAPOL, this refers to 802.1x implementations in which clients make physical Ethernet connections over Ethernet cable.

EAP over wireless   Known by the acronym EAPOW, this refers to 802.1x implementations in which clients make wireless Ethernet connections.

header   Information appended to the beginning of a packet that specifies information about a packet, including protocol, destination address, and origin address.

IGMP router and proxy   A component of Routing and Remote Access Services (RRAS) that provides support for multicast network traffic by routing multicast traffic to networks that host multicast services.

Layer 2 Tunneling Protocol (L2TP)   An industry-standard and recommended protocol for securing virtual private network (VPN) connections. L2TP works by encapsulating Point-to-Point Protocol (PPP) frames before they are transmitted across a network. It is a combination of Point-to-Point Tunneling Protocol (PPTP), developed by Microsoft, and Layer 2 Forwarding, developed by Cisco Systems.

network access control   A method of securing network access for wireless and wired network connections. Based on the PPP, this protocol is widely used for remote access and site-to-site VPN connections. The protocol was developed by a group of vendors, including Microsoft, Lucent, 3COM, and others. PPTP supports securing VPNs using 128-bit RC4 encryption.

Network Access Protection (NAP)   A framework for administrators to block external and internal network threats. NAP works by measuring network clients against specified health requirement, or policies.

network access server   A server responsible for providing network access to remote access clients such as users needing VPN or dial-in network access.

network address translation (NAT)   A feature of RRAS that allows administrators to shield internal IP address ranges from public networks by allowing internal clients to access the Internet through a shared IP address.

Network Policy Server (NPS)   A role service providing administrators with a framework for creating and enforcing network access policies for client health along with policies for authentication and authorization of connection requests.

RADIUS   An industry-standard protocol that provides centralized authentication, authorization, and accounting for network access devices, such as wireless access points and remote access servers.

RADIUS client   Any device such as a remote access server or VPN concentrator that accepts remote connections from remote access clients.

RADIUS proxy   Part of RADIUS used to route RADIUS messages between the access client and the appropriate RADIUS server.

RADIUS server   A server used on networks to perform authentication, authorization, and accounting for RADIUS clients.

router   A hardware device responsible for forwarding packets between subnets, or networks with differing IP addressing schemes.

Routing and Remote Access Services (RRAS)   A role service used to configure and manage network routing in Windows Server 2008.

Routing Information Protocol version 2 (RIPv2)   A protocol that uses partner routers, or RIP neighbors, in determining the dynamic routes it can use for forwarding packets of data. As additional routes are added to RIP-enabled routers, neighbors will share the information about remote networks.

routing table   A table that contains information used to route traffic to specific networks. Routers direct data traffic to its destination based on the information contained in a routing table.

Secure Socket Tunneling Protocol (SSTP)   A new tunneling protocol in Windows Server 2008. SSTP uses PPP to encapsulate traffic for transmission across network using a secure socket layer, or SSL, connection. SSL, often referred to HTTPS, provides authentication and encryption of its traffic across public and private networks.

supplicant   The client or device attempting to gain access to an 802.1x network.

user account database   The database used by a RADIUS server to authenticate users. This can be either an Active Directory Domain Services database or a local Security Accounts Manager database.

virtual private network (VPN)   A type of network that provides secure network access for remote clients over the Internet through the use of tunneling protocols.

Review Questions

1. _____ is the TCP/IP routing protocol supported on Windows Server 2008 running Routing and Remote Access Services that dynamically determines routes based on information from neighboring routers called _____.

2. What RRAS service is used to hide private IP address networks and provide multiple clients access to the Internet by using a single public IP address?

   a. DHCP Relay Agent

   b. NAC

   c. NAP

   d. NAT

3. _____ is the RRAS service that provides dynamic IP addresses to subnets without a DHCP server.

4. Using RRAS as a production router in large, heavily trafficked networks is a recommended practice from Microsoft. True or False?

5. All Windows Server 2008 networks that use DHCP require a DHCP relay agent to be configured using RRAS. True or False?

6. VPN connections using L2TP are often combined with _____ for a more secure VPN connection.

7. What role does an NPS or RADIUS server perform in 802.1x implementation?

   a. Supplicant

   b. Authenticator

   c. Authentication server

   d. Authorization server

8. When implementing 802.1x on a network, client computers are considered which of the following components?

   a. Node

   b. Authenticator

   c. Supplicant

   d. Receiver

9. Which of the following components of an 802.1x network is responsible for requesting the identity of a client computer?

   a. Authentication server

   b. Authenticator

   c. Authorization server

   d. Supplicant

10. _____ is the process of determining what level of access a user or client has to the network and/or resources.

11. Which of the following commands will display the current routing table on a Windows Server 2008 computer running RRAS?

    a. Show route

    b. Route -p

    c. Route print

    d. Netsh int ip show config

12. Which tunneling protocol is built to run over HTTPS?

    a. SSTP

    b. L2TP/IPSec

    c. PPTP

    d. PPP

13. Which Properties tab is used for managing NAP for VPN users connecting to a domain?

    a. VPN

    b. Remote

    c. Sessions

    d. Dial-in

14. The NPS role service requires a third-party RADIUS server to authenticate Windows XP and Windows Server 2003 clients. True or False?

15. _____ is the process of proving that a user or client is who they claim to be.

16. Routers that do not support this RFC cannot route DHCP broadcast messages between networks.

    a. RFC 2895

    b. RFC 1524

    c. RFC 1542

    d. RFC 2985

17. Which of the following is *not* performed by the NPS?

    a. RADIUS proxy

    b. RADIUS server

    c. RADIUS client

    d. NAP

18. Which of the following is *not* a tunneling protocol that can be used for VPNs deployed with Windows Server 2008?

    a. L2TP

    b. PPTP

    c. IPSec Tunneling Protocol

    d. SSTP

19. You need to add a static route to your RRAS server. All traffic going to the 10.10.10.0 /16 subnet needs to be routed to the gateway of 10.10.255.254. In addition, the route should be available if the RRAS server is rebooted. Which of the following commands will successfully create the route?

    a. Route -p 10.10.10.0 mask 255.255.255.0 10.10.255.254

    b. Route 10.10.10.0 mask 255.255.0.0 10.10.255.254

    c. Netsh rras ipv4 set router 10.10.10.0 255.255.0.0 10.10.255.254

   d. Route -p 10.10.10.0 mask 255.255.0.0 10.10.255.254

   e. Route -p 10.10.10.0 mask 255.255.255.255 10.10.255.254

20. What port does SSTP use?

   a. 3389

   b. 21

   c. 80

   d. 443

Case Projects

CASE PROJECTS

Case Project 9-1: Researching the SSTP

In this chapter, you learned about SSTP and using it as a tunneling protocol for VPNs. Research SSTP, then describe how SSTP works between a VPN client and server. In addition, research and describe the operating systems that support SSTP on the client side.

Case Project 9-2: Creating a VPN Server for Remote Client Access

Your company has just hired a new accounting firm, P.F. Cardinal & Associates. In order to perform its accounting tasks, you need to provide remote access to your network to one of their employees, Cindy Bee. You need to provide a secure method for Cindy to access the network. On CS-SRV-001, create a user account for Cindy in the Badgertech.local domain that has dial-in access and set the server up as a VPN server.

Case Project 9-3: Recommending Remote Access

You have been approached by a small company, Breakaway Brothers Touring Company, a provider of hunting excursions in northern Wisconsin. Their tour guides are equipped with notebook computers for logging tour details and communicating with the home office. Each guide requires a secure method for connecting back to the home office. Guides have mobile broadband Internet cards. However, they are often in areas without access to cellular networks and have access only to telephone lines. Based on their operation, what would you recommend Breakaway Brothers implement to meet the needs of their remote users? Explain your recommendation in detail.

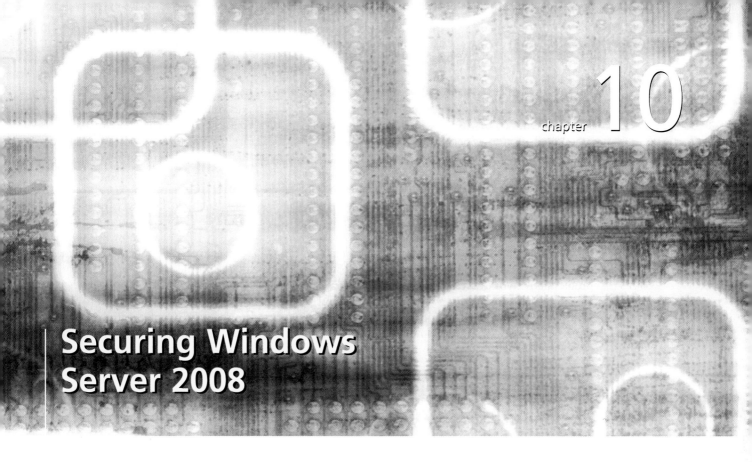

chapter 10

Securing Windows Server 2008

After reading this chapter and completing the exercises, you will be able to:

- Manage security in Windows Server 2008 with various Windows utilities
- Discuss threats to Internet Protocol Security
- Create Internet Protocol Security policies
- Discuss Network Access Protection
- Install Network Access Protection

As an administrator, security is one of your most important concerns. Without good security policies and practices, you put yourself and your company at risk. Threats such as Denial of Service attacks, viruses, and malware can wreak havoc on your network and users' data. Windows Server 2008 is designed to be more secure than any version of Windows Server to date with improvements such as the Windows Firewall. However, you can enhance the security on your servers using additional tools as well.

In this chapter, you will learn how use tools such as the Security Configuration Wizard and Windows Firewall to improve the security of your servers. Tools such as the Encrypting File System and BitLocker will be introduced so that you can use various levels of encryption to protect corporate data. The chapter also surveys Internet Protocol Security (IPSec) and how it is used to secure communications between client machines. Finally, the chapter introduces Network Access Protection (NAP), a new feature of Windows Server 2008, and the tools it provides for protecting network access and client health compliance.

Note that this chapter covers the basics of BitLocker, EFS, IPSec, and NAP as related to the Configuring Microsoft Windows Server 2008 Network Infrastructure Configuration exam (70-642). More substantial resources and details are provided elsewhere, including the Microsoft Web site (*www.microsoft.com*).

Managing Security in Server 2008

To effectively secure networks, you need to have a toolbox to implement security practices and policies. Windows Server 2008 provides a number of new and improved tools for managing your network security, including the following:

- Security Configuration Wizard
- Windows Firewall
- Encrypting File System
- BitLocker
- Microsoft Baseline Security Analyzer

Security Configuration Wizard

First introduced in Windows Server 2003 R2 and Windows Server 2003 Service Pack 2 (SP2), the Security Configuration Wizard (SCW) provides a step-by-step wizard for hardening your network servers. The SCW takes a holistic view of your server. By analyzing the baseline computer, the SCW can determine the roles and features that are installed. These findings are compared to a database of settings to determine what changes can be made to harden the server's security without compromising functionality. With this information, you can choose to create a new security policy, modify an existing policy, or apply an existing policy. You can also revert to a previous version of a policy.

After making this decision, you can choose different analysis paths depending on your selection. If you choose to create a new security policy, for example, the baseline computer will be analyzed. After analysis is complete, you can create policies for the following four areas:

- *Role-based service configuration*—This section allows you to harden services based on the roles and features in the server.
- *Network security*—This section allows you to manage the Windows Firewall with Advanced Security rules.
- *Registry settings*—This section allows you to configure protocols used to communicate with other computers.
- *Audit policy*—This section allows you to configure audit security policies.

Activity 10-1: Creating a Role-Based Security Policy

Time Required: 15 minutes

Objective: Create a security policy using the SCW.

Description: You need to continue your efforts to protect your servers against security threats. You have decided to use the SCW to create a new security policy for MSN-SRV-0XX. In this activity, you create a security policy using the SCW.

1. Log onto MSN-SRV-0XX, if necessary.

2. From the Start menu, open Administrative Tools, and then start the SCW.

3. Click **Next** on the Welcome screen.

4. Click **Next** in the Configuration Action dialog box to accept the default option of **Create a new security policy**.

5. On the Select Server window, click **Next** to accept the default of MSN-SRV-0XX as the base server.

6. Click **View Configuration Database** to open the SCW Viewer and display all the configuration settings of MSN-SRV-0XX.

7. After reviewing the settings, close the SCW Viewer and then click **Next**.

8. Click **Next** in the Role-Based Service Configuration window.

9. In the Select Server Roles window, click **Next** to accept the default selection of installed roles.

10. In the Select Client Features window, click **Next** to accept the default selection of installed features.

11. In the Select Administration and Other Options window, browse and select **Remote Desktop** in the list of options (leaving the other options unchanged), and then click **Next**.

12. In the Select Additional Services window, click **Next**.

13. In the Handling Unspecified Services window, click **Next** to accept the default selection.

14. Review the list of Changed services and then click **Next**.

15. In the Network Security window, click the **Skip this section** check box and then click **Next**.

16. In the Registry Settings window, click the **Skip this section** check box and then click **Next**.

17. In the Audit Policy window, click the **Skip this section** check box and then click **Next**.

18. In the Save Security Policy window, click **Next**.

19. Enter **NewPolicy** in the text box after the default location of C:\Windows\security\msscw\Policies\ and then click **Next**.

20. In the Apply Security Policy window, click **Next** to accept the default of **Apply later**.

21. Click **Finish** to complete the SCW.

Windows Firewall

Windows Firewall has been significantly improved in Windows Server 2008. It provides inbound and outbound traffic enforcement through two consoles: Windows Firewall and Windows Firewall with Advanced Security.

Windows Firewall   Windows Firewall provides a user-friendly interface for managing the firewall policies it provides, as shown in Figure 10-1.

Windows Firewall allows users to turn the firewall off or on. By default, Windows Firewall is turned on and allows exceptions for programs and ports. An **exception** is an instruction to open a port briefly, allow a program or service to pass information, and then close the port. They are exceptions because normally the firewall blocks all unsolicited attempts to send information. When Windows Firewall is turned on, you can also choose to block all incoming connections, as shown in Figure 10-2. Choosing this option means Windows Firewall ignores all defined firewall exceptions.

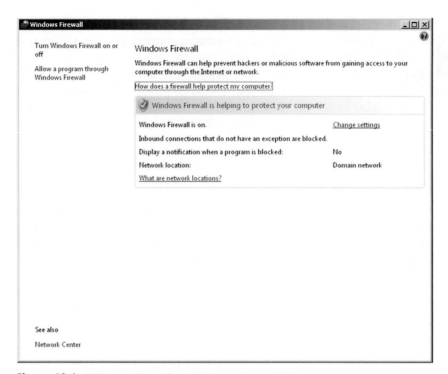

Figure 10-1   Windows Firewall on Windows Server 2008

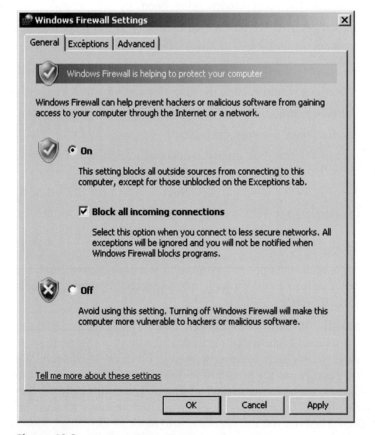

Figure 10-2   Windows Firewall status options

Blocking all incoming exceptions is rarely used on a Windows Server 2008 computer because most people run at least one service that requires an inbound connection. However, you can block all incoming exceptions if you need to quickly harden a Windows Server 2008 computer and prevent all inbound connections. For example, suppose you are running a Web server and determine that it is being attacked by external sources. With the Windows Firewall, you can temporarily block all inbound connections to your server while you work to end the outside attack. This is an aggressive defensive posture and blocks legitimate traffic as well.

You should also avoid turning off Windows Firewall. Doing so leaves your computer accessible to all inbound traffic. Use this option only in testing or troubleshooting exercises. You might also turn off Windows Firewall if your company is using a third-party firewall application; running two firewalls on a single computer is not recommended and should be avoided.

Windows Firewall Exceptions   Windows Firewall allows you to create exceptions for inbound traffic. Exceptions can be a specific program or a specific port that needs to be accessible by inbound traffic. The Exceptions tab lists the current roles, features, and applications, including their exception status, as shown in Figure 10-3.

Activity 10-2: Working with Windows Firewall

Time Required: 10 minutes

Objective: Become familiar with the Windows Firewall interface.

Description: You need to find out more information about the built-in Windows Firewall so that you can create exceptions to the current firewall settings. In this activity, you explore Windows Firewall and create firewall exceptions for specific programs installed on Windows Server 2008.

1. On the MSN-SRV-1XX computer, open the Control Panel and then double-click the **Windows Firewall** icon to open the Windows Firewall window.

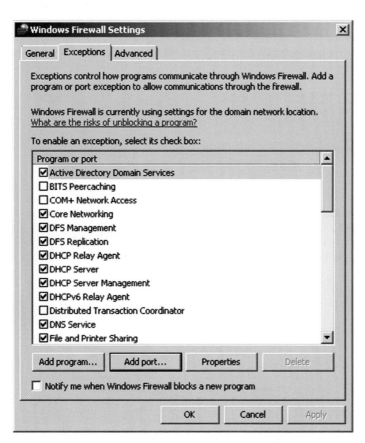

Figure 10-3   Exceptions tab in the Windows Firewall Settings dialog box

2. In the Windows Firewall window, click the **Allow a program through Windows Firewall** link to open the Windows Firewall Settings dialog box to the Exceptions tab.

3. On the Exceptions tab, scroll down the list of programs and ports and select the **Remote Administration** and **Remote Event Log Management** check boxes. Then click **Apply**.

4. Click **Remote Service Management** and then click **Properties**. A message box opens describing the effects of enabling this exception.

5. Read the description and then click **OK**.

6. On the Exceptions tab, click **Add program** to add a program to the list.

7. Click **Browse** and then search for and click **c:\windows\explorer.exe** to add Windows Explorer to the exceptions list.

8. Click **Open** to add Explorer to the list of programs on the Add a Program dialog box. Click **OK**.

9. Click **OK** to close the Windows Firewall Settings dialog box.

10. Close the Windows Firewall window.

Windows Firewall with Advanced Security

Windows Firewall with Advanced Security (WFAS) provides a more robust interface for managing the firewall policies in detail. Use this console to manage Windows Firewall based on port, services, applications, and protocols.

The WFAS console allows you to manage both inbound and outbound firewall policies, or rules. See Figure 10-4. In this context, a **rule** is a way to manage communications by checking to see if they meet certain conditions and deciding what to do with them based on those conditions. WFAS also integrates IPSec connection management.

Both versions of Windows Firewall work with the Add Roles and Add Features Wizards to protect your server. By default, Windows Firewall is enabled at startup. It has a default profile, which is hardened to prevent external attacks prior to administrative intervention. When a new role or feature is added to Windows Server 2008, the installation wizards work with the firewall to open only the ports and services necessary for the role or feature to function.

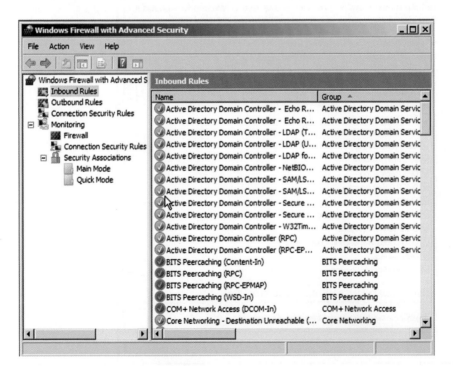

Figure 10-4   Windows Firewall with Advanced Security console

Activity 10-3: Working with WFAS

Time Required: 10 minutes

Objective: Modify an inbound rule.

Description: You need to create an inbound firewall rule on MSN-SRV-1XX that allows Remote Desktop connections from domain computers only. In this activity, you use the Windows Firewall with Advanced Security console to modify an inbound rule.

Your instructor might give you additional steps to perform depending on your lab environment. This activity is appropriate for labs on physical machines and within virtual machine applications.

1. In Server Manager on MSN-SRV-1XX, click **Configure Remote Desktop** under Server Summary.

2. Click **Allow connections only from computers running Remote Desktop with Network Level Authentication (more secure)**. A message box opens stating that an exception will be added to the Windows Firewall for Remote Desktop.

3. Click **OK** to close the message box and then click **OK** to close the System Properties window.

4. On the Start menu, point to **Programs**, click **Administrative Tools**, and then click **Windows Firewall with Advanced Security**.

5. Click **Inbound Rules**. Review the list of inbound rules to find the Remote Desktop (TCP-In) rule.

If MSN-SRV-1XX has been added into the bentech.local domain, two inbound rules are created when Remote Desktop is enabled. One rule is created for public profiles and is disabled. A second enabled rule is created for domain and private profiles.

6. Click **Remote Desktop**. Click **Action** on the menu bar and then click **Properties** to open the Remote Desktop (TCP-In) Properties dialog box.

7. On the General tab, verify that **Enabled** is checked and **Allow the connections** is selected as shown in Figure 10-5.

8. Click the **Advanced** tab. Click **These profiles** and then click **Private** to set the rule to apply only connections from computers with private network profiles.

9. Click **OK** to close the Properties dialog box and apply the changes to the rule.

10. Log onto MSN-SRV-0XX.

11. From the Start menu, start the Remote Desktop Connection program by entering **Remote Desktop Connection** in the Start Search box.

12. In the Remote Desktop Connection window, enter **msn-srv-1xx** as the computer in the text box, and then click **Connect**. After a few moments, you receive a message box stating that MSN-SRV-0XX was unable to connect. Click **OK**. Leave the Remote Desktop Connection window open.

13. Return to MSN-SRV-1XX and the Windows Firewall with Advanced Security console.

14. Open the Properties dialog box for the rule you modified in steps 6 to 9.

15. On the Advanced tab, select **Domain** under the Profiles section and click **OK**.

16. Return to MSN-SRV-0XX and click **Connect** in the Remote Desktop Connection window. This time, a Windows Security window opens requesting your user name and password.

17. Click **Cancel** and then click **Close** to exit the Remote Desktop Connection windows.

10

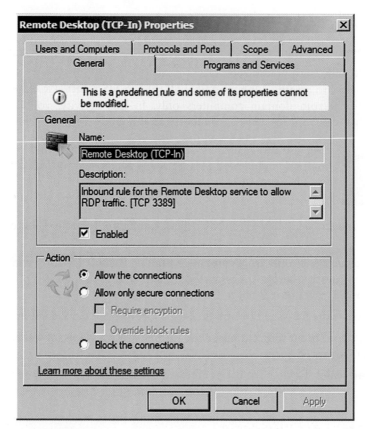

Figure 10-5   General tab for Remote Desktop (TCP-In) Properties dialog box

Windows Firewall with Advanced Security Console   Unlike the Windows Firewall console, the WFAS console provides a more detailed view of a computer's firewall settings. You can manage the following areas in the WFAS console:

- Inbound rules
- Outbound rules
- Connection security rules
- Monitoring

Inbound and outbound rules provide details about each enable and disable rule on a server. You can use the console to edit an existing rule, or you can create additional inbound or outbound rules manually. See Figure 10-6. You can then use these rules to manage connections based on a specific program, a Transmission Control Protocol (TCP) or User Datagram Protocol (UDP) port, or a predefined Windows experience, such as Active Directory Domain Services (AD DS).

Activity 10-4: Creating a New Firewall Rule

Time Required: 10 minutes

Objective: Create a firewall rule.

Description: You need to create a new firewall rule to block outbound connections to a particular Web site. In this activity, you create a firewall rule to block connections to the Microsoft Web site and then allow the connection again.

1. In Server Manager on MSN-SRV-0XX, click the **Configure IE ESC** under Security Information.

2. In the Internet Explorer Enhanced Security Configuration window, click **Off** under Administrators and then click **OK**.

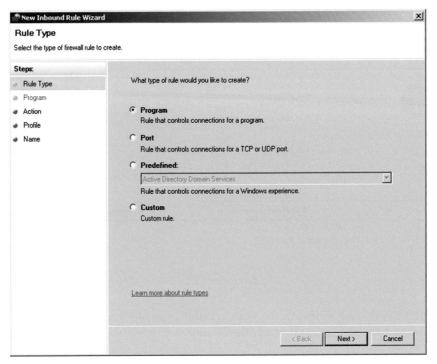

Figure 10-6 Types of inbound rules

10

3. Open Internet Explorer and browse to **www.microsoft.com**. Ensure that you reach the Microsoft Web site before continuing with this lab.

4. Close Internet Explorer.

5. Open the Windows Firewall with Advanced Security console from the Start menu.

6. Expand the console and click **Outbound Rules**.

7. In the Actions pane, click **New Rule**.

8. In the New Outbound Rule Wizard, accept the default of Program by clicking **Next**.

9. In the Program dialog box, enter **C:\Program Files\Internet Explorer\iexplore.exe** in the text box for the program path and then click **Next**.

10. In the Action screen dialog box, click **Block the connection** and then click **Next**.

11. In the Profile dialog box, accept the default of all profiles by clicking **Next**.

12. In the Name dialog box, enter **Internet Explorer** in the Name text box and then click **Finish**.

13. Verify that the Internet Explorer rule you just created is shown at the top of the Outbound Rules pane.

14. Open Internet Explorer and browse to **www.microsoft.com**. You should receive an error when attempting to connect to this site, as shown in Figure 10-7.

15. Switch to the WFAS console, select the **Internet Explorer** rule, and then click **Disable Rule** in Actions pane.

16. Switch to Internet Explorer and browse to **www.microsoft.com**. This time you should connect to the Web page for Microsoft.

17. Close Internet Explorer and the WFAS console.

The Connection Security Rules section is where you manage all your secure connections using IPSec. In previous versions of Windows Server, IPSec was managed in its own console. In Windows Server 2008, it is managed within the WFAS console. You will learn about configuring connection security rules later in this chapter.

Figure 10-7   Internet Explorer error

The Monitoring section of the WFAS console provides you with real-time information about active connections passing through the Windows Firewall. The initial pane of the Monitoring section provides you with general information, including the state of the Windows Firewall, log settings, active firewall rules, and active firewall connections. The Monitoring section is organized into three areas that are discussed in the following sections:

- *Firewall*—This section displays all the active inbound and outbound firewall rules.

- *Connection Security Rules*—This section displays all the enabled connection security rules, including detailed settings information.

- *Security Associations*—This section displays all the Main Mode and Quick Mode security associations, including detailed settings and endpoints.

Windows Firewall Profiles   A new addition to Windows Server 2008 and Windows Vista is the concept of network profiles, which are also known as network locations. Clients use a network profile to determine to what type of network they are connected. Firewall policies and other network settings, such as sharing, are defined for a client based on its profile. With WFAS, you can specify that a particular firewall rule affects only a specific profile. Windows Server 2008 uses the following network profiles:

- *Public*—This profile is used for clients accessing public networks such as WiFi hot spots or noncompany networks, such as a user's home network or another company's network. Public profiles are more hardened than private and domain profiles.

- *Private*—This profile is used for clients on any internal network that is hosted behind a firewall but does not have an Active Directory domain. This scenario assumes that the client is in a more secured network environment, so the security posture is relaxed to allow network functionality on a private network.

- *Domain*—This profile is used for clients in a domain environment. This profile is different than the other two profiles because it refers to a logical network rather than a physical network.

Activity 10-5: Configuring Firewall Rules with Network Profiles

Time Required: 10 minutes

Objective: Configure firewall rules with network profiles.

Description: You have created firewall rules for clients on your domain and need to change the settings so that they apply only to clients on your internal network hosted behind the firewall.

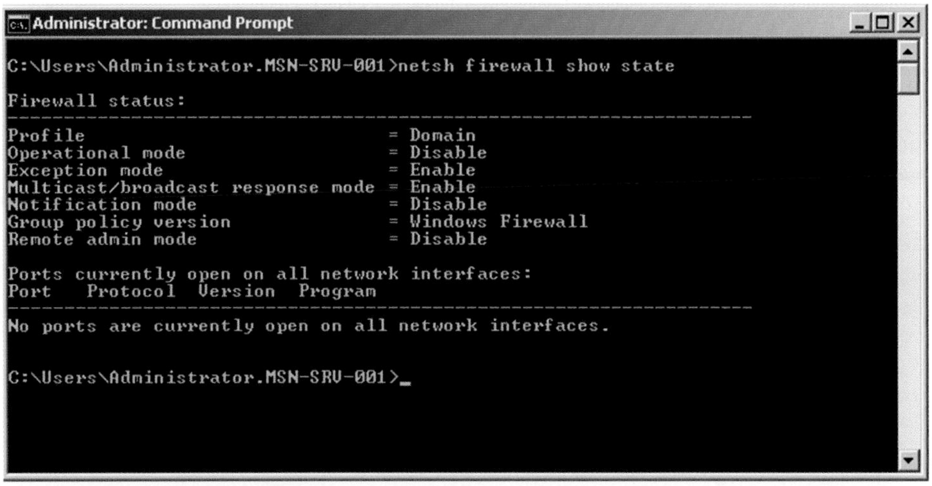

Figure 10-8   Output from netsh firewall show state command

To do so, you will change the firewall rules for the Domain profile. In this activity, you apply the rule you created in Activity 10-4 to domain-only connections.

1. On MSN-SRV-0XX, open the command prompt and enter the **netsh firewall show state** command to verify that the firewall profile is set to Domain, as shown in Figure 10-8. Close the command prompt window.

2. Start Internet Explorer and browse to **www.microsoft.com**. Ensure that you reach the Microsoft Web site before continuing with this lab. Then close Internet Explorer.

3. Open the WFAS console and click **Internet Explorer** under Outbound Rules.

4. In the Actions pane, click **Properties**. The Internet Explorer Properties dialog box opens where you can modify all the settings for this firewall rule.

5. On the Advanced tab, choose **These profiles**, select **Domain**, and then click **OK**.

6. Enable the Internet Explorer rule in the WFAS console.

7. Start Internet Explorer and browse to **www.microsoft.com**. You will receive an error and be unable to browse to the page.

8. Close Internet Explorer and switch back to the WFAS console.

9. Open the Properties dialog box for the Internet Explorer rule.

10. On the Advanced tab, change the profile used by the rule from Domain to **Private**.

11. Open Internet Explorer and browse to **www.microsoft.com**. You should reach the site.

12. Close Internet Explorer and disable the Internet Explorer rule in the WFAS console.

Deploying Windows Firewall Settings via Group Policy

As you have seen, Windows Firewall can be configured through two separate consoles on the local machine. However, you might occasionally need to configure a firewall rule for a number of network clients to establish a common level of security. This is best done with Active Directory. By creating a Group Policy object for firewall rules, you can specify firewall policies and settings centrally and distribute them automatically to all your network clients. Because WFAS is a security service, it is listed in the Security Settings section in the Group Policy Management Editor, as shown in Figure 10-9.

Although you can customize firewall rules and apply them to computer objects through the Group Policy Management Editor, the easiest way to apply firewall policies is to create them on a single machine, export the existing policy, and then import the policy into your Group Policy object. The WFAS allows you to import or export firewall policies.

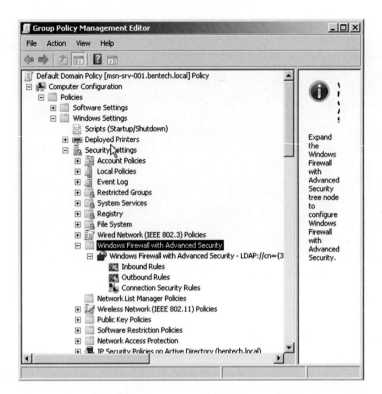

Figure 10-9   Windows Firewall settings in the Group Policy Management Editor

Activity 10-6: Working with Firewall Policies in the Group Policy Management Editor

Time Required: 15 minutes

Objective: Using Group Policy objects and firewall policies to deploy firewall settings.

Description: You have modified the firewall on MSN-SRV-0XX. Now you want to apply those policies to future servers in your environment and you plan to use Group Policy to do so. In this activity, you export the firewall policy of a local system so it can be imported into a Group Policy object later.

Prior to beginning this lab, remove the File Services Resource manager with the following command:

Servermanagercmd.exe –remove FS-Resource-Manager

Due to a bug in Windows Server 2008, you will receive an error when trying to create a GPO if you did not remove the File Services Resource Manager. For more information, search Microsoft.com for KB967358.

1. Open the WFAS console. Click **Windows Firewall with Advanced Security** in the left pane, if necessary.

2. Click **Action** on the menu bar and then click **Export Policy**. The Save As dialog box opens.

3. In the Save As dialog box, save the firewall policy to c:\70642\Chapter 10\ with the name **ServerFWPol.wfw**, and then click **Save**.

4. Click **OK** to close the Message box stating that the policy was successfully exported. Then close WFAS.

5. Open the Group Policy Management console (GPMC). In the GPMC, expand the forest until you can select **bentech.local**.

6. Click **Action** on the menu bar and then click **Create a GPO in this domain, and Link it here**. This will allow you to create a Group Policy object for the firewall policy settings that can be applied to computer objects within the domain.

7. In the New GPO dialog box, type **Firewall Policy - Servers** in the Name text box and then click **OK**.

8. Click the new Group Policy you just created, click the **Show/Hide Action Pane** button, if necessary, to display the Action pane, click **More Actions**, and then click **Edit**. The Group Policy Management Editor (GPME) starts.

9. In the GPME, expand **Computer Configuration**, then **Policies**, then **Windows Settings**, then **Security Settings**, and then **Windows Firewall with Advanced Security**. Click **Windows Firewall with Advanced Security**.

10. Click each of the rules (Inbound, Outbound, and Connection Security) and verify that they contain no entries. Click **Windows Firewall with Advanced Security** again.

11. Click **Action** on the menu bar and then click **Import Policy**.

12. Choose **Yes** in the message box. The Open dialog box opens.

13. In the Open dialog box, type **c:\70642\Chapter 10\ ServerFWPol.wfw** in the File name text box and then click **Open**.

14. After successfully importing the policy, click **OK**.

15. Click **Windows Firewall with Advanced Security**, click **Action** on the menu bar, and then click **Clear Policy**.

16. Click **Yes** and then click **OK** in the message boxes.

17. Close the GPME and then the GPMC.

Encrypting File Services

Along with providing file security through Access Control Lists, New Technology File System (NTFS) allows users to perform file-based encryption through the Encrypting File Service (EFS). EFS is Microsoft's built-in service for providing folder and file-level encryption. In general, EFS transparently encrypts files on NTFS file systems to protect data from attackers who have physical access to a computer.

EFS uses a combination of private and public key encryption for securing a user's data. A randomly created symmetric key is first used to encrypt and decrypt the file contents. **Symmetric encryption** uses a single key and is faster and more efficient than public key encryption, especially for very large files. With **public key (asymmetric) encryption**, each user has a public key that is available to everyone and a private key that is known only to the user. With the user's EFS certificate, the public key encrypts the symmetric key. The private key decrypts the symmetric key, meaning that it decrypts the files. If other users need to access the encrypted file, this unique system allows the file owner to give them access to the symmetric key. These users can then encrypt the symmetric key with their own public keys and append them to the file. Any one of the user's private keys is required to access to the file. Unlike other third-party utilities for encryption, EFS provides transparent encryption and decryption. After a file is encrypted with EFS, users do not need to manually decrypt the file every time they use it. Instead, this task is performed by the NTFS file system and the EFS service.

Recovery Agents play an important part in EFS. A user can be assigned the role of Recovery Agent to recover files encrypted by another user. If you lose your EFS private key, for example, you can use a Recovery Agent to recover encrypted files. When a file is encrypted, the file encryption key (discussed next) is also encrypted with the Recovery Agent's public key. The encrypted FEK uses a copy of the file encrypted with your EFS public key in the Data Recovery Field of the file header to become attached to the original file. Using the Recovery Agent's private key, you can decrypt the FEK, and then decrypt the file.

EFS in Windows Server 2008   EFS has been included in many versions of Windows Server and desktop operating systems (OSs). Windows Server 2008 introduces significant improvements over previous Server versions, including the following:

- EFS rekeying wizard
- Key caching
- Improved Group Policy support
- Smart card key storage
- Smart card single sign-on
- Per user encryption of offline files

Using EFS   When a user encrypts a file, a symmetric file encryption key (FEK) is generated that EFS uses to encrypt the file. The FEK is then encrypted by using the user's public key. Finally, the encrypted FEK is stored in the header information of the encrypted file.

EFS performs the following tasks to encrypt and decrypt a file:

- User begins encrypting a plain-text data file by applying their public key and the Recovery Agent's public key to the FEK.

- The encrypted FEK for each user is applied to the data file and stored in the header of the file. This header contains the list of FEKs for an encrypted file, which are stored in the Data Decryption Field and Data Recovery Field.

- When the first file for encryption is created, EFS generates the user's public-private key certificate that will be used for all EFS process. Administrators can create this key ahead of time using the Cipher utility.

- When a user accesses an encrypted file, the private key is applied to the FEK of the file. This decrypts the FEK so that it can be used to decrypt the data.

Windows Server 2008 has two tools for managing EFS: file and folder properties and Cipher. Using Windows Explorer, you can modify the encryption attribute of a file or folder by changing its properties. You access the encryption attributes by clicking the Advanced button on the General tab in the Properties dialog box for a file or folder.

Clicking the Advanced button opens a dialog box where you can select the Encrypt contents to secure data check box, as shown in Figure 10-10. EFS will then perform the initial encryption process of the resource as discussed previously.

Cipher.exe is a command-line utility that allows you to manage EFS through scripts or the command prompt. Use /E to encrypt and /D to decrypt. The following is a listing of common cipher commands:

```
cipher.exe
cipher.exe /E testfile.txt
cipher.exe /D testfile.txt
```

Activity 10-7: Working with cipher.exe

Time Required: 10 minutes

Objective: Using cipher.exe with EFS.

Figure 10-10   Advanced Attributes dialog box

Description: You need to encrypt some local files, and you decide that the easiest way to accomplish this is by using the Cipher utility. In this activity, you use cipher.exe to encrypt files and folders on a remote server.

1. Log onto MSN-SRV-1XX, if necessary.

2. Open the command prompt and enter the following commands:

```
md "C:\70642\Chapter 10\Secret Files"
md "C:\70642\Chapter 10\NonSecret Files"
md "C:\70642\Chapter 10\Secret Files 2"
cd C:\70642\Chapter 10\
```

3. At the command prompt, enter **Cipher /K** to generate a new EFS certificate for the logged-on user. The command will return the EFS Certificate Thumbprint, as shown in Figure 10-11. (The Certificate Thumbprint is the hash of the certificate used to encrypt the session key for the user.)

4. Type **cipher /e "secret files"** and then press **Enter** to encrypt the Secret Files folder.

5. To verify that the folder is encrypted, type **cipher** and then press **Enter.** You will see that an "E" appears before Secret Files. This means that the folder is encrypted.

6. Type **cd Secret Files** and then press **Enter.**

7. Type **echo This is secret information! > SecretDoc.txt** and then press **Enter.** This will create a text file called SecretDoc.txt.

8. Type **cipher** and then press **Enter.** Verify that SecretDoc.txt is encrypted.

9. Enter the following command to move the encrypted file, SecretDoc.txt, to the unencrypted folder, NonSecret Files.

```
move /Y "C:\70642\Chapter 10\Secret Files\SecretDoc.txt"
"C:\70642\Chapter 10\NonSecret Files\"
```

10. Then enter the following command to move the command prompt to the NonSecret Files directory:

```
cd C:\70642\Chapter 10\NonSecret Files\
```

11. Type **cipher** and then press **Enter.** Note that SecretDoc.txt is still encrypted even when moved to a folder not using encryption.

12. Close the command prompt.

EFS has a number of usage rules that are important to understand, including the following:

- Files copied or moved into an encrypted folder will become encrypted.

- Files copied or moved out of an encrypted folder will remain encrypted unless the destination file system is not NTFS. However, files can be moved to a non-NTFS file system disk only by a user who has decryption rights.

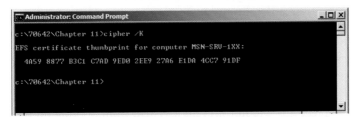

Figure 10-11 EFS Certificate Thumbprint

Activity 10-8: Using Windows Explorer to Encrypt Files with EFS

Time Required: 10 minutes

Objective: Configure file and folder encryption through the graphical user interface (GUI).

Description: You need to encrypt a few more local files. You have decided the cipher utility is not the easiest way to accomplish this, so you decide to use the GUI. In this activity, you will use Windows Explorer to encrypt files and folders on a remote server.

1. On MSN-SRV-1XX, open Windows Explorer from the Start menu.

2. In Windows Explorer, browse to c:\70642\Chapter 10 and display the folders under Chapter 10. Note that Secret Files is displayed in green text, signifying that the folder is encrypted.

3. Open the folder **Secret Files 2**, right-click a blank spot in the window, point to **New** on the shortcut menu, and then click **Text Document**. Name the new document **SecretDoc2**.

4. Right-click **Secret Files 2** and then click **Properties**. The Secret Files 2 Properties dialog box opens.

5. On the General tab, click the **Advanced** button.

6. In the Advanced Attributes dialog box, click the **Encrypt contents to secure data** check box and then click **OK**. Click **OK** to close the Properties dialog box, and then click **OK** to confirm the attribute changes.

7. In Windows Explorer, verify that Secret Files 2 and SecretDoc2.txt are encrypted.

8. Right-click **SecretDoc2.txt** and then click **Properties** to open the Properties dialog box for the file.

9. On the General tab, click the **Advanced** button.

10. In the Advanced Attributes dialog box, click the **Details** button. This will open the user access window where additional users can be given access to a document by adding their certificate to the document's properties.

BitLocker

A new addition to Windows Server 2008, **BitLocker** provides hard drive–based encryption of servers and Windows Vista computers. While EFS provides file- and folder-level encryption, BitLocker encrypts the entire Windows system volume of a computer running Windows Server 2008. This includes all the Windows system files.

BitLocker is designed to enhance protection against data theft or exposure on computers that are lost or stolen, and to delete data more securely when BitLocker-protected computers are recycled. In addition, BitLocker prevents a number of threats to Windows systems, including the following:

- *Compromised system files*—Since all of the system files are encrypted, BitLocker prevents access to system files that can be used to compromise local accounts and passwords.

- *Data access from outside the OS*—BitLocker prevents data stored on a hard disk from being accessed either from a bootable utility CD or when the drive is removed from the computer.

BitLocker prevents these threats by encrypting the entire Windows OS volume on the hard disk and verifying the integrity of early boot components and boot configuration data.

BitLocker supports four different authentication modes. Three modes are based on systems with a Trusted Protection Module (TPM) chip, and one mode is without a TPM module. A TPM is a microchip that performs basic security tasks with encryption keys. Computers that have a TPM can create cryptographic keys and encrypt them so that only the TPM can decrypt them. Following are the four authentication modes that BitLocker uses:

- *BitLocker with a TPM*—This provides drive encryption protection only. While the drive contents are encrypted, this will not prevent a system from booting up the OS. This is referred to as transparent encryption.

- *BitLocker with Universal Serial Bus (USB) flash drive in place of TPM*—This provides drive encryption protection and boot protection. Prior to boot, users are required to insert a USB flash drive before BitLocker unlocks the drive and allows the OS to boot. This is implemented without a TPM module.

- *BitLocker with a TPM and a personal identification number (PIN)*—This provides drive encryption protection and boot protection. Prior to boot, users are required to enter a PIN before BitLocker unlocks the drive and allows the OS to boot. This provides multifactor authentication, which requires two or more items for authentication.

- *BitLocker with a TPM and a USB flash drive*—This provides drive encryption protection and boot protection. Prior to boot, users are required to insert a USB flash drive before BitLocker unlocks the drive and allows the OS to boot. This provides multifactor authentication, which requires two or more items for authentication.

Using BitLocker with a TPM and a PIN or a USB flash drive is called **enhanced security mode**. This is because you are using **multifactor authentication**, which requires two or more different authentication pieces. In the preceding case, TPM provides a system integrity check for authentication, a PIN provides authentication based on a secret known by the user, and a USB key provides authentication based on an object a user has.

BitLocker does have some limitations. Currently, BitLocker supports encryption only of the system drive in Windows Server 2008. It does not support encryption of other logical or physical drives in a system. For this, you need to use EFS. Also, files are encrypted only while they reside on the BitLocker drive. Moving the files to another drive decrypts them. This is important if you store network-accessible files on a BitLocker-enabled drive. The files will be encrypted while they are on the server and accessible to authorized users. If a user copies a file from the network drive, the file will decrypt.

At startup, BitLocker performs a system check prior to booting into the OS. TPM performs this task, which is often called the system integrity authentication. If it determines that conditions represent a security risk, the drive is locked down. These changes can include hardware changes, such as moving a drive to a new computer, modifying any startup files, or changing the BIOS. The locked drive requires the user to enter the BitLocker recovery password. This password is created when you first turn on BitLocker and should be kept in a safe, secure, and available place in case it is needed.

Contrary to popular speculation, Microsoft did not create a "back door" for BitLocker in case of emergency. What that means is that if you lose your recovery password and your drive locks, you will not be able to access your drive. So make sure you have a copy of your password stored in a safe location. For environments running AD DS, Group Policy can be used to escrow, or archive, copies of the BitLocker recovery passwords for domain machines.

Installing BitLocker   The hard drive that supports BitLocker needs to be configured before installing BitLocker, which requires at least 1.5 GB of unallocated or available drive space. This space will contain the system volume, which is responsible for maintaining the unencrypted boot information necessary for the OS to start with BitLocker in use. Another volume, the boot volume, will contain the OS files and be encrypted by BitLocker. To ease the burden of configuring BitLocker, Microsoft has released the BitLocker Drive Preparation Tool, which automates the following tasks for administrators:

- Creates a second partition for the system volume in instances where this second volume does not exist.

- Moves boot files to unencrypted system volume.

- Verifies that the OS is configured correctly to find the boot files at system startup.

- Configures the system drive as the active partition on the drive for system startup.

Activity 10-9: Installing the BitLocker and the BitLocker Drive Preparation Tool in Windows Server 2008

Time Required: 15 minutes

Objective: Install the BitLocker and BitLocker Drive Preparation tool.

Description: You want to take advantage of the protection BitLocker offers, so you want to download the preparation tool and install BitLocker on your Windows Server 2008 computer.

For this activity, you need the BitLocker Drive Preparation Tool from *www.microsoft.com/downloads* (search for KB article 933246). It is available for both x86 and x64 systems.

1. At the command prompt on MSN-SRV-0XX, enter the following command to install the BitLocker Drive Encryption feature.

    ServerManagerCmd -install BitLocker -restart

2. Log onto MSN-SRV-0XX after it restarts and wait for BitLocker to finish installing.
3. On MSN-SRV-0XX, download the BitLocker Drive Preparation Tool from *http://www.microsoft.com/downloads*, if Internet access is available, or copy the file from a location provided by your instructor. Save the program file in the Downloads folder of the Administrator account.
4. Browse to the Downloads folder and double-click **Windows6.0-KB933246-x86** to start the Setup Wizard.
5. Click **OK** to install the update.
6. Click **I Accept** on the license terms page and wait for the installation to complete.
7. Click **Close** when installation is completed.
8. Open a command prompt, type **cd \program files\BitLocker** and then press **Enter**. This will place you in the directory containing the BitLocker Drive Preparation Tool.
9. At the command prompt, type **bdehdcfg -?** and then press **Enter**. This will display all the available options for running the BitLocker Drive Preparation Tool from the command line.
10. Type **bdehdcfg –driveinfo** and then press **Enter**. This will display all the information about the current hard drive similar to Figure 10-12.
11. Enter the following command:

    bdehdcfg -target c: shrink -newdriveletter x: -size 1500

12. Type **Y** when requested to continue. This will shrink the current c: drive for space recovery, create a 1500-MB drive named X:, and prepare drive X: for BitLocker, as shown in Figure 10-13. The process takes a few minutes.
13. Type **shutdown –r**, press **Enter**, and then click **Close** to restart MSN-SRV-0XX.

If **Server 2008 SP2** is installed, you will have issues installing the Drive Prep tool. Either remove SP2 or perform the following steps:

1. Download the Bit Locker Preparation Tool to the C: drive.
2. Enter the following commands at the command prompt.
    a. **expand -f:* "C:\Windows6.0-KB933246-x86.msu" %TEMP%**
    b. **pkgmgr.exe /n:%TEMP%\Windows6.0-KB933246-x86.xml**
3. Enter "C:\Program Files\BitLocker\BdeHdCfg.exe" on the Run line. This will repartition your drive to allow Bit Locker to work properly.

Figure 10-12   Viewing drive information with BitLocker Drive Preparation Tool

Figure 10-13 Preparing a drive for BitLocker

After BitLocker is installed on your computer, you need to configure it. To do so, you can use the BitLocker Drive Encryption console or the command line using the manage-bde.wsf tool. Manage-bde.wsf is a Windows Management Instrumentation script that allows you to manage BitLocker on local and remote machines.

Activity 10-10: Configuring BitLocker to Use a USB Flash Drive

10

Time Required: 15 minutes

Objective: Configure BitLocker to use a USB flash drive.

Description: Now that BitLocker is installed on your Windows Server 2008 computer, you want to configure it to use a removable drive. In this activity, you configure BitLocker to use a USB flash drive.

> This activity is designed for a physical computer or a virtual machine using VMware Workstation 6.x, not Virtual PC or other virtualization products. If you are working on a virtual machine using software other than VMware Workstation 6.x, read but do not complete the steps in this activity.
>
> This activity requires a USB flash drive. If you are using virtual machines, verify that your application supports mounting a USB flash drive. Check with your instructor for additional instructions based on your lab environment.

1. Log onto MSN-SRV-0XX.

2. From the Start menu, open **Control Panel**, and then start **BitLocker Drive Encryption**.

3. In the BitLocker window, notice a warning stating that a TPM was not found, as shown in Figure 10-14.

4. Enter **gpedit.msc** in the Start Search box on the Start menu to start the Local Group Policy Editor, and then press **Enter**.

5. In the Local Group Policy Editor, select **Local Computer Policy**, then **Computer Configuration**, then **Administrative Templates**, then **Windows Components**, and then **BitLocker Drive Encryption**.

6. In the right pane displaying the BitLocker Drive Encryption Group Policy settings, double-click **Control Panel Setup: Enable advanced startup options** to open the Properties dialog box.

7. In the Properties dialog box, click the **Enabled** option button, as shown in Figure 10-15. Then click **OK**. Close the Local Group Policy Editor.

8. At the command prompt, type **gpupdate /force** and then press **Enter** to reload the local computer Group Policy and apply the new change to BitLocker.

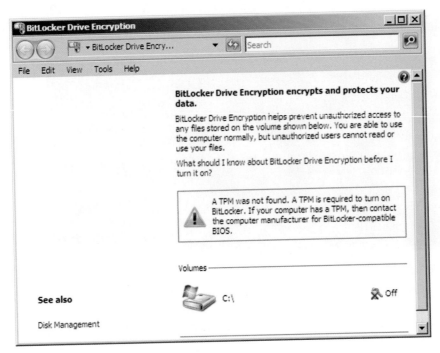

Figure 10-14 Warning for missing TPM chip

9. Type **shutdown -r** and then press **Enter** to restart your server. Click the **Close** button.

10. Log onto MSN-SRV-0XX.

11. Insert your USB flash drive in the appropriate port and verify that it is formatted and recognized by your computer. Note the drive letter used by your USB flash drive.

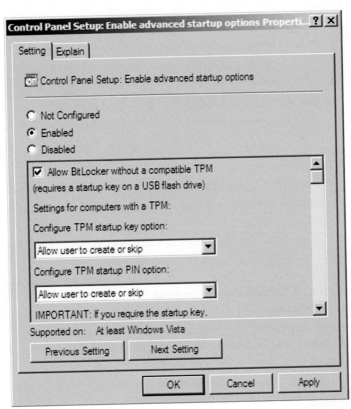

Figure 10-15 Control Panel Setup: Enable advanced startup options Properties dialog box

12. Open **Bitlocker Drive Encryption** from the Start menu and click the **Turn On BitLocker** link under c: drive.

13. Click **Continue with BitLocker Drive Encryption** in the Platform Check dialog box.

14. Click **Require Startup USB Key at every startup** in the Set BitLocker startup preferences window.

15. In the Save your Startup Key window, select the drive letter from Step 11 and then click **Save**.

16. In the Save Your Recovery Password window, select **Print the Password**, select **Microsoft XPS Document Writer** (or the name of your printer, if different), and then click **Print**.

17. In the Save the file as dialog box, type **c:\70642\Chapter 10\BitLocker Key** and then click **Save**. Click **Next**.

18. In the Encrypt the volume window, click **Continue** and then click **Restart Now** when the message box appears.

19. Log onto MSN-SRV-1XX. As BitLocker begins encrypting the drive, you will see a message box that shows the progress of the encryption process, similar to Figure 10-16.

Results will differ if you are using a virtual machine. You will be unable to encrypt your volume and will receive an error when you log on.

Microsoft Baseline Security Analyzer

Introduced in previous versions of Windows, the Microsoft Baseline Security Analyzer (MBSA) is an excellent tool for performing an initial analysis of your current security setup. The MBSA can scan single or multiple computers on a network or view existing security scan reports, as shown in Figure 10-17.

When MBSA scans a computer, it creates a report that uses current information from Windows Update and recommended configurations from Microsoft. The results of the report are organized into the following areas:

- *Security Assessment*—Provides a general assessment of a computer's security risk level based on the results from the entire report.

- *Security Update Scan Results*—Displays system status in regards to security update currency. You can see what updates are missing, and then download any needed updates.

- *Windows Scan Results*—Displays administrative vulnerabilities along with additional system information. The administrative vulnerabilities include password policies, guest and administrator account status, and Windows Firewall status. In addition, the MBSA checks for auditing, unnecessary services, and the number of available shares.

- *Internet Information Services (IIS) Scan Results*—This section is optional and should only be run on systems with IIS installed. It checks a computer's IIS configuration and notifies you if it finds security problems.

- *SQL Server Scan Results*—This section is optional and should only be run on systems with SQL installed. It checks a computer's SQL configuration and notifies you if it finds security problems.

Figure 10-16   Drive encryption progress

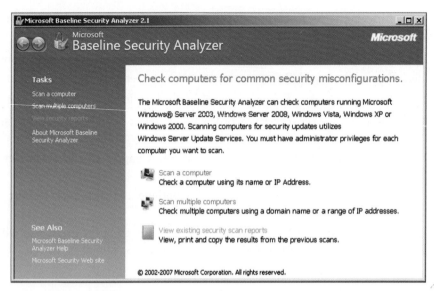

Figure 10-17   Microsoft Baseline Security Analyzer

- *Desktop Application Scan Results*—This section is used to provide information on installed Microsoft desktop applications such as Internet Explorer and the Microsoft Office suite. If the applications are installed, MBSA provides information about security risks along with a listing of needed application updates from Windows Update.

Scanning a Computer with MBSA

MBSA allows you to scan a local computer or remote computers using the following OSs:

- Windows Server 2008
- Windows Vista
- Windows Server 2003
- Windows XP
- Windows 2000

You can perform MBSA scans using the GUI-based tool, or you can use the mbsacli.exe command-line tool to perform scans from the command line or scripts. Scans can be stored for later usage or printed out for immediate review or filing. One requirement of MBSA is Internet connectivity. MBSA needs access to the Microsoft Update Web site or to Microsoft Windows Software Update Servers to create the baseline against which computers are measured. Internet access is also helpful if you want to download any of the recommended updates that MBSA identifies as missing.

You can run MBSA in offline mode using the command-line tool mbsacli.exe. However, using MBSA offline does not give you the current update status of your computer.

Activity 10-11: Working with MBSA

Time Required: 15 minutes

Objective: Analyze Windows Server 2008 with MBSA.

Description: As part of a company initiative to improve security, you decide that MBSA would be a good tool to assess your servers against current Microsoft updates and best practices. In this activity, you download, install, and run the MBSA on MSN-SRV-0XX.

Because MBSA requires access to the Windows Update services on the Internet, you need to ensure that your computer has access to the Internet.

1. Log onto MSN-SRV-0XX and download the latest version of MBSA from *http://www.microsoft.com/downloads*. Save the downloaded MBSA file to the Downloads folder on MSN-SRV-0XX.

2. Browse to the Downloads folder and double-click the MBSA file you just downloaded to start the installation.

3. On the Welcome screen, click **Next**.

4. Accept the license agreement on the next window and click **Next**.

5. On the Destination Folder window, click **Next** to use the default installation path of C:\Program Files\Microsoft Baseline Security Analyzer 2\.

This path may differ depending on the version of MBSA you are running.

6. Click **Install** to begin the installation.

7. Click **OK** to close the MBSA Setup completion message box.

8. Click the **Start** button, point to **All Programs** and then click **Microsoft Baseline Security Analyzer 2.1**. MBSA creates an icon on your desktop to access the analyzer.

9. In the Microsoft Baseline Security Analyzer window, click the **Scan a computer** link. This will allow you to analyze a computer based on its name or IP address.

10. In the next window, click **Start Scan** to accept the default settings to scan the local machine, MSN-SRV-0XX, as shown in Figure 10-18.

11. In the Report Details window, review the scan results, as shown in Figure 10-19, and then click **OK** to return to the MBSA main window.

12. Close the MBSA main window.

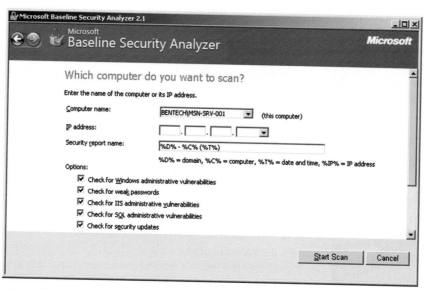

Figure 10-18   Choosing settings for MBSA scan

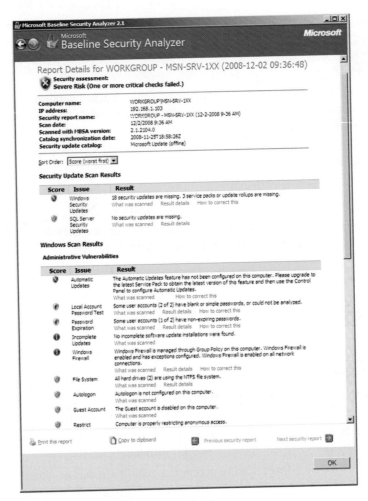

Figure 10-19   MBSA Scan report details

Internet Protocol Security

Internet Protocol Security (IPSec) is an open-standards framework for securing network communications. Built on industry standard protocols, IPSec works at the network layer of the Open Systems Interconnection (OSI) model. Unlike other security protocols, such as Secure Socket Layer (SSL) and Secure Shell (SSH), which work at higher layers, IPSec can protect Transport layer protocols and information such as TCP and UDP. In addition, applications in higher layers do not need to be designed to work with IPSec because it is transparent to them. IPSec meets three basic goals:

- *Authentication*—Verifies that the packet received is actually from the claimed sender
- *Integrity*—Ensures that the contents of the packet did not change in transit
- *Confidentiality*—Conceals the message content through encryption

While these are three distinct services, they are supported together through the IPSec suite of protocols and services. Depending on your needs from IPSec, the preceding goals can be met through different implementations of IPSec.

IPSec is a complex and intricate framework for securing networks. It requires a detailed understanding of the protocols and the mechanisms for implementing IPSec. It is beyond the scope of this text to provide in-depth information on IPSec. For more information on IPSec, refer to *http://technet.microsoft.com* and search for IPSec.

IPSec Threats

Using the components to be discussed next, IPSec provides data authentication, integrity, and confidentiality for data communications across public and private networks. Depending on the configuration of IPSec, it provides protection from the following threats:

- *Data tampering*—This threat involves the malicious modification of data stored on Web sites or in databases or being passed between two computers on a network. An example would be the defacing of a Web site by an unauthorized user. A common tactic used to gain access for data tampering is session hijacking. Hijacking a session involves capturing a regular users' session after the user has been authenticated and authorized.

- *Denial of service*—This threat involves a directed attack against a specific host or network such as a Web site like microsoft.com. Denial-of-service attacks are performed by flooding a host or a network router with more traffic than it can handle. This can cause disruption in legitimate traffic along with taking services such as a Web site offline. These type of attacks are often initiated from multiple hosts to increase the scale of the attack.

- *Identity spoofing*—This threat involves a computer masquerading as a client. This may be done by mimicking another client's IP address, Media Access Control address, or other identifying characteristics.

- *Man-in-the-middle attacks*—Often employed in wireless network scenarios, this threat involves placing a computer between two communicating computers in a network connection. This computer impersonates each machine in the transaction, giving the computer the ability to read or modify communications between the two computers.

- *Repudiation*—This threat involves users who deny that they performed a malicious action on a network, and administrators do not have a way to prove them wrong. An example of this threat would be a user accessing confidential information on a system, but the system does not have the ability to track the prohibited operation.

- *Network traffic sniffing*—This threat involves the capture of network traffic by attackers looking for important data files and to obtain passwords in order to penetrate a network. This is accomplished through the use of sniffing tools to capture data packets as they travel across the network.

How IPSec Works

IPSec is used by administrators to protect Internet Protocol (IP) communications between IPSec peers. To do so, it uses a number of protocols and mechanisms. In this section, you review the components of IPSec and how IPSec works.

IPSec Modes of Operation   For IPSec, the mode of operation is how you are going to use IPSec to secure your data communications. There are two modes of operation in IPSec:

- *Transport mode*—The **transport mode** is the default mode for IPSec. It provides end-to-end security between devices or hosts, such as between a client and server or for Layer 2 Tunneling Protocol (L2TP) virtual private network (VPN) solutions for remote access. Transport mode encrypts only the data portion, or the payload, of each packet through a header. For example, IP payloads include TCP segments that contain a TCP header and TCP segment data. In transport mode, the two participating hosts authenticate with one another and then determine what negotiation services to use to secure their communications.

- *Tunnel mode*—The IPSec **tunnel mode** provides secure communications between two networks through a single node. The more secure tunnel mode encrypts both the header and the payload. This means that new addressing information must be appended to the encrypted packet again. This method is more commonly used between a fixed, secure network and a mobile device or between two fixed, secure networks. The sending device first encrypts the packets (including the original IP address common to both end points) and

Figure 10-20 Site-to-site scenario

then appends a new header to the packet so that it can be routed over the Internet or another untrusted network. On the receiving side, an IPSec-compliant device decrypts each packet and conveys it on the network as if the source host were connected locally.

Using these two modes and IPSec, you can deploy three different scenarios for securing data communications based on need. The following three scenarios are available when deploying IPSec:

- *Site to site*—Site-to-site scenarios involve two network devices that established a secured tunnel between their respective networks. This is often used when connecting to remote networks over the Internet with an IPSec VPN, as shown in Figure 10-20.

- *Client to client*—This scenario is referred to as transport mode, or end-to-end communication. Here, clients communicate directly with each other. Examples of this include secure traffic between a Web server and a database server or securing desktop client communications with a network application server, as shown in Figure 10-21.

- *Client to site*—This scenario is most often used when a client makes a VPN connection to a private network using Remote Access, as shown in Figure 10-22.

IPSec Security Association Modes   Although IPSec is appropriate in three different scenarios, IPSec works the same for each transaction. For each transaction, IPSec uses the **Internet Key Exchange (IKE)** to negotiate security protocols each IPSec peer will use for communicating and constructing data transactions. IKE generates the encryption and authentication keys used by IPSec for the transaction. IPSec performs all transactions in two phases:

- *Main mode/Phase 1*—During this phase, hosts authenticate each other and negotiate the Main mode security associations used to define and establish the secure communication tunnel between the two IPSec peers.

- *Quick mode/Phase 2*—During this phase, the initial tunnel created in Phase 1 is used to negotiate the security protocols and lifetimes that will be used for the secure communications channel (Quick mode security associations) and establish the tunnels for secure transmission of data packets.

Creating a secure tunnel in either mode requires each IPSec peer to agree on security information and encryption algorithms used for the tunnel. After completion of the negotiation

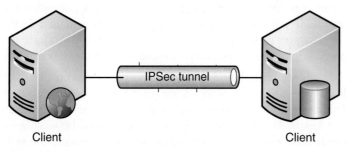

Figure 10-21 Client-to-client scenario

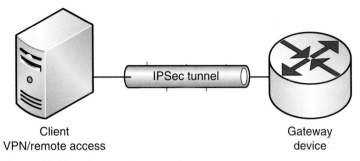

Figure 10-22   Client-to-site scenario

process, each IPSec peer creates a security association it will use with the other peer. The security association is the connection between IPSec peers that applies a security policy and keys to protect information during their transaction. The following list includes the methods used for Main mode/Phase 1 authentication:

- *Kerberos version 5*—In Active Directory domain environments, Kerberos is used by clients for host authentication. IPSec can use Kerberos as well to authenticate IPSec transactions between domain-based hosts. If both peers are in the same Active Directory forest, IPSec on computers running the Windows Server 2003 OS can also use the Kerberos protocol for the initial computer-to-computer authentication. Kerberos is appropriate if you don't have a public key infrastructure (PKI) and don't need to establish IPSec security associations between computers outside a single forest.

 Although beyond the scope of this text, Active Directory Certificate Services (AD CS) provides the necessary components for deploying a PKI to support Network Access Protection and IPSec. For more information on **NOTE** AD CS, refer to *http://technet.microsoft.com*.

- *Digital certificates*—This form of authentication uses certificates issued by a trusted authority, or certification authority (CA). A CA can be either a trusted third-party certificate vendor such as Verisign or Thawte or issued by an internal PKI. By using digital certificates issued by trusted sources, each IPSec peer will authenticate the other peer. This is the preferred method of configuring IPSec.

- *Preshared keys*—This form of authentication uses a string of characters, known as the preshared key, that is provided to all IPSec peers participating in the communications. Every peer that participates in the same security policy will need the same preshared key. Shared secrets don't remain secret for very long. Furthermore, they're stored in the Registry and are clearly visible to anyone with administrative privileges on the computer.

You can see where the methods are applied when creating a new Connection Security rule in Figure 10-23.

IPSec Security Methods   IPSec uses two security services:

- *Encapsulating Security Payload*—Encapsulating Security Payload (ESP) provides authentication, integrity, and confidentiality services, depending on how it is implemented. ESP is the default IPSec security protocol in Windows Server 2008 and is defined by RFC 4303. Figure 10-24 shows how ESP protects data in IPSec tunnel and transport modes. Note that the IP payload is encrypted with ESP to provide confidentiality for your data. Then it is signed with ESP to provide authentication and data integrity.

- *Authentication Header*—Authentication Header (AH) provides authentication and integrity services but does not provide confidentiality because data encryption is not supported. In addition, AH does not support traversing NAT devices, as the NAT translation of the IP address (private to public or vice versa) will modify the packet contents, thus

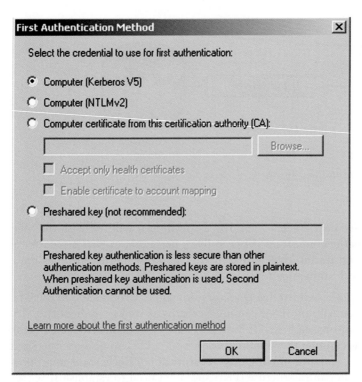

Figure 10-23 First Authentication Method dialog box for IPSec policies

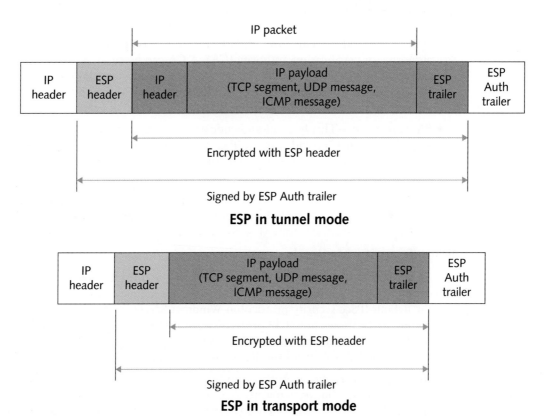

Figure 10-24 ESP used in tunnel and transport modes

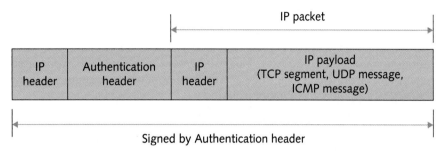

AH in tunnel mode

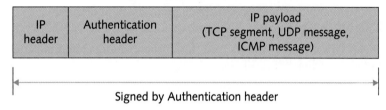

AH in transport mode

Figure 10-25   AH used in tunnel and transport modes

breaking the integrity of the transmission. Figure 10-25 shows how AH protects data in IPSec tunnel and transport modes. Note there is no encryption of the IP payload as AH provides no data confidentiality; the packet is signed to provide authentication and data integrity information.

IPSec Policies   Administrators create IPSec policies to configure IPSec security services on local computers or remote network computers. Depending on the needs of IPSec, you can configure the services at differing levels of security. You can manage IPSec policies using the following tools:

- *WFAS*—This console allows for the configuration of IPSec security services for Windows Server 2008 and Windows Vista clients only. This is done through the Connection Security Rules section of WFAS. Using WFAS would allow you to export IPSec policies for use in Group Policy.

- *IP Security Policy snap-in*—This console is used to create IPSec policies running Windows Vista and Windows Server 2008 as well as older OSs. However, it does not support the new security algorithms and other new features available to Windows Vista and Windows Server 2008.

- *Netsh*—This command-line utility allows administrators to perform all the GUI-based tasks of the previously mentioned tools, along with other advanced configurations that are available only through netsh.

- *GPME*—This console will allow you to create policies for IPSec services so that they can be applied to computer objects within your Active Directory environment. Creating connection Security Rules in the GPME follows the same process as those created in WFAS.

Windows Server 2008 has no default IPSec policies, so you need to create rules for machines running the OS. *Previous versions of Windows including Windows XP and Windows Server 2003 included default IPSec policies.* However, they might be incompatible with Windows Server 2008, so you should create your own policies. While there are no default rules, Windows Server 2008 does include four Connection Security Rule Templates, including the following:

- *Isolation*—This template creates rules that restrict network connections based on administrator-defined policies. This can be used to isolate your corporate domain computers from being able to be accessed by nondomain computers. In Activity 10-12, you create a policy for domain isolation.

- *Authentication Exemption Rule*—This template creates rules that allow specific computers, groups, or IP addresses to connect with network computers without being required to authenticate themselves.

- *Server-to-Server*—This template creates rules for authenticating communication between two computers, two groups of computers, two different subnets, or a combination of these. An example would be securing communication between a Web server and a database server. In Activity 10-13, you create a policy for server-to-server communications.

- *Tunnel*—This template creates rules for authenticating communications between gateway computers, such as IPSec VPNs.

- *Custom*—Not necessarily a template, this wizard allows administrators to create rules requiring specific settings and functionality not covered by the four default templates.

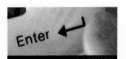

Activity 10-12: Creating an IPSec Policy for Domain Isolation

Time Required: 15 minutes

Objective: Use IPSec to isolate domain computers from nondomain computers.

Description: Domain isolation is the practice of putting security measures in place so that your domain computers are isolated from nondomain computers. You have decided to implement an IPSec policy that will prevent nondomain computers from accessing your server resources. In the activity, you create an isolation connection security rule.

1. Log onto MSN-SRV-0XX.
2. Open the Windows Firewall with Advanced Security console.
3. Click **Connection Security Rules** and then click **New Rule** under Actions.
4. In the Rule Type dialog box, click **Isolation** if necessary and then click **Next**.
5. In the Requirements dialog box, choose **Require authentication for inbound and outbound connections** and then click **Next**.
6. In the Authentication Method dialog box, click **Computer and user (Kerberos V5)** and then click **Next**.
7. In the Profile dialog box, accept the default selections by clicking **Next**.
8. In the Name dialog box, type **Domain Isolation** as the name for the new rule and then click **Finish**.
9. Verify that the new rule appears in the WFAS console Connection Security Rules pane.
10. Leave WFAS open for the next activity.

Activity 10-13: Creating an IPSec Policy for Server-to-Server Communications

Time Required: 15 minutes

Objective: Use IPSec to secure communication between two hosts.

Description: Another common connection rule is setting up secure communication between two computers, such as a Web server and a database server hosting the Web server's data to prevent data sniffing. As part of your security deployment, you want to ensure that all authentication and data passed between computers in your domain is secured. In this activity, you will create a connection security rule on MSN-SRV-0XX that requires all inbound and outbound traffic to be authenticated.

1. In the Windows Firewall with Advanced Security console, click **Connection Security Rules** and then click **New Rule** under Actions.

2. In the Rule Type dialog box, click **Server-to-server** and then click **Next**.

3. In the Endpoints dialog box, click **These IP addresses** under Which computers are in Endpoint 1? and then click **Add**.

4. In the IP Address dialog box, type **192.168.100.0/24** in the text box and then click **OK**.

5. Click **These IP addresses** under for Which computers are in Endpoint 2? and then click **Add**.

6. In the IP Address dialog box, type **192.168.100.0/24** in the text box and then click **OK**.

7. Click **Next**.

8. In the Requirements dialog box, choose **Require authentication for inbound and outbound connections** and then click **Next**.

9. In the Authentication Method dialog box, click **Advanced** and then click **Customize**.

10. In the First authentication portion of the dialog box, click **Add**, click **Computer (Kerberos V5)**, and then click **OK**.

11. Click **OK** again and then click **Next** in the Authentication Method dialog box.

12. In the Profile dialog box, accept the default selections by clicking **Next**.

13. In the Name dialog box, type **Client to Client Security** as the name for the new rule and click **Finish**.

14. Verify that the new rule appears in the WFAS console Connection Security Rules pane.

Network Authentication in Windows Server 2008

Securing network authentications is another important task in Windows Server 2008. On Windows networks with Active Directory domains, Windows Server 2008 uses Kerberos as its default authentication method in Active Directory domains. However, there may be occasions where Kerberos cannot be used such as in workgroup environments or when connections are initiated through the use of an IP address as opposed to a host name. In these cases, you need to use a NT LAN Manager (NTLM) protocol. Windows Server 2008 supports the following authentication protocols to some degree:

- *LAN Manager authentication*—Available since Windows 95 and Windows NT, this is the weakest type of the NTLM authentication and is rarely used in modern networks.

- *NTLM version 1 authentication*—This authentication protocol was introduced in Windows NT 3.51 to provide an improvement in authentication from LAN Manager.

- *NTLM version 2 authentication*—This is the most current and secure of the NTLM authentication protocols. First introduced in Windows NT 4.0 SP4, it is the replacement for NTLM version 1. It is the default NTLM authentication option in Windows Server 2008.

Administrators usually use Group Policy to manage NTLM settings in Windows Server 2008. In domain environments, NTLM settings can be delivered using a Group Policy object applied in Active Directory. For workgroup computers or stand-alone domain computers, Local Group Policy objects can be used.

All forms of NTLM use the **challenge-response protocol**. Challenge-response protocol scenarios involve a server sending a challenge question to the client. The client must provide a correct and valid response to have their logon request authenticated.

Introduction to Network Access Protection

In Windows Server 2008, Network Access Protection (NAP) provides a framework for administrators to block external and internal network threats. NAP works by measuring network client configurations and settings against a set of specified health requirements, or policies. If clients do not meet the network health standards, such as out-of-date antivirus or missing security updates, the client will be prevented from accessing the network. NAP can be broken into three parts:

- *Health policy validation*—This process involves a health examination of clients attempting to access the network. Network policies created by administrators are used for this examination. Common policies include minimum levels of antivirus, OS updates, and more.

- *Health policy compliance*—This process provides mechanisms that allow clients to become "compliant" by updating their antivirus or applying need updates.

- *Access limitation*—This process allows administrators to limit or deny clients access to network resources depending on their compliance with defined health policies.

NAP Terminology

Before you use NAP, it is important to gain an understanding of the terms used by NAP processes in Windows Server 2008. The following is a list of helpful NAP terms:

- Enforcement Client
- Enforcement Server
- Host Credential Authorization Protocol
- Health Registration Authority
- Network Policy Server
- Remediation Server
- System Health Agent
- System Health Validator

Enforcement Client   In order to use NAP policies, a client needs be a part of the NAP infrastructure on a network. This requires that the client support NAP. Currently, Windows Server 2008, Windows Vista, and Windows XP SP3 can act as an Enforcement Client because the System Health Agent is included in the OSs.

Enforcement Server   NAP is managed by an Enforcement Server (ES) responsible for maintaining and enforcing NAP policies on the network. In Windows Server 2008, the Network Policy Server (NPS) role acts as an ES, which is one of two roles making up the NPS role.

Host Credential Authorization Protocol   An industry-standard protocol, Host Credential Authorization Protocol allows Windows Server 2008 servers running NAP to work with a Cisco Network Admission Control server. This is used primarily with 802.1x clients because the NPS role can authorize Cisco 802.1x clients and enforce the network NAP policies against those clients.

The use and implementation of Cisco NAC servers is outside the scope of this textbook. For more information on Cisco and NAC, visit *www.cisco.com* and search for "Network Admission Control."

Health Registration Authority   At the core of NAP's IPSec enforcement services, the Health Registration Authority (HRA) distributes health certificates to NAP clients that comply with network health requirements. The health certificate allows a NAP client to take part in intranet communication protected by IPSec. The HRA is used as well when deploying domain and server isolation with Group Policy.

Network Policy Server   The Network Policy Server (NPS) is responsible for managing the network health and connectivity policies on a network. Administrators use the NPS console to create new health policies, manage existing policies, and work with network connections such as virtual private network (VPN) connections. On a Windows Server 2008 network, NPS acts both as a RADIUS server for authorization and authentication of NAP clients and as the NAP Health Policy Server that manages NAP policy.

Remediation Server   Part of the benefit of implementing NAP is keeping "unhealthy" computers off your network. However, you might want to provide a means for legitimate clients to update themselves so that they can access the network safely. This is the role that Remediation Servers play. Remediation Servers work with a client so that it can update itself and make its health policy compliant again. Antivirus and Windows Software Update Services are two of the common types of remediation servers you can provide in a restricted network.

System Health Agent   All clients participating in NAP require a mechanism for checking their compliance levels against the NAP policies and providing information about each client to the network's NPS. This mechanism is called System Health Agent (SHA). In Server 2008, Windows Vista, and Windows XP SP3, the SHA is known as the Windows System Health Validator (WSHV). WSHV runs as a local service. Along with communication with the network's NPS, the WSHV monitors the Windows Security Center for changes to items such as the Windows Firewall and antivirus status.

System Health Validator   The System Health Validator (SHV) is the server-based partner of the client-based SHA. The SHV works with the SHA to process client information and enforce NAP policies. Although it is a part of the Windows Server 2008 implementation of NAP, Microsoft's implementation is based on open standards, allowing integration with other NAP products.

NAP Enforcement Methods

The NPS role and NAP in Windows Server 2008 are responsible for managing network access through enforcement policies defined by administrators. Windows Server 2008 uses NAP enforcement methods to manage network access and communications. The following are the five types of NAP enforcement methods used by NAP:

- *802.1x-authenticated connections*—This method works with the 802.1x access points and switches on a network to enforce client health compliance and restrict network access for noncompliant devices.

- *Dynamic Host Configuration Protocol (DHCP) address configurations*—This method allows you to restrict network access based on the health compliance of DHCP clients. Noncompliant clients are given a DHCP configuration that limits their network access until they reach health compliance.

- *IPSec communications*—This method enforces network access by leveraging IPSec. With the use of IPSec, administrators can define health requirements for protected communications based on IP address or TCP/UDP port numbers. This allows compliant computers to be isolated from noncompliant computers on the same network.

- *Terminal Services Gateway (TS Gateway) connections*—This method allows you to restrict the network access of TS Gateway clients. New in Windows Server 2008, TS Gateway provides secure access to internal network resources by authorized users from Internet-connected Terminal Services clients.

- *Virtual Private Network (VPN) connections*—This enforcement method allows you to restrict network access based on the health compliance of computers access network resources via VPN. NAP restricts access by applying IP packet filters to the VPN connection. Noncompliant computers are restricted until they become compliant. This method also monitors the connection to ensure that the connected computer maintains compliance.

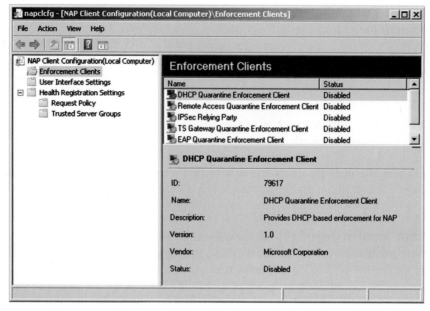

Figure 10-26   NAP Client Configuration console

By default, all the preceding methods are disabled when you install the NPS and NAP. To enable one or more of the enforcement methods, you need to access the NAP Client Configuration console and then modify the enforcement clients, as shown in Figure 10-26.

Implementing NAP

NAP was designed by Microsoft to allow you to customize it to meet the unique needs of your networks. This means that implementing and configuring NAP differs from network to network based on requirements and policies. The basic network diagram in Figure 10-27 shows how the components of NAP can be deployed to meet the following requirements:

- Health state validation
- Health Policy compliance
- Restricted network access for noncompliant computers
- Remediation for noncompliant servers
- IPSec enforcement
- 802.1x enforcement
- DHCP enforcement
- VPN enforcement

Installing NAP

NAP is part of the NPS role. To install the NAP components, you need to add the NPS role either through the Role Services Wizard or from the command line using servermanagercmd.exe.

Activity 10-14: Installing and Configuring NAP

Time Required: 10 minutes

Objective: Install NAP and configure a NAP policy.

Description: As part of your security deployment, you want to employ NAP. In this activity, you will configure NAP and the WSHV properties.

1. Open the Network Policy Server console.

2. On the Getting Started page, click **Configure NAP**.

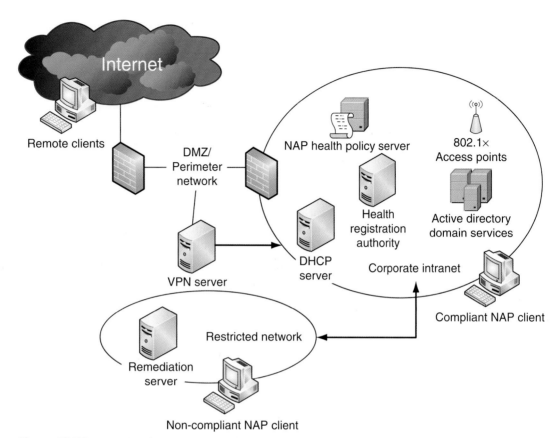

Figure 10-27   Example of NAP deployment

3. In the Select Network Connection Method For Use with NAP dialog box, choose **Dynamic Host Configuration Protocol (DHCP)** from the drop-down menu and then click **Next**.

4. Click **Next** four times until you reach the Define NAP Health Policy screen. Review the default settings, click **Next,** and then click **Finish**.

5. In the NPS console, expand **Network Access Protection** and then click **System Health Validators**.

6. Open the Actions pane, if necessary. Click **Windows Security Health Validator** in the middle pane, and then under Actions, click **Properties**.

7. In the Windows Security Health Validator Properties dialog box, click **Configure**.

8. In the Windows Security Health Validator dialog box, uncheck **Virus Protection**, **Spyware Protection**, and **Automatic updating is enabled** and then click **OK**. Click **OK** in the Windows Security Health Validator Properties dialog box to close it.

9. Open the DHCP console, expand **msn-srv-0XX.bentech.local**, and then click **IPv4**.

10. In the Actions pane, click **More Actions** and then click **Properties**.

11. In the IPv4 Properties dialog box, click the **Network Access Protection** tab, click **Enable on all scopes**, and then click **Yes** in the message box.

12. Click **OK** to close the Properties dialog box. Close the open windows and log off both servers.

Chapter Summary

- The SCW guides you through the steps of hardening your network servers. By analyzing the baseline computer, SCW can determine the roles and features that are installed. It compares these findings to a database of settings to determine what changes can be made to harden the server's security without compromising functionality. You can then choose to create a new security policy, modify an existing policy, apply an existing policy, or revert to a previous version of a policy.

- The Windows Firewall provides inbound and outbound traffic enforcement through the Windows Firewall and WFAS consoles. Windows Firewall allows you to create exceptions for inbound traffic. Exceptions can be a specific program or a specific port that needs to be accessible by inbound traffic. WFAS provides a more robust interface for managing the firewall policies in detail.

- EFS is Microsoft's built-in service for providing folder- and file-level encryption. EFS uses public key encryption for securing a user's data, meaning that a user has a public key that is available to everyone and a private key that is only known to the user. Using the user's certificate, EFS encryption is performed with the user's public key. Their private key is required for subsequent access to the document.

- BitLocker provides hard drive–based encryption of servers. While EFS provides file- and folder-level encryption, BitLocker encrypts the entire Windows system volume of a computer running Windows Server 2008. BitLocker supports four different authentication modes. Three modes are based on systems with a TPM chip, and one mode is without a TPM chip.

- At startup, BitLocker performs a system integrity authentication prior to booting into the OS. If BitLocker determines that conditions represent a security risk, the drive is locked down. These changes can include hardware changes such as moving a drive to a new computer, modifying any startup files, or changing the BIOS. The locked drive requires the user to enter the BitLocker recovery password.

- MBSA scans single or multiple computers on a network and lets you view existing security scan reports. Scans can be stored or printed for immediately review or filing. To use the MBSA, you must have Internet connectivity because MBSA needs access to the Microsoft Windows Update Servers to create the baseline against which computers are measured.

- IPSec is an open-standards framework for securing network communications and works at the network layer of the OSI model. Unlike other security protocols, such as SSL and SSH, which work at higher layers, IPSec can protect Transport layer protocols such as TCP and UDP. Applications in higher layers do not need to be designed to work with IPSec because it is transparent to them.

- On Windows networks, Windows Server 2008 uses Kerberos as its default authentication method in Active Directory domains. However, when Kerberos cannot be used, such as in work group environments or when connections are initiated through the use of an IP address as opposed to a host name, you need to use a NT LAN Manager, or NTLM, protocol.

- To use NAP policies, a client must be a part of the NAP infrastructure on a network. Currently, Windows Server 2008, Windows Vista, and Windows XP SP3 can act as an EC to verify that the client supports NAP. NAP is managed by ESs responsible for maintaining and enforcing NAP policies on the network. In Windows Server 2008, the NPS role acts as an ES.

- The HRA distributes health certificates to NAP clients that comply with network health requirements. The NPS is responsible for managing the network health and connectivity policies on a network. In addition, all clients participating in NAP use SHA to check its compliance level against the NAP policies and providing information about the client to the network's NPS.

- Configuring NAP differs from network to network based on requirements and policies. NAP is part of the NPS. Before installing the NAP components, add the NPS role using the Role Services Wizard or from the command line using servermanagercmd.exe.

Key Terms

BitLocker   A security method that provides hard drive–based encryption of servers. While Encrypting File Service (EFS) provides file- and folder-level encryption, BitLocker encrypts the entire Windows system volume of a computer running Windows Server 2008.

challenge-response protocol   A protocol used in scenarios involving a server sending a challenge question to the client. The client must provide a correct and valid response before their logon request is authenticated.

enhanced security mode   Using BitLocker with a Trusted Protection Module (TPM) and a personal identification number (PIN) or a Universal Serial Bus (USB) flash drive.

exception   An instruction to open a port briefly, allow a program or service to pass information, and then close the port. Normally, the firewall blocks all unsolicited attempts to send information.

Internet Key Exchange (IKE)   A way to negotiate security protocols each Internet Protocol Security (IPSec) peer will use for communicating and constructing data transactions. IKE generates the encryption and authentication keys used by IPSec for the transaction.

multifactor authentication   Authentication that requires two or more different authentication pieces.

public key (asymmetric) encryption   A security method for securing a user's data that provides a public key to everyone and a private key only to the user. The public key is always used to provide the encryption of files, while the private key is required for decrypting files.

rule   A way to manage communications by checking to see if they meet certain conditions and deciding what to do with them based on those conditions.

symmetric encryption   A security method for securing a user's data that provides a single key to a user.

transport mode   An IPSec mode that provides end-to-end security between devices or hosts such as for Layer 2 Tunneling Protocol (L2TP) virtual private network (VPN) solutions for remote access. Transport mode encrypts only the data portion, or the payload, of each packet.

tunnel mode   An IPSec mode that provides secure communications between two networks through a single node. More secure than transport mode, tunnel mode encrypts both the header and the payload.

Review Questions

1. Which one of the following tools allows administrators to create and manage security profiles?

   a. NAP

   b. SCW

   c. MBSA

   d. NPS

   e. Security Templates console

2. Which tool allows administrators to view security and update information for multiple network machines?

   a. NAP

   b. SCW

   c. MBSA

   d. NPS

3. Which of the following tasks cannot be performed with the SCW?

   a. Securing roles and features

   b. Encrypting folders and files

   c. Disabling unneeded services

   d. Configuring auditing policies

4. You can configure MBSA to install all missing Windows security updates. True or False?

5. Which of these features of Windows Server 2008 allows you to encrypt the entire system volume on a hard drive?

   a. EFS

   b. IPSec

   c. BitLocker

   d. NTFS encryption

6. The _____ is used to access an EFS-encrypted file.

7. What type of network profile would be applied to a workgroup server on a network protected from the Internet by a firewall?

   a. Public

   b. Workgroup

   c. Private

   d. Domain

8. Which of the following tools can be used for managing IPSec policies?

   a. Network Monitor

   b. Windows Firewall

   c. Windows Firewall with Advanced Security

   d. Netsh.exe

   e. Ipsecmgt.exe

9. Which of the following is *not* a threat mitigated by IPSec?

   a. Data tampering

   b. Social engineering

   c. Network traffic sniffing

   d. Identity spoofing

10. Transport mode is used to set up VPN connections for remote access clients in Windows Server 2008. True or False?

11. McClantz, Inc., a small publishing company, needs to install client to client IPSec to secure communications between a Web server and a database server. The network is running AD DS without a PKI infrastructure. They are running Windows Server 2008 and do not want to have to purchase additional hardware or software to implement their solution. What is the recommended authentication method this implementation?

   a. Preshared key

   b. Third-party digital certificate

   c. Kerberos version 5

   d. NTLMv2 authentication

12. Which of the following commands will encrypt the folder f:\Shared\SecureData?

    a. Cipher.exe /E SecureData

    b. Cipher.exe /E f:\Shared\SecureData

    c. EFS.exe /E f:\Shared\SecureData

    d. Cipher.exe /D f:\Shared\SecureData

13. Which of the following cannot be enforced by NAP?

    a. DHCP address configuration

    b. IPSec communications

    c. EFS file encryption

    d. VPN client health compliance

14. You have a small workgroup environment with two servers, SRV1 and SRV2. SRV1 is a Web server hosting a financial application for your users. SRV2 is a database server used to store the financial application's data. Both servers have digital certificates issued by Thawte. You need to use IPSec to secure the communication between SRV1 and SRV2. However, you want to use only components that are built into Windows Server 2008. Which of the following actions will make up part of the solution? (Choose the two best answers.)

    a. Create a transport mode IPSec policy in Routing and Remote Access

    b. Choose Kerberos version 5 for Phase 1 authentication

    c. Create a server-to-server policy in WFAS

    d. Choose digital certificates for Phase 1 authentication

    e. Choose preshared keys for Phase 1 authentication

15. AH security services is the preferred method for securing IPSec traffic, as it provides encryption of a data packet's payload. True or False?

16. Which of the following are supported by default in Windows Server 2008? (Choose the two best answers.)

    a. ESP

    b. NTLMv1 authentication

    c. AH

    d. NTLMv2 authentication

    e. LAN Manager authentication

17. In a NAP environment, a centralized antivirus server would be an example of a(n) _____.

18. By default, which policy will IPSec use for authentication?

    a. Digital certificates

    b. Preshared keys

    c. Kerberos version 5

    d. NTLM v2

19. _____ mode is used when implementing IPSec between two gateways.

20. At which layer of the OSI model is IPSec implemented?

    a. Physical

    b. Data Link

    c. Network

    d. Transport

    e. Implementation

    f. Application

Case Projects

Case Project 10-1: Securing FTP Traffic with IPSec

You need to secure all FTP traffic to your FTP server from Windows Server 2008 and Windows Vista clients on your internal network. You do not have a Public Key Infrastructure (PKI) or access to third-party certificates. You plan to use IPSec to complete this task. What steps would you take to implement this solution for clients?

Case Project 10-2: Creating a Windows Firewall Policy

After spending time custom-configuring your network servers, you have decided you would like to create a base firewall policy that applies to all your member servers in an Active Directory environment. List the process you would use to create a base firewall policy and apply it within your organization, or complete the process on a Windows Server 2008 computer.

Case Project 10-3: Network Security Recommendations

You've been asked by a local company, B.R. Hunter, LLC, to help improve their network security. They are currently running a Windows Server 2008 network with Active Directory. They have a desktop financial application that communicates with an application and database server, both Windows Server 2008, on the network. They use both desktop and mobile notebook computers. All configurations are default. No customizations have been performed beyond installing roles and features. Name and discuss at least four recommendations for increasing the security of their environment. Discuss why you believe your choices are particularly important.

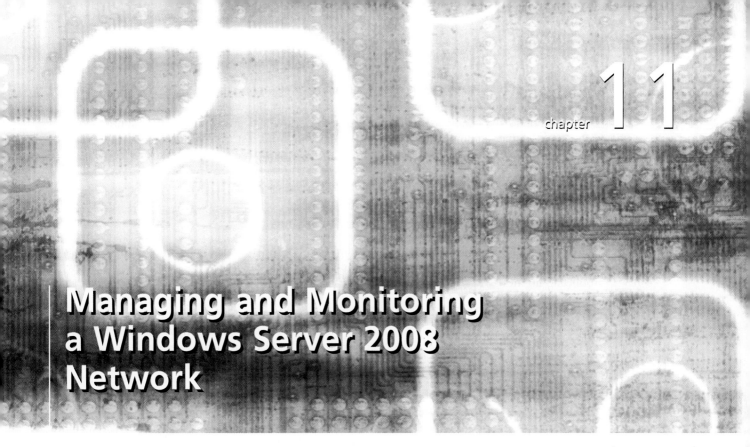

Managing and Monitoring a Windows Server 2008 Network

After reading this chapter and completing the exercises, you will be able to:

• Use management consoles to maintain Windows Server 2008

• Update and maintain your clients using Windows Server Update Service

• Monitor Windows Server 2008 using built-in and downloadable utilities

• Perform backup and restore tasks with Windows Server 2008

404 Chapter 11 Managing and Monitoring a Windows Server 2008 Network

As an administrator, much of your day-to-day activities will revolve around managing and monitoring the servers on your networks. Windows Server 2008 has a number of built-in and downloadable tools and utilities that can help streamline your administrative processes. Another common activity is applying updates and restoring files.

In this chapter, you will explore a number of tools used to manage Windows Server 2008, including Server Manager and custom management consoles, and use Windows Server Update Services 3.0 to keep Windows Server 2008 up to date.

Managing Windows Server 2008

With the introduction of Windows Server 2008, you have an arsenal of new and improved tools for managing your Windows network. In this section, you will learn about a number of new tools and utilities.

Microsoft Management Consoles

Windows Server 2008 takes full advantage of the new **Microsoft Management Console (MMC) 3.0 framework**. MMC 3.0 is an improved version of the MMC that has been used in past versions of Windows Server. Improvements to MMC 3.0 include the Action pane at the right of the console. The Action pane lists the available actions a user can perform based on the currently selected item in the console tree or results pane, as shown in Figure 11-1.

The MMC provides a framework for tools, referred to as snap-ins, to add to the console. Depending on how you use the snap-in console and your network needs, you can customize the MMC to provide a robust set of administrative tools. Many of the snap-ins allow you to manage remote computers and the local computer on which they reside.

Building Custom MMCs To suit your particular needs and streamline maintenance tasks, you can set up a custom snap-in console. For example, you can create a custom snap-in console for the following reasons:

- Centralize tools you use on a regular basis

- Provide access to users that need to use specific snap-ins to perform their jobs

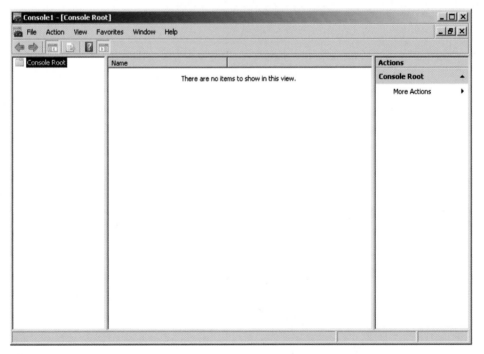

Figure 11-1 MMC 3.0 snap-in console

You create snap-in consoles through the MMC 3.0, which you can start from the command line or the Start Search box on the Start menu box. The initial MMC 3.0 snap-in console is shown in Figure 11-1.

You add snap-ins to the empty console as necessary using the Add/Remove Snap-in command on the File menu (or by pressing the shortcut key combination Ctrl+M). You can then use the Add or Remove Snap-ins window, shown in Figure 11-2, to select and add snap-ins.

This window lists the available snap-ins in the left pane, such as the Active Directory Users and Computers snap-in, which you use to simplify directory service administration, and the Computer Management snap-in, which provides tools for managing your system, storage devices, and services and applications.

Activity 11-1: Creating a Custom MMC Console

Time Required: 15 minutes

Objective: Work with snap-ins and the MMC console.

Description: You find that you spend a lot of time moving between multiple administrative consoles on a daily basis, so you decide to create your own. You want a console that gives you access to Active Directory, Domain Name System (DNS), Dynamic Host Configuration Protocol (DHCP), and Computer Management. In this activity, you create a custom MMC console.

 MSN-SRV-1XX will need to have its Firewall rules modified in order to complete this and future activivities. Enter the following command through the command prompt on MSN-SRV-1XX:

```
Netsh advfirewall firewall set rule group="remote
            administration" new enable=yes
```

1. Log onto MSN-SRV-0XX.
2. In the Start Search box on the Start menu, type **MMC.exe** and then press **Enter** to open the MMC console.
3. In the MMC console, click **File** on the menu bar and then click **Add/Remove Snap-in** to open the Add or Remove Snap-ins window.
4. In the Available snap-ins pane, click **Active Directory Users and Computers** and then click the **Add** button.
5. Click **Computer Management** on the left and then click the **Add** button.
6. In the Computer Management window, click **Finish** to select the default of managing the local computer.
7. Click **DNS** on the left and then click the **Add** button.

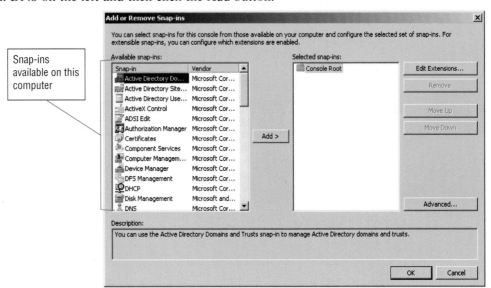

Figure 11-2 Add or Remove Snap-ins window

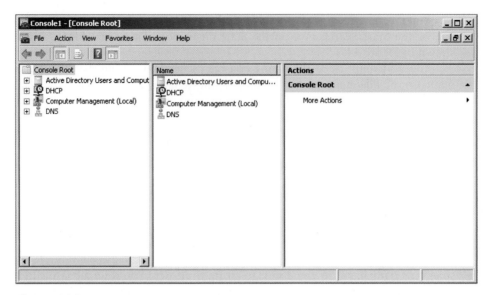

Figure 11-3   Custom MMC console with added snap-ins

8. Click **DHCP** on the left and then click the **Add** button.

9. Click **OK** to close the Add or Remove Snap-ins window. The MMC console now contains the four snap-ins you added, as shown in Figure 11-3.

10. In the MMC console, click **Computer Management** in the left pane, click **More Actions** in the right pane, and then click **Connect to another computer**.

11. In the Select Computer window, type **msn-srv-1xx.bentech.local** and click **OK**. Now your Computer Management snap-in will access the information on MSN-SRV-1XX.

12. In the MMC console, click **File** on the menu bar and then click **Save**.

13. In the Save As dialog box, type **Administrator Console** as the file name and then click **Save**.

14. Close the MMC console. If a message appears asking if you want to save the console settings, click **Yes**.

15. In the Start Search box on the Start menu, type **Administrator Console**. The Administrator Console you just created is listed on the Start menu.

16. Click **Administrator Console** to open the console.

All the built-in snap-in consoles and other tools are available from the Start menu, the graphical user interface (GUI), the command line, and the Run dialog box. Table 11-1 lists common commands that can be run from the Start Search box, the Run dialog box, and the command prompt.

Server Manager Console

Throughout this book, you have used Server Manager for managing and administering Windows Server 2008. Besides accessing roles and features installed on a computer, Server Manager lets you manage components in the following five sections:

- Roles
- Features
- Diagnostics
- Configuration
- Storage

Roles   The Roles section of Server Manager provides a single source of management for your installed roles. All snap-in consoles for currently installed roles are available in the Roles section.

Table 11-1 Shortcut commands for common Windows Server 2008 tools

Shortcut Command	Description of Tool
Appwiz.cpl	Add/Remove Programs
Compmgmt.msc	Computer Management
Control.exe	Control Panel
Dcomcnfg.exe	Component Services
Desk.cpl	Display Properties
Devmgmt.msc	Device Manager
Dnsmgmt.msc	DNS Management
Dsa.msc	ADUC (AD Users and Computers)
Eventvwr.msc	Event Viewer
Findfast.cpl	FindFast
Firewall.cpl	Firewall applet
Fsmgmt.msc	File Sharing Management
Gpedit.msc	Local Policy
Gpmc.msc	Group Policy Management Console
Napclcfg.msc	Network Access Protection Client Configuration
Ncpa.cpl	Network Properties
Pasword.cpl	Password Properties
Printers.cpl	Printers Folder
Secpol.msc	Local Security Policy
Servermanager.msc	Server Manager
Services.msc	Services
Sysdm.cpl	System Properties
Taskmgr.exe	Task Manager
Timedate.cpl	Date/Time Properties
Wbadmin.msc	Windows Server Backup
Wf.msc	Windows Firewall with Advanced Security

Along with access to snap-in consoles, a general summary of the installed roles is provided, as shown in Figure 11-4.

Each role summary includes the status of all the services and Event Viewer messages related to the role. Clicking the System Services link under Role Status provides you access to an expanded summary menu. This menu contains the following sections:

- *Events*—Provides access to all related events in the past 24 hours. You can also access the Event Viewer console from here.

- *System Services*—Displays the current status of all system services related to the role. You can start, stop, or restart any of the services from here. You can also check the status of all system services, manage the state of the services, and manage which services are monitored.

- *Role Services*—Displays the installed role services. You can also add and remove role services from this location.

- *Advanced Tools*—Includes all of the GUI and command-line tools an administrator would need to administer the role.

- *Resources and Support*—Provides access to recommended tasks, configurations, and online resources. Microsoft also provides you with best practices for the given role.

Features   Similar to the Roles section, the Features section provides you a single location for managing the installed features. All snap-in consoles for currently installed features will be

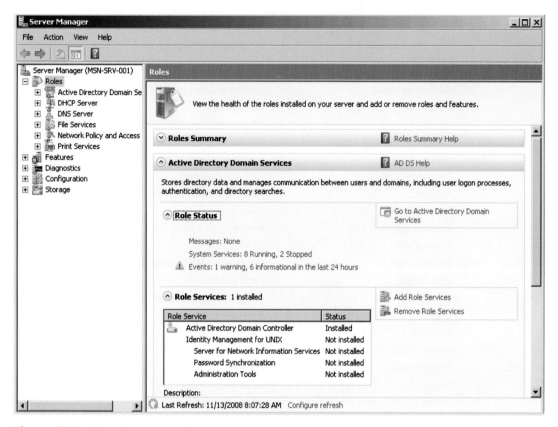

Figure 11-4 General summary of roles in Server Manager

available in this area. The Features summary section details all the installed features and gives you access to the Add Features or Remove Features wizards, as shown in Figure 11-5.

Diagnostics The Diagnostics section of Server Manager provides tools for monitoring and troubleshooting Windows Server 2008, including the following tools:

- *Event Viewer*—An MMC snap-in, this console enables you to browse and manage event logs. You will learn more about Event Viewer later in this chapter.
- *Reliability and Performance*—Allows you to collect real-time and logged data in regard to how programs affect your server's performance. You will learn more about Event Viewer later in this chapter.
- *Device Manager*—The central tool for managing installed hardware. From this console, you can add or update drivers, modify device settings, and troubleshoot device-specific issues.

Configuration The Configuration section provides access to consoles you use to configure background processes, such as scheduling tasks and managing system services. This section also lets you access the Windows Firewall for Advanced Security and the Windows Management Instrumentation Control console, as shown in Figure 11-6.

Storage The Storage section lists the tools necessary for managing disk storage and system backups, including the following consoles:

- *Windows Server Backup*—The Windows Server Backup console allows you to perform disk-to-disk system backups. You will learn more about Windows Server Backup later in this chapter.

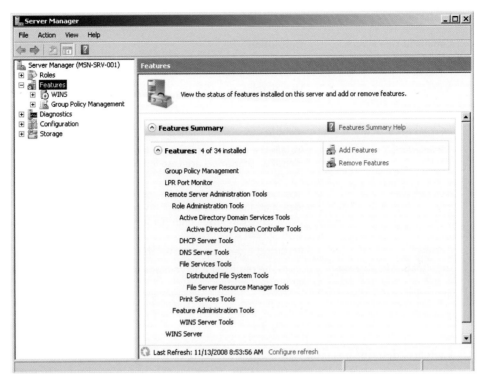

Figure 11-5   General summary of features in Server Manager

• *Disk Management*—This console provides access to the physical disk installed in a server. You can add new disks, manage existing physical disks, and manage logical volumes or partitions.

 Although Server Manager provides a single source for managing roles and features, the consoles in Server Manager do not always have the same capabilities as the stand-alone consoles.

Servermanagercmd.exe   Windows Server 2008 now lets you manage Server Manager from the command line. As you have learned throughout this book, **servermanagercmd.exe** provides a command-line utility so that you can perform automated installations or removals of roles, role services, and features. Table 11-2 lists the servermanagercmd.exe command-line

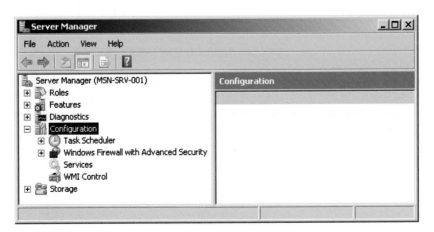

Figure 11-6   Configuration section of Server Manager

Table 11-2 Servermanagercmd.exe commands

Command-Line Switch	Description
-help or -?	Displays the help file for servermanagercmd.exe.
-query	Lists all roles, role services, and features installed and available for installation on the server, which is helpful in determining the Id variable when installing or removing components.
-version or –v	Identifies the Server Manager version number.
-install *<Id>*	Installs the role, role service, or feature specified by the Id variable or identifier; identifiers are case insensitive and can be viewed using the -query switch.
-remove *<Id>*	Removes the role, role service, or feature specified by the Id variable or identifier; identifiers are case insensitive and can be viewed using the -query switch. You can install multiple roles, role services, and features by separating each Id with a space.
-restart	Restarts the server, such as for role installations that require a reboot.
-resultpath *filename.xml*	Saves the results of a servermanagercmd.exe operation to an xml-formatted file.

switches, descriptions, and syntax options. Note that servermanagercmd.exe is available only on Full versions of Windows Server 2008. Ocsetup.exe provides similar functionality on Server Core systems.

Activity 11-2: Using servermanagercmd.exe

Time Required: 15 minutes

Objective: Use servermanagercmd.exe command switches.

Description: You are adding the Fax Server role to MSN-SRV-1XX, and you want to use the command line for the task. You do not currently know the syntax for the Fax Server role. In addition, you need to remove the File Services Resource Manager from MSN-SRV-0XX. In this activity, you will use the various switches for servermanagercmd.exe to install a new role.

1. Log onto MSN-SRV-1XX.

2. Open a command prompt, and then enter the following command to view the current version of Server Manager installed:

    servermanagercmd.exe –version

3. Enter the following command to view the list of all available and installed roles and features:

    servermanagercmd.exe –query

4. Enter the following command to install the Fax Server role:

    servermanagercmd.exe –install Fax –resultpath "c:\70642\Chapter 11\Switches.xml"

5. Enter the following command to verify that the Fax Server role is listed as installed:

    servermanagercmd.exe –query

6. Browse to **c:\70642\Chapter 11** and double-click **Switches.xml**. This will launch the results of your role installation in Internet Explorer.

7. Review the installation results and then close Internet Explorer.

8. Close the command prompt.

9. Log off MSN-SRV-1XX and then log onto MSN-SRV-0XX.

10. Open the command prompt and enter the following command to remove the Internet Information Services (IIS) and automatically restart the machine:

```
servermanagercmd.exe -remove Web-WebServer -restart
```

Updating Windows Server 2008

As you work with Windows Server 2008, you need to update your system to correct security holes, improve existing functions, and fix discovered bugs. To do so, you use **Windows Update**, which is a suite of tools and services provided by Microsoft for applying updates to systems. In this section, you will learn about the following tools for keeping your systems up to date:

- Windows Update Service
- Windows Server Update Services 3.0

Windows Update

Every Windows Server 2008 computer comes installed with the Windows Update. Windows Update is responsible for managing the download and installation process of updates from Microsoft. Windows Update requires access to the Internet because it communicates with Microsoft's Windows Update servers on a regular basis.

Located in the Control Panel, you use Windows Update to perform the following tasks:

- Check for available updates
- Change settings concerning how Windows Update checks for available updates
- View the history of updates applied to a system
- Restore and install hidden updates
- Access the Installed Updates area to uninstall an update

As shown in Figure 11-7, Windows Update displays a message when updates are available. It also provides the most recent information, including the last check for updates, last installation of updates, and Windows Update settings you have set.

You typically use Windows Update when you have a small number of servers or you want to manually manage the updates on your servers. While it can be used in larger organizations, doing so can be a time-consuming task and can consume excessive wide area network (WAN) connection bandwidth when client and server systems all attempt to access Microsoft's servers.

Windows Server Update Services

Windows Server Update Services (WSUS) centralizes the updating tasks for client and server computers and allows you to relocate them from the WAN onto the local network. (The current version is 3.0 SP1.) With WSUS 3.0, you can effectively deliver approved updates to clients and remove updates that are outdated or have caused problems with clients. In this section, you learn about the types of WSUS and how to perform the following:

- Install WSUS 3.0
- Configure client WSUS settings
- Approve and deploy updates
- Troubleshoot WSUS

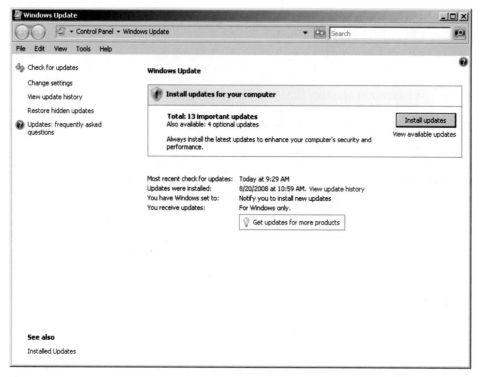

Figure 11-7   Windows Update window in Control Panel

Introducing WSUS   WSUS is a separate application you can install on Windows Server 2008. It provides a central administrative console for downloading the list of the latest updates from the Microsoft Update servers, approving updates to be deployed to network clients, and viewing reports on the status of your network clients. It can be used as a single server to provide update services to your network, or you can deploy multiple WSUS servers.

WSUS provides a number of benefits to business and organizations deploying it, including the following:

- Centralizes update management
- Minimizes effects on the WAN connection
- Improves network security and reliability
- Improves installation of relevant updates
- Targets updates to specific computers and computer groups
- Determines whether updates apply before installing them
- Updates clients automatically
- Provides more updates for Microsoft products in more categories
- Downloads updates from Microsoft Update by product and type

Installing WSUS 3.0 SP1   Before installing WSUS 3.0 SP1, you should verify that your system meets the following necessary system requirements:

- Microsoft Internet Information Services (IIS) 7.0.
- Microsoft Report Viewer Redistributable 2005, available as a free download from *www.microsoft.com/downloads*.
- Minimum of 6 GB of free space for storing downloaded updates. This is optional but highly recommended, as updates can take up a large amount of space, depending on your network clients.

- Minimum of 2 GB of free space on a New Technology File System (NTFS) drive for installing the Windows internal database unless a previously installed or external SQL database is being used.

- Internet connectivity and the ability to connect to *www.update.microsoft.com*.

Activity 11-3: Performing Preinstallation Tasks for WSUS

Time Required: 15 minutes

Objective: Prepare for the WSUS installation.

Description: You are planning to deploy WSUS on your network. To prepare for the installation, you need to install a necessary application. In this activity, you install Microsoft Report Viewer Redistributable 2005, IIS 7. You also need to update the Web Server (IIS) service so the new tools work properly.

1. Open a command prompt and enter the following command to create a directory:

```
md "c:\70642\chapter 11\WSUS"
```

2. On MSN-SRV-0XX, download **Microsoft Report Viewer Redistributable 2005** from *www. microsoft.com/downloads* and save it to **c:\70642\chapter 11\WSUS**.

3. Install **ReportViewer.exe** from c:\70642\chapter 11\WSUS and then click **Finish** when setup is complete.

4. Open Server Manager, select **Roles**, and then in the Roles pane, click **Add Roles**.

5. In the Add Roles Wizard, click **Server Roles**, select the **Web Server (IIS)** check box, and then click **Next**. If the Add features required for Web Server (IIS)? dialog box appears, click **Add Required Features**. Click **Next**.

6. Click **Next** in the Web Server (IIS) window.

7. In the Select Role Services window under Application Development, select **ASP.NET**. When a message appears about adding required role services, click **Add Required Role Services**.

8. In the Select Role Services window under Security, select **Windows Authentication**.

9. In the Select Role Services window under Management Tools, expand **IIS 6 Management Compatibility** and then select **IIS 6 Metabase Compatibility**. Click **Next**.

10. In the Confirm Installation Selections window, click **Install**.

11. In the Installation Results window, click **Close**.

12. Reboot MSN-SRV-0XX.

After installing the prerequisites for WSUS, you are ready to install WSUS 3.0. This is a free download from Microsoft and is not included with Windows Server 2008. WSUS 3.0 has a few requirements for installation, including the following:

- At least 6 GB of free space for storing downloaded updates
- At least 2 GB of free space on an NTFS drive for installing the Windows Internal Database used by WSUS

Activity 11-4: Installing WSUS

Time Required: 15 minutes

Objective: Install WSUS 3.0 SP1.

Description: You want to install WSUS 3.0 SP1 on MSN-SRV-0XX to centralize administration and deployment of updates for client computers. In this activity, you download and install WSUS 3.0 SP1.

1. On MSN-SRV-0XX, download **Windows Server Update Services 3.0 SP1** from *www. microsoft.com/downloads* and save it to **c:\70642\chapter 11\WSUS**.

11

2. Browse to **c:\70642\chapter 11\WSUS** and double-click **WSUSSetup_30SP1_x86** to begin the installation.

3. On the Welcome screen, click **Next**.

4. In the Installation Mode Selection dialog box, click **Next** to accept the default selection of a Full server installation including the Administration console.

5. In the License Agreement dialog box, click **I accept the terms of the license agreement** and then click **Next**.

6. Click **Next** in the Select Update Source dialog box to accept the default update storage location. If you receive a warning that you have less than the recommended 6 GB of space for storing updates, click **Yes** to continue.

7. In the Database Options dialog box, click **Next**.

8. In the Web Site Selection dialog box, click **Next**.

9. In the Ready to Install Windows Server Update Services 3.0 SP1 dialog box, review the configuration settings and then click **Next**.

10. Click **Finish** when setup is complete.

11. When the Before You Begin window opens, click **Cancel**. You will configure WSUS in the next activity.

Configuring WSUS   After installing WSUS, you need to configure it before you can use it regularly. You can configure WSUS by running the WSUS Server Configuration Wizard or by using the configuration components under Options in the Update Services console.

Activity 11-5: Configuring WSUS Using the WSUS Setup Wizard

Time Required: 20 minutes

Objective: Run the WSUS Setup Wizard.

Description: Before you can begin using WSUS, you need to configure it for your network. In your company, you are running only Windows Server 2008 and Windows Vista with Microsoft Office 2007. In this activity, you will use the WSUS Setup Wizard to configure WSUS.

1. On MSN-SRV-0XX, open the **Microsoft Windows Server Update Services 3.0 SP1** console from Administrative Tools on the Start menu.

2. In the Update Services console, expand **MSN-SRV-0XX** and then select **Options**.

3. In the Options pane, click **WSUS Server Configuration Wizard**.

4. In the Before You Begin window, click **Next**.

5. In the Join the Microsoft Update Improvement Program window, click **Next**.

6. In the Choose Upstream Server window, click **Next** to accept the default of synchronizing with Microsoft Update.

 If you were installing an additional WSUS server that received updates from a WSUS server on your network, this is where you specify the WSUS server internally providing update information.

7. In the Specify Proxy Server window, click **Next**.

8. In the Connect to Upstream Server window, click **Start Connecting**. This will provide the WSUS server with update information and requires access to the Internet. Connecting might take a few minutes, depending on your Internet connection.

9. Click **Next** when it becomes active.

10. Click **Download updates only in these languages**, choose **English** in the list of choices, and then click **Next**.

11. In the Choose Products window under Office, click the **Office2002/XP** and **Office 2003** boxes to remove the checkmarks.

12. In the Choose Products window, click the **Windows** box to remove the checkmark, click the **Windows Server 2008** and **Windows Vista** boxes to select them, and then click **Next**.

13. In the Classifications window, click **Next** to choose the default classes of updates.

14. In the Set Sync Schedule window, click **Next** to synchronize manually.

15. In the Finished window, click **Begin initial synchronization** and then click **Next**.

16. In the What's Next window, review the available steps and then click **Finish**.

17. Click **MSN-SRV-0XX** and wait for your server's Synchronization Status to be Idle.

18. Close the WSUS Administrative console.

Working with WSUS   The WSUS Administrative console provides you a single point for managing WSUS. You generate reports, manage updates, and monitor the computer through the console. The left pane in the Update Services console displays all the WSUS servers being administered through the console and the server's status, as shown in Figure 11-8.

When you select a server listed in the left pane, the right pane displays information about the status of the server along with a To Do list of recommended actions. See Figure 11-9.

Listed below each server in the left pane are sections responsible for different components of the WSUS server along with tools and configuration options, including the following sections:

- *Updates*—Provides information about all of the available Windows Updates. Individual sections within this area provide listings of specific updates, such as Critical Updates or Security Updates. From this area, you can find out more information about the update along with choosing whether to approve or decline a specific update, as shown in Figure 11-10.

- *Computers*—Provides information about all of the computers that are using WSUS for client updates. The computers can be placed into specific groupings, or computer groups,

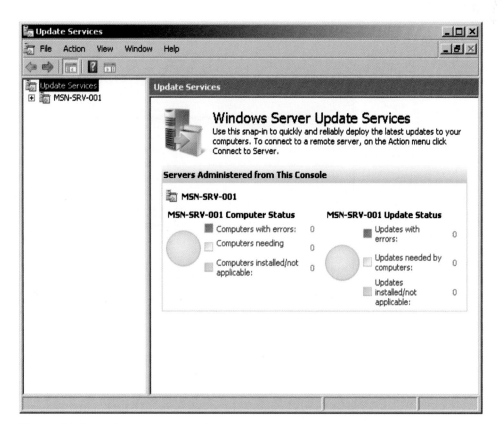

Figure 11-8   Update Services console

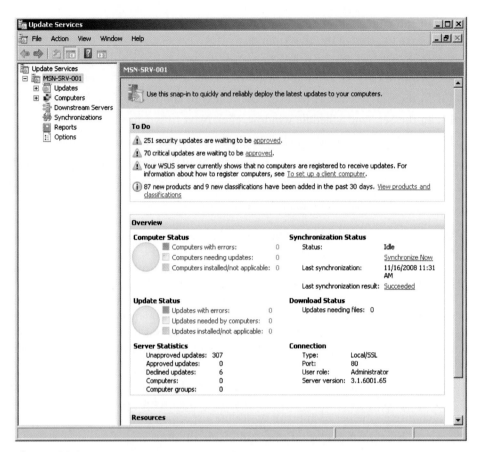

Figure 11-9   Server Status information in the Update Services console

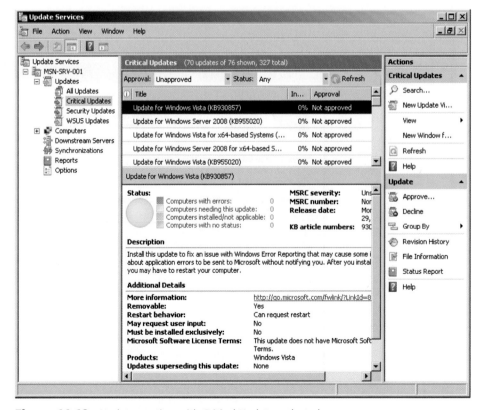

Figure 11-10   Updates section with Critical Updates selected

for more detailed update application. Computer groups allow administrators to group clients by type or function, such as Windows Servers, Windows XP desktops, and Windows Vista notebooks. Updates can be applied to one or more computer groups, depending on what the update applies to.

- *Downstream Servers*—Provides information about any downstream servers that are using a WSUS server, known as the upstream server, for update files, metadata, and approvals.

- *Synchronizations*—Provides information on all the synchronization attempts.

- *Reports*—Provides built-in reports that can be run at any time based on information gathered from the WSUS Server. Reports are broken into three groups, as shown in Figure 11-11: Update Reports, Computer Reports, and Synchronization Reports.

- *Options*—Includes additional server settings that you can configure. Along with configuration options, you can define cleanup settings and e-mail notifications here.

Activity 11-6: Working with the Update Services Console

Time Required: 15 minutes

Objective: Modify the configuration settings for WSUS.

Description: Since running the initial WSUS Setup Wizard, you have decided you need to create a computer group called Servers, add service packs to the Classification list of updates, and set all computers to determine computer group membership from group policy. In this activity, you will perform postinstallation configuration changes in the Update Services console.

1. Open the WSUS 3.0 SP1 Administrative console.

2. In the left pane, expand **MSN-SRV-0XX**, expand **Updates**, and then click **All Updates**.

3. In the All Updates pane, click the **Status** list arrow, click **Any** if necessary, and then click **Refresh** in the Actions pane to view the list of the current updates.

11

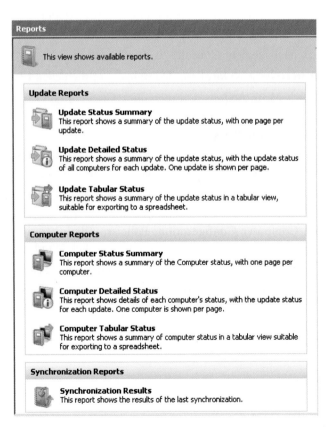

Figure 11-11   Available reports in the Update Services console

4. In the left pane, expand **Computers** and then click **All Computers**. No computers should be listed because they will be added in a later activity.

5. In the Actions pane, click **Add Computer Group**, enter **Servers** in the text box, and then click **Add**.

6. In the left pane, expand **All Computers** to display two computer groups: Unassigned Computers and Servers.

7. Click **Options** and then click **Products and Classifications** in the Options pane.

8. Click the **Classifications** tab, click the **Service Packs** check box, and then click **OK**.

9. Click the **Computers** option and change the setting to **Use Group Policy or registry settings on computers** and then click **OK**.

10. Click **Synchronizations** in the left pane and then click **Synchronize Now**. Wait for the synchronization to be completed.

11. Leave the Update Services console open.

Configuring Clients   After WSUS has been installed and configured in the WSUS console, your clients need to be configured to use the WSUS server for updates. This can be accomplished in two ways. The preferred method is through the use of Group Policy. An alternate method is to modify the Registry of a client machine. By default, the Group Policy Editor in Windows Server 2008 contains all the group policies necessary to configure WSUS clients.

Activity 11-7: Configuring Group Policy Settings for WSUS Clients

Time Required: 30 minutes

Objective: Using Group Policy to deploy WSUS client settings.

Description: You have decided you need to use Group Policy to deploy WSUS settings to your client computers. In this activity, you create a Group Policy object (GPO) and edit the WSUS-specific policies.

1. Open the Group Policy Management Console.

2. If necessary, expand **Forest: bentech.local** and **Domains**, and then click **bentech.local**.

3. In the Actions pane, click **More Actions** and then click **Create a GPO in this domain, and Link it here**.

4. In the New GPO window, type **WSUS Client settings** and then click **OK**.

5. Click **bentech.local** to view the linked GPOs and then click **WSUS Client settings** in the left pane. If a Group Policy Management console message box appears, click **OK**.

6. In the Actions pane, click **More Actions** and then click **Edit** to start the Group Policy Management Editor (GPME).

7. In the GPME, expand **Computer Configuration**, **Policies**, **Administrative Templates**, and then **Windows Components**. Under Windows Components, click **Windows Update**.

8. In the Settings pane, right-click **Configure Automatic Updates**, and then click **Properties**.

9. Click **Enabled**, click the **Configure automatic updating** list arrow, and then select **4 - Auto download and schedule the install**. Click **Next Setting**.

10. In the Specify intranet Microsoft update service location Properties dialog box, click **Enabled** and enter **http://MSN-SRV-0XX** in each text box, as shown in Figure 11-12, and then click **Next Setting**.

11. In the Automatic Updates detection frequency Properties dialog box, click **Enabled**, change the update interval to **1 hour**, and then click **Next Setting**.

12. Continue clicking **Next Setting** (seven times), reviewing each Properties dialog box, until you open the Enable client-side targeting Properties dialog box.

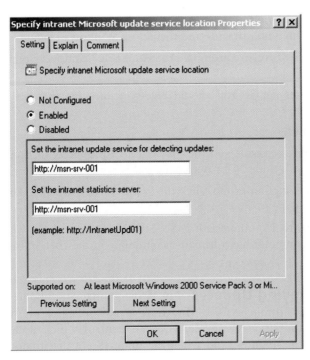

Figure 11-12 Specify intranet Microsoft update service location Properties dialog box

13. In the Enable client-side targeting Properties dialog box, click **Enabled**, enter **Servers** as the target group name, and then click **OK**.

14. Close the GPME and Group Policy Management Console.

After you have defined your WSUS settings, you can use the Update Services console to view the client computer. With GPOs, the computer applies the Group Policy settings, usually within 20 minutes. You can speed up the process by forcing Group Policy to apply to a computer using the following command:

```
gpupdate /force
```

After they are applied on the client, the updates should also be applied on Windows Server 2008. Older clients, such as Windows Server 2003 and Windows XP, might require a reboot to apply new computer configuration Group Policies. If a reboot is required, you will receive a message asking whether you would like to restart your computer.

Although you should not have to reboot Windows Server 2008 and Windows Vista to apply new Group Policy settings, rebooting can be a good idea to make sure the settings are applied properly.

Activity 11-8: Verifying Client Settings

Time Required: 30 minutes

Objective: Verify that client computers have the correct settings.

Description: Now that you have deployed your GPO, you need to verify that your client computers have the proper settings. In this activity, you verify that MSN-SRV-1XX has received the proper Group Policy settings and has contacted the WSUS server.

1. Log onto MSN-SRV-1XX.

2. Open the Control Panel, click **System and Maintenance**, and then click **Windows Update**.

3. In the Windows Update window, verify that the You receive updates setting is set to **Managed by your system administrator** and then close Windows Update.

4. Click **Check for updates**. If you are prompted to install new Windows Update software, click **Install Now**.

5. Click **Check for updates** again. You should receive a message that no new updates are available.

6. Log onto MSN-SRV-0XX.

7. Open the Update Services console and then browse to **Computers** section. Verify that you have two computers listed under All Computers and Servers, as shown in Figure 11-13.

8. Browse to the Servers computer group, click the **Status** list arrow, click **Any**, and then click **Refresh** in the Actions pane to view MSN-SRV-0XX.

9. Wait approximately 10 to 15 minutes for MSN-SRV-1XX to check in. Click **Refresh** every few minutes until the computer has a listed time and date in the Last Status Report column.

10. Review the information on MSN-SRV-1XX.

Approving and Deploying Updates
In WSUS, approving updates is probably the task you will perform most often because Microsoft usually releases many updates for its products. Using the Update Services console, you can control which updates are applied, which computers receive the updates, and when the updates are distributed. Depending on your needs, you can approve updates by selecting a computer listed under Computers or selecting an update listed under Updates. Both allow you to specify whether you want the updates to apply to All Computers, Unassigned Computers, or any computer groups you have created.

Activity 11-9: Approving Updates

Time Required: 30 minutes

Objective: Approve updates for clients.

Description: While reviewing the Update Services console, you notice that your servers need some Windows Server 2008 updates. Deploying the updates will require you to approve them. In this activity, you approve updates for WSUS.

1. On MSN-SRV-0XX, open the WSUS 3.0 SP1 Administrative console if necessary.

2. Expand **MSN-SRV-0XX**, click **Updates**, and then click **Critical Updates**.

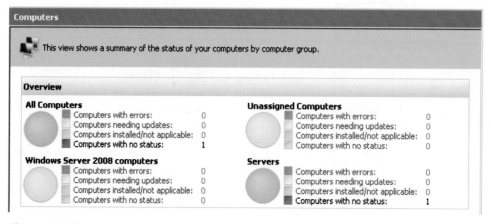

Figure 11-13   Computer groups in Update Services console

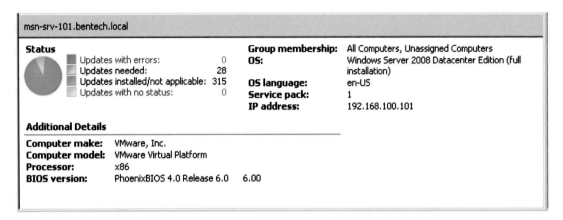

Figure 11-14   Update status window

3. Browse through the list of Critical Updates and select three for Windows Server 2008 that are not installed on either server. To determine the installation status, view the status of each update and look for Computers needing this update, as shown in Figure 11-14.

Hold down the Ctrl key while selecting updates to select multiple updates for approval.

4. Click **Approve** in the Actions pane.

5. In the Approve Updates window, click next to Servers, select **Approved for Install**, and then click **OK**.

6. When the Approval Progress window indicates the approvals are set up, click **Close**.

7. Browse to Windows Update in the Control Panel and then click **Check for updates**. You should have three updates available for installation.

8. Click **Install Updates** and wait for the updates to be installed.

9. If you are prompted to restart to finish the installation, click **Restart Now**. Otherwise, close Windows Update and log off MSN-SRV-1XX.

You also can decline updates through the Updates section of the Update Services console. By declining an update, you hide it from the default console view.

Microsoft Baseline Security Analyzer 2.1

Introduced in previous versions of Windows, the **Microsoft Baseline Security Analyzer (MBSA) 2.1** is an excellent tool for beginning to analyze your current security posture. Designed for small to medium-sized businesses, MBSA provides security recommendations from Microsoft and guidance for improving a computer's security posture. It does this by detecting missing security updates and common security holes. With the MBSA, you can analyze a local computer, remote computer, or groups of remote computers.

MBSA scans for the missing security updates for the following products:

- Windows 2000 SP4 and later operating systems and components
- Microsoft Office XP and later
- Microsoft Exchange Server 2000 and later
- Microsoft SQL Server 2000 SP4 and later

MBSA also looks for misconfigured security settings, including the following:

- Windows Firewall status
- Windows Updates status
- Weak passwords
- Accounts with nonexpiring passwords
- Excessive Administrative accounts
- Enabled Guest accounts

Table 11-3 provides a reference to current Microsoft products and how they are supported by MBSA 2.1.

 MBSA 2.1 is the most current version of this tool at the time of printing of this textbook. Updated versions may contain different functionality. Check *www.microsoft.com* for the latest version.

Working with MBSA
The MBSA is a free download from Microsoft and supported for use with multiple Microsoft operating systems, including the following:

- Windows Server 2008
- Windows Vista
- Windows Server 2003
- Windows XP
- Windows 2000 Service Pack 4

The current downloadable version of this text is MBSA 2.1. It is available in multiple languages and for x86 and x64 platforms.

Table 11-3   Microsoft Baseline Security Analyzer supported products list

Supported Product	Scan for Security Updates	Scan for Administrative Vulnerabilities
Windows 2000 Service Pack 4 and later	X	X
Microsoft Office XP and later	X	X
IIS 5.0 and above	X	X
Exchange Server 2000 and later	X	
SQL Server 7.0, 2000, 2005		X
Microsoft Office XP, 2000, 2003, 2007		X
All Windows components (such as IIS, Internet Explorer, MSXML, MDAC, Microsoft Virtual Machine, etc.)	X	
DirectX	X	
.NET Framework	X	
Windows Messenger	X	
FrontPage Server Extensions	X	
Windows Media Player	X	
Windows Script 5.1, 5.5, 5.6	X	
Outlook Express	X	
SQL Server 2000 SP4 and later	X	
64-bit Windows Operating Systems	X	x
Microsoft Windows XP Embedded (Remote Only)	X	

MBSA can be used on a local computer or to connect to one or more remote computers on your network. You have two options for running MBSA on remote computers: by domain name and by IP address range, as shown in Figure 11-15.

The domain name in Figure 11-15 needs to be specified as a NETBIOS name (such as bentech) instead of the DNS domain name of bentech.local. Another important consideration is that Windows Firewall can cause problems with fully scanning remote computers. In cases where a target computer is running a firewall, open TCP ports 135, 139, and 445 and UDP ports 137 and 138. This will allow MBSA to access, authenticate, and scan a remote machine. Group Policy is a viable option for deploying the firewall settings needed by MBSA to access clients.

Along with running MBSA through the GUI, you can use the command-line version of MBSA, mbsacli.exe. Mbsacli.exe provides the same benefits as the GUI tool and lets you script MBSA scans.

For example, you can perform a scan using the default MBSA settings by executing the following code from the command prompt:

mbsacli.exe

You can use mbsacli.exe with a number of switches. For example, you can check for security updates and patches on a target machine by executing the following code from the command prompt:

mbsacli.exe /target 192.168.100.10 /n os+iis+sql+password

Activity 11-10: Running MBSA from the Command Line

Time Required: 10 minutes

Objective: Use mbscli.exe to complete MBSA scans from the command line.

Description: You have just learned that MBSA can be run from the command line using mbsacli.exe, and you want to perform some basic tasks with the utility. In this activity, you use mbsacli.exe to scan the MSN-SRV-0XX computer.

1. On MSN-SRV-0XX, open the command prompt, type **cd \Program Files\Microsoft Baseline Security Analyzer 2** and then press **Enter** to change the location to MBSA installation directory.

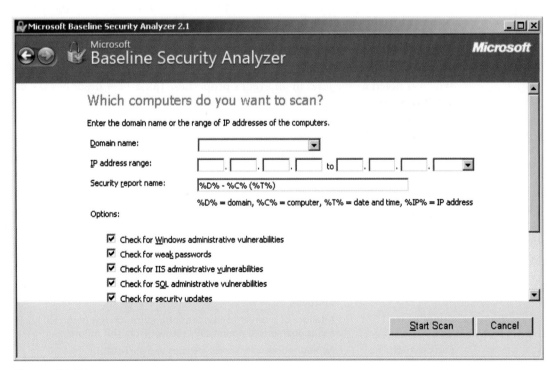

Figure 11-15   MBSA options

2. At the command prompt, type **mbsacli.exe** and then press **Enter** to run a default MBSA scan. This will take a couple of minutes to complete.

3. When the scan is complete, scroll the command window to review the results. You will see information such as missing updates and administrative vulnerabilities.

4. To view the results in a text file, type **Mbsacli.exe > "C:\70642\chapter 11\MBSAcli.txt"** at the command prompt and then press **Enter**. This will send the command output to a text file named MBSAcli.txt.

5. Use Windows Explorer to browse to c:\70642\chapter 11, and then open **MBSAcli.txt** using a text editor such as Notepad.

6. Review the contents of mbsacli.txt.

7. Close Windows Explorer and the command prompt.

Monitoring Windows Server 2008

After you deploy your Windows Server 2008 network, be proactive in managing your environment by using the tools and utilities available to monitor your systems. Your goal is to discover problems before they affect your users and your network. Windows Server 2008 provides a number of utilities for helping with this task. Those utilities include the following:

- Event Viewer
- Reliability and Performance Console
- Network Monitor
- Task Manager
- Disk Management

Working with Event Viewer

Event Viewer allows you to review and manage events for local and remote computers. Use the information provided by Event Viewer to troubleshoot computer problems and monitor the health of your servers.

Event Viewer Classifications   Each event in Event Viewer is classified by severity, which is noted as the level in an event's properties. Table 11-4 describes the classifications used by Event Viewer.

Table 11-4   Classifications used in Event Viewer

Classification	Description
Information	A change in an application or component has occurred.
Warning	A server event has occurred that is not significant but may cause future issues if not resolved.
Error	A significant server event has occurred that might affect current service or external functions.
Critical	A failure of a server component or application has occurred, known as a stop error, and is unable to automatically recover from this failure.
Success Audit	An audited security access attempt was successful.
Failure Audit	An audited security access attempt failed.

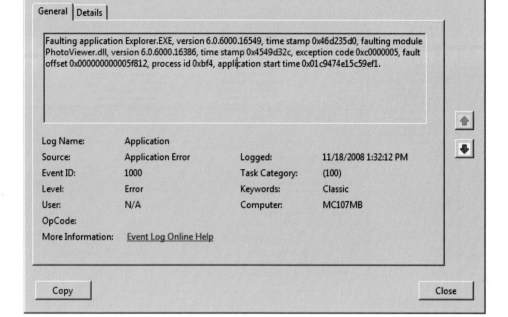

Figure 11-16 Sample Event Viewer message

The event classification along with the event details, as shown in Figure 11-16, will help you work toward resolving the related issue. The source of the event and the Event ID, a number assigned to the event, are useful information when researching an issue.

Event Viewer Console Event Viewer is organized into sections similar to other MMC consoles, as shown in Figure 11-17. Each section has its own purposes and functionality. As you work with Event Viewer, you will see the following sections:

- *Custom Views*—A new feature in Windows Server 2008, custom views allow you to create a custom event view based on the events that have been captured in the logs. The criteria for the view include all the event details and the period in which an event was logged. You can also specify multiple logs or sources to be used in your custom view. After you choose the filters for your custom view, the view is saved for current and future reference. When Windows Server 2008 is installed, a default custom view called Administrative Events is created. This view includes all of the Critical, Error, and Warning events that have occurred on the server. Event Viewer also creates a custom view for each role installed on the server. These are collected under a folder called Server Roles.

- *Windows Logs*—This is the view you are probably most familiar with. It is similar to the Event Viewer layout in Windows Server 2003 in that it contains the Application, Security, and System logs. New logs include Setup and forwarded Events logs. Each of these logs is described in Table 11-5.

- *Applications and Services Logs*—New in Windows Server 2008, this section stores event logs that are based on a single application or component running on the system. Logs available in the section may vary from server to server, depending on applications, roles, and features installed on a server. Internet Explorer, hardware events, and various Windows events are included, as shown in Figure 11-18.

- *Subscriptions*—Another new feature of Windows Server 2008 is the ability to gather event information from remote computers. This is known as creating an **event subscription**.

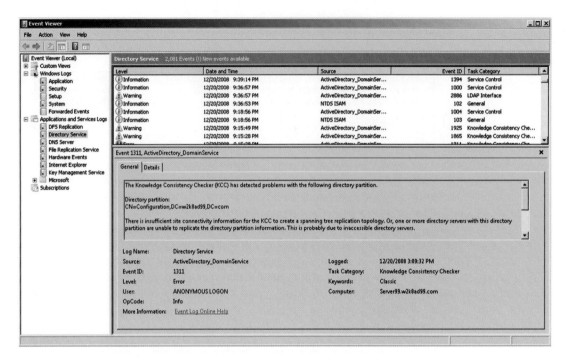

Figure 11-17   Event Viewer

With event subscriptions, you can centralize the event logs for network servers on a single server for easier reviewing and management of logs. Instead of connecting to multiple servers and reviewing logs, centralized logs allow for viewing multiple network servers in one location. They also mitigate the effect of network attacks where attackers delete server logs to hide their actions. Used with custom views, centralized logs will save you time gathering event information. Subscriptions are based on the Windows Event Collector Service.

Before working with any of the features that access remote data, you need to configure WinRM to run on each target machine, known as the source. **Windows Remote Management (WinRM)** is a command-line tool service in Windows that you use to configure a computer to accept WS-Management (Windows Remote Management) requests from other computers. You configure each machine using the WinRM quickconfig command at the command prompt. Because Windows Firewall blocks all traffic, including the traffic for remote management by

Table 11-5   Event logs in Windows Logs section of Event Viewer

Type of Log	Description
Application	Events logged by applications or programs. The developers of the application or program are responsible for determining these types of events.
Security	Events logged based on security auditing defined on the server.
Setup	Events logged and related to the setup of applications.
System	Events logged by system components. These types of events are predetermined by Windows.
Forwarded Events	Events collected from remote computers through an event subscription.

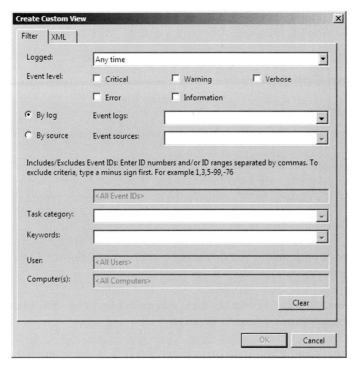

Figure 11-18 Filters available for creating Custom Views in Event Viewer

default, you need to create some exceptions on your firewall. The following exceptions allow you to collect remote event logs:

- *Remote Event Log Management*—Required for accessing remote event logs
- *Remote Service Management*—Required for event subscriptions

Activity 11-11: Preparing MSN-SRV-1XX for Remote Log Collection

Time Required: 5 minutes

Objective: Configure Windows Server 2008 Enterprise clients for remote logging and administration.

Description: To log events on MSN-SRV-1XX, you will need to make configuration changes by adding firewall exceptions and configuring WinRM. In this activity, you prepare the MSN-SRV-1XX server for remote log collection.

1. Log onto MSN-SRV-1XX.
2. Open Windows Firewall from the Control Panel.
3. Click the **Change settings** link in the Windows Firewall window.
4. In the Windows Firewall Settings dialog box, click the **Exceptions** tab.
5. On the Exceptions tab, select **Remote Service Management** and **Remote Event Log Management** and then click **OK**.
6. Open a command prompt, type **WINRM quickconfig** and then press **Enter**. When prompted, enter **Y** to complete the command.
7. Log off MSN-SRV-1XX.

To configure Server Core machines for remote log collection and management, you need to open up a firewall port to allow remote management along with configuring WinRM. Then you can connect from a Windows Server 2008 computer running the full version and access the server core machine's firewall rules remotely with a custom MMC console.

Activity 11-12: Preparing MSN-SC-0XX for Remote Log Collection

Time Required: 15 minutes

Objective: Configure Windows Server 2008 Server Core clients for remote logging and administration.

Description: To log events on a Server Core machine, you will need to make some configuration changes. After those are made, you need to access the Windows Firewall with Advance Security console remotely using a custom MMC console. In this activity, you prepare the MSN-SC-0XX server for remote log collection.

1. Log onto MSN-SC-0XX.

2. At the command prompt, enter the following command to open the firewall exception for Remote Management:

   ```
   netsh advfirewall set currentprofile settings
   remotemanagement enable
   ```

3. Type **WINRM quickconfig** and then press **Enter**. Enter **Y** when prompted to complete configuration of WinRM.

4. Log onto MSN-SRV-1XX.

5. Open the MMC console from the Start menu.

6. In the MMC console, click **File** on the menu bar and then click **Add/Remove Snap-in**.

7. On the Add or Remove Snap-ins window, click **Windows Firewall with Advanced Security** and then click **Add**.

8. In the Select Computer window, click **Another computer**, type **MSN-SC-0XX**, and then click **Finish**.

9. Click **OK**.

10. Expand the Windows Firewall with Advanced Security console and click **Inbound Rules**.

11. In the Rules pane, click each Remote Event Log Management rule (three in total) and then click **Enable Rule** in the Actions pane.

12. Click each Remote Service Management rule (three in total) and then click **Enable Rule** in the Actions pane.

13. Close the console without saving the settings.

After you have configured your other network servers for remote management and data collection, you can begin using Event Viewer to collect event logs from all your network computers.

Activity 11-13: Configuring an Event Subscription with a Remote Server

Time Required: 15 minutes

Objective: Create an event subscription.

Description: To make monitoring remote servers easier, you have decided to create an event subscription for MSN-SRV-1XX. This will allow you to collect event log data from MSN-SRV-1XX on MSN-SRV-0XX. In this activity, you configure an event subscription with a remote server.

1. On MSN-SRV-0XX, open Event Viewer from the Administrative Tools menu.

2. In Event Viewer, click **Subscriptions** and then click **Yes** when prompted by the Event Viewer message box asking to start and configure the Windows Event Collector Service automatically.

3. Click **Subscriptions** in the left pane, and then click **Create Subscription** in the Actions pane.

4. In the Subscription Properties dialog box, type **MSN-SRV-0XX** as the Subscription name.

5. Click the **Select Computers** button and then click **Add Domain Computers** to browse for domain servers.

6. In the Select Computer dialog box, type **MSN-SRV-1XX** in the Enter the object name to select text box, then click **OK**.

7. In the Computers window, click **Test** to verify the subscription connection, click **OK** in the Test Succeeded message box, and then click **OK** to close the Computers window.

8. In the Subscription Properties - MSN-SRV-0XX dialog box, click **Select Events**.

9. In the Query Filter dialog box, click **Last 7 days** for logged events.

10. Click **Critical**, **Warning**, **Error**, and **Information** event levels; click the **Event logs** list arrow; and then click the **Windows Logs** check box. Click **OK**.

11. Click **Advanced**.

12. Click **Specific User** and then click **User and Password**.

13. Enter **P@ssw0rd** in the Password text box and then click **OK**.

14. Click **OK** twice.

15. In Event Viewer, expand Windows Logs in the left pane, and then click **Forwarded Events** to verify that you have events listed. Then close Event Viewer.

Reliability and Performance Console

The **Reliability and Performance console** provides a suite of utilities for monitoring and capturing performance data for local and remote systems. Updated from the **Performance Monitor** console in Windows Server 2003, the new console is divided into the following areas:

- Resource Overview
- Monitoring Tools including Performance Monitor and Reliability Monitor
- Data Collector Sets
- Reports

Each area provides a different function for capturing and displaying performance data. Windows Reliability and Performance Monitor uses performance counters, event trace data, and configuration information. This information can be combined into **Data Collector Sets**, which are central repositories for gathering information for Reliability and Performance Monitor. They organize multiple data collection points into a single component that can be used to review or log performance.

Performance counters are measurements of system state or activity. They can be included in the operating system or as part of individual applications. Windows Reliability and Performance Monitor requests the current value of performance counters at specified time intervals.

Event trace data is collected from trace providers, which are components of the operating system or of individual applications that report actions or events. Output from multiple trace providers can be combined into a trace session, such as the Windows Kernel Trace used by Resource View to show real-time central processing unit (CPU), memory, disk, and network activity.

Configuration information is collected from key values in the Windows Registry. Windows Reliability and Performance Monitor can record the value of a Registry key at a specified time or interval as part of a log file.

Resource Overview   When you first access the Reliability and Performance Monitor, the default view shows the Resource Overview. This tool provides a real-time summary based on the

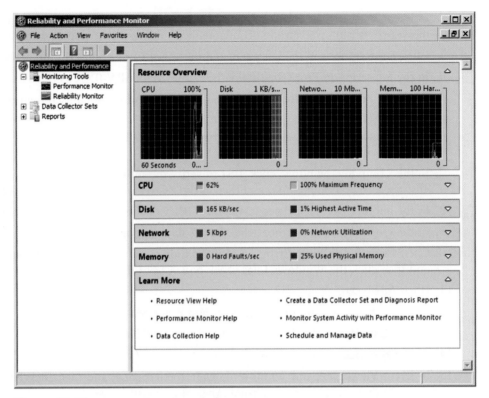

Figure 11-19   Resource Overview summary pane

four key components, or subsystems, of a Windows Server 2008 computer—CPU, disk, network, and memory—as shown in Figure 11-19.

Each area can be expanded to view more detailed information. For example, expanding the Memory section reveals each application running on a server, labeled as Image, and the memory resources being used by the application, as shown in Figure 11-20.

Performance Monitor   The Performance Monitor is similar to the System Monitor in Windows Server 2003. This utility can display real-time or historical data of local or remote computers. Data can be displayed in a report view, a histogram bar view, or a line graph view. The data displayed is based on Windows Performance counters. The counters measure system state and activity based on each Windows role, feature, and service running on a Windows Server 2008 computer.

Memory	4 Hard Faults/sec		25% Used Physical Memory			△
Image	PID	Hard Fa...	Commit (...	Working ...	Shareabl...	Private (KB)
svchost.exe (LocalSyste...	1048	1	194,416	199,552	10,808	188,744
explorer.exe	4848	0	168,376	131,624	50,132	81,492
Moe.exe	3864	0	87,320	107,644	37,252	70,392
svchost.exe (netsvcs)	1072	0	67,160	82,232	22,132	60,100
SearchIndexer.exe	2096	4	119,536	50,752	12,464	38,288
svchost.exe (secsvcs)	564	0	54,496	44,916	10,216	34,700
WINWORD.EXE	4560	0	40,136	83,164	53,732	29,432
MoeMonitor.exe	2876	0	30,948	45,720	19,664	26,056
svchost.exe (NetworkSe...	1464	0	29,476	32,256	12,480	19,776
audiodg.exe	1188	0	21,112	24,060	6,120	17,940

Figure 11-20   Example of Memory section in Resource Overview

Performance Monitor displays only the counters available for roles and services running on the target computer or those contained in a Data Collector Set being viewed. Adding other roles or features to Windows Server 2008 reveals additional performance counters related to the new roles or features.

You can add counters to the console for local or remote computers through the Add Counters window by clicking the green plus (+) sign or pressing Ctrl+I. Figure 11-21 displays the Add Counters window and some of the available counters.

Activity 11-14: Working with Performance Monitor

Time Required: 15 minutes

Objective: Learn about Performance Monitor.

Description: You need to gather some information about MSN-SRV-0XX. You decide to use Performance Monitor to capture real-time data and then create a Data Collector Set from the counters. In this activity, you perform various tasks in Performance Monitor.

1. Click **Start**, click in the Start Search box, type **perfmon**, and then press **Enter**.
2. In the navigation tree, expand **Monitoring Tools** and then click **Performance Monitor**.
3. Click the green **plus (+)** sign to open the Add Counters window.
4. Under Available counters, expand **Processor,** click **% Processor Time**, and then click **Add**.
5. Expand **Memory**, click **% Committed Bytes In Use**, and then click **Add**.
6. Expand **Logical Disk**, click **% Free Space**, and then click **Add**.
7. Click **OK** to close the Add Counters window. The counters are added to Performance Monitor and begin displaying data.
8. Click **Action** on the menu bar and then click **Properties** to open the Performance Monitor Properties dialog box.

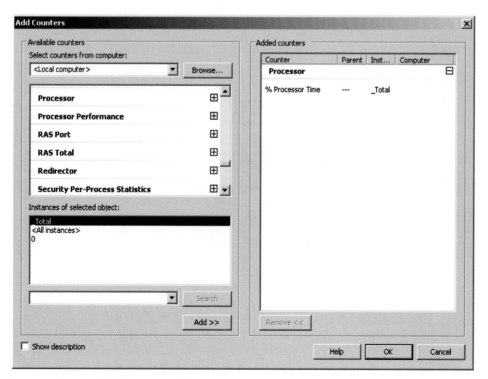

Figure 11-21   Add Counters window

9. Click the **Graph** tab, click the **View** list box, click **Histogram bar**, and then click **OK**.

10. Open the Actions pane, click **More Actions**, point to **New**, and then click **Data Collector Set**. This will open the Create new Data Collector Set window.

11. Enter **Perfmon Set** as the name in the first window and then click **Next**.

12. Type **c:\70642\chapter 11\Data Collector Sets** as the directory for the data and then click **Finish**.

Reliability Monitor   New in Windows Server 2008, the **Reliability Monitor** snap-in provides an overview of system stability by listing details about events that have affected reliability. Reliability Monitor calculates a current stability index for a server, as displayed in Figure 11-22.

This index is based on data collected over the lifetime of the machine by the RACAgent scheduled task. The RACAgent will begin running regularly after the operating system is installed.

Data Collector Sets   As mentioned earlier, the Data Collector Set acts as a central repository for gathering information for Reliability and Performance Monitor. It organizes data collection points into a single component that you can use to review or log performance in many ways, including the following:

- Create individual Data Collector Sets for recording performance data
- Add to logs with other Data Collector Sets
- Generate performance alerts
- Provide data to non-Microsoft applications

To collect the data, you can create a Data Collector Set manually through the console or by using a defined template located in the System folder. You can also use Performance Monitor.

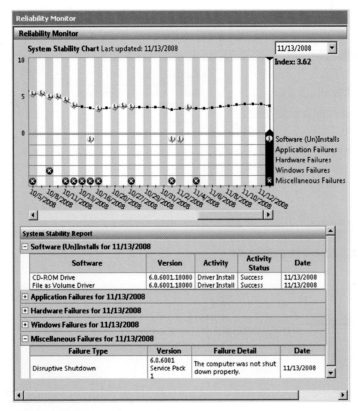

Figure 11-22   Reliability Monitor

After defining the counters you want to watch in Performance Monitor, your configuration can be used to create a Data Collector Set.

Activity 11-15: Working with Data Collector Sets

Time Required: 15 minutes

Objective: Use Data Collector Sets.

Description: While real-time data is useful, many times you need data that spans a period of time. You have decided to create some Data Collector Sets so that you can begin collecting data over a period of time to create a baseline for your server. In this activity, you complete some tasks that can be performed with Data Collector Sets.

1. In Reliability and Performance Monitor, expand **Data Collector Sets** and then click **User Defined**. You will see the Data Collector Set, Perfmon Set, which you created in the previous activity.

2. Click **More Actions**, point to **New**, and then click **Data Collector Set**.

3. In the first window, type **Template Set** for the name and choose the default of creating with a template by clicking **Next**.

4. If necessary, select the **System Performance** template and then click **Next**.

5. Type **c:\70642\chapter 11\Template Set** as the root directory and then click **Next**.

6. Click **Start this data collector set now** and then click **Finish**.

7. Click **Perfmon Set**, click **More Actions** under Perfmon Set, and then click **Start** to begin collecting data.

8. Click **Template Set** under Perfmon Set, click **More Actions**, and then click **Stop**.

9. Click **Perfmon Set** under User Defined, click **More Actions**, and then click **Stop**.

10. Expand **System** and then click **System Diagnostics** to run the built-in system diagnostics check.

11. Click **More Actions** and then click **Start**. System Diagnostics will run for a couple of minutes and then stop. Close Reliability and Performance Monitor when you are finished.

Generating Reports   The Reports section provides a central reporting location for the information gathered by the Data Collector Sets. When a Data Collector Set is run, all the data received is compiled and displayed, as shown in Figure 11-23.

Within the report, you can expand all available sections to reveal more detailed information. Each report is customized on the basis of the data it is showing. If your Data Collector Set contains only Performance Monitor counters, the view will be within Performance Monitor. Three views are available: as a report, in Performance Monitor (for performance counter data only), or in the folder that contains all the collected data.

Network Monitor

For complex network issues, you often need a tool that allows you to work with network details to troubleshoot and solve problems. **Network Monitor** is a built-in utility for capturing and viewing network traffic as it arrives or leaves a server. This is helpful for determining whether a problem, such as slow server response time, is related to the server itself or an outside source, such as a faulty router or client application. Network Monitor also helps you determine whether traffic is reaching a destination and lets you view encrypted ESP packets to verify that Internet Protocol Security policies are being properly applied. Network Monitor 3.2 has evolved into a tool that is more robust and easier to use than the one delivered with Windows Server 2003. Network Monitor is not built into Windows Server 2008, so you need to download it from the Microsoft Web site.

The current version of Network Monitor supported on Windows Server 2008 is version 3.2. It is available from the *www.microsoft.com/ downloads* by searching for Microsoft Network Monitor 3.2.

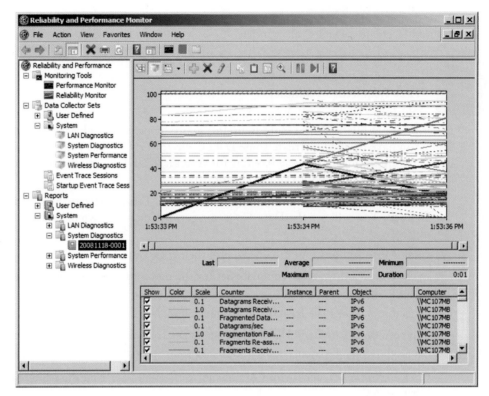

Figure 11-23   Data collected by Data Collector Set

Activity 11-16: Installing Network Monitor 3.2

Time Required: 15 minutes

Objective: Install Network Monitor 3.2.

Description: You need to gather some information about network traffic traveling to and from MSN-SRV-0XX. To do this, you need to install Network Monitor. In this activity, you download and install Network Monitor 3.2 in preparation for using Network Monitor in future activities.

Ask your instructor if a newer version of Network Monitor is available and should be used for this activity.

1. Log onto MSN-SRV-0XX.

2. Download Network Monitor 3.2 from Microsoft.

3. Double-click **NM32_x86_setup.exe** to start the Setup Wizard.

4. Click **Yes** to respond to the message box.

5. In the first Setup Wizard dialog box, click **Next**.

6. Accept the license agreement and then click **Next** in the End-User License Agreement window.

7. Click **Use Microsoft Update when I check for updates (recommended)** and then click **Next**.

8. In the Choose Setup Type window, click **Typical**.

9. In the Ready to Install window, click **Install**.

10. Click **Finish** to close the Setup Wizard.

11. Another installer starts and begins to install Microsoft Parsers 3.2.

12. Browse the Start menu to verify that Network Monitor 3.2 is installed in the All Programs menu.

After Network Monitor is installed, you can begin capturing data, as shown in Figure 11-24.

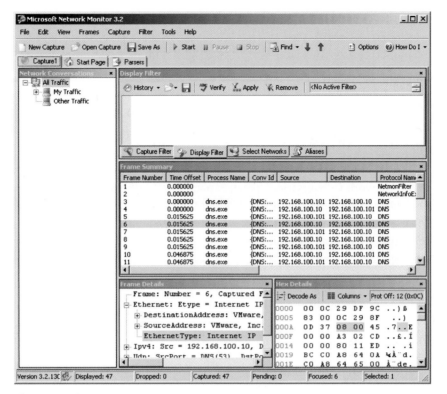

Figure 11-24   Data capture in Network Monitor

One welcome improvement is the **frame summary**. It displays a process name if one exists for traffic so that you can easily track data back to its source. By clicking individual frames, you are provided with two details panes: Frame details and Hex details. Frame details can be expanded to provide more detail about a frame, while Hex lists the hexadecimal equivalents of the frame data.

Although Network Monitor is an excellent tool, it does have some limitations. The current version allows administrators to capture only data entering or leaving a network adapter. It cannot capture traffic that is passing across the network but not destined for the server running Network Monitor. This is known as promiscuous mode.

Activity 11-17: Working with Network Monitor

Time Required: 15 minutes

Objective: Capture and save frame data with Network Monitor.

Description: You are experiencing some sporadic DNS and connectivity issues between MSN-SRV-0XX and MSN-SRV-1XX. To find out more about traffic between the two servers, you will be using Network Monitor to capture and view frame information. In this activity, you perform various tasks in Network Monitor.

1. On MSN-SRV-0XX, open **Microsoft Network Monitor 3.2** from the Start menu.

2. In the Network Monitor console, click **Internet** under Select Networks to remove the checkmark. This means that Network Monitor captures only traffic originating or arriving on your private network adapter, bentech.local.

3. On the toolbar, click the **New Capture** button.

4. In the Capture 1 window, click **Start** on the toolbar.

5. Log onto MSN-SRV-1XX.

6. Open a command prompt and enter the following command:

nslookup www.microsoft.com

7. Enter the following command:

ping 192.168.100.10

8. Log off MSN-SRV-1XX.

9. Return to MSN-SRV-0XX and click **Stop** on the toolbar.

10. In the Network Conversations pane, expand **My Traffic** and then click **dns.exe**. This lists all the back-and-forth messages when nslookup was performed on MSN-SRV-1XX.

11. Click **<Unknown>** to display messages with a protocol name of ICMP. These messages were generated when ping was initiated earlier.

12. Click **Save As** on the toolbar.

13. In the Save As dialog box, enter **c:\70642\Chapter 11\capture** and then click **Save**.

14. Close Network Monitor and log off MSN-SRV-0XX.

For a more full-featured network monitoring tool that allows for promiscuous mode, Microsoft recommends using Microsoft Systems Management Server with System Center Operations Manager. Other **NOTE** options include third-party utilities.

Disk Management

The **Disk Management console** provides a central location for administering the physical hard disks and disk-based devices attached to a server. It displays a graphical view of your hard disk storage allocation along with the health of your disk subsystems. You can complete many tasks using the Disk Management console, including the following:

• Working with disk quotas

• Resizing hard drives

• Performing disk diagnostics

• Configuring volume shadow copies

NTFS Disk Quotas   Another function of using NTFS with Windows Server 2008 is disk quotas. **Disk quotas** allow you to track disk usage by users and enforce disk space limits on disk volumes. This is done through the Quota tab located in the Properties dialog box of each disk volume, as shown in Figure 11-25.

By default, disk quotas are disabled because the feature requires system resources to run and maintain. It is recommended that you enable disk quotas only on network drives or local drives containing user data and not system drives where Windows Server 2008 is installed.

After you enable disk quotas, you have a number of options. In the most basic setup, you can choose to gather data to gauge space usage and find users who are maintaining large amounts of space. The other option is to regulate disk space for individual users to prevent them from exceeding the limits that you define. This is helpful if you need to closely manage the amount of space you have on your volumes. On the Quota tab, you first define the space limit and warning levels for the entire volume. These settings affect all users accessing the volume. A user's quota amount is measured by totaling all the files that a user owns on a volume.

When quotas are enabled, you can see the data on all the space usage on a particular volume. Each user's space usage is listed as an entry, or quota entry, in the Quota Entries table, as shown in Figure 11-26.

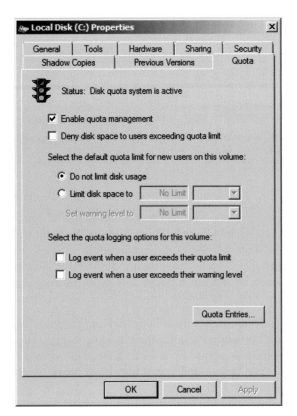

Figure 11-25 Quota tab in the Local Disk (C:) Properties dialog box

You can configure these entries for defining space limits and warning levels, allowing you to define different limits for existing users. You can also add new entries into the table if you know that particular users will be storing data on a volume in the future and you want to set specific limits for them now instead of using the default limits.

The amount of space you choose for your limits should be carefully planned. As technologies grow, the size of data grows as well, especially in the case of video, audio, and graphics files. A careful examination of your users' usage patterns along with your server's capacity should provide you with a good starting point. For more information about designing disk quotas, see the Designing a Disk Quota Strategy article at *http://technet. microsoft.com/en-us/library*.

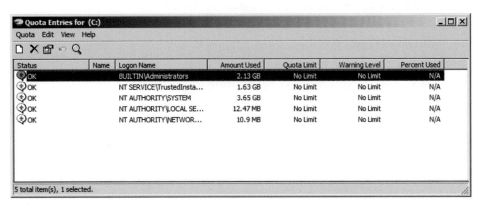

Figure 11-26 Quota Entries table

Table 11-6 Differences between disk quotas using FSRM and NTFS

Disk Quota Feature	FSRM	NTFS Disk Quotas
Quota Tracking Object	This is done by folder or by volume.	This is done by user per volume.
Disk usage calculation	This is based on actual disk space used, so compressed files are seen as their actual size.	This is based on the logical size of a file, so compressed files are seen as their uncompressed size.
Administrator notification tools	Notifications are available through e-mail, event logs, and built-in reports.	Only event logs can be used for notification.

NTFS disk quotas differ from the disk quota function available through the File Server Resource Manager console discussed in Chapter 8. The major differences in between File Server Resource Manager (FSRM) and NTFS disk quotas are listed in Table 11-6.

As stated previously in Chapter 8, NTFS disk quotas and FSRM disk quotas are two entirely separate tools, and they should not be used in tandem. For more information on FSRM disk quotas, see Chapter 8.

Volume Shadow Copy The **Volume Shadow Copy service (VSS)** is a feature of Windows Server 2008 that allows you to set up manual or automatic backup copies, known as **snapshots**, of files or folders on a specific volume at a specific point in time. This allows you to implement a file restore strategy where users can restore their own files from previous versions right from the user's desktop.

VSS is configured at the volume level but is disabled by default, so you can choose which volumes use the service and which do not. This is done on the Shadow Copies tab on the Local Disk Properties dialog box, as shown in Figure 11-27.

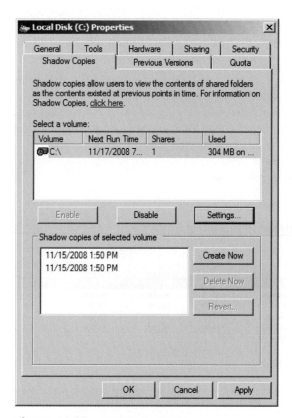

Figure 11-27 Shadow Copies tab

Using the settings on the Shadow Copies tab, you can manually create a new snapshot and view all the available snapshots on a system. VSS stores up to 64 shadow copies of a selected volume as long as there is enough disk space to store the VSS backups. Access shadow copy settings to change the size of the storage area used by VSS and customize the schedule of automatic snapshots, as shown in Figure 11-28.

Similar to other processes in Windows Server 2008, you can administer VSS from the command line using the vssadmin utility. The following example shows how you can create a manual snapshot of the c: volume:

```
vssadmin create shadow /for = c:
```

Restoring files and folders with Volume Shadow Copy is very straightforward on Windows Server 2008 and Windows Vista. The client-side service that is needed to view previous versions is part of the operating system. For other versions of Windows, download the Shadow Copy Client from *www.microsoft.com/downloads/*.

To view the previous versions of a folder, browse to the file in Windows Explorer, right-click the folder, and then click Properties to open the Properties dialog box for the folder. The process works exactly the same for files. The Previous Versions tab displays all available shadow copy versions on the server, as shown in Figure 11-29.

Activity 11-18: Working with Volume Shadow Copies

Time Required: 15 minutes

Objective: Enable VSS and restore a file from Previous Versions.

Description: You want to roll out Volume Shadow Copy on your network but need to test the functionality prior to allowing users access. In this activity, you will enable VSS, create snapshots, and restore a file from Previous Versions using the process that users usually follow.

1. Log onto MSN-SRV-0XX.

2. Open the Disk Management utility in Server Manager and click the **C:** volume.

3. Click **More Actions**, point to **All Tasks**, and then click **Configure Shadow Copies**.

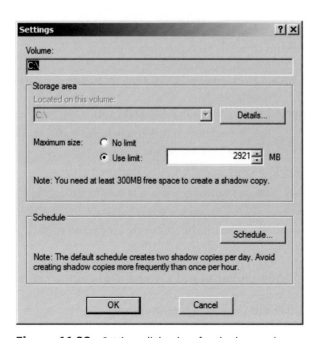

Figure 11-28 Settings dialog box for shadow copies

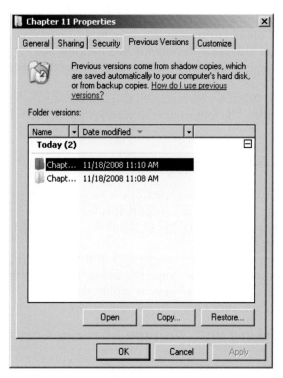

Figure 11-29   Previous Versions tab

4. In the Shadow Copies dialog box, select **C:** and then click **Enable**.

5. When a warning message appears, click **Yes** to continue enabling VSS. Once enabled, an initial snapshot will be taken, and a shadow copy will be created. Click **OK**.

6. Open a command prompt and enter the following command to delete the files in the Data Collector Sets folder:

> `del "c:\70642\chapter 11\Data Collector Sets\*.*" /Q`

7. Enter the following command to verify that the output shows no files:

> `dir "c:\70642\chapter 11\Data Collector Sets"`

8. Browse to **c:\70642\chapter 11** and then click the **Data Collector Sets** folder.

9. Click **File** on the menu bar, click **Properties**, and then click the **Previous Versions** tab in the Data Collector Sets Properties dialog box.

10. Select the most current shadow copy and then click **Restore** twice.

11. Click **OK** in the Previous Versions message box stating that the folder was successfully restored and then click **OK** to close the Data Collector Sets Properties dialog box.

12. Switch to the command prompt and enter the following command to verify that a file named system monitor log.blg appears in the directory listing:

> `dir "c:\70642\chapter 11\Data Collector Sets"`

13. Enter the following command to create another snapshot:

> `vssadmin create shadow /for = C:`

14. Enter the following command to view the currently available shadow copies and close the command prompt:

```
vssadmin list shadows
```

15. Log off MSN-SRV-0XX.

Backup and Restore in Windows Server 2008

Servers fail, data gets corrupted, and users delete needed files. These are all facts of life on a Windows network. Backup and restore procedures on a Windows network are critical functions for maintaining a stable network. Without proper backups, you will not be able to recover from network events such as server crashes, virus infections, and user deletions.

Windows Server 2008 provides two primary mechanisms for backing up and restoring data: Windows Server Backup and Volume Shadow Copy. In this section, you will learn about Windows Backup and how it can be used on your network. You will also learn how to restore data with Volume Shadow Copy.

Windows Server Backup

Windows Server Backup (WSB) is a new utility that replaces ntbackup.exe in previous versions of Windows Server. It provides backup and recovery of your files, folders, volumes, and application data on Windows Server 2008. Here is a list of improvements and changes with WSB:

- Uses the VSS to perform backups
- Uses block-level backups to improve backup speed, recovery time, and backup space usage
- Does not support tape drive backups, only disk-to-disk backups
- Provides an easy-to-use interface design for simple and reliable functionality
- Does not support individual file or folder backup

WSB works by using VSS and the Block Level Backup Engine service. Snapshots are taken of a target volume. By using VSS, you can perform backups with applications still online. These snapshots are stored using the **.vhd file format**, thus creating a **block-level backup**, which works directly with the hard disk to back up the physical disk sectors, not the actual files in the file system. Often, block-level backups are referred to as a disk image. With this change, you will see a noticeable decrease in the size of incremental backups and backup run times because only the changed blocks are backed up, not the entire changed file. Typically, the service examines blocks on a disk, compares them to the previously stored backup information, and then captures only blocks that have changed. WSB uses the current backup stored in the .vhd format to compare. In addition, WSB no longer uses the Archive bit registered at the file level to determine what to back up when performing incremental backups. Previously, the archive bit was checked by ntbackup and other third-party utilities to determine if a file had changed. Third-party backup utilities will continue to use the archive bit when performing file-level backups. WSB supports both local and remote backups through the console.

One significant change is the lack of support for tape drives. WSB supports only **disk-to-disk backup**, which means that you can back up only to a Universal Serial Bus removable drive, a network drive location, or a separate physical disk on your server. CD and DVD media are supported as well.

Installing Windows Backup Because WSB is considered a feature of Windows Server 2008, it is not installed by default. You can add this feature through the Add Features Wizard using servermanagercmd.exe on Full versions of Windows Server 2008 or using ocsetup on Server Core. Along with the WSB, you can install the WSB command-line tools to manage backup functions using the wbadmin.exe utility on both Full and Server Core versions of Windows Server 2008. You can use WSB to manage backups on remote computers that have the backup feature installed, as you will learn in the next activity.

Activity 11-19: Installing WSB and Command-Line Tools

Time Required: 15 minutes

Objective: Install WSB and command-line tools.

Description: In preparation for backing up your servers, you need to add the WSB feature along with the command-line tools. In this activity, you will install WSB on all your servers, including the command-line tools on servers that support them.

1. Log onto MSN-SC-0XX.

2. At the command prompt, enter the following command:

```
start /w ocsetup WindowsServerBackup
```

3. When the installation is finished, log off MSN-SC-0XX.

4. Log onto MSN-SRV-0XX.

5. Open a command prompt and enter the following command:

```
servermanagercmd.exe -install Backup-Tools
```

6. Enter the following commands to create a remote share location for backups:

```
md "c:\70642\chapter 11\RemoteBackup"

Net share RemoteBackup="c:\70642\Chapter 11\RemoteBackup"
/Grant:Everyone,Change
```

7. Log onto MSN-SRV-1XX.

8. In Server Manager, click **Add Features** under Features.

9. In the Add Features Wizard, click **Windows PowerShell**.

10. Click **Windows Server Backup** and **Command-line Tools** under Windows Server Backup Features and then click **Next**.

11. Click **Install** in the Confirm Installation Selections window.

12. When installations are complete, click **Close**.

Configuring Windows Backup   Unlike previous Windows Server backup utilities, WSB now has a straightforward configuration. When you open WSB, you have the following three choices, as shown in Figure 11-30.

- *Backup Schedule*—Schedule future backup jobs using the Backup Schedule Wizard. This is also referred to as a Scheduled backup.

- *Backup Once*—Configure and perform a single backup using the Backup Once Wizard. This is also referred to as a Manual backup since it is initiated by the administrator, not scheduled.

- *Recover*—Start the Recovery Wizard.

Through the console, you have the option of configuring the performance settings of WSB. This allows you to optimize a server's performance based on the type of backup job you choose. WSB supports three backup options, as shown in Figure 11-31:

- *Always perform full backup*—A **full backup** performs a complete backup of your target data set. It increases the amount of time necessary for performing your backup but does not affect the overall performance of your server or performance when restoring files.

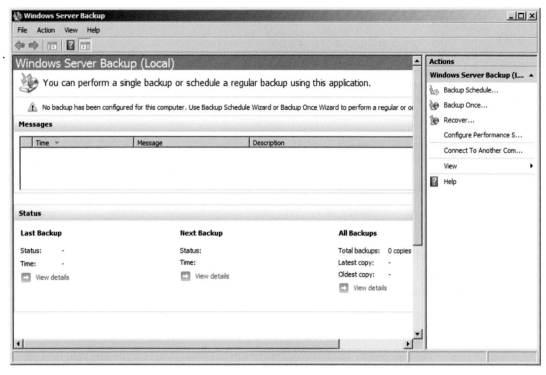

Figure 11-30   WSB console

- *Always perform incremental backup*—An **incremental backup** backs up only the blocks that have changed since the last backup was performed. This decreases your backup time but might also decrease your performance when restoring files.
- *Custom*—This type of backup allows you to configure each volume on a server separately so that you can use full and incremental backups on the same server.

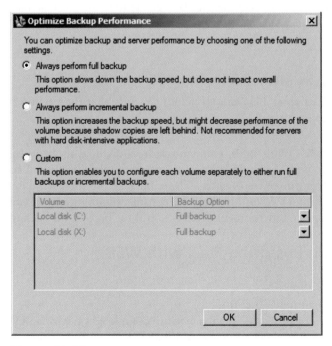

Figure 11-31   WSB console supported backup options

Activity 11-20: Running a Manual Backup on a Remote Server

Time Required: 45 minutes

Objective: Perform a remote manual backup.

Description: You want to centralize your backups on MSN-SRV-0XX and create a remote backup from MSN-SRV-0XX. In this activity, you perform a manual backup of MSN-SRV-1XX from MSN-SRV-0XX.

This activity requires at least 9 GB of free space on MSN-SRV-0XX. Depending on your lab setup, instructors may need to modify the network share location to meet the class needs.

1. Log onto MSN-SRV-0XX.

2. Open the WSB console.

3. In the WSB console, click **Connect to Another Computer** under Actions.

4. In the ComputerChooser window, click **Another computer**, type **MSN-SRV-1XX**, and then click **Finish**.

5. Once completed, click **Backup Once** under Actions.

6. In the Backup Once Wizard, click **Next**.

7. In the Select backup configuration window, accept the default of Full server by clicking **Next**.

8. In the Select destination type window, click **Remote shared folder** and then click **Next**.

9. In the Specify remote folder window, type **\\msn-srv-0XX\RemoteBackup** and then click **Next**.

10. When prompted for credentials, type **Administrator** and **P@ssw0rd** and then click OK.

11. In the Specify advanced option window, click **Next**.

12. In the Confirmation window, click **Backup**. Backing up might take a while since you are copying a large amount of data.

Ask your instructor whether you should complete an entire backup or let it partially complete, as a full backup will take some time.

13. When the backup is complete, click **Close**.

14. Browse to **c:\70642\chapter 11\RemoteBackup** to verify that the backup file is available.

15. Leave WSB console open for next activity.

Restoring with WSB   With WSB, you can restore individual files and folders, or you can restore an entire volume. WSB also supports performing bare-metal backup. A **bare-metal backup** is a process where a server can be restored to a clean machine (no installed data) in a single step. To restore, you use the Restore Wizard in the WSB console. In addition, you can restore backups using the Windows Recovery Environment. This is useful for bare-metal backups.

Activity 11-21: Restoring Files with WSB

Time Required: 15 minutes

Objective: Restore an individual file.

Description: You need to restore a file from a backup completed on MSN-SRV-1XX. You want to restore the file to an alternate location on MSN-SRV-1XX so that it does not overwrite the current file. In this activity, you use WSB to restore a file from a backup.

1. On MSN-SRV-0XX, click **Recover** in the Windows Server Backup console to open the Getting Started window.

2. In the Getting started window, choose **Another server** as the option to recover data and then click **Next**.

3. In the Specify location type window, click **Remote shared folder** and then click **Next**.

4. In the Specify remote folder window, type **\\msn-srv-0XX\RemoteBackup** and then click **Next**.

5. When prompted for credentials, type **Administrator** and **P@ssw0rd** and then click **OK**.

6. Click **Next** in the Select backup date window.

7. Click **Next** in the Select recovery type window to accept the default selection of Files and Folders.

8. In the Select items to recover window, expand **MSN-SRV-1XX** to **c:\Windows**, click **winhelp.exe** in the right pane, and then click **Next**.

9. In the Specify recovery options window, choose **Another location**, type **c:\70642\Chapter 11**, and then click **Next**.

10. In the Confirmation window, click **Recover**.

11. Once completed, click **Close**.

12. Close the WSB console and log off MSN-SRV-0XX.

13. Log onto MSN-SRV-1XX.

14. Browse to **c:\70642\chapter 11** and verify that the winhelp.exe file has been restored.

15. Log off MSN-SRV-1XX.

Chapter Summary

- MMC 3.0 provides a framework for tools, referred to as snap-ins, to add to the console. Depending on how you use the snap-in console and your network needs, you can customize the MMC to provide a robust set of administrative tools. Many of the snap-ins allow you to manage remote computers and the local computer on which they reside.

- Besides accessing roles and features installed on a computer, Server Manager lets you manage roles, features, diagnostics, configuration, and storage. You can also manage Server Manager from the command line with servermanagercmd.exe.

- Use Windows Update to update your system to correct security holes, improve existing functions, and fix discovered bugs. You typically use Windows Update when you have a small number of servers or want to manually manage the updates on your servers.

- WSUS centralizes the updating tasks for client and server computers and allows you to relocate them from the WAN onto the local network. With WSUS 3.0, you can effectively deliver approved updates to clients and remove updates that are outdated or have caused problems with clients.

- You can configure WSUS running the WSUS Server Configuration Wizard or by using the configuration components under Options in the Update Services console. After WSUS has been installed and configured in the WSUS console, your clients need to be configured to use the WSUS server for updates. The preferred method is using Group Policy. An alternate method is to modify the Registry of a client machine.

- MBSA 2.1 is a tool for beginning to analyze your current security posture. Designed for small to medium-sized businesses, MBSA provides security recommendations from Microsoft along with guidance for improving a computer's security posture. It does this by detecting missing security updates and common security holes.

- When monitoring Windows Server 2008, Event Viewer allows you to review and manage events for local and remote computers. Use the event classification and event details, such as the source of the event and the Event ID, when researching an issue.

- The Reliability and Performance console provides a suite of utilities for monitoring and capturing performance data for local and remote systems. The Resource Overview provides a real-time summary based on the four key components, or subsystems, of a Windows Server 2008 computer: CPU, disk, network, and memory. The Performance Monitor displays real-time or historical data of local or remote computers. Data can be displayed in a report view, a histogram bar view, or a line graph view. The data displayed is based on Windows Performance counters.

- Reliability Monitor provides an overview of system stability by listing details about events that have affected reliability. Reliability Monitor calculates a current stability index for a server.

- A Data Collector Set acts as a central repository for gathering information for Reliability and Performance Monitor. It organizes multiple data collection points into a single component that can be used to review or log performance.

- Network Monitor is a built-in utility for capturing and viewing network traffic as it arrives or leaves a server.

- The Disk Management console provides you with a central location for administering the physical hard disks and disk-based devices attached to a server. It provides a graphical view of your hard disk storage allocation along with the health of your disk subsystems.

- VSS allows you to set up manual or automatic backup copies (snapshots) of files or folders on a specific volume at a specific point in time.

- WSB replaces ntbackup.exe in previous versions of Windows Server and provides backup and recovery of your files, folders, volumes, and application data on Windows Server 2008.

Key Terms

.vhd file format   The format used by Windows Server Backup to store backups. It is also the format used by Microsoft virtualization products.

bare-metal backup   A process where a server can be restored to a clean machine (no installed data) in a single step, typically using a block-level backup or disk image.

block-level backup   A type of backup where an image of the target data set, or the data you've chosen to backup, is created instead of backing up file by file.

Data Collector Set   A central repository for gathering information for Reliability and Performance Monitor. It organizes multiple data collection points into a single component that can be used to review or log performance.

disk quota   Allow you to track disk usage by users. Along with tracking quota data, you can enforce disk space limits on disk volumes. Based on NTFS.

Disk Management console   A console that provides you with a central location for administering the physical hard disks and disk-based devices attached to a server. It provides a graphical view of your hard disk storage allocation along with the health of your disk subsystems.

disk-to-disk backup   A backup type where the storage location of the backup file is a disk drive that includes a Universal Serial Bus removable drive, a network drive location, and a separate physical disk on your server.

event subscription   A new feature of Windows Server 2008 that allows administrators to gather event logs from remote servers onto a single machine. Subscriptions are based on the Windows Event Collector Service.

frame summary   Displays a process name, if one exists, for traffic so that you can easily track data back to its source.

full backup   This option performs a complete backup of your target set data set. It will increase the amount of time necessary for performing your backup, but it will not affect the overall performance of your server.

incremental backup   This option backs up only the data that has changed since the last backup was performed. This will decrease your backup time but may decrease your performance.

Microsoft Baseline Security Analyzer (MBSA) 2.1   Designed for small to medium-sized businesses, MBSA provides security recommendations from Microsoft along with guidance for improving a computer's security posture.

Microsoft Management Console (MMC) 3.0 framework   The new management console used to house snap-in consoles for existing machines.

Network Monitor   A downloadable utility for capturing and viewing network traffic as it arrives at or leaves a server.

Performance Monitor   This utility displays real-time or historical data of local or remote computers. Data can be displayed in a report view, a histogram bar view, or a line graph view.

Reliability and Performance console   A suite of utilities for monitoring and capturing performance data for local and remote systems.

Reliability Monitor   A snap-in that provides a stability overview of the system along with providing details about events that have affected reliability.

Resource Overview   A tool that provides a real-time summary based on the four key components, or subsystems, of a Windows Server 2008 computer.

servermanagercmd.exe   A command-line utility that allows administrators to perform automated installations or removals of roles, role services, and features.

snapshot   The file storing previous versions of files or folders on a specific volume at a specific point in time.

Volume Shadow Copy service (VSS)   A feature of Windows Server 2008 that allows you to set up manual or automatic backup copies, known as snapshots, of files or folders on a specific volume at a specific point in time.

Windows Remote Management (WinRM)   A command-line tool service in Windows that is used to configure a computer to accept WS-Management (Windows Remote Management) requests from other computers.

Windows Server Backup (WSB)   A new utility that replaces ntbackup.exe in previous versions of Windows Server. It provides backup and recovery of your files, folders, volumes, and application data on Windows Server 2008.

Windows Server Update Services (WSUS)   A centralized tool for managing Windows Updates for client computers. With WSUS 3.0, you can effectively deliver approved updates to clients and remove updates that are outdated or have caused issues with clients.

Windows Update   A suite of tools and services provided by Microsoft to provide easy and ·reliable methods for applying updates to systems.

Review Questions

1. Windows Backup allows administrators the flexibility of saving backups to tape drives, disk-to-disk, or network backups. True or False?

2. _____ is the most effective way to deliver WSUS client settings to clients in an Active Directory domain.

3. Which of the following are *not* required for WSUS 3.0 Service Pack 1 to be installed and provide updates on a network?

    a. Internet connectivity

    b. IIS 7.0

    c. Active Directory Domain Services

    d. Microsoft Report Viewer Redistributable 2005

4. MBSA 2.1 will perform the following tasks *except*:
   a. Determine if weak passwords are being used on a computer
   b. Scan multiple computers on a domain
   c. Install security updates that are missing automatically
   d. Verify firewall and Windows Update status

5. Which of the following operating systems is *not* supported by MBSA 2.1?
   a. Windows Server 2003
   b. Windows Vista
   c. Windows Server 2000 SP3
   d. Windows XP

6. _____ is a new tool used for gathering Performance and Reliability data from multiple sources into one place.

7. Which of the following file extensions is used by the Windows Backup utility?
   a. .vss
   b. .bkp
   c. .vhd
   d. .vmxd

8. A Windows Server 2008 server running Network Monitor can capture network traffic in promiscuous mode. True or False?

9. Which of the following commands can be used to create a VSS snapshot of the E: drive on a Windows Server 2008 computer?
   a. vssadmin create snapshot /for = e:
   b. vssadmin create shadow /for = e:
   c. vssadmin /createsnapshot :e:
   d. vssadmin –snapshot e:

10. Performance Monitor provides only real-time data in Windows Server 2008. For historical data, you need to use Data Collector Sets. True or False?

11. Which of the following is the best tool for creating folder-level disk quotas?
    a. NTFS disk quotas
    b. FAT32 disk quotas
    c. FSRM disk quotas
    d. VSS disk quotas

12. Which of the following is the best choice for updating a small number of workstations in a work group environment?
    a. MBSA 2.1
    b. WSUS 3.0
    c. Windows Updates
    d. Reliability Monitor

13. Which of the following commands will display all the installed roles and features on a Windows Server 2008 computer?
    a. Ocsetup –query
    b. Servermanagercmd –list
    c. Ocsetup –list
    d. Servermanagercmd –query
    e. Servermanagercmd –?

14. When running the WSUS Configuration Wizard for the first time, which of the following updates are not chosen by default?

    a. Critical Updates

    b. Drivers

    c. Definition Updates

    d. Security Updates

Case Projects

Case Project 11-1: Recommending How to Improve Network and Windows Update Management

You have been asked to review the network of a local company, Badger Tools, Inc. Badger Tools is running Windows Server 2008 on its three servers and Windows Vista Enterprise on its 15 desktop clients. Currently, all updates are being performed manually by the system administrator. Badger Tools would like recommendations on how they can improve their network management and Windows Update procedures. Your task is to perform the following:

- List all the tools and utilities you would utilize to review their network

- Make recommendations on how they can improve the management of their network

Case Project 11-2: Researching Backup Solutions

You have been asked to provide information about other backup utilities and options available besides WSB. Research and list at least three different options available for backing up Windows Server 2008.

Case Project 11-3: Researching the wbadmin.exe Utility

For this project, you need to research the wbadmin.exe utility. As you have learned, wbadmin is the command-line utility for WSB. It is a helpful tool for performing backups to network locations or for creating backup scripts. Based on your research, list the syntax used by wbadmin to perform the following tasks:

- Perform a backup of server CS-SCSRV-001, excluding noncritical drives, and send the backup to \\CS-SRV-001\Backups without prompting for confirmation to begin backup.

- Perform a backup of CS-SRV-001, including all installed disks (c, e, f), and store the backup on an attached drive, such as h:.

- Create a scheduled backup on CS-SCSRV-001 that runs daily at 12:00 am and 6:00 pm and that backs up the c: drive and the system state to \\cs-srv-001\backups\DailyBackups.

- List the available backup versions located at \\CS-SRV-001\Backups for server CS-SCSRV-001.

- Perform a system state backup of CS-SCSRV-001 and send the backup to \\CS-SRV-001\WBadminBackupsSystemState.

MCTS 70-642 Exam Objectives

Table A-1 maps the Windows Server 2008 Network Infrastructure Configuration (70-642) exam objectives to the corresponding chapter and section title where the objectives are covered in this book. Major sections are listed in the column after the chapter number, and applicable subsections are shown in parentheses. After each objective, the percentage of the exam that includes the objective is shown in parentheses.

Table A-1   Objectives-to-chapter mapping

Objective	Chapter	Section
Configuring IP Addressing and Services (24 percent)		
Configure IPv4 and IPv6 addressing *May include but is not limited to: configure IP options, subnetting, supernetting, alternative configuration*	3	Configuring Clients for IPv4 and IPv6
Configure Dynamic Host Configuration Protocol (DHCP). *May include but is not limited to: DHCP options, creating new options, PXE boot, default user profiles, DHCP relay agents, exclusions, authorize server in Active Directory, scopes, server core, Windows Server Hyper-V*	4	Configuring the DHCP Server
Configure routing *May include but is not limited to: static routing, persistent routing, Routing Internet Protocol (RIP), Open Shortest Path First (OSPF)*	9	Configuring Routing in Windows Server 2008
Configure IPsec. *May include but is not limited to: create IPsec policy, IPsec Authentication Header (AH), IPsec Encapsulating Security Payload (ESP)*	10	Internet Protocol Security
Configuring Name Resolution (27 percent)		
Configure a Domain Name System (DNS) server. *May include but is not limited to: conditional forwarding, external forwarders, root hints, cache-only, server core, WINS and DNS integration, Windows Server virtualization*	5	Installing DNS in Windows Server 2008
Configure DNS zones. *May include but is not limited to: DNS Refresh no-refresh, intervals, DNS listserv address (NSLOOKUP), primary/secondary zones, Active Directory integration, Dynamic Domain Name System (DDNS), GlobalNames, SOA refresh*	5	DNS Zones

(continued)

Table A-1   *(continued)*

Objective	Chapter	Section
Configure DNS records. *May include but is not limited to: record types, host, pointer, MX, SRV, NS, dynamic updates, Time to Live (TTL)*	5	DNS Records
Configure DNS replication. *May include but is not limited to: DNS secondary zones, DNS stub zones, DNS scavenging interval, replication scope*	5 6	Standard DNS Zone Types Standard DNS Zone Transfers Dynamic DNS AD-Integrated DNS
Configure name resolution for client computers. *May include but is not limited to: DNS and WINS integration, configuring HOSTS file, LMHOSTS, node type, Link-Local Multicast Name Resolution (LLMNR), broadcasting, resolver cache, DNS Server list, Suffix Search order, manage client settings by using group policy*	5 6	Domain Name System Dynamic DNS
Configuring Network Access (22 percent)		
Configure remote access. *May include but is not limited to: dial-up, Remote Access Policy, Network Address Translation (NAT), Internet Connection Sharing (ICS), VPN, Routing and Remote Access Services (RRAS), inbound/outbound filters, configure Remote Authentication Dial-In User Service (RADIUS) server, configure RADIUS proxy, remote access protocols, Connection Manager*	9	Configuring Remote Access Services in Windows Server 2008
Configure Network Access Protection (NAP). *May include but is not limited to: network layer protection, DHCP enforcement, VPN enforcement, configure NAP health policies, IPsec enforcement, 802.1x enforcement, flexible host isolation*	10	Introduction to Network Access Protection
Configure network authentication. *May include but is not limited to: LAN authentication by using NTLMv2 and Kerberos, WLAN authentication by using 802.1x, RAS authentication by using MS-CHAP, MS-CHAP v2, and EAP*	10	Network Authentication in Windows Server 2008
Configure wireless access. *May include but is not limited to: Set Service Identifier (SSID), Wired Equivalent Privacy (WEP), Wi-Fi Protected Access (WPA), Wi-Fi Protected Access 2 (WPA2), ad hoc versus infrastructure mode, group policy for wireless*	9	Wireless Access Configuration in Windows Server 2008
Configure firewall settings. *May include but is not limited to: incoming and outgoing traffic filtering, Active Directory account integration, identify ports and protocols, Microsoft Windows Firewall versus Windows Firewall with Advanced Security, configure firewall by using group policy, isolation policy*	10	Windows Firewall
Configuring File and Print Services (13 percent)		
Configure a file server. *May include but is not limited to: file share publishing, Offline Files, share permissions, NTFS permissions, encrypting file system (EFS)*	7	Configuring File Services in Windows Server 2008
Configure Distributed File System (DFS). *May include but is not limited to: DFS namespace, DFS configuration and application, creating and configuring targets, DFS replication*	7	Distributed File System

Objective	Chapter	Section
Configure shadow copy services. *May include but is not limited to: recover previous versions, set schedule, set storage locations*	11	Disk Management (Volume Shadow Copy)
Configure backup and restore. *May include but is not limited to: backup types, backup schedules, managing remotely, restoring data*	11	Backup and Restore in Windows Server 2008
Manage disk quotas. *May include but is not limited to: quota by volume or quota by user, quota entries, quota templates*	11	Disk Management (NTFS Disk Quotas)
Configure and monitor print services. *May include but is not limited to: printer share, publish printers to Active Directory, printer permissions, deploy printer connections, install printer drivers, export and import print queues and printer settings, add counters to Reliability and Performance Monitor to monitor print servers, print pooling, print priority*	8	Deploying Printers and Print Services Configuring Printer Resources
Monitoring and Managing a Network Infrastructure (14 percent)		
Configure Windows Server Update Services (WSUS) server settings. *May include but is not limited to: update type selection, client settings, Group Policy object (GPO), client targeting, software updates, test and approval, disconnected networks*	11	Updating Windows Server 2008 (Windows Server Update Services)
Capture performance data. *May include but is not limited to: Data Collector Sets, Performance Monitor, Reliability Monitor, monitoring System Stability Index*	11	Monitoring Windows Server 2008 (Reliability and Performance Console)
Monitor event logs. *May include but is not limited to: custom views, application and services logs, subscriptions, DNS log*	11	Monitoring Windows Server 2008 (Working with Event Viewer)
Gather network data. *May include but is not limited to: Simple Network Management Protocol (SNMP), Baseline Security Analyzer, Network Monitor*	11	Monitoring Windows Server 2008 (Network Monitor)

A Step-by-Step Guide to Using Server Virtualization Software

Virtualization enables a school or student to get the most out of computer resources. Schools can use virtualization to turn a single server-grade computer into a virtual server that can host two, three, or more operating systems. For example, one computer can house three virtual servers running Windows Server 2008. This capability saves the school money on servers and enables more students to be able to work on their own operating systems.

Another capability of virtualization is the ability for a school or student to turn a single PC into a virtual system on which to run another operating system — without having to alter the current operating system running on the PC. A single computer lab PC or a student's home PC can be turned into a host for Windows Server 2008. This is ideal, for example, when your textbook comes with an evaluation copy of Windows Server 2008. You can install virtualization software and then install Windows Server 2008 for completing hands-on projects and activities. You can, for example, use your originally installed operating system, such as Windows XP or Vista, and also use Windows Server 2008 in a virtual "window" or "session." When you are finished learning Windows Server 2008, you simply remove the virtualization software and you're back where you started with your original operating system.

This appendix is a step-by-step guide for turning a single computer into a virtual system hosting one or more virtual machines. The main focus is on three popular virtualization systems that are available free:

- *Microsoft Virtual PC* — Intended for a workstation-grade PC to host another operating system, such as a Windows Server 2008 virtual machine

- *Microsoft Virtual Server* — Intended for a server-grade computer to host multiple virtual machines, including Windows Server 2008 and other operating systems

- *VMware Server* — Intended for server-grade computers to host multiple virtual machines, such as Windows Server 2008

For each of these virtualization systems, you learn how to:

- Obtain a free download version.
- Install it.
- Create a virtual machine.
- Install a guest operating system, such as Windows Server 2008, in the virtual machine, and then how to access that virtual machine's operating system.
- Install ISO images.
- Configure virtual networking.
- Configure hardware components.

At the end of the appendix, a brief look at VMware Workstation 6 and Microsoft Hyper-V is also provided.

455

Microsoft Virtual PC

Microsoft Virtual PC can be installed in Microsoft Windows XP, Vista, and Windows Server 2003 operating systems. At this writing, it is not adapted to be installed in Windows Server 2008. Although Microsoft Virtual PC is intended to host workstation operating systems as virtual machines, you can also use it to create a Windows Server 2008 Standard Edition virtual machine.

Microsoft Virtual PC is available from Microsoft as a free download. From a student's perspective, this is ideal for running the Windows Server 2008 Standard Edition evaluation DVD (available from Microsoft at *www.microsoft.com*) on a Windows XP or Windows Vista computer. It works equally well on Windows XP or Windows Vista computers in a student computer lab.

Requirements for Microsoft Virtual PC

At this writing, Microsoft Virtual PC 2007 with Service Pack 1 (SP1) is the most recently available version. It can be loaded on the following operating system hosts:

- Windows XP Professional with SP2 or SP3
- Windows Server 2003 Edition SP2 (x86 or x64)
- Windows Vista Business Edition (x86 or x64 versions with or without SP1)
- Windows Vista Enterprise Edition (x86 or x64 versions with or without SP1)
- Windows Vista Ultimate Edition (x86 or x64 versions with or without SP1)

The hardware requirements for Microsoft Virtual PC 2007 SP1 are as follows:

- *CPU* — Intel Celeron, Pentium II, Pentium III, Pentium 4, Core Duo, or Core 2 Duo CPU or AMD Athlon or Duron CPU (400 MHz or faster; x86 or x64).
- *RAM* — Enough RAM for at least the minimum requirements of the total number of operating systems you will be running. For example, if you are running Windows XP Professional (128 MB minimum) and want to load Windows Server 2008 (512 MB minimum) as a virtual machine, you need a minimum of 640 MB to 1 GB RAM. If Windows Vista is the host and you want to run a Windows Server 2008 Standard Edition virtual machine, you need a minimum of 1 GB RAM.
- *Disk space* — Enough disk storage for the operating systems you plan to run. For example, Windows XP requires at least 1.5 GB, Windows Vista requires at least 15 GB, and Windows Server 2008 requires at least 10 GB (but 15 GB to 20 GB is better for using different roles and services).

Virtual Machine Operating Systems Supported

After Virtual PC 2007 SP1 is loaded, you can run any of the following operating systems as virtual machines (guests) in Virtual PC 2007 SP1:

- Windows 98 and 98 SE
- Windows Me
- Windows 2000 Professional
- Windows XP Home or Professional with SP1, SP2, SP3 (or no service pack)
- Windows Vista Business Edition (x86 or x64 versions with or without SP1)
- Windows Vista Enterprise Edition (x86 or x64 versions with or without SP1)
- Windows Vista Ultimate Edition (x86 or x64 versions with or without SP1)
- Windows Server 2008 Standard Edition
- OS/2 Warp

How to Download Microsoft Virtual PC

Microsoft Virtual PC can be downloaded from Microsoft's Web site for no cost. The steps to download Microsoft Virtual PC 2007 SP1 are as follows:

1. Log on to your computer.
2. Create a folder in which to download the setup.exe file for Microsoft Virtual PC (such as a temporary folder or a folder under your Program Files folder).
3. Open a Web browser, such as Microsoft Internet Explorer.
4. Go to the URL **www.microsoft.com/downloads** or **www.microsoft.com/downloads/ Search.aspx?displaylang=en** (for English).

 Web links and specific instructions change periodically. You might need to search *www.microsoft.com* for the most current link if these links do not work.

5. Look for Microsoft Virtual PC in the Popular Downloads or Recommended Downloads sections. (Also check the New Downloads section in case a new version is available.) If you find it in one of these sections, click the link for **Microsoft Virtual PC**. If you do not see a link, click **Windows** under the Product Families heading. Click the **down arrow** in the Show downloads for list box, and click **Microsoft Virtual PC**. Click **Go**.
6. Click the link for **VPC 2007 SP1**.

 To use Microsoft Virtual PC 2007 with Windows Server 2008 or Windows Vista as the virtual machine (guest) operating system, you must use the download containing SP1.

7. Click the **Download** button for the setup.exe file that matches your computer, which is 32 BIT\ setup.exe for an x86 computer or 64 BIT\ setup.exe for an x64 computer.
8. Click the **Save** or **Save File** button.
9. Select the folder you created in which to save the setup.exe file.
10. Click **Save**.
11. Click **Close** in the Download complete dialog box.
12. Close your Web browser.

How to Install Microsoft Virtual PC

Microsoft Virtual PC 2007 SP1 is easy to install. The installation steps are as follows:

1. Browse to the folder in which you saved the setup.exe file for Microsoft Virtual PC.
2. Double-click **setup.exe**.
3. Click **Next** after the Microsoft Virtual PC 2007 SP1 Wizard starts (see Figure B-1).
4. Click the option button for **I accept the terms in the license agreement**. Click **Next**.
5. Enter your username and name of your organization (if an organization name is appropriate). Notice that the product key should already be provided. Also, if you see this option, leave **Anyone who uses this computer (All Users)** selected. Click **Next**.
6. Click **Install**. The installation process takes a few minutes.
7. Click **Finish**.

Creating a Virtual Machine and Installing a Guest OS

After Microsoft Virtual PC 2007 SP1 is installed, the next step is to create a virtual machine in which to install a guest operating system.

Figure B-1   Microsoft Virtual PC 2007 SP1 Wizard

Microsoft Virtual PC 2007 SP1 might not be compatible with hardware virtualization on some CPUs. If you experience a crash dump when configuring the virtual machine or loading the guest OS, first make sure you have enabled hardware virtualization in Step 12. If this does not work, try disabling hardware virtualization in the BIOS and restart these steps from the beginning.

The following are sample steps for setting up the virtual machine with Windows Server 2008 Standard Edition as the guest operating system:

1. From the host operating system, such as Windows XP or Windows Vista, click **Start**.

2. Point to **All Programs** and click **Microsoft Virtual PC**.

3. The New Virtual Machine Wizard opens (see Figure B-2). Click **Next**.

4. Ensure that **Create a virtual machine** is selected and click **Next**.

5. Provide a name for the virtual machine, such as **Windows Server 2008**. Click **Next**.

6. Ensure that **Windows Server 2008** is selected as the operating system to install and click Next.

Figure B-2   New Virtual Machine Wizard

7. Ensure that at least 512 MB to 1 GB RAM is allocated for the virtual machine. If necessary, click **Adjusting the RAM** and use the slider bar to allocate enough memory. Click **Next**.

8. Ensure that **A new virtual hard disk** is selected and click **Next**.

9. Make sure the virtual hard disk is sized to meet your needs, or leave the default size. (You need 15 GB for Windows Server 2008 and might use at least 20–40 GB, for example.) Click **Next**.

10. Click **Finish**.

11. You should see the Virtual PC Console open on the desktop. If it is not open, click Start, point to **All Programs**, and click **Microsoft Virtual PC**.

12. You can configure options at this point by clicking **File**, **Options** from the menu. Click each option to see what it does and configure any options as necessary. When you are finished, click **OK**. The options are as follows:

    - *Restore at Start* — Pauses a running virtual machine when you exit the console and restores the virtual machine when you reopen the console.

    - *Performance* — Specifies how CPU time is allocated to virtual machines and specifies what happens when Virtual PC is a process running in the background.

    - *Hardware virtualization* — Enable hardware virtualization, if your CPU has this capability.

    - *Full-Screen Mode* — Enables the screen resolution to be adjusted so it is the same for the host and guest OSs. (Note the previous caution if this setting is enabled.)

    - *Sound* — Configures virtual machine sound. Sound is muted by default. If you enable it, the sounds from the host and guest OS can be difficult to differentiate.

    - *Messages* — Turn off error and informational messages from Virtual PC.

    - *Keyboard* — Specifies the host key for the guest operating system. The default host key is the right Alt key. When you press this key, you can switch the mouse between the guest and host windows and you can execute guest key combinations, such as pressing Alt+Delete to send the Ctrl+Alt+Delete key combination to the guest OS for logging on.

    - *Mouse* — Specifies how the pointer is captured for use in the virtual machine window.

    - *Security* — Determines how to control access to Virtual PC functions.

    - *Language* — Specifies the language to use for Virtual PC.

13. Insert the Windows Server 2008 Standard Edition installation DVD.

At this point, you could install any of the supported guest operating systems. If you are installing a different operating system, you would insert the CD/DVD now, complete Step 14, and then Steps 15 through 30 (or whatever steps are required) would be unique to the operating system you are installing.

14. Click the **Start** button in the Virtual PC Console. This opens a second larger window, which is the Microsoft Virtual PC 2007 console. Wait a few minutes for the DVD to start loading. Click in the console to enable the mouse to operate in this window. (If necessary, you can switch the mouse movement back so that it can go all over the screen by pressing the right Alt key, which is the "host" key.)

Occasionally, the mouse might seem stuck, move slowly, or stop functioning in the active portion of the console. If this happens, close all windows and go to Step 11 to start again. Also, some installation processes take longer to install in a virtual machine. Don't close the window or stop the installation prematurely, even if you seem to be stuck on a black screen for several minutes.

15. Click the language to install, such as **English**, in the Language to install drop-down list. In the Time and currency format list box, make your selection, such as **English (United States)**. In the Keyboard or input method list box, make your selection, such as **US**. Click **Next**.

16. Click **Install now**.

17. Click **Windows Server 2008 Standard (Full Installation)** and click **Next**.

18. Read the license terms, click the **I accept the license terms** check box, and click **Next**.

19. Click **Custom (advanced)**.

20. You'll see the amount of unallocated disk space highlighted, which is the disk space you specified when you configured the virtual machine. Ensure that it is highlighted and click **Next**.

21. The installation program begins installing Windows Server 2008. You'll see progress information about copying files, expanding files, installing features, installing updates, and completing the installation. This part of the installation can take 30 minutes or longer.

22. The installation program restarts the operating system.

23. You see the message *Please wait while Windows sets up your computer*.

24. Next, you see the Install Windows window in the Completing installation phase.

25. The system restarts again.

26. You'll see the message (a red circle with a white x in it) *The user's password must be changed before logging on the first time*. Click **OK**. (You might have to click inside the active portion of the console first to have the mouse function in it.)

27. Enter a new password for the Administrator account and then enter the same password again to confirm it. Click the **blue circle** with the white right-pointing arrow inside.

If you enter a password that is not a strong password, you'll see the message (with a white x in a red circle) *Unable to update the password*. This means the value provided for the new password does not meet the length, complexity, or history requirements of the domain. Click OK and enter a different password that is more than seven characters and uses letters, numbers, and special symbols, such as &.

28. When you see the message *Your password has been changed*, click **OK**.

29. At this point, the Windows desktop is displayed and the Initial Configuration Tasks window opens.

30. You can configure Windows Server 2008 as you would in a nonvirtual environment.

31. When you close the Microsoft Virtual PC 2007 console, you can turn off the virtual machine or save its current state. Unless you want to save its state, a good practice is to shut down the server before closing the window. (Saving the state means to keep the server in its current state, without shutting it down.) When you shut down the server in this way, the Microsoft Virtual PC 2007 console closes but leaves the Virtual PC Console open. Also, to restart the virtual machine, open the Virtual PC Console, click Start, and wait for the system to boot in the Microsoft Virtual PC 2007 console.

When you log on to Windows Server 2008 from the console, the normal Ctrl+Alt+Delete key sequence does not work. Instead, click the Action menu and press Ctrl+Alt+Delete. Another alternative is to press right Alt+Delete.

Installing an OS from an ISO Image

An ISO file is an optical disc (CD/DVD) image file with the .iso file extension. An ISO file can be accessed in several ways, such as from a CD/DVD, from a hard drive, or as a shared network file. Typically, when you download an operating system, such as an evaluation copy of a Windows operating system, you download an ISO file. One advantage of using an ISO file for installing a guest operating system on a virtual machine is that the installation process can go faster. Virtual PC enables you to install from an ISO file by using the following general steps:

1. Follow Steps 1 through 12 in the previous section, "Creating a Virtual Machine and Installing a Guest OS."

2. Click the **Start** button in the Virtual PC Console.

3. After the Microsoft Virtual PC 2007 console opens, press the **right Alt** key if necessary to access the menu at the top of the window.

4. Click **CD, Capture ISO Image** from the menu.

5. Navigate to the ISO file, click the file, and click the **Open** button.

6. You return to the Microsoft Virtual PC 2007 console, and then you should restart the virtual machine.

Configuring Networking and Hardware Options

You can configure a range of networking and hardware options in Microsoft Virtual PC. For example, if the host computer has two or more NICs, you can specify which NIC to use for a virtual machine. In another example, you might need to create one or more additional virtual hard disks for a virtual machine.

Use these steps to configure networking and hardware options:

1. Open the Virtual PC Console, if it is not open. Also, ensure that the virtual machine is turned off before you start.

2. Click the **Settings** button, or click the **Action** menu and click **Settings** to open the dialog box shown in Figure B-3.

3. Click **Networking** in the left pane. If your computer has multiple adapters, you can select the specific adapter (or multiple adapters) to associate with a virtual machine.

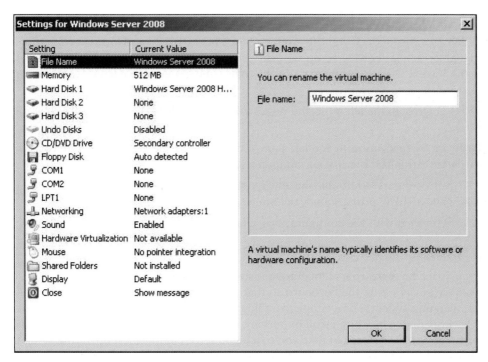

Figure B-3   Settings for a virtual machine

4. In the right pane, click the list arrow for the adapter that is selected by default. The following options are available:

   - *Not connected* — Used if you do not intend to enable the virtual machine to access a network (including the Internet) and so that it cannot be accessed from a network.

   - *Local* — If two or more virtual machines are set up, they can access each other; however, virtual machines cannot access the network.

   - *NetworkInterfaceName* — The actual name of a NIC model, such as an Intel or Broadcom NIC, that the virtual machine is directly connected to for regular network and Internet access. With this selection, network configuration tasks that apply to other network computers also apply to the virtual machine. If a DHCP server is on the network or if the network uses a router with Network Address Translation (NAT), the virtual machine's network connection can be configured to use these services. The same applies if a DNS server is set up.

   - *Shared Networking (NAT)* — Used to create a private Virtual PC network that has a virtual DHCP server and a virtual NAT-enabled router or firewall. Typically, the first virtual computer created acts as the DHCP server and provides NAT services. In this arrangement, Microsoft Virtual PC performs as a virtual DHCP server, leasing IP addresses for virtual machines in the range of 192.168.131.1 to 192.168.131.253. Further, the virtual machines appear as computers in a private NAT-protected network. A connection to the Internet is shared among the virtual machines and is protected in a way similar to a NAT-enabled router or firewall.

   - *Loopback Adapter* — You see this option if the operating system is configured to have a Microsoft loopback adapter (configured as a network adapter, such as through the Add Hardware option in Control Panel). This option is used in two contexts. One context is when no physical network connection is present, but you want to simulate network connectivity between the host and all virtual machines. A second context is when you are creating a network with many routers and firewalls as well as many virtual machines.

5. Make the networking selections that are appropriate for your situation.

6. Click **Memory** in the left pane. Notice that you can increase the memory allocation for the virtual machine by using the slider bar in the right pane.

7. In the left pane, click **Hard Disk 1** and notice that the right pane shows the path to the virtual hard disk file. Also, notice you can configure the Hard Disk 2 and Hard Disk 3 options for additional virtual hard disks. To do this, click Hard Disk 2 in the left pane, for example, and click the Virtual Disk Wizard button in the right pane. (A virtual machine can have up to three hard disks.)

8. Click **CD/DVD Drive** in the left pane and notice you can attach a CD or DVD drive via the right pane.

9. Click **Hardware Virtualization** in the left pane, and notice in the right pane that you can enable hardware virtualization, if your computer supports it.

10. Notice you can configure additional hardware, such as communication (COM) ports, a floppy disk, printer (LPT) ports, sound, the mouse, the display, and other devices.

11. When you are finished with the configurations, click **OK**.

Host Key Options

Because a virtual machine represents an operating system running inside an operating system, it is necessary to have a way to use the keyboard so that the keys you press communicate directly with the guest operating system. For example, you'll notice that pressing Ctrl+Alt+Delete opens the Windows Security dialog box or a menu of options, depending on which version of Windows is the host operating system. It does not take you to a logon screen in the guest operating system.

Microsoft Virtual PC enables you to communicate with the guest operating system by using the host key, which is the right Alt key by default. Table B-1 lists important host key combinations you can use while you are accessing a virtual machine.

Table B-1   Host key options for Microsoft Virtual PC

Keyboard combination	Result
HostKey	Enables you to move the mouse outside the window area used by the guest OS. (Move the mouse back into the guest OS display and click when you want to work in the guest OS.)
HostKey + Delete	The virtual machine OS responds to this as Ctrl+Alt+Delete.
HostKey + P	Toggles the virtual machine between pause and resume.
HostKey + R	Causes the virtual machine to reset.
HostKey + A	Selects all items in the active window in the guest OS.
HostKey + C	Copies selected text and items in the active window in the guest OS.
HostKey + V	Pastes text and items in the active window in the guest OS.
HostKey + Enter	Switches between full screen and window modes.
HostKey + down arrow	Causes the virtual machine to minimize.
HostKey + I	Enables you to install virtual machine additions.

Microsoft Virtual Server

Microsoft Virtual Server 2005 is intended to host server operating systems as virtual machines. At this writing, Microsoft Virtual Server 2005 R2 SP1 is the most recent version. This version supports hardware (integrated in the CPU) virtualization, such as AMD CPUs equipped with AMD-V and Intel CPUs with Intel VT. Other new features include the following:

- Can be installed in x64 operating systems
- Provides support for Internet Small Computer System Interface (iSCSI), which is a technology used in Storage Area Networks (SANs)
- Has the ability to cluster virtual servers on a single computer
- Provides enhanced Active Directory support by publishing Virtual Server binding data through service connection points

Other features of Microsoft Virtual Server include the following:
- Virtual disks can expand dynamically
- Supports most popular x86 operating systems
- Can mount a virtual disk on a different operating system
- Enables use of Volume Shadow Copy Service (VSS) for backups (used in newer versions of Windows operating systems, such as Windows Server 2008 and Vista)
- Offers virtual server management through the Virtual Server Web console
- Can use scripting to control virtual machine setups
- Memory access can be resized

Microsoft Virtual Server Guest Operating Systems Supported

Microsoft Virtual Server can house virtual machines for popular Windows and Linux server and workstation operating systems. The following operating systems can be guests:

- Windows Server 2008 Standard, Enterprise, Datacenter, and Web Server (x86 and x64)
- Windows Server 2003 Standard, Enterprise, Datacenter, and Web Server SP1 or SP2 (x86 or x64)
- Windows Server 2003 Standard, Enterprise, Datacenter, and Web Server R2 (x86 or x64)
- Windows Small Business Server 2003 (Standard and Premium Editions)
- Windows 2000 Server

- Windows XP Professional SP2
- Windows Vista Business, Ultimate, and Enterprise
- Red Hat Enterprise Linux versions 2.1 to 4.0
- SUSE Linux Enterprise Server 9.0
- SUSE Linux versions 9.2 to 10.0

Other operating systems can also run experimentally in Microsoft Virtual Server.

Microsoft Virtual Server Host Operating Systems Supported

Microsoft Virtual Server can be installed on the following Windows host operating systems:

- Windows Server 2008 Standard and Enterprise (x86 or x64)
- Windows Server 2003 Standard, Enterprise, and Web Server with SP1 or SP2 (x86 or x64)
- Windows Server 2003 Standard, Enterprise, and Web Server R2 (x86 or x64)
- Windows Small Business Server 2003 (Standard and Premium Editions, also R2 versions)
- Windows 2000 Server with SP3 or SP4
- Windows XP Professional (x86 and x64)
- Windows Vista Business, Ultimate, and Enterprise Editions

Requirements for Microsoft Virtual Server

The hardware requirements for Microsoft Virtual Server 2005 R2 with SP1 are as follows:

- *CPU* — Intel Celeron, Pentium III, Pentium 4, Xeon, or AMD Opteron, Athlon, Athlon 64, Althon X2, Duron, or Sempron (550 MHz or faster; x86 or x64).
- *RAM* — Enough RAM to match at least the minimum requirements of the total number of operating systems you will be running. For example, if you are running Windows XP Professional (256 MB minimum required for Virtual Server) and want to load Windows Server 2008 (512 MB minimum) as a virtual machine, you need a minimum of 768 MB to 1 GB RAM. If Windows Server 2003 R2 Standard Edition is the host and you want to run a Windows Server 2008 Enterprise Edition virtual machine, then you need a minimum of 768 MB to 1 GB RAM.
- *Disk space* — Enough disk storage for the operating systems you plan to run. For example, Windows Server 2003 R2 Standard Edition requires at least 3 GB, and Windows Server 2008 requires at least 10 GB (but 15 to 20 GB enables you to load more roles and services).

How to Download Microsoft Virtual Server

You can download Microsoft Virtual Server from Microsoft's Web site free by following these steps:

1. Log on to your computer.
2. Establish a folder in which to store the download (such as a temporary folder or a folder under your Program Files folder).
3. Start your Web browser, such as Internet Explorer.
4. Go to the URL **www.microsoft.com/downloads** or **www.microsoft.com/downloads/ Search. aspx?displaylang=en** (for English).

Web links and specific instructions change periodically. You might need to search *www.microsoft.com* for the most current link if these links do not work.

5. Look for Microsoft Virtual Server in the Popular Downloads or Recommended Downloads sections. (Also check the New Downloads section in case there is a new version.) If you find it in one of these sections, click the link for **Microsoft Virtual Server**. If you do not see a link, ensure that you set the search box near the top of the Web page to **Windows**, if Windows is not already selected. Enter **Virtual Server** in the blank text box next to the Go button, and click **Go**.

6. Click the link for **Virtual Server 2005 R2 SP1**.

7. Click the **Continue** button to register for the free download.

8. The information you provide next depends on whether you have already signed up for Windows Live ID or whether you already have an MSN Hotmail, MSN Messenger, or Passport account. If you already have an account, provide your e-mail address and password for the Windows Live ID information, click **Sign in** to verify your information (and answer any required questions), and click **Continue**. If you do not have an account or do not have a Windows Live ID, follow the steps to sign up for a Windows Live ID.

9. Click the **Download** button for the setup.exe file that matches your computer, which is 32 BIT\ setup.exe for an x86 computer or 64 BIT\ setup.exe for an x64 computer.

10. Click the **Save** or **Save File** button.

11. Select the folder you created in which to save the setup.exe file.

12. Click **Save**.

13. Click **Close** in the Download complete dialog box.

14. Close your Web browser.

How to Install Microsoft Virtual Server

The general steps for installing Microsoft Virtual Server on the host operating system are as follows:

1. Browse to the folder in which you saved the setup.exe file for Microsoft Virtual Server.

2. Double-click **setup.exe**.

3. Click **Install Microsoft Virtual Server 2005 R2 SP1** (see Figure B-4).

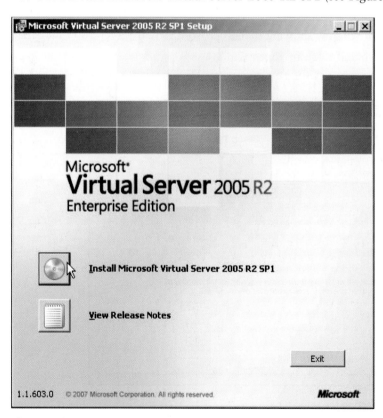

Figure B-4   Installing Microsoft Virtual Server 2005 R2 SP1

4. Click **I accept the terms in the license agreement**. Click **Next**.

5. Enter your username and the name of your organization (if you represent an organization). Notice that the product key information is provided by default. Click **Next**.

6. Ensure that **Complete** is selected in the Setup Type window, as shown in Figure B-5, and click **Next**.

7. Notice that the Virtual Server Administration Website will be added to Internet Information Services (IIS), and the default Website port is 1024. Further, if you see the option **Configure the Administration Website to always run as the authenticated user (Recommended for most users)**, ensure that it is selected. Click **Next**.

 After you click Next, you might see the informational message *The installed version of Internet Information Services (IIS) does not allow multiple websites.* The Virtual Server Administration Website will be added as a virtual directory under the default site.

8. If the Windows Firewall is enabled on your computer, you can have the setup process create firewall exceptions for Virtual Server. Make sure **Enable Virtual Server exceptions in Windows Firewall** is selected, and click **Next**.

9. Click **Install**.

10. If the required IIS components needed for the Virtual Server Administration Website are not already installed, click **Yes** to install them. Click **Install** again, if necessary. You'll see a dialog box showing that the components are being installed.

 In Step 10, if you see a message that the installation program needs to have the IIS World Wide Web service installed and there is no option to install it, this typically means the Virtual Server installation program cannot install IIS. Click OK when you see the message, click Cancel to stop the installation, and follow the steps for your host OS to install IIS. (You might need the host OS installation CD/DVD.) Start the Virtual Server installation again from Step 1.

11. You'll see a window showing that Microsoft Virtual Server 2005 R2 SP1 is being installed.

12. Click **Finish** and close any open windows.

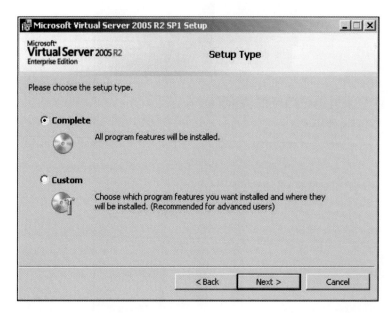

Figure B-5   Selecting the setup type

Creating a Virtual Machine and Installing a Guest OS

After Microsoft Virtual Server is installed, you can use the Virtual Server Administration Website tool to configure Microsoft Virtual Server, configure a virtual machine, and install a guest operating system.

Here are the steps for creating a virtual machine and installing a guest operating system (using Windows Server 2008 as the guest operating system):

1. Click **Start**, point to **All Programs**, and click **Microsoft Virtual Server**.

2. Click **Virtual Server Administration Website**.

3. In the Connect to dialog box, provide a username and password (for an account that has administrator privileges), and click **OK**.

4. If you are using a recent version of the Windows Firewall, you might see the Internet Explorer dialog box to enable you to add this Web site to the list of trusted sites. (You are likely to see this dialog box the first time you access the Virtual Server Administration Website tool.) Click the **Add** button. In the Trusted sites dialog box, click the **Add** button for the site you are adding and click **Close**. Also, if you see the Microsoft Phishing Filter dialog box, select whether you want to turn on the Phishing Filter (turning the filter on is recommended) and click **OK**.

5. The Virtual Server Administration Website tool is displayed through Internet Explorer, as shown in Figure B-6. Notice that the left pane contains options to navigate, create and add virtual machines, manage virtual disks, manage virtual networks, and manage the virtual server.

6. In the left pane under Virtual Machines, click **Create**.

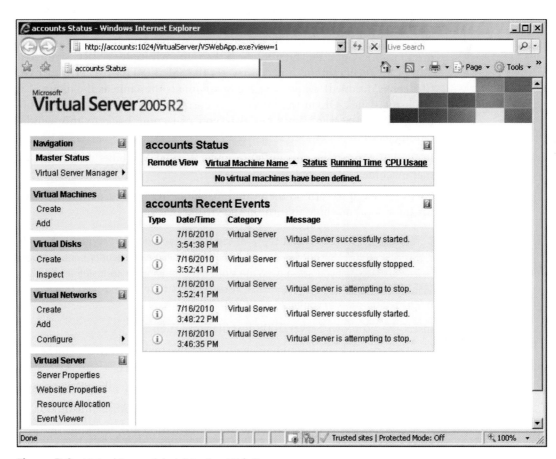

Figure B-6   Virtual Server Administration Website

7. Enter the name for the virtual machine and set the virtual machine memory. For Windows Server 2008, you should set it for at least 512 MB to 1024 MB. Also, click **Create a new virtual hard disk** and set at least 15 GB (more is better) for Windows Server 2008. Finally, specify the virtual network adapter, such as an external network interface. Click **Create**.

 The virtual network adapter options are Not connected, External Network, and Internal Network. Not connected (the default) does not provide any type of connection, so you can access the virtual machine only from the server. External Network means users can connect to the virtual machine through the computer's network interface card. Internal Network means there can be a connection between virtual machines on the same computer.

8. If you see the option to enable AutoComplete (to remember your entries in Web forms), select whether to use this feature by clicking **Yes** or **No.**

9. In the right pane, review the configuration information for your test server. Notice that you can use this pane to make changes to the configuration. (See "Configuring Networking and Hardware Options," later in this appendix, for more information about configuring these options.)

10. So that you can access a window in which to use the virtual server, click **Server Properties** under Virtual Server in the left pane.

11. In the right pane, click **Virtual Machine Remote Control (VMRC) Server.**

12. Ensure that the **VMRC server** check box is selected for the **Enable** option and that the TCP/IP address of the host server is entered. (If you have trouble connecting after entering the TCP/IP address of the host server, try leaving the TCP/IP address setting at "All unassigned.") Also, ensure that Authentication is set to **Automatic.** Click to clear the **Enable** check box for **Disconnect idle connections** (so that you are not disconnected during the OS installation). Click the **Enable** check box for **Multiple VMRC connections** and for **SSL 3.0/TLS 1.0 encryption.** If necessary, set the SSL 3.0/TLS 1.0 certificate to **Keep** or **Request** (if Keep is disabled). Make sure the hostname is the same as the name of the computer you are using. Click **OK** in the lower-right corner of the window. (If you have any problems using VMRC Server, remember that you can come back to this window to adjust any parameters.)

13. In the left pane, point to **Configure** under Virtual Machines and click the name of the virtual machine you created.

14. Next, you need to turn on the virtual machine. In the right pane, click the thumbnail image for the virtual machine to turn on the virtual machine.

 You might see a message that you need to configure Internet Explorer security to proceed. Make the necessary security configurations. Also, if you see a message from Internet Explorer to install an add-on, click the message and click Install ActiveX Control, and then follow the directions to continue.

15. Insert the Windows Server 2008 installation DVD.

16. If necessary, click the thumbnail again for the virtual machine. If you see a security message, click **Yes** to proceed.

17. Enter your username and password (using an account with administrator privileges). Click **OK.**

18. If you see another security message, such as for NTLM Authentication, click **Yes** to proceed.

19. If necessary, scroll down to view the information for working in the Remote Control window. Notice the options Pause, Save State, Turn Off, and Reset for the virtual machine.

20. Scroll back to the top of the Remote Control window.

21. You should see a beginning installation screen for Windows Server 2008. Move the mouse pointer into that screen. (The mouse pointer becomes a small black dot.) Click in the screen until you see the normal arrow for the mouse pointer. Notice that you can work only in the console for the virtual machine. Press the **right Alt** key (the default host key) to be able to use the mouse throughout the Remote Control window. Remember that you can always use the right Alt key to leave the console as needed. (Also, to work inside the console again, click the mouse inside the console.) In the upper-right corner of the Remote Control window, click the down arrow for **Remote Control**. Review the options on the menu, such as Special Keys and Connect To Server.

When you point to Special Keys, note that pressing the host key (the right Alt key) with the Delete key can be used to send the Ctrl+Alt+Delete key sequence to the virtual machine. (This is important to know later for logging on after you have installed Windows Server 2008.)

22. Move the mouse pointer back into the console and click it so that you can work in this area again. You can now proceed with the installation of Windows Server 2008.

23. In the Install Windows window, specify the language to install, such as **English**, in the Language to install drop-down list. In the Time and currency format list box, make your selection, such as **English (United States)**. In the Keyboard or input method list box, make your selection, such as **US**. Click **Next**.

24. Click **Install now**.

If your connection stops before the installation is finished, use the left arrow at the top of the window to go back to the main Status window. Click the virtual machine thumbnail to open a new connection via the Remote Control window. Respond to any security messages, log back on, and respond to any additional security messages. The installation should still be running.

25. Click **Windows Server 2008 Enterprise (Full Installation)** (or select a different full installation edition, such as Standard Edition if it is available) and click **Next**.

26. Read the license terms, click the **I accept the license terms** check box, and click **Next**.

27. Click **Custom (advanced)**.

28. You'll see the amount of unallocated disk space highlighted, which is the disk space you specified when you configured the virtual machine. Ensure that it is highlighted and click **Next**.

29. The installation program begins installing Windows Server 2008. You'll see progress information about copying files, expanding files, installing features, installing updates, and completing the installation. This process takes 30 minutes or more.

30. The installation program restarts the operating system.

31. You see the message *Please wait while Windows sets up your computer.*

32. Next, you see the Install Windows window in the Completing installation phase.

33. The system restarts again.

34. You see the message (a red circle with a white x in it) *The user's password must be changed before logging on the first time.* Click **OK**. (You might have to click inside the active portion of the console first to have the mouse function in it.)

35. Enter a new password for the Administrator account and then enter the same password again to confirm it. Click the **blue circle** with the white right-pointing arrow inside.

B

If you enter a password that is not a strong password, you see the message (with a white x in a red circle) *Unable to update the password*. This means the value provided for the new password does not meet the length, complexity, or history requirements of the domain. Click OK and enter a different password that is more than seven characters and uses letters, numbers, and special symbols, such as &.

36. When you see the message *Your password has been changed*, click **OK**.

37. At this point, the Windows desktop is displayed and the Initial Configuration Tasks window opens. From here, you can start configuring Windows Server 2008.

38. You can close the Remote Control window (the Virtual Machine Remote Control Server) or the Status window (the Virtual Server Administration Website) at any time. The virtual machine continues running in the background. Also, when in the Remote Control window, you can go back to the Administrator window by clicking the left-pointing arrow at the top of the Remote Control window.

You can shut down a server by first logging on through the Remote Control window. Also, you can use this window and the Status window to turn off a virtual machine (but make sure you shut down the server first).

To access the documentation for Microsoft Virtual Server, click Start, point to All Programs, click Microsoft Virtual Server, and click Virtual Server Administrator's Guide.

Installing an OS from an ISO Image

If you have an ISO image file for the guest operating system, you have the option to install it instead of performing a traditional installation through the installation DVD. Here are the general steps for installing an ISO image file on a virtual machine in Microsoft Virtual Server:

1. Follow Steps 1 through 13 in the previous section, "Creating a Virtual Machine and Installing a Guest OS."

2. The bottom portion of the right pane should now show the configuration options for the virtual machine.

3. Click the link for **CD/DVD**.

4. Under Virtual CD/DVD Drive 1, click the **Known image files** option button. Next, click the **Known image files** list arrow and select the image file. If the ISO image file is not listed, enter the path to the ISO image file in the Fully qualified path to file text box.

5. Click **OK** to return to the Master Status listing.

Configuring Networking and Hardware Options

The Microsoft Virtual Server Administration Website offers the ability to configure virtual networks. For example, as you learned earlier, a connected network has two default virtual network options: external network and internal network. You can customize settings for both types of networks, such as settings for a virtual DHCP server. You can also create a new virtual network with properties you define.

A virtual network is one used by virtual machines in a network and is independent of other virtual networks. In Microsoft Virtual Server, the number of virtual machines connected to a virtual network is unlimited.

The Microsoft Virtual Server Administration Website also provides options to configure hardware settings, such as adding more memory for use by a virtual server. In the next sections, you learn how to configure virtual networking and configure hardware for a virtual machine.

Configuring Virtual Networking   In the following steps, you examine how to configure virtual networking:

1. Open the Microsoft Virtual Server Administration Website, if it is not open. (Click **Start**, point to **All Programs**, click **Microsoft Virtual Server**, and click **Virtual Server Administration Website**.)

2. In the left pane under Navigation, click **Master Status**, if necessary. Access each virtual server that is running (if any) and shut it down. To do this, point to the server name (that has a right-pointing arrow) under Virtual Machine Name in the right pane, click **Turn Off**, and click **OK**. (You can configure virtual networking while virtual machines are running, but turning them off first is recommended.)

3. In the left pane under Virtual Networks, point to **Configure** and click **View All**.

4. In the right pane, point to **External Network (NICname)** and click **Edit Configuration**.

5. Review the information in the right pane.

6. In the right pane, click the link for **Network Settings**.

7. Review the properties information, including information about the NIC. Click **OK**.

8. In the right pane, click the link for **DHCP server**.

9. You can use the right pane to configure a virtual DHCP server that leases IP addresses through Microsoft Virtual Server (see Figure B-7). To enable the virtual DHCP server, click the **Enabled** check box in the right pane. When you enable the virtual DHCP server, you can configure the following:

   • *Network address* — Enter the network address for the virtual network.

   • *Network mask* — Enter the network mask.

   • *Starting IP address* — Enter the beginning address for the range (scope) of IP addresses that can be leased.

   • *Ending IP address* — Enter the ending address for the range of IP addresses that can be leased.

   • *Virtual DHCP server address* — Enter the IP address of the virtual DHCP server.

   • *Default gateway address* — Enter the IP address of a router that transports packets beyond the virtual network.

   • *DNS servers* — Enter the IP address of one or more DNS servers already on the network.

   • *WINS servers* — Enter the IP addresses of any Windows Internet Naming Service (WINS) servers (for converting NetBIOS computer names to IP addresses).

   • *IP address lease time* — Enter the amount of time that an IP address can be leased, which can be set in days, hours, minutes, or seconds. (Typically, you set it for one or more days.)

   • *Lease renewal time* — Enter the amount of time in which the client can contact the virtual DHCP server to renew a lease (in days, hours, minutes, or seconds, but with a minimum of 30 seconds).

   • *Lease rebinding time* — Enter the amount of time it takes to enable the client to contact another server to renew its lease, when the main leasing server cannot be reached (in days, hours, minutes, or seconds, but with a minimum of 45 seconds).

10. In the left pane under Virtual Networks, point to **Configure** and click **Internal Network**.

11. Review the information in the right pane for the virtual network properties.

12. Click **Network Settings** in the right pane and review the information.

13. Click the **back arrow** at the top of the window.

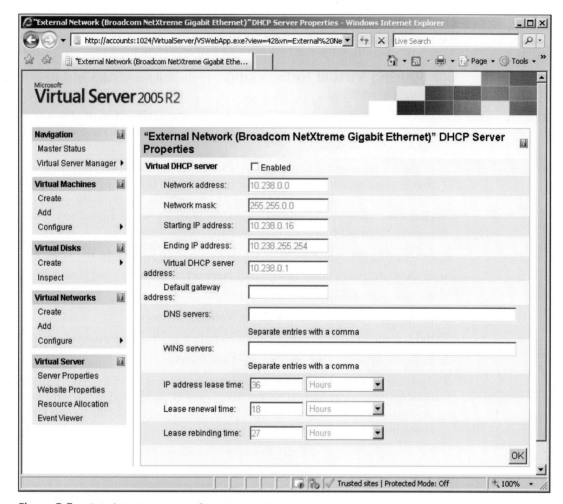

Figure B-7   Virtual DHCP server configuration options

14. Click **DHCP Server** in the right pane and notice that you can enable a virtual DHCP server and configure it.

15. Leave the window open for the next set of steps.

Configuring Hardware for a Virtual Machine

In addition to configuring a virtual network, you can configure hardware and other options for a virtual machine. In the following steps, you examine the options that can be configured:

 The virtual machine you select in the steps that follow should be turned off before you start.

1. Make sure the Microsoft Virtual Server Administration Website is open.

2. In the left pane under Virtual Machines, point to **Configure** and click the name of the virtual server you have configured.

3. Scroll to the configuration section in the right pane. Review the options that can be configured, which include the following:

  • General properties

  • Virtual Machine Additions

- Memory
- Hard disks
- CD/DVD
- SCSI adapters
- Network adapters
- Scripts
- Floppy drive
- COM ports
- LPT ports

4. In the right pane, click **General properties**. If your computer supports hardware-assisted virtualization, notice that you can enable it here. You can also specify a user account under which to run the virtual machine, and you can specify what action to take when the virtual server stops. If you make changes, click **OK** at the lower left.

5. Click the **back arrow** at the top of the window to return to the previous configuration display in the right pane.

6. In the right pane, click **Memory**. Now you can change the amount of memory allocated to the virtual machine. If you make changes, click **OK**.

7. Click the **back arrow** at the top of the window.

8. In the right pane, click the link for **Hard disks**. In the right pane, you see the configuration of the virtual disk used by the virtual machine. Notice the option "Enable undo disks." When you select this option, configuration and other changes on the virtual machine are saved so that you can undo those changes, if necessary. Also, notice that you can add a new virtual disk by clicking the Add disk button. If you make changes, remember to click **OK** so that they take effect.

9. Click the **back arrow**.

10. Click **CD/DVD** in the right pane. In the right pane, you can click the Remove check box to remove a CD/DVD drive, and you can click the Add CD/DVD Drive button to add a new drive. If you make changes, click **OK**.

11. Click the **back arrow**.

12. Click each of the remaining configuration options in the right pane to view what they cover. In particular, notice that you can add NICs by using the Network adapters option.

13. Close the Microsoft Virtual Server Administration Website when you are finished (or restart your virtual server so that it is in use).

Host Key Options

Microsoft Virtual Server designates the right Alt key as the default host key and offers host key options that are similar to those in Microsoft Virtual PC. Table B-2 lists important host key combinations you can use while you are accessing a virtual machine.

VMware Server

VMware Server enables you to set up virtual machines to run Windows or Linux operating systems. VMware Server version 2 is a major update compared with previous 1.x versions. The new features of VMware Server 2 include the following:

- Ability to manage virtual machines from the Web Access management interface or the VMware Remote Console
- Ability to configure different levels of permissions
- Ability to configure which operating systems are started when VMware is started

Table B-2   Host key options for Microsoft Virtual Server

Keyboard combination	Result
HostKey	Enables you to move the mouse outside the window used by the guest OS. (Move the mouse back into the guest OS display and click when you want to work on the guest OS.)
HostKey + Delete	The virtual machine OS responds to this as Ctrl+Alt+Delete.
HostKey + C	Displays the Connect to server dialog box for connecting to a specific virtual machine. (or if you have selected text first, it can be used to copy the text.)
HostKey + A	Toggles to the Administrator display window.
HostKey + I	Shows the VMRC Connection Properties dialog box with information about the connected virtual machine.
HostKey + B	Provides information about the VMRC client software.
HostKey + V	Pastes text and items saved in the Clipboard into the active window in the guest OS.
HostKey + H	Enables you to configure a different key as the host key.

- Editors for hardware devices
- New support for Windows Vista, Windows Server 2008, Red Hat Enterprise 5.0, and Ubuntu Linux up through version 8.x
- Ability to handle increased memory (to 8 GB) and more NICs (up to 10) in the host machine
- Supports 64-bit guest operating systems on 64-bit (x64) host computers
- Hot-add capability for new SCSI and tape devices (without shutting down a virtual machine)
- Supports VSS for backups on Microsoft guest systems
- Enables use of Firefox 3 or Internet Explorer for the Web Access management interface
- Supports hardware virtualization, such as through AMD CPUs with AMD-V capability and Intel CPUs with Intel VT
- Supports multiple monitors (to see different virtual machines on different displays)

VMware Server Guest Operating Systems Supported
VMware Server supports the following guest operating systems:
- Windows Server 2008 Standard, Enterprise, Datacenter, and Web Server (x86 or x64)
- Windows Server 2003 Standard, Enterprise, Datacenter, and Web Server with SP1 or SP2 (x86 or x64)
- Windows Server 2003 Standard, Enterprise, Datacenter, and Web Server R2 (x86 or x64)
- Windows Small Business Server 2003 (Standard and Premium Editions)
- Windows 2000 Server and Professional
- Windows XP Professional
- Windows Vista Business and Ultimate (x86 and x64)
- Red Hat Enterprise Linux Server and Desktop versions up through version 5 (x86 and x64)
- Ubuntu Linux 6.x to 8.x
- SUSE Linux Enterprise Server up to 10.x (x86 and x64)
- SUSE Linux versions up to 10.x (x86 and x64)
- Novell NetWare
- Solaris

VMware Server Host Operating Systems Supported

VMware Server 2.x runs on more different kinds of host operating systems than Microsoft Virtual PC or Server because it can run on several different Linux distributions. It also runs on x86 and x64 computers. The list of VMware host operating systems includes the following:

- Windows Server 2008 Standard, Enterprise, Datacenter, and Web Server (x86 or x64)
- Windows Server 2003 Standard, Enterprise, Datacenter, and Web Server with SP1 or SP2 (x86 or x64)
- Windows Server 2003 Standard, Enterprise, Datacenter, and Web Server R2 (x86 or x64)
- Windows Small Business Server 2003 (Standard and Premium Editions)
- Windows 2000 Server and Professional with SP3 or SP4
- Windows XP Professional and Home through the current service pack
- Windows Vista Business and Ultimate (x86 and x64)
- Red Hat Enterprise Linux Server and Desktop versions up through version 5 (x86 and x64)
- Ubuntu Linux 6.x to 8.x
- SUSE Linux Enterprise Server up to 10.x (x86 and x64)
- SUSE Linux versions up to 10.x (x86 and x64)
- Mandrake Linux up to 10.x

VMware Server also can run on other Windows and Linux distributions, such as other Windows Vista editions or Fedora Linux, but they should be considered "experimental" because they might not be fully tested.

For Windows host operating systems, you must download the VMware Server version for Windows, which is in .exe format. For Linux host operating systems, you must download the VMware Server version for Linux, which is in .tar format.

Windows Server Core is not a supported host at this writing.

Requirements for VMware Server

VMware Server has the following hardware requirements:

- *CPU* — Any standard x86 or x64 computer, including the following processors: dual- or quad-core Intel Zeon, Intel Core 2, AMD Opteron, or Athlon (733 MHz or faster)
- *RAM* — A minimum of 512 MB, but must include enough RAM for at least the minimum requirements of the total number of operating systems you'll be running (host and guest)
- *Disk space* — Enough disk storage for the operating systems you plan to run (host and guest)
- *Console Web Access* — Internet Explorer 6.0 or later (for Windows hosts) or Mozilla Firefox 2.0 or later (for Linux hosts)

VMware Server 2.x virtual machines can connect to hard, optical, and floppy drives. VMware 2.x also supports USB 2.x connections.

How to Download VMware Server

VMware Server can be downloaded from VMware's Web site at no cost by following these steps.

1. Log on to your computer.
2. Establish a folder in which to store the download (such as a temporary folder or a folder under your Program Files folder).
3. Start your Web browser, such as Internet Explorer.
4. Go to the URL **www.VMware.com/products/server**.

 Web links and specific instructions change periodically. You might need to search for the most current link at *www.vmware.com* if this link does not work.

5. Click **Download Now**.
6. Find the latest version of VMware Server (if multiple versions are listed) and click **Download** or **Download Now**.
7. If asked to provide registration information, complete the registration form.
8. Read the licensing information and click **Yes** or **Accept**.
9. Record the serial number for the Windows version (used later when you install VMware Server).
10. Click the link to download the Binary (.exe) file for VMware Server for Windows Operating Systems.
11. Click the **Save** button.
12. Select the folder you created in which to save the file.
13. Click **Save**.
14. Click **Close** in the Download Complete dialog box.
15. Close your Web browser.

How to Install VMware Server

The general steps for installing VMware Server on the host operating system are as follows:

1. If possible, connect to the Internet so that updates can be installed automatically during the installation process.
2. Browse to the folder in which you saved the install file for VMware Server.
3. Double-click **VMware-server-2.x.x-xxxxxx** (2.x.x-xxxxxx is the version of VMware Server).
4. You'll see a message box noting it is preparing for the installation, followed by the Windows Installer dialog box.
5. When the Installation Wizard for VMware Server starts (see Figure B-8), click Next.
6. Read the license agreement, click **Yes, I accept the terms in the license agreement,** and click **Next**.
7. Verify that the VMware server files will be written to the correct destination folder (or click the Change button to select a different destination). Click **Next**.
8. Verify the fully qualified domain name for the host computer, and verify that the server HTTP (port 8222) and server HTTPS (port 8333) ports are selected by default. Make any changes as needed, such as to the host and domain names (but leave the defaults for the ports). Click **Next**.
9. Make sure the shortcuts you want are selected, as shown in Figure B-9. Click **Next**.
10. Click **Install**.

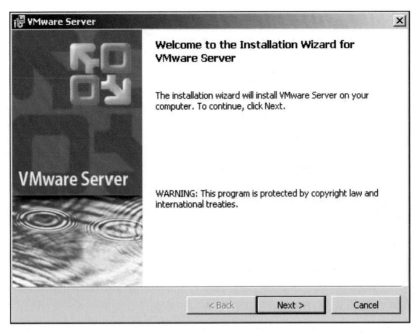

Figure B-8   The Installation Wizard for VMware Server

11. You'll see a message that the installation might take several minutes.

12. If you see any message boxes to install device software, click **Install**.

13. For the registration information, enter your name and the name of your company (or school), if appropriate. Next, enter the serial number you obtained when you downloaded the software. Click **Enter**.

14. Click **Finish**.

15. Make sure all programs are closed and click **Yes** to restart the system.

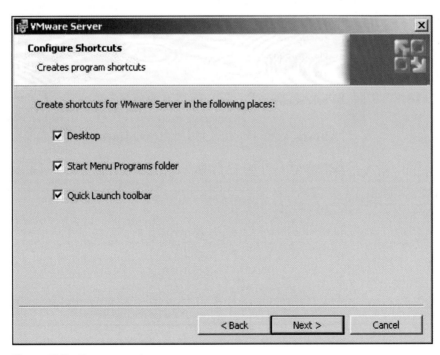

Figure B-9   Shortcut options

Creating a Virtual Machine and Installing a Guest OS

Now that VMware Server is installed, the next step is to create a virtual machine and install the guest operating system. Here are the general steps using Windows Server 2008 as the guest:

 The VMware Remote Console that you use later in these steps requires that the VMware virtual server (host computer) be resolvable through Domain Name System (DNS). Before you start, make sure your server can be resolved through DNS on your network (or that DNS is installed on the host). For example, there should be a host address (A) resource record in the DNS server for the host computer.

1. Double-click the **VMware Server Home Page** icon on the desktop or the taskbar. (Alternatively, you can click **Start,** point to **All Programs,** click **VMware Server,** and click **VMware Server Home Page.**)

 You might need to resolve security requirements for Internet Explorer, such as providing a digital certificate, answering whether to set up a phishing filter, and adding this site as a trusted site. These issues are related to Internet Explorer.

2. Log on with your host computer account name (or the administrator account) and enter the password. (Use the same account that you used to install VMware Server.)

3. You see the VMware Infrastructure Web Access window, as shown in Figure B-10.

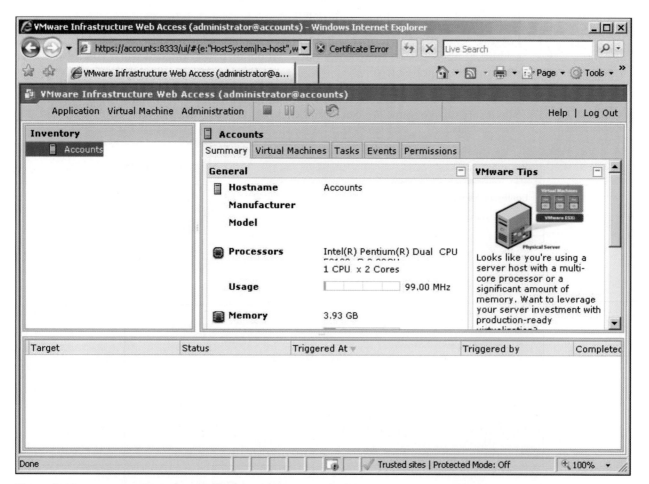

Figure B-10   VMware Infrastructure Web Access window

Notice that a certificate error is reported in Figure B-10 because this new site does not yet have a trusted certificate. If you have this problem, you might be able to import a certificate by clicking the Certificate Error box at the top of the window, clicking the link for View certificates, and clicking Install Certificate. Another option is to talk to your network administrator about importing a certificate.

4. Make sure your host computer is highlighted in the left pane.

5. Click the **Virtual Machines** tab.

6. In the right pane under the Commands heading, click **Create Virtual Machine**.

7. Enter the name for the virtual machine and click **Next**.

8. Ensure that **Windows operating system** is selected for the type of guest operating system, click the operating system (in the Version list box), and click **Next**.

9. Set the memory size to **512 MB** or higher. (1024 MB is the default when installing Windows Server 2008.) Also, if your system has a dual- or quad-core CPU or is an SMP system, you can select the number of processors to use. Notice, however, that you should not reconfigure the setting for number of processors after the virtual machine is set up. Click **Next**.

10. Select the virtual disk to use, such as by clicking **Create a New Virtual Disk** (a disk on the current computer). (The other option is Use an Existing Virtual Disk, which is a disk on a shared drive or hard disk on a different computer.) Enter the capacity for the virtual disk, such as **20 GB** (see Figure B-11). Adjust any parameters as needed, which include the following:

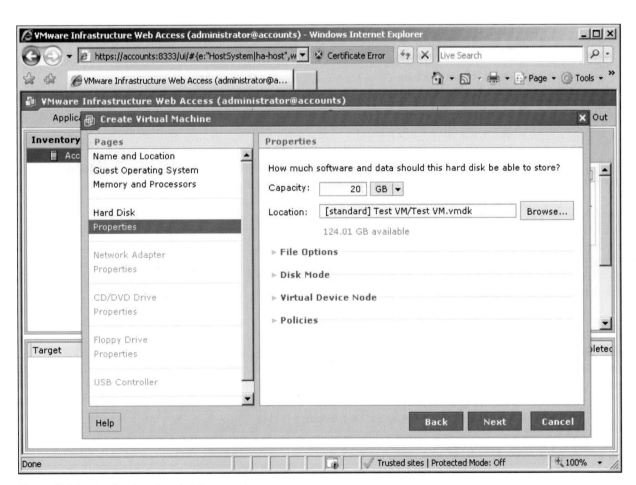

Figure B-11   Configuring virtual disk properties

- *Location for the virtual disk file* — A file location other than the default
- *File Options* — Ability to allocate disk space now and ability to split the disk into two files
- *Disk Mode* — Ability to create independent disks not affected by snapshots
- *Virtual Device Node* — Ability to select the SCSI or IDE adapter and device
- *Policies* — Ability to optimize for safety (the default) or for performance

11. Click **Next**.

12. In the next window, you can add a network adapter for access over a network. Click **Add a Network Adapter**. If you do not want to use the default settings for Network Connection (Bridged) and for Connect at Power On (Yes), configure those settings. The network settings you can configure for the Network Connection parameter are as follows:

- *Bridged* — This setting gives the virtual machine its own network identity (so that it is seen as a different computer from the host), which enables other computers on the network to communicate with it. The bridged setting also means the virtual machine can access the Internet through the local network.
- *HostOnly* — With this setting, only the host computer and other virtual machines on the same host can access the virtual machine, which means the virtual machine is not accessible through the local network.
- *NAT* — The virtual machine and host use the same IP and MAC addresses, which means the virtual machine does not have its own identity on the local network. This selection might be made if IP addresses are in short supply for the specific network or because an organization's network policy is to allow only one IP address for a specific computer.

13. Click **Next**.

14. You can configure whether to enable access to a CD/DVD drive or use an ISO image for the installation of the operating system. For this activity, click **Use a Physical Drive**. Ensure that the correct CD/DVD drive is selected, such as drive E, and ensure that Connect at Power On is set to **Yes**. Click **Next**.

15. If your computer has a floppy drive, you can configure it to provide an image for the operating system. Select the appropriate configuration options. (To install Windows Server 2008, click **Don't Add a Floppy Drive**.) Click **Next**, if necessary. (Depending on your selection, you might need to configure additional properties.)

16. In the next window, you can specify whether to add a USB controller, such as to access a flash drive. Make your selection and click **Next**, if necessary.

17. Review your configuration selections and click **Finish**.

18. In the bottom pane, you should see Success under the Status column to show that you successfully created the virtual machine.

 In some cases, if you have selected different configuration options and then clicked the Back button to go back to the preceding steps, VMware Server might give you an error message or you might not end up with an installed virtual machine. If this happens, start from scratch and avoid undoing selections you have made.

19. Insert the Windows Server 2008 installation DVD.

20. In the left pane, click the new virtual machine name under the host server name. (You might have to expand entries under the host server name first.)

21. Ensure that the **Summary** tab is selected.

22. In the right pane, scroll to the Hardware section. Click the **down arrow** next to CD/DVD Drive 1 (*drivetype*) and click **Edit**.

23. Review the parameters set for the host media (CD/DVD drive), make any needed changes, and click **OK**.

24. Click the **Console** tab.

25. Click **Install plug-in** to install the Remote Console plug-in.

> If you see a message box about noticing the Information Bar, click Close. Also, if the plug-in is not successfully installed in Internet Explorer, you might see a message at the top of the window that you must click to continue. Click the message and click to install the elements required by Internet Explorer, such as Install the ActiveX Control. Next, click Install plug-in again, and, if necessary, click Install.

26. In the right pane, click **Powered off** (which is like a switch to turn the virtual machine on or off.)

27. Click anywhere in the reduced console area in the right pane.

28. In the Install Windows window, specify the language to install, such as **English,** in the Language to install drop-down list. In the Time and currency format list box, make your selection, such as **English (United States)**. In the Keyboard or input method list box, make your selection, such as **US**. Click **Next**.

29. Click **Install now**.

30. Click **Windows Server 2008 Enterprise (Full Installation)** (or select a different full installation edition, such as Standard Edition if it is available), and click **Next**.

31. Read the license terms, click the **I accept the license terms** check box, and click **Next**.

32. Click **Custom (advanced)**.

33. You'll see the amount of unallocated disk space highlighted, which is the disk space you specified when you configured the virtual machine. Ensure that it is highlighted, and click **Next**.

34. The installation program begins installing Windows Server 2008. You'll see progress information about copying files, expanding files, installing features, installing updates, and completing the installation. This process takes 30 minutes or longer.

35. The installation program restarts the operating system.

36. You see the message *Please wait while Windows sets up your computer*.

37. Next, you see the Install Windows window in the Completing installation phase.

38. The system restarts again.

39. You see the message (a red circle with a white x in it) *The user's password must be changed before logging on the first time*. Click **OK**. (You might have to click inside the active portion of the console first to have the mouse function in it.)

40. Enter a new password for the Administrator account and then enter the same password again to confirm it. Click the **blue circle** with the white right-pointing arrow inside.

> If you enter a password that is not a strong password, you see the message (with a white x in a red circle) *Unable to update the password*. This means the value provided for the new password does not meet the length, complexity, or history requirements of the domain. Click OK and enter a different password that is more than seven characters and uses letters, numbers, and special symbols, such as &.

41. When you see the message *Your password has been changed*, click **OK**.

42. At this point, the Windows desktop is displayed and the Initial Configuration Tasks window opens. From here, you can start configuring Windows Server 2008 or log off and use the Remote Control window later to access Windows Server 2008.

43. You can close the VMware Remote Console window at any time (but note that the virtual machine keeps running).

44. Close the VMware Infrastructure Web Access window when you are finished using it. (The virtual machine continues running, unless you shut it down in the VMware Remote Console window and power it off in the VMware Infrastructure Web Access window.)

 You can access online help documentation while you are in the VMware Infrastructure Web Access window. Click the Help option near the upper-right corner of the window.

Installing an OS from an ISO Image

VMware Server supports installing an operating system via an ISO image file. The general steps for this type of installation are as follows:

1. Follow the steps to create a virtual machine.

2. In the Inventory pane of the VMware Infrastructure Web Access window, click the virtual server you have created.

3. Click the **Summary** tab.

4. Scroll down to view the Hardware section.

5. Click the **down arrow** next to **CD/DVD Drive 1** and click **Edit**.

6. Under the Connection section, click the **ISO Image** option button.

7. Enter the optical disk image path or use the **Browse** option to find and select it.

8. If necessary, select the device node in the Virtual Device Node section.

9. Click **OK**.

10. Click the **Console** tab.

11. Power on the virtual machine, if necessary.

12. Click inside the console and follow the instructions from the operating system.

Configuring Networking Options

As you learned earlier, the three network connection options are Bridged, HostOnly, and NAT. Each of these network types has a default name, as follows:

- Bridged is called VMnet0.
- HostOnly is called VMnet1.
- NAT is called VMnet8.

You can configure virtual networking, including VMnet0, VMnet1, and VMnet8, with the Virtual Network Editor. For example, you can configure VMware internal DHCP server capability for HostOnly and NAT networks. Bridged networks use an external DHCP server, such as a Windows Server 2008 server configured for this service.

To explore the Virtual Network Editor, follow these steps:

1. Click **Start**, point to **All Programs**, click **VMware**, click **VMware Server**, and click **Manage Virtual Networks**.

2. The Virtual Network Editor has the following tabs (see Figure B-12):

   - *Summary* — Provides a summary of the virtual networks, including VMnet0, VMnet1, and VMnet8

   - *Automatic Bridging* — Controls bridging between the VMnet0 network and the network adapter

   - *Host Virtual Network Mapping* — Enables you to link virtual networks to physical network adapters and virtual network adapters as well as configure subnet and DHCP properties

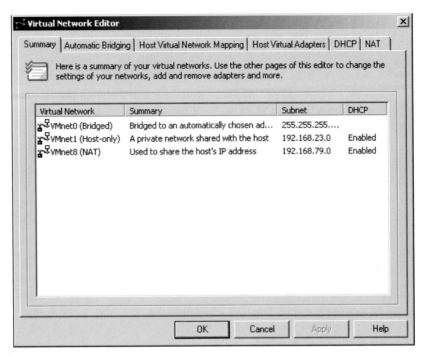

Figure B-12   Virtual Network Editor

- *Host Virtual Adapters* — Shows virtual adapter connections, virtual networks, and the status of connections
- *DHCP* — Enables you to configure DHCP for VMnet1 and VMnet8
- *NAT* — Enables you to control the NAT service and configure NAT settings

3. Click each tab to view what it does.

4. Click the **DHCP** tab again.

5. Click **VMnet1** and click **Properties**.

6. In the DHCP Settings dialog box, notice that you can configure the range of IP addresses to use. You can also configure the lease duration parameters for clients. Click **Cancel**.

7. Notice that you can start, stop, and restart the DHCP service in the DHCP tab.

8. Click the **NAT** tab. You can use this tab to associate the NAT service with a virtual network and to start, stop, and restart the NAT service.

9. Close the Virtual Network Editor when you are finished.

Configuring Hardware Options

After you set up a virtual machine, you might want to go back and configure hardware options. For example, you might change the configuration of the network and decide to go from a Bridged network to a HostOnly network.

The following steps enable you to configure hardware:

1. Open the VMware Infrastructure Web Access window.

2. In the Inventory pane, expand to view the virtual machines under the host server, if necessary.

3. Click the virtual machine you want to configure.

4. To configure hardware, you first need to ensure that the virtual machine is turned off. Use the Console tab to shut down the OS. Also, click **Virtual Machine** on the toolbar and click **Power Off**.

5. Click the **Summary** tab.

6. Scroll down to view the Hardware section.

7. Click the down arrow next to **Processors** and click **Edit.** You'll see a note that advises against changing the number of virtual processors, if you have more than one processor. Click **Cancel.**

8. Click the down arrow next to **Memory** and click **Edit.** Notice the recommended size information for memory allocation. Also, you can use the Size (in multiples of 4) text box to change the memory allocation. Click **Cancel.**

9. Click the down arrow next to **Hard Disk 1** and click **Edit.** You can increase the virtual disk capacity, configure the virtual device node, configure the disk mode, and configure policies. Click **Cancel.**

10. Click **Network Adapter 1** and click **Edit.** You can change the type of network connection, such as from Bridged to HostOnly. Information about the connection status, MAC address, and virtual device is also displayed. Click **Cancel.**

11. Click the down arrow next to **CD/DVD Drive 1** and click **Edit.** Review the properties you can set and the connection status information. Click **Cancel.**

12. Review information about any other hardware devices.

13. Restart the virtual machine when you are finished.

Installing VMware Tools

VMware Tools is an add-on that provides additional ways to manage a virtual machine and improve its performance. The elements of VMware Tools include the following:

- *VMware Tools control panel* to conveniently change virtual machine settings and connect devices

- *VMware user processes* for Linux and Solaris guest operating systems

- *Device drivers* for enhanced video, audio, mouse, network, and SCSI disk performance

- *Tools service* that provides a variety of tools for messaging, mouse performance, screen resolution, and others

When you install VMware Tools, the virtual machine must be started and you should be logged on to the guest operating system account from which you manage the Virtual Server software. This is because VMware Tools, including drivers, is installed on the guest operating system and you can access it from Control Panel in Windows Server 2008 (and other Windows operating systems).

To install VMware Tools, follow these steps:

1. Open the VMware Infrastructure Web Access window.

2. In the Inventory pane, click a virtual machine.

3. Ensure that the guest operating system is running, and if it is not, start it. Log on to the Administrator account or an account that has Administrator privileges.

4. In the VMware Infrastructure Web Access window, click **Install VMware Tools** in the Status column of the right pane for the virtual machine.

5. Click **Install.**

6. Open the virtual machine console by clicking the **Console** tab and clicking inside the console.

7. It might take several minutes for the AutoPlay message box to appear in the guest operating system desktop. Click the option **Run setup.exe.**

8. You see the Windows Installer dialog box with the message *Preparing to install.* This process might take several minutes.

9. Click **Next** in the Welcome to the installation wizard for VMware Tools window (see Figure B-13).

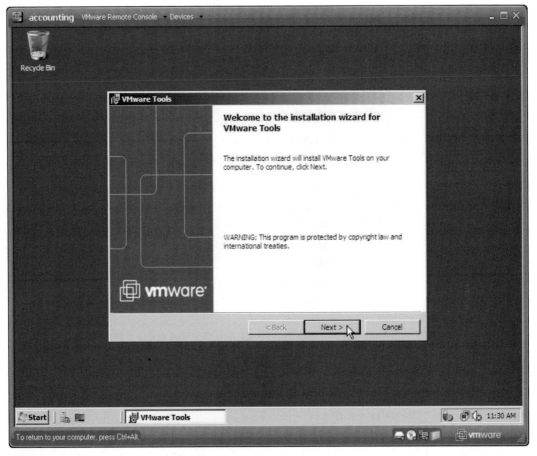

Figure B-13   Installation wizard for VMware Tools

10. Select the setup type option from the following options:

   • *Typical* — If you plan to use only VMware Server
   • *Complete* — If you plan to use VMware Server and other VMware products
   • *Custom* — If you want to choose the specific features to install

11. Click **Next**.

12. Click **Install**.

13. If you see the message *Windows can't verify the publisher of the driver software*, click the option **Install this driver software anyway**. (You might see this message several times.)

14. If you see a Windows Security dialog box asking whether you want to install this device software, click the **Always trust software from "VMware, Inc."** check box. Click **Install**.

15. Click **Finish**.

16. Save any work you have open on the virtual machine and click **Yes** to restart.

17. Log back on to the guest operating system in the console window.

18. In the guest operating system (Windows Server 2008), click **Start, Control Panel**.

19. Click **Classic View** and click the new applet **VMware Tools**.

20. The VMware Tools Properties dialog box opens, as shown in Figure B-14.

21. Click each tab to see what it does.

22. Click the **Help** button to learn more about VMware Tools capabilities.

23. Close the VMware Tools Help window when you are finished with the Help feature.

Figure B-14   VMware Tools Properties dialog box

24. Click **Cancel** to close the VMware Tools Properties dialog box.

25. Notice that a new icon is displayed on the guest operating system's taskbar, which can be used to open the VMware Tools Properties dialog box.

26. Close Control Panel in the guest operating system.

Other Virtual Systems

This appendix has focused on virtualization systems that are free. Other systems are available at a cost. On the desktop side, VMware Workstation has grown in use along with desktop virtualization. Another system is Microsoft Hyper-V, which is new to Windows Server 2008. The following sections give you a brief overview of these systems but are not intended to provide instructions about how to use them.

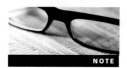 VMware Workstation is free for academic institutions approved in the VMware Academic Program. Entry in this program is free for two- and four-year degree-granting higher education institutions and accredited technical schools. For more information, visit *http://vmware.com/partners/academic*.

VMware Workstation

VMware Workstation is popular among software developers and testers because it provides a safe environment in which to write and test development software before it is released to live production. It is also used by people who need to run multiple operating systems on one workstation-class computer, including legacy operating systems. This can be useful for running old software without having to convert it for a new operating system. It's also useful for learning a new operating system.

VMware Workstation 6.04 (and later) supports Windows, Linux, and other operating systems as host and guest OSs. Newer operating systems supported as both hosts and guests include the following:

- Windows Server 2008 Standard, Enterprise, and Datacenter editions (x86 and x64)

- Windows Vista Home Basic, Home Premium, Enterprise, Business, and Ultimate (x86 and x64)

- Red Hat Enterprise Linux up to 4.6 (x86 and x64)

- Ubuntu Linux up to 7.10 (x86 and x64)

- SUSE Linux Enterprise Server 10 (x86 and x64)
- openSUSE Linux up to 10.3

VMware Workstation has several of the same new features as VMware Server, which include the following:

- Handles increased memory (to 8 GB)
- Supports 64-bit guest operating systems on 64-bit host computers
- Supports hardware virtualization, such as through AMD CPUs that have AMD-V capability and Intel CPUs with Intel VT
- Supports USB 2.0 (including on Linux operating systems)
- Supports multiple monitors (to see different virtual machines on different displays)

As with VMware Server, you can configure hardware for the virtual machine, including multiple processors, memory, hard disks, USB access, floppy access, and other hardware elements. You can also configure Bridged, HostOnly, and NAT virtual networks. A virtual DHCP server can be configured when you use HostOnly and NAT virtual networking. Setting up a virtual machine is also done with a step-by-step wizard.

Also, as in VMware Server, you can install VMware Tools, which includes specialized drivers, such as drivers for enhanced video and audio functions for the guest operating system. VMware Workstation has a console for accessing the guest operating system that resembles the VMware Server console.

VMware Workstation is specifically designed for workstation host machines and offers a wider range of host and guest operating system compatibility than Microsoft Virtual PC (at this writing). You can download a 30-day free evaluation version at *www.vmware.com/products/ws*.

Microsoft Hyper-V

Microsoft Hyper-V was released just a few months after Windows Server 2008. Unlike the other virtualization systems discussed in this appendix, Microsoft Hyper-V is intended to run only on Windows Server 2008. It is loaded through Server Manager like any other role in Windows Server 2008. In this regard, Windows Server 2008 offers perhaps the smoothest installation process of any of the virtual systems discussed in this appendix. Also, unlike the other systems in this appendix, Hyper-V runs only on x64 computers, which means the host systems include only the following:

- Windows Server 2008 Standard Edition x64
- Windows Server 2008 Enterprise Edition x64
- Windows Server 2008 Datacenter Edition x64

 For a general introduction to the features and requirements of Hyper-V, see Chapter 2.

You can purchase any of Windows Server 2008 Standard, Enterprise, or Datacenter Editions with Hyper-V (for an extra $28 at this writing) or you can purchase Hyper-V separately (also for $28). The low cost and seamless installation and integration with Windows Server 2008 are designed to make this virtualization system particularly appealing to Windows Server 2008 users.

The guest operating systems that can be installed in Hyper-V include the following:

- Windows Server 2008 Standard, Enterprise, Datacenter, and Web Server (x86 or x64)
- Windows Server 2003 Standard, Enterprise, and Datacenter (x86 or x64)
- Windows Server 2003 Web Edition
- Windows 2000 Server and Advanced Server with SP4

- Windows Vista Business, Enterprise, and Ultimate (x86 and x64)
- Windows XP Professional with SP2 or SP3 (x86)
- Windows XP Professional with SP2 (x64)
- SUSE Linux Enterprise Server 10 with SP1 or SP2 (x86 or x64)

After Hyper-V is installed as a server role, you can open Hyper-V Manager as a Microsoft Management Console (MMC) snap-in or from the Administrative Tools menu — steps familiar to Windows Server 2008 administrators. Hyper-V Manager is easy to use because it is designed in the same format as most Windows Server 2008 administrative tools. For example, to create a new virtual machine, click the New option in the right pane and follow the steps in the New Virtual Machine Wizard.

To configure hardware and management settings for a virtual machine, click Settings under the name of the virtual machine in the right pane of Hyper-V Manager. The Settings dialog box (see Figure B-15) enables you to add hardware, configure hardware, and configure management capabilities.

You can access the Virtual Network Manager dialog box from Hyper-V Manager to configure a virtual network. There are three types of virtual networks:

- *Private* — Communication only between virtual machines on the same virtual server
- *Internal* — Communication between virtual machines and the host virtual server
- *External* — Communication between virtual machines and the physical network (using a network adapter)

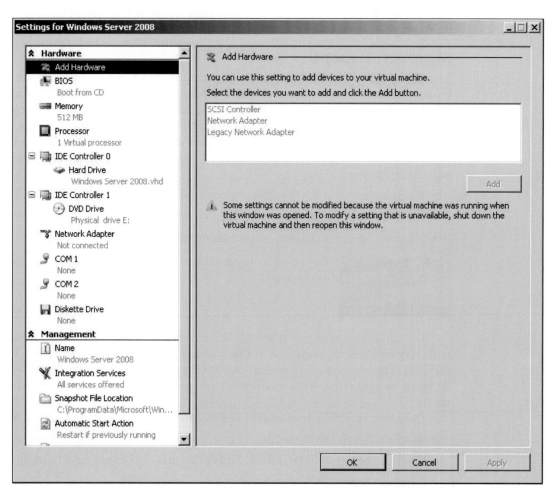

Figure B-15   Configuring settings for a virtual machine

For an external virtual network, you can specify a virtual LAN identification number. This is a unique number used for communication through the network adapter that distinguishes the virtual network from other networks.

The guest operating system appears in a console that has an Action menu from which you can send a Ctrl+Alt+Delete keystroke for logging on and start, turn off, shut down, or pause a virtual machine (as well as other options). You also can expand the console to completely fill the desktop display. The console can be started by clicking its thumbnail. When the console opens, it displays a message about how to start the guest operating system.

At this writing, Hyper-V does not include as extensive a range of guest and host operating systems as other virtualization systems. However, it is a good fit with Windows Server 2008 environments, and more guest operating systems likely will be added in the future. Windows Server 2008 administrators will find that installation and administration are consistent with how other server roles are installed and administered.

B

Glossary

.NET object A data package containing information useable by applications and services that are compatible with .NET.

.vhd file format The format used by Windows Server Backup to store backups. It is also the format used by Microsoft virtualization products.

_msdcs._forestname_ zone The Domain Name System (DNS) zone created in an Active Directory Domain Services (AD DS)–integrated zone that maintains the records of the servers responsible for the forest services.

802.1x standard A standard that provides an authentication mechanism to allow or deny network access based on port connection. It is used for most wireless 802.11 access points and is based on the Extensible Authentication Protocol (EAP), an industry-standard protocol for authentication.

access control entry (ACE) An individual permission assigned to a specific user or group on an object.

access control list (ACL) A list that defines permissions to resources. Each file and folder object on a Windows Server 2008 computer maintains an ACL.

accounting Often used along with authorization, this component logs the RADIUS processes so that access to resources can be reviewed at a later date.

activation threshold The minimum number of physical computers in a network environment needed before a Key Management Services (KMS) server begins issuing activations.

Active Directory (AD) Represents the suite of roles in Windows Server 2008 domain networks for providing directory-based management, security, and authentication. Prior to Windows Server 2008, AD represented Microsoft's version of a directory services database that provided centralized security and object management.

Active Directory Domain Services (AD DS) Stores information about objects such as users and groups on the network. This information is available so users can effectively access resources on the network and collaborate with other users. For network administrators, AD DS provides a framework for securing information and resources, along with facilitating the sharing of these resources to users.

Active Directory Domain Services Installation Wizard The second stage of the AD DS installation process where a Windows Server 2008 server is promoted to a domain controller (DC). This process is often referred to as dcpromo, which is the name of the executable for the process.

Active Directory–integrated DNS (AD DS DNS) A type of Domain Name System (DNS) available in Windows Server 2008 where the DNS database is stored within Active Directory (AD). DNS replication occurs through the normal Active Directory replication process.

AD DS sites Sites designed to limit the replication traffic across wide area network links as this traffic may affect the performance on client and user computers. Although multiple AD DS sites might not require multiple domains, each site has at least one DC for managing requests from local clients.

ad-hoc wireless A method for wireless devices to directly communicate with each other. Operating in ad-hoc mode allows all wireless devices within range of each other to discover and communicate in peer-to-peer fashion without involving central access points.

administrative share A share hidden from regular users and identified by a name ending with a dollar sign ($). For example, C$ is an administrative share used to access the C: drive of a computer.

Advanced Research Projects Agency Network (ARPANET) The original network created by the U.S. Department of Defense that is the basis for the Internet.

alias A record used to create an alias for an existing host name. Also called a canonical (CNAME) record.

alternate DNS server A DNS server that a client attempts to contact should their preferred DNS server be unavailable or unresponsive.

answer file A file used during an unattended setup to provide configuration to Setup.exe. All answer files used by Windows Server 2008 are eXtensible Markup Language based and are created by using Windows System Image Manager (WSIM).

Application layer The Open Systems Interconnection (OSI) model layer responsible for providing user services, such as file transfers, electronic messaging, e-mail, virtual terminal access, and network management. This is the layer with which the user interacts.

application programming interface (API) A set of rules and conditions created by the code writers of an operating system. Outside programmers use APIs so their applications can connect to a specific portion of the operating system. Companies such as Microsoft publish APIs for their operating systems to allow third parties to write complementary applications for their software.

attack surface In computer networking, the available ports or services a network client or server makes available to other network clients. In network security, the goal is to reduce the attack surface to the minimum allowable level.

attended installation An installation that requires a network administrator to be present to answer configuration questions presented during Windows Server 2008 installations.

Audit Mode An advance generalization mode that allows administrators to perform additional application and driver modifications to a specific image. This is one of two options available when using System Preparation tool (Sysprep) on an operating system.

authentication The first component of the RADIUS process in which the identity of a user connecting to a resource is verified.

authentication server (AS) The server responsible for authenticating a supplicant's request for network access.

authenticator A device, such as a wireless access point or a network switch, that receives a supplicant's initial connection and requests authentication information from them.

authorization Completed after authentication, this component determines what a user is allowed to do on a network or with resources.

background zone loading A new feature of AD DS–integrated DNS servers that loads DNS records as a background process to allow the server to respond more quickly to client requests after restarting the server of the DNS service.

backup domain controller (BDC) A domain controller in a Windows NT/pre-AD environment that is responsible for storing a read-only copy of the domain security database.

bandwidth The amount of data that can be carried from one point to another in a given time period. Bandwidth is normally measured in bits per second (bps).

bare-metal backup A process where a server can be restored to clean machine (no installed data) in a single step, typically using a block-level backup or disk image.

Berkeley Internet Name Domain (BIND) server The industry standard for DNS servers on the Internet and networks running DNS on Linux/UNIX systems.

binary number A number represented by either 0 or 1. Binary numbers are used in subnetting and IP address range creation.

binding time value Equal to 87.5 percent of the Dynamic Host Configuration Protocol (DHCP) lease duration, the binding time value is the number of seconds before a DHCP client attempts to renew its address lease with the DHCP server. If unsuccessful, it initiates a DHCPDiscover request to receive an IP address from any DHCP server on its network.

BitLocker A security method that provides hard drive–based encryption of servers. While Encrypting File Service (EFS) provides file- and folder-level encryption, BitLocker encrypts the entire Windows system volume of a computer running Windows Server 2008.

block-level backup A type of backup where an image of the target data set, or the data you've chosen to back up, is created instead of backing up file by file.

BOOTP An industry-standard protocol used for dynamic Internet Protocol (IP) allocation for clients prior to the proliferation of DHCP.

BOOTP relay agent Another name for a DHCP relay agent.

cache-only DNS server A DNS server that does not host any zone but is set up to perform DNS queries based on client requests. On receiving its query answers, the answers are stored on the server for a specific time period in case other DNS clients request the same information.

CD boot installation An installation of Windows Server 2008 that initiates setup.exe by using a CD, DVD, or USB drive.

challenge-response protocol A protocol used in scenarios involving a server sending a challenge question to the client. The client must provide a correct and valid response before their logon request is authenticated.

CIDR block The number of bits used for the subnet mask when using classless networks.

Classless Interdomain Routing (CIDR) A method for assigning IP addresses without using the standard IP address classes such as Class A, Class B, or Class C. CIDR allows for the more efficient usage and distribution of public IP addresses.

clean installation A complete installation of the operating system onto a new or reformatted disk drive. By their nature, clean installations, or migrations, do not transfer any settings from previous operating systems installed on a server.

client An entity that requests information or resources from another entity on a network. A client can be a computer, application, process, or hardware device.

client access license (CAL) A license that grants the right to access a server's resources to a user or computer device. You need a CAL for each client connection to a Windows Server 2008 server.

client machine identification (CMID) A unique client ID stored in the KMS database as part of activation threshold enumeration.

client-server computing A network model that describes the relationship between two computer programs in which one program, the client, makes a service request from another program, the server, which fulfills the request.

command-line interface (CLI) An administrative interface that requires the use of typed commands or scripted commands. After ending a command, a response is received from the system. The command prompt and Windows PowerShell are examples of CLIs in Windows Server 2008.

command-line switch An indication by a user that a computer program should change its default behavior. Also known as a flag, an option, or a command-line parameter.

conditional forwarding Forwarding based on a specific domain name.

connection methodology A network characteristic that defines the type of hardware technology used for connecting network nodes.

cross-domain name resolution The process where a client in a domain seeks to resolve the host name for target computer in another domain.

Data Collector Set A central repository for gathering information for Reliability and Performance Monitor. It organizes multiple data collection points into a single component that can be used to review or log performance.

Data Link layer The OSI model layer responsible for communications between adjacent network nodes. Hubs and switches operate at the Data Link layer.

datagram A packet that is sent using a networking service, such as Internet Protocol (IP) or User Datagram Protocol (UDP). IP and UDP are unreliable services because they do not inform the sender of delivery failure. Reliable services such as TCP provide senders information on failure of delivery.

DCDiag A Windows Server 2008 utility that allows administrators to perform diagnostic queries of your DCs.

delegation The process by which a DNS namespace is split so that a child, or subdomain, is stored in a different zone outside the parent, or root, domain.

demand-dial routing A type of routing that allows a server to initiate a connection only when it receives data traffic bound for a remote network.

device-based CAL A client access license (CAL) purchased for each computer accessing server resources. Because any number of users can use one device-based CAL, this is the license of choice in situations where many users access resources from a few client computers.

DFS namespace A File Services role service that creates a shared file resources entry point using a single naming convention. It is the first of two technologies that make up the Distributed File System (DFS). This central namespace makes the distributed nature of the file resources transparent to the user.

DFS replication A File Services role service that is responsible for synchronizing all the data within a DFS structure. Using a multi-master replication engine, DFS replication allows servers connected across wide area network or limited bandwidth network connections to stay current.

DHCP lease A placeholder in the DHCP database for an IP address. When a lease is issued, the IP address is removed from the available pool of IP addresses.

DHCP option A setting provided by a DHCP server to clients. Domain Name System (DNS) servers, router address, and domain name are some of the values for DHCP options.

DHCP relay agent A Windows Server 2008 server or hardware device configured to pass DHCP/BOOTP requests between clients and DHCP servers.

DHCP reservation A record on a DHCP server that provides a client with a static IP address based on the client's Media Access Control address.

DHCPAck A response from the DHCP server that confirms a DHCP client's IP address and includes configuration information and the confirmed IP address.

DHCPDiscover A broadcast message a client sends requesting an IP address from a DHCP server.

DHCPOffer A response message from a server that provides a client with an offer of an IP address.

DHCPRequest A broadcast message from a client that acknowledges the acceptance of an offered IP address from a specific DHCP server.

dial-up networking (DUN) A form of remote access that uses modems for connecting remote clients over telephone networks.

Disk Management console A console that provides you with a central location for administering the physical hard disks and disk-based devices attached to a server. It provides a graphical view of your hard disk storage allocation along with the health of your disk subsystems.

disk quota Allows you to track disk usage by users. Along with tracking quota data, you can enforce disk space limits on disk volumes. Based on NTFS.

disk-to-disk backup A backup type where the storage location of the backup file is a disk drive that includes a Universal Serial Bus removable drive, a network drive location, and a separate physical disk on your server.

Distributed File System (DFS) A set of client and server services that allows companies to deploy their shared file resources, known as targets, as a single file structure, while distributing the resources across multiple servers and multiple network locations.

DNS client Any computing device that requests DNS information via DNS queries. Also known as a DNS resolver.

DNS Client service The service that Windows Server 2008 uses to manage DNS client processes.

DNS domain The portion of the DNS namespace to the right of the host name.

DNS namespace A top-down hierarchical structure based on domain names.

DNS query process The process that DNS resolvers and DNS servers perform when they request information from each other.

DNS server A server that hosts one or more DNS domains.

DNS suffix The portion of the DNS namespace to the right of the host name. It is used by DNS clients to resolve unqualified DNS queries, or those that only contain a host name.

DNS zone A group of one or more DNS domains that contain the authoritative records for the member domains.

domain In the client-server computing model, a group of users and computers that are managed by the same security database.

domain controller (DC) A server responsible for holding a domain security database in an AD domain environment.

domain controller locator A service that runs at logon to provide the client with the location of a DC that can authenticate its requests.

Domain Name System (DNS) A system that matches a domain name to an Internet Protocol (IP) address based on a client query for information. Besides providing domain names, DNS provides information necessary for services such as e-mail to route mail to the proper destination. In an AD environment, DNS provides information to clients so they can connect with necessary network services.

domain-based namespace A namespace stored on one or more servers as part of Active Directory Domain Services (AD DS). Because of its integration with AD DS, this namespace provides increased scalability and availability, as it can be spread across multiple servers.

Dynamic DNS A feature of DHCP and DNS where DHCP servers work with DNS servers to create, modify, and delete DNS name records for clients in its environment.

Dynamic Host Configuration Protocol (DHCP) An industry-standard communications protocol that provides automatic IP addressing for Windows clients. Administrators use DHCP to ease the burden of maintaining IP addresses on small and large networks.

dynamic protocol A protocol that routes traffic based on information it discovers about remote networks from other routers.

EAP over local area network (LAN) Known by the acronym EAPOL, this refers to 802.1x implementations in which clients make physical Ethernet connections over Ethernet cable.

EAP over wireless Known by the acronym EAPOW, this refers to 802.1x implementations in which clients make wireless Ethernet connections.

enhanced metafile (EMF) The default print job format for use with Windows 2000, Windows XP, and Windows Server 2003 clients. With this format, application data is converted into an EMF file using the printer driver assigned to the printer.

enhanced security mode Using BitLocker with a Trusted Protection Module (TPM) and a personal identification number (PIN) or a Universal Serial Bus (USB) flash drive.

Ethernet A protocol and set of cabling specifications for local area networks (LANs) based on the IEEE 802.3 standard.

event subscription A new feature of Windows Server 2008 that allows administrators to gather event logs from remote servers onto a single machine. Subscriptions are based on the Windows Event Collector Service.

exception An instruction to open a port briefly, allow a program or service to pass information, and then close the port. Normally, the firewall blocks all unsolicited attempts to send information.

exclusion An IP address or range of addresses that are reserved for routers, printers, or other network devices.

eXtensible Markup Language (XML) A standard specification for annotating and formatting data exchanged between applications.

feature A function that enhances or supports a role or provides a stand-alone service.

fiber optics A form of telecommunication media that uses glass fibers for transmitting data via light.

file server The server responsible for sharing and managing data resources on a Windows Server 2008 computer.

File Sharing Wizard A wizard in Windows Server 2008 you use to configure both the New Technology File System (NTFS) permissions and the shared permissions simultaneously, depending on the type of access you give users or groups.

filter screening A feature that allows administrators to block specific types of files from being stored in Windows Server 2008 file directories. Filters can be defined by using built-in templates or custom-created templates or by specific file type.

forest One or more domains with noncontiguous namespaces that are related to each other by trust relationships.

forward lookup DNS zones A DNS zone that performs host name–to–IP address resolution.

forwarder An IP address of a server that a DNS server queries when it receives domain name requests for zones in which it is not authoritative.

frame A unit of data transferred between a sender and a receiver on a network. Frames are Data Link layer data units.

frame summary Displays a process name, if one exists, for traffic so that you can easily track data back to its source.

full backup This option performs a complete backup of your target set data set. It will increase the amount of time necessary for performing your backup, but it will not affect the overall performance of your server.

full zone transfer (AXFR) A zone transfer request where the slave is requesting the entire zone be reloaded.

fully qualified domain name (FQDN) The entire name for a specific host, or the DNS name, that needs to have a DNS record created so that users can use the FQDN to get the host's IP address.

generalization A process performed by Sysprep to prepare a computer running Windows Vista or Windows Server 2008 for imaging. The computer security identifier (SID), computer name, user profiles, and hardware information are removed during generalization.

global catalog A domain controller that holds a master searchable database of information about every object in every domain in a forest. The global catalog contains a complete replica of all objects in AD for its host domain and contains a partial replica of all objects in AD for every other domain in the forest.

global catalog (GC) server A DC in an AD DS forest that maintains a database containing objects from the entire forest, not just specific domains along with the directory services database.

Global Logs folder The folder located in the DNS console that stores a subset of Windows Events encompassing events based on DNS.

global name zone (GNZ) A feature of Windows Server 2008 DNS that provides single name–to–Internet Protocol (IP) address resolution by creating CNAME records in a special DNS zone. If a global name zone is created, a DNS server looks to the global name zone prior to failing over to Windows Internet Name Service.

Group Policy A method for implementing specific configurations for users and computers within an AD domain. Group Policy settings are contained in Group Policy objects, which are linked to the following AD service containers: sites, domains, and organizational units.

header Information appended to the beginning of a packet that specifies information about a packet, including protocol, destination address, and origin address.

high-performance computing (HPC) The use of supercomputers and computer clusters, or computing systems made of multiple processors linked together in a single system, to perform computing tasks requiring large amounts of resources.

host A computer on the Internet that provides a specific resource is called a host. This host is most often a Web server responsible for supplying Web-based information or applications. Hosts can also be network entry points for a company's network such as a firewall or a router.

host name A name given to a computer, or host, to make connecting to it easier.

host (A) record A record that is used to map a host name to an IP address.

host-based stateful firewall A local application that blocks incoming and outgoing connections based on its configuration.

hub The most basic of the hardware devices that interconnect multiple nodes. Hubs have multiple ports to which nodes connect. When a packet arrives at one port, it is broadcast to all the ports of the hub.

IGMP router and proxy A component of Routing and Remote Access Services (RRAS) that provides support for multicast network traffic by routing multicast traffic to networks that host multicast services.

image A collection of files stored in a single file. Windows Server 2008 uses the .wim file format for images. Typically, an image represents a file that is used to deploy new operating systems to computers.

image file A file that stores one or more images. In Windows Server 2008, the .wim file format is used. Windows Server 2008 uses single-instance storage to minimize the size of an image file containing multiple images.

image-based installation An installation of Windows Server 2008 that requires you create a customized image and apply it to each computer you are deploying. You use ImageX to create this customized installation. The image can include applications as well as the operating system. You use Windows PE to initiate the connection with the remote share, often via an unattend.xml file.

ImageX A command-line tool that enables organizations to capture, modify, and apply file-based disk images for rapid deployment.

incremental backup This option backs up only the data that has changed since the last backup was performed. This will decrease your backup time but may decrease your performance.

incremental zone transfer (IXFR) A zone transfer request where the slave is requesting only the updates since its last successful update.

installation script A file that automates the installation of services and features that you would normally enter manually during the process.

Internet A global network of networks used to exchange information using Transmission Control Protocol/Internet Protocol (TCP/IP). It allows for electronic mail and the accessing and retrieval of information from remote sources.

Internet Corporation for Assigned Names and Numbers (ICANN) The organization that oversees the distribution of public IP addresses, along with the maintenance of Domain Name System and domain name registrations.

Internet Key Exchange (IKE) A way to negotiate security protocols each Internet Protocol Security (IPSec) peer will use for communicating and constructing data transactions. IKE generates the encryption and authentication keys used by IPSec for the transaction.

Internet printing Windows service based on Internet Information Services 7.0 where users can add printers to their client as well as manage the printers on the print server through a Web browser.

Internet Protocol (IP) A set of rules to send and receive messages at the Internet address level. IP is the basis for network addressing on the Internet, the World Wide Web, and almost every network around the world.

Internet Protocol version 4 (IPv4) A version of IP whose address scheme is based on 32-bit addresses. IPv4 is the current standard, though available public addresses are becoming limited.

Internet Protocol version 6 (IPv6) A version of IP whose address scheme is based on 128-bit addresses.

Internet service provider (ISP) A company that provides public network access to the Internet for private networks.

iterative query When a DNS client requests the best answer that its DNS server can provide. If the DNS server has the answer cached, it will provide it with the address. If the DNS Server does not have it cached or it is not authoritative for the zone, it will provide a referral.

Kerberos The computer security protocol used by AD DS clients and servers for secure communications. It is based on mutual authentication. The name comes from the three-headed dog that guarded the gates of Hades in Greek mythology.

Kerberos Key Distribution Center (KDC) The security accounts database stored within the AD DS database responsible for managing and storing security account information.

kernel code The programmatic logic, or code, that makes up the kernel.

Key Management Services (KMS) An internal service for activating all computers within an enterprise network without the computers contacting Microsoft.

KMS client A server or computer that contacts the KMS host for activation and assignment of a client machine ID.

KMS host A server or computer hosting the KMS service and database.

label Each part of a fully qualified domain name.

Layer 2 Tunneling Protocol (L2TP) An industry-standard and recommended protocol for securing virtual private network (VPN)

connections. L2TP works by encapsulating Point-to-Point Protocol (PPP) frames before they are transmitted across a network. It is a combination of Point-to-Point Tunneling Protocol (PPTP), developed by Microsoft, and Layer 2 Forwarding, developed by Cisco Systems.

lease duration The amount of time the client keeps an IP address before releasing it.

license The right to install an instance of Windows Server 2008 you purchased on a single physical computer.

Line Printer Daemon (LPD) service The server-based service that allows access to shared printers from computers that use the Line Printer Remote (LPR) service. This is often used for UNIX-based clients.

Line Printer Remote (LPR) port monitor A feature needed by your Windows Clients to print to a print server that uses the LPD protocol.

link-local multicast name resolution (LLMNR) A new protocol whereby Windows 2008 member servers, Vista clients, and Windows 2003 member servers can resolve names on the local subnet even when the DNS server is down.

local area network (LAN) A network covering a small geographic area, such as a home, office, or building. Current LANs are usually based on Ethernet technology.

locally attached printers This type of printer is connected directly to a physical computer port. Typical port examples include universal serial bus (USB) and parallel port.

locator DNS resource records To find DCs in a domain or forest, a client queries DNS for the SRV and A DNS resource records of the DC. The resource records provide the client with the names and IP addresses of the DCs.

logical layout Defines how nodes communicate over a network.

mail exchanger (MX) record A record containing DNS and IP information specifically designed to allow Internet mail servers to relay electronic messages.

mail server preference value A value starting from 0 that designates the order in which mail servers should be attempted. The lowest number has first priority and so on.

managed code Computer program code that executes under the management of a virtual machine, unlike unmanaged code, which is executed directly by the computer's central processing unit.

master server A server responsible for providing DNS database updates and responding to Start of Authority (SOA) queries and IXFR/AXFR queries.

Media Access Control (MAC) A low-level network addressing system designed to be globally unique and allow clients to communicate on certain networks. MAC addresses work on Layer 2 of the OSI model.

membership status A setting indicating whether a network computer belongs to a workgroup or a domain.

mesh network A LAN in which each node has a direct network connection to every other node on the network or at least two routes of travel from a single node to other nodes.

Microsoft Baseline Security Analyzer (MBSA) 2.1 Designed for small to medium-sized businesses, MBSA provides security recommendations from Microsoft along with guidance for improving a computer's security posture.

Microsoft Management Console (MMC) 3.0 framework The new management console used to house snap-in consoles for existing machines.

modularization A design of the basic architecture of the Windows operating system so that it uses modules and provides a selective capability to customize Windows Server 2008 by swapping out modules.

module An independent unit of programming logic.

multicast A communications technology that allows multiple computers to receive a communication simultaneously.

multifactor authentication Authentication that requires two or more different authentication pieces.

multilayer switch (MLS) A computer networking device that switches on OSI Layer 2 like an ordinary network switch and provides extra functions on higher OSI layers. A common usage is a Layer 3 switch, which allows routing based on IP address as well as Layer 2 switch functionality.

multimaster environment An environment where more than one server is responsible for providing current information and changing information. In an AD DS environment, DCs are multimaster and AD DS-integrated DNS servers are multimaster.

multimaster replication A form of replication used by domain controllers (DCs) that allows them to maintain the same read and write security databases. With multimaster replication, no DC is more authoritative than any other, and all DCs can respond to client requests.

Multiple Activation Key (MAK) A key you can use to activate individual computers or a group of computers within your environment. Each computer communicates with special servers at Microsoft responsible for managing and maintaining activation records for its customers. By design, a computer can be activated only a limited number of times before activations are no longer allowed.

name resolution The process of resolving a host name to an IP address or some other piece of information stored in a DNS database.

name server (NS) record A record that denotes a DNS name server that is authoritative for a particular zone.

net share A Windows utility that allows you to create and manage shared folder resources and that contains many switches for assigning permissions.

NetBIOS The naming convention of choice for Windows nodes prior to the use of DNS. Every node on a Windows Server 2008 network is assigned a NetBIOS name at installation. This name is normally the same as the computer name, but it does not have to be. NetBIOS names are limited to 15 characters.

NetBIOS Name Server (NBNS) A server responsible for providing NetBIOS name–to–IP resolution for network clients.

netlogon service The client service responsible for finding AD DS resources such as DCs and GC servers.

network A group of two or more network nodes or computers and hardware devices linked together for sharing data.

Network Access Control (NAC) A computer networking concept and set of protocols used to explain how to secure network clients before the clients access the network.

network access point A private point of access to shared network resources.

Network Access Protection (NAP) A service that protects networks, both public and private, from malware such as viruses and spyware.

network access server A server responsible for providing network access to remote access clients such as users needing VPN or dial-in network access.

network address translation (NAT) A feature of RRAS that allows administrators to shield internal IP address ranges from public networks by allowing internal clients to access the Internet through a shared IP address.

network architecture A characteristic of networks that categorizes needs on the basis of the functional relationships between the nodes.

network attached printers A printer that is attached to the network by either a network adapter or a hardware print server. This type of printer is connected directly to the network, not to a physical port on a computer.

network distribution share installation An installation of Windows Server 2008 that initiates setup.exe via a distribution share located on the network or network distribution share. Windows Preinstallation Environment (PE) is used to initiate the connection with the remote share often via an unattend.xml file.

network distribution share A share configured through WSIM to store drivers and packages that can be added to Windows Vista during installation.

network interface card (NIC) A hardware card installed in a computer so that it can connect to a physical network.

Network layer The OSI model layer responsible for establishing paths for data transfer through the network. Routers operate at the Network layer.

Network Monitor A downloadable utility for capturing and viewing network traffic as it arrives at or leaves a server.

Network Policy Server (NPS) A role service providing administrators with a framework for creating and enforcing network access policies for client health along with policies for authentication and authorization of connection requests.

network protocol The special set of rules that end points in a telecommunication connection use when they communicate.

network scale A characteristic of networks that defines how they occupy geographic space.

network topology A characteristic of networks that describes the physical and logical relationship that devices have to one another.

networking The practice of designing, implementing, and managing a collection of computers and devices, or a network.

New Technology File System (NTFS) The default file system used by Windows Server 2008. NTFS provides file-level security for its resources along with other features, such as file compression and file and folder encryption.

Next-Generation TCP/IP stack A new implementation of the Transmission Control Protocol (TCP)/IP protocol by Microsoft that contains full support for Internet Protocol version 4 (IPv4) and Internet Protocol version 6 (IPv6).

node A computer or hardware device that participates in a network.

No-refresh interval The time between the most recent refresh of a record time stamp and the moment when the time stamp may be refreshed again.

OEM licensing OEM copies of Windows are installed on a specific system, and the license is linked to that specific hardware. This means that OEM copies of Windows cannot be reinstalled on a new piece of hardware.

Offline Files A feature in Windows Server 2008 that makes shared file resources available to clients when they are not connected to the network.

Open Systems Interconnection (OSI) model A seven-layer model responsible for detailing end-to-end network traffic and communication.

original equipment manufacturer (OEM) A company that originally produced a piece of hardware.

out-of-box experience (OOBE) A feature that removes the SIDs, unique characteristics, and applications from an OS. This allows it be more easily imaged and deployed to new clients. OOBE is one of two options available when performing Sysprep on an operating system.

packet A unit of data routed between a sender and a receiver on the Internet or any other packet-switched network. Packets are Network layer data units.

partition A storage area within AD where parts of the AD DS database are stored.

Per Server mode The CAL type where a separate Windows CAL is required for each device or user that accesses the resources on specific server, not all network servers.

Per User or Per Device mode The CAL type where a separate Windows CAL is required for each device or user that accesses the resources on any network server.

Performance Monitor This utility provides displays real-time or historical data of local or remote computers. Data can be displayed in a report view, a histogram bar view, or a line graph view.

Physical layer The OSI model layer responsible for bit-level transmission between network nodes. Cabling and connection types are defined at this layer.

physical layout In a network, defines how the cables are arranged and how the computers are connected.

pointer record (PTR) A record used by reverse lookup zones. It maps an IP address to a host name.

Preboot eXecution Environment (PXE) An industry standard that allows PXE-compliant computers to boot the network using their network card, and install an operating system to facilitate processes such as imaging.

preferred DNS server The first DNS server listed in the DNS search order. It is the first server that a client will use in performing a DNS query.

Presentation layer The OSI model layer responsible for defining the syntax that two network hosts use to communicate.

primary DNS zone The zone that is authoritative for a domain and its records.

primary domain controller (PDC) A central domain controller in a Windows NT/pre-AD environment that has a readable and writable copy of the domain security database. There can be only one PDC.

primary read-only zone Read-only domain controllers running AD-integrated DNS hold a primary read-only zone only for the forestDNSzones and DomainDNSzones.

print device This is the physical printer hardware that is connected either locally or on the network.

print job A document that is prepared and submitted by a client computer to a logical printer for process to a physical printer.

print server This is the computer that hosts one or more printers for use by network clients. The print server is responsible for the queuing and submitting print jobs to the print device.

printer A logical device created on a computer to allow output to physical media, such as paper.

printer driver This is the software provided by the printer's manufacturer that allows clients to prepare a document for printing.

printer pool A single printer that sends jobs to multiple print devices.

private network A network with an address range that is not routable on the Internet.

product activation A process put in place by Microsoft to reduce piracy. Unique information about your computer is sent to Microsoft to ensure that operating systems such as Windows Server 2008 are installed on only the allowable number of systems. Activation is usually done over the Internet, but you can activate via a telephone connection if necessary.

product key group A group of products that identify the type of MAK or KMS key required to install specific operating system editions.

protocol suite A group of interconnected network protocols from different layers of the OSI model that work together to provide network services. An example of a protocol suite is TCP/IP.

Public folder sharing When enabled, a feature that allows users to share files with all the users logged on locally or on the network.

public key (asymmetric) encryption A security method for securing a user's data that provides a public key to everyone and a private key only to the user. The public key is always used to provide the encryption of files, while the private key is required for decrypting files.

RADIUS An industry-standard protocol that provides centralized authentication, authorization, and accounting for network access devices, such as wireless access points and remote access servers.

RADIUS client Any device such as a remote access server or VPN concentrator that accepts remote connections from remote access clients.

RADIUS proxy Part of RADIUS used to route RADIUS messages between the access client and the appropriate RADIUS server.

RADIUS server A server used on networks to perform authentication, authorization, and accounting for RADIUS clients.

read-only domain controller (RODC) An AD DS domain controller that contains a read-only copy of the AD DS database and can answer client requests. Changes cannot be made to AD DS via the RODC.

Receive Window Auto-tuning A feature of TCP that allows the network interface receive window to be optimized based on the type of traffic that it is receiving.

recursive query A query where the client requires an answer from its DNS server. In this case, it receives a positive or a negative answer. It either receives an answer or is told it cannot be resolved, and no answer will be given to the client.

referral An answer provided to the client of the DNS server that can provide a better answer than it can provide. Also, a pointer to a DNS server authoritative for a lower level of the domain namespace.

Refresh interval The interval from the point that the No-refresh interval expires. It is number of days Dynamic DNS waits for the client to refresh its record before it becomes stale.

Reliability and Performance console A suite of utilities for monitoring and capturing performance data for local and remote systems.

Reliability Monitor A snap-in that provides a stability overview of the system along with providing details about events that have affected reliability.

renewal time value Equal to 50 percent of the DHCP lease duration, the renewal time value is the number of seconds before a DHCP client attempts to renew its lease with the DHCP server that issued its current IP address.

repeater A hardware device that receives a signal and resends the signal at a higher level or higher power so that it can go longer distances between the start and end points of communication.

Request for Comment (RFC) A document that describes the specifications for a recommended technology. RFCs are used by the Internet Engineering Task Force and other standards bodies.

Resource Overview A tool that provides a real-time summary based on the four key components, or subsystems, of a Windows Server 2008 computer.

resource record A record that contains details about a specific portion of the domain name.

retail licensing OEM copies of Windows are installed on a specific system, and the license is linked to that specific hardware. This means OEM copies of Windows cannot be reinstalled on a new piece of hardware.

reverse lookup DNS (rDNS) zone A DNS zone that performs IP address–to–host name resolution.

role A major function or service that a server performs.

root domain The first domain created when AD DS is installed and configured on the first domain controller on the network.

root hint A referral server for the root domain. Root hints provide IP address pointers to top-level DNS servers and are kept current on the computer via Microsoft Update.

round-robin DNS A feature of Windows Server 2008 DNS that allows multiple IP addresses to be assigned to a single host name.

router A hardware device responsible for forwarding packets between subnets, or networks with differing IP addressing schemes. Routers work on Layer 3 of the OSI model.

Routing and Remote Access Services (RRAS) A role service used to configure and manage network routing in Windows Server 2008.

Routing Information Protocol (RIP) version 2 A routing protocol that uses hop count to determine which path to use for sending packets so that they reach their destination.

routing table A table that contains information used to route traffic to specific networks. Routers direct data traffic to its destination based on the information contained in a routing table.

rule A way to manage communications by checking to see if they meet certain conditions and deciding what to do with them based on those conditions.

scavenge To use time stamps to determine when DNS records can update themselves and whether a record has exceeded the length of time records can exist without an update. You can scavenge manually or automatically in Windows Server 2008.

scope A pool of IP addresses created on a DHCP server from which the server responds to requests for addresses.

scope option A setting defined per scope that applies only to the scope to which it is added.

secondary DNS zone A read-only version of the DNS records for a zone.

Secure Sockets Layer (SSL) An established industry standard that encrypts the channel between a Web browser and Web server to ensure the privacy and reliability of data transmitted over this channel. SSL does not, however, provide ways to validate the identities or banking accounts of the parties exchanging this data.

Secure Socket Tunneling Protocol (SSTP) A new tunneling protocol in Windows Server 2008. SSTP uses PPP to encapsulate traffic for transmission across networks using a secure socket layer, or SSL, connection. SSL, often referred to HTTPS, provides authentication and encryption of its traffic across public and private networks.

security identifier (SID) A unique name given to objects in a Windows environment. The SID is used for managing security and access in a Windows environment.

serial number A number stored in the SOA record that increments by 1 for every change occurring in a DNS zone. This is used during the zone transfer process.

server An entity that responds to requests for information and resources on a network. A server can be a computer, application, process, or hardware device.

Server Core Available in Windows Server 2008, Server Core is a minimal server installation option designed to run a limited set of server roles and features and to provide a reduced attack surface.

Server Message Block (SMB) A protocol that clients use to access shared resources.

server option A setting defined per server that applies to all scopes on a specific DHCP server.

servermanagercmd.exe A command-line utility that allows administrators to perform automated installations or removals of roles, role services, and features.

service locator (SRV) record A record used to resolve the location of specific services available within a DNS zone. SRV records are used by DNS clients to find resources in an Active Directory environment.

Session layer An OSI model layer responsible for establishing process-to-process communications between networked hosts.

share-level permission A permission defined at the shared resource level that allows clients access to network shares. Also called a share permission.

single-instance storage (SIS) A process that eliminates data duplication by allowing multiple users, computers, or processes to use the same files and data. A WIM image uses SIS to reduce its size by allowing multiple image instances within a single WIM file to share files.

single-master environment An environment where one server holds the writable copy of a database such as the DNS database. Standard Primary DNS zones are single master.

slave server A server responsible for requesting DNS database updates and initiating SOA queries and IXFR/AXFR queries. Also called a secondary server.

snapshot The file storing previous versions of files or folders on a specific volume at a specific point in time.

stale record A DNS record that is out of date or no longer valid. These can occur when the Dynamic DNS process does not delete records out of DNS properly.

stand-alone namespace A namespace stored on a single server and restricted to the space and availability of that server.

standard file sharing A type of file sharing that makes files and folders accessible from a network location. In Windows Server 2008, standard file sharing is permitted only on NTFS volumes and partitions.

star network LAN topology in which each node on a network is connected directly to a central network hub or switch.

Start of Authority (SOA) record A DNS record that contains important zone information including the serial number, default TTL value, and authoritative name servers for the zone.

stub zone A read-only copy of a zone that obtains its resource records from the name servers that are authoritative for a particular zone. Unlike a secondary zone, a stub zone only contains only SOA, NS, and A records for a zone.

subnet A subnetwork; a separate part of an organization's network.

subnet mask A 32-bit number used to determine the host and network portions of an IP address.

subnetting The process of creating multiple smaller networks, or subnets, from the network address of an IP network.

supplicant The client or device attempting to gain access to an 802.1x network.

switch A network device that works at Layer 2 of the OSI model and forwards frames between ports based on MAC address. However, a switch is a more intelligent Layer 2 device because it forwards frames only to the ports involved in sending and receiving a datagram.

symmetric encryption A security method for securing a user's data that provides a single key to a user.

System Preparation tool (Sysprep) A tool that prepares an installation of Windows for imaging and deployment by modifying a system to create a new SID and other unique information the next time it starts. Sysprep also removes user and computer-specific information that should not be transferred to new images. Often, this process is referred to as generalization.

Teredo An IPv6 transition technology that provides address assignment and host-to-host automatic tunneling for unicast IPv6 traffic when IPv6/IPv4 hosts are located behind one or more IPv4 network address translators.

Terminal Services A group of technologies that enable users to access Windows-based programs that are installed on a terminal server or to access the Windows desktop itself from almost any computing device.

thin client A client computer or client software in a client-server network that depends primarily on a network server for processing activities and focuses mainly on conveying input and output between the user and the remote server.

token An object attached to a user's account that validates the user's identity and privileges they have to resources.

transitive trust A trust between domains in a tree, which is automatically created during the domain creation process.

Transmission Control Protocol (TCP) A set of rules to exchange messages with other Internet points at the information packet level. TCP guarantees the delivery of packets. This is the reason it is paired with IP for the basis of modern network communications.

Transmission Control Protocol/Internet Protocol (TCP/IP) A suite of protocols that provides the backbone for the Internet and most modern networks. TCP/IP is made up of protocols from the Network and Transport layers of the OSI model.

Transport layer The OSI model layer responsible for delivering messages between networked hosts. User Datagram Protocol and TCP function at this layer.

transport mode An IPSec mode that provides end-to-end security between devices or hosts such as for Layer 2 Tunneling Protocol (L2TP) virtual private network (VPN) solutions for remote access. Transport mode encrypts only the data portion, or the payload, of each packet.

tree One or more domains related to each other by trust relationships and a shared namespace.

Trivial File Transfer Protocol (TFTP) The protocol used for transferring images across the network. TFTP is a key component of the PXE, the backbone of Windows Deployment Services. Based on the UDP, TFTP traffic is connectionless in nature, meaning it does not guarantee sequencing or even arrival of data packets, or datagrams.

tunnel mode An IPSec mode that provides secure communications between two networks through a single node. More secure than transport mode, tunnel mode encrypts both the header and the payload.

unattend.xml An answer file used during the installation of Windows Server 2008. It is specifically sought out during installation phases to provide information for automating an installation.

unattended installation An installation that does not require an administrator's input because it uses answer files and scripts for automation.

upgrade installation An installation that migrates all of the settings from an existing operating system to Windows Server 2008.

user account database The database used by a RADIUS server to authenticate users. This can be either an Active Directory Domain Services database or a local Security Accounts Manager database.

User Datagram Protocol (UDP) A core IP suite protocol that provides connectionless transport with no guarantees for delivery and no protection from duplication. Because UDP does not check for delivery success or failure, it is a faster and more efficient protocol for applications requiring speed instead of guarantee of delivery. Multicast and DNS are two services that use UDP.

user-based CAL A CAL that allows one user to access server resources from unknown or multiple devices.

user-level permission A permission defined at the file level. On Windows Server 2008 computers, user-level permissions are based on NTFS.

virtual license A license to install an operating system within a virtual machine (VM) guest.

virtual private network (VPN) A type of network that provides secure network access for remote clients over the Internet through the use of tunneling protocols.

virtualization A broad term that refers to presenting computing resources to users by hiding the physical characteristics of computing resources. This is done by providing an intermediary program responsible for managing communication between users and resources.

VM guest An instance of an operating system like Windows Server 2008 that is running within a software-based workspace provided by a virtualization application such as Hyper-V.

VM host A computer running a virtualization application that provides software-based workspaces for VM guests. Examples include Virtual Server 2005 R2 and Hyper-V.

Volume Activation 2.0 (VA 2.0) The latest volume activation process used by Windows Server 2008 and Windows Vista.

Volume Activation Management Tool (VAMT) A tool used for proxy activation of a MAK, allowing activation of a group of computers with a single connection to Microsoft. VAMT activates your MAK with Microsoft while it manages the activations of your network clients internally in its database.

volume licensing A licensing model where you can use an individual key to license multiple installations of an operating system. Volume licensing is often used by business, government, and education institutions because it provides price discounts based on the application type, quantity, and applicable subscription term.

Volume Shadow Copy service (VSS) A feature of Windows Server 2008 that allows you to set up manual or automatic backup copies, known as snapshots, of files or folders on a specific volume at a specific point in time.

Web server A network resource that hosts applications and information available through a Web browser or Web-based application.

wide area network (WAN) A network connecting computers within very large areas, such as states, countries, and the world.

Windows 2000 Server mode A domain-based namespace that requires a domain to be running in Windows 2000 mixed AD DS functional mode and all namespace servers are running at least Windows 2000 Server.

Windows Automated Installation Kit (WAIK) A suite of tools that helps OEMs, system builders, and corporate IT professionals deploy Windows onto new hardware through automation of the installation process.

Windows Deployment Services (WDS) A server-based framework used to automate the deployment of operating systems over the network from a centralized server.

Windows Imaging Format (WIM) A file-based image format developed by Microsoft to create and manage WIM files

using ImageX. WIM allows you to mount your image files and add drivers, applications, or files directly to your image through Windows Explorer.

Windows Internet Name Service (WINS) A Microsoft-developed name server that resolves Windows network computer names (also known as NetBIOS names) to Internet IP addresses, allowing Windows computers on a network to easily find and communicate with each other. WINS has been replaced by DNS for most name resolution since Windows 2000. However, some legacy computers and application that do not support DNS require WINS to function mostly in older NT networks.

Windows Management Instrumentation Command-line (WMIC) An improved tool for managing WIM in Windows Server 2008.

Windows Preinstallation Environment (Windows PE) A limited 32-bit operating system based on the Windows Server 2008 and Windows Vista SP1 kernel code. Not to be used as a stand-alone operating system, Windows PE is designed for installation, troubleshooting, and recovery of Windows Server 2008 and Windows Vista.

Windows Recovery Environment (Windows RE) A new recovery environment built into Windows Server 2008 and based on Windows PE 2.0. Windows RE is a complete diagnostic and recovery solution as well as a platform for building your own recovery solutions.

Windows Remote Management (WinRM) A command-line tool service in Windows that is used to configure a computer to accept WS-Management (Windows Remote management) requests from other computers.

Windows Server 2008 mode A domain-based namespace that requires a domain to be running in Windows Server 2008 AD DS functional mode, and all namespace servers are running at least Windows Server 2008.

Windows Server Backup (WSB) A new utility that replaces ntbackup.exe in previous versions of Windows Server. It provides backup and recovery of your files, folders, volumes, and application data on Windows Server 2008.

Windows Server Update Services (WSUS) A centralized tool for managing Windows Updates for client computers. With WSUS 3.0, you can effectively deliver approved updates to clients and remove updates that are outdated or have caused issues with clients.

Windows System Image Manager (WSIM) A utility used to create answer files for Windows Server 2008 unattended installations. WSIM can also create distribution shares and configuration sets.

Windows Update A suite of tools and services provided by Microsoft to provide easy and reliable methods for applying updates to systems.

wireless LAN A network that uses radio frequencies to transmit data between nodes. Wireless networks do not use cables except for their connections to wired networks.

workgroup A network model where each member has its own locally stored Security Account Manager database, which controls user and group membership and access to its local resources.

World Wide Web (WWW) A part of the Internet designed to allow easier navigation of the network through the use of graphical user interfaces and hypertext links between different Universal Resource

Locators. Also called the Web. Often mistaken for the Internet, the WWW is actually a service of the Internet, like e-mail.

WS-Management protocol A public standard for exchanging management data remotely by any device implementing the protocol, making it non–vendor specific.

XML paper specification (XPS) This format is a new format in Windows Server 2008 and Windows Vista. XPS is a platform-independent document format does not require the job file to be converted at different steps of the process like EMF jobs.

zone transfer A process used by standard DNS servers to replicate changes in the DNS database.

Index

Numbers